A2 LAW FOR AQA

Visit the *A2 Law for AQA* Companion Website at **www.pearsoned.co.uk/russell** to find valuable **student** learning material including:

- Links to relevant sites on the web
- Regular updates of major changes in the law affecting the book
- Answers and suggested approaches to the self test questions and tasks in the book

We work with leading authors to develop the strongest
educational materials in law, bringing cutting-edge
thinking and best learning practice to a global market.

Under a range of well-known imprints, including Longman,
we craft high quality print and electronic publications which
help readers to understand and apply their content, whether
studying or at work.

To find out more about the complete range of our
publishing, please visit us on the World Wide Web at:
www.pearsoned.co.uk

A2 LAW FOR AQA

Sally Russell

PEARSON
Longman

Harlow, England • London • New York • Boston • San Francisco • Toronto
Sydney • Tokyo • Singapore • Hong Kong • Seoul • Taipei • New Delhi
Cape Town • Madrid • Mexico City • Amsterdam • Munich • Paris • Milan

Pearson Education Limited

Edinburgh Gate
Harlow
Essex CM20 2JE
England

and Associated Companies throughout the world

Visit us on the World Wide Web at:
www.pearsoned.co.uk

First published 2007

ISBN (13): 978-1-4058-0741-8
ISBN (10): 1-4058-0741-5

British Library Cataloguing-in-Publication Data
A catalogue record for this book is available from the British Library

10 9 8 7 6 5 4 3 2 1
10 09 08 07 06

Typeset in 9.5/12.5pt Stone Serif by 35
Printed and bound by Ashford Colour Press Ltd. in Gosport

The publisher's policy is to use paper manufactured from sustainable forests.

Contents

Preface   xi
List of abbreviations   xiv
Table of cases   xvi
Table of statutes and statutory
    instruments   xxvi
Acknowledgements   xxix

PART 1
MODULE 4 CONTRACT LAW

Introduction to Part 1   3

Study Block 1
FORMATION OF A CONTRACT   5

Unit 1 Offer   6
Bilateral and unilateral offers   6
Invitations to treat   7
Collateral contracts   9
Termination of an offer   10
Summary   13
Self-test questions   14

Unit 2 Acceptance   15
Acceptance must match the offer   15
Communication of acceptance   16
Acceptance by post   18
Summary   20
Self-test questions   20

Unit 3 Consideration   21
Executed and executory consideration   22
Part-payment of a debt   26
Summary   28
Self-test questions   28

**Unit 4 Intention to create legal
    relations**   29
Social and domestic agreements   29
Commercial agreements   31

Summary   32
Self-test questions   32

Study Block 1 Summary   33

Study Block 2
CONTRACT TERMS   37

Unit 5 Express and implied terms   39
Express terms   39
Collateral contracts   41
Implied terms   41
Summary   45
Self-test questions   45

**Unit 6 Conditions, warranties and
    innominate terms**   46
Summary   49
Self-test questions   50

Unit 7 Exclusion clauses   51
What is an exclusion clause?   51
Common law rules   51
Statutory rules   54
Summary   56
Self-test questions   57

Study Block 2 Summary   58

Study Block 3
VITIATING FACTORS   61

Unit 8 Mistake   62
Types of mistake   62
Common mistake   63
Mutual mistake   66
Unilateral mistake   66
Rectification   68
Non est factum   69
Summary   70
Self-test questions   71

Contents

Unit 9 Misrepresentation   72
What is a misrepresentation?   72
An untrue statement   73
A statement of *fact*   73
Induced the other to enter the contract   74
Types of misrepresentation   75
Remedies   76
Exclusion of liability   79
Summary   79
Self-test questions   80

Study Block 3 Summary   81

**Study Block 4
DISCHARGE AND REMEDIES**   85

**Unit 10 Discharge by agreement
   and performance**   87
Discharge by agreement   87
Discharge by performance   88
Summary   92
Self-test questions   93

Unit 11 Discharge by frustration   94
Nature and purpose of frustration   94
Limits to the rule   97
Effect of frustration   99
Summary   101
Self-test questions   102

Unit 12 Discharge by breach   103
Types of breach   103
Effect of breach   105
Summary   108
Self-test questions   108

Unit 13 Remedies   109
The purpose of damages   109
Equitable remedies   115
Summary   116
Self-test questions   116

Study Block 4 Summary   117

Examination practice for Part 1   120

**PART 2
MODULE 4 CRIME
OFFENCES AGAINST THE PERSON**

Introduction to Part 2   125

**Study Block 5
ACTUS REUS, MENS REA AND
   MURDER**   127

**Unit 14 *Actus reus* 1: Conduct and
   circumstances**   128
What makes an action criminal?   128
Summary   132
Self-test questions   132

**Unit 15 *Actus reus* 2: Consequences
   and causation**   133
Consequences   133
Causation   133
Summary   138
Self-test questions   138

Unit 16 *Mens rea*   139
Intention   139
Recklessness   144
Transferred malice   146
Coincidence of *actus reus* and *mens rea*   146
Summary   147
Self-test questions   147

Unit 17 Murder   148
Actus reus   148
Causation   149
Mens rea   151
Summary of the rules and how they
   apply   152
Self-test questions   153

Study Block 5 Summary   154

**Study Block 6
VOLUNTARY MANSLAUGHTER**   157

**Unit 18 Voluntary manslaughter
   under Homicide Act s. 3:
   provocation**   158
The test for provocation   159
Summary   164
Self-test questions   164

**Unit 19 Voluntary manslaughter
   under Homicide Act s. 2:
   diminished responsibility**   165
What is diminished responsibility?   165
Summary   169
Self-test questions   169

Unit 20 Voluntary manslaughter under Homicide Act s. 4: suicide pact — 170

Study Block 6 Summary — 172

Study Block 7
INVOLUNTARY MANSLAUGHTER — 177

Unit 21 Constructive or unlawful act manslaughter — 178
Actus reus — 178
Mens rea — 182
Summary — 183
Self-test questions — 183

Unit 22 Gross negligence manslaughter — 184
Reckless manslaughter – does it exist? — 185
The rules — 186
Corporate killing and reforms — 189
Summary — 190
Self-test questions — 190

Study Block 7 Summary — 191

Study Block 8
NON-FATAL OFFENCES AGAINST THE PERSON — 195

Unit 23 Common assault: assault and battery — 196
Assault — 197
Battery — 200
Summary — 202
Self-test questions — 202

Unit 24 Assault occasioning actual bodily harm (ABH) under s. 47 of the Offences Against the Person Act 1861 — 203
Actus reus — 203
Mens rea — 205
Summary — 207
Self-test questions — 207

Unit 25 Grievous bodily harm (GBH) and wounding under s. 20 and s. 18 of the Offences Against the Person Act 1861 — 208
Actus reus — 208
Mens rea — 211

Summary — 213
Self-test questions — 213

Study Block 8 Summary — 214

Study Block 9
DEFENCES — 219

Unit 26 Consent — 221
Activities to which you can consent — 222
Consent and sex — 224
Consent and other offences — 226
Summary — 227
Self-test questions — 227

Unit 27 Insanity and automatism — 228
Insanity — 228
Automatism — 233
Summary — 235
Self-test questions — 235

Unit 28 Intoxication — 236
Involuntary intoxication — 237
Voluntary intoxication — 237
The 'Dutch courage' rule — 239
Intoxicated mistakes — 239
Public policy — 240
Summary — 241
Self-test questions — 241

Unit 29 Self-defence and mistake — 242
Self-defence — 242
Mistake — 245
The overlap — 247
Summary — 248
Self-test questions — 248

Study Block 9 Summary — 250

Examination practice for Part 2 — 253

PART 3
MODULE 5 CRIME
OFFENCES AGAINST PROPERTY

Introduction to Part 3 — 257

Study Block 10
THEFT, ROBBERY AND BURGLARY — 259

Contents

Unit 30 Theft: *actus reus*   260
Appropriation s. 3(1)   261
Property s. 4(1)   264
Belonging to another s. 5(1)   265
Summary   268
Self-test questions   268

Unit 31 Theft: *mens rea*   269
Dishonesty s. 2(1)   269
Intention to permanently
    deprive s. 6(1)   273
Summary   275
Self-test questions   275

Unit 32 Robbery   276
Steals   276
Immediately before or at the time
    of doing so   277
In order to do so   277
Uses force on any person or puts or seeks
    to put any person in fear   278
Being then and there subjected to force   279
Mens rea   279
Summary   280
Self-test questions   280

Unit 33 Burglary   281
Actus reus   281
Mens rea   284
Actus reus and *mens rea* of the ulterior
    offence   285
Summary   287
Self-test questions   287

Study Block 10 Summary   288

Study Block 11
DECEPTION OFFENCES, MAKING
OFF WITHOUT PAYMENT AND
CRIMINAL DAMAGE   291

Unit 34 Deception offences   292
The common elements   292
Obtaining property by deception
    s. 15(1) Theft Act 1968   294
Obtaining services by deception
    s. 1(1) Theft Act 1978   295
Evasion of liability by deception
    s. 2 Theft Act 1978   297
Reform   299
Summary   299
Self-test questions   300

Unit 35 Making off without payment   301
Actus reus   301
Mens rea   302
Summary   304
Self-test questions   304

Unit 36 Criminal damage   305
Criminal damage   305
Actus reus   305
Mens rea   308
Destroying or damaging property with
    intent to endanger life   308
Arson   309
Summary   310
Self-test questions   311

Study Block 11 Summary   312

Study Block 12
DEFENCES   315

Unit 37 Necessity, duress and
duress of circumstances   317
Necessity   318
Duress   319
Duress of circumstances   321
The overlap   323
Limits to the availability of the defence
    of duress   324
Criticisms and reform   324
Summary   325
Self-test questions   326

Study Block 12 Summary   327

Examination practice for Part 3   329

PART 4
MODULE 5 TORT

Introduction to Part 4   333

Study Block 13
NEGLIGENCE   335

Unit 38 Duty of care: physical harm   337
Duty   337
Summary   343
Self-test questions   343

Unit 39 Duty of care: economic loss and negligent misstatement 344
Negligent misstatements 345
Economic loss by acts 349
Summary 350
Self-test questions 351

Unit 40 Duty of care: psychiatric harm 352
What is meant by psychiatric harm? 352
Primary and secondary victims 354
Rescuers 355
The control mechanisms 356
Law Commission proposals for reform 358
Summary 359
Self-test questions 360

Unit 41 Breach of duty 361
How to assess what is 'reasonable' 361
Objective standard? 363
Summary 365
Self-test questions 365

Unit 42 Causation 366
Causation in fact: the 'but for' test 366
Causation in law: remoteness of damage 368
Summary 371
Self-test questions 371

Study Block 13 Summary 372

Study Block 14 OCCUPIER'S LIABILITY 375

Unit 43 Occupier's liability 1: lawful visitors 376
The duty 376
The occupier 377
Lawful visitors 377
Warning s. 2(4)(a) 381
Breach of duty and causation 382
Exclusions s. 2(1) 382
Defences 383
Summary 383
Self-test questions 384

Unit 44 Occupier's liability 2: non-visitors 385
What is meant by occupier's liability for non-visitors? 385

The duty s. 1(3) 386
Warnings s. 1(5) 387
Defences 388
Breach of duty and causation 389
Summary 389
Self-test questions 390

Study Block 14 Summary 391

Study Block 15 NUISANCE, STRICT AND VICARIOUS LIABILITY 395

Unit 45 Nuisance 396
What is nuisance? 396
Statutory nuisance 396
Public nuisance 397
Private nuisance 397
Claimants: who can sue? 400
Defendants: who can be sued? 401
Causation 403
Defences 403
Remedies 404
Overlap 405
Summary 406
Self-test questions 406

Unit 46 Rylands v Fletcher 407
The rule in Rylands v Fletcher 407
Is liability strict? 411
Defences 411
Summary 413
Self-test questions 413

Unit 47 Vicarious liability 414
What is vicarious liability? 414
Why is it needed? 414
Status: test for an employee 415
In the course of employment 416
Summary 418
Self-test questions 419

Study Block 15 Summary 420

Study Block 16 DEFENCES AND REMEDIES 423

Unit 48 Contributory negligence and consent 424
Contributory negligence 424
Breaking the chain of causation 426

Contents

Consent 426
Summary 429
Self-test questions 429

Unit 49 Remedies 430
Damages 430
Injunction 431
Summary 433
Self-test questions 433

Study Block 16 Summary 434

Examination practice for Part 4 437

PART 5
MODULE 6 CONCEPTS OF LAW

Introduction to Part 5 441

Study Block 17
CONCEPTS OF LAW 443

Unit 50 Law and morals 444
Diversity of moral views 445
The relationship between law and
    morals 447
Legal enforcement of morality 450
Summary 452
Self-test questions 453

Unit 51 Law and justice 454
The meaning of justice 454
Theories of justice 455
How far does the law achieve justice? 459
Summary 462
Self-test questions 462

Unit 52 Balancing conflicting
    interests 463
Identification of different interests:
    public and private interests 463
The substantive law 465
The legal process 469
Sanctions and remedies 470
Current affairs examples 470
Summary 472
Self-test questions 472

Unit 53 Fault 473
What is fault? 473
The importance of fault in criminal law 473
Liability without fault in criminal law 476
Should there be liability without fault
    in criminal cases? 476
The importance of fault in civil law 477
Liability without fault in civil law 479
Should there be liability without fault
    in civil law? 480
Summary 482
Self-test questions 482

Unit 54 Judicial creativity 483
Do judges make law? 483
How do judges make law? 484
Should judges make law? 488
The balance between the roles of
    Parliament and the courts 489
Summary 490
Self-test questions 491

Study Block 17 Summary 492

Websites 500
Glossary G-1
Index I-1

Supporting resources
Visit **www.pearsoned.co.uk/russell** to find valuable online resources

Companion Website for students
- Links to relevant sites on the web
- Regular updates of major changes in the law affecting the book
- Answers and suggested approaches to the self test questions and tasks in the book

For more information please contact your local Pearson Education sales representative or visit **www.pearsoned.co.uk/russell**

My main aim has been to combine accuracy with a style that is accessible to all students. The writer's background of professional and academic law qualifications together with teaching qualifications and experience has hopefully produced the right mix – only you can tell!

This book is designed to match the AQA syllabus for A2, but also provides a sound base for first-year LLB, ILEX and other courses. It covers all the crime, contract and tort needed for the AQA syllabus as well as all the material for concepts of law. Everything you need is in this book, however, the Companion Website (**www.pearsoned.co.uk/russell**) will contain further material where space has not allowed for inclusion here. These may be of benefit for those with a particular interest or who intend studying law at a higher level. The site will also contain updates.

The Parts, each covering a module in the AQA syllabus, are divided into Study Blocks and Units for clarity. Each Study Block has a summary of the main points covered, a task, key criticisms (in more detail where the area is popular for essay questions) and some ideas for connecting the law to the wider issues studied in Module 6. At the end of each Part is an examination question and guide.

Each Unit contains **Examples** to help you see how the law relates to real-life situations, and also **Tasks** and **Self-test questions**, designed to help you check your understanding. Do these on a separate sheet if it isn't your book – or better still, work with a partner testing each other. Tasks will sometimes ask you to jot down a few thoughts for use in an essay question, so keep these. The answers to the self-test questions can be found within the text but are also available on the Companion Website.

Criminal cases are usually in the form *R v the defendant*. It is quite acceptable to just use the name so if the case is **R v Miller** I have called it **Miller**. If another form is used, e.g. **DPP v Miller**, then I have used the full title, as you may want to look up the case for further information.

Civil cases are between the *claimant* and the *defendant*; however, you will still see the use of the word *'plaintiff'* in quotes from older cases as it only changed to claimant in 1999. Other than in quotes, I have used the word claimant throughout the book.

Module 6 is synoptic. This means you need to relate the law that you have learnt over the whole course, including the three AS Modules, to such concepts as morals, fault and justice. A brief guide on connecting the law that you have learnt to the concepts in Module 6 is given in the summaries at the end of each Study Block. This is merely a taster to get you thinking about the wider issues in the law and it is fully covered in Part 5 (Module 6) itself.

Further reading is not specifically recommended as this book should contain all you need. However, it is always a good idea to get a different perspective so explore other sources too. In particular the House of Lords (HL) website should be borne in mind as recent cases will help you see how the law is developing. This and other useful – and free – sites are listed on page 500.

A word about exams

Module 4 and 5 papers are $1^1/_4$ hours each. Each paper contains two problem questions (scenarios), of which you must answer one. These are similar in form to Module 3 but more complex. Each question has three parts, two on the application of the law and the third requiring an evaluation of a particular area, in essay form. Module 6 is only essay questions and is $1^1/_2$ hours. The paper contains four questions and you must answer two of them. What you need for problem and essay questions cannot be divided completely but there is a difference. For both, it is important to know and understand cases well. Problem questions require you to use the current legal tests, which come from cases. Some crimes (including murder) are common law offences so *all* the law comes from cases, and even if the law comes from a statute, that statute has to be *interpreted* by judges. **Key cases** are used to highlight those which are particularly important. You can then apply just the law that is both current and relevant to the given facts – if you ask a solicitor for advice, they won't tell you everything they know, they will pick out the law that suits your case. You have to do the same in a problem question. Don't write down everything you know just to prove that you have learnt it. Being selective is a skill in itself. Use the **Examination pointers** and **Key cases**, plus the **diagrams** or **Summaries** at the end of each unit as a guide for problem questions. An answer to a problem scenario should be rounded off with a conclusion as to liability. This need not be, *nor should it be*, a firm conclusion. It is unlikely to be clear-cut, especially in criminal cases where a jury may be making the decision. Never start (or even finish) an answer with 'D will be guilty of . . .'. Identify the appropriate area of law, apply the relevant rules, consider whether a defence is available and conclude along the lines of 'D may therefore be charged with/liable in . . . but may be successful in pleading the defence of . . .'. In civil law also mention what remedy will be appropriate.

Essays require more discussion and evaluation of the law. The **Food for thought** sections are designed to help with this, and a summary including **Key criticisms** is found at the end of each Study Block. If appropriate, some Units will also have diagrams to show case law developments as a guide for essays, some areas are more popular with examiners than others. Each Unit opens with a **quote** so use these too – examiners like them. I have included an example essay question in the summary for each Study Block to give you an idea of the type of thing you will get. Where marked with an asterisk, they also appear in the full question and guide section at the end of each Part (there because the 'problem' parts can cover any of the law in the Module). The dates are on all exam questions so you can look at the AQA site for the mark schemes. For Module 6, you need to connect your existing knowledge from Modules 1 to 5 to several conceptual issues. Some ideas to get you thinking are contained in the Study Block summaries.

Finally, if you are confused by a case, or you see cases which conflict, don't despair. Just say to yourself, 'I can use that in an essay question when asked for a critique of the law'. If there is confusion or uncertainty then there will be a valid case for arguing that the law is not fully satisfactory.

Examination essentials

In precedent, you learnt that the important part of a case is the *ratio decidendi*, the reasoning behind the judge's decision. As you read a case, think about this and look for the legal principle. For problem questions try to summarise the facts in a few words. It is valuable when it comes to exams and time is short. Don't be tempted to write all you know about the area. An examiner won't be able to give you marks for stuff that isn't relevant even if it is correct.

It is important to:

- explain a case briefly but show that you understand the principle;
- show that you understand the law well enough to be selective.

DO BOTH!

List of abbreviations

All these abbreviations are commonly used. You may use them in an examination answer, but write them in full the first time, e.g. write 'actual bodily harm (ABH)' and then after that you can just write 'ABH'.

Case names are in full the first time but shortened in later use, e.g. **Donoghue v Stephenson** is later referred to as **Donoghue**. Also note that in shipping cases it is common to use the name of the ship, not the full case name (which can be very long), e.g. **The Wagon Mound** case on remoteness of damage is actually **Overseas Tankship (UK) Ltd v Morts Dock & Engineering Co. (1961)**.

General

ABH	Actual bodily harm
C	Claimant
CA	Court of Appeal
CCRC	Criminal Cases Review Commission
D	Defendant
Draft Code	A Criminal Code for England and Wales (Law Commission No. 177), 1989
GBH	Grievous bodily harm
HL	House of Lords
V	Victim

Acts

s.	Section; thus, s.1 Theft Act 1968 refers to section 1 of that Act and s. 1(2) means section 1 subsection 2 of an Act (section numbers don't need to be written in full)
OAPA	Offences against the Person Act 1861
OLA	Occupier's Liability Act

In cases

(These don't need to be written in full)

AHA	Area Health Authority
BC	Borough council
CC	(at beginning) Chief constable
CC	(at end) County council
DC	District council
LBC	London borough council

Judges and other legal personnel

(These don't need to be written in full)

AG	Attorney General
CPS	Crown Prosecution Service
DPP	Director of Public Prosecutions
J	Justice
LC	Lord Chancellor
LCJ	Lord Chief Justice
LJ	Lord Justice
VC	Vice Chancellor

Table of cases

A v UK (1998)   *223*

A (Conjoined twins), *re*   *317, 318, 323, 325, 326, 327, 328, 450, 454, 460*

AG v PYA Quarries (1975)   *397*

Adams v Linsell (1818)   *18, 20, 34, 35, 487*

Adams v Ursell (1913)   *399, 406, 478*

Addie v Dumbreck   *487*

Addis v Gramophone Co Ltd (1909)   *113, 487, 490*

Airedale NHS Trust v Bland (1993)   *129, 149, 155, 156, 450, 471*

Alaskan Trader, The   *104, 105, 107*

Alcock v CC of South Yorkshire (1991)   *354, 356, 357, 358, 359, 360, 372, 434, 438, 487*

Allard v Selfridge Ltd [1925]   *503*

Allen v Gulf Oil (1981)   *403, 406*

Amalgamated Investment & Property Co Ltd v John Walker & Sons (1977)   *68, 97*

André et Cie v Tradax [1983]   *502*

Anglia Television v Read (1972)   *110, 116, 118*

Anns v Merton LBC (1978)   *338*

Appleson v Littlewoods Pools (1939)   *31*

Atkinson v Seghal (2003)   *357*

Attorney-General's Reference (No 6 of 1980) (1981)   *221, 222, 223, 226, 227, 251*

Attorney-General for Jersey v Holley (2005)   *162, 163, 163, 172, 173, 175, 254, 486*

Attorney-General for Northern Ireland v Gallagher (1963)   *236, 239*

Attorney-General's Reference (Nos. 1 & 2 of 1979)   *286*

Attorney-General's Reference (No. 1 of 1983)   *267*

Attorney-General's Reference (No. 2 of 1992) (1994)   *234*

Attorney-General's Reference (No. 3 of 1994) (1997)   *152*

Attwood v Small (1838)   *74, 121*

Avery v Bowden (1855)   *97, 104*

B v DPP (2000)   *247, 248, 252, 476*

BP Exploration v Hunt (1982)   *100*

B & S v Leathley (1979)   *283*

Baker v James [1921]   *504*

Balfour v Balfour (1919)   *29, 30, 34, 120, 459, 487, 490*

Bannerman v White (1861)   *40, 45, 58, 72*

Barnett v Chelsea & Kensington HMC (1968)   *366, 373, 391, 434*

Barrett v MOD (1995)   *428, 429, 436*

Barry v Davies (t/a Heathcote Ball & Co) (2000)   *9, 112*

Barry v Heathcote Ball & Co (Commercial Auctions) Ltd *see* Barry v Davies (t/a Heathcote Ball & Co)

Beale v Taylor (1967)   *42*

Beard v LGOC (1900)   *417*

Becke v Smith (1836)   *502*

Bell v Lever Bros (1932)   *64, 65, 70, 81*

Bettini v Gye (1876)   *47, 49, 58, 86, 106, 108, 118*

Bisset v Wilkinson (1927)   *74*

Blackpool and Fylde Aero Club Ltd v Blackpool BC (1990)   *9*

Blyth v Birmingham Waterworks Co (1856)   *361*

Bolam v Friern HMC (1957)   *363, 434*

Bolitho v City & Hackney HA (1998)   *364, 372, 434*

Bolton v Mahadeva (1972)   *89, 90, 118, 119*

Bolton v Stone (1951)   *362, 363, 364, 396, 397, 399, 400, 406, 478*

Bottomley v Todmorden Cricket Club (2003)   *380, 382, 392*

Bourhill v Young   *335, 340, 343, 353, 359, 485*

Bratty v Attorney-General for Northern Ireland (1963)   *229, 231, 232, 233, 252, 466*

Brinkibon v Stahag Stahl und Stahlwarenhandels GmbH (1983)   *17, 18, 20*

British Railways Board *v* Herrington (1972) *386, 388, 393, 451, 461, 487*

Britvic Soft Drinks *v* Messer UK (2001) *42*

Broome *v* Perkins (1987) *234, 250, 251, 252*

Bunge Corporation *v* Tradax Export SA (1981) *46, 48, 59*

Burrell *v* Harmer (1967) *223*

Butler Machine Tool Co *v* Ex-cell-o Corp (England) (1979) *16*

Byrne & Co *v* Leon Van Tien Hoven & Co (1879–80) *11, 12, 13, 14, 15, 18, 19, 20, 34*

C *v* Eisenhower (1983) *209, 211, 213, 215, 252*

Cambridge Water Co Ltd *v* Eastern Counties Leather Plc (1994) *403, 410, 411, 413, 420, 421, 422, 480, 482, 487, 489*

Candler Crane *v* Christmas (1951) *344*

Caparo *v* Dickman *335, 338, 339, 340, 342, 343, 345, 347, 348, 350, 352, 353, 356, 360, 372, 373, 392, 434*

Carlill *v* Carbolic Smoke Ball Co (1892) *6, 7, 12, 13, 14, 16, 20, 31, 32, 34, 110, 112*

Carty *v* Croydon LBC (2005) *348, 414*

Casey's Patents, *re* (1892) *23, 35*

Castle *v* St Augustine's Links (1922) *397, 399*

Central London Property Trust Ltd *v* High Trees Ltd [1947] *503*

Chadwick *v* BTC (1967) *355, 427, 435*

Chamberlain *v* Lindon (1998) *307, 314*

Chapelton *v* Barry UDC (1940) *52, 56*

Chappell & Co Ltd *v* Nestle Co Ltd (1960) *23, 28, 120*

Chaudry *v* Prabhakar (1989) *347, 351, 374*

Cheney *v* Conn [1986] *502*

Chester *v* Afshar (2004) *367*

Christie *v* Davey (1893) *400, 406, 468, 478*

City of Westminster Properties Ltd *v* Mudd (1959) *41, 45*

Clea Shipping Corp *v* Bulk Oil International (*The Alaskan Trader*) (No. 2)(1984) *104, 105, 107*

Collins *v* Godefroy (1831) *24, 34*

Collins *v* Wilcock (1984) *201, 202*

Commissioner of Police of the Metropolis *v* Charles (Derek Michael) (1977) *293, 313*

Condon *v* Basi (1985) *427, 429, 436*

Condor *v* The Barron Knights (1966) *95*

Cooper Brookes Ltd *v* FCT (1981) *502*

Corcoran *v* Anderton (1980) *278, 279, 280, 289*

Corocraft *v* Pan Am Airways [1969] *502*

Cotton *v* Derbyshire Dales DC (1994) *381, 392*

County Ltd *v* Girozentrale Securities (1996) *110*

Couturier *v* Hastie (1856) *63, 64, 70, 81, 82, 504*

Crown River Cruises Ltd *v* Kimbolton Fireworks Ltd (1996) *410, 413, 421*

Cundy *v* Lindsay (1878) *67, 68, 70*

Currie *v* Misa *see* Misa *v* Currie

Customs and Excise Commissioners *v* Barclays Bank (2004) *348, 351*

Cutler *v* United Dairies (1933) *427*

Cutter *v* Powell (1795) *88, 92, 100, 117*

D&C Builders Ltd *v* Rees (1966) *27, 35*

Dacas *v* Brooke Street Bureau (2004) *416*

Dann *v* Hamilton (1939) *427, 504*

Darby *v* National Trust (2001) *381, 383, 388, 392*

Daulia Ltd *v* Four Millbank Nominees Ltd (1978) *16*

Davidge *v* Bunnett (1984) *267*

Davis Contractors *v* Fareham UDC (1956) *94, 96, 97, 98, 102, 117, 477*

Davis *v* Johnson [1978] *503*

Dawson and James (1978) *278*

Delaware Mansions Ltd *v* Westminster City Council (2001) *396, 405, 406*

Denny, Mott & Dickson *v* James B Fraser & Co Ltd (1944) *97, 117*

Derry *v* Peek (1889) *75, 121, 477*

Dick Bentley Productions *v* Harold Smith Motors Ltd (1965) *40, 41, 43, 45, 60, 74, 467*

Dickinson *v* Dodds (1875–76) L.R. 2 Ch. D. 463, CA *11, 13, 14, 34*

Dimmock *v* Hallett (1866) *73*

DPP *v* A (2000) *211*

DPP *v* Bedder (1954) *161, 163*

DPP *v* Bell (1992) *322*

DPP *v* Blake (1993) *307, 314, 450*

DPP *v* K (1990) *201, 202, 214*

DPP *v* Morgan (1976) *246, 247, 248*

DPP *v* Ray (1974) *292, 293, 294, 296, 299, 313*

DPP *v* Smith (Jim) (1960) *144, 151, 152, 155, 156, 254, 474*

Donachie *v* Chief Constable of Greater Manchester (2004) *355*

Donoghue *v* Stevenson (1932) *333, 337, 338, 339, 340, 342, 343, 345, 372, 373, 374, 387,*

413, 434, 451, 452, 459, 461, 483, 487, 490, 493, 497

Douglas v Hello (2005)   471, 486

Doyle v Olby (Ironmongers) (1969)   78

Dudley v Stephens (1884)   318

Dulieu v White (1901)   353, 355, 359

Dunlop Pneumatic Tyre Co Ltd v Selfridge & Co Ltd (1915)   21

Dunnachie v Hull CC (2004)   113, 116, 119, 487, 490

Duport Steels Ltd v Sirs (1980)   484, 488

Edginton v Fitzmaurice (1885)   72, 74

Edwards v Ddin (1976)   266

Edwards v Skyways Ltd (1964)   31, 34

Elliott v C (a Minor) (1983)   146, 310, 495

Entores Ltd v Miles Far East Corp (1955)   17, 20

Erlanger v New Sombrero (1878)   77

Errington v Errington and Woods (1952)   12

Esso Petroleum v Marden (1976)   76, 345, 350

Fagan v Metropolitan Police Commissioner (1969)   129, 131, 132, 146, 155, 201, 214, 277, 503

Fairchild v Glenhaven Funeral Services Ltd (2002)   366, 367, 373

Fardon v Harcourt-Rivington (1932)   361

Farley v Skinner (2001)   109, 114, 119

Faulkner v Talbot (1981)   200

Felthouse v Bindley (1862)   17, 20

Fibrosa Spolka Akcyjna v Fairbairn Lawson Combe Barbour Ltd (1943)   99, 119

Fisher v Bell (1961)   6, 8, 13, 34, 487, 490, 497 502

Foakes v Beer (1883–84)   27, 34, 35

Froom v Butcher (1976)   424, 425, 429, 436

FW Moore & Co Ltd v Landauer & Co (1921)   89

Gabriel v Kirklees Metropolitan Council (2004)   369, 370

Gannon v Rotherham MBC (1991)   425, 426, 429, 436, 479

Gemmell and Richards (2003)   145, 146, 154, 156, 186, 308, 311, 312, 313, 314, 459, 460, 469, 474, 486, 490

General Cleaning Contractors v Christmas (1953)   379, 392

George Mitchell (Chesterhall) Ltd v Finney Lock Seeds Ltd (1983)   55

George Wimpey UK Ltd v V I Construction Ltd (2005)   68, 70

Gibbins and Proctor (1918)   148, 156, 450

Giles v Walker (1890)   408

Gillick v West Norfolk and Wisbech AHA (1986)   445

Gillingham Borough Council v Medway Docks (1993)   403

Glasbrook Bros Ltd v Glamorgan CC (1925)   25

Glasgow Corporation v Taylor (1922)   377, 378, 381, 385, 386, 391, 392

Godley v Perry (1960)   42, 43, 60, 479

Goldman v Hargrave (1967)   401, 403

Gorringe v Calderdale MBC (2004)   341

Grant v Australian Knitting Mills (1936)   497

Great Peace Shipping Ltd v Tsavliris Salvage (International) Ltd (2002)   65, 70, 71, 81, 82, 83, 487

Greatorex v Greatorex (2000)   356, 374, 451

Gregg v Scott (2005)   367, 374

Gwilliam v West Hertfordshire Hospitals NHS Trust (2002)   380

Hadley v Baxendale (1854)   110, 111, 113, 116, 118, 121, 478

Hale v Jennings (1938)   410, 412

Hall v Lorimer (1994)   416

Hallam and Blackburn (1995)   267

Hambrook v Stokes (1925)   353, 354

Hardman v Chief Constable of Avon Somerset Constabulary (1986)   306, 313, 314

Harlingdon & Leinster Enterprises Ltd v Christopher Hull Fine Art (1990)   42, 59

Harris v Sheffield United Football Club (1988)   25

Harrow LBC v Shah (1999)   476

Hartley v Ponsonby (1857)   25

Harvey v Facey (1893)   8, 10

Haseldine v Daw (1941)   380, 391, 393

Haughton v Smith [1975]   502

Haynes v Harwood (1935)   427

Hedley Byrne v Heller (1964)   76, 345, 346, 347, 350, 372, 374, 434

Henderson v Merrett Syndicates (1995)   344, 347, 348

Herne Bay Steamboat Co v Hutton   95, 96, 118

Heydon's Case (1584)   *502*

Hibbert *v* Mc Kiernan (1948)   *266*

Hill *v* Baxter (1958)   *234, 494*

Hill *v* Chief Constable for West Yorkshire (1988)   *340, 342, 461, 468, 489*

Hochster *v* De la Tour (1853)   *104, 108, 118, 467*

Holbeck Hall Hotel *v* Scarborough Borough Council (2001)   *402*

Hollier *v* Rambler Motors Ltd (1972)   *53, 56*

Holwell Securities Ltd *v* Hughes (1974)   *18, 20*

Hong Kong Fir Shipping Co Ltd *v* Kawasaki Kisen Kaisha Ltd (1962)   *47, 48, 49, 50, 58, 59, 60, 106, 108, 460, 467*

Hönig *v* Isaacs (1952)   *89, 90, 91*

Household Fire & Carriage Accident Insurance Co Ltd *v* Grant (1878–79)   *18, 479*

Howard Marine and Dredging Ltd *v* Ogden & Sons Ltd (1978)   *76, 477*

Hudson *v* Taylor (1971)   *320*

Hughes *v* Lord Advocate (1963)   *368, 369, 371, 373*

Hunter *v* Canary Wharf (1997)   *398, 401, 402, 421, 468*

Hyam *v* DPP (1975)   *141, 142, 144*

Hyde *v* Wrench (1840)   *10, 13, 15, 20, 34*

Inco Europe Ltd *v* First Choice Distribution [2000]   *502*

Ingram *v* Little (1961)   *67, 68, 83, 467*

Interfoto *v* Stiletto Visual Programmes Ltd (1988)   *52*

JEB Fasteners Ltd *v* Mark Bloom (1983)   *346, 347, 350*

J Lauritzen AS *v* Wijsmuller BV (*The Super Servant Two*) (1990)   *97, 11, 478*

Jackson *v* Horizon Holidays (1975)   *113*

Jackson *v* Royal Bank of Scotland (2005)   *109, 111, 112, 114, 116*

Jaggard *v* Dickenson (1981)   *246, 248, 307, 308, 314, 316*

Jarvis *v* Swan Tours (1973)   *113*

Jolley *v* Sutton LBC (2000)   *366, 369, 370, 371, 378, 382, 383, 386, 391, 392, 438*

Jones *v* Gallagher (2005)   *114*

Jones *v* Livox Quarries (1952)   *424, 429, 435*

Junior Books *v* Veitchi (1983)   *349*

Kennaway *v* Thompson (1981)   *431, 432*

Khorasandjan *v* Bush (1993)   *401, 402*

King *v* Phillips (1952)   *353, 354*

King's Norton Metal Co *v* Eldridge Merrett & Co (1897)   *67, 68*

Knuller *v* DPP (1973)   *448*

Krell *v* Henry (1903)   *95, 96, 117, 118*

LMS International Ltd *v* Styrene Packaging & Insulation Ltd (2005)   *409*

L'Estrange *v* Graucob (1934)   *52, 56*

Lampleigh *v* Braithwaite (1615) Hob. 105   *22, 23*

Latimer *v* AEC (1952)   *363, 373, 374, 468*

Leaf *v* International Galleries (1950)   *64, 65, 77, 82*

Leakey *v* National Trust (1980)   *402, 403*

Leicester *v* Pearson (1952)   *128, 131, 474*

Lewis *v* Averay (No. 1) (1972)   *66, 67, 75, 77, 83, 467*

Limpus *v* London General Omnibus Company (1862)   *417*

Lister *v* Helsey Hall (2001)   *414, 417, 418, 419, 421, 422, 437, 473, 480, 488*

Liverpool City Council *v* Irwin (1977)   *44, 45*

Lloyd's Bank *v* Waterhouse (1990)   *69, 83*

London and Northern Bank *ex p.* Jones, *re* (1900)   *18*

London Street Tramways Co *v* LCC [1898]   *503*

Lynch *v* DPP for N Ireland (1975)   *497*

McArdle, *re* (1951) Ch. 669; (1951)   *22, 28, 34, 35*

McCrae *v* Commonwealth Disposals Commission (1951)   *63, 64, 65, 82, 83*

McDonnell *v* Holwerda (2005)   *364*

McFarlane *v* Caledonia Ltd (1993)   *356*

McKinnon Industries *v* Walker (1951)   *400*

McLoughlin *v* O'Brien (1982)   *353, 356, 357, 358, 359, 434, 438, 487, 489*

McNaghton's Case *see* R *v* McNaughten

McNicholl *v* Ministry of Agriculture [1988]   *502*

Maguire *v* Harland & Wolff Plc (2005)   *362, 365, 373*

Malnik *v* DPP (1989)   *243*

Malone *v* Laskey (1907)   *400, 401*

Marcic *v* Thames Water Utilities Ltd (2003)   *403*

Mason *v* Levy Autoparts (1967)   *408*

Mattis v Pollock (2003) *418*
Meade and Belt (1823) *198*
Meah v Roberts (1977) *476*
Meli v Queen, The (1954) *146, 183*
Merritt v Merritt (1970) *30, 31, 34, 120, 459, 487, 490*
Mersey Docks Harbour Board v Coggins and Griffiths (Liverpool) Ltd (1947) *416*
Metropolitan Water Board v Dick Kerr & Co Ltd (1918) *98*
Miller v Jackson (1977) *399, 400, 404, 405, 406, 430, 431, 436, 461, 463, 464, 468, 470, 472*
Ministry of Sound (Ireland) Ltd v World Online Ltd (2003) *105*
Misa v Currie (1875–76) *21*
Mock v Pensions Ombudsman (2000) *502*
Moore & Co and Landauer & Co, *re see* FW Moore & Co Ltd v Landauer & Co
Morphitis v Salmon (1990) *306*
Morris v Murray (1990) *427, 429*
MPC v Caldwell *see* R v Caldwell (James) (1982) *310, 495*
MPC v Charles *see* Commissioner of Police of the Metropolis v Charles (Derek Michael)
Mullin v Richards (1998) *363, 372, 478*
Murphy v Brentwood BC (1990) *338, 349, 350, 351*
Mutual Life and Citizen's Assurance Co v Evatt (1971) *345, 350*

Nelson Group Services Ltd v BG Plc (2002) *74*
Nettleship v Weston (1971) *363, 364, 372, 373, 374, 461, 478, 504*
Network Rail v Morris (2004) *398, 400, 421*
New Zealand Shipping Co Ltd v AM Satterthwaite & Co Ltd (*The Eurymedon*) (1975) *26*

Nichols v Marsland (1976) *412, 422*
Norfolk Constabulary v Seekings and Gould (1986) *283*
North Glamorgan NHST v Walters (2003) *358*

Ogwa v Taylor (1988) *379, 381, 382, 392*
Olley v Marlborough Court Hotel (1949) *52, 56, 57*
Orange v CC of West Yorkshire Police (2001) *341*

Oscar Chess Ltd v Williams (1957) *40, 45, 60, 72, 74, 460, 467*
Overseas Tankship (UK) Ltd v Morts Dock & Engineering Co (*The Wagon Mound*) (1961) *368, 369, 370, 373, 378, 391, 403, 405, 411, 420, 430, 434, 437, 438, 479*
Oxford v Moss (1978) *265*

Page One Records v Britton (1968) *115*
Page v Smith (1995) *352, 354, 355, 356, 359, 360, 438*
Pao On v Lau Yiu Long (1980) *23, 28, 34*
Paradine v Jane (1647) *94, 119*
Paris v Stepney BC (1951) *362, 363, 372*
Partridge v Crittenden (1968) *7*
Payne v Cave (1789) *9*
Peekay Intermark Ltd v Australia and New Zealand Banking Group Ltd (2005) *75*
Pepper (Inspector of Taxes) v Hart (1993) *485, 490*
Pharmaceutical Society of Great Britain v Boots Cash Chemists (Southern) Ltd (1952) *7, 502*
Phelps v Hillingdon BC (2001) *348, 351, 414*
Phillips v Brooks Ltd (1919) *66, 67, 68, 70, 77, 81, 115, 460, 477*
Phipps v Rochester Corporation (1955) *376, 378, 386, 391, 392, 393*
Pickfords Ltd v Celestica Ltd (2003) *10, 11, 13, 34*
Pilbrow v Pearless de Rougemont & Co (1999) *103, 107, 108, 118*
Pinnell's Case (1602) *21, 26, 27, 28, 35, 88*
Planché v Colbourn (1831) *90, 92, 115, 117, 504*
Polemis, *re* (1921) *368*
Pollock & Co v MacRae (1922) *53, 56*
Poussard v Spiers and Pond (1876) *47, 49, 58, 86, 106, 108, 118*
Powell v Lee (1908) *17*
Practice Statement (HL: Judicial Precedent) (1966) *145, 308, 459, 460, 469, 485, 486, 487, 490*
Pretty v United Kingdom (2002), ECHR *129*
Production Technology Consultants v Bartlett (1988) *77*

Qualcast Ltd v Haynes [1959] *503*
Quintavelle v Human Fertilisation and Embryology Authority (2005) *449, 453, 485*

R v A (a minor) (1978)   306
R v Abdul-Hussain (1999)   320, 323
R v Acott (1997)   158, 159, 166, 172, 254
R v Adomako (1994)   184, 185, 186, 187, 188, 189, 190, 191, 193, 254, 474, 495
R v Ahluwalia (1992)   160, 168, 173
R v Aitken (1992)   224, 225, 450
R v Allen (1872)   490
R v Allen (1985)   303, 304, 313, 314
R v Allen (1988)   237
R v Aziz (1993)   302, 304
R v Bailey (1983)   234, 235, 241
R v Bailey (2002)   167, 168, 173, 175
R v Baillie (1995)   160
R v Barnes (2004)   223, 227, 252
R v Beard (1920)   237
R v Beckford (1988)   496
R v Billingshurst (1978)   223, 226
R v Bilton (2005)   230, 252
R v Blaue (Robert Konrad) (1975)   133, 134, 137, 150, 154, 155, 156, 466, 495
R v Bowen (1996)   321, 328
R v Briggs (2004)   263
R v Brooks (Edward George); R. v Brooks (Julie Ann) (1983)   301, 304
R v Brown (1985)   282
R v Brown (1993)   498
R v Brown (1994)   209, 217, 222, 224, 225, 226, 227, 251, 252, 448, 449, 450, 453, 460, 466, 485, 486, 488, 492
R v Burgess (1991)   230, 231, 252
R v Byrne (1960)   165, 166, 169, 172
R v Cahill (1993)   274
R v Caldwell (James) (1982)   145, 146, 185, 186, 308, 310, 459, 474, 495
R v Campbell (1987)   167
R v Camplin (1978)   161, 162, 163, 486
R v Cato (Ronald Philip) (1976)   181, 183
R v Chan Fook (1994)   205, 207, 215
R v Cheshire (David William) (1991)   134, 135, 137, 150, 152, 154, 155, 254
R v Church (1967)   178, 179, 183, 191, 193
R v Clarence (1888)   209, 210, 224, 225
R v Clarke (1927)   7
R v Clarke (1972)   229
R v Clouden (1987)   278, 279, 288, 289, 330
R v Cocker (1989)   160, 173
R v Codere (1916)   232
R v Collins (1972)   282, 284, 285, 288

R v Collis-Smith (1971)   293, 299, 313
R v Coney (1882)   223
R v Constanza (1997)   198
R v Conway (1988)   321, 324
R v Cooke (1997)   296, 314
R v Corbett (Christopher) (1996)   136, 150
R v Courtie (1984)   203
R v Cox (1992)   149
R v Cunningham (Anthony Barry) (1981)   152
R v Cunningham (Roy) (1957)   145, 146, 147, 152, 154, 156, 200, 211, 279, 474, 495
R v Dalby (1982)   181, 183
R v Dawson (1985)   179, 180
R v Denton (1982)   310
R v Derek   254
R v Dias (2002)   181, 182, 193
R v Dica (2004)   209, 210, 215, 225, 227, 250, 251, 252
R v Dietschmann (2003)   166, 167, 169, 173
R v Doughty (1986)   159, 254
R (on the application of Pretty) v DPP (2002), HL 129
R v Duffy (1949)   159, 166, 254
R v Dytham (Philip Thomas) (1979)   130
R v Feely (1971)   269
R v Fenton (1975)   166, 167
R v Firth (1990)   298, 299
R v Galasso (1993)   262
R v Ghosh (1982)   270, 271, 272, 273, 274, 275, 288, 289, 294, 295, 296, 299, 303, 304, 313, 329, 330
R v Gibson (1991)   449, 450
R v Gill (1963)   320
R v Gittens (1984)   166, 167
R v Goldman (1997)   293, 295, 296, 299
R v Gomez (1993)   262, 263, 268, 278, 288, 330
R v Gotts (1992)   318, 324, 325, 327
R v Graham (1982)   319, 320, 321, 324, 325, 327
R v Halai (1983)   296, 299, 313
R v Hale (1979)   277, 279, 280, 288, 330
R v Hall (1973)   267
R v Hancock (Reginald Dean); R. v Shankland (Russell) (1986)   141, 144, 178, 179, 181, 193
R v Hardie (1984)   234, 236, 238, 241
R v Hasan (2005)   319, 320, 321, 322, 323, 324, 325, 326, 327, 328
R v Hatton (2005)   247
R v Haystead (2000)   201, 215

R v Hennessy (1989)   230, 241

R v Hinks (1998)   260, 263, 268, 330

R v Holt (Victor Reginald); R v Lee (Julian Dana) (1981)   298, 313

R v Howe (1987)   318, 324, 325, 328, 497

R v Humphries (1995)   160, 161

R v Husseyn (1977)   286

R v Ireland (Robert Matthew); R. v Burstow (Anthony Christopher) (1997)   197, 198, 199, 202, 203, 204, 205, 207, 208, 210, 213, 214, 215, 217

R v Jackson (1983)   297

R v Jones (1988)   224, 225, 252

R v Jones (John); R. v Smith (Christopher) (1976)   281, 284, 288

R v Jordan (1956)   497

R v K (2001)   247, 248, 250

R v Kelly (1998)   264

R v Kemp (1957)   230

R v Kennedy (1999)   181

R v Kennedy (2005)   182, 183, 191, 193, 459

R v Khan (Rungzabe); R. v Khan (Tahir) (1998)   178, 181, 182, 185, 187, 188, 189, 190, 191, 193, 254

R v Kingston (1994)   237, 238, 241, 250, 251, 252, 327

R v Laing (1995)   284

R v Lamb (1967)   178, 191

R v Lambie (1981)   293

R v Larsonneur (1983)   131, 156

R v Latimer (1886)   146, 147

R v Lavender (1994)   273

R v Lawrence (1971)   261, 262, 263, 268, 289

R v Leach (1969)   221, 226

R v Lidar (2000)   185, 190

R v Lipman (1970)   233, 234, 237, 238, 241

R v Lloyd (1967)   167, 169, 172

R v Lloyd (1985)   273, 274, 330

R v Lockley (1995)   277

R v Luc Thiet Thuan (1996)   161, 162, 163

R v Madeley (1990)   140, 229, 269, 474

R v Majewski (1977)   238, 239, 240, 241, 250, 251, 252, 327, 330, 475

R v Marshall (1998)   265, 273

R v Martin (1988)   322, 328

R v Martin (2001)   168, 244, 247, 248, 250, 252

R v Matthews (Darren John): R. v Alleyne (Brian Dean) (2003)   143, 144, 152

R v Mazo (1996)   262, 263

R v McDavitt (1981)   302, 303, 313

R v McInnes (1971)   243

R v Mellor (Gavin Thomas) (1996)   135

R v Miao (2003)   159

R v Miller (1954)   205, 207, 215

R v Miller (James) (1983)   131, 494

R v Misra (2004)   186, 188, 189, 190, 191, 254, 44

R v M'Naughten (1843)   229, 252, 496

R v Moloney (Alistair Baden) (1985)   141, 144

R v Morhall (1995)   161, 162, 163, 173

R v Morris (1984)   261, 262, 263, 268, 289

R v Mowatt (1968)   211, 213, 214, 217, 252

R v Nedrick (Ransford Delroy) (1986)   139, 142, 143, 144, 147, 151, 152, 153, 154, 156, 179, 181, 182

R v Newell (1980)   158, 161

R v O'Grady (1987)   240, 247, 248, 252, 466

R v Pagett (David Keith) (1983)   135, 150, 151, 152, 153, 179, 180, 181, 503

R v Palmer (1971)   242, 244, 249

R v Pearson (1992)   159

R v Pittwood (1902)   128, 129, 156, 187, 474

R v Pommell (1995)   322

R v Preddy (1996)   294, 295, 296, 313

R v Prince (1875)   495

R v Quayle (2005)   317, 319, 323, 325, 326, 327, 328

R v Quick (1973)   230, 231, 234, 235

R v R (1991)   443, 446, 447, 461, 483, 486, 488, 496, 498

R v Rai (2000)   293

R v Registrar General, ex p. Smith (1990)   498

R v Richardson (1999)   224, 225, 226

R v Rimmington (Anthony); R. v Goldstein (Harry Chaim) (2005)   397, 406, 420, 422, 478, 487

R v Roberts (David) (1971)   134, 136, 150, 152, 154, 155, 199, 204, 205, 206, 207, 214, 217

R v Robinson (1977)   276, 279

R v Rogers (2003)   181, 193

R v Rossiter (1992)   159

R v Ryan (1996)   282, 289

R v Safi (2003)   323, 324

R v Salisbury (1976)   209, 210

R v Saunders (1985)   151, 156, 210, 213

R v Savage (1991)   200, 203, 204, 206, 207, 210, 212, 214, 217

R v Savage (Susan); R. v Parmenter (Philip Mark) (No.1) (1992)   200, 206, 210, 211, 212, 213, 214, 215, 252
R v Seymour (1983)   185
R v Sharp (1987)   321, 322, 324, 327
R v Shayler (2001)   317, 320
R v Shepherd (1987)   321, 322
R v Shivpuri (1987)   503
R v Sibartie (1983)   298, 313
R v Small (1987)   246, 270, 274, 289
R v Smith (1961)   210, 211, 213, 215
R v Smith (1974)   306
R v Smith (Morgan James) (2000)   161, 162, 164, 173, 175, 486
R v Smith (Unlawful wounding) (1959)   134, 135, 148, 150, 495, 497
R v Sofrinou (2003)   296
R v Staines (1974)   293
R v Steer (1987)   309
R v Stone (John Edward); R. v Dobinson (Gwendoline) (1977)   130, 148, 155, 156, 181, 185, 187, 188, 254, 450
R v Sullivan (1984)   230, 231, 251, 252
R v Sutcliffe (1981)   168, 173, 175
R v Tandy (1989)   167
R v Thomas (1985)   196, 200, 202
R v Thornton (1992)   159, 160, 168, 169, 172, 173, 175, 466
R v Thornton (1996)   160, 161, 168, 169, 172, 173, 175
R v Tolson (1889)   246, 247
R v Turner (1971)   266, 329
R v Turner (1974)   297, 314
R v Valderrama-Vega (1985)   319
R v Velumyl (1989)   273, 274
R v Wacker (2003)   187, 190, 191
R v Walker (John Charles); R. v Hayles (William) (1990)   143, 144
R v Walkington (1979)   283, 284
R v Watson (1989)   179, 475
R v West (1999)   276, 278
R v White (1910)   134, 150, 152, 154, 254, 495
R v Williams (2005)   223
R v Williams (Barry Anthony); R. v Davis (Frank O'Neill) (1992)   136
R v Williams (Gladstone) (1987)   244, 246, 247, 248, 251, 324, 327
R v Willoughby (2004)   184, 187, 188, 192
R v Wilson (1955)   198, 202, 215

R v Wilson (1984)   209, 210, 217
R v Wilson (1996)   224, 226, 449, 450, 466
R v Windle (1952)   228, 232
R v Woodman (1974)   266, 288
R v Woollin (Stephen Leslie) (1998)   139, 142, 143, 144, 147, 151, 154
Raffles v Wichelhaus (1864)   *66, 70, 81*
Ramsgate Victoria Hotel Co Ltd v Montefiore (1865–66)   *12, 13*
Ratcliff v McConnell (1999)   *387, 390, 428*
Read v Lyons (1947)   *408, 410*
Ready Mixed Concrete v Minister of Pensions (1968)   *416, 418, 421*
Reardon Smith Line Ltd v Hansentangen (1976)   *87, 89*
Rees v Skerrett (2001)   *402*
Reeves v MPC (1999)   *340, 341, 342, 368, 370, 428, 436*
Rickards v Lothian (1913)   *408, 412*
Robinson v Kilvert (1889)   *400, 406*
Rodger v Rose (1998)   *323*
Roe v Kingerlee (1986)   *306*
Roe v Ministry of Health (1954)   *361, 362, 372*
Roles v Nathan (1963)   *379, 383, 391, 437*
Rose v Plenty (1976)   *417*
Ross Smyth and Co Ltd v Bailey, Son & Co (1940)   *103, 106*
Ross v Caunters (1980)   *347*
Routledge v Grant (1828)   *11, 28*
Routledge v MacKay (1954)   *40, 45, 72*
Rowland v Divall (1923)   *42, 58, 60*
Royscott Trust v Rogerson (1991)   *78*
Ruxley Electronics and Construction Ltd v Forsyth (1995)   *103, 107, 108, 114*
Rylands v Fletcher   *333, 336, 395, 396, 403, 404, 407, 408, 409, 410, 411, 412, 413, 420, 421, 422, 423, 435 461, 479, 480, 482, 487*

Samuel v Stubbs (1972)   *305*
Sandhar v Department of Transport (2004)   *341, 468*
Saunders v Anglia Building Society (1971)   *69, 70*
Sayers v Harlow UDC (1958)   *425, 429*
Schawel v Reade (1913)   *40*
Scotson v Pegg (1861)   *26*
Scott v Shepherd (1773)   *201, 503*
Scutts v Keyse (2001)   *425*
Sedleigh Denfield v O'Callaghan (1940)   *401, 402, 421*

Selectmove, *re* (1994)   *27*

Shanklin Pier Ltd *v* Detel Products Ltd (1951)
9

Shaw *v* DPP (1961)   *448*

Shelfer *v* City of London Electric Lighting Co
(1985)   *404, 406, 432, 436*

Shirlaw *v* Southern Foundries Ltd (1939)   *44,
45*

Shogun Finance Ltd *v* Hudson (2003)   *62, 67,
68, 70, 71, 81, 82, 83*

Shuey *v* US (1875)   *12*

Sigsworth, *re*   *484*

Simpkins *v* Pays (1955)   *30*

Smith *v* Baker (1891)   *426, 429, 435, 436, 461*

Smith *v* Bush (1990)   *55, 346, 350, 351*

Smith *v* Chief Superintendant of Woking Police
Station (1983)   *198, 199*

Smith *v* Hughes (1960)   *490*

Smith *v* Leech Brain (1962)   *370, 372, 374*

Smith *v* Littlewoods (1987)   *368*

Smith *v* Manchester Corporation (1974)
430

Solle *v* Butcher (1950)   *64, 65, 487*

Southwark London Borough *v* Williams (1971)
317, 318

Spartan Steel and Alloys Ltd *v* Martin & Co
(1973)   *349, 351*

Spicer *v* Smee (1946)   *399*

Spring *v* Guardian Assurance plc (1993)   *346*

Spring *v* National Amalgamated Stevedores
(1956)   *44, 351*

Spurling *v* Bradshaw (1956)   *43, 45, 51, 52, 53,
56*

St Helen's Smelting Co *v* Tipping
(1865)   *399*

Staples *v* West Dorset CC (1995)   *381*

Startup *v* Macdonald (1843)   *90, 93*

Stevens *v* Gourley (1859)   *283*

Stevenson Jaques & Co *v* McLean (1879–80)
10, 11, 16

Stilk *v* Myrick (1809)   *25, 26, 28, 34, 487*

Stone and Dobinson *see* R *v* Stone (John
Edward); R *v* Dobinson (Gwendoline)

Sturges *v* Bridgman (1879)   *399, 404, 406, 421,
422*

Sumpter *v* Hedges (1898)   *89, 90*

Super Servant II, The see J Lauritzen AS *v*
Wijsmuller BV (*The Super Servant Two*)

Sutherland Shire County *v* Heyman (1985)
338, 343

Sweet *v* Parsley   *460, 476*

Taylor *v* Caldwell (1863)   *94, 95, 96, 119, 480,
486, 487*

Taylorson *v* Shieldness (1994)   *357*

Tetley *v* Chitty (1986)   *401, 402, 404, 405, 431,
432*

The Alaskan Trader see Clea Shipping Corp *v* Bulk
Oil International

The Eurymedon see New Zealand Shipping Co Ltd
v AM Satterthwaite & Co Ltd

The Moorcock (1889)   *43, 45, 58, 60, 450, 460,
467, 487*

The Wagon Mound see Overseas Tankship (UK)
Ltd *v* Morts Dock & Engineering Co

Thomas *v* Thomas (1842)   *23, 34*

Thornton *v* Shoe Lane Parking (1971)   *52*

Tomlinson *v* Congleton Borough Council (2003)
385, 387, 388, 389, 390, 391, 392, 393

Transco Plc *v* Stockport BC (2004)   *409, 410,
411, 412, 413, 421, 480, 488*

Trollope & Colls Ltd *v* NW Metropolitan RHB
(1973)   *39, 44*

Trotman *v* North Yorkshire CC (1999)   *417,
418, 488*

Troughton *v* MPC (1987)   *302, 304*

Tsakiroglou & Co Ltd *v* Noblee & Thorl GmbH
(1962)   *96, 97*

Turbeville *v* Savage (1669)   *199, 214*

Tweddle *v* Atkinson (1861)   *24, 28, 34*

Twine *v* Bean's Express (1946)   *417, 421*

Ultramares *v* Touche (1931)   *344*

Union Eagle Limited *v* Golden Achievement Ltd
(1997)   *49, 50, 59*

Vellino *v* CC of Greater Manchester (2001)   *341*

Vernon *v* Bosley (1997)   *358*

Viasystems (Tyneside) Ltd *v* Thermal Transfer
(Northern) Ltd (2005)   *416, 421, 422*

Victoria Laundry Ltd *v* Newman Industries Ltd
(1949)   *111, 118*

Vowles *v* Evans (2002)   *364*

Vowles *v* Evans (2003)   *342*

Walker *v* Boyle (1982)   *79*

Watkin *v* Watson-Smith (1986)   *115, 118, 460*

Watson *v* British Boxing Board (2000) *342*

Watt *v* Hertfordshire CC (1954) *362, 373, 374, 468*

Watts *v* Morris (1991) *114, 226*

Wheat *v* Lacon (1966) *377, 383*

Wheeler *v* Saunders (1995) *403*

White and Carter *v* McGregor (1962) *104, 105, 107, 108, 113, 118, 119*

White *v* CC of South Yorkshire (1999) *355, 356, 359, 374*

White *v* Jones (1995) *347, 348, 350, 351, 374, 434, 438, 451*

Wickman Machine Tools Sales Ltd *v* Schuler AG (1973) *48, 50*

Williams *v* Roffey Bros & Nicholls (Contractors) Ltd (1990) *25, 26, 27, 28, 34, 35, 467, 487*

Winzar *v* Chief Constable of Kent (1983) *131, 155, 156, 474, 494, 496*

With *v* O'Flanagan (1936) *73*

Wood and Hodgson (2003) *187, 190, 191*

Woodar Investment Development *v* Wimpey Construction (UK) Ltd (1980) *106, 108*

Woodward *v* Mayor of Hastings (1945) *380, 391, 414, 421*

Woolridge *v* Sumner (1963) *427, 428, 435, 436*

Yachuk *v* Oliver Blais Ltd (1949) *425, 426, 429, 438*

Yates (1982) *51*

Yates Building Co Ltd *v* RJ Pulleyn & Sons (York) Ltd (1975) *18*

Young *v* Bristol Aeroplane (1944) *497, 503*

Table of statutes and statutory instruments

Statutes

Access to Justice Act 1999 *459*
Adoption Act 1976
  s.51 *498*
Anti-social Behaviour Act 2003 *396*

Children Act 2004 *223, 451*
Children and Young Persons Act 1933 *220*
Civil Partnership Act 2004 *451*
Consumer Protection Act 1987 *3, 413,*
  480, 493
Contracts (Rights of Third Parties) Act 1999
  24
Countryside and Rights of Way Act 2000
  385
Crime and Disorder Act 1998 *220*
Crime (Sentences) Act 1997 *496*
Criminal Damage Act 1971 *131*
  s.1 *305, 312*
  s.1(1) *305, 309, 310*
  s.1(2) *305, 309, 310, 311*
  s.1(2)(a) *309*
  s.1(2)(b) *309*
  s.1(3) *305, 309, 310, 311*
  s.5 *311*
  s.5(2) *226, 246, 314, 316*
  s.5(2)(a) *307, 311*
  s.5(2)(b) *307, 318*
  s.10(1) *306*
Criminal Justice Act 1967 *239*
  s.8 *140, 141, 144*
Criminal Justice Act 1988
  s.39 *196, 197*
Criminal Law Act 1967
  s.3 *243*
  s.3(1) *242*
Criminal Procedure (Insanity) Act 1964 *228*
Criminal Procedure (Insanity and Unfitness to
  Plead) Act 1991 *228, 232*
  s.1 *229*

Dangerous Dogs Act 1991 *498*

Education Act 1996 *223*
European Communities Act 1972
  s.3(1) *503*

Homicide Act 1957 *174, 232, 233, 475, 486,*
  496
  s.2 *157, 158, 165, 166, 169*
  s.2(1) *165*
  s.2(3) *168*
  s.3 *157, 158, 159, 160, 164, 254*
  s.4 *157, 170, 171, 173*
  s.4(1) *170*
  s.4(2) *170*
  s.4(3) *170*
Human Fertilisation and Embryology Act 1990
  446, 449
Human Rights Act (1998) *308, 455, 457, 469,*
  472, 486
  s.2 *503*

Law Reform (Contributory Negligence) Act 1945
  424, 435, 436
  s.1(1) *425, 429*
Law Reform (Frustrated Contracts) Act 1943
  119
  s.1(1) *100*
  s.1(2) *99, 100, 101, 102, 117*
  s.1(3) *100, 101, 102, 117*
Licensing Act 2003 *471*

Misrepresentation Act 1967 *75, 121, 477*
  s.2(1) *76, 78, 79, 81*
  s.2(2) *76, 77, 78, 79, 81*
  s.3 *79*

Occupiers Liability Act 1957 *375, 378, 385,*
  386, 387, 388, 390, 434, 478
  s.1(1) *376, 382*

s.2   *376*
s.2(1)   *380, 382, 391*
s.2(2)   *376, 385, 386, 391*
s.2(3)   *383, 391*
s.2(3)(a)   *377, 383, 391, 437, 438*
s.2(3)(b)   *379, 380, 383, 437*
s.2(4)(a)   *381, 383, 391*
s.2(4)(b)   *379, 380, 421*
s.2(5)   *383, 391*
Occupiers Liability Act 1984   *375, 378, 381,*
   382, 385, 390, 392, 393, 434, 437, 438, 461,
   487
s.1(3)   *386, 387, 388, 389, 391*
s.1(4)   *389*
s.1(5)   *387, 389, 391*
s.1(6)   *388, 391*
Offences against the Person Act 1861   *485, 486,*
   498
s.18   *195, 208, 209, 210, 211, 212, 213, 214,*
   215, 216, 221, 227, 238, 253
s.20   *195, 208, 209, 210, 211, 212, 213, 214,*
   215, 216, 217, 222, 224, 225, 227, 238, 253
s.23   *182*
s.47   *195, 199, 203, 204, 205, 206, 209,*
   210, 211, 212, 213, 214, 216, 217, 222,
   227, 253
Official Secrets Act 1989   *317*

Pharmacy and Poisons Act 1933   *8*
Protection from Harassment Act 1997   *401*

Road Traffic Act 1988   *130*
s.4(2)   *502*
s.149   *427*

Sale and Supply of Goods Act 1994   *41, 42*
Sale of Goods Act 1979   *3, 44, 450*
s.6   *63*
ss.12–15   *45*
s.12   *41, 42, 43, 58*
s.13   *41, 42, 43, 58*
s.14   *41, 42, 43, 54, 58, 479*
s.15   *41, 42, 43*
Sexual Offences Act 1967   *448*
Suicide Act 1961
s.2   *171, 173*

Theft Act 1968   *240*
s.1   *260, 263, 264, 268, 288, 292*

s.1(1)   *260, 269*
s.1(2)   *264, 272*
s.2   *226, 260, 261, 268, 270, 272, 274, 275,*
   279, 280, 288, 289, 292
s.2(1)   *272, 276, 279*
s.2(1)(a)   *269, 270, 272, 273*
s.2(1)(b)   *269, 270, 272, 273, 275*
s.2(1)(c)   *270, 272, 273, 329*
s.2(2)   *272*
s.3   *260, 261, 264, 268, 275, 288*
s.3(1)   *261, 264*
s.4   *260, 261, 264, 268, 275, 288*
s.4(1)   *260, 264, 265*
s.4(3)   *265*
s.4(4)   *265*
s.5   *260, 261, 266, 268, 275, 288*
s.5(1)   *265*
s.5(3)   *266, 267*
s.5(4)   *267*
s.6   *260, 261, 268, 273, 274, 275, 288, 329*
s.6(1)   *273*
s.8   *276, 288, 330*
s.8(1)   *276, 277*
s.9   *283*
s.9(1)   *281*
s.9(1)(a)   *281, 282, 285, 286, 287, 288*
s.9(1)(b)   *281, 285, 287, 288, 315*
s.9(2)   *281*
s.9(4)   *283*
s.15   *261, 292, 295, 296, 299, 300, 312,*
   330
s.15(1)   *294*
s.15(4)   *292*
s.15A   *295, 300*
s.16   *291*
Theft Act 1978   *291, 299, 308*
s.1   *296, 300, 312*
s.1(1)   *295*
s.1(2)   *295*
s.1(3)   *296*
s.2   *293, 296, 297, 312, 313*
s.2(1)   *297*
s.2(1)(a)   *297, 300*
s.2(1)(b)   *297, 298, 300, 312, 314, 329*
s.2(1)(c)   *297, 298, 300, 312*
s.2(3)   *298*
s.3   *266, 293, 296, 301, 302, 303, 304, 312,*
   314, 330
Theft (Amendment) Act 1996   *295, 296, 313*

Unfair Contracts Terms Act 1977   *346, 382, 383, 391, 392, 460*
  s.2(1)   *54, 56*
  s.2(2)   *54, 56*
  s.3   *55*
  s.6   *56, 82*
  s.6(2)   *54, 57*
  s.6(3)   *54, 57*
  s.11   *79*
  Sched.2   *55*

Vaccine Damage Payments Act 1979   *480*

Statutory Instruments

Civil Procedure Rules 1998 SI 1998 No 3132
  r.2.3(1)   *503*

Electronic Commerce Directive (Financial Services and Markets) Regulations 2002 SI 2002 No 1775   *18*

Sale and Supply of Goods to Consumers Regulations 2002 SI 2002 No 3045   *41, 42, 43*

Unfair Terms in Consumer Contracts Regulations 1999 SI 1999 No 2083   *54, 55, 56, 57*

Acknowledgements

We are grateful to the following for permission to reproduce copyright material:

The Assessment and Qualification Alliance for twenty AQA examination questions.
Note: Where worked solutions to, and/or commentaries on AQA questions or possible answers are provided it is the author of this title who is responsible for them; they (a) have neither been provided or approved by AQA and (b) do not necessarily constitute the only possible solutions.

Pearson Education Ltd for extracts from L.B. Curzon (2002) *Dictionary of Law*, Sixth Edition. Copyright © 2002.

Part 1

MODULE 4 CONTRACT LAW

Study Block 1 FORMATION OF A CONTRACT

Study Block 2 CONTRACT TERMS

Study Block 3 VITIATING FACTORS

Study Block 4 DISCHARGE AND REMEDIES

Introduction to Part 1
MODULE 4 CONTRACT LAW

General principles of contract law

Arising from the concept of *'laissez-faire'*, which flourished in the nineteenth century, the main principle underlying all contract law is that of 'freedom of contract'. *Laissez-faire*, simply translated means 'leave alone', and as far as the law of contract was concerned people were left to make their own bargains, without interference. This is still to some extent the case, especially in commercial contracts where certainty is so important. There are times, however, when this principle has had to give way to the principle of protection, in the interests of justice. Although people should be able to choose their own terms, and would usually take care of their own interests, it became clear that with the rise of big businesses and globalisation there was an imbalance. No longer were people making agreements on equal terms, and the need to protect 'the little guy' became apparent. What had started as freedom of choice could easily become freedom to oppress. Much protection of the consumer is now governed by statute laws such as the **Sale of Goods Act** and the **Consumer Protection Act**, but where there is no statutory protection the courts may 'interfere' in a contract in order to protect a weaker party.

What is a contract?

Simple contracts are agreements that can be spoken or written (although there are some which *have* to be in writing, such as hire purchase agreements).

Speciality contracts are agreements that cannot just be spoken or written, but must be created by deed. These include house purchases. The difference is that consideration (something in exchange) is not necessary to support an agreement if it is made by deed.

An agreement is based on an offer by one party and acceptance of that offer by the other. A contract is an agreement that the law will enforce.

So when does an agreement become enforceable in law?

When it is backed up with something of value (consideration) and there is an intention to create an enforceable agreement. You probably make dozens of contracts every day without even noticing. If you bought a bus ticket, packet of crisps or magazine then you had a contract. You accepted an offer to sell you something and you provided consideration (money) in return. Any transaction like this will involve an intention to create legal relations as it is a business deal. The first Study Block will cover *formation* of a contract and look at all these elements.

We will then look at the different *terms* that can be included in a contract. Not all statements become terms of the contract. Also, the law imposes certain terms regardless of what the people making it decide to include.

Once a contract is validly formed it may still be unenforceable because of a *mistake* or a *misrepresentation* by someone. These are called *vitiating factors*. Vitiating factors will invalidate a contract even though it was validly formed.

Example   You agree to buy a magazine, called *ROCK!* because the newsagent told you that it was about rock music (a misrepresentation). It turns out to be about geology. The newsagent cannot make you pay even though you had an agreement.

The last Study Block covers the different ways to *terminate* a contract, and *remedies* for breach. It is usually only when an agreement is broken that the law will get involved. If the magazine was about rock music but the pages are blank, you can sue for breach of contract and be compensated with a refund.

Study Block 1
FORMATION OF A CONTRACT

Unit 1   Offer

Unit 2   Acceptance

Unit 3   Consideration

Unit 4   Intention to create legal relations

This Study Block covers the formation of a contract. To be validly formed a contract must have all the following elements:

- **an agreement** (an offer by one party and acceptance of that offer by the other);
- **consideration** (something of value provided by each party, unless the contract is made by deed); and
- **an intention to create legal relations** (the parties to the contract intend to create a legally enforceable agreement).

Example You offer to buy a television from an electrical store for £300. Once the cashier accepts your offer and takes your money you have a contract. There is an offer and acceptance of the offer. The consideration from you is the £300 and the television is the shop's consideration. Finally there is an intention to create legal relations as this is a business transaction. Both you and the shop intend the agreement to be legally enforceable so that if you don't pay or they don't give you the television there is a right to sue for breach of contract.

Offer and acceptance are dealt with separately in the first two Units because, although they go together to constitute an agreement, there are special rules on each. You also need to know how an offer can come to an end and the rules on acceptance by post.

The third Unit looks at consideration. In my example of the money and the television it is clear and there is no problem, but consideration includes many other things that may have a value, such as doing, or promising to do, something. The courts may have to decide whether this is good enough to support a contract.

Finally we look at intent to create legal relations and the situations when the courts may presume that intention even when it is not clear, and also the times when the courts may presume that there is no such intention, such as family agreements.

Offer

... the display of an article with a price on it in a shop window is merely an invitation to treat. It is in no sense an offer for sale the acceptance of which constitutes a contract.

Lord Parker, **Fisher v Bell (1961)**

> **By the end of this Unit you should be able to:**
> - Explain the rules on making and ending an offer
> - Distinguish an offer from an invitation to treat
> - Identify problems with the law in order to attempt an evaluation

An offer is the first step towards making a contract. One person makes an offer and when that offer is accepted an agreement is reached. If both parties provide something of value, called *consideration*, then it becomes a legally enforceable contract. The person making an offer is called the *offeror* and the person to whom it is made is the *offeree*. An offer has to consist of a definite intention to be bound by the terms of the offer once accepted, and must be communicated.

Bilateral and unilateral offers

Most contracts are bilateral. This means both parties to the agreement have obligations to perform, i.e. do what they 'offered' to do.

Some contracts are unilateral, or 'one-sided'. Here only one party has obligations: to do something if certain conditions are met. Such offers can be made to a specific person or group or the world at large. When someone comes forward and performs the conditions, i.e. *accepts* the offer, it ripens into a contract. Nobody is *obliged* to perform the conditions, but if somebody does then the person making the offer is obliged to keep the promise made.

Example   I offer to sell you my law textbook for £5. You agree to give me £5. This is a *bilateral* agreement. We *both* have obligations. I am obliged to sell it to you, and you are obliged to give me £5.

If, however, I offer to sell the book to anyone in the class who gives me £5, this is a *unilateral* offer. Only *I* have an obligation. Nobody is obliged to give me £5, but if somebody does, then I am obliged to give them the book.

The best-known example of a unilateral offer is the case of **Carlill v Carbolic Smoke Ball Co. (1892)**.

Key case

In **Carlill**, a company had put an advertisement in the paper offering a 'Smokeball' for sale. They said that it would prevent the user getting flu and backed this up by saying they would pay £100 to anyone who used it and did get flu. Mrs Carlill bought one and used it according to the instructions. When she got flu she claimed the £100. The company argued, among other things, that there was no contract as nobody can contract with 'all the world'. The CA held that it wasn't a *contract* with the world, but an *offer* to the world, which ripened into a contract with anybody who came forward and performed the conditions. The buying and using of the Smokeball amounted to acceptance by Mrs Carlill. The company were obliged to keep their promise to pay £100.

Rewards

An offer of a reward implies an intent to be bound by the offer, and C is entitled to the reward by performing the conditions. However, C must be aware of the offer in order to 'accept' it. In **R v Clarke (1927)** a man claimed a reward for giving information leading to the conviction of a murderer. He failed. Although he had seen the offer of a reward, the evidence was that he had forgotten all about it, and merely given the information to clear his own name, not in exchange for the offer.

Example I have lost my dog. I put notices up on the trees nearby offering '£50 reward for the return of Fluffy'. Sue reads this and later she sees my dog. She returns Fluffy and claims £50. I have made a unilateral offer to 'all the world', which turns into a contract when it is accepted by Sue's performance. She is entitled to £50. If, however, she had not seen the advertisement but had merely seen and returned Fluffy then she is not entitled to it. I *may* give it to her but I don't *have* to. This is because the return of Fluffy was not in response to my offer.

Invitations to treat

An offer must be certain and must be distinguished from an **invitation to treat**. An offer becomes an agreement once accepted. An invitation to treat is an attempt to stimulate interest without any intention to be bound, it is an invitation to *make* an offer (to treat), thus it cannot be 'accepted'. There are several examples.

Goods on display

Goods in a shop window or on a supermarket shelf are an invitation to treat, not an offer.

Example I see a leather jacket in a shop window and the price tag mistakenly says £15 instead of £150. I have been 'invited' to make an offer to buy it. I can't insist the shop sells it to me for £15. However, if I offer £15 and the shop assistant accepts it (e.g. by ringing it up on the till), we have a contract. There is a valid agreement (my offer, the shop's acceptance) and we both provide something of value (the jacket and the £15). I can now have the jacket for the £15.

In **Pharmacuetical Society of Great Britain v Boots Ltd (1952)** a chemist had been charged under the **Pharmacy and Poisons Act 1933** with offering certain medicines for sale without a pharmacist being present. The court held that while the goods were on the shelf there was only an invitation to treat. The offer was made by the customer at the checkout and accepted by the cashier, at which point a pharmacist was present so Boots had not broken the law. In **Fisher v Bell (1961)** a shopkeeper had flick-knives in his shop window but was found not guilty of offering weapons for sale, as this was also seen as an invitation to treat. Lord Parker made the remark opening this Unit and then said that 'according to the ordinary law of contract' the matter was clear.

Food for thought

You may have looked at **Fisher v Bell** when doing statutory interpretation and the literal rule. Taken literally, under contract law, the flick-knife in the window was not an offer so the verdict was 'not guilty'. This does not seem to be what Parliament intended when passing the **Restriction of Offensive Weapons Act 1954**. Should the judges have been a bit more creative? The Act could have been interpreted purposively, looking at what it aimed to achieve or what 'mischief' it aimed to remedy. As the purpose of the Act was presumably to reduce the availability of weapons to the public, this could lead to a conviction.

Advertisements and mere 'puffs'

Advertisements do not usually amount to offers. In **Partridge v Crittenden (1968)** an advertisement 'offering' protected birds for sale was held not to contravene the **Protection of Birds Act** as it was seen as an invitation to treat. Although this particular case can be criticised, it makes sense. If you advertise your car for sale you don't want a binding agreement with everyone who sees the advertisement and accepts your 'offer' – you only have one car! It is therefore regarded as an invitation to treat, to invite people to make you offers, which you can then accept or reject.

Advertisements making claims like that in **Carlill** are usually regarded as boasts or mere 'puffs', not to be taken seriously. Otherwise people could sue when that moisturising cream doesn't make them look 10 years younger! This argument failed in **Carlill** because the company had said that they had deposited £1,000 to cover claims and the court felt this showed a serious intention to be bound by the offer.

Supplying information

What looks like an offer may only be supplying information. In **Harvey v Facey (1893)** a potential buyer wrote to the owner of a property asking, 'Will you sell Bumper Hall Pen? Telegraph lowest cash price'. They replied, 'Lowest price £900'. The buyers then tried to 'accept' this. It was held to be a statement of the price that would apply *if* they decided to sell, in effect an invitation to treat. It was not an offer so could not be accepted.

Auctions

In **Payne v Cave (1789)** it was confirmed that an auctioneer's call for bids is an invitation to treat. The bidder makes the offer, which is then accepted by the fall of the hammer. It is at this point that it becomes a legally enforceable agreement. However, in **Barry v Heathcote Ball Ltd (2000)** the CA held that where goods at an auction were advertised as 'without reserve' (where there is no lower limit placed on the amount which will be accepted), then a collateral (secondary) agreement exists to accept the highest bid, whatever it is. The auctioneers were therefore in breach of this second contract when they rejected the claimant's bid because it was too low.

Tenders

These are treated in a similar way. If someone invites tenders, or quotes, for the supply of goods or services, this is an invitation to treat. The person who submits the tender is making the offer. The person requesting the tender can then accept the preferred offer and reject the rest. As with auctions, a collateral contract can arise here too. In **Blackpool and Fylde Aero Club Ltd v Blackpool BC (1990)** the council invited tenders to run an airport, stating that all tenders must be in by noon on a certain date. C put a tender in the council's letter box before noon, but the box was not emptied. The CA held that although the council did not have to *accept* any particular tender, there was a collateral contract to *consider* all tenders, which it had not done. The council was in breach of this second contract.

Collateral contracts

We saw above with auctions and tenders that collateral contracts can arise. These are where there is a secondary agreement to the main contract between two parties. In some cases a collateral contract arises where there is an agreement involving a third party. In **Shanklin Pier Ltd v Detel Products (1951)** the pier company (SPL) arranged with X to have the pier painted. A paint manufacturer, D, persuaded them to add a condition to their contract with X, to the effect that certain paint must be used (you guessed it, D's), saying it would last 10 years. When it only lasted a few months, SPL sued D, which argued that there was no contract between them. The court held that although the main contract (for the sale of the paint) was between D and X, there was a collateral contract between D and SPL, that in return for SPL adding the condition, D guaranteed the quality of the paint.

Termination of an offer

An offer can be terminated by:

- acceptance
- counter-offer or rejection
- revocation
- lapse of time
- death

Acceptance

As soon as the offer is accepted it ceases to be an offer. It is a binding agreement with the person accepting it and nobody else can now do so. The rules on acceptance are discussed in the next Unit.

Counter-offer or rejection

If the offeree rejects an offer then it ends. This also applies to the introduction of new terms, or a counter-offer. In **Hyde v Wrench (1840)** D offered a house for sale for £1,000 (it was a long time ago!) and C replied with a counter-offer of £950. D rejected this so C offered the full price, which D now refused. C sued for breach of contract but the court held the counter-offer destroyed the original offer, so there was no contract. A counter-offer is not acceptance but another offer, which the original offeror can either accept or reject. Of course if it is accepted then a contact will have been created based on the new terms. In **Pickfords Ltd v Celestica Ltd (2003)** Pickfords offered to relocate D at a price per unit moved. Later that month a second offer was made quoting a fixed sum for the whole relocation. D sent a fax headed 'confirmation', adding that the price of the work should not exceed £10,000. The relocation was performed and D paid as per the first offer. Pickfords claimed the fixed sum on the basis that communication of the second offer revoked the first offer, so D had accepted the second offer. The CA confirmed an offer could be revoked at any time before acceptance either by express words or if the offeror acted inconsistently with the offer. Here the second offer was inconsistent with the first, so the first was revoked. However, it was clear D was accepting the first offer because reference was made to a maximum price. D's 'acceptance' was therefore a counter-offer, on the same terms as the first offer plus the new term that the cost would not exceed £10,000. This was accepted by Pickfords' conduct in carrying out the relocation. It could not claim the fixed sum.

If the offeree asks for further information this will not usually amount to a counter-offer. This is similar to the rule that a mere supplying of information will not amount to an offer (**Harvey v Facey**). Thus in **Stevenson v McLean (1880)** D had offered to sell goods to C, who asked if he could pay over two months, or if not then what period would be acceptable. He did not get a reply but then accepted the offer as it stood, for payment in cash. In the meantime the goods had been sold to someone else. D had taken the letter as a counter-offer, but the court held that it was merely a request for information and did not terminate the original offer. This offer had been accepted so there was a valid agreement and D was in breach of contract.

Food for thought

It may not always be clear what amounts to a counter-offer, and what will be treated as merely a request for information. In **Stevenson** the question about credit could arguably be taken as a new term, and thus a counter-offer or rejection of the original offer, as indeed it was by the seller. This leaves the law somewhat uncertain in an area where certainty is vital: buying and selling goods.

Revocation

As we saw in **Pickfords**, the offeror can revoke, i.e. withdraw, the offer at any time up to acceptance. This applies even if there is a promise to hold the offer open, unless there is a separate agreement supported by consideration. In **Routledge v Grant (1828)** D offered his house for sale and promised to keep the offer open for six weeks. The court said that this was not enforceable because the offeree had not 'bought' the option to have it kept open. If he had provided something of value in return (consideration) he would have been able to sue for breach of this second contract.

The revocation must be communicated to the offeree, although this can be through a third party. In **Dickinson v Dodds (1876)** D had offered his house for sale to C. D then sold it to someone else and C was told about this by a third (or in this case fourth) party. At this point C wrote a letter 'accepting' the offer and then sued for breach of contract. The court said that he knew that the offer was no longer open as clearly as if he had been told by D himself. The revocation was therefore valid and his attempted acceptance was too late.

Food for thought

It would seem that this leaves the offeror free to change his mind without telling the offeree on the basis that he will hear about it from someone, but it probably applies only if this is a reliable source and is not just a matter of gossip. It may not always be easy to judge this though, and each case will have to be decided on its own facts. Certainty and clarity in the law is important and it could be argued that a rule that revocation be made personally would not be too hard on the offeror and would protect the offeree. Contract law is an area where the courts are often reluctant to interfere, on the basis that people should be free to make their own bargains.

In **Byrne & Co. v Leon Van Tien Hoven & Co. (1879–80)** it was held that revocation is not 'communicated' until it *reaches* the offeree. This means that if revocation is by letter, the offer stays open until the offeree has received the letter.

Key case

In **Byrne**, D was a company in Cardiff and offered to sell some tin plates to C in New York. D sent a letter revoking the offer on 8 October. On 11 October C sent a letter accepting the offer. D argued that the offer was already revoked, but the court held that revocation did not take place until C *received* the letter, and this was not until 20 October. Acceptance was therefore valid and a contract existed.

There is no clear English authority on communication of revocation of a unilateral offer to the world, but you can't write to everyone! In an American case, **Shuey v US (1875)**, it was said that 'reasonable steps' to revoke should be taken. This could mean, for example in a case like **Carlill**, putting an advertisement in the same paper as the original offer. One English case is **Errington v Errington and Woods (1952)**, although not an offer to the world. A promise was made by a father to his daughter and son-in-law to transfer a house to them if they paid all the instalments on the mortgage. This was a unilateral contract because *they were not obliged* to pay, but if they did so then *the father was obliged* to transfer the house. Although they had not finished paying the instalments, the CA held that once performance had *commenced* the father's promise was binding. He could not revoke his offer while they continued to pay the instalments.

Food for thought

The issue of revocation is difficult in unilateral contracts made with the world and accepted by performance, both in relation to communication and that revocation can occur at any time up to *completion* of performance. If a newspaper promises £100 to anyone who swims the Channel, it would be unfair if they could revoke when you reached the entrance to Calais harbour. It seems that a unilateral offer cannot be revoked once performance is *commenced*, but **Errington** was not an offer to the world so clearer authority is needed on the issue.

Lapse of time

An offer may be extinguished through lapse of time. If it is an offer only for a certain period then it will end on the due date. If there is no time limit then the offer will end after a 'reasonable time' and the courts may have to decide what is reasonable in the circumstances. In **Ramsgate Victoria Hotel v Montefiore (1866)**, shares were offered in June but not 'accepted' until November. The court said that the offer had ended due to lapse of time. Much will depend on the subject matter. An offer to sell shares will clearly have a short time span as prices can fluctuate so much. The same would apply to perishable items like food. Something more stable might be different.

Death

If the *offeree* dies before acceptance the offer ceases, as only the person to whom the offer is made can accept it. If the *offeror* dies before acceptance it will depend on whether the offeree knows about the death. If so, then it is likely to be the same as for **Dickinson *v* Dodds** – knowledge will end the offer and it will be too late to accept. If acceptance occurs before knowledge of the death then it is likely that a contract exists and the deceased's estate will have to fulfil it.

Examination pointer

Always bear in mind that there is rarely a straightforward 'yes' or 'no' answer. Look at the facts given in the question, applying the law as you go through the issues. It may be that you need to make a 'best guess' as to how it applies. For example, an advertisement may be classed as an offer, or only an invitation to treat. The most important thing is to back up your answer with reasons and case authorities.

Task

Answer the following questions, using cases in support.

1 John offers to sell Mary a painting for £250. Mary says she'll give him £225 for it but later changes her mind and agrees to pay the full £250. If he decides not to sell, can she sue for breach of contract?

2 Karen offers to sell Susan her stamp collection and agrees to give her a week to decide. After three days Susan hears from Paul that Karen has already sold it to someone else. Susan writes a letter 'accepting' the offer. Is this acceptance valid?

Summary

Essentials of an offer:	
An offer must be certain and must be communicated. This can be to one person, a group or to the world at large	**Carlill *v* Carbolic Smoke Ball Co.**
The offer must be distinguished from an 'invitation to treat'	**Fisher *v* Bell/Pharmaceutical Society of Great Britain *v* Boots**
An offer may be terminated by:	
Acceptance	If offer is made to several people then the first acceptance terminates it
Rejection or counter-offer	**Hyde *v* Wrench/Pickfords**
Revocation (which must be communicated)	**Dickinson *v* Dodds** **Byrne & Co. *v* Leon Van Tien Hoven & Co.**
Lapse of time	**Ramsgate Victoria Hotel *v* Montefiore**
Death	Depends on knowledge of the death

Self-test questions

1 Why is it important to distinguish between an offer and an invitation to treat?

2 Why was the advertisement treated as an offer in **Carlill**?

3 What is a unilateral contract?

4 How does an offer come to an end?

5 What point about revocation was made in:
   (i) **Dickinson v Dodds**?
   (ii) **Byrne & Co. v Leon Van Tien Hoven & Co.**?

 For further resources and updates please go to the Companion Website accompanying this book at **www.pearsoned.co.uk/russell**

Unit 2

Acceptance

. . . where an offer is made and accepted by letters sent through the post, the contract is completed the moment the letter accepting the offer is posted, even though it never reaches its destination.

Lindley LJ, **Byrne & Co.** *v* **Leon Van Tien Hoven Co. (1879–80)**

By the end of this Unit you should be able to:
- Explain the rules relating to acceptance of an offer
- Explain the operation of the postal rule and when it may be avoided
- Show how the law has developed by reference to cases
- Identify problems with the law in order to attempt an evaluation

Contract law is based on agreement. An agreement is shown by the fact that there is an offer and an acceptance. We know that an offer must be certain and be communicated to the offeree. There are similar rules with acceptance. An offer can be revoked right up until acceptance, so it is important to know at what time acceptance has occurred. This is not always clear.

Example I offer to sell you my car for £700. You say you will ring back but when you do I am out. You leave a message saying that you accept my offer and will call the next evening to collect the car and pay me £700. I forget to check my messages when I come home and so do not hear yours until after I have sold the car to someone else. I can revoke my offer up until acceptance so I really need to know if this happened when you rang, or when I heard the message. If it was when you rang then I am in breach of contract.

Acceptance must match the offer

We saw in **Hyde** *v* **Wrench** that if new terms are introduced this may be seen as a counter-offer. This means that it is not an acceptance but a new offer; the original offeror now becomes the offeree, and can accept or reject the new terms.

Example If your message had been that you would give me £650 for my car then this is a counter-offer, or rejection, of my offer and terminates it. I can decide whether to accept or reject this new offer.

We also saw in **Stevenson _v_ McLean** that a request for information is not usually seen as a rejection and so the original offer can still be accepted. If your message had said that you wanted to know if you could pay by cheque, this would not be seen as a rejection.

A problem can arise where standard forms are used. If business A offers goods to business B on a form containing its standard terms, and business B accepts on _its_ standard terms, whose should apply? It is particularly difficult where negotiations are lengthy, referred to as the 'battle of the forms'. The general rule is that each 'form' is a counter-offer, not an acceptance. Thus the last form would be an offer, accepted by, for example, delivery of goods.

Food for thought

The courts have not fully resolved the issue of the 'battle of the forms'. In **Butler Machine Tool Company _v_ Ex-Cell-O Corporation (1979)** the last form was held not to be a counter-offer, but an acceptance. This indicates that a case may be decided on its own facts, which leaves the area uncertain.

Communication of acceptance

Acceptance must be unconditional and must be communicated to the offeror. This can be by words or conduct. In unilateral contracts, performance is the usual method of acceptance. Communication is implied by the act of performance. Thus in **Carlill**, Mrs Carlill buying and using the smokeball amounted to acceptance. This would also apply to, for example, the return of a lost dog where a reward had been offered. It is not fully clear whether acceptance occurs only when the performance is complete. As we saw when considering offers, this could be unfair if someone has commenced a lengthy task. In **Daulia Ltd _v_ Four Millbank Nominees (1978)** there were obiter dicta in the CA that once the offeree has commenced performance it would not be open to the offeror to revoke. However, it was also said that this did not mean acceptance had occurred, only that completion of the performance would not be prevented.

Example I offer a group of students £50 if they complete a 5000-word essay. They are not obliged to do anything, as it is a unilateral offer, but writing the essay would be acceptance by whoever chooses to do it. I am not obliged to give anyone £50 until they have completed the essay, but it is likely that I cannot revoke my offer once they have started, even though acceptance won't be complete until the essay is finished.

There is a general rule that silence does not usually amount to acceptance.

Key case

In **Felthouse v Bindley (1862)** a man wrote to his nephew offering to buy one of his horses for £30, and added, 'if I hear no more about him, I consider the horse mine at that price'. Although the nephew intended to keep the horse for his uncle, it was sold by mistake by his auctioneer. The uncle sued the auctioneer on the basis that the horse belonged to him, and so should not have been sold. The court held that there was no acceptance; therefore, ownership of the horse had not passed to the uncle.

The exception to this rule is where conduct is enough. Many contracts for buying and selling goods are concluded this way. Say you buy a newspaper: you *offer* the price of it, and this is *accepted* by the newsagent handing over the paper. No words are necessary.

Communication must be by the offeree or via an authorised third party. If the third party is not authorised, there will be no acceptance. In **Powell v Lee (1908)** an applicant for the job of headmaster was told by one of the school managers that he had got the job. When someone else was appointed instead, he sued for breach of contract. It was held that as the manager was not authorised to tell him that he had been appointed, there was no valid acceptance.

The general rule is that acceptance is not communicated until it is *received* by the offeror. Although not usually a problem when the parties are face to face, something could prevent acceptance being communicated. An example was given by Lord Denning in **Entores Ltd v Miles Far East Corporation (1955)**. He said,

> *'Suppose, for instance, that I shout an offer to a man across a river or a courtyard but I do not hear his reply because it is drowned by an aircraft flying overhead. There is no contract at that moment. If he wishes to make a contract, he must wait till the aircraft is gone and then shout back his acceptance so that I can hear what he says. Not until I have his answer am I bound.'*

In **Entores Ltd** the question was where exactly a contract was made in the case of instantaneous communications. An offer had been made by a London company to a firm in Amsterdam. The acceptance was sent by telex from Amsterdam to London. The CA held that the contract was formed when the acceptance was *received* (in London). This was confirmed by the HL in **Brinkibon v Stahag Stahl (1983)**.

Key case

In **Brinkibon** a telex was received in office hours, in Vienna, so the contract was formed in Vienna. However, the HL said if it was sent outside office hours it may be different. Does acceptance occur when it is received in the *office* or when it is actually read by a *person*? This could be several hours, or even days, later. This question was left for future cases. It is therefore not clear what would happen in the case of a fax or email. Although such communications seem instantaneous, they could be received out of office hours, particularly where the parties are in different countries, or different time zones.

Food for thought

It is still unclear when the acceptance takes place in the case of electronic communications that are not actually read or heard by anyone. This could apply to the answerphone message you left me in my example. The HL in **Brinkibon** suggested that if the telex had been sent out of office hours, its decision might have been different, but it did not give any definite guidance on this. Anyway, what if a communication responding to an offer is sent during office hours but not seen by anyone? Is there a valid contract? Can the offer still be revoked? In the interests of certainty these questions need to be answered.

Further problems arose with the advent of the Internet. If you were buying something on the net you would need to know whether, and when, the contract is actually made. This is now governed by the **Electronic Commerce Regulations 2002**. If you order something via the Internet, the service provider must provide you with certain information and its acknowledgement of your order, i.e. its acceptance of your offer to buy is not treated as communicated until you are able to access it.

So that's acceptance by electronic means, but what about letters? Is an acceptance sent by post effective when *sent* or when *received*? Although the above rules seem to suggest the latter, different rules apply when using the post.

Acceptance by post

It was established in **Adams *v* Linsell (1818)** that once the offeree has posted acceptance it is too late to revoke an offer. This rule was not without its critics and at first it was distinguished in cases where the letter of acceptance was posted but did not arrive. However, in **Household Insurance *v* Grant (1879)** it was confirmed that acceptance by post is complete as soon as it is posted, *even if it doesn't arrive*. Following this, Lindley LJ in **Byrne & Co. *v* Leon Van Tien Hoven & Co. (1879–80)** said, '*It may be taken as now settled where an offer is made and accepted by letters sent through the post, the contract is completed the moment the letter accepting the offer is posted, even though it never reaches its destination.*'

There are some further refinements to the rule. One is that the posting must be valid, the letter must be properly stamped and addressed. Also, in **Re London & Northern Bank (1900)** it was held that handing a letter to a postman who is delivering is not a valid posting. Most importantly, the offeror can exclude the rule by stipulating a particular form of acceptance. In **Holwell Securities *v* Hughes (1974)** the offeror said that acceptance must be 'by notice in writing to the vendor' and this was held to indicate that it must *reach* him. If an offer is made by post then acceptance can be by post *unless* the offeror specifies some other method for acceptance. However, any equally effective method is enough. In **Yates Building Co. Ltd *v* R J Pulleyn (1975)** acceptance was required to be by recorded or registered post. It was actually sent by ordinary post, but the court said that this sufficed because the requirement was only to ensure receipt, and this had happened.

Example	Let's go back to my offer of the car. If I had sent my offer to you by post then you can reply by post and your letter will be valid acceptance as soon as you post it. However, if I had said to you that your acceptance must reach me, then even if you had followed up your message with a letter, neither the message nor the letter would suffice until I actually *received* one of them. Until then I can revoke my offer and sell to someone else.

Food for thought

The postal rule is something that can be criticised. Nowadays, when it is possible to guarantee next-day delivery of post (for a price!), and with fax, email, mobile phones and texting all providing a means of instantaneous communication, it is arguable that the postal rule is outdated and should be abolished. On the other side of the argument, it can be said that the offeror always has the opportunity to state that the acceptance must be in a particular form, and/or must be received and that this protects both sides.

Finally, remember that the postal rule only applies to acceptance; it does not apply to revocation – **Byrne & Co.** *v* **Leon Van Tien Hoven & Co.**

Examination pointer

Look carefully for any clues in a problem question, such as times or dates. This will be particularly important when letters are exchanged. The following task involves an application of the rules you have seen so far and is the type of thing that could be included in a given scenario.

Task

Smith and Jones Ltd send an offer to buy 200 keyboards to Computer Bitz Ltd in Glasgow on 1 October. On 3 October they change their mind and send a revocation of the offer, also by post. Computer Bitz Ltd receives the offer on 4 October and imme-diately emails their acceptance. They follow this up with a letter posted the next day. The letter of revocation reaches Computer Bitz Ltd on 6 October and the letter of acceptance reaches Smith and Jones Ltd on 7 October.

Applying the rules relating to offer, revocation and acceptance, decide whether there is a binding contract and, if so, when it was created. Say which case(s) will sup-port your answer, and how.

Summary

Acceptance can be by words or conduct	**Carlill *v* Carbolic Smoke Ball Co.**
Acceptance must match the offer	**Hyde *v* Wrench**
Silence does not usually amount to acceptance	**Felthouse *v* Bindley**
Acceptance must be communicated	**Entores Ltd *v* Miles Far East Corporation**
Postal rule may apply . . .	**Adams *v* Linsell**
Unless a particular method is required	**Holwell Securities *v* Hughes**
Postal rule does not apply to electronic communications	**Brinkibon *v* Stahag Stahl**
The postal rule does not apply to revocation	**Byrne & Co. *v* Leon Van Tien Hoven & Co.**

Self-test questions

1 Which case supports the principle that silence cannot amount to acceptance?

2 How is a unilateral offer usually accepted?

3 What is the postal rule and when can it be excluded?

4 What cases can support your previous answer?

5 Do you think the postal rule should be extended to cover electronic communications or abolished altogether?

For further resources and updates please go to the Companion Website accompanying this book at **www.pearsoned.co.uk/russell**

Consideration

Payment of a lesser sum on the day in satisfaction of a greater sum cannot be satisfaction of the whole . . . but the gift of a horse, hawk or robe etc. in satisfaction is good.

The rule in **Pinnell's Case (1602)**

By the end of this Unit you should be able to:
- Explain the rules on consideration and how it supports a contract
- Show how the law has developed by reference to cases
- Identify problems with the law in order to attempt an evaluation

A contract is based on the idea of a bargain. Offer and acceptance show that there is agreement, but this will not be enforceable (unless made by deed) unless each party provides something to support the bargain. This new element is called *consideration*. Each party to a contract must give and receive something of value. The law will not enforce a bare promise, i.e. one that is not supported by consideration. Although often referred to as the 'price' it is wider than this. It can include a promise or an act, as well as a payment. One person is 'buying' the other's act or promise by doing, or promising to do, something in return for it. The person making the promise is called the *promisor*; the person to whom the promise is made is called the *promisee*.

Example   John promises to mow Dave's lawn. He doesn't do so. Dave cannot enforce John's promise as he offered nothing in return for it. If Dave had said, 'I'll pay you £5', then this is no longer a bare promise. Both sides have provided something of value; either can therefore enforce the agreement. Dave has a right to sue if John doesn't mow the lawn. John has a right to sue if he does mow it, but Dave doesn't pay. In this example it is unlikely they will take any such action, but the point is that they *can*.

The classic definition of consideration came from **Currie *v* Misa (1875)** and was based on *benefit* and *detriment*. In my example, the benefit to John is £5; the detriment is the work he has to do. The benefit to Dave is a nice lawn; the detriment is paying out £5. This has now given way to the more popular notion of a bargain. Sir Frederick Pollock, in his book *Principles of Contract*, described consideration as '*an act or forbearance of one party, or the promise thereof, for which the promise of the other is bought, and the promise thus given for value is enforceable*'. This definition was adopted by the HL in **Dunlop *v* Selfridge (1915)**, and since then consideration has been based on each party *buying* the act or promise of the other.

Executed and executory consideration

A promise given for a promise received is called *executory* consideration; it means that performance occurs in the future. Thus John's offer to mow the lawn was executory consideration, as was Dave's promise of £5. Both promises are enforceable. Once performance has occurred, this is *executed* consideration. Once John fulfils his promise and mows the lawn, Dave is obliged to fulfil his by paying £5.

There are several rules on whether consideration is good enough to support a contract (*see* Figure, below). It is important to know these.

Consideration must not be past
Consideration must be sufficient but need not be adequate
Consideration must move from the *promisee*
Consideration must be more than an existing obligation

Consideration must not be past

An act or promise by one party must be *in return for* the act or promise by the other. This means it must be causally related to it. If performance occurs *before* the promise is made, it is not enforceable. This is called *past consideration* and is not valid consideration.

Example Let's go back to John and Dave. If John had mowed the lawn and then *afterwards* Dave had promised to pay him £5, John cannot enforce the agreement. The act of mowing the lawn was *past* in relation to Dave's promise of £5, not *in return for* it.

In **Re McArdle (1951)** a husband left his wife a life interest in their house, which would then go to their children when she died. The wife made improvements to the house and, after she had done so, the children signed a document promising her £488 'in consideration of your carrying out alterations and improvements'. As this promise was made *after* the work had been done it was not enforceable.

There is an exception where the person making the promise has previously requested the action. Say Dave had asked John to mow the lawn without offering money, but John mowed it expecting to be paid. Dave's later promise of £5 may be enforceable in these circumstances. A seventeenth-century case shows that in such circumstances the prior request and later promise are treated as one transaction. In **Lampleigh v Braithwaite (1615)** Braithwait had killed a man and had asked Lampleigh to obtain a pardon from the King on his behalf. This was done and Braithwait then promised him £100. The court held that Lampleigh could enforce this promise because the act had been requested. This request was connected to the later promise. In effect, there was an implied promise of some reward at the time of the original request.

This blurs the distinction between executed consideration and past consideration. In order to avoid this, the principle was developed in **Re Casey's Patents (1892)**. Here, the owners of some patent rights promised to give a share in the patents to a manager in return for services already performed. The court held the promise was enforceable, but made clear that for this to be the case the parties must have assumed throughout negotiations that the services were to be paid for. In **Pao On v Lau Yiu Long (1980)** the facts were somewhat complicated, but the principle was restated in clear terms. An act done prior to a later promise could amount to consideration for that promise where:

- the act was done at the *promisor*'s request; and
- the parties understood that the act was to be paid for.

Examination pointer

Watch for the timing of any promise to pay for an act. If the act is past, i.e. already done before any promise to pay for it, then it may not be valid consideration. You may then have to consider whether the exceptions apply. In a business relationship where an act has been requested, there is more likely to be an implied promise that it will be paid for. This would mean that any later promise to pay would be enforceable. Use *Lampleigh* and *Pao On* to support such a conclusion.

Consideration must be sufficient but need not be adequate

Although the word bargain is often used in relation to a contract, the law is not usually interested in whether a person has made a good deal or not. If I want to sell my shiny new car for £10 I may be seen as crazy, but the person who agrees to buy it will be able to enforce the agreement. It may not be *adequate* in terms of economic value, but it is *sufficient* in law.

In **Thomas v Thomas (1842)** Mrs Thomas paid rent of £1 per year to her husband's estate to carry on living in their house. This was held to be *sufficient* in law to constitute consideration, even though not *adequate* in terms of market value. In **Chappell & Co. v Nestlé (1960)** chocolate bar wrappers were held to be sufficient to support a contract, even though they had no real value. The company was therefore obliged to keep its promise to supply a record to people who sent in the wrappers.

Consideration must move from the promisee

A person can only enforce a contract if that person has provided consideration. The rule is that consideration must move from the *promisee*, although it does not necessarily have to move to the *promisor*. The rule applies even if the contract was made for the benefit of the person concerned.

<table>
<tr><td>**Example**</td><td>Dave promised John that if John mowed the lawn then he would give John's father £5. John's father cannot enforce this promise because he gave nothing in return for it. No consideration moved from him to Dave.</td></tr>
</table>

In **Tweddle** *v* **Atkinson (1861)** the fathers of a bride and groom promised *each other* that they would pay the groom a sum of money following the marriage. The bride's father did not do so, and when he died the groom sued the estate. Although the agreement between the two fathers had expressly included a clause giving him the right to sue, the court held that he was unable to enforce the promise because he had provided no consideration. Wightman J said, '*No stranger to the consideration can take advantage of a contract, although made for his benefit.*' Also known as *privity of contract*, this means that only the parties to a contract can sue or be sued on that contract.

The rule is now subject to the **Contracts (Rights of Third Parties) Act 1999**, which provides that a person not party to an agreement can sue under the contract either where the agreement *expressly allows for this* or where it *confers a benefit* on the third party. Both requirements were met in the **Tweddle** case, so a situation like that would now be covered by the Act.

Examination pointer

Although Parliament has changed the law on third party rights, cases are still important in relation to contracts made prior to 11 May 2000, as only contracts made on or after this date are affected. Cases would also be needed where one of the two requirements is not met.

Task

Applying the rules that you have learnt, answer the following questions. If you think the answer could go either way explain why, using cases in support.

1 Pete bought a computer from Simon, who then said that because he had paid so promptly he would give him some extra software. If he doesn't do so, can Pete sue for breach of contract?

2 Bob asks his friend Martin, who is a car dealer, to sell his car for him. Martin does so and Bob is so pleased with the deal he gets that he says he will give him £50 for his trouble. Can Martin enforce this promise?

Consideration must be more than an existing obligation

If there is an existing obligation or duty to do something, then doing it will not usually be deemed 'sufficient' consideration. This may be a public duty or a contractual duty.

Public duty

In **Collins** *v* **Godefroy (1831)** a witness in a court case was promised money by the defendant in return for attending court. This promise could not be enforced because there was a legal duty to attend, thus doing so was no more than doing what he was already obliged to do. This was not sufficient consideration in return for the promise.

If the act is more than the existing duty, it may be sufficient. In **Glasbrook Bros *v* Glamorgan CC (1925)** the police provided protection at a mine during a strike, at the mine-owner's request. This was sufficient consideration to support the owner's promise to pay for the special protection of his property. The mine-owner argued that the police had a public duty to protect property, but the court held that they had gone beyond what they were obliged to do by providing extra men. Similarly, in **Harris *v* Sheffield Football Club (1988)** the police were able to charge for policing a football ground because the special police presence was more than the normal police cover, which they had a public duty to provide.

Contractual duty

Two early cases with similar facts illustrate this. In **Stilk *v* Myrick (1809)** two crew members deserted a ship and the captain promised to share their wages between the other crew if they worked the ship home short-handed. When he did not pay, one of them sued for breach of contract. He failed. The court held that the crew had done no more than they were already obliged to do by their contracts, i.e. work the ship home. In **Hartley *v* Ponsonby (1857)** most of the crew deserted a ship. This left the ship so short-handed that the voyage home was very dangerous. The court held that this meant the remaining crew were discharged from their old contract and free to make a new one. Their consideration (also working the ship home) *was* sufficient to support this new contract, including the promise of the extra wages. The position was reconsidered in **Williams *v* Roffey (1990)**, which had considerable impact at the time as it seemed to change the principle that performance of an existing obligation cannot amount to sufficient consideration.

Key case

In **Williams *v* Roffey**, contractors were refurbishing some flats. Williams was sub-contracted to do the carpentry work on 27 flats but he under-quoted for the work. He then got into financial difficulties and the contractor offered him an extra payment of £575 per completed flat if he got the work finished on time. He carried on but didn't get paid, so he stopped and claimed the extra payment. The contractors argued that there was no consideration; the carpenter was only doing what he had been contracted to do. Based on **Stilk**, one would expect the court to agree. However, in the CA, Glidewell LJ said that if:

A enters a contract with B to do work in return for payment, and

B sees A can't complete his side of the bargain, and

B promises additional payment, and

B receives a benefit in return (or obviates a disbenefit), and

the promise is not given due to economic duress or fraud, then

the benefit to B is capable of being consideration for B's promise, and so the promise is legally binding.

▶

The benefit here was the avoidance of a 'penalty clause'. This was a clause in the main contractor's agreement with the owners of the flats which would have meant that the contractors would lose a lot of money if they finished late.

Food for thought

Williams is hard to reconcile with **Stilk v Myrick**, which Glidewell LJ said it 'refined'. The case never went to the HL, so the area is still open to some extent. It may be hard to distinguish between genuine cases and cases where a promise is made under duress. For example, if Williams had threatened, 'I won't finish on time unless you pay me more, and you'll lose a lot of money', then he would probably have failed in his claim. It may be hard to prove this one way or the other though.

On the other hand, it may be that the courts are merely recognising the reality of the situation. It is arguably better for the contractor to get the flats finished and pay extra than have to pay a penalty for finishing late. So there is no reason the carpenter shouldn't be able to enforce any agreement to do this.

Duty to a third party

Sometimes performance of an existing duty to perform *for someone else* is sufficient consideration. In **Scotson v Pegg (1861)** C had a contract with X to deliver some coal to D. D then agreed with C that he would unload it at a certain rate, and was sued by C when he didn't. He argued that C was already obliged to deliver so there was no consideration. The court held that there was, although the reasoning is not entirely clear. The decision of the Privy Council in **The Eurymedon (1975)** was clearer, although the facts were somewhat complex. Essentially, the act of unloading C's goods from a ship was held to be sufficient consideration, even though D was obliged under his contract with the shipper to do so. He could therefore rely on C's promise not to hold him liable if anything was damaged. This would appear to be a recognition of commercial reality. In non-commercial cases the courts may be more reluctant to 'find' consideration.

Part-payment of a debt

A final issue on the sufficiency of consideration is the principle that paying part of what is owed cannot amount to consideration for a promise to forgo the rest. This is often referred to as *'the rule in Pinnel's Case'*, from the 1602 case of that name, although the rule actually originated even earlier than this.

Key case

In **Pinnell's Case (1602)** the question arose as to whether paying part of a debt early was consideration for the agreement to accept this in full satisfaction of a larger amount. The court decided that although *'Payment of a lesser sum on the day in satisfaction of a greater sum cannot be satisfaction of the whole'*, it could be where the sum was either paid early or was a different *type* of payment, for example *'the gift of a horse, hawk or robe etc. in satisfaction is good'*.

Example You owe me £15 and are due to pay by the end of the month. I am short of cash and say if you pay me £10 now I will forgo the rest. By paying me early you have provided sufficient consideration in return for me forgoing the £5. Similarly, if I say I'll accept your silk shirt instead because I have always liked it, then this a different type of payment and again sufficient.

The 'rule in **Pinnell's Case**' was not challenged until **Foakes v Beer (1884)**, where it was upheld, with an arguably unfair result. Mrs Beer was owed around £2,000 from a court judgment and agreed with the debtor, Dr Foakes, to take £500 at once and the rest by instalments. Interest is payable on court judgments, but no mention of interest was made in their agreement. Dr Foakes paid everything as agreed, but Mrs Beer then claimed interest on the debt. She succeeded in her claim on the basis of the rule.

In **D & C Builders v Rees (1966)** a small firm had done some work for Mr Rees and had not been paid the £482 due. After some months of being asked for payment Mrs Rees, acting on behalf of her husband, offered to pay them £300. She knew they badly needed the money and told them it was that or nothing. They successfully sued for the balance because she had not provided sufficient consideration. (Perhaps she should have enclosed a hawk or a robe with her cheque!) The case also shows that the courts will not enforce a promise made under duress.

Food for thought

The rule may appear harsh in such cases as **Foakes**, where the debt appeared to be fully paid as agreed, but it is fair in situations like **Rees**, where there is a 'take it or leave it' threat. In **Foakes**, Lord Blackburn disagreed with the majority and thought business people would recognise the advantage of prompt, rather than full, payment. This is a fair point. It may, however, be hard to distinguish between a genuine agreement to take a lesser sum and one induced by threats. It is at the latter situations that the rule was aimed.

The issue was considered again in **Re Selectmove (1994)**, where the Inland Revenue agreed that tax owed by a company could be paid in instalments. They then demanded payment in full. The company argued, using **Williams v Roffey**, that the Revenue had gained a benefit. The CA held that the rule in **Pinnel's Case**, as applied in **Foakes v Beer**, had not been affected by **Williams v Roffey**. This meant that, as there was no consideration in return for the Revenue's promise to accept payment in instalments, they had every right to ask for the full amount owed.

Task

Read the above cases on part-payment of a debt. Using cases, write a paragraph on whether you believe the rule in **Pinnel's Case** to be a necessary protection, or whether you think it should be abolished. Would business people benefit from its abolition, as suggested by Lord Blackburn in **Foakes**, or suffer unwanted pressure as in **Rees**? Should the Inland Revenue have been able to change their minds and demand payment in full in **Selectmove**?

A promise to keep an offer open is not enforceable unless the offeree gives some further consideration. We saw this when looking at offers, in **Routledge *v* Grant (1828)**.

Example | I am selling my car to Pete and I tell him that I'll keep the offer open until the weekend. There is nothing he can do if I sell it to someone else on Thursday. However, if he had told me that if I keep the offer open he'll pay me £50 more than I was asking for the car then he has provided sufficient consideration to 'buy' my promise.

Summary

Consideration must not be past . . .	Re McArdle
Unless there was a request	Pao On *v* Lau Yiu Long
Consideration need not be adequate but must be sufficient	Chappell *v* Nestlé
Consideration must move from the *promisee*	Tweddle *v* Atkinson
Performance of an existing obligation is not sufficient consideration . . .	Stilk *v* Myrick
But receiving a 'benefit' can amount to sufficient consideration	Williams *v* Roffey
Part-payment of a debt is not sufficient consideration	Re Pinnell's Case

Self-test questions

1 What is the difference between executory consideration, executed consideration and past consideration?

2 What is meant by the phrase 'consideration must be sufficient but need not be adequate'?

3 When might it be possible to enforce a promise made *after* something is done?

4 Why couldn't the groom sue his father-in-law in **Tweddle**?

5 Explain the rule in **Pinnel's Case** and when it may not apply.

For further resources and updates please go to the Companion Website accompanying this book at **www.pearsoned.co.uk/russell**

Intention to create legal relations

. . . one of the most usual forms of agreement which does not constitute a contract appears to me to be the arrangements which are made between husband and wife.

Atkin LJ, **Balfour *v* Balfour (1919)**

By the end of this Unit you should be able to:
- Explain the rules on social and commercial agreements
- Show how the law applies by reference to cases
- Identify problems with the law in order to attempt an evaluation

Once you have an agreement supported by consideration you would seem to have a legally enforceable contract. In commercial agreements this will usually be true; however, there are some agreements which the law will not enforce. If this were not the case then the law would get involved in all sorts of trivial issues, such as a mother's promise to pay her son £1 to tidy his room.

Social and domestic agreements

There are many agreements made every day between people where offer, acceptance and consideration may all be present. These agreements are not usually a matter for the courts.

Example   You offer a friend a lift into town and they say that they will pay for the petrol. There is an offer ('Do you want a lift?'), an acceptance ('Sure do, it's raining'), and consideration ('I'll pay for the petrol in return for the lift'). This is really something that should remain a matter between you and your friend. There may be a moral obligation to pay, but there is not a legal one.

It is presumed, therefore, that in social or domestic agreements there is no intention to create legal relations. This presumption can be rebutted, or shown to be false, by evidence to the contrary. Two case examples illustrate this.

Key cases

In **Balfour v Balfour (1919)** a husband and wife made an agreement whereby he would pay her £30 per month while she stayed in England for health reasons and he returned to his work abroad. The marriage later broke up and he stopped paying. The CA held that although consideration was present, there was no evidence of an intention to create a binding contract. It was merely a temporary domestic arrangement. She was therefore unable to claim for breach of contract.

In **Merritt v Merritt (1970)** the husband and wife were living apart but met to discuss financial arrangements. They wrote down what was agreed and both signed the paper. One of the matters agreed was that she would pay the mortgage out of his maintenance payments, and when it was fully paid he would transfer the house to her. When he failed to do so she sued. The CA held that the signed document was sufficient evidence to rebut the presumption that there was no intention to create a legally binding contract.

Food for thought

In **Balfour**, Atkin LJ, made the opening statement that '. . . *one of the most usual forms of agreement which does not constitute a contract appears to me to be the arrangements which are made between husband and wife*', and continued that '. . . *they are not contracts because the parties did not intend that they should be attended by legal consequences*'. Do you think this is true in a case like Mrs Balfour's? When the arrangement was made they were living together. However, it could be argued that had they foreseen the marriage break-up, then they may have thought differently. Do you think the courts now recognise the fact that some apparently domestic agreements are intended to be binding? Is this a good thing? Much will depend on the circumstances surrounding the agreement.

Outside the husband and wife cases, the court will have to look carefully at the facts to decide whether there is sufficient evidence to rebut the presumption that there was no intention to create a legally binding contract. In **Simpkins v Pays (1955)** an agreement between a house-owner, her granddaughter and their lodger was held enforceable. They took part in a weekly newspaper competition to which they all contributed. The entries were done in the owner's name and there was no specific agreement as regards payment of postage and other incidental expenses. When they won £750 she kept the lot. The lodger sued and the court held that although family arrangements would not normally constitute a contract, the presence of an outsider, the lodger, was evidence of an intention to be bound.

Task

You agree with a colleague to take her to work while her car is in the garage. She offers to pay £25 to cover the petrol as you are doing all the driving. You both sign an agreement which states that you will drive her to work for a month, and at the end of the month she will pay £25. Your colleague refuses to pay. Decide whether you can enforce this agreement and which case(s) you can use to support your argument. Which case will your colleague use to argue that she needn't pay?

Commercial agreements

There is a different presumption made in commercial and business agreements. This is that there *is* an intention to create legal relations. However, this presumption can also be rebutted if evidence is produced to counter it. One way to do so is for the parties to expressly provide that they do not intend to create legal relations, but merely intend their agreement to be morally binding. These are called 'honour' clauses and are often used for competitions; for example, on a pools coupons there is a clause which says 'binding in honour only'. It was held in several pools cases, for example **Appleson v Littlewood Pools (1939)**, that this means the agreement between the pools company and the entrant is not enforceable in court. The clause rebuts the presumption that there is an intention to be legally bound. This would also apply to lottery tickets and magazine competitions.

In order to rebut the presumption the evidence must be pretty compelling. In **Carlill v Carbolic Smoke Ball Company**, we saw that the company failed to convince the court that they were not bound by the agreement to pay out £100. This was partly because of the fact that they had deposited £1,000, which showed an intention to be bound by the agreement. Not all advertisements will be binding though. Many television advertisements include wild claims of the sensational effects of a particular product. These are likely to be taken as mere 'puffs' and not binding. A specific promise may be though.

Example You see an advertisement that says 'Eat Crunchy Wheatos every morning and you'll feel great for the rest of the day'. You eat them for breakfast every day for a month but still feel moody and depressed. You cannot sue for breach of this 'promise'. However, if the advertisement says 'Does not contain nuts' and you find that it does then, if you have an allergy to nuts and become ill, you can sue for compensation.

If there is any ambiguity in the clause attempting to rebut the presumption then it is unlikely to be effective. Thus in **Edwards v Skyways Ltd (1964)** a pilot who claimed a payment under an agreement with his employers was successful. The clause on which the employers had relied was ambiguous and the court refused to accept that it rebutted the presumption.

Examination pointer

If you are expected to discuss either of these presumptions there will usually be an indication in the scenario. Look for words like 'friend', 'brother', 'colleague' or 'business partner'. You will almost always be expected to consider whether the relevant presumption can be rebutted, so make sure you know a case on each of these.

Summary

The following questions should be asked when addressing a problem question:
Is there an intention to be legally bound by the agreement?
Is the agreement a purely social one?
Is it a business agreement?
If a presumption that there was no intention to create a legally binding contract applies, can it be rebutted?

Self-test questions

1 Explain how each presumption works.

2 Give, and briefly explain, a case example for one of them.

3 How was the presumption rebutted in **Merritt**?

4 What is an 'honour clause' and how may it affect a business agreement?

5 We saw the **Carlill** case earlier; what happened in this case?

For further resources and updates please go to the Companion Website accompanying this book at **www.pearsoned.co.uk/russell**

An offer must be communicated, but this can be to the world	
An offer must be certain and distinguished from an invitation to treat	
An offer may be terminated by: ● acceptance ● rejection or counter-offer ● revocation, which must be communicated ● lapse of time ● death	
Acceptance must be communicated but can be by words or conduct	
Acceptance must match the offer	
Postal rule may apply	
The postal rule does not apply to revocation	
Consideration must not be past	
Consideration must be sufficient but need not be adequate	
Consideration must move from the *promisee*	
An existing obligation is not sufficient consideration	
Part-payment of a debt is not sufficient consideration	
Intent to create legal relations is presumed in business contracts, but can be rebutted by evidence	
Intent to create legal relations is not presumed in social agreements	

Task

Add the following cases to the above table as appropriate (in pencil if it isn't your book!):

Adams *v* Linsell   Foakes *v* Beer
Balfour *v* Balfour   Hyde *v* Wrench
Byrne & Co. *v* Leon Van Tien Hoven & Co. (x 2)   Re McArdle 1951
Carlill *v* Carbolic Smoke Ball Co. (x 2)   Merritt *v* Merritt
Collins *v* Godefroy   Pickfords *v* Celestica
Dickinson *v* Dodds   Thomas *v* Thomas
Edwards *v* Skyways   Tweddle *v* Atkinson
Fisher *v* Bell

Key criticisms

- Displaying flick-knives in a shop window was seen as an invitation to treat in **Fisher *v* Bell**. This does not seem to be what Parliament intended.
- It may not always be clear what amounts to a counter-offer.
- Clearer authority is needed on the issue of revocation in unilateral contracts.
- It is still unclear when the acceptance takes place in the case of electronic communications.
- It is arguable that the postal rule is outdated and should be abolished.
- The 'battle of the forms' causes difficulties.
- The courts may 'find' consideration where there is little evidence of it: **Williams *v* Roffey**.
- **Williams** is hard to reconcile with **Stilk**.
- The rules on past consideration may be unfair, e.g. in **Re McArdle**.
- But in business cases the courts are more likely to accept an implied promise to pay – **Pao On**.
- In **Foakes *v* Beer** no mention of interest was made in their agreement but he was obliged to pay it.
- The presumption that there is no intent in domestic cases is arguably outdated. Many couples now sign 'pre-nuptial' agreements before marriage. Should these be enforceable as they are in the USA?

Examination practice

January 2005*
Agreement is an important aspect in the formation of a contract. How satisfactory are the rules that determine when an agreement has taken place?   *(25 marks)*

Module 6 connections

Morals	Refusing to allow payment of a lesser sum where it was due to duress shows that the courts are reluctant to allow improper pressure to enforce a contract	**D & C Builders** *v* **Rees**
	However, in commercial contracts there is less of a moral issue	**Williams** *v* **Roffey**
Justice	Allowing past consideration where there is an expectation of payment ensures justice	**Re Casey**
	However, injustice is caused by a stricter application of the rules	**Re McArdle**
	The strict rule in *Pinnell's* Case can lead to injustice	**Foakes** *v* **Beer**
Conflicting interests	Most contract cases involve balancing the interests of the parties with the need to allow freedom of contract	
	In presuming intent in business relationships, but presuming no intent in domestic ones, the courts balance the need to protect people, by enforcing agreements, with the reality of the situation	
Fault	The connection between contract and fault mainly lies in the vitiating factors and breach of contract, dealt with later	
Creativity	The establishment of the postal rule	**Adams** *v* **Linsell**
	The finding of a benefit to support a promise to pay	**Williams** *v* **Roffey**

For further resources and updates please go to the Companion Website accompanying this book at www.pearsoned.co.uk/russell

Study Block 2
CONTRACT TERMS

Unit 5   Express and implied terms
Unit 6   Conditions, warranties and innominate terms
Unit 7   Exclusion clauses

Terms of a contract are the rights and obligations that the parties to the agreement have: what each has promised. In many contracts these are clear; however, if negotiations have been long and complex then it may be difficult to know exactly what is, and what is not, included.

The first Unit looks at *express terms* and compares these to representations to decide what part of any discussions has become part of the contract. However, some terms are automatically included in certain contracts by law, even though not expressly agreed between the parties. These are called *implied terms*.

Whether express or implied, terms are not all of equal importance. The second Unit covers the two main types of terms, *conditions* and *warranties*, the difference being the *importance of the term itself*. We then look at a third type, called *innominate terms*, which are classed as either conditions or warranties, depending on the *consequence of a breach* of the term.

Example   You book a two-week package holiday to Greece. The travel agent shows you a brochure stating that the hotel is in a seaside resort and that all rooms have television. These are express terms. There will also be an implied term that the holiday fits the description in the brochure. The hotel turns out to be in the town centre, miles from the beach, with no TV. The promise of a seaside resort is likely to be a condition as it is important; you can sue for breach of contract and treat the contract as ended, claiming a full refund. The television is likely to be seen as a warranty. This is a less important term, so you can sue for breach of contract but cannot treat the contract as ended, just claim compensation for the lack of a television. If the travel agent also promised that a tour rep would visit every day to offer excursions, this is likely to be seen as an innominate term as it could be breached in two ways, with different consequences. If the rep misses just one visit, the consequence of this breach is small, so the term will be treated as a warranty. If the rep never shows up at all and you don't have the opportunity to go on any excursions, the consequence is more serious and so may be treated as a condition.

The last Unit in this Study Block covers **exclusion clauses**. These are terms where one party tries to avoid, or limit, their liability. Say the travel brochure stated that 'no liability is accepted for any changes to the accommodation'. It may seem that you cannot sue when the hotel is in town, but these clauses are governed by both the common law and statute, and a term which is unreasonable or unfair may not be allowed. Although the syllabus only requires you to know these rules in outline, this Unit is a useful source for considering conflicting interests for Module 6. The law tries to achieve a balance between protection of a consumer dealing with a big business, and allowing the parties freedom to make agreements on their own terms.

Express and implied terms

. . . an unexpressed term can be implied if and only if the courts find that the parties must have intended that term to form part of their contract . . . it must have been a term that went without saying, a term necessary to give business efficacy to the contract.

Lord Pearson, **Trollope & Colls Ltd** *v* **NW Metropolitan RHB (1973)**

By the end of this Unit you should be able to:

- Explain the difference between a term and a representation
- Explain the three ways that a term can be implied into a contract
- Refer to the cases and statutes that govern implied terms
- Identify problems with the law in order to attempt an evaluation

Express terms

If there is a later dispute about what was agreed by the parties, it will be necessary to know whether a statement made orally, or in writing, is included in the contract. A distinction is made between *terms* and *representations*. Many discussions can take place before an agreement is finally made. Not all that is discussed becomes a term of the contract. This distinction is important because of the effect it has for the wronged party. A term is part of a contract, so if a party does not do as agreed by that term, there is a breach of contract and the other party can sue. If it is only a representation then the situation is different. There won't be a breach of contract. (There may be a case for 'misrepresentation' which is dealt with in Unit 9.)

Example I get a quote from Bill to paint my bathroom. He confirms he will charge £550 to paint it blue, with a white ceiling. He says he thinks this will make the room look bigger. If Bill uses the wrong colour paint or charges a different amount he is likely to have breached a term of the contract. His comment about the size is probably only a representation, and he will not be in breach of contract if it is untrue.

In order to decide whether a statement, made orally or in writing, is a term or merely a representation, the court will look at the intention of the parties. This is an objective test: would a reasonable person see it as a term? There are several matters to consider.

Timing

The longer the gap between making a statement and finalising the contract, the less likely it is to be a term. In **Routledge v Mackay (1954)** a week passed between the statement regarding the age of a motorbike and the contract for sale. This was held to be too long, so the buyer could not sue for breach when it turned out to be older. No mention of the age was made at the time of the contract.

This case can be compared to **Schawel v Reade (1913)**, where the seller of a horse had assured the buyer that it was sound and he need not examine it further. The price was agreed within a few days but the sale was not concluded until three weeks later. The HL held that the statement was made 'at the time of sale' and therefore was part of the contract.

Importance

In **Bannerman v White (1861)** a buyer of hops asked the seller whether any sulphur had been used in their treatment, making clear that if so he wasn't interested in buying. The seller said it hadn't but it turned out that it had been used in the cultivation of a small percentage of them. Even though only a small proportion was affected, the buyer wouldn't have bought the hops if he had known this, so the statement was vital. It was therefore regarded as a term of the contract.

Special knowledge

If one party has a particular skill, or knowledge, then a statement will carry more weight. In **Oscar Chess Ltd v Williams (1957)** a statement by a seller as to a car's age was held not to be a term. He wasn't an expert but was selling to a garage, which did have specialist knowledge. Also, the garage may have bought it anyway, regardless of the age. They could therefore not sue the seller for the £115 difference in price between a 1939 model and a 1948 one.

In **Dick Bentley Productions v Harold Smith Motors Ltd (1965)** the CA distinguished **Oscar Chess**. A representation that a car had only done 20,000 miles was held to be a term. Here the seller was a garage, and thus the party with specialist knowledge. The buyer was able to sue when the car was unsatisfactory and the mileage higher than stated.

Food for thought

In **Oscar Chess**, the court found against the buyer, which was a garage. This protects an individual, but is it justified? If we apply the above tests then it can be argued that the statement was made at the time of sale, and a car's age is important as it affects the price quite dramatically. They may have bought it anyway, regardless of the age, but would they have paid the extra £115? The decision was heavily influenced by the fact that it was the buyer that had the skill, and should have known better. In contrast, in **Dick Bentley Productions**, the seller had the specialist knowledge. The two cases are not easy to reconcile.

Collateral contracts

The court may find a second contract, collateral to the main contract, and find that a statement is a term of this. This is seen in **City & Westminster Properties Ltd v Mudd (1959)**, where a tenant signed a new lease in relation to a small room where he slept above a shop. Although the lease contained a clause which restricted the use of the premises to showrooms and offices, he was assured that he could continue to sleep there. The landlord later tried to evict him for breach of this clause. The court held that the assurance was a collateral contract, i.e. 'if you sign the lease I promise not to enforce the clause about the property only being used as a shop'. Cheshire, Fifoot and Furmston, in their *Law of Contract*, suggest that this approach could have been used in **Dick Bentley**. There was a recognition of it in the case itself, when Salmon LJ said that there was effectively a second agreement that if the buyer enters into the contract, the seller guarantees the mileage.

Task

Make a table or chart showing all the matters relevant to whether something will be treated as part of a contract – a term. Add a case on each and a line on the facts. Finally, add a comment of your own on whether you agree with the court.

Implied terms

Apart from the terms expressly agreed between the contracting parties, other terms may be implied by:

- statute
- custom or trade usage
- the courts

Statute

Parliament has recognised that there is a need to protect consumers where freedom to contract could become freedom to oppress. For example, a customer has little strength against a huge company when buying things, so the **Sale of Goods Act 1979 (SOGA)**, as amended by the **Sale and Supply of Goods Act 1994** and the **Sale and Supply of Goods to Consumers Regulations 2002**, implies certain terms into all contracts for the sale of goods to a consumer. The most important implied terms are contained in **ss. 12–15**:

- **s. 12** – the seller has a right to sell, i.e. has, or will have, title;
- **s. 13** – in a sale by description, the goods will correspond with that description;
- **s. 14** – if the goods are sold in the course of business, they must be of satisfactory quality and be fit for the purpose for which they were bought;
- **s. 15** – in a sale by sample, the bulk will correspond with the sample.

Example   BFN Motors advertise a car in the local paper as being two years old, white and with 16,000 miles on the clock. These are express terms. In addition there are further implied terms that BFN Motors is the rightful owner, that the car is of satisfactory quality and that it is fit for driving (its purpose). If any of these are breached, the company can be sued in exactly the same way as if an express term is breached.

Let's have a further look at these terms.

S. 12 protects a buyer from loss where the goods turn out to be stolen, because if this is the case they will have to return them to the true owner. Thus in **Rowland *v* Divall (1923)** the buyer of a used car could rely on the then equivalent of s. 12 when he discovered, three months later, that the car was stolen. He could sue the seller to recover the money he paid for it.

S. 13 can apply even if a buyer actually sees and selects the goods, i.e. it can still be a sale by description. In **Beale *v* Taylor (1967)** a buyer looking over a car was influenced by the description of it as a '1961 Triumph Herald'. It turned out to be a mix of two cars welded together, one of which was an earlier model. The buyer successfully argued breach of **s. 13**. Much may depend on the relative expertise of the parties and how much the description influenced the purchase. In **Harlingdon & Leinster Enterprises Ltd *v* Christopher Hull Fine Art (1990)** a painting had been described as by the artist Munter but, unknown to either party, this was not the case. Here the seller had less expertise than the buyer, so the statement was held not to be a 'description' of the painting.

S. 14 only applies where goods are sold in the course of business. The **1994 Act** amends **s. 14** from 'merchantable' quality to 'satisfactory' quality. This section also applies to second-hand goods but a lower standard applies. If you buy a new book and find several of the pages are dog-eared then the quality is not satisfactory. This would not be the case with a second-hand book. Whether goods are 'satisfactory' is decided by looking at any description, the price and all other relevant circumstances. The **2002 Regulations** add that any statement by the seller or their representative is a 'relevant circumstance'.

Under the second part of **s. 14**, there is a further requirement that goods are fit for the purpose for which they are commonly supplied. Thus, if the book had half the pages missing then clearly it would not be fit for the purpose – of reading. In **Godley *v* Perry (1960)** a young boy lost an eye when the catapult that he had bought snapped. The catapult was neither of satisfactory quality nor fit for the purpose for which it was supplied – catapulting things. In **Britvic Soft Drinks *v* Messer UK (2001)** gas supplied for making soft drinks was contaminated so could not be used in food production. It was not of satisfactory quality, nor fit for its purpose.

S. 14 applies unless the defects were brought to the buyer's attention, or the goods were examined and the defect should have been noticed. Many sale goods are reduced due to a small defect, such as a button missing. If the buyer is told of this, or it is really obvious, then **s. 14** cannot be relied on.

S. 15 applies where a buyer looks at a sample and then buys in bulk, the bulk must correspond with the original sample. Also, the buyer must have reasonable opportunity to compare the bulk with the sample and the goods must be free from any defect. In **Godley *v* Perry (1960)**, after being sued under **s. 14**, the shop-keeper sued the supplier under **s. 15**, because he had bought a box of the catapults after seeing a sample.

Task

Make a table of the sections discussed above. Add a note of how the courts have applied them in particular cases. Keep this for use in a problem scenario.

Food for thought

In some cases it may be hard to sue the seller under **s. 12**, so it is still 'buyer beware'. If you buy something in a car boot sale and it turns out to be stolen, you have to return it to the original owner, but would probably have trouble finding the person who sold it to you. The two cases seen under **s. 13** are hard to reconcile. The fact that a painting is by a particular artist would seem to be important to many people. It is also confusing that such a statement *could* be taken as an express term, as in the **Dick Bentley** case. The **2002 Regulations** amend **SOGA** so that any statement by the seller or their representative is a 'relevant circumstance' under **s. 14**. This may solve some of the issues relating to 'representations', discussed above.

Custom

Sometimes terms may be implied by custom or where there has been a usual course of dealing between the parties. This means that the 'usual' terms will be implied into any later contracts. These are not very common these days. An example is **Spurling *v* Bradshaw (1956)**, where, because a contract had been made several times before on similar terms, those terms were implied into a new agreement.

The courts

Although the courts are reluctant to 'write' contracts, they recognise that they may have to intervene to ensure that the parties get what they expected. Terms may be implied in order to achieve 'business efficacy'. **The Moorcock (1889)** is an early example.

Key case

In **The Moorcock**, there was an agreement between the owners of a boat and the owners of a jetty to moor the boat. It turned out that the mooring was not safe and the boat was damaged when the tide went out and it grounded. The CA held that there was an implied undertaking that the river bottom was not dangerous to ships. Such terms are implied into business transactions to give the contract 'business efficacy'. This expression has often been used and just means that the contract would not make sound business sense without the term.

In **Trollope & Colls Ltd _v_ NW Metropolitan RHB (1973)** Lord Pearson again said that a term could only be implied if it was '_necessary to give business efficacy to the contract_'.

Another way of referring to it is as the 'officious bystander' test. This expression was used by MacKinnon LJ in **Shirlaw _v_ Southern Foundries Ltd (1939)**. If a bystander listened in while the parties were discussing matters and said 'what about such and such', the parties to the contract would have answered that 'of course' such and such was included. It was so obvious it went without saying. It is based on implying those terms into a contract which the parties are presumed to have intended, but didn't include. However, MacKinnon LJ made clear that the courts should use their power sparingly.

Food for thought

Do you think that the courts _should_ imply terms into business contracts? Arguably it is for the parties themselves to decide on the terms, and they have the opportunity to make things clear if they wish. On the other hand, if a term is omitted through mere forgetfulness then it could be seen as fair for the courts to intervene.

If one party didn't know of the matter on which the term is to be based, it can't be implied; _both_ parties must have intended the term to be part of the contract. Thus in **Spring _v_ National Amalgamated Stevedores (1956)** a union tried to argue that there was an implied term in a member's contract because it was normal. Applying the 'officious bystander' test, if the member had been asked about the matter he would _not_ have answered 'of course' (although the union might have).

The courts may imply a term into a contract but then go on to find that it was not breached. In **Liverpool City Council _v_ Irwin (1977)** due to vandalism there were problems with the lifts, stair lights and rubbish chutes in a block of flats. A tenant withheld rent from the council on the basis that there was an implied term that the council would keep these services in good repair, and that this term had been breached. The council argued there was no such implied term. The HL held that there _was_ an implied term, but only to take reasonable care to keep the common parts in reasonable repair. The council had not breached this term, and it was not right to impose an absolute obligation to maintain these services.

Examination pointer

If answering an 'essay'-type question, you may have to discuss not only how terms can be implied, but also whether they should be. In a problem scenario you will need to look carefully to see if the examiner has referred to anything to indicate that a term may be implied, such as a purchase in a shop (**SOGA**) or a business agreement (efficacy test).

Summary

Express terms: *The distinction between terms and representations*	Case(s)
Timing	**Routledge v Mackay**
Importance	**Bannerman v White**
Knowledge	**Oscar Chess/Dick Bentley**
Collateral contract	**City & Westminster Properties Ltd**
Implied terms: *Terms can be implied by*	Statute/case

Statute:
   terms relating to:
     – title
     – description
     – satisfactory quality
     – corresponding with bulk
	**Sale of Goods Act 1979
	ss. 12–15**

Custom or trade usage	**Spurling v Bradshaw 1956**
The courts: to give a contract 'business efficacy'	**The Moorcock 1889 Shirlaw v Southern Foundries Ltd**

Self-test questions

1 Why is it important to make a distinction between terms and representations?

2 What does it mean to say a term is 'implied' into a contract?

3 Briefly explain each of the terms implied into contracts by **ss. 12–15**.

4 The court was prepared to imply a term into a tenancy agreement in **Liverpool City Council v Irwin**, so why did the tenants fail in their claim?

5 In what case was the 'officious bystander' test referred to, and what does it mean?

For further resources and updates please go to the Companion Website accompanying this book at **www.pearsoned.co.uk/russell**

Conditions, warranties and innominate terms

In suitable cases the courts should not be reluctant, if the intentions of the parties as shown by the contracts so indicate, to hold that an obligation has the force of a condition.
Lord Wilberforce, **Bunge Corporation v Tradax Export SA (1981)**

By the end of this Unit you should be able to:
- Explain the two main types of contract term: conditions and warranties
- Explain how the law has added a third type of contract term
- Identify problems with these classifications, and how they apply, in order to attempt an evaluation

Terms of a contract are not only seen in formal, written contracts. Spoken agreements also contain terms. If two people agree between them to exchange goods for money, i.e. to trade, they will agree certain matters between them. These would include the price, when payment is due, the condition of the goods, whether they will be delivered, a delivery date, etc. All these are *terms of the contract*. Not all terms in a contract are of equal importance. Contract terms are divided into two categories: conditions and warranties. A third classification has arisen through case law; these terms are called innominate (or intermediate) terms. The classification applies to all terms, whether express or implied.

It is important to identify what type of term it is because the consequences of any breach depend on this. A condition is a major term in a contract, something that 'goes to the root of the contract', i.e. it is fundamental to it. If a condition is breached, the injured party can treat the contract as ended, as well as claim damages. A warranty is a minor term and will not affect the main purpose of the contract. If a warranty is breached, the only remedy is damages. The contract remains in force. There are also intermediate terms; they are neither conditions nor warranties until they are breached. If a breach does occur then the court will look at the effect of this breach and decide whether the term should be seen as a condition or warranty.

Example Sue sells a car to Steve, telling him it has only done 15,000 miles and is in very good condition. It turns out to have done 80,000 and is in poor condition. This is pretty fundamental and Steve is entitled to treat the contract as at an end. He will be entitled to any deposit back and can return the car to Sue. However, if the car is in good condition but has done 17,000 miles, this is likely to only be a warranty. The effect of this breach is fairly minor. Steve may be able to sue for damages, e.g. if there is a loss in value between a car with 15,000 miles on it and one with 17,000 miles on it, but must go ahead with the agreed purchase.

Examination pointer

Take care with who may want to sue whom in exam scenarios. As you read the cases on this area note that it is often the person who has breached the contract who is suing. This seems odd; usually it is the person in breach, the one who has broken their promise, who is sued. The reason for this apparent role reversal is that although the other person has broken a term, the injured party wants the contract to continue. In the above example, Sue has breached the contract as the car has done more than 15,000 miles. However, Sue still wants to sell the car so she can sue Steve for breach of contract for refusing to go ahead with the purchase. She will fail if it was a condition because he is entitled to treat the contract as over. If it is only a warranty, she will succeed.

A comparison of two similar cases will illustrate the difference between conditions and warranties.

In **Poussard v Spiers and Pond (1876)** C was contracted to take the lead role in an opera that was due to start on 28 November. She was unable to attend until 4 December and the role was given to someone else. She argued that, as this was only a *warranty*, the Ds could not treat the contract as ended. The court held that her failure to attend amounted to a breach of a *condition* and so they were entitled to treat the contract as ended.

In **Bettini v Gye (1876)** C was contracted to take part in an opera and had agreed to attend rehearsals prior to the performance. She arrived two days late for the rehearsals. The rehearsal clause was held to be a warranty so the theatre company could not treat the contract as ended, but could claim damages for the two missing days.

If the parties to a contract do not identify the importance of a term, it is for the court to decide whether it allows a party to rescind the contract or not. This has led to a third type of term, known as *intermediate*, or *innominate*, terms. In most cases, the court will decide their status by looking at the effect of any breach. The question will be whether breach of a term 'goes to the root of the contract' (is fundamental, and so a *condition*), or has only a minor effect (and so is a *warranty*). Thus, if the court has to decide the status of the term, it will adopt a 'wait and see' approach. It will look at the *consequence* of the breach, rather than the term itself. If the consequence of the breach is serious then any innominate term is more likely to be considered a condition rather than a warranty. This approach was first taken in the following 'Key case'.

Key case

In **Hong Kong Fir Shipping Co Ltd v Kawasaki Kisen Kaisha Ltd (1962)** C chartered a ship to D for 24 months. A clause in the contract stated that it was to be 'in every way fitted for ordinary cargo service'. As it turned out, the engines were old and the crew was less than able. This caused delays, with the result that it became clear D would lose several months' use. D therefore repudiated (rejected) the contract, arguing that the promise that the ship would be fitted for ordinary cargo ▶

service was a condition, which C had broken. The charterers then sued D for breach for pulling out of the agreement. The CA held that the term was an intermediate (innominate) term and looked at the consequence of the breach. The effect of the delay was that the ship was still available for 19 out of the 24 months; therefore, the breach did not go to the root of the contract. This meant it was a warranty and D could not treat the contract as at an end, only claim damages caused by the delay.

In **Bunge Corporation *v* Tradax Export SA (1981)** the HL held the **Hong Kong Fir** approach was not always suitable in mercantile (trading) cases. Giving 13 instead of 15 days' notice to load a ship was found to be a condition, even though the effect was minor. The comment in the opening quote was made by Lord Wilberforce, who felt a clause as to timing would usually be a condition.

Food for thought

So, the **Hong Kong Fir** case has not been without its critics. It arguably leads to uncertainty in an area of law which requires particular clarity, that of business trading. If there is a breach of contract, the parties need to know what their rights and obligations are. This is recognised by the HL in **Bunge Corporation *v* Tradax**. However, treating a term as a condition because of its seeming importance, e.g. where a time is agreed, may mean a contract can be rescinded even though breach of a term leads to only a minor inconvenience. This can be unfair. Look at the following example. Is this fair to Jim?

Example Jim and John agree the terms of a contract for the sale to John of Jim's motorbike. These include delivery by van to John's house, 20 miles away, at 5 p.m. the next day. Jim arrives with the bike at 5.05 p.m. and John refuses to go through with the deal. If the 'time clause' is seen as a condition, this would mean that John can rescind the contract. Jim has wasted his time.

There are ways to avoid the uncertainty. If the parties expressly state in the contract which terms they consider to be of fundamental importance, then the court will be bound by their express intention. Just naming a clause as a condition is not enough though; it must be clearly shown that breach of the term entitles the other to reject the contract.

In **Wickman Machine Tools Sales Ltd *v* Schuler AG (1973)** D had appointed C as an agent to sell goods for them. There was a term in their contract which stated that it was a 'condition' to visit six customers each week. C missed some visits and D ended the contract for breach. The HL held that 'condition' could have several meanings. They decided that the parties could not have intended such serious consequences as losing the whole agency to result from an apparently minor breach. The breach did not entitle D to end the contract. It seemed on the facts that D was using the breach of a relatively minor term as an excuse to end the contract. However, if it is clear in the agreement that breach of the term entitles the other to reject, then this is conclusive. This can also cause problems, as we see in the next case.

In **Union Eagle Limited *v* Golden Achievement Ltd (1997)** C had agreed to purchase a flat and had paid a 10 per cent deposit. The contract stipulated a time for completion of the transaction. There was a further term which stated that failure to comply with any of the conditions in the contract would result in the loss of the deposit. The buyer was ten minutes late for the completion transaction and the seller refused to complete the sale, and kept the deposit. The Privy Council held the buyer had failed to comply with a condition in the contract so the seller could treat the contract as ended.

Food for thought

John would have been able to reject the bike on this basis. The **Hong Kong Fir** approach would seem fairer in circumstances like this, and those in my example; the effect of the breach is minor and could be treated as a warranty. This would allow for damages, for example if John was late for work and lost five minutes' pay, but he would not be able to end the contract. If it was a commercial contract, e.g. for delivery of 500 motorbikes to a dealer, then the need for certainty *might* outweigh the seeming unfairness.

Task

Write a paragraph explaining the 'wait and see' approach used in **Hong Kong Fir**. Look at the other cases and use these to discuss how fair (or not) it is to both the parties to a contract. Add a comment on the relative importance of certainty and fairness. Keep this for essay practice.

Summary

Type of term	Explanation	Effect of breach
Conditions	Fundamental and go to the 'root' of the contract: **Poussard *v* Spiers**	Allows the other party to rescind the contract
Warranties	Not so important terms: **Bettini *v* Gye**	Damages only
Innominate terms	In-between terms that may be one or other of the above depending on the seriousness of any breach: **Hong Kong Fir**	Allows rescission and/or damages depending on whether it is deemed a condition or a warranty

??? Self-test questions

1 Why is it important to distinguish between a condition and a warranty?

2 How do the courts treat an innominate term?

3 Why was the condition treated as a warranty in **Wickman Machine Tools Sales Ltd v Schuler**?

4 Why in **Union Eagle Limited v Golden Achievement Ltd** was a term concerning an apparently minor matter held to be a condition?

5 In what type of case is the **Hong Kong Fir** approach not always suitable?

For further resources and updates please go to the Companion Website accompanying this book at www.pearsoned.co.uk/russell

Unit 7

Exclusion clauses

Some clauses which I have seen would need to be printed in red ink on the face of the document with a red hand pointing to it before the notice could be held to be sufficient.

Denning LJ, **Spurling v Bradshaw (1956)**

By the end of this Unit you should be able to:

- Explain the rules relating to terms which attempt to exclude or limit liability
- Show how the law has developed through both common law and statute
- Apply the rules to a factual situation

What is an exclusion clause?

An exclusion clause was defined in **Yates (1982)** as a term in a contract which '. . . *appears to exclude or restrict a liability or a legal duty which would otherwise arise*'. Although called 'exclusion' clauses, some clauses attempt to exempt a party from liability for breach of contract altogether, while others merely try to limit liability.

Example A notice at the entrance to a car park says, 'The management accepts no responsibility for damage to cars left in this car park'. This is an exclusion clause. It is excluding liability for any damage. If the notice said, 'The management accepts no responsibility for damage to cars left in this car park which is in excess of £500', then this, although usually referred to as an exclusion clause, doesn't exclude liability altogether, but limits any claim to £500.

Although many exclusion clauses are now governed by statute, much of the development of the rules has been through case law. Earlier cases are still important as they will be used when interpreting the statutes, and will also apply to contracts which the statutes do not cover. We will look at the common law rules first.

Common law rules

In determining whether an exclusion clause is valid the courts will examine a number of factors.

Examination pointer

You should be able to refer to a case for each of the following matters. It is usual for a problem scenario to include specific issues which the examiner will want you to pick up on. I have not identified particular 'key' cases here, because the rules have been developed and refined through many cases over the years. They are mostly of equal importance.

Signing

Terms contained in a signed document are usually binding on the person who signed it. In **L'Estrange *v* Graucob (1934)** C was unable to sue for breach of contract because she had signed an agreement containing a clause which excluded liability, even though she hadn't read it. Where there is no signed document, the courts will ask a number of questions in order to decide whether the exclusion clause is part of a contract.

Is the clause in a contractual document?

The document must be one that can reasonably be expected to have contractual terms. In **Chapelton *v* Barry UDC (1940)** C was injured when a deckchair collapsed. The council argued that an exclusion of liability was printed on the ticket given to him when he hired it. The CA held that no reasonable person would expect the ticket to be any more than a receipt for his payment. It could not be expected to contain contractual terms so the clause was not binding.

Was it brought to the notice of the other party – and when?

Reasonable steps must be taken to bring the clause to C's notice. The more onerous or unusual the clause, the greater the notice expected. In **Spurling *v* Bradshaw (1956)** Denning LJ made the point in the opening quote. This was approved in **Interfoto *v* Stiletto Visual Programmes Ltd (1988)** in relation to a clause which allowed a photographic library to charge £5 + VAT per day for each photographic transparency which was returned late by the borrower. An advertising agency returned some transparencies two weeks late and was faced with a bill of £3,783.50! The CA held that the agency did not have to pay this amount. The term had not been sufficiently brought to their notice. Although this was not an exclusion clause, it was expressly stated in this case that the point applied to '*any particularly onerous clause in a printed set of conditions*'.

An exclusion clause will only be part of a contract if notice of it is given *before, or at the time, the contract is made*. In **Olley *v* Marlborough Court Hotel (1949)** a couple booked into a hotel and paid on arrival. Some furs were later stolen from their room and the hotel tried to rely on a notice in their room which excluded liability. The CA held that it was communicated too late to be part of the contract.

In **Thornton *v* Shoe Lane Parking (1971)** a clause excluding liability for injury on a ticket to park, issued from a machine, was not valid. Lord Denning – yes, same judge, but he is now a Lord – said, '*The customer pays his money and gets his ticket. He cannot refuse it. He cannot get his money back. He may protest to the machine,* *even swear at it, but it will remain unmoved . . . He was committed at the very moment when he put his money into the machine. The contract was concluded at that time'.* Again, it was communicated too late and so could not be relied on.

Course of dealing

Even in unsigned documents which are not specifically brought to a person's attention in advance, an exclusion clause *may* be valid if there has been a consistent course of dealing between the parties. In **Spurling Ltd v Bradshaw**, the court said that because a similar contract had been made several times before, C had implied notice of the terms. Much will depend on the circumstances. In **Hollier v Rambler Motors Ltd (1972)** it was held that a customer dealing with a garage three or four times over five years did not constitute a course of dealing.

Task

Can Jack, Jerry and Jill claim for their losses in the following situations?

- Jack buys some paint. It is faulty and damages his wall. The company points out that he signed the invoice which stated, 'We accept no liability for loss or damage caused by our products'.

- Jerry also buys some of this duff paint, but by telephone. The paint arrives the next day with the invoice containing the exclusion clause. He also wants to claim for damage caused.

- Jill buys a cinema ticket but while watching the film her seat collapses and she is badly bruised. The cinema tells her she has no claim because the ticket says on the back that liability is excluded.

After establishing that a clause is part of a contract, it is then necessary for the courts to decide whether a clause is applicable in the particular circumstances. A number of further rules have developed.

Ambiguity

If a clause is ambiguous the courts will apply what is called the *contra proferentem* rule. This means that they will look at any ambiguity against (*contra*) the person relying on it, and in favour of (*proferentem*) the person injured or affected by it. In **Hollier v Rambler Motors Ltd** a term said, 'the company is not responsible for damage caused by fire to customers' cars'. C's car was damaged by fire due to D's negligence. Applying the *contra proferentem* rule, the CA held that the clause could have meant only excluding liability not caused by negligence. It was therefore ambiguous and the garage could not rely on it.

The main purpose rule

If the exclusion clause is in direct contradiction to the main purpose of the contract it will have no effect. In **Pollock & Co. v MacRae (1922)** a clause excluding liability for defective materials and workmanship could not be relied on when the materials were so defective that they could not be used at all. This was held to be contrary to the main purpose of the contract, which was to build and supply engines, presumably ones that worked.

Food for thought

There are many rules on exclusion clauses which have developed through case law. This restricts the ability of people to negotiate their own terms. Do you think the courts are interfering too much or are these rules a necessary protection? You are studying law and, hopefully, now know more about your rights. Most people are probably unaware of these protections, so one can also ask how far such rules are useful in reality. Perhaps law should be compulsory in schools!

Statutory rules

The main statutory controls governing exclusion clauses in consumer contracts are contained in the **Unfair Contract Terms Act 1977 (UCTA)** and the **Unfair Terms in Consumer Contracts Regulations 1999 (UTCCR)**.

Unfair Contract Terms Act 1977

UCTA makes the following ineffective:

- **s. 2(1)**: any term or notice excluding or restricting liability for death or personal injury caused by negligence;
- **s. 6(2)**: any clause that tries to exclude the terms implied into a contract by the **Sale of Goods Act 1979** (as amended) in consumer contracts.

UCTA applies mainly to attempts by businesses to exclude liability, not to individuals. It is intended to *protect* individuals. **Section 6(2)** applies to businesses selling to consumers but under **s. 6(3)**, where the contract is with another business, liability may be excluded if the term is reasonable.

Example | 'Traders Ltd' sells five cars to Cars-are-Us Ltd, which then sells one to John. John sells his old car to Jane. In all three sales, the seller attempts to exclude liability for the goods being found unsatisfactory. **Section 14 Sale of Goods Act 1979** implies a term into all contracts for the sale of goods that they are of a satisfactory quality. This term can be excluded by Traders Ltd when selling to Cars-are-Us if it is seen as reasonable. It cannot be excluded by Cars-are-Us when dealing with John as they are a business and John is a private customer. The implied term *can* be excluded by John selling privately to Jane. Here, the old maxim **caveat emptor** (buyer beware) still applies.

As well as **s. 6(3)** above, the following clauses are valid only if reasonable:

- **s. 2(2)**: any clause which tries to exclude liability for damage to goods caused by negligence;

- **s. 3**: any clause which tries to exclude liability for breach of contract, or for non-performance or substantially different performance, in any consumer contract or any contract made on standard terms.

What is 'reasonable'?

The test for reasonableness is decided by reference to guidelines laid down in **Schedule 2** to the **Act**. These include whether the customer knew of the term, whether they were given an inducement to agree to it (e.g. a discount) and whether the goods were made especially for them. Much is left to the court's discretion. In **George Mitchell (Chesterhall) v Finney Lock Seeds Ltd (1983)** a farmer bought some cabbage seeds which cost less than £200. The seeds were defective and he lost his whole crop, a loss of over £60,000. The sellers relied on a clause limiting liability to the amount paid for the seed. The court held that it was unreasonable on the basis of:

- the size of the loss;
- the relative bargaining powers of the parties;
- the fact that the sellers had been negligent;
- the fact that they had negotiated settlements with other farmers in similar circumstances; and
- the fact that they could – and should – insure against such claims.

In **Smith v Bush (1990)** the HL said that the various factors should be balanced against each other. They confirmed that the relative bargaining powers of the parties was an important factor, as was insurance, and these should be balanced against the difficulty of the task for which liability is being excluded, and the likely effect of finding the clause reasonable.

Task

Look around at school, work or college, or when you next go shopping. See how many notices excluding liability you can spot. Which ones do *you* think would be valid?

Unfair Terms in Consumer Contracts Regulations 1999 (UTCCR)

These regulations were passed in response to **European Directive 93/13**. They govern *all* clauses in contracts, not just exclusion clauses. They apply to contracts between a business and a consumer which have not been individually negotiated, i.e. contracts based on a business's own terms and not specifically negotiated between the parties (called 'standard form contracts'). **UTCCR** complement both **UCTA** and the common law rules, but the emphasis is on 'unfairness'. In particular, all terms must be in 'plain, intelligible language'. Examples of terms which may be considered unfair are found in **Schedule 2**. They include terms which exclude or limit liability for death or personal injury, terms providing excessive compensation if the consumer fails to fulfil their obligations, and terms excluding liability for non-performance of the contract. The Regulations also provide that any ambiguous terms should be read in favour of the consumer. As you can see, there is considerable overlap with **UCTA** and the common law.

Food for thought

The rules are very complex and contained in several places. It is hard enough for lawyers to understand, so it is arguable that consumers, at whom the rules are aimed, have very little idea of what the law is. UTCCR did not replace UCTA but merely added to it – and to the confusion. In 2005 the Law Commission published a draft bill on the subject. This aims to provide a unified set of rules governing contract terms.

If a term is deemed unfair under UTCCR it is not binding on the consumer. If the rest of the contract can stand without the unfair term, the other terms will be valid.

Examination pointer

When applying the rules to a situation, look at the common law rules. Is the clause in a contractual document? Was it brought to the notice of the other party before or at the time the contract was made? Is the clause ambiguous? Is it in contradiction to the main purpose of the contract? Then apply **UCTA** and/or **UTCCR**. This shows the examiner that you appreciate that exclusion clauses are governed by both common law and statute. Use the summary below as a guide to these points and to the relevant cases to use.

Summary

Common law rules	
A party is bound by a signed agreement	**L'Estrange v Graucob**
The clause must be in a contractual document . . .	**Chapelton v Barry UDC**
And brought to the notice of the other party before or at the time the contract is made	**Olley v Marlborough Court Hotel**
If it is particularly onerous, greater efforts must be made to bring it to the notice of the other party	**Spurling v Bradshaw**
If the clause is ambiguous, it is interpreted against the person relying on it	**Hollier v Rambler Motors Ltd**
If it is in direct contradiction to the main purpose of the contract, it is not valid	**Pollock & Co v MacRae**
Statutory rules	
Liability for death or personal injury caused by negligence cannot be excluded	**UCTA s. 2(1)**
Liability for other damage caused by negligence can be excluded if reasonable	**UCTA s. 2(2)**
Implied terms under Sale of Goods Act cannot be excluded in consumer contracts	**UCTA s. 6**
Contracts with consumers must be in 'plain, intelligible language'	**UTCCR 1999**

Self-test questions

1 In what case did Denning LJ make the opening quote, and what did he mean?

2 What happened in **Olley v Marlborough Court Hotel (1949)**?

3 What is the *contra proferentem* rule?

4 What is the difference between **s. 6(2)** and **s. 6(3)** of **UCTA**?

5 State three of the areas in which **UTCCR** overlap with **UCTA** and/or the common law.

 For further resources and updates please go to the Companion Website accompanying this book at **www.pearsoned.co.uk/russell**

Study Block 2 Summary
CONTRACT TERMS

Terms may be express Whether a statement is a term or a representation is based on timing, importance of the term and knowledge	**Or implied** ● by statute: **SOGA** ● by the courts: **The Moorcock** ● by custom
Terms may be: Conditions Warranties Innominate	Breach of a condition is fundamental and the contract may end – **Poussard v Spiers** Breach of a warranty only allows for an award of damages – **Bettini v Guy** The effect of breach will indicate whether the term is a condition or a warranty – **Hong Kong Fir**
Exclusion clauses Attempt to limit or exclude liability	Are governed by statutory rules and the courts
Exclusion clauses are needed in outline only	

Task

Add the principle and brief facts to the cases and answer the questions

Case	Principle	Facts
Bannerman *v* White		
Rowland *v* Divall		
The Moorcock		

Hong Kong Fir		

1 What is the difference between **Poussard _v_ Spiers** and **Bettini _v_ Guy**?

2 Briefly explain **s. 13** and **s. 14** of **SOGA**.

Key criticisms

- In deciding whether a statement is a term or a representation the court will look for the intention of the parties, but they use an objective test to do this, i.e. what the reasonable person, not the parties themselves, would think.

- Should the courts imply terms into a contract or should this be left to Parliament? There are plenty of statutes offering protection to consumers so it can be argued that the courts should leave parties to make their own agreements in non-consumer cases.

- A statement as to the artist was found not to be part of the description of a painting in **Harlingdon**, which seems odd as most people would regard this as a critical matter.

- **Hong Kong Fir** may mean justice is done on the facts, but arguably leads to uncertainty as the parties will not know what a term is until it is breached. The parties need to know their rights and obligations.

- **Bunge Corporation** shows the courts recognise the approach may not be suitable in mercantile (trading) cases and the need for certainty is more important.

- **Union Eagle** also shows timing may well be seen as a condition even though the effect is minor.

Examination practice

Essay questions on this area alone are rare. Most commonly it comes into a problem question, so look at the examination question at the end of Part 1. The most common areas for essays are formation and vitiating factors, and also discharge. An essay on misrepresentation (a vitiating factor) may well require a discussion of terms, and in particular the difference between a term and a representation. Exclusion clauses are only needed in outline so are unlikely to come up in an essay.

Module 6 connections

Morals	Implied terms prevent an unscrupulous business taking advantage of a weaker party, where freedom of contract could become freedom to oppress The same can be said of the rules on exclusion clauses	SOGA
Justice	Implied terms and the rules on exclusion clauses can be used by the courts to do justice in the particular circumstances	**The Moorcock**
Conflicting interests	Taking specialist knowledge into account tips the balance in favour of the non-expert Protection of the consumer is balanced against the rights of a business, by certain terms being implied by statute into all consumer contracts	**Oscar Chess/ Dick Bentley** **SOGA**
Fault	If a car is stolen, the buyer has to return it, and even though s. 12 allows for recovery of the money this is only useful if the seller can be found, so the buyer may well be out of pocket without being at fault in any way A breach of **SOGA** implied terms allows the buyer to end the contract but the seller may not be at fault	**Rowland _v_ Divall** **Godley _v_ Perry**
Creativity	The CA in **Dick Bentley** distinguished **Oscar Chess** so that the buyer was protected The courts will imply terms into a contract in order for it to make sound business sense Innominate terms allow the court to look to the effect of the breach to decide the status of a term	 **The Moorcock** **Hong Kong Fir**

For further resources and updates please go to the Companion Website accompanying this book at www.pearsoned.co.uk/russell

Study Block 3
VITIATING FACTORS

Unit 8 Mistake

Unit 9 Misrepresentation

Once a contract has been formed it may still be found imperfect, and so not binding. The two factors you need to know about are *mistake* and *misrepresentation*. These are called *vitiating* factors and may invalidate an otherwise properly formed contract. Mistake occurs where one or both of the parties to a contract have made a mistake in regard to some aspect of it. We looked at representations in Unit 5. A *mis*representation is an untrue statement by one party which has persuaded the other to enter a contract.

The important difference between *mistake* and *misrepresentation* is the *effect* they have on the contract. Mistake makes a contract **void**. Misrepresentation makes it **voidable**. A void contract means there *never was a contract*. This means that neither party can enforce it, and third parties cannot acquire rights under it. A voidable contract is where *there is a contract* but the innocent party has a right to reject it, i.e. 'avoid' it. Until that time the contract stands. Third parties can acquire rights under a voidable contract up until the time it is avoided. The difference between void and voidable contracts is therefore very important.

| Example | I sell you my car for £700. You sell it to George for £800. If the contract is *void* for mistake then it never existed. The car must be returned to me, and the £700 to you. Poor old George cannot get title to (ownership of) the car, because you never acquired title so cannot pass it on. If the contract is *voidable* for misrepresentation, e.g. I told you that it had only done 30,000 miles but it had done 130,000, then you have a right to reject it. You can do this before selling it on, but not afterwards. In this case George will have title. This is not a problem if you are an honest person. I have £700, you have £800 and George has a car. The problem comes when you are a crook and disappear before you pay me. Either I will lose out or George will. If the contract is *void* George has to return the car. He loses £800. If it is *voidable* he does not. I lose a car and don't have the £700 either. |

Mistake

In the case of a face-to-face sale, where the sale is over a counter or between two individuals, the law is well established that the mere fact that the vendor is under the misapprehension as to the identity of the person in front of him does not operate so as to render the contract void for mistake, it being a mere unilateral mistake as to a quality of the purchaser.

Browne-Wilkinson VC, **Shogun Finance Ltd *v* Hudson (2003)**

By the end of this Unit you should be able to:

● Explain the rules on how and when mistake may invalidate a contract

● Show how the law has developed by reference to cases

● Identify problems with the law in order to attempt an evaluation

The fact that one or both parties to a contract have made a mistake does not as a general rule affect the validity of a contract. Even if it means that one or other of the parties is not really agreeing to what was expected, a mistake will not make a contract void unless it is *fundamental*.

Types of mistake

There are three main types of mistake:

● common mistake – both parties are making the *same mistake*;
● mutual mistake – the parties are making *different* mistakes;
● unilateral mistake – only *one* party is making a mistake.

Example Roger is selling a car to Rob. Unknown to either of them it has been destroyed on the way to Roger's garage. This is a *common mistake*; they are both making the same mistake (that the car exists). As it is fundamental (no car) the contract is likely to be void for mistake. Roger does not have to provide the car and Rob does not have to pay for it. However, if Roger intends selling his estate car but Rob believes he is getting a sports car, this is a *mutual mistake*. They are making different mistakes (Roger that the contract is for an estate car, Rob that it is for a sports car). Again, the contract may be void. Third, if Roger thinks, wrongly, that Rob is a famous actor and so is happy to allow him time to pay, this is a *unilateral mistake*. Only Roger has made a mistake. A mistake as to the identity of the other will not usually render the contract void, especially where it is made face to face.

Let's look at each in a little more detail.

Common mistake

This occurs where both parties are thinking alike but both are wrong. They may be wrong about:

- the existence of the subject matter
- the quality of the subject matter

The existence of the subject matter

A mistake as to the existence of the subject matter (*res extincta*), may make a contract void.

Key case

In **Couturier v Hastie (1856)** a buyer contracted to buy some corn to be delivered by ship to England. Unknown to the parties, the corn had begun to go off in transit, and so was sold by the shipper. As the corn no longer existed the HL held that the buyer did not have to pay for it. The seller had not delivered as agreed. Although not specifically based on mistake, it has been taken as the leading case on non-existent subject matter.

This area is now to some extent covered by **s. 6** of the **Sale of Goods Act 1979**, which provides that if goods have perished, the contract is void. However, it is not fully clear whether **s. 6** would apply to goods which *never existed*, as it refers to goods which 'have perished'. Also, mistake will not make a contract void if the parties have made provision for the issue in the contract, e.g. they have allocated the risk to one party. In this case that party bears the risk and cannot claim mistake.

Example

If the contract between Roger and Rob had contained a clause saying that any risk passes to the buyer once the contract is made, then Rob should take care to insure against the possibility of the car being destroyed. He has accepted the risk and so will have to pay for the car.

In the Australian case of **McCrae v Commonwealth Disposals Commission (1951)** the Commission had accepted a tender by C for the salvage of a tanker, but it turned out that the tanker did not exist. By the time this was discovered C had spent a considerable amount of money in preparation for the salvage. The court held that damages should be awarded to C for breach of an implied term that the tanker existed.

Food for thought

The facts of **McRae** were not dissimilar to those of **Couturier** but produced a different result. The decision may seem fair in the circumstances, but conflicts with the **Couturier** principle that there can be no contract for something which does not exist. The **Sale of Goods Act** seems to favour the **Couturier** decision but refers to goods which have perished, not to goods which never existed as in **McRae**.

The quality of the subject matter

A mistake as to the quality or value of the subject matter is not usually fundamental enough to render a contract void. In **Leaf v International Galleries 1950**, a buyer and seller of a picture both believed it to be by Constable (a *common* mistake). Some five years later the buyer discovered it wasn't. Although the case was based on misrepresentation rather than mistake, the CA confirmed that the contract could not have been void for mistake, because it was only as to the *quality* of the picture.

Examination pointer

If a contract is not void for mistake there may be a second argument that it is voidable for misrepresentation, as in **Leaf**. This is discussed in the next Unit. You will often need to discuss both. If the contract is voidable, the innocent party has a right to reject it, but note that the right doesn't last indefinitely. Thus in **Leaf** the right to reject was lost due to the five-year delay. A void contract means there never was a contract so third parties cannot acquire rights. If the contract had been void and he had sold the painting, the new buyer would have to return it.

The leading mistake case on 'quality' is **Bell v Lever Bros (1932)**.

Key case

In **Bell**, a company agreed to pay compensation for terminating the contracts of the chairman and vice chairman following an amalgamation. It later turned out that they had breached their contracts so could have been dismissed without compensation. The company argued that the contract was void for mistake and claimed a return of the money. The HL held that the contract was not void as the mistake only related to the *quality* of the contract, which was not a fundamental mistake. The company got what it bargained for, a termination of the service contract. Termination with compensation was not *fundamentally* different from termination without compensation.

In **Solle v Butcher (1950)** the CA had held that if the contract was not void for mistake at common law, equity could step in to grant rescission in order to do justice. Thus a common mistake that the **Rent Act** did not apply to a tenancy agreement did not void the contract, but equity could allow rescission on terms

– that the rent did not exceed the maximum allowed under the Act, meaning C could stay in the flat. Although this approach was followed in several other cases, the CA made clear in **Great Peace Shipping Ltd v Tsavliris Salvage (International) Ltd (2002)** that **Solle** was wrongly decided. It is now clear that the law on mistake is governed solely by the common law and equity has no role.

Key case

In **Great Peace**, D, a salvage company, had hired C's vessel to stand by to save the crew of a damaged ship if it became necessary before its own salvage tug could arrive. The contract provided for a right to cancel, but with an obligation to pay a cancellation fee. Both parties believed that the vessel and the damaged ship were only a few hours apart. In fact, they were 39 hours apart. When D discovered this, instead of immediately cancelling the contract it looked for a closer vessel. Only after finding one did D cancel, and C claimed the cancellation fee.

D refused to pay, arguing the contract was void for mistake. The CA rejected this argument, noting that the fact that D did not cancel the contract until after another, closer, vessel had been found showed that it had not believed that C's services were 'something essentially different' from those originally envisaged. The contract was valid, D had a right to cancel, but was obliged to pay the cancellation fee as agreed.

D further argued that if not void for mistake, then equity could provide relief following **Solle v Butcher**. This was also rejected. The CA felt bound by the HL decision in **Bell** and said that **Solle** was wrongly decided.

The law on common mistake was summarised by the CA in **Great Peace**. Mistake will not apply:

- unless unforeseen circumstances make performance of the contract impossible or 'something essentially different' from that agreed by the parties;
- if one of the parties has guaranteed the existence of the subject matter;
- if one of the parties has accepted the risk (that the subject matter will exist);
- if the non-existence of the subject matter is the fault of either party (e.g. in **McRae** the Commission were at fault in not checking the tanker was where they said it was).

Food for thought

The decisions in **Solle** and **Bell** left it unclear as to when, and whether, the common law or equity would apply. Having two sets of rules made the law uncertain, a point recognised by the CA in **Great Peace**. This case has perhaps clarified this area of law, but the involvement of equity allowed for a fairer solution. The common law rules are very strict, as can be seen in **Leaf**. If you mistakenly believe a painting is by a famous artist surely this is 'something essentially different' to a painting by someone else? The CA indicated that it was for Parliament, not the courts, to amend the common law.

Mutual mistake

This is similar to common mistake, but here the parties are thinking differently, i.e. they are at cross-purposes. The courts rarely find such a mistake renders the contract void. It is looked at objectively. What would a reasonable person infer from the behaviour of the parties? If it is impossible to do this, the contract may be void. In my example, a reasonable person is unlikely to be able to say whether the contract is for an estate car or a sports car, so the contract may be void for mistake.

In **Raffles v Wichelhaus (1864)** a buyer of cotton was expecting delivery on a ship called *Peerless* sailing from Bombay in October. In fact there were two different ships called *Peerless*, and the seller sent the cotton on the ship sailing in December. The court held that the buyer was entitled to reject the cotton. A reasonable person would be unlikely to find that there was an agreement. One person intended the October ship and the other intended the December one.

Unilateral mistake

A unilateral mistake is one made by only one party. It often arises in mistaken identity cases involving the sale of goods to crooks who then vanish without paying. The seller will argue the contract is void because if the goods have been sold on they can then be reclaimed.

Mistake as to identity

A mistake as to identity is rarely fundamental enough to render a contract void. A mistake as to some *quality* of a person will not suffice. The other party must have intended dealing with someone else entirely. This is best explained by looking at some cases.

In **Phillips v Brooks Ltd (1919)** a crook went to a jeweller's and pretended to be someone called Sir George Bullough, giving a London address. The jeweller checked the telephone book, saw that such a person did live at that address, and allowed him to take a ring worth £450 before clearing his cheque. The crook pawned the ring. The cheque bounced and the jeweller argued mistake, claiming the return of the ring from the pawnbroker. The court rejected this argument and said the shopkeeper had contracted to sell the ring to the person who came into his shop, i.e. the person who pretended that he was Sir George Bullough. This was what he had done; his mistake was merely as to whether the man was creditworthy (a quality), not his particular identity. The contract was therefore valid. It was also made clear that identity will not be deemed significant if it is not raised until the contract is concluded, especially if dealing face to face. Here it was *after* the contract that the issue was raised, when it was time to pay.

The same approach was taken in **Lewis v Averay (No. 1) (1972)**. Here a crook buying a car pretended to be the actor Richard Greene. He was therefore allowed to pay by cheque, but the cheque bounced. By this time the car had been sold to Mr Averay. Again, it was held that the contract was not void, so Mr Averay obtained good title to the car.

This seems clear, but doubts had been raised in the case of **Ingram v Little (1961)**. Here two elderly sisters were selling a car. They refused to take a cheque until the buyer said that he was a particular person and, as in **Phillips**, they checked this in the telephone book. This time the court held that the contract was void and they could reclaim the car, which had again been sold to a third party.

Task

Compare **Ingram v Little** and **Lewis v Averay (No. 1)**. The facts are very similar. It is unclear why the court held the contract void in **Ingram**. Make a note of the facts and which decision you think is the better one.

So, the person arguing mistake must show:

- an intention to deal with someone else;
- that the identity was important; and
- that reasonable steps were taken to verify it.

If dealings are carried on by post, similar rules apply, although it may be easier to show someone's identity was important when they are not standing in front of you. In **Cundy v Lindsay (1878)** a crook called Blenkarn signed an order for goods to look like 'Blenkiron & Co.', a company that actually existed. This contract was held to be void because the supplier had intended to deal with Blenkiron & Co., not Blenkarn. This can be compared to **King's Norton Metal Co. v Edridge Merrett & Co. (1897)**. Here a crook ordered goods using headed notepaper with a false name. The supplier failed to show that the contract was void because they had intended dealing with the person who ordered the goods. These issues were discussed at length in **Shogun Finance Ltd v Hudson (2003)**.

Key case

In **Shogun**, a crook had signed a hire-purchase agreement for a car, pretending to be someone else. There was some argument about whether this was a face-to-face arrangement or not. The crook had dealt with the car dealer face to face, but not the finance company. The finance company had done a credit check on the person he claimed to be and told the dealer to release the car. The HL treated this in the same way as **Cundy**, rather than as a face-to-face contract. Because the finance company believed they were dealing with someone else entirely, the contract was void for mistake. The finance company could therefore reclaim the car from Mr Hudson, to whom the crook had sold it.

In **Shogun**, Browne-Wilkinson VC said, '*only in cases where the identity of the purchaser is of direct and important materiality in inducing the vendor to enter into the contract is a mistake of that kind capable of avoiding the contract*'.

So the essential difference is whether the crook pretends to be someone else who actually exists, or just uses a false name. In the first case, the contract may be void for mistake (**Cundy, Shogun**); in the second, it is not (**Phillips, King's Norton**).

Food for thought

Although the HL decided in **Shogun** that this was not a face-to-face situation, the case law on these was discussed at some length. The opening quote from Browne-Wilkinson VC in the CA was approved by the majority in the HL. The only case out of line with the principle is **Ingram v Little**. The HL felt that **Ingram** was wrongly decided. Perhaps the fact that the sellers in **Ingram** were elderly and vulnerable had influenced the decision. However, it can be argued that cases should be based on clear principles of law, not individual circumstances. These cases raise difficult issues. There are usually two innocent parties so the decision is likely to be unfair to someone. It is arguable that in **Shogun** the finance company was at fault in not checking properly. The decision left Mr Hudson seriously out of pocket. Do you think justice was done?

In all cases the mistake must be made *before* the contract and have *induced* one party to enter the contract. In **Amalgamated Investment & Property Co. Ltd v John Walker & Sons (1977)** a property sold for redevelopment became listed the day after the contract for sale was made, drastically reducing the value. The buyer argued mistake (that it was not listed) but as it was listed *after* the contract, he failed.

Task

Read the cases in this Unit so far. Make up a diagram showing the different types of mistake with a case example of each. Note where the courts might find a contract void, and where they will not. Keep this for revision and exam practice.

Rectification

This is an equitable remedy, which only applies to written contracts where the parties have agreed on a term but left it out of the document by mistake. The court will attempt to discover the common intention of the parties and rectify the document accordingly. As there must be an agreement it will rarely apply to a unilateral mistake. In **George Wimpey UK Ltd v V I Construction Ltd (2005)** D had allowed C to enter a contract knowing C was mistaken about the terms. The High Court ordered rectification and D appealed. The CA allowed the appeal and held that a unilateral mistake would usually only lead to rectification where the other party had been dishonest.

Non est factum

This is Latin for 'it is not my deed'. It occurs when a person has signed a document believing it to be something completely different. As mistake makes a contract void, the courts take a narrow view of the doctrine. Mistaken signing of a document will only render a contract void where it is:

- fraudulently induced
- a fundamental mistake (as to subject matter of document)
- not negligent

If someone induces another to sign a document by fraud it will still only be void if the document signed is *radically different* from that intended and if there is *no negligence* on the part of the person signing. In **Saunders v Anglia Building Society (1971)** a widow was tricked into signing a document in the belief that she was transferring the title of her house to her nephew so that he could get a loan. In fact the document transferred it to a friend of her nephew's, who mortgaged it and kept the money. She argued *non est factum*. The HL rejected the argument on two counts. First, she had not signed a *radically different* document. What she thought she was signing, and what she did sign, was a transfer of title of her house to enable her nephew to raise funds. The fact that his friend had been dishonest did not change the object of the exercise. Second, she had been *negligent*. She had not bothered to read the document because she had broken her glasses.

This can be contrasted with **Lloyd's Bank v Waterhouse (1990)**, where a plea succeeded. Here a person had signed a document at a bank. He did not read it because he was unable to read. The evidence was that he had asked several questions in relation to what he was signing and so had not been negligent.

Examination pointer

Where the situation involves fraud there may be an argument for mistake and misrepresentation. Look again at the introduction for the effect of each. Make sure you can explain these, especially if goods have been passed on to a third party. Misrepresentation may not help the person defrauded unless the contract has been avoided before this happens, because there is nobody around to sue. Mistake would be the preferred option.

Summary

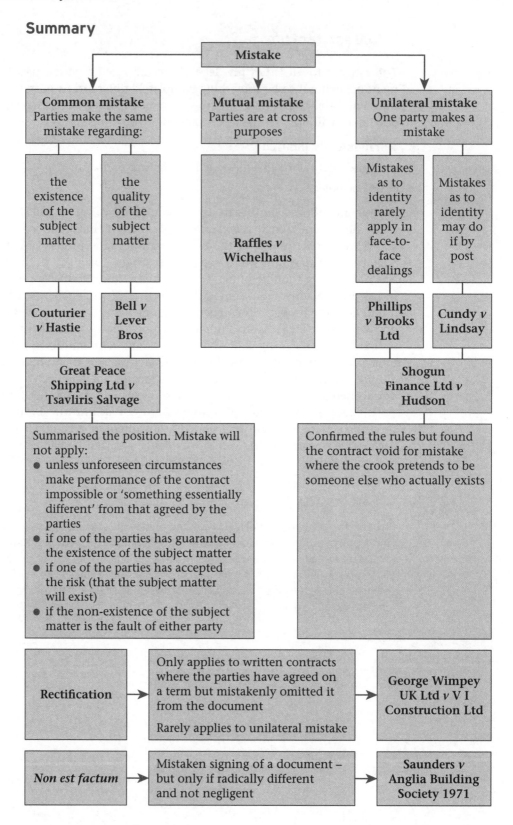

Self-test questions

1 Explain the difference between common mistake, mutual mistake and unilateral mistake.

2 The CA in **Great Peace** gave four instances where mistake will not apply. What are they?

3 What were the facts of **Shogun**?

4 When does rectification apply?

5 What are the three essentials for a successful plea of *non est factum*?

For further resources and updates please go to the Companion Website accompanying this book at **www.pearsoned.co.uk/russell**

Misrepresentation

The state of a man's mind is as much a fact as the state of his digestion.

Bowen LJ, **Edginton *v* Fitzmaurice (1885)**

By the end of this Unit you should be able to:

● Explain what a misrepresentation is

● Show how the law treats misrepresentations by reference to cases

● Identify problems with the law in order to attempt an evaluation

What is a misrepresentation?

A misrepresentation is an untrue statement of fact, made before the contract, which induces a person to enter into the contract. We saw when looking at express terms that to decide if a pre-contractual statement is a term or a representation the courts will look at:

● timing

● the importance of the statement

● the relative expertise of the parties

If it is a term, the wronged party can sue for breach of contract. If it is not a term but a representation then it is necessary to see whether it is actionable, i.e. is there a remedy in court? There may be if the representation was not true – if it was a *mis*representation.

Task

Look up the following cases. Which would you use to illustrate each of the three bullet points above?

Oscar Chess Ltd *v* Williams (1957)

Routledge *v* Mackay (1954)

Bannerman *v* White (1861)

For a statement to be actionable three requirements need to be satisfied. The statement must:

● be *untrue*;

● be a statement of *fact*, not opinion;

● have *induced* the other to enter the contract.

An untrue statement

Although referred to as 'statements', representations may be by words or conduct. However, silence cannot normally amount to a representation.

Example
> Sam is buying a car from Gary. Gary does not tell Sam that the engine has been playing up. Sam cannot sue for breach of contract when he finds that the car won't start. He should have asked about it or checked for himself – the legal rule is *caveat emptor*, or 'buyer beware'.

There are exceptions. Keeping silent may amount to a representation when:

- not admitting to a change in previous statement;
- where there is a partial disclosure;
- where material facts are omitted.

Not admitting to a change in previous statement

In **With *v* O'Flanagan (1936)** a doctor had told a buyer what the annual income from his practice was worth. He then became ill and his income dropped considerably as his patients left the practice. His failure to tell the buyer of the change in circumstances amounted to a misrepresentation.

Where there is a partial disclosure

In **Dimmock *v* Hallett (1866)** a seller of land which had tenant farmers on it told the buyer that the farms were let (thus producing an income). He omitted to add that the tenants had been given notice to quit. This type of half-truth amounts to a misrepresentation. Essentially you can say nothing at all, but if you *do* say something it should be the whole truth.

Where material facts are omitted

Certain types of contract require 'utmost good faith'. In such cases omitting a material fact may amount to a misrepresentation, e.g. in a contract of insurance where non-disclosure could affect the premium.

Example
> Con applies for life insurance and does not tell the insurance company of an existing illness. This would be a contract which required 'utmost good faith'. His silence could therefore amount to a misrepresentation.

A statement of *fact*

A mere statement of opinion has no legal effect.

Key case

In **Bisset v Wilkinson (1927)** a seller of land told the buyer that he thought it would support 2,000 sheep. The land had not been used as a sheep farm before so his statement was one of opinion rather than fact. The relative expertise of the parties will be important in assessing whether something said is opinion or fact.

In **Nelson Group Services Ltd v BG plc (2002)** a statement as to the likely future sales figures of a business was held to be one of fact because it was based on factual knowledge, unlike **Bisset**, where the seller was not an expert and had no knowledge of the matter.

Task

Compare the two cases of **Oscar Chess Ltd v Williams (1957)** and **Dick Bentley Productions v Harold Smith Motors Ltd (1965)** (see p. 40). Why was a statement held to be a term in one case but only a representation in the other?

A statement of intention, i.e. a promise to do something in the future, is not usually treated as one of fact. However, it can be if the maker of the statement *knows* it is untrue.

Key case

In **Edginton v Fitzmaurice (1885)** a prospectus was issued inviting loans from the public, and stating the money was intended for improving and extending the business. The company actually intended to use the money to pay off some debts. This was held to be a misrepresentation because it was not a statement of what *might* happen, but a statement of what *would* happen. The statement of intention in the prospectus was one of fact because the company *knew* (a state of mind) that something else was intended.

Induced the other to enter the contract

If the statement does not persuade the other person to enter the contract it does not matter how untrue it is.

Example

I see a lovely red sports car advertised in the local paper. I fall in love with it at first sight and pay the asking price happily. The seller tells me it has only had one owner. If this turns out to be untrue I cannot argue that it is a misrepresentation because it did not influence my decision to buy the car.

A case example is **Attwood v Small (1838)**, where a buyer was unable to sue for misrepresentation because he had not relied on the seller's statement, but had done his own survey. The statement need not be the *only* reason for entering into a contract, but it must be *part* of the reason. This was stated in **Edginton**, where the person investing in the company had partly relied on the prospectus and partly on what he believed he would gain. This was sufficient.

If a person *knows* a statement is not true then that person cannot be said to have relied on it, and will have no remedy. However, it was confirmed in **Peekay Intermark Ltd v Australia and New Zealand Banking Group Ltd (2005)** that the fact that the truth can be checked will not prevent an action. Here, pre-contract misrepresentations about an investment were made but had been corrected in a later document which the investor signed. The court held that the original statement had induced the investor to enter the contract and he was entitled to expect that the material facts remained unchanged. He could therefore sue for misrepresentation, even though he could have discovered the truth if he had read the later document.

Types of misrepresentation

There are three types of misrepresentation, with different remedies:

- fraudulent – a false statement made *knowingly*;
- negligent – a statement made *negligently* which is untrue;
- innocent – a false statement made *in the reasonable belief it was true.*

Fraudulent misrepresentation

Fraudulent misrepresentation comes under the common law tort of deceit. It was defined in **Derry v Peek (1889)** as a false statement made knowingly, without belief in its truth, or recklessly, careless as to whether it is true or false. Here, a statement in a company prospectus was not fraudulent because the company believed it was true when it was made. We saw the case of **Lewis v Averay** in the previous Unit. That would be a fraudulent misrepresentation because he *knew* he wasn't Richard Greene.

Examination pointer

Be prepared to discuss both mistake and misrepresentation. If mistake succeeds, a contract is void, as if it had never existed. If the contract in **Lewis v Averay (No. 1)** had been void for mistake, ownership of the car would not have passed to the third party and the seller would have got it back. If the contract is not void for mistake, then misrepresentation can be relied on. This makes the contract voidable, which means taking steps to avoid it. This cannot be done once the property has passed on, so in **Lewis** the seller could not reclaim the car. You should discuss mistake first because if the fraudster has disappeared there is no one to sue for misrepresentation.

Negligent misrepresentation

This comes under both the common law tort of negligence and the **Misrepresentation Act 1967**:

Tort: a statement made negligently which is untrue is called a *negligent misstatement*. This was established in **Hedley Byrne v Heller (1964)**. It is a false statement made honestly but without grounds for belief in it. It is up to C to prove that the statement was made negligently. There is also a need to prove a special relationship. A special relationship exists where it is foreseeable that someone will rely on the statement, and it is reasonable to do so. Knowledge is important here. If one party has superior knowledge then it is foreseeable and reasonable for the other to rely on a statement. In **Esso Petroleum v Mardon (1976)** a statement by Esso's sales representative as to the likely income from a petrol station was held to be a negligent misstatement because he had the relevant expertise. It was reasonable for the tenant to rely on his statement.

If a contract has been entered into, the usual course of action is under statute.

Statute: Under **s. 2(1) Misrepresentation Act 1967**, if one party enters a contract because of a misrepresentation then that party can claim damages. There is no need to prove a relationship and the burden of proof moves from C to D. D must prove the statement was *not* negligently made. In **Howard Marine and Dredging Ltd v Ogden & Sons Ltd (1978)** Bridge LJ said, '*the statute imposes an absolute obligation not to state facts which the representor cannot prove he had reasonable ground to believe*'. Thus, even though the statement (as to the carrying capacity of two barges hired by C) was honestly made, the hirer was held to have made a negligent misrepresentation because he should have checked his information on such an important matter.

Innocent misrepresentation

This is a false statement made in the reasonable belief it was true. Until **Hedley Byrne** there was no negligent misstatement, so if a statement was not fraudulent it was treated as innocent. Now, though, an innocent statement is one made *entirely* without fault. Any fault on the part of the maker of the statement (e.g. not checking the facts in **Howard Marine**) means the action will come under negligence.

Food for thought

Should there be an action for a completely innocent misrepresentation? If the statement was made entirely without fault it is arguably unfair to D. However, C has also acted without fault so it is perhaps fair because usually D will just be put back to the pre-contract position and won't actually lose money.

Remedies

Remedies are discussed in a separate Unit, but included here because there are differences in the remedies for the various types of misrepresentation. Both rescission of the contract and damages are available for fraudulent and negligent misrepresentations. For innocent misrepresentations rescission is the normal remedy, with damages under **s. 2(2)** as an alternative at the discretion of the court.

Rescission

This is where the parties to the contract are returned to their pre-contract position. In the case of a sale this would mean the goods are returned and the money repaid. It is an equitable remedy and this means that it is at the discretion of the court. It is not available as of right. If it would be unfair, e.g. to an innocent third party who has acquired title to goods, the court will award damages under **s. 2(2)** of the **Act** instead. Thus in **Lewis v Averay**, where ownership of the car had passed to the third-party buyer, the court refused rescission on the grounds that it would not be fair to the person who had bought the car in good faith.

The right to rescission can be lost by:

- affirmation
- lapse of time
- impossibility to return the parties to the pre-contract position
- third-party rights

Affirmation: if C has agreed to continue with the contract after discovering the misrepresentation there is no action for rescission. Agreement can be by words or conduct, e.g. continuing to use the goods. It was confirmed in **Production Technology Consultants v Bartlett (1988)** that although the right to rescind is lost, damages may still be claimed.

Lapse of time: this may not apply where a misrepresentation is fraudulent but will if negligent or innocent. In **Leaf v International Galleries (1950)**, (see p. 64) a painting described as by Constable was found some five years later not to be so. The court held that it was too late to rescind the contract because the buyer had had plenty of time to check for himself. Again, although the right to rescind may be lost, damages can be claimed. If the statement is innocent, this is discretionary and not as of right.

Impossibility: if it is impossible to restore the parties to their original position then rescission cannot be awarded. However, rescission may be granted where restoration can only be partial. In **Erlanger v New Sombrero (1878)** a mine had been partly worked so could not be returned in the same state as when sold. The court awarded rescission, with damages as compensation for the reduction in value of the mine.

Third-party rights: if someone else has acquired rights in the subject matter of the contract then returning the contracting parties to their original position would be unfair to this third party. We saw examples of this in **Lewis v Averay**, **Phillips v Brooks** etc.

Food for thought

Do you think that the courts achieve a fair balance in relation to rescission? In cases such as **Lewis** and **Phillips** there are often two innocent parties, so any decision will mean one of them suffering loss.

Damages

Damages are available as of right for fraudulent and negligent misrepresentations. For innocent misrepresentations damages under **s. 2(2)** *may* be awarded, at the discretion of the court. Different rules apply to the different types of claim.

Fraudulent misrepresentations: This would be a claim in tort and the rule is that an award of damages should return C to the position held before the misrepresentation was made.

<table>
<tr><td>Example</td><td>Brian buys a painting from Tim for £2,000. Tim told him it is by a well-known artist and well worth the price. This persuaded Brian to buy it, but it later turns out to only be worth £200. Returning Brian to his earlier financial position (he had £2,000) means he will get £1,800 damages (this plus a painting worth £200 = £2,000). If Brian chooses rescission of the contract he will get £2,000 and give the painting back to Tim.</td></tr>
</table>

Although tort claims are usually based on whether the losses were foreseeable, where the misrepresentation was fraudulent the courts have allowed unforeseeable loss to be claimed. In **Doyle *v* Olby (Ironmongers) (1969)** Lord Denning said, '*it does not lie in the mouth of a fraudulent person to say that they [the losses] could not reasonably have been foreseen*'.

Negligent misrepresentations at common law: this would again be a claim in tort. However, here the normal rules apply so only foreseeable losses can be claimed.

Negligent misrepresentations under the Misrepresentation Act 1967: a claim under **s. 2(1)** of the **Act** would appear to be the same as for fraudulent misrepresentation. The **Act** does not provide a test for damages but in **Royscott Trust *v* Rogerson (1991)** the CA held that damages should be based on the rules governing fraudulent misrepresentation. This indicates that unforeseeable loss can be claimed.

Innocent misrepresentations: according to **s. 2(1)** damages cannot be claimed if D can show that the statement was made in the reasonable belief that it was true. In such a case *only* rescission is available. The remedy for an innocent misrepresentation is *either* damages *or* rescission, not both. If the court does decide that damages are appropriate, it will make an award under **s. 2(2)** of the **Act**. Here again, loss can only be claimed if it is foreseeable.

Indemnity

A further remedy may be available by way of an indemnity. This is not an award of damages but an amount of money to cover expenses incurred due to obligations created by the contract. Now that claims for damages can be made at common law and under the **Act** this remedy is of less significance. It could be useful where the court refuses damages for an innocent misrepresentation and C has been obliged to expend money on the contract.

Examination pointer

Misrepresentation makes the contract voidable, not void. Thus it is valid unless and until it is set aside by the person to whom the statement is made. That person may affirm the contract and sue for damages for any losses, or reject it and sue for damages. However, remember that the court may not allow rescission if there is a third party involved and that you may need to discuss both remedies.

Exclusion of liability

Under **s. 3** of the **Misrepresentation Act 1967** liability can only be excluded if it is reasonable. The test for reasonableness comes under **s. 11** of the **Unfair Contract Terms Act 1977**. In **Walker v Boyle (1982)** a seller of a house had told the buyer that there were no boundary disputes. In the contract of sale was a clause attempting to exclude liability for any errors or misstatements. The court held that although the statement was made innocently the buyer was entitled to rescind the contract, because the clause was unreasonable.

Summary

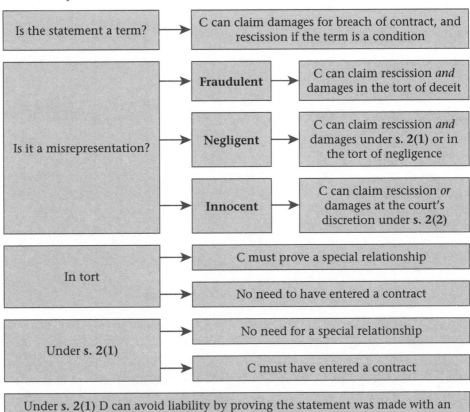

Self-test questions

1 What three things do the courts look at when deciding if a statement is a term or a representation?

2 What three requirements need to be satisfied for a statement to be a misrepresentation?

3 Give two ways the right to rescission can be lost.

4 What is the rule on excluding liability?

5 How else can D avoid liability?

 For further resources and updates please go to the Companion Website accompanying this book at **www.pearsoned.co.uk/russell**

Study Block 3 Summary
VITIATING FACTORS

The two factors which may invalidate a contract are mistake and misrepresentation. Look back at the introduction for a reminder of the *effect* each of these has on a contract.

There are three main types of **mistake**	Mistake makes a contract **void**
Common mistake	Parties make the same mistake: as to the existence of the subject matter – **Couturier v Hastie/Great Peace** as to the quality of the subject matter – **Bell v Lever Bros**
Mutual mistake	Parties are at cross purposes – **Raffles v Wichelhaus**
Unilateral mistake	Unilateral mistake as to identity rarely makes a contract void – **Phillips v Brooks** – but may do where the crook pretends to be someone else who actually exists – **Shogun**
Mistaken signing of a document is governed by the rules on *non est factum*	
A **misrepresentation** must be distinguished from a term	If a **term** then C can claim damages for breach of contract, and rescission if the term is a condition
There are three types of **misrepresentation**	Misrepresentation makes a contract **voidable**
Fraudulent	C can claim rescission *and* damages in the tort of deceit
Negligent	C can claim rescission *and* damages under s. 2(1) **Misrepresentation Act 1967** or in the tort of negligence
Innocent	C can claim rescission *or* damages at the court's discretion under s. 2(2)

Task

Fill in the gaps:

The law on common mistake was summarised by the CA in **Great** _____. Mistake will not apply:

● unless _____ circumstances make performance of the contract impossible or 'something _____ different' from that agreed by the parties;

● if one of the parties has _____ the existence of the subject matter;

● if one of the parties has _____ the _____ (that the subject matter will exist);

● if the non-existence of the subject matter is the _____ of either party.

A misrepresentation is an _____ statement of _____, made before the contract, which _____ a person to enter into the contract. Three requirements need to be satisfied. The statement must:

● be _____

● be a statement of *fact* not _____

● have *induced* the other to _____ the _____

Silence may amount to a representation when:

● not admitting to a change in _____ _____

● where there is a _____ disclosure

● where _____ facts are omitted

Key criticisms

● The facts of **McRae** were not dissimilar to those of **Couturier** but produced a different result.

● It is not fully clear whether **s. 6** would apply to goods which *never existed*, as it refers to goods which 'have perished'.

● **Great Peace** has perhaps clarified the law on mistake, but arguably equity allowed for a fairer solution.

● Mistakenly believing a painting is by a famous artist is arguably 'something essentially different' to a painting by someone else – **Leaf**.

● It is arguable that in **Shogun** the finance company was at fault in not checking properly.

Examination practice

January 2005

Outline and comment critically on the rules on **either** misrepresentation **or** mistake in contract.

(25 marks)

Module 6 connections

Morals	It is questionable that the courts are taking a moral view in certain mistake cases, taking into account who the victim is rather than applying strict legal principles	Ingram *v* Little
	The *non est factum* rules mean the courts won't enforce a contract induced by fraud. Also, the courts will protect someone with a vulnerability	Lloyd's Bank *v* Waterhouse
Justice	There are often two innocent parties in mistaken identity cases so the decision is likely to be unfair to someone. Was justice done in **Shogun**?	
	Is it just to allow a claim for misrepresentation when it was made in all innocence?	
Conflicting interests	Do you think the courts achieve a fair balance when deciding a contract made face to face is not void for mistake? Two innocent parties have competing claims on goods in such cases	Lewis *v* Averay (No. 1) Shogun
	Misrepresentation takes the interests of the third-party buyer into account	
Fault	Where fault is involved the contract will not be void for common mistake	McRae Great Peace
	There are different types of misrepresentation with varying degrees of fault and different remedies	
Creativity	The CA indicated that it was for Parliament, not the courts, to amend the law on mistake	Great Peace

For further resources and updates please go to the Companion Website accompanying this book at www.pearsoned.co.uk/russell

Study Block 4
DISCHARGE AND REMEDIES

Unit 10   Discharge by agreement and performance
Unit 11   Discharge by frustration
Unit 12   Discharge by breach
Unit 13   Remedies

Discharge of contract is where the contract comes to an end. This can occur by performance, agreement, frustration and breach. Although referred to as discharge of contract, it is more correctly discharge of *obligations* under the contract. Discharge connects with remedies because if the contract is discharged by incomplete performance or by breach, the innocent party will claim the remedy of damages. In some cases rescission of the contract may be available too. This is where the innocent party is excused from any further obligations under the contract. In the case of discharge by frustration, both parties are excused performance. This is where neither party is at fault but something unexpected has made performance impossible.

Example   I offer to paint your bathroom.

- I do it but forget the window frame. This is incomplete performance. I can claim payment, but you can claim an amount to remedy the defect.

- I paint one wall and then walk out as I have been offered a better job elsewhere. This is non-performance and it amounts to breach of contract. You can sue me for any payments made in advance and expenses incurred as a result of my breach.

- I don't do it because I am struck down by a mystery virus and confined to bed. Here the contract is frustrated. Through no fault of mine – or yours – the contract is impossible to perform.

The usual remedy for breach of contract is damages. Damages are available as of right once breach of contract has been proved. In addition there may be an equitable remedy, such as rescission of the contract. This is awarded at the court's discretion.

Example Remember **Bettini** *v* **Gye (1876)** and **Poussard** *v* **Spiers and Pond (1876)**? In the first case the clause was held to be a *warranty* so when it was breached the theatre company could not treat the contract as ended. They could only claim damages for the two missing days. In the second case the court held that her failure to attend amounted to a breach of a *condition* and so the company were entitled to treat the contract as ended. They had no further obligation to perform, i.e. to employ her and the contract was *discharged*, or *rescinded*.

Discharge by agreement and performance

[the rule on performance of a contract] is excessively technical and due for examination in this House.

Lord Wilberforce, **Reardon Smith Line Ltd v Hansentangen (1976)**

By the end of this Unit you should be able to:

- Explain how parties to a contract can agree to end it
- Explain how a contract can be ended by performance
- Show how the law on both these applies by reference to cases
- Identify problems with the law in order to attempt an evaluation

Discharge by agreement

A contract is made by agreement and so can be ended by agreement. Where both parties agree to end the contract and both receive a benefit, there is a *bilateral* discharge. If only one party receives a benefit but has persuaded the other to agree to end it, this is a *unilateral* discharge. We saw that to support an agreement, to make it enforceable, both parties must provide consideration, i.e. one party buys the act or promise of the other (see Unit 3). It is the same with an agreement to terminate. In a bilateral agreement there is usually no problem; each party 'buys' the promise of the other not to enforce the contract. However, if one person has performed, or 'acted', the other party now has an obligation to act. Any agreement to release them from this obligation must be purchased, or it will not be enforceable (unless it is made by deed). This is referred to as 'accord and satisfaction'. The 'accord' is the agreement and the 'satisfaction' is the consideration which makes it enforceable. A few examples may help to make things clear.

Example I agree to sell you my car for £500. We both then agree not to go ahead. This is a *bilateral* agreement. The promise by each of us not to enforce the contract is *executory* consideration. I give up the right to £500 and you give up your right to the car.

Example You ask me to sell you a motorbike instead and I agree to change the contract in this way. This is a *unilateral* agreement as I have not received a benefit. If I change my mind and decide not to sell you a bike instead, you cannot enforce my promise to do so. Your obligation under the contract remains: you owe me £500 for the car. You must buy my agreement to change the contract.

Example

I agree to sell you my car and you agree to pay me £500. I deliver it but you no longer want it. Here, my consideration is *executed*. I have performed my part of the contract. If you want me to agree to end the contract (I will get the car back and you won't have to pay £500) then you need to provide some consideration to buy my agreement. Take me out for dinner perhaps.

If both parties have partly performed, they can each enforce any agreement to discontinue as this is sufficient consideration.

Example

I have half decorated your house and you have half paid me. You are short of cash and want to finish it yourself. I have been offered a much better job elsewhere. Agreeing to forego full performance is consideration from both of us. We both receive a benefit. If I change my mind and want to carry on, you can enforce my promise not to continue with the contract.

Under the rule in **Pinnell's Case**, a promise to release someone from a debt will not suffice, unless a new factor is added (e.g. paying early).

A final point. Some contracts require certain formalities to be satisfied. These include contracts for the sale of land. If a contract has to be evidenced in writing then an agreement to vary the terms of that contract must also be evidenced in writing.

Discharge by performance

If both parties perform then there is no problem; the contract is completed. I sell you my car; you pay me £500 for it. We have discharged the contract by performing our obligations. However, problems arise where one party has partly performed or performs late. This ties in with discharge by breach (see Unit 12) because if one person has not performed then there may be a breach of contract. This allows the other to sue for damages, and in some cases discharges the other party from any further obligations.

The basic rule: exact and complete performance

The basic rule is that performance must be *exact and complete*, i.e. '*part performance is no performance*'. This can be harsh, as can be seen in **Cutter v Powell (1795)**.

Key case

In **Cutter**, a sailor had a contract to work on a ship from the West Indies to Liverpool. He died on the voyage and his widow claimed the wages due to the date of death. She was entitled to nothing, as the contract had not been fully performed. The strict approach applies to all 'entire' contracts. These are contracts where there is no obligation on one party to perform until the other has fully performed. The most common examples are contracts for the sale of goods.

In **Re Moore & Co. and Landauer & Co. (1921)** part of a consignment of tinned fruit came in cases of 24 tins, rather than the agreed 30 tins. The correct quantity was received overall, but the buyer was allowed to reject the whole order. This somewhat inflexible approach has been criticised. In **Reardon Smith Line Ltd v Hansentangen (1976)** Lord Wilberforce made the comment opening this Unit. The courts have sought to introduce exceptions to mitigate the rule, so it may not apply where there is:

- substantial performance by one party;
- a severable contract;
- partial performance by one party which has been accepted by the other;
- prevention of performance by one party;
- tender of performance by one party which has been refused by the other.

Substantial performance

Where the contract has been substantially performed it may be possible to claim payment for that performance. In **Hönig v Isaacs (1952)** a decorator had refurbished a flat but the owner refused to pay the balance due of £350 as the work was not exactly as agreed. The court found the contract had been substantially performed. The defects were minor and so payment for the work completed could be claimed, with a reduction for the cost of putting the defects right. This can be compared to **Bolton v Mahadeva (1972)**. In this case a central heating system was installed which was defective. The plumber was entitled to nothing because there were so many defects that the court could not find the contract had been substantially performed. In **Sumpter v Hedges (1898)** a builder stopped work after only partly completing two buildings and stables. He had completed over half the work and claimed payment for this. The court found that he had not substantially performed. He could only claim for the materials that he had left on site, used by the owner to finish the job. By using these, the owner had implied that he would pay for them.

Food for thought

Do you think it fair that in cases like **Bolton v Mahadeva** a person who has done quite a lot of work receives nothing? In **Sumpter v Hedges** the builder may have been at fault in not finishing, but he had completed more than half the work, but received nothing. In 1983 the **Law Commission (Report 121)** proposed changes to the rule but these have not been accepted. An argument in favour is that in big building contracts there will be payment by instalments so the builder will get something for work done so far, but this may not be the case in smaller contracts. Say you have some builders to do some work and they get a better offer elsewhere. If the rule were abolished, it may not be possible to persuade them to finish the job, as they know that they will be paid for work done so far.

Severable contracts

If the contract is not *entire*, but can be divided up, then payment can be claimed for any goods delivered or work done so far. These are called *severable*, or *divisible*, contracts.

Example A building is constructed in several stages, with payments being due at the end of each stage. The builder becomes ill and can't finish the work. Here the instalments due after each stage can be claimed, even though the entire contract is not complete. It would also apply in employment contracts where payment is usually weekly or monthly. An employee who leaves is entitled to payment for any weeks already worked even if the contract was for longer.

Task

Compare **Hönig v Isaacs** and **Bolton v Mahadeva**. Why did one claim fail and the other succeed?

Partial performance

If one party accepts partial performance of the contract, this may avoid the strict rule that performance must be complete. There must be an option to accept or reject, so it would not apply in a case like **Sumpter** because there was no real choice. The owner could not reject because he couldn't tell the builder to take away the half-built buildings, so there was no genuine acceptance. If a party accepts part performance then payment will be due on what is called *quantum meruit*, which means payment of a reasonable price for the work done.

Example You order a case of 12 bottles of wine but only 10 bottles are sent. You have a choice whether to reject the lot or accept 10 and pay a reasonable price for those received.

Prevention of performance

If performance is not complete due to the fault of the other party, a claim on *quantum meruit* can be made. In **Planché v Colbourn (1831)** a writer had done as asked in preparing a manuscript, but the editor had then cancelled the series of which it was to form part. The writer was entitled to be paid for the work done, i.e. the part which he had already performed.

Tender of performance

If one party tenders, or offers, to perform but this is refused by the other, the same applies. In **Startup v Macdonald (1843)** D refused delivery of some goods from C, which arrived at 8.30 on a Saturday evening, on the last day on which delivery had been promised. C succeeded in claiming damages as he had done all he could to deliver and had done so within the contractual time. It is possible that this would be differently decided today, as legislation on the sale of goods stipulates that delivery must be at a reasonable hour.

Task

Chris agrees to take 10 tonnes of potatoes to Glasgow for Danny in return for £50. He gets three-quarters of the way to Glasgow and stops there. Can he claim the £50? Would your answer be different if he got to Glasgow but with only 3 tonnes?

Two further issues need to be considered:

● time; and
● vicarious performance.

Time

If performance is complete, but late, much depends on whether timing is seen as a condition or a warranty (see Unit 6). If a stipulation about timing is 'of the essence', i.e. a fundamental part of the contract, then it is a condition and late delivery will entitle the other party to reject altogether. If timing is not 'of the essence' then the other party cannot reject, but can claim damages for any loss suffered. Whether time is of the essence may be expressed in the contract or implied by circumstances. If no time is stated the court will consider what is 'reasonable time' in the circumstances.

Example   Sadie orders and pays for a birthday cake for a party. The baker promises to deliver it by 5 p.m. If it doesn't arrive until 9 p.m., Sadie can refuse to accept the cake and demand a refund.

Time will usually be fundamental, and thus a condition, where the contract is for the sale of perishable goods. Getting a delivery of milk two days late is no good to the buyer, but a pair of shoes may be different, unless they were promised in time for a special occasion.

Examination pointer

You may need to discuss conditions and warranties when looking at discharge by performance. If a condition has not been performed correctly then rescission of the contract as well as damages are possible. If it is a warranty then only damages can be claimed. In *Hönig* v *Isaacs* performance was substantial so he had to go on with the contract, but could claim damages for putting the defects right.

Vicarious performance

It may be possible to perform through a third party. Thus in the task, if Chris is ill but asks a friend to take the potatoes to Glasgow then the contract has been performed. This is not possible if it is a contract for personal services; there is no point in sending Fred Smith to perform a contract for George Michael! If performance is through a third party it is still the original parties to a contract who are liable. This is a basic rule of contract – only the parties to a contract can sue or be sued. Thus if Chris's friend doesn't deliver the potatoes, Danny will sue *Chris* for non-performance.

Summary

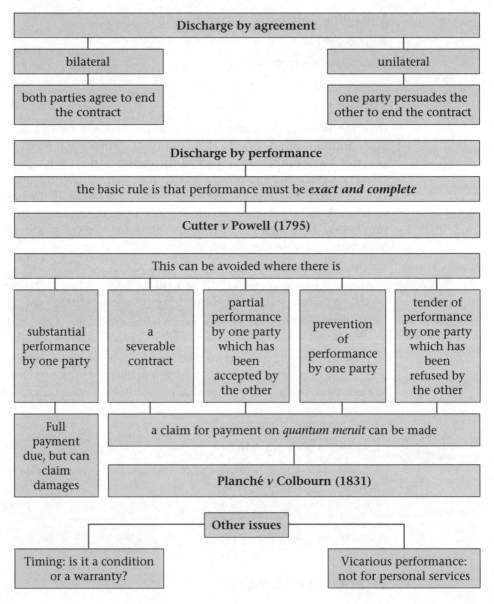

Self-test questions

1 What is the difference between a bilateral agreement and a unilateral agreement?

2 What is the basic rule for discharge by performance?

3 State two ways this rule may be avoided, with case examples.

4 Why might **Startup *v* McDonald** be decided differently today?

5 What does *quantum meruit* mean?

 For further resources and updates please go to the Companion Website accompanying this book at **www.pearsoned.co.uk/russell**

Discharge by frustration

'... frustration occurs whenever the law recognises that without default of either party a contractual obligation has become incapable of being performed because the circumstances in which performance is called for would render it a thing radically different from that which was undertaken by the contract'.

Lord Radcliffe, **Davis Contractors v Fareham UDC (1956)**

By the end of this Unit you should be able to:
- Explain the rules on frustration of a contract
- Explain the effect of frustration
- Show how the law has developed and how it applies by reference to cases
- Identify problems with the law in order to attempt an evaluation

In certain cases a contract is said to be frustrated. This is a legal term, not what you might think of as frustration.

Example | Mike contracts with Mitch for the delivery of some computer software. Mitch does not deliver it on time and Mike is very frustrated that he cannot get on with the work he wanted to do. This is not legal frustration. Mitch will be in breach of contract but the contract still stands.

Mitch does not deliver because there is a fire at his warehouse and the software is destroyed. This is legal frustration and the contract is discharged. Neither party have to meet their obligations. Mitch does not have to deliver the software and Mike does not have to pay for it.

The old rule was that even if performance was impossible the parties retained their obligations under the contract. There was no excuse for non-performance. This could cause injustice. In **Paradine v Jane (1647)** D rented some land which was then occupied by an enemy army. He was sued for the rent and claimed that he could not use the land so should not have to pay rent. The court rejected his argument and held that if he wished to be excused from his obligations he should have made provision for this in the contract.

This harsh rule remained until the concept of frustration was established in **Taylor v Caldwell (1863)**.

Nature and purpose of frustration

Frustration automatically ends the contract and excuses both parties from further performance. The courts tend to uphold contracts where possible, so the doctrine of frustration has been kept within strict limits. It will only apply where neither party is at fault (see quote) and something has prevented the contract being performed.

> **Key case**
>
> In **Taylor v Caldwell**, a concert hall hired for four concerts burned down six days before the first one. The hirer sued for breach of contract and claimed damages for wasted advertising expenses. He failed on the basis that there was an implied term that the hall would continue to exist until performance. As it had not done so the contract was frustrated on the grounds of impossibility. Thus the contract ends and there is no obligation on either party to perform. This means that neither can sue for breach of contract. This case abolished the old rule and established the idea of an implied term that if a contract became impossible all obligations ceased.

There are essentially three ways a contract will be frustrated. Where events make performance:

- impossible
- radically different
- illegal

Impossibility

Where a contract is for personal services, illness or death will frustrate it as performance will be impossible. Thus in **Condor v The Barron Knights (1966)** a contract was frustrated when the drummer of a pop group was ill and couldn't perform for the agreed number of days.

In **Krell v Henry (1903)** D rented rooms to watch the coronation procession of Edward VII in 1901. This was postponed due to illness, but he was sued for the rent. The contract was held to be frustrated because although it was still possible to rent the rooms, the foundation of the contract was to watch the procession and *this* was impossible.

The clearest case of impossibility is **Taylor v Caldwell**. However, matters are not usually so clear-cut. It is more usual for the subject matter to be unavailable or delayed rather than destroyed altogether. In these cases the contract will not be frustrated unless it becomes *radically different*.

Radical difference

Here, performance is not impossible but events have occurred which would radically alter the nature of the contract. The case of **Krell v Henry** could come under this heading. The nature of the contract was radically altered by the events (the postponement of the coronation). The contract will not be frustrated unless the whole foundation of it becomes radically different. Thus in **Herne Bay Steamboat Co. v Hutton (1903)**, also based on the postponement of the coronation, a contract for the hire of a boat to take people to watch the review of the fleet by the King, and to cruise round the fleet, was not frustrated. Although the review was cancelled, the fleet was still there. D could still organise the cruise so the purpose of the contract was not completely lost.

Task

Compare the cases of **Krell v Henry** and **Herne Bay Steamboat Co. v Hutton**. Make a note of why one was frustrated and the other not.

The leading case on radical difference is **Davis Contractors v Fareham UDC (1956)**.

Key case

In **Davis Contractors**, a building firm had a contract to build 78 houses. The work had cost a lot more than the contract price due to delays and labour shortages. The builders claimed frustration so they could avoid taking the price agreed and obtain payment on a *quantum meruit* basis (for the work done), which would have been more. The HL held that extra expense or inconvenience was not enough to frustrate a contract, it must be rendered *'radically different'*. Lord Radcliffe reformulated the doctrine. Rather than using the idea of an implied term, as in **Taylor**, which would not always be possible, he said that a contract would only be frustrated where the circumstances had rendered performance *'a thing radically different from that which was undertaken by the contract'*.

Food for thought

Krell v Henry and **Herne Bay Steamboat Co. v Hutton** are similar cases with different outcomes. This shows that there is a very fine line between circumstances which render performance impossible or radically different and those which do not. Suppose I organise a work's outing by coach to London to do some shopping and see a play. I find that the play is cancelled so I want to cancel the coach. If the play is not seen as a fundamental then I may still be obliged to go ahead with the contract. If **Krell** were followed I may be OK, but if **Herne Bay** were followed (on the basis that the shopping is still possible) I would be obliged to go ahead with the contract. It is unsatisfactory that I could not be sure enough of the law to know whether or not I could safely reject the contract for the hire of the coach. I may be obliged to pay for it anyway.

Closure of the Suez Canal in 1956 produced a number of cases claiming frustration, because it meant a longer and more expensive trip via the Cape of Good Hope. An example is **Tsakiroglou & Co. Ltd v Noblee & Thorl GmbH (1962)**, where a consignment of groundnuts was due to be shipped via the canal. When it closed, the shipper did not deliver and claimed that the contract was frustrated by the closure of the canal. The HL held that the method of performance (the longer trip) was not *'a thing radically different'* from that contracted for. It may have been different if the longer journey had meant that the groundnuts deteriorated, but this was not the case. The shipper had therefore breached its contract.

Examination pointer

Note that if the contract is not frustrated then performance is still required. This means that if one party does not perform there will be a breach, as in *Tsakiroglou*. You will need to discuss frustration first, and then go on to breach if you conclude it is unlikely the contract has been frustrated.

Cases involving trade, or other business dealings, are classed as commercial. In **Davis Contractors** it was made clear that inconvenience and increased expense will not be enough, so commercial frustration is rare. It may occur where performance in a contract has become illegal, however.

Illegality

Where, subsequent to the making of a contract, a government prohibition makes performance illegal, the contract may be frustrated. This would include contracts to buy or sell goods, where their sale has become illegal, e.g. by the outbreak of war. In **Denny, Mott & Dickson *v* James Fraser (1944)** controls on the sale of timber due to the war meant a contract involving the lease of a timber yard and the sale of timber was frustrated. In **Avery *v* Bowden (1855)**, D chartered a ship and agreed to provide cargo within 45 days. Before the deadline came war was declared and the contract was frustrated. D was not obliged to supply the cargo, so could not be sued for breach when he did not do so.

Examination pointer

Look out for indications of timing. If an event occurs before the contract is concluded there may be an argument that the contract is void for mistake. In **Amalgamated Investment & Property Co. Ltd *v* John Walker & Sons 1977**, see p. 68, a buyer of property for redevelopment argued both frustration and mistake. The property became listed the day after the contract was made and thus drastically reduced the value. This was not enough to make it radically different, so the frustration argument failed. The building was listed after the contract so the mistake argument also failed. Had it been listed before the contract was concluded, the buyer might have succeeded.

Limits to the rule

We have already seen that the doctrine is limited, as in **Davis Contractors** and **Amalgamated Investment**, where extra expense and loss in value was held not to be sufficient to frustrate a contract. There are further limits to the rule.

Self-induced frustration

As we saw in the opening quote, frustration only occurs *'without default of either party'*. If one party is at fault, frustration is deemed to be self-induced. In **The Super Servant II (1990)** D contracted to carry a drilling rig for C. D had two vessels but one was promised for another contract. The remaining vessel sank and

D claimed frustration. This was held to be self-induced because D didn't *have* to use the remaining vessel for the other, more lucrative, contract. Also, the other contract had been finalised *after* the one which D was claiming was frustrated. There was no frustration and D was in breach of contract.

Foreseeability

Frustration only applies where the supervening event is not foreseeable. For example, in **Davis Contractors** it could be foreseen that delays might occur during the building of the houses, so the contract was not frustrated. If an event is foreseeable then the parties are expected to make their own provisions for it. Commercial contracts often include wide terms for the suspension or discharge of the contract in the event of *unforeseen* difficulties. These provisions are known as **force majeure** clauses. The doctrine of frustration can only apply if there is no clause to cover the occurrence; it cannot displace express provisions. The courts are unwilling to rewrite contracts, especially commercial ones.

However, although the courts will not usually override express provisions, they may interpret them so that frustration applies. In **Metropolitan Water Board v Dick Kerr & Co. Ltd (1918)** a contract to build a reservoir within six years was frustrated by a government requisition during the war. There was a clause allowing for an extension of time in the event of '*difficulties, impediments or obstructions*', but this was held not to cover such a major event. The delay would be so long as to make it unreasonable to hold the parties to their obligations. The only other time such clauses will not be effective is when performance would be illegal. Illegality will frustrate the contract despite any express clause.

Food for thought

In **Davis Contractors**, Lord Radcliffe rejected the idea of an implied term, recognising the difficulty in arguing the parties could even impliedly have made provision for something completely unforeseeable. However, at least the implied term theory appeared to be giving effect to the intentions of the parties. The alternative of imposing a term when the contract has become radically different may do justice, but it can be argued that the courts should not interfere in contracts in this way. The parties could make provision for the occurrence by including a *force majeure* class. Do you think the courts should intervene where something unexpected has occurred which is the fault of neither party? If so, should they do it despite an express provision, as in **Metropolitan Water Board**?

Task

Oasis are booked to appear at a venue in Brighton, but they fail to appear because:

- one of them has flu
- one of them has a bad hangover
- the van they were using to get to the concert wouldn't start

Decide whether the contract is frustrated or not. Use a case to support each answer.

Effect of frustration

If the contract is frustrated, it is discharged, i.e. terminated, from the time of the event which causes the frustration. This discharge is automatic and not under the control of either party and the effect is that no obligations remain. (Unlike a case of breach where the innocent party has a choice whether to continue or not.)

The old rule at common law was that '*loss lay where it fell*'. This meant at the point of frustration and could be harsh, especially where payments had been made, or work done, in advance. This is because any rights and obligations which already existed were still binding.

Example
I hire a room and agree to pay *in advance*. If the contract is frustrated I cannot recover any payment made. Even if I had not paid as agreed, I would be liable to do so, because the obligation already exists.

I contract for the building of a house with payment due *on completion*. If the house is destroyed by fire and the contract frustrated the day before it is finished I won't have to pay a penny; there is no obligation to pay until completion. This is fine by me, but the builder won't be too happy.

To avoid the harshness of the rule, the law was qualified in the **Fibrosa** case in 1943.

Key case

In the **Fibrosa** case (full name **Fibrosa Spolka Akcyjna *v* Fairbairn Lawson Combe Barbour Ltd**), the HL held that advance payments could be recovered in cases where there was a total failure of consideration. Here, an agreement to supply machinery was frustrated due to the war. No machinery had been supplied at all so the other party was able to claim the return of the £1,000 paid in advance. This approach was still not fully satisfactory, as it would not apply where some consideration had been given. If even a small amount of machinery had been delivered, nothing would be recoverable. Also, it could be unfair to a party that may have commenced work or incurred expenses in preparation of the contract (as happened in **Fibrosa**).

This case was followed by statutory reform, which made further changes.

The Law Reform (Frustrated Contracts) Act 1943

The two main changes are that money paid in advance can be recovered even where there is no consideration, and a party that has provided a benefit can claim payment for this.

Essentially, **s. 1(2)** provides that:

● money paid before frustration is recoverable;

● money not yet paid ceases to be payable;

- expenses may be retained or recovered up to the amount payable or paid before frustration.

Section 1(3) provides that:

- where a benefit has been obtained a sum may be payable in respect of that benefit.

Section 1(2) covers advance payments. Thus, in my example, if I had paid a deposit it would be recoverable, and if I had not then I would not be liable to do so. **Section 1(3)** would cover part-performance cases, e.g. **Cutter v Powell** (see p. 88). It means that if work has been done then payment may be recoverable. However, the provision is not without its problems. In **BP Exploration v Hunt (1982)** the HL indicated that whether a valuable benefit has been received is decided *after* the frustrating event. This would mean that, in my example, where a fire destroyed the building just before it was finished, the builder would still not recover anything. I did not receive a valuable benefit.

Under **s. 1(1)** certain types of contract are excluded from operation of these rules. These include contracts:

- for the sale of specific goods which have perished
- of insurance
- for the carriage of goods by sea
- where the parties have expressly dealt with the matter

Food for thought

Do you think the law is now satisfactory? The **Act** certainly adds a degree of fairness but there are several situations which fall outside it. Also, expenses are only recoverable *up to the amount payable or paid before frustration*, so if no advance payment was agreed, none will be due unless **s. 1(3)** applies. Even this may not provide for payment for work done unless a benefit has been received.

Note that the **Act** does not deal with frustration itself, only the *effect* of it. This means the courts will still use the rules seen above in deciding *whether* a contract has been frustrated.

Task

Dave is an electrician and you employ him to rewire your house. He buys several items in anticipation of the work, amounting to £150. The house burns down before he arrives to do the work. Using cases and the **Act** in support, answer the following questions:

Is the contract frustrated?

Can he recover the £150?

Would your answer be different if you had paid him a deposit of £500?

What if you agreed to pay a deposit but had not done so?

Summary

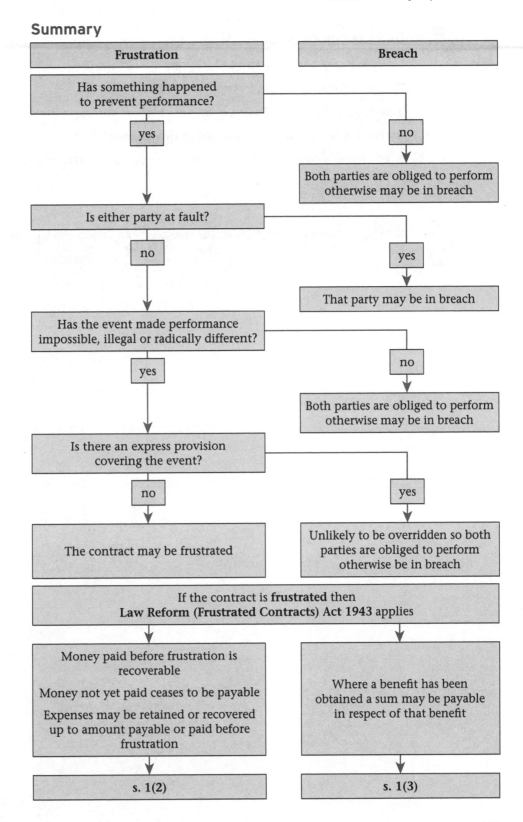

Self-test questions

1 In which case was the doctrine of frustration established?

2 When will illness or death frustrate a contract?

3 What were the facts of **Davis Contractors** and why was the contract not frustrated?

4 What is self-induced frustration? Give a case example.

5 What is the effect of **s. 1(2)** and **s. 1(3)** of the **Law Reform (Frustrated Contracts) Act 1943**?

 For further resources and updates please go to the Companion Website accompanying this book at **www.pearsoned.co.uk/russell**

Discharge by breach

... a mere honest misapprehension, especially if open to correction, will not justify a charge of repudiation.

Lord Wright, **Ross Smyth and Co. Ltd** *v* **Bailey, Son & Co. (1940)**

By the end of this Unit you should be able to:

● Explain the different types of breach of contract

● Explain the effects of these

● Show how the law applies by reference to cases

● Identify problems with the law in order to attempt an evaluation

If one party to a contract does not do what was agreed there will be a breach of contract by that person. This may be due to non-performance or improper performance, so this Unit ties in with that on discharge by (agreement and) performance.

Types of breach

Breach may be *actual* or *anticipatory*.

Actual breach

This is where a breach has actually occurred, either due to *improper performance* or *non-performance*. In **Ruxley Electronics and Construction Ltd** *v* **Forsyth (1995)** D had a swimming pool built but it was not as deep as he had stipulated. It was a safe depth, but he had particularly asked for it to be deeper. He was awarded damages for breach of the term regarding the depth of the pool to compensate him for not feeling safe diving into this depth. This is *improper performance*. In **Pilbrow** *v* **Pearless de Rougemont & Co. (1999)** a man had arranged to see a solicitor. His case was handled by someone who was neither a solicitor nor a legal executive, although the advice given was up to the standard of a competent solicitor. The man refused to pay the full bill and the solicitors sued for the balance. The CA held that the contract was to provide legal services by a solicitor, and no such services had been provided. The firm had breached the contract. This was *non-performance* as no services by a solicitor had been given.

Anticipatory breach

An *anticipatory* breach is where a party to a contract has made it clear *in advance* that the contract will be *repudiated*, i.e. the contractual obligations will not be honoured. If this happens the other party need not wait until the time for performance is due; an action for breach of contract can be commenced straight away.

Key case

In **Hochster *v* De la Tour (1853)** a courier was able to sue for breach as soon as he was told his employment contract was cancelled, even though he was not due to start work for a couple of months. By cancelling, the company was in *anticipatory* breach of contract.

The choice is with the injured party so instead of suing immediately, as in **Hochster**, the contract can be kept alive until performance is due. This can be seen in **White and Carter *v* McGregor (1962)**. D owned a garage and contracted with C for advertising his business on litterbins around the town for three years. Later the same day he changed his mind and told C he no longer wanted the advertisements. C had a choice whether to sue for breach immediately or to continue with the contract for the agreed three years. They chose to continue and were held by the HL to be able to claim the full contract price for the advertising.

Continuing with the contract may be unwise though. It is possible for a contract to be frustrated by events (see Unit 11). In **Avery *v* Bowden (1855)** D chartered a ship and agreed to provide cargo within 45 days. He then told C that he had no cargo and that the contract was not going to be fulfilled, an anticipatory breach. However, C kept his ship available at the port, hoping for a change of mind. Before the deadline came, war was declared and the contract was frustrated. This automatically discharges the contract, so no performance was due, and D was not in breach.

Examination pointer

You may need to discuss discharge by frustration as well as breach if there is a question of something preventing performance, or discharge by performance if there is a partial performance. Be prepared for more than one issue to arise. You should also explain the available remedies.

In **White and Carter**, Lord Reid said the rule on continuing with the contract would not apply where there was no genuine, legitimate reason for doing so. In **Clea Shipping *v* Bulk Oil International (1984) (The Alaskan Trader)** the charterers of a ship repudiated the contract before the end of the charter, saying they no longer needed it. The owners continued to crew the ship and keep it standing by and in repair, at a cost of £800,000, for the whole period of the hire. They then sold it for scrap and sued for the full contract price. The court held that they had no *legitimate reason* to continue to perform, and had merely tried to increase the amount of damages. They could therefore only sue for damages for their actual loss, not for the full amount of the charter period.

Task

Compare this to **White and Carter v McGregor (1962)**. Which decision do you think is the better?

Although **The Alaskan Trader** suggests the courts are unwilling to allow one party to increase damages by continuing, **White and Carter** was followed in **Ministry of Sound (Ireland) Ltd v World Online Ltd (2003)**. Ministry of Sound agreed to market World Online's Internet service for two years. In breach of contract, World Online stopped supplying the necessary Internet access CDs after six months. Ministry of Sound could therefore no longer perform its part of the contract, but sued for the full amount due. The court felt that the decision in **White and Carter** was correct because otherwise a party in breach could force an innocent party to treat a contract as at an end. The claim was allowed.

Food for thought

Do you think it is sensible that someone can continue with a contract as in **White and Carter**? It meant that the garage had to pay for advertising that they didn't want. On the other hand, as made clear in **Ministry of Sound**, not to allow this could mean the party not in breach is forced to end the contract.

Example | Tony rents a boat for a week. After two days of bad weather he is bored and wants to end the contract. The argument is that he should not be able to force the people who rented him the boat to breach their own obligations by non-performance (not renting the boat to Tony for the week), and so be unable to claim the full payment. Following **White and Carter**, Tony could be obliged to pay for the entire week.

Effect of breach

Whether actual or anticipatory, if there is a breach by one party the other is entitled to damages as of right. In some cases the innocent party may also be released from further performance. This is not so common and only arises where there is:

- a repudiatory breach, or
- a fundamental breach.

Repudiatory breach

Repudiatory breach occurs where a party to a contract refuses to perform as agreed. This may be at the time performance is due or, more commonly, in advance, i.e. an *anticipatory* breach, as discussed above. Repudiation by one party allows the other to rescind (end) the contract, so the courts are slow to find a repudiation. Lord Wright, in **Ross Smyth and Co. Ltd *v* Bailey, Son & Co. (1940)**, called it a *'serious matter, not to be lightly found or inferred.'*

> **Example** June refuses to do some photocopying for her boss, Wendy. Wendy sacks her and June claims unfair dismissal. Wendy argues that June repudiated the contract by refusing to perform her contractual obligations. It is unlikely that a court would find that June's refusal is sufficient to allow Wendy to treat the contract as ended.

It may be that refusing to meet the contractual obligations is due to an honest mistake and thus may not amount to a repudiation. In **Ross Smyth**, Lord Wright made the point in the opening quote.

Key case

In **Woodar Investment Development *v* Wimpey Construction (UK) Ltd (1980)** the HL refused to find repudiation. Here, the buyers of some land misinterpreted the contract and thought they had a right to rescind. The sellers argued this was a repudiatory breach. The HL disagreed. The main reason seems to be that there was some time between the alleged repudiation and the time performance was due, thus giving time to correct the 'misapprehension'. Lord Wilberforce said, *'Repudiation is a drastic conclusion which should only be held to arise in clear cases of a refusal, in a matter going to the root of the contract, to perform contractual obligations'*. This brings us to the last point.

Fundamental breach

Although breach of *any* term allows the injured party to sue for damages, it does not always allow that person to rescind. We saw that repudiation can give the right to rescind. This usually happens with an *anticipatory breach*. Where an *actual breach* has occurred the usual remedy is damages, unless the breach is *fundamental*. This will occur with:

- breach of a condition
- breach of an innominate term if the result is serious

Task

Look up **Bettini *v* Gye** and **Poussard *v* Spiers and Pond**. Which involved breach of a condition and why? What was the effect of the breach for the innocent party in each case?

In the case of an innominate term, rescission depends on whether the *consequence* of the breach is sufficiently serious. If so, the term is seen as a condition and both damages and rescission are available. If not, it is seen as a warranty and only damages are available. In **Hong Kong Fir Shipping Co. Ltd,** (see Unit 6) the ship was still available for 19 out of the 24 months, so the CA held that the breach did not 'go to the root' of the contract. This meant it was a warranty and D could not treat the contract as at an end, only claim damages caused by the delay.

Examination pointer

Look for clues in the scenario when applying the law. If there is an anticipatory breach, whether the other party can sue for the full contract price or not may depend on whether there is a genuine reason for continuing performance. Use **White and Carter** and **The Alaskan Trader** to discuss this. You may also have to discuss terms, because the remedy depends on whether there is a breach of a condition, or only of a warranty.

If rescission is unavailable then performance is still required.

Example   In **Ruxley Electronics** D was awarded damages for breach of the term regarding the depth of the pool but he had to continue with the contract, i.e. meet his own obligations under it. This meant paying for the pool. Had he been able to rescind he would not have had to pay anything and would be able to treat his obligations as at an end.

Food for thought

Rescission is a drastic measure. In **Pilbrow**, for example, no payment was due at all because the solicitors had not performed as agreed – a fundamental breach. That is why the courts are reluctant to allow rescission unless there is a clear refusal to perform (repudiatory breach) or breach of a condition (fundamental breach). Do you think they have achieved the right balance?

Summary

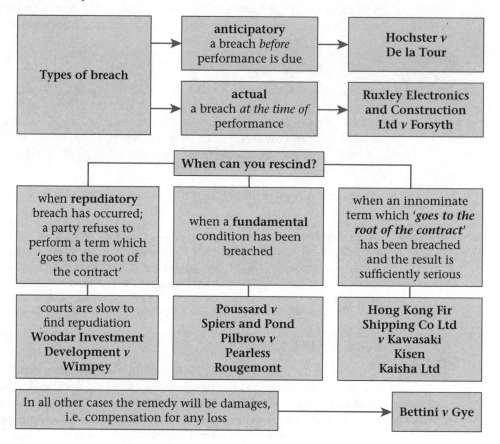

 Self-test questions

1 Name two cases of actual breach which you have seen elsewhere than in this Unit.

2 What is an anticipatory breach?

3 What is the difference in effect between breach of a condition and breach of a warranty?

4 What happened in **White and Carter**?

5 In **Woodar Investment Development,** Lord Wilberforce said repudiation should only apply when?

 For further resources and updates please go to the Companion Website accompanying this book at **www.pearsoned.co.uk/russell**

Remedies

. . . a property offering peace and tranquillity was the raison d'être of the proposed purchase. He wanted to be reasonably sure that the property was not seriously affected by aircraft noise.

Lord Steyn, **Farley *v* Skinner (2001)**

By the end of this Unit you should be able to:

● Explain how the courts assess the amount of compensation given to C

● Show how the law on causation and quantification has developed

● Apply the law and identify problems using cases in support

Compensation is the usual remedy in contract cases. This remedy is called *damages,* and is available as of right once breach of contract has been proved.

The purpose of damages

The courts will look at the position the parties would be in if D had performed as agreed. In **Jackson & another *v* Royal Bank of Scotland (2005)** the HL said an award of damages is intended *'to put them in the same position as they would have been if there had been no breach of contract'*. There are several issues to consider:

● the basis of the claim

● the rule on remoteness

● quantification of damages

The basis of the claim

There are two bases for a claim:

● Expectation loss – what C *expected* to gain from the contract being performed.

● Reliance loss – what C spent in *reliance* on the contract.

Expectation loss

Damages are normally based on what C would have expected to gain from the contract.

Example In **Carlill v Carbolic Smoke Ball Co.** Mrs Carlill would 'expect' the £100 offered by the company. This is what she would be awarded in damages.

You will see more about how this applies when we look at quantification of damages.

Reliance loss

Compensation can sometimes be based on putting C in a position as if the contract had *never been made*, rather than made and not breached. This is called reliance loss. It is most often seen where the contract is extremely speculative and it is hard to put a price on what C would have gained from it. An example is **Anglia Television v Read (1972)**. A film project was abandoned when the actor pulled out, in breach of contract. It would have been hard to assess what profits the film company would have made, so an amount for expenses they incurred *in reliance on the contract* was awarded.

The rule on remoteness

There are limitations on what can be claimed in that the loss must:

● Be *caused* by the breach;
● Not be too *remote*.

Causation

Causation in fact is usually reasonably straightforward. Was the breach of contract by D the main cause of the loss to C or 'but for' D's breach would the loss have occurred? It was confirmed in **County Ltd v Girozentrale Securities (1996)** that as long as it is the *main* cause, it need not be the *only* cause of C's loss.

Remoteness

Even if C can prove causation, if D was liable for *all* damage resulting from a breach this could impose an impossible burden.

Example I refuse to honour an agreement to sell you my car for £500. As a result of this breach of contract you have to get a bus home. Running for the bus you fall and break a leg; this means that you lose an important contract to play the lead role in a play. In turn you cannot pay your mortgage, and your house is repossessed. You might argue all these losses were caused by my breach of contract, but this would seem unfair to me. The courts have therefore developed rules to limit the amount you can claim, based on foreseeability.

If the loss is not foreseeable, it is said to be '*too remote*' (from the breach) and will not be allowed. The test comes from **Hadley v Baxendale (1854)**.

Key case

In **Hadley**, a mill owner had ordered a crankshaft which was not delivered on time. It was usual for owners to have a spare, but he didn't, and so was unable to operate the mill. He failed in his claim for loss of his profits. It was laid down by Baron Alderson that:

'*Where two parties have made a contract which one of them has broken, the damages which the other party ought to receive in respect of such breach of contract should be such as may fairly and reasonably be considered either **arising naturally, i.e. according to the usual course of things**, from such breach of contract itself, or such as may reasonably be supposed to have been **in the contemplation of both parties**, at the time they made the contract, as the probable result of the breach of it'.*

arising naturally: is an objective test, what loss would *normally* be expected.

or: indicates that it is **either** what is normal **or** what is contemplated by the parties.

in the contemplation of both parties: is subjective, what is *foreseeable* by **both** parties. Although the owner would have foreseen the loss, D would not have foreseen that he would be unable to operate the mill if the contract was breached.

at the time they made the contract: means the test is applied at the time of the agreement, not with hindsight.

In **Victoria Laundry Ltd *v* Newman Industries Ltd (1949)** D had failed to deliver a boiler to a laundry company. They claimed for loss of profits from the normal day-to-day business, and for loss from a special contract, which D did not know about. Only the first was recoverable. Asquith LJ said the aggrieved party is only entitled to recover 'such part of the loss actually resulting as was *at the time of the contract reasonably foreseeable* as likely to result from the breach'.

So, if the loss is not *natural*, or normal, it:

- must be foreseeable by both parties;
- at the time they made their contract.

Examination pointer

Knowledge is an important factor. Look out for comments like 'he told him that...' or 'as usual...' This will help you to apply the rule. Had the mill owner told D the crankshaft was vital, or had they done business before so that D knew he had no spare, then the loss would have been in the contemplation of both parties.

The HL, in **Jackson & another *v* Royal Bank of Scotland (2005)**, confirmed that the starting point for any application of **Hadley *v* Baxendale** is to look at the extent of the *shared* knowledge of both parties *at the time the contract is made*.

Key case

In **Jackson**, a business relationship between a supplier and its principal customer came to an end as a result of a breach of contract, for which the Bank was responsible. The supplier claimed for the loss of the opportunity to earn further profits from that relationship. The HL held that *but for* the Bank's breach, C would *in fact* have been the other company's supplier in the following years. Also, that the loss of repeat orders from their customer was *foreseeable* so it was not *too remote* from the Bank's breach. The claim was allowed.

Task

Bill runs a bakery. The electricity to the ovens is cut off by a faulty wire, so he rings Eric the electrician, who promises to be there in an hour. Eric doesn't turn up until six hours later, by which time Bill is unable to supply his usual customers and loses a day's profit. He also loses money he expected from an order for some speciality cakes for a party. Can Bill claim for any of his losses?

OK, so C can prove that D's breach of contract caused the loss and was not too remote, the question now is how much will C get?

Quantification of damages

Usually C will claim what was *expected* from the contract, and in many cases this will be clear, e.g. the £100 in Mrs Carlill's case. However, sometimes the amount will require assessing by the court. This will usually be done using what is known as the market price rule.

Market price rule

Under this rule, mainly applicable to the sale or auction of goods, damages would be the difference between the contract price and the market price.

Example Steve offers to sell Tim his car for £3,000. He then gets a better offer so breaches the contract and refuses to sell to Tim. Say the market price for this type and age of car is £3,500. Tim can buy one for this price and sue Steve for the difference between the contract price (£3,000) and the market price (£3,500), i.e. £500. If the market price is £3,000 or less then Tim has not lost anything – he can pick up a car for this amount if he wants to buy one. He will win his case, but is unlikely to be awarded anything but nominal damages.

In **Barry *v* Davies (2000)** (see p. 9) the expectation of people attending an auction 'without reserve' would be that the highest bidder would get the items at the price bid for them. The CA held that damages would be the same as where a seller refused to deliver goods, i.e. the difference between the price he had bid for the items (the contract price) and their market price.

Consequential loss

C can claim for consequential or indirect loss as long as that loss is foreseeable (under the test in **Hadley v Baxendale**).

Example Don buys a new TV, which blows up. As a *consequence*, damage is caused to the furniture and Don is burnt by sparks. The TV is clearly faulty. He can claim breach of contract and get his money back; he can also claim compensation for the damage and the injury caused by the breach as it is *foreseeable*.

Task

A pop group contracts with Ron's Roadies to take them to concerts in a van. On one occasion the van fails to turn up and the group misses the concert. They don't get paid their fee. They are told that as they are unreliable a second date is also cancelled. In addition they were expecting a record producer to be in the audience and claim that because of the breach of contract they have lost a recording contract. Can they claim for any of the three losses?

Mitigation

C must take reasonable steps to minimise the loss. This is called *mitigation*. Thus in a case involving dismissal in breach of an employment contract, C could reasonably be expected to look for alternative work. A claim for loss of earnings may be reduced if this is not done. However, mitigation only arises *following* a breach. Thus in cases of anticipatory breach it does not apply. In **White & Carter v McGregor** (see p. 104) D failed in the argument that C should not have carried on making and displaying the advertisements.

Food for thought

This was hardly decisive, only a 3–2 majority in the HL. Lord Keith thought it was 'startling'. He has a point. It allows C to substantially increase the loss, and therefore increase the amount of damages awarded.

Non-pecuniary loss

Non-pecuniary loss is loss which is not easily quantifiable, such as distress. The courts are reluctant to award an amount for non-pecuniary loss in contract cases. In **Addis v Gramophone Co. Ltd (1909)** the HL refused to allow an amount for distress and loss of reputation in a case where an employee was dismissed in breach of a contract. In **Dunnachie v Hull CC (2004)** the HL confirmed that in unfair dismissal cases no damages for non-pecuniary loss, such as hurt feelings, should be awarded. There are, as always, exceptions. It was accepted in **Jarvis v Swan Tours (1973)**, where a holiday fell far below expectation, that in cases where enjoyment is an essential part of the contract, an amount could be awarded for 'disappointment'. In **Jackson v Horizon Holidays (1975)** this was extended to claims for disappointment from members of the family (who were not parties to the contract). Even so, the amount is usually kept to a minimum. In **Watts v Morris (1991)** the CA held that any such amount should be 'modest' and reduced an award from £4,000 to £750.

Key case

In **Farley v Skinner (2001)** C claimed for 'discomfort' after buying a house which his surveyor had incorrectly reported would not be affected by aircraft noise. He was awarded £10,000 because peace and tranquillity was the main reason he bought it. The HL confirmed that non-pecuniary loss could be awarded in cases where the object of the contract was 'pleasure, relaxation or peace of mind'. They suggested that this amount would be at the very top end of the scale though. The HL treated C's discomfort as a *consequential* loss arising from the breach. They approved **Ruxley Electronics and Construction Ltd v Forsyth (1995)**, that C could claim where deprived of something of value. In **Ruxley** (see p. 107) D was awarded £2,500 for 'loss of amenity' to compensate him for not feeling safe diving.

In **Jones v Gallagher (2005)** C had had many problems with the installation of a kitchen. Only £500 was awarded for non-pecuniary loss, for the inconvenience suffered. It would therefore seem that any claim for non-pecuniary loss will be limited.

Food for thought

Do you think it is right to limit non-pecuniary loss in this way? If you have suffered a great deal of anxiety and inconvenience because of the breach should you be able to claim for this or not? Should employment cases be treated differently? In **Dunnachie**, the CA allowed the claim, but the HL reversed the decision, suggesting the situation is by no means clear.

Loss of *opportunity* may sometimes be claimed; it is a type of non-pecuniary loss. We saw it in **Jackson**. The supplier did not just claim for loss of expected *profit*, but for loss of the *opportunity* to make a profit.

Examination pointer

There will be no claim for damages unless there is a valid contract. This may involve a discussion of formation, e.g. is there a valid offer and acceptance? There must also be a breach of a term of the contract, so terms and representations may need discussing. Look in the question for clues as to which area you are being directed to. The more cases you know, the easier it is to pick up clues because you may recognise a similar scenario.

Other factors which may affect an award of damages

Liquidated damages and penalty clauses: The parties may have agreed in the contract that a fixed (liquidated) sum would be payable in the event of breach, e.g. if there is a breach, damages will be set at £500. C gets £500 whether or not the *actual* loss is more or less. They are often called 'penalty' clauses, but it is only where they are excessive that they will be classed as penalties and not valid. A genuine estimate of what loss would result from the breach, made at the time of the contract, will be enforceable.

Quantum meruit: A claim on *quantum meruit* means a claim for a reasonable sum rather than a precise one. It is often awarded where there is no fixed sum in a contract for goods or services. Another example is **Planché v Colbourn (1831)**, where a writer was entitled to be paid for the work done before the contract was cancelled.

Equitable remedies

These are awarded at the court's discretion, unlike damages which are as of right. The courts will not allow an equitable remedy if it will be unfair to another party.

There are several different remedies, the main ones are:

- Specific performance
- Injunction
- Rescission
- Rectification

Specific performance and injunction

These are court orders to do something (specific performance) or not to do something (injunction). Such remedies are only granted where damages would be inadequate. An order for specific performance in relation to the sale of a house could be used to force the sale if one party has pulled out, in breach of contract. It will not be granted if this would be unfair, thus in **Watkin v Watson-Smith (1986)** the court refused such an order after an elderly seller had offered his bungalow at £2,950 instead of £29,500 by mistake, and then – understandably – refused to honour this price.

Both specific performance and injunction are rare in cases where the contract is for performance of personal services. In **Page One Records v Britton (1968)** the agent and manager of the Troggs pop group had a 5-year contract with them. When they tried to replace him (in breach of this contract) he applied to get an injunction to stop them doing so. The court refused it.

Rescission

This is where a wronged party can treat the contract as at an end. Both parties are returned to the position they would be in if the contract had *never existed*; unlike damages where they are put in a position as if it *existed* but was not *breached*. Rescission is possible where there is breach of a *condition*, but not breach of a *warranty*. Again, as an equitable remedy, it will not be awarded if it would be unfair. In **Phillips v Brooks** (see p. 66, Unit 8) the shop could claim damages (if they could find the crook) but not rescind the contract, because to put them in their pre-contract position would mean the pawnbroker returning the jewellery.

If one party refuses to do as agreed, i.e. *repudiates* the contract, the other is entitled to treat the contract as at an end. Repudiation is sometimes referred to as a remedy, because repudiation by one party allows (the remedy of) rescission by the other.

Rectification

This *only* applies to contract cases. In some cases the court will make an order that a contractual document is amended (rectified) to correct a mistake (see Unit 8).

Summary

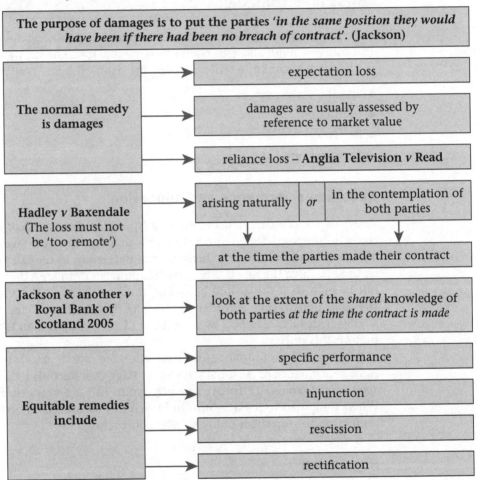

The purpose of damages is to put the parties *'in the same position they would have been if there had been no breach of contract'*. (Jackson)

The normal remedy is damages	→ expectation loss
	→ damages are usually assessed by reference to market value
	→ reliance loss – **Anglia Television v Read**

| **Hadley v Baxendale** (The loss must not be 'too remote') | → arising naturally *or* in the contemplation of both parties ↓ at the time the parties made their contract |

| **Jackson & another v Royal Bank of Scotland 2005** | → look at the extent of the *shared* knowledge of both parties *at the time the contract is made* |

Equitable remedies include	→ specific performance
	→ injunction
	→ rescission
	→ rectification

 ## Self-test questions

1 What is the test in **Hadley v Baxendale**?

2 Which case was followed in **Dunnachie v Hull CC** and on what basis?

3 What decision did Lord Keith think was 'startling'?

4 What is the market price rule?

Study Block 4 Summary
DISCHARGE AND REMEDIES

Once a contract is validly formed, and there are no vitiating factors, it will continue until discharged. This can be done by agreement, performance, frustration or breach. Once the contract is discharged a remedy may be sought if one party has been wronged.

Discharge	Rules	Remedy
Agreement	The parties can agree to end the contract, either bilaterally or unilaterally	No further obligations arise under the contract, but if unilateral the other must provide consideration
Performance The basic rule is that performance must be *exact and complete* – **Cutter v Powell (1795)**	**Unless there is:** Substantial performance by one party A severable contract Partial performance which has been accepted Prevention of performance Tender of performance which has been refused	The contract price is paid less the cost of putting any defect right Payment is made for the part that is completed A claim for work done can be made on *'quantum meruit'* – **Planché v Colbourn (1831)** Damages can be claimed by the person still offering to perform
Frustration Something has happened to prevent performance which is the fault of neither party	The event makes performance impossible, illegal or radically different – **Krell, Denny, Mott & Dickson, Davis Contractors**	**Law Reform (Frustrated Contracts) Act 1943** has special rules: S. 1(2): Money paid before frustration is recoverable Money not yet paid ceases to be payable Expenses may be retained or recovered up to amount payable or paid before frustration S. 1(3): Where a benefit has been obtained a sum may be payable in respect of that benefit

Discharge	Rules	Remedy
Breach		
May be *anticipatory*	**Hochster v De la Tour**	Gives the other party the right to sue for damages immediately
A breach of a condition is *fundamental*	**Poussard v Spiers**	The contract can be rescinded and damages claimed
Breach of a warranty	**Bettini v Gye**	Remedy will be damages only

Task

Add the principle and brief facts to the case. Then answer the questions.

Case	Principle	Facts
Hadley v Baxendale		
Victoria Laundry v Newman		
Anglia Television v Read		
Watkin v Watson-Smith		

1 Briefly explain these equitable remedies:

- specific performance
- injunction
- recission
- rectification

2 What is the market price rule?

Key criticisms

- In cases like **Bolton v Mahadeva** a person who has done a lot of work receives nothing.
- The rules on breach allow C to substantially increase the loss, and therefore increase the amount of damages awarded. In **White and Carter** the garage had to pay for advertising that they didn't want.
- In cases of fundamental breach rescission is allowed, but this is a drastic measure. In **Pilbrow**, for example, no payment was due at all for the work done.
- There is a fine line between circumstances which render performance impossible or radically different, and those which do not – **Krell v Henry** and **Herne Bay Steamboat**.

- There are several situations which fall outside the **Law Reform (Frustrated Contracts) Act 1943**.

- When non-pecuniary loss is claimable is unclear. It was extended from 'holiday' cases in **Farley**, but **Dunnachie** confirmed it is not allowed in employment cases.

Examination practice

June 2004

Select any **one** method of termination of a contract (breach, frustration, performance, agreement) and outline and critically evaluate the relevant rules.   (*25 marks*)

Module 6 connections

Morals	All contracts are based on the idea of an exchange of promises. If one person breaks their promise the law will step in to correct any wrongdoing by providing a remedy	Use any case on breach or remedies
Justice	Discharge by breach can be discussed. It may not be just to allow the other to continue and thus increase the amount of damages. On the other hand, the party that has not performed is at fault so this can be discussed with fault too. Discharge by performance, especially the 'all or nothing' rules on substantial performance, can be unjust.	White and Carter
	The remedy of rescission is used to achieve justice and won't be available where unfair, e.g. to a third party	Bolton/Sumpter
Conflicting interests	Remedies attempt to balance the interests of the parties by putting both parties in the position which they would have been had the contract been performed. Breach of warranty only allows damages, parties must continue with performance thus taking all interests into account.	Use any case on remedies
	The courts need to balance the interests of both parties in frustration cases as neither is at fault	Taylor *v* Caldwell
Fault	Discharge by frustration only applies where there is no fault on either side	Super Servant II
	Remedies for breach take into account that D is at fault in breaching the contract	
Creativity	The creation of the doctrine of frustration avoids the problem of the strict rules	Paradine/Taylor
	The **Fibrosa** case amended the common law and this then led to statutory intervention	

January 2005

Jay sometimes had a drink with Karl, a property developer. Karl mentioned that he needed some heavy iron gates removed by next weekend from a house about to be redeveloped. He told Jay that he could have them free of charge if Jay promised to remove the gates. Jay readily agreed. He then rang a number of van-hire companies to enquire about hire prices, and arranged to hire a van from Laura, who quoted the cheapest daily rate.

Having paid £150 to hire the van for two days, Jay turned up at the house only to discover that the work had already commenced, and that the gates had been removed and sold. Jay then discovered that he could have hired a van for £40 less for the two days from other hirers. It had not been made clear to him that the favourable price quoted by Laura was based on a weekend hire of three days.

(a) Consider whether Jay and Karl made a contract in respect of the iron gates, and consider the rights and remedies which may be available to Jay. *(25 marks)*

(b) Having regard to the rules of misrepresentation, consider the rights and remedies which may be available to Jay against Laura. *(25 marks)*

(c) Agreement is an essential aspect in the formation of a contract. How satisfactory are the rules which determine when an agreement has taken place? *(25 marks)*

Guide

(a) Main issues: offer and acceptance, consideration and intention to create legal relations, as well as remedies for breach of contract.

Explanation and application of the rules on each.

An agreement existed in that Karl offered the gates and Jay accepted that offer.

There is evidence of consideration by Karl promising to give away a pair of valuable gates. Even though 'free of charge', Jay promised to remove them so would expend energy and effort, and possibly money, in doing so; thus, his consideration is 'sufficient' even if arguably not adequate (**Chappell & Co. *v* Nestlé**).

This leaves intention to create legal relations to discuss in more detail. It was arguably a social occasion. It is ambiguous, as although indicating Jay and Karl had a social relationship, it is not clear whether the discussion actually took place over a drink. Discuss the presumption that there is no intention to create legal relations in social situations, but also that there is an argument which may rebut the presumption. Karl was a property developer so arguably acting in a business capacity when he made the deal with

Jay. Compare **Balfour** and **Merritt**.

If a contract was made between them, it seems that Karl was in breach by selling to someone else.

Remedies: Jay would be able to claim foreseeable loss under the **Hadley v Baxendale** rules. Damages would be based on the market price. He would claim sufficient compensation to enable him to buy an equivalent set of gates on the open market. He may be able to claim for the hire of the van, if such loss was reasonably foreseeable, but arguably it was not in Karl's contemplation, nor in the 'normal course of things' **(Hadley)**.

(b) Main issues: types of misrepresentation and remedies.

Explanation of the difference between terms and representations. It is arguably a term as Laura has superior knowledge, but you are directed to misrepresentation so move quickly to this. It is likely that a misrepresentation has taken place, as the rate quoted by Laura applied only to a three-day hire, and this was not made clear to Jay.

Explain the need to prove Jay was 'induced' to enter the contract, i.e. relied on the statement **(Attwood v Small)**.

Explanation of the different types of misrepresentation. It appears to be at least a negligent misrepresentation, and may have been fraudulent if made 'knowingly, without belief in its truth' **(Derry v Peek)**.

Remedies: discussion of the remedies for the different types of misrepresentation under the common law and **Misrepresentation Act**. Possible rescission (he returns the van and gets his £150 back) and/or damages. Note damages for misrepresentation are based on the tort measure, to put him in the position he would have been before she made the statement. This is £40 (£40 plus two days' worth of van at £110 hire puts him in his original financial position). Jay will want to claim rescission as he no longer has any use for the van.

(c) This allows for a detailed treatment over a narrow range of issues or a more superficial treatment over a broad range. You could discuss:

- issues arising out of the meaning of an offer, such as the distinction between offers and invitations to treat;
- the distinction between counter offers and requests for further information;
- the ways in which offers may terminate, especially the rules on revocation;
- acceptance issues such as the postal rule and the restrictions on this mode of acceptance;
- the difficulties experienced by the courts in adapting traditional rules to new technology and instantaneous communications;
- standard form contracts and problems with the 'battle of the forms'.

Look at the key criticisms and 'Food for thought' boxes for more ideas.

DON'T FORGET CASES TO ILLUSTRATE!

Part 2

MODULE 4 **CRIME**
OFFENCES AGAINST THE PERSON

Study Block 5 *ACTUS REUS, MENS REA* AND MURDER

Study Block 6 VOLUNTARY MANSLAUGHTER

Study Block 7 INVOLUNTARY MANSLAUGHTER

Study Block 8 NON-FATAL OFFENCES AGAINST THE PERSON

Study Block 9 DEFENCES

Introduction to Part 2
MODULE 4 CRIME
OFFENCES AGAINST THE PERSON

This module covers homicide, which includes murder and manslaughter, and looks at the connection between these two offences. It also looks at five non-fatal offences, often referred to as the 'assaults', and some of the problems with the law in this area, with the proposed reforms. Several defences are covered in this module; some of these, although not all, are required for Module 5 as well.

A word of warning. Please don't be tempted to skip the first units on the basis that you know them – you don't! Hopefully you have got a good base to build on, but you need a much greater depth to your knowledge at this level. It is worth reading these units carefully; when you come to study murder you will then find that you know most of it already. I have used many murder cases to illustrate Units 14–16. These Units also contain cases on manslaughter as well as the non-fatal offences which you will have studied for Module 3. Again you need more detail here, so that you can apply them and any defences to them, as well as produce an evaluation of this area of law. Another reason for looking at these issues again is that when you come to Module 6 you will see that this is based on the material in *all* other modules. In particular, the Unit on 'Fault' relates directly to *mens rea*, the fault element in crime.

Study Block 5
ACTUS REUS, MENS REA AND MURDER

Unit 14   *Actus reus* 1: Conduct and circumstances
Unit 15   *Actus reus* 2: Consequences and causation
Unit 16   *Mens rea*
Unit 17   Murder

As you know from your study of Module 3, most offences are made up of two elements, *actus reus* and *mens rea*. Although you have already studied these concepts as part of your AS course, you need a much greater depth now. You should concentrate on developing and evaluating what you know. I have split *actus reus* into two parts as causation is an area of law in its own right; it is crucial in crimes such as murder, and you need to know it well. *Mens rea* is also needed in depth, as it is this element that distinguishes murder and manslaughter. In the final Unit in this Study Block we will look at how these elements apply in cases of murder. Murder, the killing of a human being with intent to kill or seriously injure, is probably the most socially unacceptable crime. It carries a mandatory life sentence, which means the judge has no discretion when passing sentence. By the time you reach this Unit you will be familiar with many of the cases, as I have used many murder cases to illustrate Units 14–16.

Example	Jane picks up a knife and stabs Jenny, who dies. Jane has the *actus reus* of murder as her act has caused Jenny's death. She also has the *mens rea* because she intended to kill, or at least seriously harm, her. Jane will be sentenced to life imprisonment.

Actus reus 1: Conduct and circumstances

... there was gross and criminal negligence, as the man was paid to keep the gate shut and protect the public ... a man might incur criminal liability from a duty arising out of a contract.

Wright J

By the end of this Unit you should be able to:

- Identify the two main elements of a criminal offence
- Explain the term *actus reus* in relation to acts, omissions and circumstances
- Explain how the law on *actus reus* applies in practice by reference to cases
- Identify possible criticisms

What makes an action criminal?

There are two elements which need to be proved for most offences. These are known by the Latin terms *actus reus* and *mens rea*. *Mens rea* involves the state of mind of D at the time of the offence and we will deal with this in Unit 16. First we will look at *actus reus* which involves everything else (other than the mental element) that makes up the crime.

Although in simple terms *actus reus* means a guilty act or wrongful conduct, there is more to it than this. It may include:

- conduct (which is voluntary)
- circumstances
- a consequence (which is caused by D's conduct)

It is very important to identify each element of the *actus reus* of a crime because there can be no crime unless the *actus reus* is complete. This does not necessarily mean D will be acquitted. If part of the *actus reus* of an offence is not proved then *that* offence is not committed, but there may well be a connected offence or an attempt. We will look at conduct and circumstances here, and consequences in Unit 15.

Conduct

As a rule the conduct must be voluntary. This is seen in **Leicester v Pearson (1952)**, where a car driver was prosecuted for failing to give precedence to a pedestrian on a zebra crossing. It was shown that his car had been pushed on to it by another car hitting him from behind. He was acquitted. He had not acted voluntarily. (Another example of involuntary acts will be looked at under general defences: automatism, p. 233.)

Conduct can consist of an act, an omission or a state of affairs. An **act** is usually straightforward, e.g. hitting someone. An **omission** is a failure to act. In criminal law this will not usually make you guilty unless you have a duty to act in the first place. An example is failing to look after your child. A **state of affairs** is where you can commit an offence by just being in a certain state, e.g. 'being *drunk* in charge of a motor vehicle'.

Act or omission?

In **Fagan *v* Metropolitan Police Commissioner (1969)** D accidentally drove on to a policeman's foot while parking. He didn't move his car when asked; in fact he used some fairly colourful language which I will not repeat here. He was promptly arrested for, and convicted of, assaulting a police officer in the execution of his duty. He argued that there was no *mens rea* at the time of the act (driving on to his foot) and that the refusal to move was only an omission, not an act. The court held that there was a *continuing act* which started with the driving on to the policeman's foot and continued up to the refusal to move. Thus, not moving when asked to was part of the original act rather than an omission. At this time he did have *mens rea*. This is one way in which a judge can interpret the law to suit the case. Having decided that this type of assault could not be committed by omission the CA used the idea of a continuing act to overcome the problem. This case also reaffirms the point that *actus reus* and *mens rea* must be contemporaneous (i.e. coincide or happen at the same time).

Key case

A case illustrating the distinction between an act and an omission is **Airedale NHS Trust *v* Bland (1993)**. Tony Bland, who was 17, had been badly injured in the Hillsborough football stadium disaster. He was in what is called a persistent vegetative state and had no hope of recovery. The family and doctors wanted to turn off the life support machine. The HL confirmed a court order allowing this. They drew a distinction between a positive act that killed (such as administering a lethal injection) which could never be lawful, and an omission to act which allowed someone to die (e.g. not providing life-saving treatment).

The cases of **Diane Pretty** and **Ms B** in 2002 also illustrate this distinction. In the first, Mrs Pretty wanted her husband to help her commit suicide and took her case to the HL and then the European Court of Human Rights. She wanted a court order that he would not be prosecuted for assisting her suicide. She failed as this would be a positive act. In the latter case Ms B wanted treatment discontinued and succeeded in obtaining a court order to allow this, even though it meant she would die.

So we can see that there is generally no criminal liability for not doing something. Exceptions occur when there is a duty to act. This can occur when:

- Parliament has expressly provided for it by statute.
- There is a contractual duty.
- A relationship of responsibility gives rise to a common law duty.
- D has created a dangerous situation.

In these cases an omission to act is enough.

> **Example** You see someone drowning and are a good swimmer but leave them to die. You are not guilty of any crime. However, as I said above, there are exceptions. I will come back to this as we look at the exceptions.

Statutory duty to act

The **Road Traffic Act 1988** makes it an offence for a driver involved in a road accident to fail to stop and give a name and address when asked or to fail to report the accident to the police. Failing to stop/report (an omission) is thus part of the *actus reus* of those crimes.

Contractual duty to act

In **Pittwood (1902)** D was employed as a gatekeeper by a railway company. His job was to keep the gate at the crossing shut whenever a train passed. One day he forgot to close the gate. A haycart crossed the track and was hit by an oncoming train. One person was killed and another seriously injured. D was under a contractual duty of employment to keep the gates to the crossing shut and to safeguard people using the crossing. His failure to act was in breach of his contractual duty and so amounted to the *actus reus* of manslaughter. The quote at the beginning came from this case.

In my example, if you were a lifeguard you would have a contractual duty to act, so could be liable.

Similar to this is a duty where you hold a public office. Thus in **Dytham (1979)** a policeman who failed to act when he saw D kicking someone to death was liable. Here, though, he was not guilty of homicide, only of misconduct in a public office.

Relationship of responsibility

In **Stone and Dobinson (1977)** Stone, who lived with Dobinson, allowed his sister Fanny to come and live with them. Fanny was anorexic, and often took to her bed for days at a time, refusing food and any other form of assistance. Her condition seriously deteriorated. After inadequate efforts to obtain medical assistance, Fanny was found dead in her bed. The court held that Stone and Dobinson had undertaken the duty of caring for Fanny and they had been grossly negligent in their failure to fulfil their duty. This failure had caused Fanny's death and so they were guilty of manslaughter.

In my example, if you were the parent of the swimmer you would have a duty to act, so could be liable. Also if you had taken on responsibility for them, as with Dobinson.

Creating a dangerous situation

In **Miller (1983)** D was squatting in an unoccupied house. One night he fell asleep while smoking. When he awoke he realised he'd set fire to the mattress but did nothing to extinguish it; he merely moved to another room. The house caught fire and damage was caused. He was convicted of arson under s. 1 **Criminal Damage Act 1971**. The HL upheld his conviction on the basis that if a defendant has unintentionally caused an event, and then realises what has happened, he has a duty to take appropriate action.

In my example, if you pushed them in you created the dangerous situation, so have a duty to take appropriate action. Again you could be liable.

Task

Compare **Fagan** (p. 129) and **Miller**. Could Miller have been found guilty on the 'continuing act' theory?

State of affairs

A few crimes can be committed without any apparent voluntary act by the accused. In **Larsonneur (1933)** a Frenchwoman was deported against her will from Ireland and brought to England by the police. She was convicted under the **Aliens Order 1920** of being found in the UK without permission. The state of affairs amounting to the *actus reus* was 'being found', so as soon as she landed in the UK without the required permission she committed the offence. This law has since been repealed but a similar situation is seen in **Winzar v Chief Constable of Kent (1983)**. A drunk was told to leave a hospital and didn't. He was removed by the police, who put him in their car, which was parked on the highway. The police then arrested him for being found drunk on the highway, for which he was later convicted. The state of 'being found' was again enough.

Food for thought

Think about whether there should be liability for omissions. Use the above cases to support your arguments. There is no 'right' answer. It can be argued that there is a moral duty to act if it will save a life; consider whether there should also be a legal duty. Do you think the court made the right decision in the Tony Bland case? It can be said that turning off the machine was an act, but the court viewed it as an omission. On the other hand, in **Fagan** it could be said there was only an omission but the court found a 'continuing act'. Do you think judges have too much discretion, for example, to distinguish precedents? Is it better to have certainty in the law or to ensure justice is done in a particular case?

Also the 'state of affairs' cases can be criticised. One of the arguments for imposing liability without having to prove fault is that it saves lengthy investigations and court time, but is it fair to D? Should someone be convicted just for being in the wrong place at the wrong time as in **Winzar** and **Larsonneur**? Compare these cases to **Leicester v Pearson (1952)**, page 128.

Examination pointer

All the matters above are ones that can be discussed in an essay, using the cases to illustrate what you say. There are valid arguments on both sides so don't strive to write what you think examiners want to see; they will be much more impressed with a balanced argument. By all means have an opinion, but look at the issue from the other point of view too - this shows you have considered the arguments before reaching your own opinion.

Circumstances

Many crimes are committed only if the conduct is carried out in particular circumstances. The *actus reus* of theft is the appropriation (taking) of property belonging to another. 'Appropriation' is the conduct, that it is 'property' and 'belongs to another' are both circumstances. *All* these must be proved or it is not theft. Many of the offences against the person have the word 'unlawful' in their definition. If D acted in self-defence, this makes it lawful and the *actus reus* is not satisfied.

Task

Make a separate folder for the more detailed material you need for essays. As you read cases, start to question what is satisfactory - or not - about the law and add your thoughts to the folder. Look out for articles from newspapers or law journals on any of the issues you are discussing. Cut them out and put them in the folder, adding a few of your own comments.

Summary

A summary and exercises on *actus reus* follow Unit 15.

Self-test questions

1 What '3 Cs' may be included in the *actus reus* of a crime?

2 On what basis did the court find liability in **Fagan**?

3 Give two examples of when an omission can result in criminal liability.

4 From which case did the quote at the beginning of the unit come from?

For further resources and updates please go to the Companion Website accompanying this book at **www.pearsoned.co.uk/russell**

Actus reus 2: Consequences and causation

. . . those who use violence on other people must take their victims as they find them.

Lawton LJ

> **By the end of this Unit you should be able to:**
> - Explain how *actus reus* may involve circumstances and consequences
> - Explain how causation is proved by reference to cases
> - Identify possible criticisms

We saw in Unit 14 that *actus reus* can involve conduct, circumstances and consequences. We have dealt with the first two of these; now we will look at the last one.

Consequences

Crimes where a particular consequence is part of the *actus reus* are called **result crimes**. Murder is an example. For a murder conviction the death must be as a result of D's act. Homicide is the unlawful killing of a human being. The *actus reus* involves not just killing (conduct) but also that it is unlawful and of a human being (circumstances) and that death occurs (the consequence).

Note that the difference between murder and manslaughter is the mens rea, not the actus reus, and the word homicide applies to both.

So, as well as the consequence itself, it must be proved that D's act *caused* this consequence. Causation is an important issue in many crimes.

Causation

Many of the cases on causation involve a homicide because it is a result crime. As causation is also relevant to other crimes it is dealt with here rather than with a particular offence. The prosecution must prove causation both **factually** and **legally**.

Factual causation

Factual causation is traditionally referred to as the *'sine qua non'* rule. This phrase is defined in Chambers as 'an indispensable condition'. It means D's action must be a *'sine qua non'* or an 'indispensable condition' of the result. More simply put, the result would not have occurred without D's action. It is more commonly called the 'but for' test. The prosecution must show that 'but for' D's conduct, the victim would not have died (or been injured).

Key case

In **White (1910)** D put cyanide in a drink intending to kill his mother, who was found dead shortly afterwards with the drink three parts full. In fact, the mother had died of a heart attack unconnected with the poison. The son was found not guilty of murder. He had the *mens rea* (he intended to kill her) but not the *actus reus* (his act didn't cause her death). He didn't get away with it altogether though; he was guilty of attempted murder.

White illustrates the situation where D's act has not factually caused death. Any of the following cases on legal causation could also be used for illustrating causation in fact. As you read them, ask the question 'but for D's act would the victim have died/been injured?' If the answer is 'no' then causation in fact is shown. Causation in fact can be very wide.

Example | I ask a college student to stay on for half an hour to finish a project. She therefore misses her bus and walks home. On the way she is attacked and injured. It can be argued that 'but for' my asking her to stay late she would not have been attacked and so I am liable for her injury. To avoid such a wide liability the courts have built up some rules on how far someone should be liable for the consequences of their actions. This is causation in law.

Legal causation

This is based on what is called the 'chain of causation'. It means proving an unbroken link, or chain, between D's action and the end result, for example death in homicide cases. When something has occurred after D's original act, then it may be argued that the chain of causation is broken. We will look at some cases to explain how this works but, in summary, the chain of causation will not be broken if:

● D's action makes a 'significant' contribution to the death (**Smith/Cheshire**).

● Any intervening act was foreseeable (**Roberts**).

● The victim has a particular weakness and a normal person may not have died. This is known as the 'thin skull' rule (**Blaue**).

In my example, I will argue that the chain has been broken by the attacker. I did not make a significant contribution to the harm, and the attack was not foreseeable. I have not legally caused the injuries.

Task

Use my example above but this time apply it to the attacker. Decide whether the attacker legally caused death in the following situations:

1 The attacker left her badly injured and lying in the road. She is run over by a car and killed.

2 The attacker left her badly injured but a passer-by stops and calls an ambulance. She is taken to hospital and starts to recover. However, the treatment is wrong and she dies.

3 She was only slightly injured but (not a good day!) she is struck by lightning as she recovers from the attack.

Now we'll look at some cases.

In **Smith (1959)** a soldier stabbed in a fight was dropped twice on the way to the treatment centre and then left untreated for some time. Although the court recognised that this contributed to the death, it found Smith, who had stabbed him, guilty of murder. As Lord Parker LCJ put it, his act was 'still an operating cause and a substantial cause' of the death.

Key case

In **Cheshire (1991)** due to negligent treatment by the hospital, complications arose after an operation on the victim of a shooting. The victim subsequently died. The person accused of the murder argued that his act had not caused the death of the victim, the hospital had done so. The court rejected the argument, following **Smith**, stating that as long as D's action was a 'significant and operative' cause of the death it need not be the sole cause. The jury should not regard hospital treatment as excluding D's responsibility unless it 'was so **independent of his acts**, and in itself so **potent in causing death**, that they regard the contribution made by his acts as insignificant.'

This principle was followed by the CA in **Mellor (1996)**. An elderly man was taken to hospital following an attack in which he suffered broken ribs and other injuries. He died from bronchial-pneumonia brought on by his injuries. The hospital had failed to give him oxygen which may have saved him. D's conviction for murder was upheld. The word 'operating' is used in the sense of still having an effect on – nothing to do with the fact that it was a surgical operation! It is clear from these cases that the courts are reluctant to allow medical treatment to break the chain of causation and thus prevent D being found guilty of the killing.

In **Pagett (1983)** D armed himself with a shotgun and took a pregnant girl hostage in a flat. Armed police called on him to come out. He eventually did so, holding the girl in front of him as a human shield. He then fired the shotgun at the police officers, who returned fire, killing the girl hostage. The actions of the police did not break the chain because shooting back at D was held to be a 'natural consequence' of his having shot first. D was convicted of manslaughter.

Key Case

In **Roberts (1971)** D – in a moving car – committed an assault on the victim by trying to take off her coat. She jumped out and was injured. He was charged with actual bodily harm. The court held that the only question was whether the assault caused the victim's action. Only if it was something that no reasonable person could foresee would the chain of causation be broken, and in this case it wasn't. A jury may take into account that the victim may do the wrong thing on the spur of the moment.

It had been recognised in **Roberts** that V may do the wrong thing in the agony of the moment. In **Williams and Davis (1992)** the CA said that only if V does something 'so daft or unexpected' that no reasonable person could be expected to foresee it would the chain of causation be broken. In **Corbett (1996)** the victim was trying to escape an attack by D, when he fell and was hit by a car. V died so it was a homicide case, but the same principle applies. His action came within a foreseeable range of consequences so did not break the chain.

Before looking at the final rule on causation, what did you decide in the task? Remember legal causation turns on how significant a contribution the attack made and whether the 'intervening act' (the car, the hospital treatment or the lightning) was foreseeable. You can therefore ask:

1 Whether it is foreseeable that a car will come along and hit her – yes, she is lying in the road. The chain is not broken by the car.

2 Whether it is foreseeable that hospital treatment may be inappropriate – yes, it happens enough for it to be foreseeable. The chain is not broken by the hospital treatment.

3 Whether it is foreseeable that she is struck by lightning – not likely; it is very rare. Also, as she was only slightly injured the attack did not make a significant contribution. The chain is broken by the lightning.

Note in (3) that this does not mean the attacker gets off. He will still be liable for the attack, but not the death.

The 'thin skull' rule

This appears to be an exception to the 'foreseeability' rule. The term 'thin skull' means something which makes V more vulnerable than other people. If a particular disability in the victim means that they are more likely to be harmed, or die, D is still liable. As Lawton LJ said in the opening quote, 'those who use violence on other people must take their victims as they find them'.

Key case

This comment was made in **Blaue (1975)**. Lawton LJ went on to say, 'This in our judgment means the whole man, not just the physical man'. The victim was stabbed repeatedly and rushed to hospital where doctors said she needed a blood transfusion to save her life. She was a Jehovah's Witness and so refused to have one. She consequently died. D was convicted of manslaughter. The 'disability' is more often physical (like a pre-existing medical condition such as a 'thin skull') but here it was the fact that she was a Jehovah's Witness.

Food for thought

If you were on the jury would you know what acts should be considered 'independent' or 'potent' enough to break the causation chain? How significant is significant? What amounts to a 'daft' act by the victim? There may be a thin line between doing 'something wrong in the agony of the moment' and doing something 'daft'. It could be argued that the courts could use the thin skull rule to resolve the issue. If V is easily scared and does something 'daft' then there is arguably a vulnerability that is no different to having a thin skull, or being a Jehovah's Witness, as in **Blaue**.

Another discussion point is whether D should be liable for a serious crime like manslaughter if someone, or something, else was the immediate cause of the death.

Examination pointer

In a problem question look out for anything that D can argue broke the chain. For example, D attacks someone and as they are running away they are hit by a car or bus. **Roberts** can be used to say that this is unlikely to break the chain. Look out for words like 'near the road' or 'in the bus station'. These suggest it is foreseeable. If V refuses treatment you may need the thin skull rule. Here, look out for the reason. If it is a completely idiotic decision then *Blaue* may be distinguished; if it is due to religious beliefs, it will be followed.

Task

Match the term with the brief explanation of it. If it isn't your book, do it on a piece of paper, or it could be criminal damage! The first one is done for you.

actus reas	the 'but for' test
factual causation	Cheshire
mens rea	you take your victim as you find them
'thin skull' rule	guilty act
'significant contribution' principle	guilty mind

Draw a diagram like the one in the summary for your files. Add a case to each of the principles and keep it as a revision guide.

Summary

Actus reus				
Conduct		Circumstances	Consequences	
Act	Omission	Seen in the actual definition of a crime	Causation	
voluntary	only if a duty		factual	legal
			'but for' test	D made a significant contribution/ intervening act was foreseeable/chain of causation not broken

Self-test questions

1 D has to make what type of contribution to the result?

2 What is the thin skull rule?

3 If the victim does something foreseeable will it break the chain of causation?

4 From which case did the quote at the beginning of this unit come?

For further resources and updates please go to the Companion Website accompanying this book at **www.pearsoned.co.uk/russell**

Mens rea

*I attach great importance to the search for a direction which is both clear and simple . . .
I think that the **Nedrick** direction fulfils this requirement admirably.*

Lord Hope

By the end of this Unit you should be able to:

● Explain the term *mens rea*

● Explain how the law on *mens rea* has developed and how it applies in practice

● Identify possible criticisms

Mens rea basically means a guilty mind and refers to the state of mind of the accused at the time the *actus reus* is committed. Thus *mens rea* and *actus reus* must exist at the same time.

There are two main types of *mens rea*. These are:

● Intention

● Recklessness

Other types of *mens rea* can be seen in particular offences. **Knowledge** comes into many of the property offences, as does **dishonesty**, and these are dealt with along with those crimes. **Gross negligence** is the *mens rea* for one type of manslaughter only, which has a unit to itself.

It is important to be able to identify both the *actus reus* and the *mens rea* of each offence when answering a problem question. Each and every part of a crime has to be proved beyond reasonable doubt.

Crimes are sometimes divided into 'specific intent' and 'basic intent' offences. This can seem misleading as basic intent offences don't require intent to be proved. Essentially, specific intent crimes are those requiring a *mens rea* of intention and nothing less. Basic intent crimes are those where the *mens rea* is intention *or* recklessness. Don't worry about this for now. It is mainly relevant to the defence of intoxication, and is discussed with this defence.

Intention

This is the highest form of *mens rea*. It applies to, for example, theft and murder. The *mens rea* of theft is intention to deprive someone of property permanently.

If it can be shown that the property was taken absent-mindedly, D can argue that there was no *mens rea*.

> **Example** You borrow your friend's mobile phone because you have run out of credit. You forget to give it back. You have no *mens rea* so are not guilty of theft. If you borrowed it, took it home and put your own SIM card into it, this would be evidence that you intended to deprive your friend of it permanently. In these circumstances you could be guilty of theft. Think of your own example and make a note now.

A case example is **Madeley (1990)**. The host of the *Richard and Judy* television show was charged with shoplifting. He was able to show that he was suffering from stress and merely forgot to pay for the goods. The court accepted his argument and found him not guilty.

The *mens rea* for murder is an intention to kill or seriously injure someone. Many cases dealing with intention are homicide cases. This is because it is essentially the *mens rea* that differentiates murder from manslaughter. It is only murder where the killing is intentional. Intention can be direct or oblique (indirect).

Direct Intent

Here the result is D's aim or purpose. This is what most of us would understand by intention. If you pick up a loaded gun and fire it at someone with the aim of killing them it can be said without any difficulty that you intended to do so. The courts have given the concept of intention a wider meaning, however. This is referred to as oblique, or indirect, intent.

Oblique intent

The consequence isn't your aim but is 'virtually certain' to occur as a result of your actions.

> **Example** One night, two animal rights activists set fire to a shop which sells fur coats. The shop is closed but a security guard dies in the fire. Are they guilty of murder? They do not have the *mens rea* of *direct* intent as their purpose is to make a political point, not to kill. They may have *oblique* intent. This will depend on the evidence. We will come back to this. For now, just make a note of what you think.

The issue of intent has been problematic. **Section 8 Criminal Justice Act 1967** provides that the jury *'shall not be bound in law to infer that D intended or foresaw a result of his actions by reason only of its being a natural and probable consequence of those actions'*. It also requires the jury to refer to *'all the evidence, drawing such inferences from the evidence as appear proper in the circumstances'*.

Example Don fires a gun. The bullet kills someone. So, according to **s. 8**, what do the jury have to do?

The first bit means that just because it's likely to happen, it does not mean that the jury should infer that D intended it to happen. If Don fired into a crowded room, the jury may think death is a likely result, but this is *not enough by itself* to *prove* that Don intended it.

The second bit means that the jury must look at everything else. Where did it happen? What time of day was it? Did Don know there were people about? This will help them to decide what Don 'intended'. There is a difference between firing a gun into the air in the middle of an empty field and doing the same thing in a schoolroom. Even in the latter case, it may be that the school is closed and Don is the caretaker shooting at a rat, not realising anyone is about. There is no answer that's always going to be right. That's what juries are for.

There has been a long line of cases on intent. Words like 'foreseeable', 'probable', 'likely' and 'natural' have all been used along the way. In **Smith (1960)** the HL had said that whether a result was probable was an objective test (what the reasonable person would '*contemplate as the natural and probable result*'). **Section 8** makes the test subjective, whether the *defendant* saw it as probable. In **Hyam v DPP (1975)** a woman poured petrol through the letterbox of a rival and set fire to it. Two children died. She argued that she had only intended to frighten the other woman. The HL rejected her appeal but made clear the test was subjective. It was whether *she* saw the result as 'highly probable'. However, they also suggested that this was proof of intent, not just evidence of it. This point was rejected in **Moloney (1985)**. It is now only a matter of evidence, not proof in itself.

Key case

In **Moloney**, D and his stepfather were having a drunken competition to see who could load and draw a shotgun the quickest. D won, and his stepfather said, 'I didn't think you've got the guts, but if you have, pull the trigger.' D said he didn't aim the gun but just pulled the trigger. His murder conviction was quashed. The judge had directed the jury that they could find intent if D foresaw the result as 'probable' and the HL said that this was not enough; it needed to be a certainty. Lord Bridge gave an explanation of intent in terms of 'moral certainty'. However, in his later summing up he said that a consequence was 'virtually certain' if it was a 'natural consequence'. Hardly the same thing at all. Many 'natural' consequences are far from certain. Death from a lightning strike is a natural consequence of a storm, but not very likely – let alone certain!

In **Hancock and Shankland (1986)** two striking miners had pushed concrete blocks off a bridge to prevent a miner going to work. They said they only intended to scare him, but the driver of the taxi in which he was travelling was killed. Their conviction for murder was quashed. Both the CA and HL held that 'natural consequence' was misleading and that even awareness of the consequence as 'virtually certain' was only evidence and not proof of intent.

The law on oblique intent was clarified somewhat by the HL in **Woollin (1998)**, which confirmed the direction given by the CA in **Nedrick (1986)**.

Key cases

In **Nedrick**, D poured paraffin through V's letterbox, circumstances not unlike those in **Hyam**, and set it alight. He said he only intended to scare her, but her child died in the resulting fire. He was convicted of murder and appealed on the basis of lack of *mens rea*. The CA quashed his conviction because the jury had not been properly directed on intent. A conviction for manslaughter was substituted. The court provided a standard direction for the jury as to intent in a murder trial in all cases of oblique intent. Lord Lane said,

> '*The jury should be directed that they are not entitled to infer the necessary intention unless they feel sure that death or serious bodily harm was a* **virtual certainty** *(barring some unforeseen intervention) as a result of the defendant's actions and that the* **defendant appreciated** *that such was the case . . . The decision is one for the jury to be reached on a consideration of all the evidence.*'

The opening quote comes from the HL in **Woollin**. A father was convicted of murder after throwing his baby son across the room in a fit of temper. He argued that he had thrown the baby towards his pram but had not intended to kill him. His conviction was again substituted for one of manslaughter, this time by the HL. They confirmed the **Nedrick** direction. Thus, for murder, the two questions the jury must consider are:

● Was death or serious bodily harm a virtual certainty?

● Did the defendant appreciate that such was the case?

If the answer to both these questions is 'yes' then the jury may find intent. Although the HL used the word 'find' instead of 'infer', this seems of little import.

One other point. In some appeal cases you may feel that the jury would have found intent. You could well be right. Many appeals are allowed because the jury was misdirected, not necessarily because intent could not be proved. The jury may have found sufficient evidence of intent, but were not directed correctly on the law.

Example If the defence can show that the two animal rights activists thought the shop was empty then the jury are unlikely to be convinced they appreciated that anyone's death or serious injury was a virtual certainty. They could be convicted of manslaughter but not murder. If the prosecution can prove that they knew there was a guard on duty this will be evidence for the jury that they did appreciate that death or serious injury was a virtual certainty, so a conviction for murder is possible.

You should know both **Nedrick** and **Woollin** for several reasons. First, the law was *established* by the CA in **Nedrick**, but *confirmed* by the HL in **Woollin**, and a **precedent** carries greater weight once the HL has approved it. Second, the **Nedrick** test has not been followed consistently. In **Walker and Hayles (1990)**, although the CA held the test to be correct, they said that the use of the phrase 'a very high degree of probability' sufficed. More confusion! In **Woollin** itself there was some confusion in the CA as to the application of the test (perhaps caused by the **Walker** decision). Finally, the Law Commission produced its report and **Draft Code**, in which it had given a definition of intent, after **Nedrick** but before **Woollin**. There was therefore some doubt as to whether, if a case reached the HL, that definition would be preferred. Apparently not.

Food for thought

The **Draft Code** definition is that D acts intentionally with respect to a result *'when he acts either in order to bring it about or being aware that it will occur in the ordinary course of events'*. In **Woollin**, Lord Steyn referred to the **Draft Code** but thought the **Nedrick** test was 'very similar'. It is arguable that the HL should have adopted this if they thought it so similar. It seems quite clear and would become the law if the **Code** were ever adopted.

The test was followed again in **Matthews and Alleyne (2003)**. The Ds had thrown V from a bridge into a river. He drowned. There was evidence that he had told them he couldn't swim. They appealed against their conviction for murder. The CA rejected their appeal but again said that foresight of death as a virtual certainty does not automatically prove intent, it is merely evidence (often very strong evidence) for the jury.

Examination pointer

When applying the law you need only use **Nedrick** and **Woollin**, and only then in cases of oblique intent, not where it is direct. This was made clear in **Woollin**. D's knowledge will be an important factor. Look carefully at the facts for information such as 'they knew that . . .' or 'unknown to them . . .' These comments will help you to apply the test as in my example. The cases leading up to **Woollin** would be useful for an essay question on either mens rea or murder generally. A summary of these follows.

Summary of the development of the law on intent

Case	Development	Probable, possible or certain?	Objective/subjective Proof or evidence?
DPP *v* Smith (1960)	HL held that the *mens rea* for murder is intention to kill or cause grievous bodily harm	Foresight of death or serious injury as a natural and probable result	Objective (what the 'reasonable man or woman' would contemplate)
Hyam (1974) (similar facts to **Nedrick**)	Changed to a subjective test by HL	Foresight of death or serious injury as highly probable	Noted that s. 8 had amended this to subjective It proved intent (this seems to contradict s. 8 which refers to evidence)
Moloney (1985)	HL disapproved **Hyam** Foreseeing death as 'probable' was not proof of intent	Foresight of death or serious injury as a moral certainty or natural consequence	Foresight was *evidence* of intent rather than *proof* of intent
Hancock and Shankland (1986)	**Moloney** guidelines were followed but HL held that 'natural consequence' was misleading	The greater the probability, the more likely it was foreseen and thus intended	Evidence
Nedrick (1986)	CA provided a new test	Death or serious injury was a virtual certainty and D appreciated this	Evidence from which the jury can 'infer' intent
Walker and Hayles (1990)	CA followed **Nedrick** but added	Very high degree of probability sufficed	As above
Woollin (1998)	HL confirmed **Nedrick** test	Death or serious injury was a virtual certainty and D appreciated this	Evidence from which jury can 'find' intent
Matthews and Alleyne (2003)	Applied **Nedrick** test	Death or serious injury was a virtual certainty and D appreciated this	Evidence of intent is not proof of intent

Recklessness

There were two types of recklessness. Subjective recklessness is used for most crimes as an alternative *mens rea* to intent. Objective recklessness was used for criminal damage until 2003, but is now abolished. Subjective means looking at what was in the *defendant's* mind. Objective means looking at what the *reasonable person* would think. You need to know a little about this for use in an essay on the developments.

Key case

Cunningham (1957) provides the test for subjective recklessness. D ripped a gas meter from a basement wall in order to steal the money in the meter. Gas escaped and seeped through to an adjoining property where an occupant was overcome by the fumes. D was charged with maliciously administering a noxious substance and argued that he did not realise the risk of gas escaping. The CA quashed his conviction, having interpreted 'maliciously' to mean with subjective recklessness. The prosecution had failed to prove that D was aware that his actions might cause harm. The test for subjective recklessness is therefore that **D is aware of the existence of a risk (of the consequence occurring) and deliberately goes ahead and takes that risk.**

Objective recklessness was defined in **Caldwell (1982)**. D, while drunk, set fire to a chair in the basement of the hotel where he worked. He was charged with arson (a type of criminal damage) endangering life. He argued that in his drunken state he had not thought about the fact that there could be people in the hotel. In the HL Lord Diplock extended the meaning of recklessness to include the situation where either:

- D saw a risk and ignored it (as in **Cunningham**, subjective); or
- D gave no thought to a risk which was obvious to a reasonable person. A new meaning: objective.

In **Gemmell and Richards (2003)** the HL held that the **Caldwell** test was wrong and that the *defendant* had to have recognised that there was some kind of risk.

Key case

In **Gemmell and Richards (2003)** two boys aged 11 and 13 set light to some papers outside the back of a shop. Several premises were badly damaged. They were convicted of arson on the basis of **Caldwell**, i.e. that the risk of damage was obvious to a reasonable person. In other words, objective recklessness. Their ages were therefore not taken into account. They appealed. The CA cannot overrule a decision of the HL and D's argument under the Human Rights Act also failed. They appealed further to the HL, which used the **1966 Practice Statement** to overrule its previous decision. The *mens rea* for criminal damage is now subjective (**Cunningham**) recklessness.

Thus, to prove recklessness it must be shown that *D is aware of a risk, but deliberately goes ahead and takes it.*

Food for thought

Consider whether **Caldwell** or **Gemmell** is to be preferred. **Caldwell** itself can be supported on the basis that being drunk shouldn't mean you can get away with a crime. There were other cases that followed it which are harder to justify though.

▶

In **Elliott (1983)** a 14-year-old girl, who was in a special needs class at school, set fire to a shed, not realising the risk of lighting white spirit. The magistrates acquitted her. However, the prosecution successfully appealed on the basis of **Caldwell**. A reasonable person would have seen the risk that she took, so she had sufficient *mens rea*. This case shows the difficulties of applying the objective test to a child, or a person who lacks the capacity of a 'reasonable person'. However, **Gemmell** solves this problem.

Examination pointer

For a problem question involving recklessness you only need to discuss subjective (**Cunningham**) recklessness. This is now the law as stated by the HL in **Gemmell**.

Task

Using the summary of the developments above, draw up a diagram and add a column to it. Use this column for a brief comment of your own, either on the principle or the facts. Keep the diagram as a guide for essays. It might look nice on the bedroom wall.

Transferred malice

Mens rea can be transferred from the intended victim to the actual victim. This means that if you intend to hit Steve but miss and hit Joe you cannot say 'but I didn't intend to hit Joe so I had no *mens rea*'. In **Latimer (1886)** D aimed a blow at X with his belt but missed and seriously wounded V. He had the intent (*mens rea*) to hit X, and this intent was transferred to the wounding (*actus reus*) of V. Thus he had both the *mens rea* and the *actus reus* of wounding. Although usually referred to as 'transferred intent' it applies to *mens rea* generally, both to intention and recklessness. The *actus reus* and *mens rea* must be for the *same* crime.

Example I throw a brick at someone but it misses and breaks a window. I had *mens rea* for an assault and *actus reus* for criminal damage. This *mens rea* can't be transferred. I am not guilty of either crime. If I throw the brick at someone but it hits someone else then this *mens rea* can be transferred. I had *mens rea* and *actus reus* for the *same* offence.

Coincidence of *actus reus* and *mens rea*

We saw in **Fagan** (p. 129) that *actus reus* and *mens rea* must coincide, but the court may view the *actus reus* as **continuing**. A similar reasoning can be seen in **Thabo Meli (1954)**. Planning to kill him, the Ds attacked a man and then rolled what they thought was his dead body over a cliff, to make it look like an accident. He was only unconscious at this point, and the actual cause of death was exposure.

The Ds were convicted of murder and argued that there were two separate acts. The first act (the attack) was accompanied by *mens rea* but was not the cause of death (so no *actus reus*). The second act (pushing him over the cliff) was the cause of death, but was not accompanied by *mens rea*. The *mens rea* of murder is intention to kill or seriously injure. They said there could be no such intention if they thought that the man was already dead. The court said that it was 'impossible to divide up what was really one **series of acts** in this way' and refused their appeal.

Summary

Level of *mens rea*	Explanation	Case	Example crimes
Direct intention	D's aim or purpose		Murder, theft, grievous bodily harm and wounding with intent
Indirect intention	Result is a virtual certainty and D appreciates this	**Nedrick (1986) CA Woollin (1998) HL**	Murder, theft, grievous bodily harm and wounding with intent
Subjective recklessness	D recognises a risk and goes on to take it	**Cunningham (1957)**	All other assaults, criminal damage

Self-test questions

1 From which case did the quote at the beginning of this unit come?

2 What are the two types of intent?

3 What is the **Nedrick** test for oblique intent?

4 Is recklessness now a subjective or objective test and in which case was this decided?

5 What is the principle in **Latimer**?

For further resources and updates please go to the Companion Website accompanying this book at **www.pearsoned.co.uk/russell**

Murder

... if at the time of death the original wound is still an operating cause and a substantial cause, then the death can properly be said to be the result of the wound, albeit that some other cause of death is also operating.

Lord Parker LCJ

By the end of this Unit you should be able to:
- Identify the *actus reus* and *mens rea* of murder
- Explain how the law on causation (*actus reus*) applies in murder cases
- Explain how intent (*mens rea*) is proved by reference to cases
- Identify possible criticisms of the current law on murder

There are definitions of what does and does not constitute murder going back to the eighteenth century and beyond – a famous one is by Sir Edward Coke – but, because murder is a common law offence, its definition has changed through case law. You really only need the current law.

Actus reus

The *actus reus* is essentially the same for both murder and manslaughter. The modern definition of murder is the **'unlawful killing of a human being under the Queen's peace'**.

Unlawful

Most killing will be unlawful. However, killing in self-defence (see Unit 29) may make the act lawful and so not murder.

Killing

People generally think of murder as involving an action (conduct) such as shooting or stabbing someone. However, it would seem that murder can be committed by omission. We saw the case of **Stone and Dobinson** (p. 130). That was manslaughter. In **Gibbins and Proctor (1918)**, a similar case resulted in a conviction for murder. Here the Ds lived together with the man's daughter. They failed to give her food and she died. The court held that where food was withheld with intent to cause grievous bodily harm then it would be murder if this caused death. The CA upheld their conviction for murder.

However, we have also seen that the courts draw a distinction between an act and an omission. In **Airedale NHS Trust *v* Bland (1993)** discontinuing medical treatment was treated as an omission rather than a positive action. This was a civil case so is not strictly binding on the criminal courts. It will be highly persuasive though. It can be compared to **Cox (1992)**, where a doctor gave an injection to a patient begging for help to die. This is a positive act, and so amounts to murder. (On the facts it was only attempted murder as the cause of death was not clear.) Intentionally accelerating death is still murder. Thus, even if someone is going to die anyway you will be guilty of murder if you intentionally shorten their life. The only exception is what is known as the *de minimis* rule. If D's act is so small that it cannot be said to play a significant part in the death, there is no liability for murder.

Example
V is in severe pain from an incurable illness. The doctor gives her a huge overdose of painkillers in order to end her suffering. Before these take effect V's husband gives her two more painkillers.

The doctor's act would be murder. The husband's *could* be murder as it probably hastened the death, but the court might treat it as '*de minimis*'.

Food for thought

Any intentional act which causes death will be murder. Thus, 'mercy killing', or euthanasia, would be murder. You might argue that you were easing the suffering of someone incurably ill, but this argument will not succeed. Accelerating death is still murder. The motive for a crime is rarely relevant (it is as much theft to steal a loaf of bread for a starving child as it is to steal a £5,000 music system). The motive could affect the sentence, but with murder the judge has no choice in this.

This is why the **Bland** case went to the House of Lords. Without a court order it could have been murder. A Bill was produced in 2005 to allow assisted suicide in certain circumstances. Is it better to have a law that allows euthanasia as, for example, in Belgium? These issues are difficult and there is unlikely to be agreement across society.

A related issue for an essay is the sentence for murder. One argument against a mandatory life sentence is that if the jury see the killing as morally justified they may be reluctant to find someone guilty of murder. They would know that it would mean a life sentence and that the judge would be unable to take the circumstances into account. In May 2005 the DPP, Ken Macdonald, recommended that a more flexible system should be introduced, similar to that in America, where there are different degrees of homicide. This change would mean that not all killings would be treated in exactly the same way, and could solve some of the difficulties for both judges and juries.

Causation

Murder is a result crime so it must be proved that death resulted from D's actions. If D caused death then the charge can be murder or manslaughter depending on the *mens rea*. If D did not cause death then it can only be one of the non-fatal offences or an attempt. We have seen that the prosecution must show **factual causation**: 'but for' the defendant's conduct the victim would not have died. Also **legal causation**: that D's act was a 'significant' cause of death and there was no intervening act.

> ## Task
>
> Before going any further, look up the following cases. Make a note of the facts.
>
> **White**
>
> **Roberts**
>
> **Smith**
>
> **Cheshire**
>
> **Pagett**
>
> Now add a note of the causation issue in each. Then read on to check these principles.

OK, let's have a quick recap of the causation principles involved.

Factual causation

R *v* White (1910)	'But for' his actions would she be alive? No, she would have died anyway, so he did not cause that death

Legal causation

R *v* Smith (1959)	If D's act was an **operating and substantial** cause of death there is no break in the chain of causation
R *v* Cheshire (1991)	Following **Smith**, if D has made a **significant contribution** to the death then hospital treatment will only break the chain of causation if it is **independent of the original act** and a potent cause in itself
Roberts (1971) The prosecution relied on this case in **Corbett (1996)** to find that D caused the death of a victim who was hit and killed by a car when trying to escape from D's attack	If the *victim's* act is **foreseeable** it will not break the chain of causation, as long as it is not 'daft'
R *v* Pagett (1983)	If a *third party's* act is **foreseeable** it will not break the chain of causation and the police returning fire was a **natural consequence** of D's actions

These cases could also be used to explain factual causation. In **Pagett** you would ask 'but for' his actions would she have died? No, so he factually caused death. (Note this test is sometimes reversed but the effect is the same: 'but for' his actions would she be alive? Yes, so he caused death.)

Food for thought

If V is easily scared and does something 'daft' then there is arguably a vulnerability that is no different from having a thin skull or being a Jehovah's Witness, as in **Blaue**. **Blaue** itself is somewhat controversial. If the victim does not have a life-threatening injury but refuses treatment, should D be liable for the resulting death?

Mens rea

In Coke's eighteenth-century definition of murder the unlawful killing must be done with *'malice aforethought'*. This expression is still used but has been interpreted as meaning with intention.

In **DPP *v* Smith (1960)**, the HL held that the *mens rea* for murder is satisfied by either an intention to kill, or an intention to cause grievous bodily harm. They said that grievous bodily harm should be given its ordinary and natural meaning, that is to say, 'really serious bodily harm'. In **Saunders (1985)** it was said that the word 'really' did not add anything. Thus the *mens rea* of murder is **intent to kill or seriously injure**.

Task

Look up the cases of **Nedrick** and **Woollin**. Make a note of the facts, and whether the murder charge succeeded, and why/why not.

Knowledge of the development of the law (set out in Unit 16) is needed for a critique but, for a problem question, it is the current law that is important. We saw that this comes from the CA in **Nedrick (1986)**. It was confirmed by the HL in **Woollin (1998)** as being the correct direction for oblique intent. There is *evidence* of intent if:

- death or serious bodily harm was a virtual certainty as a result of the defendant's actions;
- the defendant appreciated that such was the case.

Key case

In **Woollin**, the jury had to consider whether D appreciated that it was a virtual certainty the baby would be killed or seriously injured by being thrown in the direction of the pram. The HL confirmed the point that this is only evidence of intention, not proof. The jury should be directed on the **Nedrick** test and told to take into account *all* the circumstances.

The **Nedrick** test was followed again in **Matthews and Alleyne (2003)**. The CA confirmed the test and that foresight of death as a virtual certainty does not automatically *prove* intent; it is merely *evidence* (often very strong evidence) for the jury.

Food for thought

The *mens rea* of murder is intent to kill or seriously injure (**Smith, 1960**). This means you can be guilty of murder even if you did not intend to kill. This point was confirmed in **Cunningham (1981)** (not to be confused with the 1957 case of the same name on recklessness). The HL criticised the rule but has refused to overrule it in several cases, preferring to leave that to Parliament.

The Law Commission has also criticised it but no government has yet suggested amending the law. In **Attorney-General's Reference (No. 3 of 1994) 1997**, the HL, although not overruling it, refused to apply it so as to find someone guilty of murder where there was only intent to cause serious injury; however, this was a case of transferred malice so may be of limited application.

Murder is the most serious offence, so it is vital that the law is clear. Look at the development of intent in the summary in Unit 16. Has it produced a clear meaning of intent? Pretend you are on a jury. Could you decide what degree of probability is virtually certain? The **Cunningham** test for recklessness is that D knowingly takes a foreseeable risk. The **Nedrick** test for intent is foresight of something as a virtual certainty. At what stage does a foreseeable risk become a certainty?

The above can be discussed in an essay question on *mens rea* or a more general one on homicide. To practise for a problem question look at a case you are familiar with and apply the law you have learnt. Let's try this with **Pagett**.

Summary of the rules and how they apply

Facts

1 D shot at the police while holding the girl in front of him.

2 The police returned fire.

3 The girl was killed.

Application with cases in support:

Actus reus

There is an unlawful killing but did D cause it?

'**But for**' his action she would not have died (**White**). He factually caused death.

He also made a '**significant contribution**' (**Cheshire**) to the girl's death. The intervening act of the police shooting back was **foreseeable** and so did not break the **chain of causation** (**Roberts**). He legally caused death.

We have *actus reus* but is it murder or manslaughter?

Mens rea

Was D's **aim** to **kill or seriously injure** the girl? No, so there is no direct intent. Was death or serious injury a **'virtual certainty'** and did D **appreciate** this (**Nedrick**)? If the jury find this not to be the case there is no indirect intent. He will *probably* be found not guilty of murder due to lack of *mens rea*. However, if the jury believe that D intended to kill or seriously injure the police, whether directly or by appreciating it as a virtual certainty, then the principle of transferred malice means that this intent is transferred from them to the girl and he may be found guilty.

Examination pointer

It is quite OK to say 'probably' in a conclusion. You can't be expected to play judge and jury. It is better than 'D will be guilty (or not) of . . .' – it is rarely that simple! Decide what seems most appropriate, and then use the law to prove it. You could say 'D could be charged with murder, but it may be hard to prove intent so a manslaughter charge may be more appropriate'. Then go on to discuss involuntary manslaughter. However, read the question carefully. If you are only asked to discuss murder, don't go on to manslaughter.

Task

Practise your application of the law using my example with **Pagett** as a guide. Choose a case you know quite well and go through the stages step by step. This will produce the kind of logical structure you need for problem exam questions in other areas too. Use it as a template for the exam questions at the end of each Part.

Self-test questions

1 What is the *actus reus* and *mens rea* of murder, and how have the courts interpreted the latter?

2 What is a result crime and what is the significance in terms of *actus reus*?

3 Can you explain the law on causation using two murder cases?

4 In which CA case was the 'virtual certainty' test for *mens rea* established and which HL case confirmed this?

5 Have you achieved the aims not only of this Unit, but of the units on *actus reus* (causation) and *mens rea* (intent) too?

For further resources and updates please go to the Companion Website accompanying this book at www.pearsoned.co.uk/russell

Study Block 5 Summary
ACTUS REUS, MENS REA AND MURDER

Actus reus

- conduct (which is voluntary)
- circumstances
- a consequence (causation)

The prosecution must prove causation both **factually** and **legally**.

Factually	The 'but for' test (**White**)
Legally	D's action made a 'significant' contribution to the result (**Cheshire**)
	Any intervening act was foreseeable (**Roberts**)
The 'thin skull' rule	Where V has a particular weakness D will be liable for the full consequences (**Blaue**)

Mens rea

Intention Nedrick test confirmed in Woollin	Direct: D's aim or purpose Indirect: was the result a virtual certainty? Did D appreciate this?
Subjective recklessness **Cunningham (1957)** **Gemmell and Richards (2003)**	D is aware of a risk, but deliberately goes ahead and takes it
Other types include knowledge, dishonesty and gross negligence	These are used for specific crimes

Murder

Actus reus	the unlawful killing of a human being under the Queen's peace
Mens rea	Malice aforethought, i.e. intention to kill or seriously injure

Task

Add the principle and brief facts to the case (in pencil if it isn't your book!).

Case	Principle	Facts
Fagan		
Stone and Dobinson		
Roberts		
Cheshire		
Blaue		
DPP v Smith		

Key criticisms

- D is not usually liable for an omission but can be in certain circumstances; there is a degree of uncertainty in such cases, e.g. **Bland, Fagan**.
- State of affairs crimes mean D can be guilty without being at fault, e.g. **Winzar**.
- The rules on what will break the chain of causation may be difficult for a jury to understand.
- The law on intent has developed but is arguably still unclear.
- Murder is a common law offence. Should there be a statutory definition?
- The *mens rea* for murder is intent to kill *or seriously injure*; for such a serious crime should it only be intent to kill?

Examination practice

Essay questions may be specific to a particular area or may be quite general. Always read the question carefully to ensure you cover what's required. The first question is very wide and leaves you the choice of covering a few areas in detail, or several areas less thoroughly. How you deal with such a question will depend on how confident you are on the area. If you are not very confident, or do not know the cases very well, then the latter approach may be better. Leave this question until you have covered the other types of homicide; it is here to show you the types of question you might get.

> **January 2005***
> What criticisms would you make of the current law of homicide? *(25 marks)*

This next one is more specific, so you will only need to discuss murder. However, this includes the *actus reus* issues of causation, and the *mens rea* issue in relation to malice aforethought and intent.

> **June 2004**
> Discuss the suggestion that the current law of murder is satisfactory and does not require any modification. *(25 marks)*

The final one is even more specific so you should only discuss *mens rea*.

> **January 2002**
> How satisfactory is the current law on malice aforethought (the *mens rea* of murder)?
> *(25 marks)*

Module 6 connections

Morals	Killing is usually both immoral and illegal; is it always immoral? Discuss omissions, e.g. where a failure to act causes death, and/or euthanasia cases	**Stone and Dobinson/ Gibbins and Proctor Pittwood Bland**
Justice	Is it just to convict someone for a 'state of affairs'? Is the thin skull rule just to D? Should a murder conviction be possible where D only intends serious harm, rather than death?	**Winzar/Larsonneur Blaue DPP *v* Smith/ Saunders**
Conflicting interests	Look at *any* cases and ask not only 'was justice done', but also whether, and how, the judge balanced the interests involved, e.g. those of the victim and society, as well as D	**Cunningham/ Nedrick**
Fault	*Mens rea* is the 'fault' element in criminal law so use any of the Unit 16 material. Look at the different levels of fault required for different crimes. Refer back to Module 3 for crimes where no fault is required, those of strict liability. The cases on omissions/state of affairs can be used to show that in some cases there is a very low degree of fault	**Stone and Dobinson/Winzar/ Larsonneur**
Creativity	'Judicial creativity' ties in with the rules of precedent and statutory interpretation, so look to see if any cases are setting a precedent, or have been widely interpreted. *Any* new cases can be used for a discussion of how far judges can use their discretion. As can any where you think the law *should* have changed and didn't	**Gemmell and Richards**

Study Block 6
VOLUNTARY MANSLAUGHTER

Unit 18   Voluntary manslaughter under Homicide Act s. 3: provocation
Unit 19   Voluntary manslaughter under Homicide Act s. 2: diminished responsibility
Unit 20   Voluntary manslaughter under Homicide Act s. 4: suicide pact, and summary of all three special defences

Three specific defences to murder are found in the **Homicide Act 1957**. If successful they reduce murder to what is called 'voluntary manslaughter', and thus allow sentencing to be at the discretion of the judge. They *only* apply to a murder charge. Other defences to murder also apply to other crimes so are dealt with under general defences.

We look at provocation in Unit 18. This is where D has killed in reaction to something done or said by the victim. Unit 19 covers situations where at the time of the killing D was suffering from diminished responsibility and Unit 20 covers the much rarer defence of killing as a result of a suicide pact.

Example | Taking the example I used in the last introduction, Jane stabs Jenny, who dies. This is murder. If Jenny had taunted Jane in some way, Jane may be able to use the defence of provocation. If she is suffering from severe depression at the time, Jane may argue diminished responsibility. Finally, if Jane and Jenny had agreed to kill each other in a suicide pact but Jane survives, she can use the suicide pact defence. If any of the defences succeed Jane will be convicted of manslaughter, not murder. The judge can choose the sentence.

The **Homicide Act** does not *define* murder. Murder, somewhat surprisingly, is not a statutory offence. It comes from the common law, not an Act of Parliament. The **Act** merely provides three special defences to a murder charge. Murder and voluntary manslaughter both have the same *actus reus* and *mens rea*. The difference lies in these defences. The other type of homicide, *involuntary* manslaughter, is often referred to as murder without *mens rea*, but this is a little misleading. It does require *mens rea*, just a different type. More on this later.

A final point. 'Voluntary' and 'involuntary' are terms used to distinguish between manslaughter following a murder charge, and manslaughter as a separate charge. There is no such charge as 'voluntary manslaughter' or 'involuntary manslaughter'. The first would be charged as murder, the second as manslaughter.

Voluntary manslaughter under Homicide Act s. 3: provocation

Would a sober man, in relation to that drunken observation, batter his friend over the head with a nearly two pound-weight ashtray?

Trial Judge, **Newell (1980)**

By the end of this Unit you should be able to:

● Explain the main legal requirements in proving the s. 3 defence

● Explain how the law on provocation applies in practice by reference to cases

● Identify possible criticisms

I said in the introduction that the three special defences under the **Homicide Act 1957** reduce a murder charge to what is called 'voluntary manslaughter'. Here we look at provocation.

The **Act** did not create a new defence. Unlike diminished responsibility (see next Unit), provocation already existed as a common law defence. Cases before the **Act** are still important. However, the statutory defence is wider.

The **Homicide Act s. 3** provides:

'Where on a charge of murder there is evidence on which the jury can find that the person charged was provoked (whether by things done or by things said or by both together) to lose his self-control, the question whether the provocation was enough to make a reasonable man do as he did shall be left to be determined by the jury; and in determining that question the jury shall take into account everything both done and said according to the effect which, in their opinion, it would have on a reasonable man.'

Don't be daunted by the length of the section, you needn't learn it by heart! It has been interpreted by the courts, and the test you need to apply was restated by the HL in **Acott (1997)**:

There must be some evidence of provocation and, if so, the judge puts two questions to the jury:

1 Did the accused lose self-control due to the provocation? and

2 Would a reasonable person with similar characteristics have also lost self-control in those circumstances and done as D did?

Note that if D raises provocation it is then up to the prosecution to prove beyond reasonable doubt – the criminal standard of proof – that the case is *not* one of provocation.

Examination pointer

Remember these three defences only apply to a murder charge. Don't try to apply them to other crimes. Where there is a death combined with an intent to kill you can deal with the murder issues and then look at these defences. If intent and causation are clear you don't need to discuss these in detail; go straight on to the defences, having said that the charge is likely to be murder. Only if the facts indicate it is necessary, for example, if there is a possible break in the chain of causation, or if intent may be hard to prove, should you discuss these. Examiners know you cannot discuss everything in the time allowed so questions are usually set which address specific issues. Be selective!

The test for provocation

Let's take each of the **Acott** points in turn.

Evidence of provocation

This is a matter for the judge. If there is evidence of provocation the judge will put it to the jury. The CA said in **Rossiter (1992)** that *any* evidence, 'however tenuous', that D was provoked meant the judge had to put it to the jury. However, in **Acott**, Lord Steyn said it wasn't necessary to leave it to the jury where it was a mere 'speculative possibility'. In **Miao (2003)** the CA said that its decision in **Rossiter** could not survive Lord Steyn's comments in the HL.

If there is evidence of provocation the judge may put it to the jury even if D does not raise it as a defence. This was seen in **Thornton (1992)**, discussed below.

So what sort of thing will amount to provocation? The Act introduces 'things done and said', so provocation can be caused by both actions and words. In **Doughty (1986)** the crying of a baby was said to amount to provocation. This case also shows that since the Act the provocation need not be directed at D. Provocation by or to another person will be enough. In **Pearson (1992)** a boy killed his father because of the father's ill treatment, not of himself but of his brother. The defence succeeded.

D lost self-control

This is subjective, i.e. did D lose control? The loss of control must be 'sudden and temporary'. This comes from the earlier case of **Duffy (1949)** but has been confirmed in later cases, including **Acott**.

In several cases women who had suffered years of abuse killed their partners. Accused of murder, they argued the provocation defence. Many failed on the 'sudden and temporary' point because there was a 'cooling-off' period between the provocative conduct and the killing.

Key case

In **Thornton (1992 and 1996)** Sara Thornton had gone to the kitchen to calm down after a violent argument. While there she picked up a knife and sharpened it. She then went to where her husband was lying on the sofa and stabbed him. She didn't raise provocation at her original trial but the judge put it to the jury and it was rejected. The evidence was that she had cooled down by the time she stabbed him. Her conviction for murder in 1990 was upheld by the CA in 1991. In a later appeal in 1995 fresh medical evidence was introduced which showed she had a personality disorder and 'battered woman syndrome'. The CA held that the jury should have been allowed to consider whether a reasonable woman with these characteristics would have acted as Mrs Thornton did. They made it clear, however, that the sudden and temporary rule still applied. Lord Taylor said, '*a defendant, even if suffering from [battered woman syndrome] cannot succeed in relying on provocation unless the jury consider she suffered or may have suffered a **sudden and temporary loss of self-control** at the time of the killing.*'

A retrial was ordered. This took place in the Crown Court in May 1996 and she was convicted of manslaughter.

(I have included the dates as this case and its various appeals and retrials may seem confusing. 1992 and 1996 are the dates the case was reported (All England Law Reports.))

In **Ahluwalia (1992)** D set fire to her husband's bed when he was asleep. The defence of provocation again failed on the 'sudden and temporary' point. At both subsequent retrials the defence under **s. 2**, diminished responsibility, succeeded so we will look at these cases again in the next Unit.

Humphries (1995) was an abuse case in which the provocation defence succeeded. She had killed after abuse and taunts from her boyfriend. The courts made clear that the time factor was a matter for the jury and that the response to the provocation did not necessarily have to be *immediate*, as long as it was *sudden*. In **Baillie (1995)** D found out that a drug dealer was threatening his son. He went into a rage then armed himself with a shotgun, drove to V's house and killed him. The CA said that there was evidence he was out of control during the whole episode so provocation should have been left to the jury.

There must be loss of *control* not just *self-restraint*. In **Cocker (1989)** D had finally given way to his wife's entreaties to ease her pain and end her life. His defence failed as the evidence showed he had not lost control.

Food for thought

In **Thornton** the trial judge directed the jury on provocation and then added '*it may be difficult to come to the conclusion that that was, and I use the shorthand, a reasonable reaction*'. He then went on to suggest it wasn't reasonable to stab someone when '*there are other alternatives available, like walking out or going upstairs*'.

Do you think his comments influenced the jury too much? Many people say abused women should simply walk away but life is rarely simple. Arguably issues of fact like this should be left to the jury alone.

The question was whether a reasonable woman would have done the same in her position, which brings us to the last question.

Would a reasonable person do as D did?

This is objective. Would a *reasonable person* do as D did? What characteristics can be attributed to the reasonable person in order to decide this second question has caused many problems. In **DPP v Bedder (1954)** the jury was told that the reasonable man shared none of the peculiarities of the accused. However, this was before the **Act**.

Key case

In **Camplin (1978)** a 15-year-old boy hit V with a chapati pan after being homosexually assaulted and then taunted about it. V died and he was charged with murder. The HL said the question was whether a person of his *age* and *sex* would have done as he did, and the **Act** overruled **Bedder**.

It was not fully clear from **Camplin** whether characteristics other than age and sex could be taken into account. Earlier cases centred on physical characteristics; this was later extended to mental ones. In **Humphries**, the long period of abuse as well as her immaturity and attention-seeking characteristics were taken into account. One of the reasons for ordering a retrial in **Thornton** was that this development had occurred since her original trial.

At one time characteristics had to be both *relevant* and *permanent*. In **Newell (1980)** alcoholism was not allowed as a characteristic as it wasn't related to the taunt, which was about his girlfriend. The fact that he was drunk wasn't attributable because it was a temporary state. The court asked the jury the question in the opening quote.

In **Morhall (1995)** glue-sniffing was said by the CA not to be a characteristic to be attributed to the reasonable man but this was reversed by the HL. It was held that as D was addicted this would be attributable, in the same way that alcoholism is, but being drunk isn't. D had been taunted by V about his addiction and they got into a fight, during which he stabbed V.

In **Luc Thiet Thuan (1996)** the Privy Council took a more restrictive view. D killed his girlfriend after she teased him about his sexual prowess. He relied on **s. 3** and there was evidence he was mentally unstable and had difficulty controlling his impulses. The Privy Council held that such mental factors could not be attributed to the reasonable man for the second, objective, question.

However, in **Smith (2000)** the HL was more liberal. D and a friend, both alcoholics, spent the evening drinking. D accused the friend of stealing his work tools and selling them to buy drink. They argued and D picked up a kitchen knife and stabbed his friend to death. At his murder trial he argued provocation and said the jury should take into account the fact that he had been suffering from severe depression which reduced his powers of self-control. The judge rejected this argument but the HL accepted D's appeal. Lord Hoffman said that if the jury thought that there was some characteristic which affected the degree of control which society could reasonably have expected of him it would be unjust not to take it into account. However, he did carry on to say that characteristics such as jealousy and obsession should be ignored, and Lord Clyde added '*exceptional pugnacity or excitability*'.

So, the reasonable man is getting quite a number of possible characteristics. We can have a fat, abused wife with a big growth and one leg who is also depressed (unsurprisingly!) and addicted to sniffing glue. In **Smith** itself Lord Hoffman referred to 'monsters' being produced by attributing characteristics like glue-sniffing to the reasonable man. The decision was only by a 3–2 majority. In particular, Lord Hobhouse produced a lengthy and reasoned argument against the decision.

Food for thought

That this is a problematic defence is clear. In 2003 the Law Commission said '*its defects are beyond cure by judicial development of the law*'. The proposals for reform are now in **Consultation Paper 177 (2004)**.

Groups such as Justice for Women have long argued that the defence of provocation favours men as it can be used only by those strong enough to fight back. The women who suffer years of abuse and finally kill in desperation – but not in the heat of the moment – will fail on the 'sudden and temporary' requirement.

The second question for the jury has always been objective but with so many characteristics it can be argued you no longer have a reasonable man, you have the defendant. This makes it subjective. The Law Commission thought that the HL in **Smith** failed to achieve any clarity and left the law confused. If they are confused, what hope is there for ordinary people?! However, interpretation of **s. 3** has narrowed again. Read on.

The Privy Council looked at the issue again in **AG for Jersey *v* Holley (2005)**. Although this was an appeal from a trial in Jersey, decisions of the Privy Council are highly persuasive on English law because the judges are Law Lords.

Key case

In **Holley (2005)** D, who was an alcoholic, killed his girlfriend with an axe while drunk. The CA substituted his conviction for murder for one of manslaughter, on the basis that the jury was misdirected on provocation. The prosecution appealed to the Privy Council, who held that **s. 3** of the **Homicide Act** provided that provocation should be judged by one standard, not a standard that varied from D to D. **Smith** was held to be wrong on this point. Lord Nicholls said that Parliament had altered the common law when passing the **Homicide Act**, so it was not up to judges to depart from the Act. D was to be judged against the standard of a person having 'ordinary powers of self-control', not against the standard expected of a particular D in the same position. Alcoholism is therefore no longer a 'relevant matter' for the jury when deciding whether a reasonable person would have done what D did. Note that Lord Hoffman dissented, but as his was the leading judgment in **Smith**, this is not surprising. It would seem that the law is back to **Luc Thiet**.

Task

Go to the Law Commission's website and see what they say in regard to homicide. You will find lots of information which you can refer to in an essay.

Let's take a quick look at the test again:

- **Is there evidence of provocation?** Was something done or said that could cause a reaction? If so, there are two questions:

  1 **Was D provoked to lose control?** Was there a sudden reaction to what was done or said? This is subjective so the jury should take into account *any* particular characteristics which could affect the *gravity of the provocation* to D.

  2 **Would a reasonable person have done as D did?** This is objective so the jury should not take mental characteristics, which might have *made losing control more likely*, into account.

Example

I am very embarrassed about a big growth on my back. Recently the doctor told me I needed an operation and I am very depressed and upset. While drinking in the kitchen at a party someone calls me a hunchback. I pick up a large knife and stab them. I am charged with murder and argue that I was provoked.

There is evidence of provocation by 'things said'. I clearly lost control. But would a reasonable person have acted like this?

The reasonable person will have a growth. This affects **the gravity of the provocation** to me – **Camplin**. If the reasonable person has no growth they won't be upset by the comment.

Following **Holley**, depression may no longer be allowed as a characteristic in relation to **the amount of control I was expected to exercise**. The jury will have to ask what an ordinary person would have done. It *could* relate to the gravity of the provocation, but I am not taunted about this. Also the reasonable person will not be drunk. This cannot be taken into account unless I am addicted to drink, i.e. an alcoholic – **Morhall**.

The jury will have to decide whether a depressed person of my age and sex with a big growth would have lost control, then whether an ordinary person of my age and sex with a big growth would have done the same.

Examination pointer

Look for clues like 'goaded by what X said' or 'in reaction to what X did'. You will not be expected to reach a firm conclusion because the most difficult issues are for the jury to decide. State and apply the law and then say, 'D may be charged with murder, but if the jury are satisfied that a reasonable person would have done the same they can convict of manslaughter.'

Summary

Note what characteristics can be attributed to the 'reasonable person' in relation to the second question for the jury (Would a reasonable person do as D did?).

Bedder (1954) – no particular characteristics attributed to the reasonable person
S. 3 Homicide Act (1957) – *'the jury shall take into account everything both done and said according to the effect which, in their opinion, it would have on a reasonable man'*
DPP *v* Camplin (1978) – age and sex attributable
Morhall (1993) – CA said glue-sniffing was not a characteristic to be attributed to the reasonable person, but this was reversed by HL
Luc Thiet Thuan (1996) – mental factors could not be attributed
Smith (2000) – everything but excitability, jealousy, obsession and exceptional pugnacity could be attributed
AG *v* Holley (2005) – jury should not take into account D's mental state

Self-test questions

1 To what charge does the **Homicide Act** apply?

2 What three things need to be proved for **s. 3**?

3 The loss of control has to be sudden and what?

4 State two 'characteristics' which are not attributable to the reasonable man.

5 What did the Privy Council decide in **AG *v* Holley (2005)**?

For further resources and updates please go to the Companion Website accompanying this book at **www.pearsoned.co.uk/russell**

Unit 19

Voluntary manslaughter under Homicide Act s. 2: diminished responsibility

... a state of mind so different from that of ordinary human beings that the reasonable man would term it abnormal.

Lord Parker CJ, **Byrne (1960)**

By the end of this Unit you should be able to:

- Explain the main legal requirements in proving diminished responsibility
- Explain how the law applies in practice by reference to cases
- Identify possible criticisms

What is diminished responsibility?

Diminished responsibility comes under the **Homicide Act 1957 s. 2(1)** which provides:

> *'Where a person kills or is a party to the killing of another, he shall not be convicted of murder if he was suffering from such **abnormality of mind** (whether **arising from a condition of arrested or retarded development of mind or any inherent causes or induced by disease or injury**) as **substantially impaired his mental responsibility** for his acts and omissions in doing or being a party to the killing.'*

This is quite a mouthful! Don't panic – we'll take each part in turn. The main requirements are:

- abnormality
- due to one of the specified causes
- which substantially impairs D's responsibility

Examination pointer

First, note that there is an overlap with provocation, so you may well have to apply both. Look at the example.

Example A man's wife is dying and in terrible pain. Over a period of several months she begs him to end her suffering. He is getting very upset and severely depressed. One night she screams at him, 'For once in your life act like a man and help me die'. He finally

▶

snaps and smothers her. This could be provocation so you would apply the test in **Acott**. There is evidence of loss of control, by things 'said or done', he has lost control and the 'reasonable man' will be someone who had gone through several months of being tormented by such requests and so arguably would act in the same way. What if he had spent a couple of days thinking about it, trying to find the courage? He may fail due to the 'sudden and temporary' rule (**Duffy**). So you can refer to his 'severe depression' and bring in **s. 2** as an alternative.

Abnormality of mind

As this expression indicates, there is an overlap with the general defence of insanity. It covers more than 'defect of reason' though, which is the test for insanity. The leading case on diminished responsibility is **Byrne (1960)** where Lord Parker CJ defined abnormality of mind as '*a state of mind so different from that of ordinary human beings that the reasonable man would term it abnormal*'. In **Byrne** D was described as a sexual psychopath. While suffering from powerful urges he strangled and then mutilated a young woman. These urges did not prevent him knowing what he was doing (he would have therefore failed on insanity) but he found it difficult, if not impossible, to control them. His defence came within **s. 2** and he was acquitted of murder.

Whether D is suffering from an abnormality of mind is a matter for the jury based on the medical evidence. In my example there may not be sufficient abnormality; however, juries are often sympathetic in such cases.

Due to one of the specified causes

The abnormality of mind must be due to one of the specified causes, though there are several so it is quite wide. The **Act** says: '. . . *arising from a condition of arrested or retarded development of mind or any inherent causes or induced by disease or injury*'. Let's take a look at what these could include:

- **Arrested or retarded development** could include a low mental age.
- **Inherent causes** would be something internal such as depression or stress.
- **Disease** would be internal. Examples would include epilepsy or a clot on the brain.
- **Injury** could be external such as concussion from a blow to the head.

In my example, 'severe depression' would come within the 'inherent causes'.

Diminished responsibility and intoxication

Abnormality caused by external factors such as taking drugs or drink would not be enough alone. If D is intoxicated *as well as* suffering from one of the above causes the defence may succeed. This was stated in **Fenton (1975)**, confirmed in **Gittens (1984)** and approved by the HL in **Dietschmann (2003)**. It is thus a well-established rule.

Key case

In **Dietschmann**, D had savagely attacked someone while suffering depression following the death of his girlfriend. He was also drunk. The HL made clear that D had to show that even without the drink he had sufficient 'abnormality of mind' (as in **Fenton** and **Gittens**). However, they added that he did not have to show that he would have killed even if not intoxicated, because the 'abnormality' did not have to be the *only* cause of the killing. This means D only needs to satisfy the jury that, as well as (but not *because of*) being drunk, he had an abnormality which substantially impaired his responsibility. He need not show he would still have killed even if he had been sober. The jury must ask themselves whether D had satisfied them that, *despite the drink*, his mental abnormality substantially impaired his responsibility. *'If he has satisfied you of that, you will find him not guilty of murder but you may find him guilty of manslaughter. If he has not satisfied you of that, the defence of diminished responsibility is not available to him.'*

Abnormality caused by alcoholism (a disease) may be accepted. In **Tandy (1989)** D was an alcoholic who strangled her 11-year-old daughter after learning that she had been sexually abused. She had drunk almost a whole bottle of vodka and was clearly suffering from an abnormality of mind at the time of the killing. The CA upheld the conviction for murder and held that the abnormality had to be caused by the disease of alcoholism rather than by the voluntary taking of alcohol. It could succeed if the first drink was involuntary but on the evidence this was not the case.

Food for thought

These are difficult issues. Not least if you happen to be on the jury! You will have to try to ignore the intoxication and determine whether the other causes were enough to substantially impair responsibility. Not an easy task. The **Dietschmann** case highlights the difficulties. Does it solve any? Would you be able ignore the intoxication in such cases if you were on the jury?

If alcoholism is argued as the cause you will have to decide if the first drink taken was voluntary or involuntary.

Substantially impaired his mental responsibility

The judge will usually direct the jury as to the meaning of 'substantial' in relation to the facts of the case. In **Lloyd (1967)** the court said the impairment need not be total but must be more than trivial or minimal. In **Campbell (1987)** the medical evidence was that D had epilepsy which could make him *'vulnerable to an impulsive tendency'*. The defence failed because 'vulnerable to' indicates that it was not substantial.

Referring again to my example, even if 'abnormality' is found, it may not have 'substantially impaired' the man's mental responsibility. However, on similar facts in **Bailey (2002)** the defence succeeded. In **Bailey**, a 74-year-old man killed his wife, who had motor neurone disease (the same disease that Diane Pretty had) and who was in great pain. The defence of diminished responsibility was successful.

Task

Go to the Law Commission website and look at the 2004 report, number 290. Quotes and discussions from this will enhance an essay.

Other examples

More recently acknowledged disorders such as post-traumatic stress disorder, Gulf War syndrome, paranoid personality disorder, battered woman's syndrome and pre-menstrual stress may now give rise to a plea of diminished responsibility. We looked at **Thornton** in Unit 18. She was suffering from 'battered woman's syndrome' and killed her drunken and abusive husband. At the retrial in 1996 the jury accepted the defence of diminished responsibility. Her life sentence was reduced to the time she had already served. Similarly, in **Ahluwalia**, the retrial resulted in murder being reduced to manslaughter on the grounds of diminished responsibility.

In 2003 a woman who killed her two severely disabled sons succeeded in arguing diminished responsibility. She had cared for them for 23 years without a break and had contacted social services several times for help. In March 2005 a man who had smothered his severely disabled son also used this defence.

In **Martin (2001)** a Norfolk farmer was convicted of murder after killing an intruder. His plea of self-defence failed as there was evidence that the intruder was trying to get away. He later succeeded in arguing diminished responsibility due to paranoid personality disorder.

Burden of proof

Unlike provocation, where the prosecution has to show that D was not provoked, under **s. 2(3)**, it is D who must prove diminished responsibility. The standard of proof is the balance of probabilities, i.e. the civil standard. Remember there will need to be medical evidence to support the claim that D was suffering from diminished responsibility.

Food for thought

Some difficulties arise where a jury decides on the basis of what they feel is justified rather than by using the legal tests. The success of the defence is sometimes dependent on whether the killing was morally wrong.

Examples can be seen in cases of 'mercy killings'. A jury may accept a plea of diminished responsibility even where there is little evidence for it, as in **Bailey (2002)**. One reason is sympathy for the accused. The other, connected, reason is the mandatory life sentence. If the defence fails, the sentence will be life for murder. Thus, accepting the defence means that a discretionary sentence can be given, taking into account the circumstances. While this may 'do justice' in a particular case, it is arguably stretching the law to fit the facts.

It also works both ways. It failed in **Sutcliffe (1981)**. This was the 'Yorkshire ripper' case where D had committed a series of brutal murders. The defence of diminished responsibility was rejected by the jury (on the direction of the judge) despite strong medical evidence to the contrary and the fact that both the defence and prosecution accepted it. This indicates that it can succeed or fail for policy reasons, rather than legal ones.

An argument for abolishing the mandatory life sentence for murder could follow a discussion of this if appropriate. It would avoid the uncertainty of relying on the jury's sympathy or revulsion.

Examination pointer

Remember that there is an overlap between provocation and diminished responsibility. Look back at cases like **Thornton**. Long-term abuse may be a 'characteristic' or an 'inherent cause'. You may well have to discuss both defences. Look carefully at the given facts and watch for words like 'abuse' or 'depression'.

In an essay question you may be asked whether the law is satisfactory. You should form your own opinion but could include some of the food for thought. At the end of the Study Block there is a summary of the problems with the **Homicide Act** defences.

Summary

Abnormality of mind	A state of mind so different from that of ordinary human beings that the reasonable man would term it abnormal – **Byrne (1960)**
Due to one of the specified causes	
Substantially impaired his mental responsibility	Impairment need not be total but must be more than trivial or minimal – **Lloyd (1967)**
If D is intoxicated *as well as* suffering from one of the above causes the defence may still succeed	**Dietschmann (2003)**

Self-test questions

1 Have you achieved the aims set out at the beginning of the Unit?

2 What type of evidence will be required for an **s. 2** defence?

3 Who has the burden of proving the defence?

4 Give a possible cause of abnormality arising from:
   (i)   **Arrested or retarded development**
   (ii) **Inherent causes**
   (iii) **Disease**
   (iv) **Injury**

There is a summary critique of all the Homicide Act defences at the end of this Study Block.

Voluntary manslaughter under Homicide Act s. 4: suicide pact

We have not been requested to consider and report on s. 4 of the 1957 Act (killing by survivor of a suicide pact) ... Such cases are rarely encountered.

Law Commission Report No. 290: Partial Defences to Murder

By the end of this Unit you should be able to:

- Explain the main legal requirements in proving the s. 4 defence
- Produce an evaluation of the Homicide Act defence
- Prepare an exam question

As is indicated by the opening quote, this is by far the least common of the defences. It arises where two or more people act together in an agreement to kill each other.

The **Homicide Act 1957 s. 4(1)** provides:

'It shall be manslaughter, and shall not be murder, for a person acting in pursuance of a suicide pact between him and another to kill the other or be a party to the other ... being killed by a third person.'

Section 4(2) adds:

'Where it is shown that a person charged with the murder of another killed the other or was a party to his ... being killed, it shall be for the defence to prove that the person charged was acting in pursuance of a suicide pact between him and the other.'

Section 4(3) defines suicide pact:

'For the purposes of this section 'suicide pact' means a common agreement between two or more persons having for its object the death of all of them ...'

As with diminished responsibility, *D* must prove the defence on the *balance of probabilities*, i.e. the civil standard of proof.

For the defence to apply there must be a reciprocal arrangement. Two or more people agree to kill each other.

Example   Mickey and Minnie are heavily in debt and very depressed. They buy two guns and say to each other, 'I'll shoot you and you shoot me. One, two, three – GO!' They both fire but Mickey's gun jams. This means Minnie survives. She could be charged with Mickey's murder, but can use **s. 4** to reduce it to manslaughter.

Note that the Diane Pretty case mentioned in Unit 14 was not a case that would come under this section. In Ms Pretty's case she wanted her husband to help her to kill herself because she was too weak to do it. There was no reciprocal arrangement for her to kill him. He could have been charged with aiding and abetting a suicide, which is an offence under **s. 2** of the **Suicide Act 1961**.

Food for thought

Until the **Suicide Act 1961** suicide was itself an offence. It seemed rather odd that you could kill yourself and then be charged with a crime! It mostly arose when you didn't succeed because then you remained within reach of the law. Also, someone guilty of 'self-murder' lost all their property. This meant that the people who actually suffered were often the family of the deceased, so arguably the law is better now. However, there is a fine line between the offences under the two Acts. In my example, if Minnie and Mickey had agreed to shoot themselves instead of each other, then Minnie would be charged under the **Suicide Act**. Encouraging another person to commit suicide would be an offence under **s. 2**. So a lot depends on how the agreement is carried out. Prepare poison together and give it to each other, and the survivor is charged under **s. 4** of the **Homicide Act**. Prepare poison together and drink your own, and the survivor is charged under **s. 2** of the **Suicide Act**.

That's it on suicide pacts. In reality there are very few charges brought under **s. 4**, so no self-test questions for you! Make sure you look at the summary though – the **Homicide Act** is another popular area for essay questions.

Study Block 6 Summary
VOLUNTARY MANSLAUGHTER

s. 3 provocation

Is there evidence of provocation? Acott	Was something done or said that could cause a reaction? If so there are two questions:
Was D provoked to lose control? Thornton	Was there a sudden reaction to what was done or said? The jury should take into account any particular characteristics which could affect the gravity of the provocation to D
Would a reasonable person have done as D did? Holley	The jury should not take mental characteristics, which might have made losing control more likely, into account

s. 2 diminished responsibility

Abnormality of mind **Byrne**	A state of mind so different from that of ordinary human beings that the reasonable man would term it abnormal
Due to one of the specified causes	
Substantially impaired his mental responsibility **Lloyd**	Impairment need not be total but must be more than trivial or minimal

Task

From which cases did the following principles come?

1 That the crying of a baby could be evidence of provocation.

2 That the loss of self-control must be sudden and temporary.

3 That an 'abnormality of mind' for diminished responsibility is one that reasonable people would term abnormal.

4 An abnormality caused by alcoholism may be accepted as diminished responsibility.

5 Impairment of responsibility need not be total but must be more than trivial.

Key criticisms

Provocation

- The requirement for a 'sudden and temporary' loss of control arguably discriminates against women. Men can react violently to a woman's abuse but not the other way round, owing to lack of physical strength.
- **Morhall** shows a disagreement between the CA and the HL. Many people, including those on a jury, may feel that a reasonable man wouldn't sniff glue!
- The **Law Commission** argues that **Smith** has not clarified the law on provocation. Does the test for what characteristics the jury should take into account need to be clearly set down?
- Does the decision in **AG for Jersey *v* Holley (2005)** improve matters? The Privy Council felt that **Smith** was wrong and D's act should be judged by one standard, not a standard that varied from D to D.

Diminished responsibility

- Diminished responsibility is not a satisfactory alternative for abused women as it indicates they are mentally unbalanced.
- Where there is evidence of intoxication as well as another cause of 'abnormality' the jury has to perform an almost impossible task of separating the one from the other – **Dietschmann**.
- 'Mental responsibility' and 'abnormality of mind' are difficult concepts for the jury to understand and medical evidence is often complex and contradictory.
- Diminished responsibility is sometimes dependent on whether the killing was morally wrong – **Bailey/Sutcliffe**.

Suicide pact

- Arguably there is too fine a line between **s. 4** of the **Homicide Act** and **s. 2** of the **Suicide Act**.
- Should the law be amended to take into account cases like Ms Pretty's?

General

- Success may depend on which defence is raised in the first place. Provocation failed in the case of **Cocker (1989)** but diminished responsibility succeeded in **Bailey (2002)** in similar circumstances.
- There is an overlap between diminished responsibility and provocation where the killing has been due to a mental state such as depression or long-term abuse (**Ahluwalia** and **Thornton**).

173

- Should the mandatory life sentence be abolished? If it was then it could be argued that these defences would not be necessary. On the other hand, abolishing them and leaving the issue as one of sentencing would remove the role of the jury. It is arguably better for a jury to decide, for example, how a 'reasonable man' would act.

- The difficulties of these defences for the jury could lead to inconsistency. Juries may differ in their decisions.

- Murder is still a common law offence. Should there be a statutory definition?

- If so, should it contain more than one degree of murder as in the USA? This could again remove the need for the special defences.

In 2004, the Law Commission published a report, *'Partial defences to Murder'* (No. 290). In May 2005 the DPP recommended the introduction of different degrees of homicide and the Law Commission published a consultation paper, *'A new Homicide Act for England and Wales?'* (No. 177), in December 2005. The consultation paper incorporates suggestions for the reform of murder, as well as the partial defences (voluntary manslaughter).

Task

Pick out a few of the criticisms which make sense to you. Add a few sentences to expand on each of the points you choose. Where possible refer to cases to support your comments. You'll soon find you have a good base for an exam question.

Examination practice

An answer to this question could cover any law relating to murder, including the **Homicide Act** defences. This means you can discuss the problems seen in Study Block 4 as well as, or instead of, the problems with voluntary manslaughter.

June 2004

Discuss the suggestion that the current law of murder is satisfactory and does not require any modification. *(25 marks)*

Module 6 connections

Morals	Diminished responsibility may succeed or fail depending on whether the killing was morally wrong	**Bailey/Sutcliffe**
	Jealousy and obsession are not taken into account in provocation as these characteristics are seen as morally blameworthy	**Smith**
Justice	The law on provocation discriminates against women	Battered women cases such as **Thornton**
	The defences allow for a discretionary sentence so the judge can achieve justice in the particular circumstances	
Conflicting interests	Does allowing the defence of diminished responsibility in killing a disabled child or the terminally ill give a green light to kill? Are the victim's interests being considered?	
Fault	The defences recognise that there is a lower level of fault in some killings	
Creativity	Judges became quite creative in their interpretation of s. 3 and accepted most characteristics could be attributed to the reasonable man	This may have slowed following **Holley**

For further resources and updates please go to the Companion Website accompanying this book at www.pearsoned.co.uk/russell

Study Block 7
INVOLUNTARY MANSLAUGHTER

Unit 21 Constructive or unlawful act manslaughter

Unit 22 Gross negligence manslaughter

If intent cannot be proved then there is no *mens rea* for murder. In this case manslaughter will be the appropriate charge. There are two types, constructive manslaughter (also called unlawful act manslaughter) and gross negligence manslaughter. We will also look at a third possibility, reckless manslaughter.

Example Jane throws a brick at a passing car. The driver swerves to avoid it and hits a lamppost, killing herself. This would be constructive manslaughter. Throwing a brick at the car is unlawful and has caused the driver's death.

Jenny is driving her motorboat at great speed and hits another boat, killing the occupants. This would be gross negligence manslaughter, and at one time would have been reckless manslaughter. Jenny has been criminally negligent in not taking more care, even though she has not acted unlawfully.

The problems of both types of manslaughter are considered at the end of this Study Block, along with reforms. This is because an essay question would normally be on both. Areas of law where there are problems and/or where there are current proposals for reform are popular examination topics so look carefully at these issues.

Constructive or unlawful act manslaughter

. . . such as all sober and reasonable people would inevitably recognise must subject the other person to, at least, the risk of some harm resulting therefrom, albeit not serious harm.

The definition of *dangerous* from **Church (1967)**

By the end of this Unit you should be able to:

- Explain the three legal requirements in proving constructive manslaughter
- Explain how the law applies in practice by reference to cases
- Identify possible criticisms

This type of manslaughter is 'constructed' from an act which is both unlawful and dangerous and which causes death. You can refer to it as either constructive manslaughter or unlawful act manslaughter.

Actus reus

There are three separate issues to address in the *actus reus*:

- an unlawful act;
- which is dangerous;
- which causes death.

Unlawful act

An act is only unlawful for the purposes of constructive manslaughter if it is a crime. Criminal damage is a common example, as in **Hancock and Shankland**. Assault is another.

In **Lamb (1967)** D pointed a loaded gun at V, his friend, as a joke. Because they did not understand how a revolver works, they thought that there was no danger in pulling the trigger. D did so and V died. The court said the unlawful act must be a crime and so he was not guilty.

It must be an act, not an omission. This was confirmed in **Khan (1998)**, discussed below.

Task

Look up these cases and identify the unlawful act. Then make a note of how causation in fact and in law is proved and how these apply.

Hancock and Shankland (1986)
Pagett (1983)
Nedrick (1986)

Which is dangerous

The unlawful act must also be dangerous. This is an objective test. It means that a reasonable person would realise that it was likely to cause harm, however slight. This was stated to be the case in **Church (1967)**.

Key case

In **Church**, D had knocked a woman unconscious and then, wrongly believing her to be dead, threw her in the river to dispose of the 'body'. The CA gave the definition seen in the opening quote and held that it did not matter that D did not see any risk of harm. In this case D did not see any such risk as he thought she was dead! So, the principle is that if reasonable people would see the risk of harm, this will be enough. D was guilty of manslaughter; reasonable people would see that throwing someone into a river risks harm.

In **Dawson (1985)**, during an attempted robbery of a garage, the Ds had frightened the victim with an imitation pistol. He suffered from a heart condition and subsequently died. They were found not guilty of manslaughter because a reasonable person would not have been aware of the heart condition, and so would not see the act as dangerous. The court recognised that fear could be foreseen, but as physical harm could not be, the act was not dangerous in the true sense.

Food for thought

Both **Church** and **Dawson** show that for an act to be deemed dangerous there must be a risk of physical harm. It appears that it does not include fear or psychiatric harm. In many other areas of law physical harm has been extended to include psychiatric. It can be argued that 'dangerous' should include an act which could cause psychiatric harm. **Dawson** can be criticised on the basis that a robbery with imitation firearms could be construed as dangerous. The reaction of a victim to such a robbery could be unpredictable. Someone might decide to 'have a go' and this would certainly be dangerous, whether the guns were real or not. **Dawson** was *distinguished* in the next case.

In **Watson (1989)** burglars entered a house and saw an elderly man, but continued with their act of burglary. They were charged with manslaughter when he died of a heart attack. The man's frailty was obvious and the Ds saw this. Their knowledge could be attributed to the reasonable man who could therefore see the danger of the act, thus **Dawson** could be distinguished. (Note that on the facts their conviction was quashed on the causation issue, because there was not enough evidence that the shock of seeing burglars caused death.)

Examination pointer

Take care when applying the rules in a problem scenario. Students often misunderstand the point of **Dawson** and confuse it with the thin skull rule. This rule may well be relevant but it will only apply once the act is found to be unlawful and dangerous. It is a causation issue. In **Dawson** the question was whether the act was dangerous. The answer was 'no' because a reasonable person would not know of the heart condition. If the act had been dangerous then D would 'take the victim as he finds him'. Thus D would be liable for the death even though a person without a heart condition would not have died.

Example Consider the following imaginary cases:

1 You are angry and wave your fist at Cathy. She is of a very nervous disposition and dies of fright.

2 You are angry and throw a brick at Kate, which misses. She is of a very nervous disposition and dies of fright.

In the first case your action may be unlawful, but would it be seen as dangerous? If not, and much may depend on whether you know she is of a nervous disposition, you are not guilty of Cathy's manslaughter. It ends there.

In the second it is both unlawful and dangerous. The next question is whether you caused Kate's death. You cannot argue that most people would not have died, and that Kate's nervous disposition caused her death. You must 'take your victim as you find her'. You are guilty of manslaughter.

Food for thought

Whether the unlawful act is dangerous is an objective test, based on what a reasonable person would see as dangerous. It is not relevant that D didn't see it as dangerous. For such a serious offence it can be argued that a subjective test should be used.

Which causes death

As the unlawful act must be the cause of death, the cases on causation are relevant to both 'unlawful act' and 'causes death'. The usual rules apply, i.e. D must make a significant contribution and the chain of causation must not be broken. Let's look at the cases in your task: the first two are pretty clear on causation but **Pagett** is more indirect.

Example	**Hancock and Shankland** – throwing concrete blocks onto a taxi would be criminal damage, thus unlawful. Throwing concrete blocks off a bridge is dangerous. The damage caused the driver's death.
	Nedrick – setting fire to something belonging to someone else is a type of criminal damage (arson) and so again unlawful. It is also clearly dangerous and the fire caused death.
	Pagett – shooting at the police is both unlawful and dangerous. D made a significant contribution to the girl's death and the police didn't break the chain of causation by firing back because it was a natural reaction (foreseeable). The shooting caused death.

Causation is not always easy to prove and problems have arisen in several cases. Compare the following two decisions.

1 In **Cato (1976)** D supplied, and assisted V to take, heroin which resulted in death. It was held that he had unlawfully administered a drug which caused death and so was guilty of manslaughter.

2 In **Dalby (1982)** the CA quashed the conviction because although D had supplied drugs (an unlawful act) this had not caused death. V had injected himself and this broke the chain of causation.

In **Cato** D actually injected V so there was no break in the chain of causation. In **Dalby**, V's own act broke the chain. In **Kennedy (1999)** the unlawful act itself is hard to discover. Here, D mixed the drug and handed the syringe to V and this sufficed even though, as in **Dalby**, V injected himself.

Key case

Another case involving drugs is **Khan and Khan (1998)**. It is a case worth knowing because constructive manslaughter, omissions and gross negligence manslaughter were all discussed. The Ds had supplied drugs to a young prostitute. She went into a coma but they left her and when they returned the next day she had died. This would be a failure to act, an *omission*. The CA held that constructive manslaughter required an act. An omission is not enough. D can only be liable for manslaughter by omission if there is a pre-existing duty, as in **Stone and Dobinson**. This would be gross negligence manslaughter, discussed in the next Unit. The court held there was no such duty between a drug dealer and a client.

In **Dias (2002)** V injected himself, as in **Dalby**. The CA quashed D's conviction on the issue of causation and criticised the decision in **Kennedy**. However, they made it clear that a person who actively participated in the injection process may be convicted of manslaughter. There were also suggestions that in certain circumstances there could be a duty and thus a conviction for gross negligence manslaughter. In **Rogers (2003)** V again injected himself, but here D had 'actively participated' by applying a tourniquet to V's arm and the conviction for manslaughter was upheld. The conflicting case law led to the CCRC referring **Kennedy** back to the CA on the issue of causation.

Key case

In **Kennedy (2005)** the CA said causing your own death was not unlawful, so nor was encouraging another to. However, *participating* in the administration of a 'poison' or 'noxious thing' is a crime under **s. 23 OAPA**, and so forms the basis for a manslaughter charge.

Food for thought

It is not an offence to inject yourself, so an unlawful act is hard to find in some of these cases. Also, conflict at this level leaves the law uncertain and the 'unlawful' issue is confused with the 'causation' issue. These problems may have been solved by the CA in **Kennedy (2005)**. By participating in the taking of the drugs D commits an unlawful act. This arguably makes a 'significant contribution' to the death, so even if V actually performs the injection it won't break the chain, satisfying the causation test as well. There may still be a problem in finding evidence of participation. If so, **Dias** may pave the way for the courts to distinguish **Khan** and find a duty in such circumstances. This would mean a charge of gross negligence manslaughter could be pursued.

Before going on to *mens rea*, let's recap with an imaginary scenario.

Example Vic decides to kill himself and jumps off a tall building, checking before he does so that no one is underneath. Dave is a resident of the building who is having a violent row with his wife. He fires a gun at her and misses, hitting Vic as he passes the window. Vic is thrown off course by the blow and lands on a pedestrian, Sue, killing her. Vic survives. Can anyone be charged with manslaughter?

Look at the three requirements. Vic's act is *dangerous* and *caused her death*, but is not *unlawful*. Vic is unlikely to be found guilty of manslaughter. Dave's act is both *dangerous* and *unlawful*. However did it *cause death*? Unlikely; Vic's jumping would be the cause. Dave won't be found guilty of manslaughter either.

Mens rea

There is no special *mens rea* for this type of manslaughter. It is the *mens rea* for the unlawful act. There is therefore no need to prove *mens rea* as regards the death, only the unlawful act. Let's take one of the earlier examples a step further.

Example Going back to **Nedrick**, the unlawful act was arson, i.e. criminal damage. The *mens rea* for this is intent or recklessness. For a manslaughter charge, there is no need for D to intend, or to recognise a risk of, death, only to intend or see a risk of the damage. Here arson was clearly intended so *mens rea* is easy to prove.

The only other point on *mens rea* is to remember that it must coincide with the *actus reus*. As we saw, this is widely interpreted. Thus in both **Thabo Meli** and in **Church**, the Ds were guilty of unlawful and dangerous act manslaughter on the basis of a 'series of acts'.

Food for thought

The Law Commission has criticised the fact that the *mens rea* for this type of manslaughter may be for some quite different offence. Manslaughter is a very serious offence but the *mens rea* may be for a minor crime. Do you think it should have a *mens rea* of its own? At one time subjective reckless manslaughter existed, but it has been abolished and replaced by gross negligence manslaughter. This is discussed in the next Unit.

Task

Refer to the last task you did in the Unit on murder, where you followed my examination pointer as a guide to applying the law. Now go on to apply the rules you have just learnt on manslaughter. Use the summary, but be sure to add cases.

Summary

The three parts of the *actus reus* are:

An unlawful act	→	Which is dangerous	→	Which causes death

The *mens rea* is:

Whatever *mens rea* is required for the unlawful act

Self-test questions

1 What is the main difference between murder and manslaughter?

2 What were the facts and principle in **Church**?

3 What is the difference between **Cato** and **Dalby**?

4 When can an omission amount to manslaughter?

5 What did the CA decide in **Kennedy (2005)**?

For further resources and updates please go to the Companion Website accompanying this book at **www.pearsoned.co.uk/russell**

Gross negligence manslaughter

A verdict of manslaughter may, depending on the circumstances, be appropriate both by reason of an unlawful and dangerous act, and by reason of gross negligence.

Rose LJ, **Willoughby (2004)**

> **By the end of this Unit you should be able to:**
> - Explain the legal requirements in proving gross negligence manslaughter
> - Explain how the law applies in practice by reference to cases
> - Use cases to identify the many problems
> - Explain the proposals for reform

The second type of involuntary manslaughter is *gross negligence manslaughter*. This occurs when someone owes a duty to another person, but is 'grossly negligent', with the result that the person dies.

Example Kylie is looking after a 2-month-old baby for the evening. She gets very drunk and falls over while carrying the baby. Kylie passes out and the baby is smothered. If the baby dies then Kylie may be guilty of gross negligence manslaughter. She will owe a duty to the baby in her care, and getting so drunk while looking after such a young child is likely to be sufficiently negligent.

The rules on gross negligence manslaughter were restated and clarified by the HL in **Adomako (1994).**

Key case

In **Adomako** an anaesthetist had failed to monitor a patient during an operation. The patient later died as a result. He was accused of manslaughter.

The CA held that in order to prove gross negligence manslaughter there must be the usual *actus reus* of homicide plus:

- A risk of death
- A duty of care
- Breach of that duty
- Gross negligence as regards that breach, which must be sufficient to justify criminal liability

The CA also gave examples of the type of conduct which might amount to such negligence. When the case went to the HL, they confirmed the test but rejected the idea of setting out particular examples. Lord Mackay said that the jury would have to decide whether, *'involving as it must have done a risk of death,'* D's conduct fell below the standard expected to the extent *'that it should be judged criminal'*. On the facts this was the case here, and the conviction was upheld.

It seems that this replaces reckless manslaughter, which was said by Lord Mackay in **Adomako** no longer to apply. However, he also said, *'I consider it perfectly appropriate that the word reckless be used in cases of involuntary manslaughter'*. This left the matter somewhat uncertain. Before looking at the rules on gross negligence manslaughter we'll have a brief look at this issue.

Reckless manslaughter – does it exist?

In several cases in the 1980s an objective recklessness test was used for manslaughter. An example is **Seymour (1983)**, where D was driving recklessly and killed his girlfriend by crushing her between his lorry and a car. The HL said that the question was whether there was an 'obvious and serious' risk of injuring someone. This is **Caldwell** recklessness.

Many of the cases on reckless manslaughter had involved driving incidents and as there is now a statutory offence of causing death by dangerous driving, then arguably manslaughter is not needed. However, there were some cases outside the 'motor manslaughter' category which are not covered by any statute. In spite of this, the HL seemed to reject reckless manslaughter in **Adomako**. Lord Mackay LC stated that **Caldwell** reckless manslaughter no longer existed. As this was a unanimous HL decision it could be taken as a statement of the current law. The judgment was, however, somewhat complex and matters were further complicated by his reference to the word 'reckless'. **Khan and Khan** (see p. 181) seemed to clarify the issue. At their trial for manslaughter, the judge had referred to 'manslaughter by omission' and found them guilty. The CA allowed the appeal and stated that there were only two types of involuntary manslaughter, unlawful act manslaughter and gross negligence manslaughter. An omission is enough for the latter, but only if there is a pre-existing duty, as in **Stone and Dobinson**. No such duty was found. The point made by the CA about there only being two types of manslaughter confirmed **Adomako**, i.e. that reckless manslaughter no longer existed. Or did it? Doubt was again cast on this in **Lidar (2000)**.

In **Lidar** a group of men had a fight in the car park of a pub. When two of them got in a car and started to drive off, a third leant in the window of the car and the fight continued. They drove off with him half in the window and at some point he fell off and suffered serious injuries from which he died. The driver was convicted of manslaughter. On appeal the CA held that following **Adomako**, the jury could properly be directed in terms of recklessness. They seem to have relied on Lord Mackay's reference to it being 'perfectly appropriate' to use the word reckless.

Food for thought

For such a serious crime it is less than satisfactory that there is still confusion about whether reckless manslaughter exists, and if it does, whether the test is subjective or objective. Since **Gemmell and Richards** overruled **Caldwell** on recklessness as the *mens rea* for criminal damage it would appear that the HL prefers the subjective test. Arguably it is time the matter was addressed, either by the HL or by Parliament.

Task

Reckless manslaughter was rejected in **Adomako**, leaving only constructive/unlawful act and gross negligence manslaughter. Do you think reckless manslaughter should exist and, if so, should it be a third category or replace gross negligence manslaughter? Write a few sentences on this and keep it for essay practice.

The rules

In **Misra (2004)** it was argued that the uncertainty in the law of gross negligence manslaughter meant that it infringed the **European Convention on Human Rights**. The CA rejected this argument and confirmed the **Adomako** requirements. These were that death had occurred as a result of a **breach of a duty owed by D** to the deceased, that the victim was exposed to a **risk of death**, and that the conduct amounted to **gross negligence**. As regards the second and third points, they said that it had been clearly established that a risk of death was needed; a risk of bodily injury or injury to health was not enough. The question was then for the jury to decide whether D's conduct was grossly negligent and therefore criminal. This was a question of fact, not law. The CA felt that the offence had been sufficiently clearly set out in **Adomako** so there was no uncertainty. Let's have a quick look at the **Adomako** requirements again:

- risk of death
- duty owed by D
- breach of that duty
- gross negligence

Risk of death

In **Misra (2004)** the CA confirmed that a risk of death was needed, not just a risk of harm. This will still be quite wide. Activities which are dangerous in themselves, such as taking people mountaineering or white-water rafting, would be included. Ordinary activities which have the potential to be dangerous could also involve a risk of death. This would cover driving a train or ferry. Such activities are not dangerous in themselves, but if a train or ferry is driven negligently or is poorly maintained, there is a risk of death, so the driver or company may be liable.

Duty and breach of duty

This is a matter for the jury. The judge will direct the jury as to whether the facts were capable of giving rise to a duty. In **Khan** the CA refused to find that a duty was owed by a drug dealer to a client. However, they did suggest that such a duty *could* arise. If the facts were capable of giving rise to a duty then the judge should give the jury *'an appropriate direction which would enable them to answer the question whether on the facts as found by them there was such a duty'*.

Task

Look back at Unit 14 and reread the following manslaughter cases. What type of duty was seen? How was it breached?

Stone and Dobinson (1977)
Pittwood (1902)

It was not made fully clear in **Adomako** whether the ordinary civil test for duty is enough. Later cases suggest that it is. In **Wacker (2003)** the Ds were transporting about 60 illegal immigrants in a lorry. For some time during the journey there was no ventilation. Most of the immigrants died. At their trial for gross negligence manslaughter the judge referred to **Adomako** and the 'ordinary principles of the law of negligence'. The CA confirmed that they had assumed a duty of care for the victims and rejected their appeal against conviction.

Breach of duty means D has not reached the standard expected of a reasonable person; however, only if D is *grossly* negligent will there be criminal liability.

In **Wood and Hodgson (2003)** a 10-year-old girl was visiting the Ds. She found some ecstasy tablets hidden in a cigarette packet and took some. She later died in hospital. They were charged with gross negligence manslaughter. There was evidence that the Ds had hidden the tablets and had attempted to treat her, although they did not call an ambulance for some time. It was found that they owed her a duty, but as they had not shown a sufficiently high level of negligence they were not guilty of *gross negligence* manslaughter.

In **Willoughby (2004)** D was the owner of a disused public house in Canterbury. He had recruited a local taxi driver to help him set fire to the building for financial purposes. The taxi driver was killed when the building collapsed and D was convicted of gross negligence manslaughter. On appeal, the CA said that the judge should have directed the jury on unlawful act manslaughter rather than gross negligence manslaughter. They made it clear that either may be appropriate, depending on the circumstances. On the facts the jury had accepted that D had committed arson. There was therefore an unlawful act, which caused death, so the manslaughter conviction could not be considered unsafe.

Food for thought

Although on the facts the conviction in **Willoughby** was upheld, it does highlight the difficulties. The overlap is not always clear. If the judge has trouble identifying whether it is gross negligence or unlawful act manslaughter then arguably the law is still too uncertain, as argued in **Misra**. It is also unclear whether the civil test for duty is enough. It would *seem* so, but if it is, then another criticism is that it should not be. The functions of the criminal and civil law are very different.

You could also consider how far the law should impose a duty on a drug dealer to his client. Although the CA declined to find there was a duty in **Khan**, there could arguably have been a common law duty, as in **Stone and Dobinson**. The decision may be one of policy rather than law. Taking on responsibility for an invalid is sufficient; responsibility for a prostitute to whom D had supplied drugs is not. This is another area that needs clarification.

The conduct amounted to gross negligence

This question is also one for the jury to decide. According to **Adomako**, they must look at the circumstances and decide whether D's conduct was sufficiently grossly negligent to be deemed criminal. This was also confirmed in **Misra (2004)**.

Food for thought

In **Adomako** the CA had set out a list of what type of conduct might be deemed sufficiently negligent. The HL rejected this on the basis that it could confuse juries who might think that only those situations would suffice. They thought it better to leave it to the jury to decide on the facts whether the conduct was sufficiently bad to be deemed criminal. It is therefore not at all clear what exactly *does* amount to criminal negligence. Do you think you would be able to decide what was sufficiently negligent if you were on the jury?

Examination pointer

For a problem question look for clues in the scenario – you may need to discuss both types of manslaughter. The CA in **Adomako** indicated that it could also be gross negligence manslaughter where, for example, an electrician caused a death by faulty wiring. This was obiter dicta because it was not relevant on the facts of the case. It could be referred to if the given scenario involved such circumstances, or something similar. Although not binding, obiter dicta can be used as persuasive precedent.

As we saw in **Willoughby**, the two types of manslaughter overlap. If you think it is constructive manslaughter, discuss this first, but if, for example, there is doubt as to whether there is an act or omission, or whether the act is unlawful, go on to gross negligence manslaughter as an alternative. If, as in **Willoughby**, there is some doubt as to whether a duty is owed, you could start with gross negligence manslaughter and go on to constructive manslaughter as an alternative.

So, as a quick recap, the **Adomako** requirements as confirmed in **Misra** are:

- a risk of death
- a duty owed by D and breach of that duty
- gross negligence

Task

Refer to the tasks you did in the Unit on murder and followed up on in manslaughter, where you used my examination pointers as a guide to applying the law. Make up a new scenario and apply the pointers as before, then add these new rules. Keep the whole thing as a guide for problem questions on homicide.

Corporate killing and reforms

Where death is due to the negligence of a company, rather than a specific individual, the prosecution need to find a 'controlling mind' on which to pin a duty. There are many high-profile cases which illustrate the problem with this. The enquiries following the *Herald of Free Enterprise* ferry disaster and the King's Cross fire, both in 1987, showed a high level of negligence within the companies involved. Attempts at prosecution, however, were unsuccessful because it was impossible to find a senior individual on whom to place the duty. Similarly, the Hatfield rail crash in October 2000 caused four deaths and over 100 injuries. At the trial of Balfour Beatty in October 2005 charges of manslaughter were dismissed, although the company was fined for its poor safety procedures. Cases such as this have produced a demand for changes in the law.

It is an area which has long been in need of clarification and reform. The Law Commission published a consultation paper on manslaughter in 1994, followed by a report in 1996: *Legislating the Criminal Code: Involuntary Manslaughter* (Report 237). They looked at corporate manslaughter, motor manslaughter and involuntary manslaughter in general. They suggest that involuntary manslaughter should be abolished and replaced with three new offences:

- Corporate killing (similar to killing by gross carelessness but death is due to management failure);
- Reckless (subjective) killing (D sees a risk of death or serious injury);
- Killing by gross carelessness (the risk of death or serious injury was obvious and the conduct fell far below what was expected).

This would simplify and clarify the law. Having such a serious crime relying on the common law for its development is questionable. The courts themselves have indicated it is the role of Parliament to create the law on such a major issue. The offence of killing by gross carelessness would solve the **Khan**-type problem, as there would be no need to prove a duty.

The government accepted the Law Commission Report, and the proposals (and more) became the **Corporate Homicide Bill** in 2000. However, the Bill suffered many delays. Following the Queen's Speech in 2004, the **Corporate**

Manslaughter Bill was finally published in Spring 2005. This deals specifically with organisational and management failure to take care of employees or the public, rather than the wider issues covered by the earlier Bill. It would make employers and suppliers of goods and services liable for death caused by management failure, where the conduct falls below *'what can reasonably be expected in the circumstances'*.

Watch out for the next stage on the long road to reform.

Examination pointer

The courts have indicated that the whole concept of gross negligence manslaughter is due for reform by Parliament. The public have long called for change. The Law Commission proposals are no longer new. All these problems and calls for reform make this area a popular essay question.

Food for thought

One argument on both types of involuntary manslaughter is that they cover such a wide range. The level of fault involved can vary enormously from something just short of intent to the virtually accidental.

Another point that can be made is that in 'corporate manslaughter' cases the bigger the company, the harder it is to find a 'controlling mind'. Result? A small family business may be successfully prosecuted, where a larger one may escape liability.

Finally, we saw that change can be proposed and accepted but still take years to become law.

Summary

Risk of death – not just harm – Misra

Duty owed by D – ordinary principles of the law of negligence – Wacker

Breach of that duty – D has not reached the standard expected of a reasonable person

Gross negligence – sufficiently negligent to be deemed criminal – Wood and Hodgson/Adomako/Misra

Self-test questions

1 What are the elements required to prove gross negligence manslaughter?

2 Can you commit either type of manslaughter by omission?

3 What was the problem in **Lidar** and whose earlier speech had caused this?

4 Do you think **Khan** could have been decided differently?

Study Block 7 Summary
INVOLUNTARY MANSLAUGHTER

Involuntary manslaughter covers two separate offences.

Constructive or unlawful act manslaughter requires:

Actus reus	
An unlawful act	Must be a crime – **Lamb (1967)** Not an omission – **Khan (1998)**
Which is dangerous	An objective test – **Church (1967)**
Which causes death	Usual rules on causation apply and if D 'actively participates' in the act which caused death the chain of causation will not be broken by V – **Kennedy (2005)**
Mens rea	The *mens rea* for the unlawful act

Gross negligence manslaughter requires:

Risk of death	Not just a risk of harm – **Misra (2004)**
Duty owed by D	Ordinary principles of the law of negligence *probably* apply – **Adomako (1994)/Wacker (2003)**
Breach of that duty	D has not reached the standard expected of a reasonable person – **Wood and Hodgson (2003)**
Gross negligence	Sufficiently negligent to be deemed criminal – **Wood and Hodgson (2003)/Misra (2004)**

Key criticisms

- Involuntary manslaughter covers a wide range of behaviour.
- It is hard to find an unlawful act and/or causation in some of the decisions on unlawful act manslaughter.
- The *mens rea* for unlawful act manslaughter may be for a quite different offence.
- Whether the unlawful act is dangerous is an objective test, it can be argued that a subjective test should be used for such a serious offence.
- Identifying whether it is gross negligence or unlawful act manslaughter can be difficult, even for a judge – **Willoughby (2004)**.
- It is not fully clear what *gross negligence* amounts to.
- In 'corporate manslaughter' cases it is hard to find a 'controlling mind'.

Reforms

The Law Commission, in *Legislating the Criminal Code: Involuntary Manslaughter* (Report 237), suggests that involuntary manslaughter should be abolished and replaced with three new offences:

- corporate killing
- reckless (subjective) killing
- killing by gross carelessness

The **Corporate Manslaughter Bill** was published in spring 2005. This would make employers and suppliers of goods and services liable for death caused by management failure, where the conduct falls below *'what can reasonably be expected in the circumstances'*.

Task

Revise all the Units on homicide and prepare a commentary on how satisfactory the law is in each area. Use the 'Food for thought' boxes, as well as anything you wrote down for previous tasks. Make sure you include cases, as well as your own thoughts and ideas. Add a little on any proposed reforms and in particular make a note of any which may solve the problems you have discussed. Keep your notes in your file for planning an essay.

Examination practice

This question allows you to choose which area of law you discuss. Note that the question asks for *either* involuntary manslaughter *or* the non-fatal offences. Don't discuss both because the examiner will only be able to award marks for one of these, and much of your hard work will be wasted.

> **June 2005**
> In relation **either** to the offence of involuntary manslaughter **or** to the non-fatal offences against the person, discuss the suggestion that the current law is essentially satisfactory.
>
> *(25 marks)*

Module 6 connections

Morals	Should a drug dealer owe a duty to a prostitute?	Khan
Justice	Arguably the test for what is dangerous should be subjective, what the particular D saw as dangerous, not what the reasonable person would	Church
	Conflicting cases means the law is uncertain, and arguably unjust	Dias/Rogers
	The CCRC referred **Kennedy** to the CA in 2005	Kennedy
Conflicting interests	The public interest, as well as that of the victim, is taken into account, society needs protecting from people whose acts may cause harm	
Fault	D need only have *mens rea* for the unlawful act, which may be a low level of 'fault'. Should manslaughter have its own *mens rea*?	**Hancock and Shankland**
	Is there a sufficiently clear distinction between negligence and *gross* negligence?	**Adomako**
Creativity	Cases have been distinguished but there is little creativity here as the courts have indicated it is for Parliament to amend the law, and there are ongoing proposals for reform	

For further resources and updates please go to the Companion Website accompanying this book at www.pearsoned.co.uk/russell

Unit 23   Common assault: assault and battery

Unit 24   Assault occasioning actual bodily harm (ABH) under s. 47 of
          the Offences Against the Person Act 1861

Unit 25   Grievous bodily harm (GBH) and wounding under s. 20 and
          s. 18 of the Offences Against the Person Act 1861

The five different offences against the person contained in this Study Block are commonly called 'the assaults'. However, they are separate and distinct offences, with different rules on each. The offences of assault and battery come from the common law, the others from an Act of Parliament. As well as this the police and Crown Prosecution Service have agreed what types of harm should be charged under the various offences. This is called the **Joint Charging Standards**. In 1.1 it says:

> *'The purpose of joint charging standards is to make sure that the most appropriate charge is selected at the earliest opportunity.'*

Example   Jane threatens Jenny, who is scared and hits her head as she tries to run away. The threat is an assault, and Jane caused Jenny to hit her head, which is a battery. If Jenny cuts herself it would amount to actual bodily harm (**s. 47**) and possibly wounding (**s. 20**). If she is seriously hurt or cut badly it would be grievous bodily harm or wounding (**s. 20**). If Jane *intended* to seriously harm her it would be grievous bodily harm or wounding with intent (**s. 18**).

Note the date of the **Act**. It is very old and in need of reform. Reforms have been suggested but not implemented and this is a popular area for examination questions. At the end of the Study Block I have added a full summary of all the offences together with criticisms and a note of some of the proposed reforms.

To look at the Joint Charging Standards go to **http://www.cps.gov.uk/index.html** then click on 'legal guidance' and then 'offences against the person'.

Common assault: assault and battery

There could be no dispute that if you touch a person's clothes while he is wearing them that is equivalent to touching him.

R v Thomas (1985)

By the end of this Unit you should be able to:

- Explain the *actus reus* and *mens rea* of assault and battery
- Explain the differences between them
- Explain how the law applies in practice by reference to cases

The Joint Charging Standard says in 4.1:

> 'An offence of common assault is committed when a person either assaults or inflicts a battery upon another person.'

Thus common assault includes two separate offences, assault and battery. It is called common assault because it comes from the common law. This means that assault and battery are not defined in any statute so the rules come from cases. The **Criminal Justice Act 1988 s. 39** classifies them as summary offences (triable only in the magistrates' court) so they are charged under this section.

Examination pointer

It is better not to say they are offences under **s. 39 Criminal Justice Act**. They are common law offences charged under the **Act**. Think of common assault as an umbrella under which the two crimes of assault and battery sit. They frequently occur together. If you need to discuss both then refer to common assault and then describe assault and battery in turn.

So the law on these offences comes from:

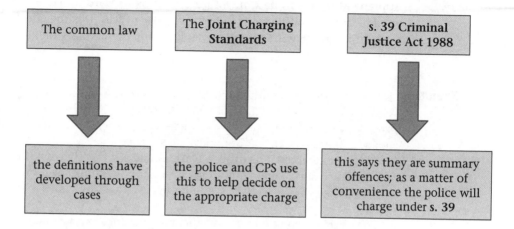

The common law	The **Joint Charging Standards**	s. 39 Criminal Justice Act 1988
the definitions have developed through cases	the police and CPS use this to help decide on the appropriate charge	this says they are summary offences; as a matter of convenience the police will charge under s. 39

Assault and battery are also trespass to the person, which is a civil matter, a tort. Here we are only dealing with *criminal* assault:

- **Assault** is to cause someone to apprehend immediate and unlawful personal violence.
- **Battery** is the unlawful application of force to another.

> **Example** Fred raises his fist and threatens Simon with a punch on the nose. This is an assault because Simon 'apprehends', or fears, violence. If Fred then follows up the threat there is both an assault and a battery. You may also have actual bodily harm but we'll come to that later.

We will look at assault and battery in turn.

Assault

The definition of assault is 'an act by which a person **intentionally or recklessly causes another to apprehend immediate and unlawful violence**'. As the definitions are not written down in an Act and come from cases they have changed slightly over the years. This definition was used by the CA in **Ireland (1996)** (discussed below) and confirmed by the HL the following year, in the twin appeals of **Ireland and Burstow (1997)**.

Actus reus

The *actus reus* is to:

- cause the victim to apprehend;
- immediate and unlawful violence.

Cause the victim to apprehend

Apprehend means to become aware of or look forward to. Here it is not look forward to in the positive sense but with a sense of fear. It is the effect on the victim that is important with assault. Assault is not the actual violence but the *threat* of it.

Example

D walks into a bank pointing a banana concealed in a bag and saying, 'I have a gun. Give me the money or I'll shoot you.' The cashier is very frightened and does as D says. This is an assault. The fact that there *is* no possibility of carrying out the threat doesn't matter. V is in fear of immediate violence.

D walks into a bank pointing a real gun and saying, 'Give me the money or I'll shoot.' The cashier knows him from college and she thinks he is doing it as a joke. This is unlikely to be assault. V doesn't believe that any violence is about to take place.

Whether it amounts to assault therefore depends on whether or not V thinks that violence is about to take place.

Can words alone constitute an assault?

Early cases indicated that words would not amount to assault unless accompanied by some threatening gesture (like raising your fist). In **Meade and Belt (1823)** it was said that 'no words or singing are equivalent to an assault'. This has changed over the years and in **Wilson (1955)** 'get out the knives' was said to be enough for assault. Also in **Constanza (1997)**, a case of stalking, the CA held that words alone could amount to an assault. Even silence is now capable of amounting to an assault. In **Smith v Chief Superintendent of Woking Police Station (1983)** a 'peeping Tom' assaulted a woman by looking at her through her bedroom window at night. He had caused her to be frightened.

Food for thought

It is the effect on the victim that is important, thus it seems right that words – or even silence – should amount to assault if they put the victim in fear of harm. The law has arguably become more satisfactory over the years, at least on this point.

Key case

In **Ireland**, D had repeatedly made silent telephone calls, accompanied by heavy breathing, to three women. In the appeal to the HL in 1997 Lord Steyn confirmed that words would be enough for assault. He said,

'The proposition that a gesture may amount to an assault, but that words can never suffice, is unrealistic and indefensible. A thing said is also a thing done. There is no reason why something said should be incapable of causing an apprehension of immediate personal violence, for example, a man accosting a woman in a dark alley saying "come with me or I will stab you." I would, therefore, reject the proposition that an assault can never be committed by words.'

Can words prevent an assault?

If D accompanies the threat with words that indicate that no violence will take place then there is no assault. An example of this is seen in a very old case. In **Turbeville v Savage (1669)** D was having an argument with V and placed his hand on the hilt of his sword. This would indicate an assault. He then said, 'If it were not assize time, I would not take such language from you.' There was held to be no assault. The statement was held to indicate that he would *not* assault V because it was assize time and the judges were in town.

Example	You say to John, 'I would hit you if it were not your birthday.' This indicates you won't do so (assuming it is his birthday!). No assault has taken place.

Immediate and unlawful violence

The threat must be of 'immediate' violence. This means if you threaten someone just as you are about to get on the train it won't be enough. You can't carry out your threat 'immediately'. The term is widely interpreted though. In **Smith v Chief Superintendent of Woking Police Station** V was scared by D looking at her through her bedroom window at night. She was frightened of what he might do next. The CA held this was sufficient.

In **Ireland (1997)** D argued that the 'immediacy' requirement was lacking. The CA held it was satisfied because by putting himself in contact with the victims D had caused them to be in immediate fear.

Food for thought

Is immediate fear the same thing as fear of immediate harm? The CA in **Ireland** seemed to think so. The appeal to the HL did not focus on this issue so it remains unclear. If D phones V and says, 'I have planted a bomb in your house. It is set to go off in five minutes,' there is no problem. Both the fear and the harm are immediate. However, if D says, 'I have planted a bomb in your house. It is set to go off in a week,' then it is a different matter. V may be in immediate fear, but is not in fear of immediate harm.

On a positive note the courts appear to be reacting to the reality of the times. In **Ireland** the HL agreed with the trial judge, Swinton Thomas LJ, who had said, 'We must apply the law to the conditions as they are in the twentieth century.'

It is now the twenty-first century and the law will hopefully be applied taking into account the latest methods of communication, which are much more 'immediate'.

Note that in many of these cases some actual harm was also caused. This means they can come under the statutory offence of an assault occasioning actual bodily harm under **s. 47 Offences Against the Person Act 1861**, as happened in **Roberts** (see p. 136). They are discussed here as well as in the next Unit because for **s. 47** to be satisfied an assault or battery must take place first.

Food for thought

A good argument that words should suffice is that they can sometimes be just as threatening as a gesture, as in the 'bomb' example I used earlier. Also, in a society that has a sophisticated communications network the immediacy issue is more easily satisfied.

Mens rea

In **Savage (1991)** Lord Ackner said, 'the mental element of assault is an intention to cause the victim to apprehend unlawful and immediate violence or recklessness whether such an apprehension be caused'. That recklessness for all assaults is **Cunningham** (subjective) recklessness (see p. 145) was confirmed in the joint appeals of **Savage and Parmenter (1992)**.

Applying the *mens rea* rules to assault

- For **direct intent** the prosecution must prove that it was D's aim or purpose to cause the victim to apprehend unlawful and immediate violence.
- For **indirect intent** it must be proved that it was a virtual certainty that V would apprehend immediate and unlawful violence and that D appreciated this.
- For **recklessness** it must be proved that D recognises a risk that V would apprehend immediate and unlawful violence and goes ahead and takes that risk.

Battery

Battery is the unlawful application of force to another. As noted earlier, it often follows the assault. Assault and battery therefore go together in many, but not all, cases.

Example In my earlier example of the punch on the nose, there would be both. Simon saw the punch coming, so he was in fear of harm. If Fred hit Simon from behind, there would only be a battery. No assault would have occurred because Simon was not in fear.

Actus reus

The *actus reus* is the unlawful application of force to another. It can be slight because the law sees people's bodies as inviolate. Lane LCJ said in **Faulkner and Talbot (1981)** that it was '*any intentional touching of another person without the consent of that person and without lawful excuse. It need not necessarily be hostile, or rude, or aggressive, as some of the cases seem to indicate.*'

In **Thomas (1985)** the court said, '*if you touch a person's clothes while he is wearing them that is equivalent to touching him.*'

Unlawful

Part of the *actus reus* is that the force must be unlawful. In **Collins v Wilcox (1984)** a police constable who took hold of a woman's arm was acting unlawfully. If there had been a lawful arrest this would not have been the case.

Consent may make the application of force lawful. This would include things like surgery and sports. Consent may be implied. Everyday jostling and most sports contacts are not battery because there is implied consent to touching. This would not be the case if unreasonable force was used. A small nudge in the cinema queue is fine; an elbow in the ribs would not be. In a game of rugby, a tackle within the rules is fine, but a punch would not be. As both *actus reus* and *mens rea* must be proved in their entirety, there is no offence if an element is missing. Consent means the 'unlawful' element of the *actus reus* is missing. Self-defence also makes a battery lawful, but again not if unreasonable force is used.

The two defences of consent and self-defence are commonly used in the non-fatal offences against the person. However, they apply to other crimes too, so are discussed again under 'Defences'.

Application of force

There is a requirement that force is applied. This means battery cannot be caused by an omission; there must be an act. This was confirmed in **Fagan** (see p. 129). D argued that not moving off was an omission, not an act. The court held that although battery could not be committed by omission, there was a continuing act. The *actus reus* was the driving on to the policeman's foot and staying there.

Direct or indirect force?

Some early cases suggest that the force had to be direct but this is unlikely to be the case now. In **DPP v K (1990)** a schoolboy put acid in a hot air drier. Later another pupil used the drier and was badly scarred by the acid. This was held to be a battery. The case raised another issue. The boy had been using the acid in an experiment in class and was merely trying to hide it. He did not have *mens rea* when he put it in the machine. He did have *mens rea* when he failed to do anything about it. We saw above that a battery cannot be committed by omission. In K, omitting to rectify what he had done was held to be enough though.

In **Haystead (2000)** the harm appeared to be indirect. Here, D punched his girlfriend, who was holding her baby. She dropped the baby, resulting in the baby hitting his head on the floor. The defendant was convicted of battery on the baby.

Food for thought

Although in **Haystead** it seemed to be indirect force, it may just be a widening of the meaning of direct. The court held that direct can include via another person or a weapon. Thus, setting a dog on someone can be seen as direct force. This is reasonable as it is unlikely to be argued that throwing a brick at someone was not direct and there is little real difference. In civil law indirect actions have long been held to be a battery. In **Scott v Shepherd (1773)** D threw a squib into a market place. Someone picked it up and tossed it away to avoid being harmed. A second person then did the same. The third was not so quick and was injured when the squib exploded. The court held this to be a battery by D on the third person.

Mens rea

As with assault, the *mens rea* is intent or recklessness. Here it is as to whether force is applied.

Task

Look back at the application of the rules on intent and recklessness to an assault. Apply the same rules for a case of battery.

Summary

Assault: *Actus reus*	
To cause the victim to apprehend	What is the effect on the victim?
Immediate and unlawful personal violence	**Ireland**
Words may be enough, or even silence	**Wilson/Ireland**
Battery: *Actus reus*	
Unlawful application of force to another	**Collins *v* Wilcox**
Can include touching V's clothes	**Thomas**
May include indirect force	**DPP *v* K**
Assault and Battery	
Mens rea	Intent or subjective recklessness

Self-test questions

1 What is the current definition of assault?

2 Can words alone constitute an assault? Use a case to support your answer.

3 What is the *mens rea* for assault?

4 Does a battery have to be hostile? Use a case to support your answer.

5 What two defences may make a battery lawful?

For further resources and updates please go to the Companion Website accompanying this book at **www.pearsoned.co.uk/russell**

Assault occasioning actual bodily harm (ABH) under s. 47 of the Offences Against the Person Act 1861

It has been recognised for many centuries that putting a person in fear may amount to an assault. The early cases predate the invention of the telephone. We must apply the law to the conditions as they are in the twentieth century.

Swinton LJ

By the end of this Unit you should be able to:

- Explain the *actus reus* of ABH as an assault or battery which causes harm
- Explain the *mens rea* of ABH
- Explain how the law applies in practice by reference to cases

This offence is charged under **s. 47 Offences Against the Person Act (1861)**. It is commonly known as ABH. **Section 47** provides:

*'whosoever shall be convicted on indictment of any **assault occasioning actual bodily harm** shall be liable to imprisonment for not more than five years.'*

Until 1984 it was thought that the **Act** merely provided for a greater penalty where an assault resulted in harm being caused. It is now clear that a new offence was created – **Courtie (1984)**. In fact in **Savage** Lord Ackner indicated that it created two offences. An assault occasioning ABH and a battery occasioning ABH.

The offence has the *actus reus* and *mens rea* of assault or battery plus the further *actus reus* of some harm being caused. Let's look at this in more detail.

Actus reus

There are three parts to this.

- **Assault** – the conduct;
- **Occasioning** – a matter of causation;
- **Actual bodily harm** – the consequence.

Assault

Before anyone can be charged with **s. 47** there must be a prior assault. This is shown by the wording of the offence: an *assault* occasioning actual bodily harm. Assault in **s. 47** covers both assault and battery. This is clear from **Savage**, where Lord Ackner referred to both.

Key case

In **Savage (1991)** a girl threw a glass of beer over another girl. As she did so, she let go of the glass which broke, resulting in a cut to the other girl's wrist. The throwing of the beer was enough for a battery. Lord Ackner said, '*It is of course common ground that Mrs Savage committed an assault upon Miss Beal when she threw the contents of her glass of beer over her.*' He is referring to assault but describing battery. When he discusses the *mens rea* for the offence he describes assault. This is further proof that the word assault in **s. 47** includes both assault and battery.

There was no proof she intended to throw the glass and she said it was an accident. She did, however, intend to throw the beer. The throwing of the beer was enough for the *actus reus* of battery. As she intended to do this there was *mens rea* too. In order for her to be convicted under **s. 47** the prosecution merely had to prove the 'assault', i.e. the battery, had 'occasioned' (caused) the harm.

In **Ireland (1997)** it had been argued there was no assault through silent telephone calls. As you can see from the opening quote, this was rejected.

Occasioning

This means bringing about, or causing. **Section 47** is a result crime, so the prosecution must show that the assault or battery caused the result. Thus D's actions must make a significant contribution to the harm and the chain of causation must not be broken.

Task

Look back at Unit 15 on *actus reus* and causation. Read **Roberts** (p. 136) to remind yourself of the facts. The question was whether the battery by D caused the harm. Why did the action by the victim not break the chain of causation? What type of action might do so?

In **Savage**, the issue of causation arose because D argued she hadn't intended any harm. The HL said that once the assault was established, the only remaining question was whether the victim's conduct was the natural consequence of that assault. According to Lord Ackner, '*the word "occasioning" raised solely a question of causation, an objective question which does not involve inquiring into the accused's state of mind.*'

Examination pointer

Causation is a common issue in a problem question, especially where ABH is involved. If harm has occurred you may need to discuss all three of these offences. You will certainly have to discuss two of them because **s. 47** cannot happen without one of the others. You will need to define and explain assault and/or battery. Then define harm. Finally show that the assault (or battery) caused the harm. Use a case like **Roberts** or **Savage** to explain this and apply it to the facts given. If those facts remind you of a more relevant case, use that instead.

Actual bodily harm

In **Miller (1954)** this was held to be any hurt or injury calculated to interfere with someone's health or comfort. It was made clear it could include a mental injury. In **Chan Fook (1994)** the CA qualified this a little. Psychiatric injury was enough but not 'mere emotions' such as fear, distress or panic. This will exclude really trivial or insignificant harm. Some type of identifiable medical condition will be needed.

Thus it is clear that harm is not confined to physical injury.

Key case

In **Ireland (1996)** silent phone calls which caused psychiatric harm was held to come under **s. 47**. D's argument was that there was no assault because there was no fear of 'immediate' harm. This would mean that there could be no assault occasioning actual bodily harm. This argument failed as the court found sufficient 'immediacy' in a telephone call. The CA also relied on **Chan Fook** to confirm that psychiatric harm was enough for 'bodily harm'. The opening quote came from the CA and was approved in the HL.

The Joint Charging Standards (see introduction) differ from what would legally constitute a particular offence. For example, a small cut or bruise would be charged under battery. Legally this could amount to actual bodily harm. Paragraph 4.7 says:

'Where battery results in injury, a choice of charge is available . . . Thus, although any injury can be classified as actual bodily harm, the appropriate charge will be contrary to section 39 where injuries amount to no more than the following.'

The types of injuries mentioned include a graze, a scratch and a black eye.

According to 7.3 psychiatric injury which is more than fear, distress or panic; the breaking of a tooth; extensive bruising; and minor, but not merely superficial, cuts should normally be prosecuted under **s. 47**.

Mens rea

D need not intend, or be reckless as to, any harm, only the assault or battery. This was held to be the case by the CA in **Roberts (1971)**. D argued that he did not intend to cause harm and nor was he reckless. He was found guilty because he had the *mens rea* and the *actus reus* for the battery, plus harm had been caused. This was enough for **s. 47**. Despite this seemingly clear principle of law there was conflict in several cases over the next 20 years.

Key case

The issue was finally put beyond doubt by the HL in the joint appeals of **Savage and Parmenter (1992)**. These two cases had been decided differently in the lower courts. The principle of **Roberts** had been followed in **Savage** but not in **Parmenter**.

In **Savage and Parmenter** the HL held **Roberts** to be the correct law. The throwing of the beer with intent to do so was enough for a battery. The question for the court was whether a further mental state had to be established in relation to the bodily harm element of the **s. 47** offence. Lord Ackner said, '*Clearly the section, by its terms, expressly imposes no such requirement.*'

This means that if D has *mens rea* for the assault and harm occurs it can amount to the more serious charge under **s. 47**. Think about it as an equation:

$$\text{Assault (AR + MR)} + \text{harm (AR)} = \text{s. 47}$$

Example Sandra shouts threateningly at Tara. Tara is scared that Sandra will hit her. She jumps back and hits her head, causing severe bruising. This will be enough for a charge under **s. 47**. There is the *actus reus* of an assault (Tara is in fear of immediate violence) plus *mens rea* (Sandra intends to frighten her) and this assault occasioned (caused – jumping back and falling is foreseeable, as in **Roberts**) ABH (severe bruising).

So, the *mens rea* for **s. 47** is intent or subjective recklessness as to the assault only, not the harm. The prosecution will have to show one of the following:

- **Direct intent.** Causing fear of violence or the application of force is D's aim or purpose.

- **Indirect intent.** D appreciates that it is virtually certain that V will fear violence, or D appreciates that the application of force is virtually certain.

- **Subjective recklessness.** D is aware of the risk of V being in fear, or is aware of the risk of force being applied, and goes ahead anyway.

Food for thought

One problem with **s. 47** is that the *mens rea* does not match the *actus reus*. For the *actus reus* of **s. 47** you need ABH to have occurred; the *mens rea* is only for assault or battery though (**Roberts, Savage**). This is confusing, and arguably unfair. Should D be guilty of causing ABH where there was only intent to scare someone? On the other hand, should D get away with harming someone when the attempt to scare them caused harm?

Summary

Actus reus	
Assault	Assault or battery (**Savage**)
Occasioning	Causing (the assault or battery must cause the harm) (**Roberts, Savage**)
Actual bodily harm	Discomfort (**Miller**) but not trivial harm (**Chan Fook**) Includes psychiatric harm (**Ireland**)
Mens rea	
Intent or recklessness	As to the assault or battery (**Roberts, Savage**)

Self-test questions

1 From which case did the quote at the beginning of this unit come?

2 What are the three parts to the *actus reus*?

3 For which part of this is *mens rea* needed?

4 According to **Roberts**, what sort of action by V could break the chain of causation?

5 In which case did the HL finally confirm that the principle in **Roberts** was correct?

For further resources and updates please go to the Companion Website accompanying this book at www.pearsoned.co.uk/russell

Grievous bodily harm (GBH) and wounding under s. 20 and s. 18 of the Offences Against the Person Act 1861

In the context of a criminal act therefore the words 'cause' and 'inflict' may be taken to be interchangeable.

Lord Hope, **Ireland and Burstow (1997)**

By the end of this Unit you should be able to:

- Explain the *actus reus* of wounding and GBH in **s. 20** and **s. 18**
- Explain the difference in the *mens rea* between the two sections
- Explain how the law applies in practice by reference to cases
- Compare all the different offences as they are now, and explain the proposed reforms
- Identify possible criticisms

Section 20 makes it an offence to:

'unlawfully and maliciously wound or inflict any grievous bodily harm upon any other person, either with or without any weapon or instrument.'

Section 18 makes it an offence to:

'unlawfully and maliciously by any means whatsoever wound or cause any grievous bodily harm to any person with intent to do some grievous bodily harm to any person.'

These two offences are commonly called malicious wounding (**s. 20**) and wounding with intent (**s. 18**). However, there are actually two separate offences under each section:

- Unlawfully and maliciously wounding;
- Unlawfully and maliciously inflicting/causing grievous bodily harm.

There is very little difference in the *actus reus*; both need **either** a wound (open cut) **or** serious injury. We will deal with the two together for this and then look at the different *mens rea* for each.

Actus reus

Let's split the *actus reus* up into manageable chunks. I have left out 'malicious' for the moment as this has been treated as relating to *mens rea*.

Unlawfully

If the act is done lawfully then no offence has occurred. Thus if D has acted in self-defence then this makes it lawful, so part of the *actus reus* is missing. Consent may also make it lawful.

In **Clarence (1888)** D, knowing he had a sexually transmitted disease, had sex with his wife. She caught the disease. This amounted to grievous bodily harm. D's conviction was quashed on the basis that the sex was by consent and it made no difference that the wife did not know about the disease.

This is more limited now. In **Brown (1994)** the House of Lords decided that consent of the victim could no longer be a defence if serious harm was *intended*. In **Dica (2004)** D had consensual sex with two women, knowing he was HIV positive. They both became infected with HIV and he was convicted under s. 20 with recklessly inflicting grievous bodily harm. On appeal, the CA confirmed the point in **Brown** that consent was not a defence to intentional harm. However, as the charge was *recklessly* inflicting grievous bodily harm, they held that the issue of consent should not have been withdrawn from the jury. A retrial was ordered.

Consent is discussed further in 'Defences.'

Wound

Key case

In **C v Eisenhower (1983)** a wound was defined as being 'any puncture of the skin'. The case involved a child firing an air gun. The pellet hit V in the eye but did not break the skin. It was held that internal bleeding caused by the rupture of an internal organ was not a wound. Therefore something that does not break the skin, such as an abrasion, bruise or burn would not amount to a wound.

Inflict and cause - is there a difference?

The *actus reus* of s. 20 is to unlawfully and maliciously wound or *inflict* grievous bodily harm. The *actus reus* of s. 18 is the same except it says '*cause*' not 'inflict'. In **Clarence** the word 'inflict' was held to mean that a prior assault was required, as for s. 47. Other cases seem to have ignored this requirement. In **Wilson (1984)** the HL held that a person could be charged under s. 20 without an assault. They relied on the Australian case of **Salisbury (1976)** where it was said that 'inflict' does not imply assault. However, it was said that the word 'inflict' did mean that *direct* application of force was needed. It was therefore narrower than the word cause.

Food for thought

This uncertainty has been clarified. Both **Salisbury** and **Wilson** were approved by the HL in **Ireland and Burstow (1997)**. In the CA Lord Bingham had said it would be 'an affront to common sense' to distinguish between the two offences in this way. The HL confirmed that liability for GBH could occur without the application of direct or indirect force, and rejected the argument that 'inflict' was narrower than 'cause'. **Clarence** was referred to as a 'troublesome authority'. In **Dica**, the CA again confirmed that there was no requirement of assault for a charge under **s. 20**.

A factor that is worth noting (as it was by the HL) is that the **1861 Act** consolidated several different Acts. Therefore the difference in the two sections is not as significant as it would be had they been written at the same time.

A final criticism is that if there is no requirement of assault in **s. 20** then it is hard to justify convicting D of *assault* occasioning actual bodily harm as an alternative, as was confirmed again in **Savage and Parmenter**.

Grievous bodily harm

This is commonly known as GBH. In **Smith (1961)** grievous was interpreted by the HL to mean 'really serious'. In **Saunders (1985)** the CA held that the word 'really' was unnecessary. Thus GBH will include *any* serious harm. In **Burstow (1996)** a campaign of harassment by D, which led to V suffering severe depressive illness, was charged under **s. 20**. In the joint appeals to the HL in **Ireland and Burstow (1997)** the HL confirmed that psychiatric harm can come under **ss. 47, 18** or **20**.

The Joint Charging Standards states in 8.5 that grievous bodily harm means serious bodily harm. Examples of this include injuries resulting in a substantial loss of blood or lengthy treatment, broken bones and compound fractures. Psychiatric harm is included but requires 'appropriate expert evidence'.

A wound may occur without GBH. Conversely, GBH may occur without a wound.

Example

Let's reconsider two cases we saw when looking at **s. 47**.

In **Savage** the glass broke and cut the other girl. This is technically a wound as the skin has been broken. She could have been charged with wounding under **s. 20**. It would not be 'serious' harm though, so no charge of inflicting GBH would succeed.

In the joint appeals of **Ireland and Burstow** the HL said psychiatric harm could amount to GBH. This type of harm could not be a wound though.

Examination pointer

Look for clues in the scenario. If it refers to a cut then discuss wounding under either **s. 18** or **20**. If it is only a small cut you could discuss **s. 47**. If a serious internal injury is mentioned then discuss GBH. In all cases the prosecution must establish a chain of causation. D's act must make a significant contribution to the wound or harm (see Unit 15).

Section 20 refers to 'with or without any weapon or instrument'. Section 18 refers to 'by any means whatsoever'. Remember, these offences came from different Acts and were not written at the same time. It doesn't matter *how* D inflicts or causes the harm. However, the use of a weapon may help in establishing intent to cause serious harm, and so point you at s. 18.

Mens rea

It is important to be able to identify the different *mens rea* in s. 18 and s. 20. There are two differences. The type of *mens rea* and the type of harm that the *mens rea* relates to.

Both sections contain the word 'maliciously'. This does not mean spite or ill-will, as we might view the word. As regards s. 20, the CA interpreted it in **Cunningham (1957)** as meaning intent or subjective recklessness (see Unit 16). For s. 18, it would appear that the word maliciously is unnecessary. In **Mowatt** the court said, 'In s. 18 the word "maliciously" adds nothing'.

Mens rea for s. 20

As noted above, this is intent or subjective recklessness. However, D need not intend or recognise the risk of serious harm. Intending or seeing the risk (*mens rea*) of *some* harm is enough as long as the result (*actus reus*) is serious harm. This was confirmed by the CA in **Mowatt (1968)** and later approved by the HL in **Savage and Parmenter (1992)**.

Key case

In **Parmenter** D threw his baby into the air and caused GBH when he caught it. His argument that he lacked *mens rea* succeeded. He had not seen the risk of *any* injury (he'd done it before several times with older children) so he was not guilty.

It is only necessary to prove that D foresaw some harm *might* occur. It is not necessary to prove that D foresaw that some harm *would* occur. This point was confirmed in **DPP v A (2000)**. Here, a 13-year-old boy shot his friend while they were playing with two air pistols. His argument that he lacked *mens rea* was rejected. The case is similar to **Eisenhower**.

Food for thought

Sections 18 and 20 involve *either* GBH *or* wounding. The first has been interpreted as 'really serious' harm (**Smith**); however, wounding has been interpreted as an 'open cut' (**Eisehower**), which could be quite trivial. The prosecution failed to prove D had inflicted a wound in **Eisenhower** because there was no open cut and thus no 'wound'. This case highlights the need to get the charge right. A charge of GBH could have succeeded. Another issue is that, as for s. 47, the *mens rea* does not match the *actus reus*. For s. 20 you need serious harm to have occurred, but the *mens rea* is only for some harm (**Mowatt**).

Application of *mens rea* for s. 20

- **Direct intent**: It is D's aim to cause *some harm*.
- **Indirect intent**: *Some harm* is a virtual certainty and D appreciates this.
- **Subjective recklessness**: D recognises the risk of *some harm* and goes ahead anyway.

Mens rea for s. 18

The *mens rea* for **s. 18** is specific intent, i.e. intent only. Note **s. 18** says *'with intent to do some grievous bodily harm'*. It was confirmed in **Parmenter** that for **s. 18** D must intend *serious harm*. This is the vital difference and makes **s. 18** much more serious, leading to a possible maximum life sentence. **Section 20** is a maximum of five years.

Food for thought

If **s. 18** requires serious harm in both *actus reus* and *mens rea*, then arguably so should **s. 20**. There is still a difference in the *mens rea* because **s. 18** requires intent *only* to be proved.

Another issue is sentencing. The maximum sentences for **s. 20** and **s. 18** are very different. The maximum for **s. 20** is the same as **s. 47**, i.e. five years. This seems strange to many people. Life for **s. 18** can be justified in that intent to seriously injure is also the *mens rea* for murder. Which charge is brought will depend on the chance factor of whether the victim dies or not. The same sentence for **s. 47** and **s. 20** is harder to justify. In **Parmenter**, the CA noted there was an overlap between **s. 47** and **s. 20** but indicated that **s. 20** was a more serious offence. The Law Commission proposes a maximum of five years for **s. 47**, as now, but a maximum seven years for **s. 20**. This seems more realistic – but the reforms may be a long way off becoming reality.

A further recommendation by the Law Commission is that **s. 18** would be 'intentional serious injury' and **s. 20** would be 'reckless serious injury'. This would clear up the problem of the *mens rea*. It is arguably unfair to charge someone with GBH when they only had the *mens rea* for some harm. A final criticism of the current law is that there are two different offences in each section. This makes four offences in all, which is unnecessarily complicated.

Application of *mens rea* for s. 18

- **Direct intent**: It is D's aim or purpose to cause *grievous bodily harm*.
- **Indirect intent**: *Grievous bodily harm* is a virtual certainty and D appreciates this.

Note that it was confirmed in **Savage** that a jury may bring in **s. 20** as an alternative verdict when someone is charged under **s. 18** and **s. 47** as an alternative to **s. 20**.

Examination pointer

This means you may need to discuss all three statutory offences. Explain the actus reus of either GBH or wounding as appropriate, using cases in support. Note carefully the difference in the mens rea as this may help you to decide which section is most appropriate. Thus, if you go for **s. 18**, explain and apply the law (with cases) but then say that if the prosecution can't prove intent to cause GBH then D may be convicted of **s. 20** instead. If you go for **s. 20** you can then discuss **s. 47** if you feel the harm may not be serious enough.

Summary

Actus reus	
Inflict or cause	Mean the same thing (**Ireland**)
Wound	Open cut (**Eisenhower**)
Grievous bodily harm	Serious harm (**Smith/Saunders**)
Mens rea	
S. 20 Intent or recklessness	To cause some harm (**Mowatt**)
S. 18 Intent only	To cause serious harm (**Parmenter**)

Self-test questions

1 How has 'wound' been interpreted?

2 How has 'grievous bodily harm' been interpreted?

3 Which cases can you use to support your answers to the above two questions?

4 What is the difference in the *mens rea* between **s. 20** and **s. 18**?

5 What are the maximum sentences for **s. 20** and **s. 18** respectively?

For further resources and updates please go to the Companion Website accompanying this book at **www.pearsoned.co.uk/russell**

Study Block 8 Summary
NON-FATAL OFFENCES AGAINST THE PERSON

Note in particular the *mens rea* for each offence.

Assault
• *Actus reus*: To cause the victim to apprehend *immediate* and unlawful personal violence
• *Mens rea*: Intent or subjective recklessness to cause fear of harm
• Cases: **Turbeville *v* Savage (1669)/Ireland (1996)**
Battery
• *Actus reus*: Unlawful application of force to another
• *Mens rea*: Intent or subjective recklessness to apply force
• Cases: **Fagan (1969)/DPP *v* K (1990)**
Assault occasioning actual bodily harm – s. 47 OAPA 1861
• *Actus reus*: An assault (or battery) which causes some harm
• *Mens rea*: Intent or subjective recklessness for the assault or battery only
• Cases: **Roberts (1971)/Savage (1991)/Ireland (1996)**
Malicious wounding – s. 20 OAPA 1861
• *Actus reus*: Unlawful and malicious wounding or inflicting grievous bodily harm
• *Mens rea*: Intent or subjective recklessness to inflict some harm
• Case: **Mowatt (1968)**
Wounding with intent – s. 18 OAPA 1861
• *Actus reus*: Unlawful and malicious wounding or causing grievous bodily harm
• *Mens rea*: Intent (only) to cause grievous bodily harm
• Case: **Parmenter (1991)**

Task

Match the principle to the case and check your answers.

Wilson (1955)	Silence may be enough for an assault
Ireland (1996)	Grievous means really serious harm
C v Eisenhower (1984)	Words may be enough for an assault
Miller (1954)	A battery can be via another person
Haystead (2000)	Actual bodily harm is anything that causes discomfort
Smith (1961)	Mere emotions such as fear, distress or panic are not enough for actual bodily harm
Chan Fook (1994)	Wound means an open cut

Key criticisms

We have seen many problems while looking at the individual offences, and it is clear the **Offences Against the Person Act 1861** is in need of reform. There are also more general issues:

Language: the Act is very complicated and was written in 1861, so much of the language is obscure. Lawyers and juries have struggled to understand the complexities of the different offences. The courts also have difficulty interpreting words such as 'occasioning', 'actual bodily harm', 'grievous' and 'maliciously' as they are not used in the same sense today. This can result in conflicting case law and injustice. The word 'maliciously' has been interpreted as meaning recklessly (**Parmenter**). However, it appears in **s. 18** as well as **s. 20** and the *mens rea* for **s. 18** is intent only. In **Parmenter**, the judge had difficulty explaining 'maliciously' to the jury. He said that it meant that it was enough that D *should have foreseen* that some harm might occur. This sounds very like objective rather than subjective recklessness. In fact, on appeal, this was said to be a misdirection. It highlights the fact that these words need to be clearly explained.

Common law: assault and battery are outside the Act. Clarity would require all the offences to be together in one place. However, an alternative argument is that the common law can keep them up to date, as in **Ireland**, where it was recognised that an assault could be via a telephone.

So, there are plenty of problems. What is being done about them?

Proposed reforms

The Law Commission has been considering codification of the criminal law for some time. This was a huge task and so it was decided it would be better to work on a series of self-contained bills to deal with different parts of the criminal law. In 1993 the Commission produced a report (No. 218) and draft Bill on the non-fatal offences against the person. This never received parliamentary time but in 1998 the government produced its own Bill incorporating most of the recommended changes. The offences are redefined and in all of them the *mens rea* matches the *actus reus*.

Name of proposed offence	Explanation of proposed offence	Current offence
Intentional serious injury	Clause 1: intentionally causing serious injury	S. 18
Reckless serious injury	Clause 2: recklessly causing serious injury	S. 20
Intentional or reckless injury	Clause 3: intentionally or recklessly causing injury	S. 47
Assault	Clause 4: intentionally or recklessly applying force to or causing an impact on the body of another; or intentionally or recklessly causing another to believe force is imminent	Common assault (assault and battery)

In each case the word 'cause' is used. The Bill also defines injury to include both physical and psychiatric harm. It excludes any harm caused by disease except for Clause 1. This is in line with **Dica**. The Bill has not yet received parliamentary time – something you can add to your critique.

Examination practice

What criticisms would you make of the current law on non-fatal offences against the person? (25 marks)

Module 6 connections

Morals	Should judges decide cases on a moral basis rather than a legal one?	Compare **Brown** to **Wilson**
Justice	Natural law and utilitarian theories	Discuss these using **Brown**
Conflicting interests	Is the law achieving a just balance?	**Brown** (balancing protection of society with individual rights) Compare to **Wilson** (individual rights upheld)
Fault	Should D be liable for a more serious offence than that intended?	**Roberts, Savage, Mowatt** on the *mens rea* for **s. 47** and **s. 20**
Creativity	Developing the law to meet changes in technology	**Ireland**
	Developing the law to reflect society's needs	**Brown**

For further resources and updates please go to the Companion Website accompanying this book at **www.pearsoned.co.uk/russell**

Study Block 9
DEFENCES

Unit 26   Consent

Unit 27   Insanity and automatism

Unit 28   Intoxication

Unit 29   Self-defence and mistake

This Study Block covers general defences. Unlike the specific defences (which only apply to murder), these apply to most offences. The summary at the end of this Study Block will compare the defences and the different effect of each for the person using them. These defences may apply to any of the crimes in Module 4; however, for examination purposes, consent and self-defence are most commonly seen with the non-fatal offences against the person, whereas insanity and automatism are seen with homicide. Intoxication comes in pretty much anywhere, but rarely succeeds.

Example   Jane and Jenny are playing football and Jenny is hurt. If Jane is charged with an offence she can argue consent on the basis that Jenny consented to play a game which could result in an injury.

   If Jane hears voices in her head which tell her to kill someone, she will argue insanity. If she is concussed by a blow to the head which causes her to lose control and she kills someone, this may be automatism as she is acting 'automatically'. If she is drunk or under the influence of drugs the defence would be intoxication, although, as I said, this rarely succeeds. Finally, if she believes, wrongly, that someone is being attacked and she hits the supposed attacker, she can use the defences of mistake and self-defence, and possibly prevention of crime.

The defences of duress, necessity and duress of circumstances are not needed for Module 4. For those students who are also studying crime in Module 5, you will find them in Unit 37.

Note that you no longer need to discuss defences in essay questions, i.e. there is no requirement for an evaluation of them. However, I have included 'Food for thought' boxes as this is a good area for tying in with Module 6. Defences often relate to issues of fault and morality (some defences excuse, or justify, the commission of a crime; some are limited for ethical reasons); they are taken into account when balancing the conflicting interests of D and the wider community; and they are used as a way of achieving justice – and in some cases not doing so.

Infancy is not on the syllabus now, but you may see references to it, so here is a brief explanation. It is a full defence and, under the **Children and Young Persons Act 1933**, a child under 10 cannot be criminally liable. Since the **Crime and Disorder Act 1998**, a child over 10 is fully liable. The defence of infancy now *only* applies to children under the age of 10. The only difference between a child over 10 and an adult is in the form of trial and in sentencing. That's it.

Consent

We think that it can be taken as a starting point that it is an essential element of an assault that the act is done contrary to the will and without the consent of the victim.

Lord Lane CJ

By the end of this Unit you should be able to:

● Explain the defence of consent
● Discuss some of the issues relating to this defence
● Apply it to the different non-fatal offences
● Refer to appropriate case examples

This defence is mainly relevant to non-fatal offences against the person. There are limits on how far an individual is free to consent to being harmed. Consent is never a defence to some offences, e.g. murder. Thus we saw in Unit 14 that Diane Pretty was unable to get immunity from prosecution for her husband if he helped her to die. For the non-fatal offences the courts will look at the nature and degree of harm consented to, as well as whether harm was intended. Consent can also be both express or implied.

Example A woman is dying and in pain. She asks her doctor to give her an injection to help her die. Even though she has clearly consented, her consent is not available as a defence to a murder charge if the doctor agrees to give her the injection.

A player is injured by an opponent's tackle during a game of rugby. The defence can be used to a charge of battery or actual bodily harm, and probably to grievous bodily harm. This consent is implied in such games.

In **Leach (1969)** a man asked to be crucified on Hampstead Heath. He survived and the people who had nailed him to the cross were charged under **s. 18 Offences Against the Person Act**. Their defence that he consented failed. The degree of harm and the fact that the act carried no social benefit influenced this decision.

Consent can provide a defence to common assault. In **AG's Reference (No. 6 of 1980) 1981** Lord Lane CJ made the comment that lack of consent was an essential element of an assault. The case is important as the CA gave guidelines on the types of activities where there would be implied consent to an assault.

Activities to which you can consent

These were set out in the following case, which gives a guide on what activities a person may consent to, expressly or by implication.

Key case

The public interest was also referred to in **AG's Reference (No. 6 of 1980) 1981**. A fight between two youths resulted in one of them suffering a bloody nose. The other was charged with actual bodily harm. The CA said it was not in the public interest that people should cause each other actual bodily harm for no good reason. They gave a list of circumstances which would be lawful even if harm occurred. These were *'properly conducted games and sports, lawful chastisement or correction, reasonable surgical interference, dangerous exhibitions, etc.'* In these circumstances consent is implied.

It had been argued by the Attorney General that the consent defence should fail because the fight had occurred in public. The CA held that it made no difference whether it occurred in public or not. The issue was that they intended harm.

Another influence on the courts appears to be a moral one. A leading case on consent to physical harm is **Brown (1994)**.

Key case

In **Brown**, consenting homosexuals engaged in sado-masochistic behaviour in a private home. Injuries were caused and they were charged under **s. 47** and **s. 20 Offences Against the Person Act**. They were convicted even though they all consented. The case went to the HL. The decision to uphold their convictions was only by a 3–2 majority. One reason appears to be the extent of the harm caused. Another was that the harm was intentional. The case raised moral issues too. Lord Templeman said, *'pleasure derived from the infliction of pain is an evil thing'*. The two dissenting judges may have agreed but Lord Mustill thought that this was no reason to bring such behaviour within the criminal law. Lord Slynn thought the issue was whether the act was done in public or not. As it was in private, the law should not interfere.

Food for thought

In **Brown**, Lord Slynn thought the issue was whether the act was done in public or not. This had already been rejected in **AG's Reference (No. 6 of 1980)**. There the CA held that the issue was whether D intended harm. Which argument do you prefer? Should private actions be within the law regardless of whether harm was intended?

Let's look at some of the different types of activity mentioned in **AG's Reference (No. 6 of 1980)**.

Properly conducted games and sports

Sport is seen as having a social benefit. In **Coney (1882)** it was held that a blow in sports such as boxing with gloves or wrestling would not amount to an assault, but a fistfight would do. Such fighting is not socially acceptable, so the consent defence is likely to fail, as in **AG's Reference (No. 6 of 1980)**. Where D's conduct is not within the rules of the game, the position was unclear. In **Billingshurst (1978)** consent was accepted even though the injury suffered was serious and D was acting outside the rules of rugby, but in several later cases it failed. The position was clarified in **Barnes (2004)**.

Key case

In **Barnes (2004)** D had been found guilty of grievous bodily harm after a late tackle in a football match. The conviction was quashed and the CA held that criminal cases should be reserved for times when the conduct was *'sufficiently grave to be categorised as criminal'*. People taking part in sport consented to the risk of injury. It now seems that the defence can be used in all but extreme sporting cases.

Lawful chastisement

Corporal punishment in schools has been illegal since 1986. The ban did not extend to parents smacking their own children, however. In **A v UK (1998)** a stepfather successfully used the defence of lawful chastisement to a charge of actual bodily harm. He had beaten the child with a stick over a period of time. However, the case went to the **European Court of Human Rights**, which held that this violated **Article 3** of the **Convention** prohibiting torture and inhuman and degrading treatment.

In **Williams (2005)** the House of Lords had to consider the earlier ban on corporal punishment in schools. It had been claimed that it did not apply where the parents had expressly given permission to the school to chastise their children. The HL rejected this argument. They held that the **Education Act 1996** made it clear that corporal punishment was banned whether the parents had consented or not.

In 2004 a general ban on smacking was discussed in Parliament. An outright ban was rejected and a compromise was reached. Under the **Children Act 2004** smacking is no longer lawful if it causes bruising or cuts. Reasonable chastisement or punishment is, however, still a defence to common assault and this has been criticised in a Council of Europe report released in 2005.

Reasonable surgical interference

Most surgical treatment would amount to a battery if carried out without the patient's consent. It is generally accepted that consent must be real. Thus consent by a child or consent induced by fraud may not be valid. In **Burrell and Harmer (1967)** the defence failed. A 12 and 13-year-old were not deemed to have consented to the actual bodily harm caused by tattooing.

In **Richardson (1999)** a dentist who had been suspended carried out treatment on several people, one of whom complained to the police. The prosecution argued that consent to the treatment was not real because the patients did not know the full facts. Had they known she had been struck off they would not have consented. The CA rejected this argument and held that they had consented to the treatment, and this was enough.

In **Wilson (1996)** a husband branded his initials on his wife's buttocks. It was done at her request. The CA held that this came within the exceptions. The defence of consent was allowed.

Task

Compare the different approaches adopted in **Brown** and **Wilson**.

Should consenting individuals be permitted to make their own decisions about their private behaviour without fear of prosecution? Alternatively, should the law be more protective of the victim? Write a paragraph on your thoughts and file it for essay practice.

Rough horseplay

Case law has long viewed 'manly sports' and 'manly diversions' as lawful activities. The question is how far this includes activities that are arguably not 'sport'.

In **Jones (1988)** a group of boys tossed two other boys 10 feet into the air, resulting in a ruptured spleen and a broken arm. This was construed as 'rough horseplay' and the defence allowed. In **Aitken (1992)** drunken RAF officers doused a fellow officer with white spirit and set fire to him. They were found not guilty of grievous bodily harm because it was assumed that the victim consented to '*rough and undisciplined horseplay*'.

Food for thought

These situations could be construed as violent bullying but the defence of consent was allowed. Do you think this goes too far? How far do you think the victims truly consented?

Lack of intent to cause injury seems to have influenced the decision in **Jones**. As the *mens rea* for **s. 20** includes recklessness, this is also something that you could discuss as less than satisfactory. The Ds must surely have recognised the risk that throwing someone 10 feet in the air could cause 'some harm'.

It can be argued that it is inconsistent to allow consent in cases like **Aitken** and not in cases like **Brown**. However, it appears from these cases that consent is a defence to reckless harm, but not to intentional harm. Do you think Parliament should legislate on the issue of consent?

Consent and sex

In **Clarence (1888)**, a man who infected his wife with a sexual disease was charged under **s. 20**. She did not know he had the disease. At this time it appeared an assault was required for a charge of grievous bodily harm to succeed. As she had consented to sexual intercourse the court held there was no assault and the case was dismissed.

Food for thought

Is consent to sex the same as consent to a disease? Hardly. A different view can be seen in more recent cases. The law now requires that consent is not just to the act, but to the 'quality' of the act.

In **Dica (2004)** D was convicted under s. 20 with recklessly inflicting grievous bodily harm. He had consensual sex with two women, knowing that he was HIV positive, and they both became infected with HIV. The CA referred to both **Clarence** and **Brown**. They said that on the point that consent to sexual intercourse was the same as consent to the risk of a consequential disease, **Clarence** was no longer good law. The question was whether there was consent to the risk of harm, not just consent to sex. They added that since **Brown**, D could no longer use consent to a charge of grievous bodily harm if such harm was intentional.

Food for thought

Is this decision a sign of a change of heart by the judiciary? **Brown** has been interpreted by some academics as rejecting the defence of consent based on the amount of harm. Others argue it is based on whether the harm was intended. The judgment itself is complicated and the reasoning somewhat obscure. In **Dica** the CA distinguished **Brown** because the prosecution had not alleged intent, so the defence of consent should have been left to the jury. A retrial was ordered. The CA held that although the defence would fail where grievous harm was intentional, it could succeed where such harm was inflicted recklessly, but only if the victim had consented to the risk of harm, not just the act itself. This means a case like **Clarence** could be decided differently today. It is not clear whether **Jones** or **Aitken** would be. It would seem that if harm was recklessly inflicted, then whether the defence succeeds will depend on whether the victim had consented to the risk of harm, not just to the activity itself.

Task

Do you think that the 'patients' truly consented in **Richardson**? Is the idea that the victim must be consenting to the harm or 'quality' of the act, not just the act itself, a better interpretation of consent? Look back at **Richardson** and compare to **Dica**. Write a paragraph with your views of these decisions.

Examination pointer

Much of the above can be used in an essay on the problems of the non-fatal offences generally. It also relates to law and morals.

Task

Match the case to the comment and keep it for revision.

Leach (1969)	The injury suffered during a game of rugby was serious
AG's reference (No. 6 of 1980) 1981	A husband branded his initials on his wife's buttocks
Brown (1994)	A dentist who had been suspended carried out treatment on several people
Billingshurst (1978)	A man asked to be crucified on Hampstead Heath
Richardson (1999)	The CA gave a list of circumstances which would be lawful even if harm occurred
Wilson (1996)	Consenting homosexuals engaged in sado-masochistic behaviour

Consent and other offences

This has been dealt with here in relation to the non-fatal offences against the person. For other crimes the issue is treated a little differently depending on the offence. It has therefore been dealt with in the Units on the particular offences. Here is a quick summary of how consent applies to these offences as well as to the non-fatal offences against the person.

Offence	Application of consent
Murder	Cannot use the defence of consent
Theft and related offences	Consent may be a defence but see **Morris** on consent and appropriation. Belief in the owner consenting is a defence under **s. 2 Theft Act 1968** in that it means D is not 'dishonest' and so negates *mens rea*
Criminal damage	Belief in the owner consenting is a defence under **s. 5(2) Criminal Damage Act 1971**
Assault	Can be a defence as it will make an assault lawful, e.g. in sports
Battery	Can be a defence as it will make a battery lawful, e.g. in sports

Offence	Application of consent
Assault occasioning actual bodily harm under **s. 47 Offences Against the Person Act**	As above, it may make the assault lawful but not if harm was intended: **AG's Reference (No. 6 of 1980)**
Wounding or grievous bodily harm under **s. 20 Offences Against the Person Act**	Can be a defence if D acted recklessly but not if harm was intended: **Brown**
Wounding or grievous bodily harm with intent under **s. 18 Offences Against the Person Act**	Cannot use the defence of consent: **Dica**

Summary

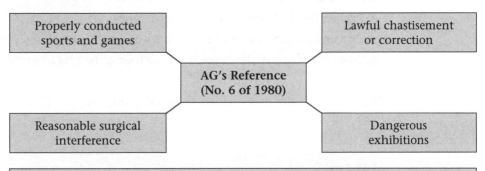

Properly conducted sports and games

Lawful chastisement or correction

AG's Reference (No. 6 of 1980)

Reasonable surgical interference

Dangerous exhibitions

BUT no consent to grievous bodily harm if such harm was intentional (**Brown**)

 ## Self-test questions

1 What point is made in **Brown** regarding consent to intentional grievous bodily harm?

2 State two of the activities where consent is implied as stated in **AG's Reference**.

3 Name one of the cases involving 'rough horseplay' where the defence was allowed.

4 Why was the conviction quashed in **Barnes (2004)**?

5 From which case did the quote at the beginning of this unit come?

 For further resources and updates please go to the Companion Website accompanying this book at **www.pearsoned.co.uk/russell**

Insanity and automatism

... and it would be an unfortunate thing if it were left to juries to consider whether some particular act was morally right or wrong. The test must be whether it is contrary to law...

Lord Goddard

By the end of this Unit you should be able to:

- Explain the different parts of these defences
- Explain how the rules on both insanity and automatism apply in practice
- Compare the two defences and explain their differences by reference to cases

There is an overlap between these two defences so we will look at them in the same Unit.

Insanity

Insanity can be relevant at three points in time. While awaiting trial, at the time of trial or at the time of the offence. The first two are not strictly defences as they mean D does not stand trial at all. It is the last one that concerns us here.

The burden of proving insanity to the jury is on D, on the balance of probabilities. The prosecution may raise insanity, in which case it must be proved beyond reasonable doubt.

Under the **Criminal Procedure (Insanity) Act 1964** the result of a successful plea of insanity was committal to a secure hospital for an indefinite period. The **Criminal Procedure (Insanity and Unfitness to Plead) Act 1991** amends the 1964 Act. The judge has increased powers and there are now four possibilities. A hospital order (indefinite or specified time), a guardianship order, a supervisory treatment order or an absolute discharge. If the charge is murder a hospital order is the only option.

Examination pointer

If the defence is successful then there is a special verdict. This is 'not guilty by reason of insanity'. When discussing the effect of a plea of insanity you should refer to the judge's powers under the **1991 Act** as 'orders'. Avoid calling them sentences. Technically, D has been found not guilty.

The defence is based on **M'Naghten's Case (1843)**.

Key case

M'Naghten fired his gun at the Tory Prime Minister Robert Peel but killed his secretary. Medical opinion showed that M'Naghten was suffering from 'morbid delusions'. He was found not guilty. Due to the public reaction to both the crime and the outcome the House of Lords formulated a set of rules. The **M'Naghten Rules** are still used today. There are two main propositions of law.

First, everyone is to be presumed to be sane until proved otherwise.

Second, insanity may be proved if, at the time of committing the act, D was *'labouring under such a defect of reason, from disease of the mind, as not to know the nature and quality of the act he was doing, or if he did know it, that he did not know he was doing wrong.'*

Let's break this defence down into the different parts.

Defect of reason

There has to be a complete deprivation of the powers of reason rather than simply a failure to exercise them. This is shown in **Clarke (1972)**. Here, D claimed that, due to depression, she had absent-mindedly put some items in her bag and so was not guilty of theft. The judge ruled that this argument amounted to insanity. She promptly changed her plea to guilty (because this was before the **1991 Act** and it would have meant being sent to a mental hospital). The CA quashed her conviction and said temporary absent-mindedness was not a defect of reason, it merely denied *mens rea*.

Lack of self-control or willpower isn't insanity – or those of us who just can't walk past a chocolate shop without buying something would be classed as insane.

Task

Look back at Unit 16 on *mens rea* and the case of **Madeley**, where the host of a TV show had a similar argument. The court decided he was not guilty. What was the reason in that case?

Disease of the mind

The defect of reason must be caused by a disease of the mind. The meaning of 'disease of the mind' is a legal question for the judge to decide rather than a medical one. However, D will need medical evidence from two experts. This is a requirement of **s. 1 Criminal Procedure (Insanity and Unfitness to Plead) Act 1991**.

So what is it then? In **Bratty v AG for Northern Ireland (1963)** Lord Denning said a disease of the mind was *'any mental disorder which has manifested itself in violence and is prone to recur'*.

In **Kemp (1957)** Devlin J said, *'the condition of the brain is irrelevant and so is the question of whether the condition of the mind is curable or incurable, transitory or permanent'*. This indicates a temporary state can still be insanity. It would appear, though, that it is more often accepted where the disease is of a permanent nature or, in Lord Denning's words, 'prone to recur'.

A lot of case law turns on this issue of 'disease'. This has led to a distinction between *internal* factors and *external* factors. If the 'defect of reason' is caused by an internal factor (a disease) it is likely to be insanity. If it is caused by an external factor (like a blow to the head and concussion) then it is likely to be automatism. The distinction is most easily explained by looking at some cases.

Kemp (1957) – D had arteriosclerosis (narrowing of the arteries which reduces the flow of blood to the brain). This caused occasional lapses of consciousness. During one such period he killed his wife by striking her with a hammer. His defence was treated as insanity.

Quick (1973) – A diabetic nurse at a psychiatric hospital attacked one of the patients. He argued that this was because at the time he was suffering from hypoglycaemia as a result of failing to eat after taking his insulin. The CA held the 'defect' was caused by an external factor, i.e. the insulin itself. This would be automatism, not insanity.

Sullivan (1984) – D hit out at someone trying to help him during an epileptic fit and was convicted of actual bodily harm. The HL confirmed that the appropriate defence would be insanity and that epilepsy was a 'disease of the mind' which had caused a 'defect of reason'.

Hennessey (1989) – D was a diabetic. He had taken a car and driven while disqualified. He argued automatism caused by failure to take his insulin. The CA upheld the judge's finding of insanity on the basis that the cause was the disease itself.

Burgess (1991) – D claimed he was sleepwalking when he hit V over the head with a bottle. He was charged with wounding with intent and raised the defence of automatism. The judge held that the cause was an internal factor and so it was a disease of the mind. He was found not guilty by reason of insanity and detained in a mental hospital. However, in **Bilton (2005) (unreported)**, the defence of automatism was successfully used when D raped a girl while sleepwalking.

Task

Look at the sequence of events in the diagram. If you take out any 'non-events' it is easier to see what caused the defect of reason. On the left it is the insulin (external) and on the right the diabetes (internal). Do the same for **Quick** and **Hennessey** and then write a summary of each, highlighting the differences.

D has diabetes	Both these are non-events so can be ignored. If you take them out then on the left you would go from insulin (external) to defect. On the right from diabetes (internal) to defect	D has diabetes
D takes insulin		
⬇		⬇
D fails to eat (a non-event)		D fails to take insulin (a non-event)
D has a defect of reason		D has a defect of reason
Caused by the insulin, which is an external factor		Caused by the diabetes itself, an internal factor, so a disease of the mind
Automatism		**Insanity**

A 'defect of reason' caused by external factors (automatism) would usually be temporary whereas if caused by internal factors (insanity) it may be more permanent. This would need treating in order to protect the public, so a hospital order may be appropriate. In **Bratty**, Lord Denning said a disorder which led to violence and was prone to recur was *'the sort of disease for which a person should be retained in hospital rather than be given an unqualified acquittal'*. **Burgess** shows that a temporary state can amount to insanity so there is a fine line between the two defences.

Food for thought

In cases like **Bratty** and **Kemp** the defence of insanity may be appropriate. D's acts were to some extent purposeful and there is a danger to the public. The case of an epileptic thrashing out and hitting someone during a fit would be less easy to justify. There is a problem with finding insanity in respect of people whose conditions are not normally associated with mental disorder. Use the 'diabetes' cases to support a discussion of these problems. **Burgess** is also arguably too wide a definition. Should a sleepwalker be classed as insane? It leads to a second issue. Once insanity is raised – and remember this can be by the prosecution or the judge as well as D – D will often change their plea to guilty to avoid the insanity verdict. This is what happened in **Sullivan**. He pleaded guilty after the judge ruled the defence was insanity and was convicted of actual bodily harm. In **Quick**, on the other hand, the defect was held to be caused by the insulin itself. D's appeal succeeded because the defence of automatism should have been left to the jury.

A final point is that the stigma of an insanity verdict may also mean people who genuinely do have a mental problem do not plead the defence.

Does not know the nature and quality of the act

In **Codere (1916)** this was held to mean the physical nature of the act, not its moral nature.

In **Bratty**, a man who killed a girl with her stocking was found not guilty by reason of insanity because it was held that his epilepsy may have prevented him knowing the 'nature and quality' of the act.

If D is suffering from insane delusions he will not succeed in the defence of insanity if he knows the nature of what he is doing.

Example | D hears imaginary voices telling him to kill someone. He does this. The defence will fail if he knew that he was killing someone when he obeyed the voices in his head.

Does not appreciate that it is wrong

If D knows that the act is wrong then there is no defence. It is a question of whether D realises it is *legally* wrong, not whether D believes it is morally right or wrong. In **Windle (1952)** D killed his wife with an overdose of aspirin. There was evidence of mental illness but on giving himself up he said, 'I suppose they will hang me for this', thereby indicating he knew that what he had done was legally wrong. In the CA Lord Goddard said, '*It would be an unfortunate thing if it were left to juries to consider whether some particular act was morally right or wrong. The test must be whether it is contrary to law.*' The conviction was upheld.

Example | Jack goes on a killing spree and murders several young prostitutes. He believes clearing the streets of prostitutes is morally justified. This would be outside the rules. Jack knows it is against the law to kill.

Examination pointer

There is an overlap with diminished responsibility so in a murder case you may need to discuss both. Until the **1991 Act** the only possible order following a successful insanity defence was detention in a mental hospital. It was therefore mainly used in murder cases. Now there are four possible orders, it may be used for other crimes more often.

The defence of diminished responsibility under the **Homicide Act 1957** is wider though.

Food for thought

The defence originates from an 1843 case and it could be argued that because of medical advances it should be updated. Judges themselves have called for Parliament to look at the insanity defence.

There are arguments that the law could breach Article 5 of the European Convention on Human Rights, which states that a person of unsound mind can only be detained where proper objective medical expertise has been sought.

The **1953 Royal Commission on Capital Punishment** recommended the abolishment of the M'Naghten Rules.

The **Homicide Act 1957** introduced diminished responsibility shortly after this which addresses some of the criticisms made. In 1975 the **Butler Committee** favoured replacing the rules with a new verdict of 'mental disorder'. This would arise where D was suffering from 'severe mental illness' or 'severe mental handicap'. The burden of proof would also move to the prosecution. The **Law Commission's Draft Code** adopts many of Butler's recommendations. If this were to be implemented it would allow automatism for sleepwalking and spasms.

Insanity and intoxication

If the defect of reason comes about through intoxication, it won't be insanity. If it comes from alcoholism it could be as this can be classed as a 'disease'. In **Lipman**, D had taken LSD and had a hallucination where he thought he was fighting snakes. He killed his girlfriend by stuffing a sheet down her throat. He did not know the quality of his act but, as the LSD was external, it would not be insanity. He was convicted of manslaughter.

Examination pointer

The defences of insanity and automatism are closely linked so you may need to discuss both. However, note that the automatism defence would be better as it results in an acquittal.

Automatism

We saw in Unit 14 that the *actus reus* must be voluntary. The defence of automatism arises where D's act was 'automatic' and so was not voluntary. Thus it is negating *actus reus* rather than *mens rea*. It is also referred to as 'non-insane automatism' to distinguish it from insanity, which can be called 'insane automatism'. Automatism is a very limited defence but if successful it leads to a complete acquittal, so it would be preferred to pleading insanity.

D has to show:

● the act was involuntary;

● this was due to an external factor.

The act was involuntary

Automatism was defined by Lord Denning in **Bratty *v* Attorney General for NI (1963):**

'. . . *automatism means an act which is done by the muscles without any control by the mind such as a spasm, a reflex action or a convulsion or an act done by a person who is not conscious of what he is doing* . . .'

Thus D is arguing lack of control over bodily movements. There must be no control at all.

Key case

In **Attorney General's Reference (No. 2 of 1992) 1994**, D killed two people when his lorry crashed into a car on the hard shoulder of the motorway. He pleaded automatism on the grounds that driving for so long on a motorway had resulted in a 'trance like' state and he was suffering from what is called 'driving without awareness'. On referral to the CA it was held that this did not amount to automatism because his lack of awareness was not total. Thus if D's behaviour is only partly automatic, there is no defence. This confirmed **Broome v Perkins (1987)** where a diabetic, suffering from hypoglycaemia, hit another car. It was held that, as D was able to exercise *some* control, automatism was not available.

This was due to an external factor

The essence of automatism is that the crime was the result of an external factor causing an involuntary act on the part of the defendant. If it was an internal factor then the defence is insanity. As we saw with insanity, this distinction has produced some fairly bizarre cases.

External factors would include being hit over the head or attacked by a swarm of bees. The latter was given as a hypothetical example in **Hill v Baxter (1958)**. It was said, *obiter*, that if D was attacked by a swarm of bees while driving a car, causing him to lose control, the defence of automatism would succeed.

Automatism and intoxication

As D must be acting involuntarily the defence cannot be relied upon if the automatism was self-induced, e.g. by drinking or taking drugs, as in **Lipman**, above.

In **Quick**, Lawton LJ said, 'A self-induced incapacity will not excuse . . . nor will one which could have been reasonably foreseen as a result of either doing, or omitting to do something, as, for example, taking alcohol against medical advice after using certain prescribed drugs, or failing to have regular meals while taking insulin . . .' It would appear from this that if you knew you had a heart condition and then drove, you could not argue automatism if you had a heart attack and crashed into someone. However, the 'self-induced' rule does not seem to have been applied very consistently.

In **Hardie (1984)** D set fire to a bedroom after taking Valium. The court held that he could successfully plead automatism even though the pills were not prescribed by a doctor. A distinction was made between drugs which are meant to calm you and ones which are likely to lead to aggressive or unpredictable behaviour.

In **Bailey (1983)** D was suffering from hypoglycaemia due to a failure to eat properly. He hit his ex-girlfriend's new boyfriend over the head with an iron bar. The CA rejected his appeal as there was clearly not a complete loss of control over his bodily movements (going to the man's house armed with an iron bar was a bit of a giveaway!). They made clear that self-induced automatism by voluntarily consuming drink or drugs would not be acceptable. However, they indicated that a case such as his could have been, even though his state was arguably self-induced, because he could have eaten something.

Food for thought

The CA in **Quick** implied that failing to eat makes automatism self-induced. It was not fully clear as they merely held that the defence of automatism should have been left to the jury. In **Bailey** the same court suggested that while drink or drugs would mean the defect is self-induced, failing to eat would not. This leaves the law insufficiently clear.

More food for thought

The rules on insanity and automatism have led to sleepwalkers and diabetics being labelled insane – sometimes. The difference between not taking insulin and taking it but not eating properly are small but lead to a huge difference for D. The result is either that D is found insane or goes free.

Do you agree with Lawton LJ? In **Quick** he said the defence was a *'quagmire of law seldom entered nowadays save by those in desperate need of some kind of defence'*. Not very reassuring!

Summary

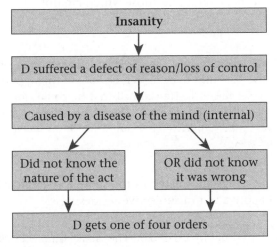
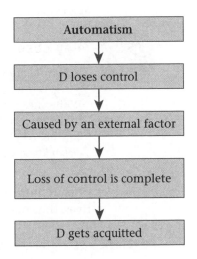

Insanity
↓
D suffered a defect of reason/loss of control
↓
Caused by a disease of the mind (internal)

Did not know the nature of the act	OR did not know it was wrong

D gets one of four orders

Automatism
↓
D loses control
↓
Caused by an external factor
↓
Loss of control is complete
↓
D gets acquitted

Self-test questions

1 From which case do the insanity rules come?

2 From which case did the quote opening this unit come?

3 Which defence applies when the cause is external?

4 Which defence applies when the cause is internal?

5 Give a case example for each of these defences to show this difference.

Intoxication

If a man, whilst sane and sober, forms an intention to kill... he cannot rely on this self-induced drunkenness as a defence to murder.

Lord Denning

By the end of this Unit you should be able to:
- Distinguish between voluntary and involuntary intoxication
- Explain how the courts treat different types of drug
- Explain the difference between specific intent and basic intent
- Show how the defence applies by reference to cases

Although traditionally this defence only applied to drink it is now clear that the rules on intoxication apply to both drink and drugs. In cases regarding drugs a distinction has been made between those which are commonly known to cause aggressive or dangerous behaviour and those which are not.

Key case

In **Hardie (1985)** D was trying to get his ex-girlfriend to get back together with him. She gave him a sedative (Valium) to calm him down and then left him in her flat. While she was out he set fire to it. He claimed that he could not remember anything after he had taken the drug. The CA allowed his appeal against conviction and held Valium was *'wholly different from drugs which are liable to cause unpredictability and aggressiveness'*.

Thus 'unpredictable' drugs are treated in the same way as alcohol. With sedatives, the courts will apply a test of subjective recklessness.

Example

D is given antidepressant drugs by his doctor. They make him feel sick and he doesn't eat for several days. Together with the pills, lack of food has the effect of making him prone to outbursts of violence. During one such period he lashes out at someone and is charged with assault. He argues intoxication as a defence.

The question will be whether he was reckless, i.e. appreciated the risk that taking the drug would lead to such aggressive and unpredictable behaviour. If he was not told about any possible side effects then it is unlikely he will be seen as reckless. However, if the doctor had warned him to eat regularly to avoid any side effects then his defence will probably fail.

Intoxication is only a defence if it can be shown that due to the intoxication D was incapable of forming the necessary intent. This was established many years ago in **Beard (1920)**. The rules for the defence differ depending on whether D was drunk voluntarily or not.

Involuntary intoxication

This would occur where D did not knowingly take alcohol or drugs. An example would be drinking orange juice which someone had 'spiked', e.g. added vodka to. The intoxication must do more than make D lose their inhibitions, though. It must remove *mens rea*.

Key case

In **Kingston (1994)** D was given drinks which had been laced with drugs. He was then photographed indecently assaulting a 15-year-old boy. He admitted that at the time of committing the offence he had the necessary intent, but said that he would not have acted in that way had he been sober. The HL overturned the decision of the CA and held that intoxicated intent was still intent. Intoxication is therefore no defence if the defendant had the necessary *mens rea*, even if it is formed while involuntarily intoxicated.

In **Allen (1988)** the CA made it clear that the intoxication had to be completely involuntary. Thus, not knowing the strength of what you are drinking would not be enough. Here, D had drunk home-made wine, not realising it was very strong. He then pleaded involuntary intoxication when charged with indecent assault. The CA held that he had freely been drinking wine, knowing it to be wine. It was therefore voluntary intoxication.

Task

Refer back to the Unit on insanity and automatism. Read the facts of **Lipman** again. Make a note of which defence was argued and which succeeded. Why was this? We will come back to this case later to see the overlap between the defences.

Voluntary intoxication

The basic rule on intoxication is that it can provide a defence to crimes of specific intent but not those of basic intent. In simple terms the distinction is this: if a crime can only be committed intentionally then it is a crime of specific intent. If it can be committed with some other form of *mens rea*, e.g. recklessness, it is a crime of basic intent.

Key case

This distinction was made in **Majewski (1977)** where the HL held that intoxication could not negate the *mens rea* where the required *mens rea* was recklessness. Essentially, getting drunk was seen as reckless in itself. D had been charged with an assault after a pub fight. He argued that he was too drunk to know what he was doing. The HL upheld his conviction and stated that evidence of self-induced intoxication which negated *mens rea* was a defence to a crime requiring specific intent but not to any other crime.

Example

While drunk, Sue takes someone's bag and is charged with theft. This is a specific intent crime. Sue's intoxication defence can succeed if she can show that she lacked *mens rea*. The *mens rea* for theft is 'intent to permanently deprive' another. She might show that because she was drunk she thought it was hers and so she had no intent to deprive anyone else of it.

If she destroyed the bag she could not use the defence to a charge of criminal damage. This offence can be committed by 'intending . . . or being reckless as to whether property is destroyed'. The fact that this can be done by 'being reckless' makes it a basic intent crime.

Note that if you plead intoxication to a specific intent crime then you will still be guilty of any related basic intent crime. If charged with murder this would be manslaughter. If charged with **s. 18 Offences Against the Person Act 1861** the result would be a conviction under **s. 20**. This is because you are using intoxication to negate the *mens rea* of intention. **Majewski** shows, however, that you will still be deemed 'reckless'. If there is no related basic intent crime then D may be acquitted. An example would be theft.

Examination pointer

Look carefully at the facts and at how D became intoxicated. First decide if it is voluntary or not. If it is then use **Majewski**, if not then use **Kingston**. You may need both if the matter isn't clear. Look at the type of intoxicant; if it is a drug you will need to look at the distinction made in **Hardie**, between drugs likely to cause aggression and sedatives. Taking unpredictable drugs is likely to be seen as voluntary intoxication.

Did you do the task on **Lipman**? It can help identify the overlap between defences. Let's take a look at how:

A possible defence is insanity. He clearly had a 'defect of reason' and he did not know 'the nature and quality' of his act. He thought he was fighting snakes, not strangling his girlfriend. However, the defect was not caused by a 'disease of the mind' but by the LSD. This is an external factor so consider automatism. The defence of automatism fails because the loss of control was self-induced (taking LSD). It was not involuntary. The defence of intoxication can be argued. The effect of the drug meant he did not have the required *mens rea* for murder. There was no proven intent so the conviction was for manslaughter, not murder. The specific intent crime (murder) became a basic intent crime (manslaughter).

Food for thought

As we saw when looking at *mens rea* in Unit 16, the **Criminal Justice Act 1967** requires the jury to decide whether D did 'intend or foresee' the result by reference to 'all the evidence'. **Majewski** seems to dispense with this requirement. If D is drunk then that is enough to prove recklessness. No other evidence is required. This favours the prosecution who will not have the usual job of proving *mens rea*. It is also wider than the usual test for recklessness. Usually the prosecution must prove that 'D recognised a risk and went ahead anyway'. Not quite the same as D was drunk.

The 'Dutch courage' rule

What if D forms the required *mens rea* and *then* gets drunk and commits an offence? This may occur where D becomes intoxicated in order to summon up the courage to commit the offence. This is called the 'Dutch courage' rule.

In **Attorney General for Northern Ireland *v* Gallagher (1963)** D decided to kill his wife. He bought a knife and a bottle of whisky. He drank the whisky and then stabbed her. The HL held that once a person formed an intention to kill then the defence would fail. Lord Denning made the main speech and also gave two examples of when intoxication might succeed: where a nurse at a christening got so drunk that she put the baby on the fire in mistake for a log and, second, where a drunken man thought his friend, lying in bed, was a theatrical dummy and stabbed him to death. Lord Denning said that in both cases D would have a defence to a murder charge. This latter is not dissimilar to **Lipman**, where D thought he was fighting snakes and ended up strangling his girlfriend.

Food for thought

In **Gallagher**, the HL held that once a person formed an intention to kill then the defence would fail. At first glance this seems fine. After all, D did have *mens rea* because he planned to kill her and went and bought a knife. That he was too intoxicated to possess intent when the act was carried out is arguably irrelevant. It can be seen as inconsistent with the normal rules of law though. The usual requirement is that *mens rea* and *actus reus* occur together.

Lord Denning's examples show that intoxication and mistake are closely linked. We will deal with mistake separately but for the moment let's just look at the overlap.

Intoxicated mistakes

Often intoxication is relied on to support a defence of mistake. There are conflicting cases here. It would seem that if the offence allows for a particular belief to be a defence (e.g. the **Theft Act** allows that if D believed the owner would consent to the taking there is no theft) then even a mistake arising from intoxication can be used. It is clear from the Act and subsequent case law that such a belief does not have to be reasonable so there is some sense in this. However, where there is no such defence, e.g. in common law crimes such as murder and assault, then it seems that intoxication cannot support a defence of mistake.

We will look at some cases when covering the defence of mistake, but here's an example.

Example

Tom has been to a party and is drunk. He can't cope with walking home but doesn't have money for a taxi. Without bothering to ask he takes £10 from someone's bag. He is charged with theft. He argues that in his drunken state he thought the owner wouldn't mind. He has a defence if he can convince the jury this belief was genuine, even if it was unreasonable.

Vicky is walking home from the same party. Someone approaches and as she is drunk she has trouble focusing. She thinks she is going to be attacked. She hits out with her umbrella. It turns out it was a friend from the party coming to offer her a lift. Her defence to an assault charge will fail because her mistake was caused by the intoxication.

Public policy

Public policy is one reason why the courts will not allow intoxicated mistake as a defence. It is not in the public interest to allow people who get drunk and then commit an offence to be able to rely on intoxication as a defence. In **O'Grady (1987)** (see p. 247) the CA refused to allow the defence and said:

'There are two competing interests. On the one hand the interest of the defendant who has only acted according to what he believed to be necessary to protect himself, and on the other hand that of the public in general, and the victim in particular who, probably through no fault of his own, has been injured or perhaps killed because of the defendant's drunken mistake. Reason recoils from the conclusion that in such circumstances a defendant is entitled to leave the court without a stain on his character.'

Food for thought

The law is complex and juries are confused by the different rules. The **Majewski** 'rules' are less than exact. It is not fully clear which crimes are specific intent and which are basic. The jury will have to decide whether D was knowingly taking an 'unpredictable' drug or a sedative. This distinction is also unclear.

The law on intoxication and mistake is also a problem. As we saw in my example, you cannot rely on a drunken mistake – except where statute provides that a certain belief will be a defence.

Task

Draw up a flow chart or diagram using the following cases. Note for each whether insanity, automatism or intoxication applied and why.

Lipman (1970)   Bailey (1983)   Hardie (1984)   Hennessy (1989)

Summary

D is intoxicated by drink or drugs			
Voluntary		**Involuntary**	
Knowingly intoxicated or takes unpredictable drugs		Unknowingly intoxicated or takes sedatives	
Majewski rules		Defence will succeed only if it negates *mens rea* – **Kingston**	
Specific intent crime	Basic intent crime	D has *mens rea*	D does not have *mens rea*
Defence succeeds in part. Reduces to any connected basic intent crime	No defence	No defence	Defence succeeds
Note the 'Dutch courage' rule. Even in specific intent crimes if D forms an intent and then gets intoxicated the defence will fail. Mens rea *already exists.*			

Self-test questions

1 What is the difference between specific and basic intent?

2 Name a crime for each type.

3 What is 'Dutch courage' and will it provide a defence?

4 If D successfully pleads intoxication to a specific intent crime such as murder what is the result?

5 From which case did the quote at the beginning of this unit come?

For further resources and updates please go to the Companion Website accompanying this book at www.pearsoned.co.uk/russell

Self-defence and mistake

. . . a person defending himself cannot weigh to a nicety the exact measure of his necessary defensive action.

The Privy Council in **Palmer (1971)**

By the end of this Unit you should be able to:
- Explain the defences of self-defence, defence of another and prevention of crime
- Explain the defence of mistake
- Identify the principles on which these defences rely and how they overlap
- Refer to appropriate case examples

These two defences are discussed together because there is a big overlap between them and many cases apply to both.

Self-defence

The law allows a defence where D is doing something that would otherwise be an offence, but is acting to protect certain public and private interests. The term 'public and private defence' is used to cover prevention of crime, self-defence, defence of another and defence of property. It is commonly just called self-defence, but this term actually only covers defending yourself or another. Prevention of crime is a statutory defence and self-defence is a common law one. There is a clear overlap because in many cases defending yourself may well also be preventing a crime. The principles which have developed are essentially the same so we will look at the rules after a brief explanation of each defence.

Prevention of crime

This defence is found in **s. 3(1)** of the **Criminal Law Act 1967**, which provides that a person:

*'may use **such force as is reasonable in the circumstances** in the prevention of crime, or in effecting or assisting in the lawful arrest of offenders or suspected offenders or of persons unlawfully at large.'*

| Example | I see a man snatch someone's handbag. I chase him and use a rugby tackle to stop him getting away. This causes severe bruising as he falls. If I am charged (unlikely) with an assault I can use **s. 3**. I was using 'reasonable' force to make a citizen's arrest. Had I tackled him as he grabbed it then I can argue I used 'reasonable' force to prevent a crime. |

The main point here is that the defence is only available if the force used is *reasonable in the circumstances*.

Self-defence and defence of another

Self-defence applies when force is used in protection of a person, whether oneself or another. In my example above I am also defending the person whose bag was snatched and so could use self-defence as an alternative argument, even though I am not defending myself, but someone else. It is a common law defence, which has been developed by the courts. The burden is on the prosecution to satisfy the jury that the defendant was *not* acting in self-defence. There are various issues to consider.

The rules

Three main questions arise:

- Should D have retreated?
- Did D honestly believe the action was justified? (What D thought; a subjective question);
- Was the degree of force reasonable in the circumstances? (What a *reasonable person* would do; an objective question).

Should D have retreated?

Early cases indicated that in order for the defence to succeed, D should show there was no possibility of retreat. It is now clear, however, that this is just one factor for the jury to take into account in deciding whether the force was reasonable. In **McInnes (1971)** the CA said that a person is not obliged to retreat from a threat in order to rely on the defence, but that this may be evidence for the jury when considering whether force was necessary, and if so whether it was reasonable.

There must, however, be an imminent threat. The defence failed in **Malnik v DPP (1989)**. D had armed himself with a martial arts weapon and gone to visit a man whom he believed had stolen some cars. He was arrested when approaching the house. He argued that the man was known to be violent, so having the weapon to protect himself was justified. The court held that the defence was not available because he had put himself in danger by going to the house. There had been no imminent threat.

Example | I disturb a burglar in my house and, feeling rather brave, hit him over the head with a china vase. While he lies unconscious at my feet I kick him in the ribs a few times to punish him for daring to enter my house. The first action may be self-defence. The second is not. There is no threat and I am merely exacting revenge.

In **Martin (2001)** the jury had rejected a plea of self-defence by a farmer who shot and killed a burglar and seriously injured another. According to evidence, they were retreating and posing no threat.

The subjective and objective questions are now the main issues for the jury. The first is whether D believed that the action which made up the offence was justified. The second relates to whether the action taken was reasonable. The prosecution will have to convince the jury that either the action was *not* justified or that *unreasonable* force was used.

Did D honestly believe the action was justified?

As we saw in the opening quote, in **Palmer (1971)** it is recognised that D 'cannot weigh to a nicety the exact measure of his necessary defensive action'. Thus, use of excessive force may be acceptable if D 'honestly and instinctively' thought it necessary in the circumstances. This is a subjective test. It is what D *believes* is necessary that is important. This ties in with the defence of mistake, discussed below. If D mistakenly believes someone is being attacked or threatened then self-defence may still be relied on, even if there was no actual threat. This can be seen in **Williams (Gladstone) (1987)**. A man saw a woman being robbed by a youth and struggled with him. D came on the scene and believed the youth to be under attack. He punched the man and was charged with actual bodily harm. His defence succeeded. The court held that D was to be judged on the facts *as he saw them*.

Was the degree of force reasonable in the circumstances?

This is a matter for the jury to decide based on the circumstances of the case, and the nature of the threat. The test here is objective. After some doubt this was confirmed in **Martin (2001)**.

Key case

In **Martin** the defence failed because the jury thought that using a pump-action shotgun to kill a 16-year-old burglar was excessive force in the circumstances. In the CA, Woolf LCJ confirmed that the farmer was entitled to use reasonable force to protect himself and his home, but that the jury were '*surely correct in coming to their judgment that Mr Martin was not acting reasonably*'.

He confirmed that the jury could only convict if either:

● they did not believe his evidence that he was acting in self-defence or
● they thought that Mr Martin had used an unreasonable amount of force

Referring to the subjective and objective questions, he went on to say:

'*As to the first issue, what Mr Martin believed, the jury heard his evidence and they could only reject that evidence, if they were satisfied it was untrue. As to the second issue, as to what is a reasonable amount of force, obviously opinions can differ . . . it was for the jury, as the representative of the public, to decide the amount of force which it would be reasonable and the amount of force which it would be unreasonable to use in the circumstances.'*

Food for thought

It can be argued that the law on self-defence should be made statutory and clarified. In early 2005 the Conservative Party called on the government to act. They argued that all bar 'grossly disproportionate' action could be justified as self-defence. The government argued that the law as it stood gave householders the protection they needed. However, they recognised that people did not understand this, and had a leaflet produced by the police and CPS in an attempt to clarify the issue.

Task

Go to the CPS website (http://www.cps.gov.uk/legal/section5/chapter_d.html) and look at the leaflet. Make some notes on what is said about reasonable force. This can be used in an evaluation of the law. Also look at the case examples given and add to your notes.

Examination pointer

If the defence of self-defence succeeds then D is acquitted. The defence either negates mens rea or means actus reus is not proved. As with consent, self-defence most often goes with the non-fatal offences against the person. For example, battery is the unlawful application of force. If you can show that D acted in self-defence and did not use excessive force, then the 'unlawful' part of the actus reus is missing. D may be found not guilty. It should not be forgotten, however, that self-defence can also apply to murder. The main issue would be whether killing someone was using excessive force. This will be a question for the jury based on the circumstances or, if mistake is also present, the circumstances as D believes them to be.

Mistake

Before looking at the overlap with self-defence we will take a brief look at its own rules.

Mistake as to the law is never a defence. You cannot say 'I did not know that what I did was against the law'. Mistake as to a fact can be used as a defence in two ways:

- where it negates *mens rea*;
- where it is used to justify an action.

If successful, the defence will result in an acquittal. This is because either the *mens rea* or the *actus reus* have not been proved.

Mistake and *mens rea*

In some crimes mistake is relevant to *mens rea*. Thus, in theft, an honestly held belief in a right to take property negates the *mens rea* of dishonesty, even if that belief was mistaken.

> **Example** In **Small (1987)** D had taken a car which had been left for over a week with the keys in the ignition. He argued that he believed that it had been abandoned and so he had a right to take it. This meant he was not dishonest, and so had no *mens rea*. The CA quashed his conviction.

Mistake and justification

A mistake may excuse or *justify* an act. For example, **s. 5(2)** of the **Criminal Damage Act 1971** allows a defence of 'lawful excuse' where D believed that the owner would consent to the damage, even if that belief was mistaken. Thus in **Jaggard v Dickenson (1981)** D broke into a house mistakenly believing that it belonged to a friend and that her friend would have consented to the damage caused. This justified her actions and thus provided a 'lawful excuse'. Mistake is commonly seen along with self-defence in relation to the non-fatal offences against the person.

> **Example** I mistakenly believe I am about to be attacked. I hit my supposed assailant over the head with my umbrella. If I am charged with battery or actual bodily harm, I will use the defence of mistake to *justify* the 'application of force'.

In **Williams (Gladstone) (1987)**, above, D argued that his actions were justified because he believed he was defending the youth. He successfully argued self-defence based on this mistaken belief.

Does the belief have to be reasonable?

It was held in the bigamy case of **Tolson (1889)** that the defence could only be relied upon if D could establish that the mistake was a *reasonable one* to make. However, in **DPP v Morgan (1976)** this case was distinguished.

Key case

In **Morgan**, an RAF officer invited three men back to his home to have sex with his wife. He told them that she would protest but that this was all part of her sexual fantasy. They were found guilty of rape. It would only be rape if it occurred without the woman's consent. They argued that they *believed* she did consent. The jury did not accept this argument. When the case reached the HL it was held that a mistake does not have to be *reasonable*, but must be *honestly held*. On the facts the HL found that the jury would have convicted anyway and upheld the conviction. However, the point of law established was that *the mistake need not be reasonable*. It may help to convince a jury if it is though, because the less reasonable the mistake then the more likely it is that the jury will not believe it was honestly made.

In **B v DPP (2000)** the HL implied that the decision in **Tolson** was no longer good law. This was a sexual offence case where D had argued a mistaken belief that the girl in question was over 16. The HL held that, as established in **Morgan**, it was not necessary for the mistake to be reasonable. In **K (2001)** this unanimous HL judgment was approved. D had been charged with indecent assault on a girl of 14. He argued a mistaken belief that she was over 16. The HL accepted that as long as his mistake was honest, it need not be reasonable. Although **Tolson** has not been overruled it would now appear that it is confined to its own facts, i.e. it only applies to bigamy cases.

The overlap

Mistake is often used in conjunction with self-defence, as we saw in **Williams (Gladstone) (1987)**. D may use a mistake to justify the use of force, thus making it reasonable.

In **Martin (2001)** Woolf LCJ confirmed:

> '*In judging whether the defendant had only used reasonable force, the jury has to take into account all the circumstances, including the situation as the defendant honestly believes it to be at the time, when he was defending himself. It does not matter if the defendant was mistaken in his belief as long as his belief was genuine.*'

Intoxication

An intoxicated mistake will not provide a defence, even though the mistake may have been honestly made. Thus a mistake can be an unreasonable one, but not a drunken one.

In **O'Grady (1987)** D hit his friend over the head in the mistaken belief that the friend was trying to kill him. Both of them were drunk at the time. He was convicted of manslaughter and appealed. The CA rejected his appeal and said he could not rely on a drunken mistake to justify his actions. It was not fully clear whether this would apply to specific intent crimes such as murder, but in **Hatton (2005)** the CA said the rule applied whether the charge was murder or manslaughter.

Food for thought

The courts are reluctant to allow intoxicated mistake as a defence for public policy reasons. In **O'Grady**, the CA said that the interests of the public and the victim should be balanced against those of the defendant and '*Reason recoils from the conclusion that in such circumstances a defendant is entitled to leave the court without a stain on his character*'.

It has often been said that policy issues are a matter for an elected government and Parliament, not the courts. A related problem is that, if successful, mistake and self-defence lead to an acquittal, 'without a stain on his character'. Arguably the law on self-defence, mistake and intoxication need some clarification by Parliament.

Task

Discuss what defence(s) Amy should use in the following situations, using a case to support this and explaining whether it is likely to be successful and, if so, the effect it will have.

1   Amy is walking down the street one dark and rainy night when a young man steps out of a doorway right in front of her. Being a paranoid sort of person she thinks she is being attacked and strikes out in alarm, cutting his cheek. In fact he was just coming from his own house.

2   Walking home from the pub in a drunken haze Amy sees what she thinks is a man with a weapon coming towards her. She picks up a brick and hits him over the head, causing severe concussion and a nasty cut. It turns out he is from the local radio and is interviewing people on the streets for their views on violence at closing time.

3   Amy is walking down the street when she sees someone whom she believes is assaulting a young man. She intervenes and attacks him but he promptly arrests her. It turns out he is a policeman in plain clothes.

Examination pointer

Note that mistake occurs either to negate mens rea or to justify an act. In the latter case you will often need to discuss self-defence. Self-defence can, for example, make a battery lawful, therefore taking away part of the actus reus.

Summary

D is judged on the facts as they are believed to be, even if that belief is mistaken

Did D honestly believe that self-defence was justified? (**Williams (Gladstone)**)

Was the force reasonable in the circumstances? (**Martin**)

Mistake can remove *mens rea* (**Small/B *v* DPP**)

Mistake can justify an act (**Jaggard *v* Dickenson**)

Mistake need not be reasonable (**Morgan/K 2001**)

D can't rely on a drunken mistake (**O' Grady**)

Self-test questions

1   What are the two ways in which the defence of mistake can be used?

2   Why was self-defence rejected by the jury in **Martin**?

3 Which phrase from the case of **Palmer** was used in the government leaflet on self-defence?

4 Can you use the following types of mistake when arguing that you were using self-defence:
   (a) **a mistake of law?**
   (b) **an unreasonable mistake?**
   (c) **a drunken mistake?**

For further resources and updates please go to the Companion Website accompanying this book at **www.pearsoned.co.uk/russell**

You will not need to evaluate the law on defences so this summary merely looks at the application of the law. An important thing to note is the *effect* of defences. This will help you decide which one is most appropriate.

Defence	Main points	Which crimes	Effect
Consent	Must consent to the harm **Dica**	Not intentional GBH/wounding or murder	Acquittal
Insanity	Defect of reason caused by disease of the mind (internal factor) **M'Naghten** Rules	All	Not guilty by reason of insanity
Automatism	Must be a total loss of control (caused by an external factor) **Broome *v* Perkins**	All	Acquittal
Intoxication – involuntary	Must remove *mens rea* **Kingston**	All crimes requiring *mens rea*	Acquittal
Intoxication – voluntary	**Majewski**	Specific intent crimes Basic intent crimes	Reduces to basic intent crime Guilty
Self-defence	Force must be reasonable **Martin**	All	Acquittal
Mistake	Must be genuine but need not be reasonable **K (2001)**	All	Acquittal

Task

Add the principle and brief facts to the case

Case	Principle	Facts
AG's Reference (No. 6 of 1980) 1981		
Brown		
Dica		
Sullivan		
Broome v Perkins		
Kingston		
Majewski		
Williams (Gladstone)		

Key criticisms

You no longer need to evaluate these defences but look at the Module 6 connections for how you might relate the problems to the wider concepts.

Examination practice

There is no longer an essay question on defences so for examination practice look at the problem questions at the end of this Part. You will need to consider the appropriate defences in any application of the law.

Module 6 connections

Morals	Insanity and automatism can be used where D does not recognise the act is wrong or is not in control Some of the cases on consent seem to be decided on moral rather than legal grounds Is bullying immoral? It seems that the 'boys will be boys' view prevails	M'Naghten Bratty Broome *v* Perkins Brown Jones
Justice	Is it just to find a diabetic insane? Also sleepwalking has come under insanity although the defence of automatism was successfully used when D raped a girl while sleepwalking	Sullivan Burgess Bilton (2005) (unreported)
Conflicting interests	The restrictions on intoxication recognise that there are competing interests between D, the public and the victim. This is especially clear in 'drunken mistake' cases where D acts according to a mistaken belief but the interests of the public and the victim outweigh D's	Kingston O'Grady
Fault	If a defence removes *mens rea*, there is no fault. In other cases, there may be fault but this is in some way excused, e.g. by consent In intoxication D is seen as at fault in getting drunk so this defence rarely succeeds	B *v* DPP Barnes Majewski
Creativity	HL refused to allow consent to intentional GBH Consent to sex is no longer true consent	Brown Dica

 For further resources and updates please go to the Companion Website accompanying this book at www.pearsoned.co.uk/russell

January 2005

Ali, who was aged 55, had been on bad terms with Bill, aged 32, over an alleged attack by Ali on Bill's young daughter. By chance, they found themselves together in the house of a mutual friend. Bill was heard to say, 'I am going to do that pervert.' Shortly afterwards, encouraged by his friend Colin, Bill began punching and kicking Ali. As he was falling to the floor, Ali took a knife from his pocket and slashed Bill's arm. Bill reeled backwards, bleeding heavily.

Ali, who was suffering from a broken nose and broken ribs, got up and followed Colin out of the house. As Colin turned to face him, Ali screamed with rage and thrust the knife into Colin's groin. Colin staggered away and collapsed in an alleyway. Some minutes later, Derek, a qualified first-aider, passed by and saw Colin. Having tried to make Colin comfortable and having promised to get help, Derek panicked and went away without doing anything. Colin bled to death.

(a) Discuss Bill's criminal liability for the injuries to Ali, and Ali's criminal liability for the injury to Bill. *(25 marks)*

(b) Discuss Ali's liability for the murder of Colin, and discuss Derek's liability for the manslaughter of Colin. *(25 marks)*

(c) What criticisms would you make of the current law of homicide? *(25 marks)*

Guide

(a) Bill: *Actus reus*: Explanation and application of ABH under **s. 47** of the **Offences Against the Person Act 1861**, and GBH under **s. 20** and **s. 18**. The level of injury suffered by Ali is more likely to amount to GBH (broken nose and ribs is 'serious' – **Saunders**) but ABH is also arguable.

Mens rea: Given Bill's comment beforehand, there is little doubt that he intended *some* harm, (**s. 20/Mowatt**) and arguably he intended *serious* injury (**s. 18/Parmenter**).

Ali: *Actus reus*: Ali clearly inflicted an 'open cut' (**Eisenhower**), so has *actus reus* for wounding under **s. 20** or **s. 18**.

Mens rea: Again, he may be charged with a **s. 18** offence if intention to cause *serious* injury can be established.

Defence: There is a possible defence of self-defence, as Ali slashed Bill with the knife in response to a serious attack.

Explanation and application of self-defence. Was the force used reasonable in the circumstances or excessive (**Martin**)? Given the level of violence involved in the attack by Bill it is probably not excessive.

(b) Ali: *Actus reus* and *mens rea*: Explanation and application of murder, especially malice aforethought. The use of the knife is evidence Ali's aim or purpose was, at the very least, serious injury (direct intent). This is sufficient *mens rea* for murder (**DPP v Smith**). Assuming he is charged with murder, the issue of provocation arises.

Defence: Explanation and application of the test for provocation (**Homicide Act s. 3 + Acott**). There is evidence of provocation by 'things done or said'. Note the provocation need not come from the victim (**Doughty**) but here, as well as evidence of provocation from other sources (Bill's attack), there is some evidence of provocation by Colin as he 'encouraged' Bill's attack on Ali. The slight time delay indicates a need to discuss the 'sudden and temporary' requirement (**Duffy**) in respect of his loss of self-control, although it is likely to be satisfied. A reasonable person with Ali's characteristics (**Holley**) may have done the same but this is a matter for the jury so you can argue it either way. It may be seen purely as a revenge attack, in which case the defence will fail.

*There is arguably a minor issue of causation in relation to Colin's death, though it is likely that Ali has made a significant contribution (**Cheshire**) and that nothing broke the chain of causation, so do no more than mention this briefly.*

Derek: *Actus reus* and *mens rea*: Explanation and application of the test for gross negligence manslaughter (**Adomako/Misra**). Did Derek owe Colin a duty? Maybe not (**Khan**) but arguably he had voluntarily assumed responsibility for Colin (**Stone and Dobinson**).

If so, is there a breach and *gross* negligence? Although he was a qualified first-aider the jury may not treat his conduct as 'so bad in all the circumstances' that it should be classed as criminal. Even if there is a breach, did it cause Colin's death? As he was seriously injured he may have died anyway, so the 'but for' test would fail (**White**). It is anyway unlikely that his contribution is 'significant' (**Cheshire**).

(c) This allows for a very wide range of matters to be discussed. The broader the approach you take, the less detail that is needed. If you limit the range you will need a much more detailed analysis. Whichever approach you take you should deal with **at least** two areas of homicide. You can discuss:

- the mandatory sentence of life imprisonment for murder does not allow for discretion;
- the difficulties in defining intention;
- intention to cause serious injury is sufficient *mens rea* for murder;
- interpreting the requirements of diminished responsibility is difficult for juries;
- the conflict in the higher courts on the issue of 'characteristics' in provocation;
- the difficulties in deciding whether D's negligence is bad enough 'in all the circumstances' to be deemed 'gross';
- the confusion of unlawful act and causation, and conflicting cases on what *is* an unlawful act.

Look at the key criticisms and 'Food for thought' boxes for more ideas, as well as the Law Commission's criticisms.

DON'T FORGET CASES TO ILLUSTRATE!

Part 3

MODULE 5 **CRIME**
OFFENCES AGAINST PROPERTY

Study Block 10   THEFT, ROBBERY AND BURGLARY

Study Block 11   DECEPTION OFFENCES, MAKING OFF WITHOUT
PAYMENT AND CRIMINAL DAMAGE

Study Block 12   DEFENCES

Introduction to Part 3
MODULE 5 CRIME
OFFENCES AGAINST PROPERTY

This Module covers offences against property and the defences to these.

The first Study Block looks at *theft, robbery and burglary*. These three offences are very closely connected. Once you have studied theft you will only need a little more for robbery and will also have much of what you need for burglary.

The second Study Block covers the *deception offences*, where, for example, someone is deceived into handing over goods or providing services. It also covers making off without payment, which is similar but requires no deception. The final Unit of the second Study Block covers criminal damage, which is another property offence.

The final Study Block looks at the *defences* of necessity, duress and duress of circumstances. These are the defences which are on the syllabus in Module 5 but not Module 4. If you are not studying crime in Module 4 you will need to refer to the Units on intoxication, self-defence and mistake in the last Study Block in Part 2 as these are also needed for Module 5 but have not been replicated here.

Study Block 10
THEFT, ROBBERY AND BURGLARY

Unit 30 Theft: *actus reus*

Unit 31 Theft: *mens rea*

Unit 32 Robbery

Unit 33 Burglary

This Study Block covers the main three property offences. Theft is a big area so I have split it into two parts. The first two Units will cover *actus reus* and *mens rea* respectively. Once you have done theft, however, you will find that you have almost all you need for robbery and most of what you need for burglary, which are covered in the following two Units.

The terms 'theft', 'robbery' and 'burglary' are used rather indiscriminately in newspaper reports, which can be confusing. Simply put, theft covers what most people would think of as stealing, like taking property belonging to someone else without their consent. The offences of robbery and burglary are theft with an added ingredient. Robbery is theft using force, or a threat of force. Burglary is theft from a building.

Example	• I steal a bicycle from outside the railway station. This is theft.
	• I tell the owner I will beat him up if he doesn't give me the bike. This is robbery.
	• I take the bike from someone's back yard. This is burglary.

We will look at the different ways a theft may be committed. Although my example is valid, theft is wider than just taking something and can include, for example, merely using something belonging to someone else. Robbery is fairly straightforward but you need to understand what amounts to 'force', so we will discuss this in more detail in Unit 32.

The offence of burglary also includes more than theft from a building. For example, damaging property can amount to burglary, so we will also look at the wider issues of this offence in Unit 33.

Theft: *actus reus*

... in a prosecution for theft it is unnecessary to prove that the taking is without the owner's consent ...

Lord Steyn, **Hinks (1998)**

> **By the end of this Unit you should be able to:**
> - Explain the *actus reus* of theft
> - Explain how the law applies in practice by reference to cases
> - Identify possible criticisms

As you can see from the quote, theft is wider than just taking something without permission. It is defined in the **Theft Act 1968 s. 1(1)** which says a person is guilty of theft:

> *'if he dishonestly appropriates property belonging to another with the intention of permanently depriving the other of it.'*

The offence of theft comes under **s. 1**. The following sections then explain each part of the *actus reus* and the *mens rea* in the definition. You will need to learn these too.

Task

There are three parts to the *actus reus* and two to the *mens rea*. Read the definition again and try to identify each of them before going on.

Examination pointer

Giving sections of Acts will enhance your answer. One way to remember them is to note that they are in order. **Section 1** is the offence itself and then 'dishonestly (**s. 2**), appropriates (**s. 3**), property (**s. 4**), belonging to another (**s. 5**), with the intention of permanently depriving the other of it (**s. 6**)'. **Subsection 1** of each of these explains each term. Further subsections may then add to this.

So you could say 'D may be charged with theft under **s. 1(1)** of the **Theft Act 1968**. The actus reus is the appropriation of property belonging to another. It could be argued here that the items are not property. This is further defined under **s. 4(1)** which states ...'

We'll look at each part of the *actus reus* and then the *mens rea*. Did you spot which was which?

The *actus reus* is:

- appropriates **s. 3** (conduct);
- property **s. 4** (circumstance);
- belonging to another **s. 5** (circumstance).

The *mens rea* is a bit more difficult. It involves:

- dishonesty **s. 2**; and
- the intention of permanently depriving the other of it **s. 6**.

In this Unit we will look at each part of the *actus reus*.

Appropriation s. 3(1)

This term covers many more types of conduct than 'take'. It is defined in **s. 3** as

'any assumption by a person of the rights of an owner.'

Assumption here means take over, e.g. you 'assume' someone's identity if you pretend to be them.

The best way to approach this is to consider what rights an owner has in the first place. If you own something you have a right to do what you like with it. So you can use it, alter it, damage it, destroy it, lend it, sell it, give it away, etc. If someone else does any of these things with it then they may well have *appropriated* it because they have 'assumed' your rights.

At one time it was thought that you could not appropriate something if you had authorisation from the owner, i.e. consent. This caused problems – and much case law.

In **Lawrence (1971)** the HL held there could still be an appropriation even if the owner consented. They found a taxi driver guilty of theft after he took more money than the correct fare (about £7 instead of 55p) from a foreign student. The student had offered him his wallet after he said £1 wasn't enough. He argued it could not be theft because the student gave him the wallet. The House disagreed. The decision was not without its critics. There is an offence under **s. 15** of the Act of 'obtaining property by deception' which would have covered this type of conduct. Why then, it has been argued, did the House need to interpret **s. 3** so widely? The next case appeared to complicate matters further.

In **Morris (1984)** the Ds switched labels on goods in a supermarket with intent to pay the lower price. The question was, had appropriation taken place? The CA held that appropriation took place when the Ds assumed *any* of the rights of the owner, so it occurred as soon as the goods were removed from the shelf with intent to pay the lower price. It could therefore be appropriation even before they switched labels. The HL's interpretation was narrower. Although Lord Roskill said that **s. 3** meant interference with *any* of the rights of the owner, he later made clear that there must be 'an *adverse* interference' with those rights. Thus, appropriation only took place when D did something unauthorised in this case switching labels. In the case of someone swapping labels for a joke, Lord Roskill said that they would have 'appropriated', but would not have the *mens rea* of dishonesty or intent to permanently deprive and so would not be guilty of theft.

Food for thought

This seems to contradict **Lawrence**, which allowed for an appropriation even with the owner's consent or authorisation. In **Morris**, Lord Roskill said appropriation *wouldn't* occur if the owner had expressly or impliedly consented – and goods are removed from a supermarket shelf with the owner's consent. The House did not need to decide on the issue because both Ds had done something 'adverse' by switching labels; the owner did not authorise label switching. The student consented in **Lawrence**, so which case do you think is to be preferred? Another matter for discussion is the difficulty for juries, the practical joker example shows how far appropriation (*actus reus*) and dishonesty (*mens rea*) are linked.

So, according to **Morris**, it can be theft even if you don't take anything. *Mens rea* may be harder to prove before D gets to the checkout, but if, as in **Morris**, you intend to pay less than you should, then you intend to permanently deprive the owner of the difference in price. This is also likely to be seen as dishonest. The HL considered the matter again in the next case.

Key case

In **Gomez (1993)** D was the assistant manager of a shop. He was asked by an acquaintance to obtain some goods in exchange for two stolen cheques. Knowing that the cheques were stolen, D got the shop manager to authorise the sale of the goods to the acquaintance. The CA allowed his appeal against a conviction for theft because the manager had consented. On the basis of **Morris**, there was no appropriation and so no theft. The prosecution appealed to the HL. The appeal raised the question of whether – and how – the earlier two cases could be reconciled. The House decided to revert to **Lawrence**. They held that it was a clear decision that an act could be an appropriation even if done with consent. They declared **Morris** to be incorrect on this point. Lord Keith said that although a customer putting items into a shopping basket is not a thief, the customer has appropriated those items.

So has **Gomez** made the issue certain? Maybe not. In **Galasso (1993)**, the same year, the CA seemed to view **Gomez** as not going as far as Lord Keith suggested. Later cases were not always consistent. A narrow interpretation of **Gomez** was seen in **Mazo (1996)**. The CA accepted that an appropriation could take place with the owner's consent, but only if that consent had been induced by deception or fraud. In this case, although there was evidence that V did not have full mental capacity, it was held that a gift of a number of cheques she had made to D, her maid, was valid; there was insufficient evidence of any deception. There was therefore no appropriation and D's appeal against her conviction for theft succeeded. However, the next case shows a wider interpretation.

Key case

In **Hinks (1998)** the CA again held that appropriation did not depend on whether there was consent, and said that consent was only relevant to the issue of dishonesty. Here, a man of limited intelligence had been persuaded to give Mrs Hinks, who claimed to be his 'carer', £60,000 over a period of a few months. The CA upheld the conviction for theft. Her appeal was rejected by the HL. Lord Steyn made the point in the opening quote, confirming the *ratio decidendi* of **Lawrence**, and continuing that it went 'to the heart of' the present case. Thus even a gift could amount to an appropriation. It should be noted that the HL decision was only a 3–2 majority and Lords Hutton and Hobhouse argued strongly that there was no appropriation.

In **Briggs (2004)** the CA considered another case where V had been deceived into parting with money. D was dealing with the purchase of a house on behalf of elderly relatives. The relatives gave authority for money for the purchase to be transferred to the seller's solicitor. They believed they were getting title to the property but in fact title was transferred to D. Their consent to the transfer was therefore induced by fraud. D argued that property was not appropriated where, by fraud, an owner was induced into parting with it. The CA agreed. They noted that if there could be an appropriation in such cases there would be little need for many of the deception offences.

Food for thought

It can be argued that the interpretation of appropriation in **Gomez** and **Hinks** was too wide. As the CA pointed out in **Briggs**, it means that many of the deception offences would be redundant. It is unlikely that Parliament would have legislated on these if they had intended appropriation to include situations where V is deceived into parting with something. Maybe the minority argument in **Hinks** was correct. However, a case like **Mazo**, where there was not enough evidence of deception and no appropriation, would come under neither offence. A prosecution against **Briggs** would probably have succeeded had D been charged with one of the deception offences.

Hinks makes clear that consent is not relevant to appropriation, but is to dishonesty. Thus, the fact that V has consented may be relevant to whether D was dishonest. Otherwise you could be guilty of theft of a genuine gift. Lord Keith intimated this in **Gomez** when he referred to Lord Roskill's joker in **Morris**. There may be appropriation in such cases, but if it isn't done dishonestly and with intent to permanently deprive then *mens rea* won't be proved. We will look at *mens rea* in Unit 31.

Examination pointer

It follows from *Gomez* that where consent is obtained by deception the charge may be theft under **s. 1**. As the matter is not fully clear you may need to refer to, for example, **Briggs** to support the alternative argument that there is no appropriation. Then go on to look at mens rea – even if there is an appropriation a prosecution may fail on this issue.

If you come by something innocently but then deal with it dishonestly, this can be theft. As we saw, **s. 3(1)** defines appropriation as being *'any assumption by a person of the rights of an owner'* and it continues *'and this includes, where he has come by the property (innocently or not) without stealing it, any later assumption of a right to it by keeping or dealing with it as owner.'* It would apply if you picked up a mobile phone by mistake, but after getting home decided to keep it.

Section 1(2) provides *'it is immaterial whether the appropriation is made with a view to gain or is made for the thief's own benefit'*. This means taking and destroying something is still appropriation. Taking something and giving it away would also come within this section.

Examination pointer

A problem question will usually involve one or two particular issues, e.g. it may be arguable whether there is an 'appropriation' or whether the property 'belongs to another'. As I pointed out earlier, **s. 1** defines theft. The other sections merely expand on each part of the definition. They aren't offences in themselves. So you should avoid statements like 'D will be guilty of appropriation under **s. 3**'. All five elements have to be proved. If they are then D will be guilty of theft under **s. 1**. If any one of them can't be proved, D is not guilty of theft.

Task

You pick up a watch in a jeweller's, intending to steal it. You see a shop assistant looking over at you and put it back. Are you guilty of theft? Think about this as you read this Unit. We'll come back to it.

Property s. 4(1)

This includes:

> *'money and all other property, real or personal, including things in action and other intangible property.'*

Real property relates to land; personal would be anything else. Tangible property is something you can touch, such as a book or a car. Intangible means things you can't touch, such as the right to the balance in a bank account or the copyright on a song. These are called 'things in action' because they are rights which can only be enforced by a court action, e.g. by suing someone for stealing the lyrics of a song and making a record. The section goes on to say that (with a few exceptions) land can't normally be stolen. Just about everything else can be though.

In **Kelly (1998)** an artist was given access to the Royal College of Surgeons to draw specimens. He took some body parts and when accused of theft argued that it was not 'property'. You can't own someone's body. The CA held it was theft and that parts of a body could come within **s. 4** if they had been treated in some way, e.g. by preserving them for medical purposes.

In **Marshall (1998)** the Ds acquired underground tickets from travellers and then sold them. On appeal they argued the tickets were not property belonging to another. The CA held that there was appropriation of property (the tickets themselves) belonging to London Underground (which 'owned' them).

In **Oxford v Moss (1978)** an examination paper was taken by a university student prior to the exam. This was not theft of the paper, as he intended to return it. Knowledge of what was on the paper was appropriated, but this was held not to be property. Take note though; it may not be theft but it is still cheating, so not to be taken to mean you can nick the law papers!

So you can steal most things including money and rights. However, **s. 4(3)** excludes wild plants (unless taken for *'reward or sale or other commercial purpose'*) and **s. 4(4)** excludes wild creatures (unless they have been tamed or kept in captivity).

Example

While exercising his rights of access to open land under the **Countryside and Rights of Way Act 2000**, Chris picks some wild mushrooms and then sells them to the local restaurant. He also takes home a rabbit to show his kids. The first is theft (from whoever owns the land); the second isn't. However, if the rabbit had been the landowner's pet then this would also be theft.

Examination pointer

Watch for references to the subsections in a problem question. In my example above you would need to pick up on the fact that although **s. 4(1)** includes most things, you can't normally steal wild plants. Then go on to say it may be 'property' in this case because selling them would be for a 'reward or sale or other commercial purpose' under **s. 4(3)**. As regards the rabbit, this would not be theft if it is wild, but if 'tamed' it can be - **s. 4(4)**. Don't worry too much if you can't remember the numbers of all the subsections though - no one's perfect!

Belonging to another s. 5(1)

This is also wide and is not confined to property actually owned by another, having possession or control of it can suffice. **Section 5(1)** states:

'Property shall be regarded as belonging to any person having possession or control of it, or having in it any proprietary right or interest . . .'

Example

You lend a coat to a friend, Sue, for the evening. While she is dancing someone takes it. They have appropriated property belonging to you, as you owned it. They have also appropriated property 'belonging to' Sue, as she had possession at the time.

You can have control of property without knowing of its existence. Thus such property can be stolen. In **Woodman (1974)** the owner of a disused business premises sold a load of scrap metal. He didn't know the buyers had left some behind. D went on to the property and took some of the remaining scrap. He was convicted of theft. The owners of the premises no longer owned the metal, as they had sold it, but they did have 'control' of it.

There is a difference between something which is lost and something which is abandoned. The first belongs to someone, so keeping it could be theft; the second does not, so can't be.

> **Example** You have some old books which you don't want any more. You leave them at college hoping someone may find them useful. You have abandoned them so they cannot then be stolen.

In **Hibbert and McKiernan (1948)** it was held that taking lost golf balls on a golf course was theft. They had been lost, not abandoned.

It is even possible to steal your own property if someone else has a right to it. **Section 5** says *'having in it any proprietary right or interest'*. This is illustrated by **Turner (1971)**, where a garage had a right to hold D's car until their bill was paid. Turner was thus guilty of theft when he took it back without paying the repair bill.

Examination pointer

Look out for situations where someone else has possession or it is debatable whether something has been abandoned. These are seen quite often in a problem question. Note that the definition is 'belonging to another'. It doesn't say you have to appropriate it from a particular person.

Problems occurred where, in contract law, title to property had already passed; for example, in **Edwards v Ddin (1976)** D obtained petrol at a self-service station and *then* decided to leave without paying. At the time he appropriated the petrol he had no *mens rea* and when he formed the *mens rea* there was no *actus reus* as title had passed when the petrol entered the tank, so it was not 'property belonging to another'. This situation has now been dealt with under **s. 3 Theft Act 1978**, with the offence of 'making off without payment' (see Unit 35), which would also apply to leaving a restaurant without paying for a meal.

Obligation to deal with the property in a certain way

Section 5(3) provides:

> *'Where a person receives property from or on account of another, and is under an obligation to the other to retain and deal with that property or its proceeds in a particular way, the property or proceeds shall be regarded (as against him) as belonging to the other.'*

Example   Your mother gives you £20 and asks you to do the shopping tomorrow. You *received* property, the £20. You are *obliged* to *retain* it until tomorrow, and to *deal with* it by doing the shopping. You may have been given the £20, but under **s. 5(3)** it *belongs* to your mother.

In **Davidge and Bunnett (1984)** D was given money by her flatmates to pay bills. She spent it on Christmas presents. She was found guilty of theft as she had an obligation to deal with it in a certain way (pay the bills) and had not done so.

In **Hallam and Blackburn (1995)** investment advisers were convicted of theft when they did not invest sums entrusted to them. There must be an obligation to deal with it in a particular way and thus there was no conviction in **Hall (1973)**. A travel agent paid deposits for flights into his firm's account and was later unable to repay the money. He was not guilty of theft as there had been no special arrangements for the deposits to be used in a particular way.

Property received by mistake

Section 5(4) provides:

'Where a person gets property by another's mistake, and is under an obligation to make restoration (in whole or in part) of the property or its proceeds or of the value thereof, then to the extent of that obligation the property or proceeds shall be regarded (as against him) as belonging to the person entitled to restoration, and an intention not to make restoration shall be regarded accordingly as an intention to deprive that person of the property or proceeds.'

Put simply – and it needs to be! – this means that if you are given something by mistake (and so have an obligation to give it back), keeping it can be theft. It would cover overpayments of wages, as in **AG's Reference No. 1 of 1983**, where D knew she'd been overpaid and simply left the money in her account. Similarly, if you buy goods from a shop and are given too much change by mistake. Essentially the excess belongs to the shop so you are obliged to give it back. Keeping it is theft of that amount.

Task

Look at the following situations. Decide if the *actus reus* of theft has occurred and explain the significance of any particular sections in each case.

1 Sam gets home from college to find she has picked up the wrong coat by mistake. She decides to keep it.

2 Peter buys a book to read on his journey home and thinks it is such rubbish he leaves it on the train in disgust. Susan picks it up and takes it home.

3 Simon pays a local builder £100 to buy sand to build a patio; the builder buys himself a second-hand dishwasher instead.

4 Mary buys a CD and gives a £20 note. She is given change from a £50 note and keeps it.

Summary

Theft: S. 1 Theft Act 1968				
Actus reus			*Mens rea*	
Appropriates s. 3	Property s. 4	Belonging to another s. 5	Dishonesty s. 2	Intent to permanently deprive s. 6
Even if with owner's consent – **Gomez**	Money and all other property	Includes those with possession or control	See Unit 31	See Unit 31

So you may be found guilty of theft in the Task on page 264. The *actus reus* is the appropriation (by picking it up – **Gomez**) of property (the watch) belonging to another (the shop). You also have *mens rea* – you intended to permanently deprive the shop and your actions were dishonest. We look at *mens rea* next.

Self-test questions

1 When can wild plants or animals be classed as property?

2 Did **Gomez** follow **Morris** or **Lawrence** on the issue of consent?

3 What was appropriated in **Hinks**?

4 What are the two parts to the *mens rea* of theft?

For further resources and updates please go to the Companion Website accompanying this book at **www.pearsoned.co.uk/russell**

Theft: *mens rea*

We can see no reason why, when in a jury box, they should require the help of a judge to tell them what amounts to dishonesty.

The CA in **Feely (1971)** on the role of a jury

By the end of this Unit you should be able to:

● Explain both the *actus reus* and *mens rea* of theft
● Explain how the law applies in practice by reference to cases
● Identify possible criticisms

We saw that theft is defined in the **Theft Act 1968 s. 1(1)** which says that a person is guilty of theft if:

*'he **dishonestly** appropriates property belonging to another with the **intention of permanently depriving the other** of it.'*

You learnt that 'appropriates' 'property' and 'belonging to another' relate to the *actus reus*. 'Dishonesty' and 'intent to permanently deprive' relate to *mens rea*. Every one of these elements must be proved or the prosecution will fail.

In **Gomez** the distinction was made between an honest shopper and a thief. A person who takes an item off a supermarket shelf appropriates it. Only the fact that a shopper means to pay the right price stops them being a thief. This is because they are not being dishonest. They have no *mens rea*. In **Madeley (1990)** (see p. 140) Richard Madeley was not guilty of theft because he lacked any intention to permanently deprive. The prosecution could not prove *mens rea*.

Dishonesty s. 2(1)

The **Act** does not define dishonesty but it does provide three specific situations where the person is *not* deemed dishonest:

1 S. 2(1)(a) *'A person's appropriation of property belonging to another is not to be regarded as dishonest if he appropriates the property **in the belief that he has in law the right to deprive the other of it**, on behalf of himself or a third person.'*

2 S. 2(1)(b) provides that it is not dishonest if a person *'appropriates the property **in the belief that he would have the other's consent** if the other knew of the appropriation and the circumstances of it.'*

3 S. 2(1)(c) provides that a person is not dishonest if he '*appropriates the property in the belief that the person to whom the property belongs cannot be discovered by taking reasonable steps.*'

The belief does not have to be reasonable, just *honestly held*. It is a subjective question, it is *D's* belief that is important. However, D will need to persuade a jury that you believed it was honestly held. The less reasonable it is, the harder it will be to convince a jury of this.

> **Example**
>
> You're having coffee with a friend. She goes to the loo, leaving her coffee and her handbag on the table. You wait for a while, but need to leave to catch your bus. You drink her coffee and take £50 from her bag (some friend). Can you rely on **s. 2(1)(b)**? You'll need to convince a jury that she would have consented in the circumstances. This may not be hard in relation to the coffee; after all, it was going cold. It will be a lot harder to convince the jury that you believed your friend would consent to taking the £50 though.

In **Small (1987)** D had taken a car which had been left for over a week with the keys in the ignition. Two issues arose. He argued it had been abandoned and so he believed he had a right to take it – **s. 2(1)(a)**. The CA quashed his conviction. They made clear that the issue under **s. 2** is whether a belief is *honestly* held, not whether it is reasonable. The second issue was not pursued, but if the car *was* abandoned then it did not 'belong to another'. Thus there would be no *actus reus* and no need to look at dishonesty at all.

> **Example**
>
> You take a bicycle which belongs to a friend. You could argue under **s. 2(1)(a)** that the friend owed you money so you believed you had a legal right to it. Alternatively you could argue under **s. 2(1)(b)** that you believed the friend would have consented in the circumstances. Under **s. 2(1)(c)** you could argue that you thought the friend had left the country and so couldn't be traced by taking reasonable steps.
>
> In a case such as **Small**, **s. 2(1)(c)** could also have been argued, although with a car it would be harder to convince a jury he honestly believed he couldn't trace the owner.

Note that **s. 2** relates to *mens rea*, not *actus reus*. So a *belief* that you could not trace the owner by taking reasonable steps would be sufficient. You do not actually have to *take* reasonable steps to find the owner.

The Ghosh test

In addition to **s. 2**, which merely shows when D is *not* dishonest (and despite the opening quote), the courts have developed a test for dishonesty. It comes from the case of **Ghosh (1982)**.

Key case

In **Ghosh** a surgeon claimed fees for operations he had not performed. The question was whether the prosecution had proved that he had acted dishonestly. The CA laid down what is now known as the 'Ghosh test'.

Lord Lane said that the jury must determine whether:

'according to the ordinary standards of reasonable and honest people what was done was dishonest. If it was not dishonest by those standards, that is the end of the matter and the prosecution fails. If it was dishonest by those standards then the jury must consider whether the defendant himself must have realised that what he was doing was by those standards dishonest.'

This means that there are two questions for the jury:

- Was D's act dishonest by the ordinary standards of reasonable and honest people? If not, stop here.

If so, ask the second question.

- Did D realise the act would be regarded as dishonest by such people?

If the jury can answer 'yes' to both parts, D is dishonest.

As is often the case it is a twofold test with both a subjective and an objective element. The first, 'objective' test, is what reasonable and honest people would have thought about D's actions. The jury will look at what D did and ask themselves whether they think that action was dishonest. The second, 'subjective' test, is what D believed reasonable and honest people would think. Here the jury will have to decide what *D* was thinking in relation to that action. This is harder.

Food for thought

Does the **Ghosh** test make things clear for a jury? Is it too wide? In this sort of case, where D claims fees for operations he has not performed, the question is probably not a difficult one for the jury to answer. It may be harder where D's actions have some 'do-good' element. Might a jury decide on moral rather than legal grounds? Writers often refer to the Robin Hood-type scenario. If D (Robin) takes from the rich and gives to the poor the jury may not consider this conduct dishonest. The problem is that members of the jury will probably differ on what they regard as dishonest. This could result in different verdicts, depending on the composition of the jury. A jury with several people on it who believe in animal rights may not regard removing animals from a laboratory as dishonest, for example. The answer to the first question would therefore be 'no'. Whatever D thinks is then irrelevant; once the first is answered in the negative there is no need to consider the second question. Motive is not normally relevant in criminal law (except in sentencing) but it may matter to a jury. Let's reverse the facts in the Robin Hood case. This time Robin steals from the poor and gives to the rich. Now would the jury think it dishonest? Quite likely. Morally this may be OK, but legally it means that the same facts can lead to a conviction or acquittal depending not only on motive, but also on who the victim is. Arguably, taking from one person should not be any different from taking from another.

▶

The CA noted the lack of clarity in the law and attempted to put it right in **Ghosh**. It is by no means certain that they have done so. The second part of the test is only partly subjective. It is what D (subjective) thinks ordinary people (objective) would regard as dishonest. It is hard for the jury to know what D thought reasonable people *would* regard as dishonest. D's own circumstances and upbringing would be reflected in the subjective part of the test. D may have some very odd ideas about what is regarded as dishonest. So, it isn't only a hard question for the jury to answer, the test is complicated in itself. However, for the moment we are stuck with it.

We saw in Unit 30 that **s. 1(2)** provides '*it is immaterial whether the appropriation is made with a view to gain or is made for the thief's own benefit*'. This touches on dishonesty as well as appropriation. It means that the Robin Hood argument should fail even though Robin isn't gaining a benefit.

Examination pointer

When discussing the mens rea of theft you may need to look at both **s. 2** and **Ghosh**. Look for clues in the scenario set, e.g. any reference to being owed money should point you to **s. 2(1)(a)**, taking from a friend or colleague to **s. 2(1)(b)**, something found to **s. 2(1)(c)**. Reference to D's age or mental capacity requires you to discuss that it is what D believes that is important, not what is reasonable. If these don't apply, or may not succeed, then discuss and apply the **Ghosh** test.

Task

Look at the following situations. State which belief under **s. 2(1)** you can argue and whether you think you'll convince the jury you honestly held that belief.

1 You find a football in your garden and keep it.

2 You take some money from a friend's bag in an emergency.

3 You find a £2 coin in the street and keep it.

4 You find a handbag containing a wallet and credit cards in the street and keep it.

Note that under **s. 2(2)** the fact that you are willing to pay for the property does not mean you are acting honestly. At first glance you may think it unfair to find D guilty of theft in such a case but compare the following two situations:

1 D takes a bottle of milk from a neighbour's doorstep and leaves more than enough money to replace it.

2 D is a very rich employer and really likes a vintage car belonging to an employee. One day D takes the car and leaves double what it is worth.

In (1) you may think it is unfair to find D guilty but if it wasn't for **s. 2(2)** the employer wouldn't be guilty either. Anyone could take anything they wanted as long as they could pay for it. Also in (1) D could use the **s. 2(1)(b)** defence.

Summary of dishonesty

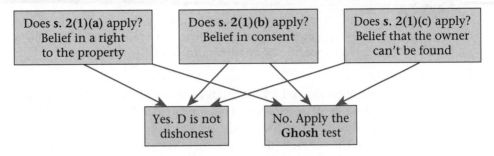

Does s. 2(1)(a) apply? Belief in a right to the property

Does s. 2(1)(b) apply? Belief in consent

Does s. 2(1)(c) apply? Belief that the owner can't be found

Yes. D is not dishonest

No. Apply the **Ghosh** test

Intention to permanently deprive s. 6(1)

Section 6(1) provides that this will exist where D's '*intention is to treat the property as his own to dispose of regardless of the other's rights*'. It will also exist where property is borrowed '*for a period and in circumstances making it equivalent to an outright taking or disposal*'. This means it is not usually theft if you mean to return the item. This would apply to borrowing but could be different if you have used it and so reduced its value.

Example   You borrow a month's season ticket intending to return it later. You use it for three weeks and are charged with theft. You can argue that you had no intention to permanently deprive the owner of it. This argument is likely to fail. The use of it for this period will make it 'equivalent to an outright taking' and so come within **s. 6**.

In **Lloyd (1985)** D borrowed some films from the cinema where he worked and copied them. The CA held **s. 6** would apply if D used something so that '*all the goodness or virtue is gone*'. On the facts this was not the case, so there was no liability. This narrow interpretation of **s. 6** has been seen as rather too generous to D and later cases have shown a significant widening of it.

In **Velumyl (1989)** D took money from his employer's safe, intending to return it. The CA held that this was sufficient as he had treated the money as his own. It was also made clear that as he would be unable to replace the exact notes taken he had intended to deprive the owner of those notes. D's best hope in a case like this is to convince the jury that the intention to put them back showed the conduct was not dishonest.

The broader approach is seen again in **Lavender (1994)** and **Marshall (1998)**.

In **Lavender** D took some doors from his flat, which belonged to the council. He hung them in his girlfriend's flat, which belonged to the same council. Arguably he hadn't intended to permanently deprive the council of the doors as he merely moved them around. The court held D had treated the doors as his own to dispose of regardless of the other's rights.

In **Marshall** the CA held that acquiring underground tickets from travellers and then selling them was within the scope of **s. 6**. The Ds had treated the tickets as their own to dispose of regardless of London Underground's rights.

Food for thought

It can be argued that the **Lloyd** approach is too narrow but the wider approach in these later cases can also be criticised. It means that D is liable even where there does not appear to be any intent to permanently deprive.

Another case which illustrates **s. 6** is **Cahill (1993)**. Very early one morning D took a pile of newspapers from a newsagent's doorstep on his way home. He was very drunk at the time and couldn't fully explain what he intended to do with them. His conviction was quashed because the judge's direction to the jury only went as far as *'to treat the property as his own'* and did not add *'to dispose of regardless of the other's rights'*. Had the direction been given correctly he may have been found to have *mens rea*. It would depend if he dumped them close by or not. The newspapers would be worthless after the end of the day. If they didn't find their way back to the shop then 'all the goodness or virtue' would be gone.

Examination pointer

If given a scenario like **Velumyl** you could argue that D may not be dishonest under **s. 2**. Suggest D may have believed that the owner would have consented (perhaps borrowing from the employer had been allowed before). Or D believed they had a right to it (perhaps they were owed wages). Alternatively rely on the **Ghosh** test. The jury may consider that by intending to return the money, D was not dishonest by ordinary standards.

A final point. In *Small (1987)* D had taken a car. It may be hard to prove intention to permanently deprive in such a case because a car is easily traceable. (It was for this reason that a separate offence of taking without consent was later added to the **Theft Act**.) You should look for clues in the type of property that has been taken.

Task

Consider the following situations and decide if **s. 6** is satisfied:

- Dave takes Steve's tickets for that night's pop concert and returns them the next day.

- Frank takes £10 from his mother's purse and puts it in his pocket. His sister sees him and says she will tell if he doesn't return it. He puts it back.

- Ellie borrows a book from a friend and reads it. She then throws it away.

Recap

Let's look back at the Task in Unit 30 where you took a watch and put it back.

You appropriated (by picking it up) property (the watch) belonging to another (the shop). You have the *actus reus* for theft. Do you have *mens rea*? It may be difficult to find evidence but you know you acted dishonestly. You know 'ordinary reasonable people' would regard the fact that you only put it back because someone was watching as dishonest. You can argue that you didn't keep it so haven't permanently deprived anyone. This actually doesn't matter. It is *intent* to do so that makes it theft. Intent relates to *mens rea* (what you think), not *actus reus* (your actual conduct). Again it will be hard to prove, but yes, technically, you have committed theft. As has Frank in the above task, although he may be able to argue under **s. 2(1)(b)** that he believed his mother would have consented in the circumstances.

Summary

Actus reus			Mens rea	
Appropriates s. 3	Property s. 4	Belonging to another s. 5	Dishonesty s. 2	Intent to permanently deprive s. 6
Even if with owner's consent – **Gomez**	Money and all other property	Includes those with possession or control	S. 2 + **Ghosh** test	Can include borrowing

Self-test questions

1 What are the three statutory beliefs in **s. 2**?

2 Do these beliefs have to be reasonable?

3 What is the **Ghosh** test?

4 When can borrowing amount to an intent to permanently deprive?

5 Can you state all the section numbers dealing with each part of the *actus reus* and *mens rea*?

For further resources and updates please go to the Companion Website accompanying this book at www.pearsoned.co.uk/russell

Robbery

What is a robbery, ladies and gentlemen? Well, in very crude terms, it is a theft that has been carried out through violence.

R *v* West (1999)

> **By the end of this Unit you should be able to:**
> - Explain the *actus reus* and *mens rea* of theft and what turns it into robbery
> - Explain how the law applies in practice by reference to cases
> - Identify possible criticisms

Robbery is essentially a type of aggravated theft. **Section 8** of the **Theft Act 1968** makes it a more serious offence if D uses force (or the threat of force) in order to steal. **Section (8)(1)** provides that:

> *'A person is guilty of robbery if he steals, and immediately before or at the time of doing so, and in order to do so, he uses force on any person or puts or seeks to put any person in fear of being then and there subjected to force.'*

It is an indictable offence and carries a maximum life sentence.

Let's take a look at each part of this offence to clarify what is needed – it's easier than it might look.

Steals

You will need to examine the theft requirements *plus* the force element. It is therefore necessary to prove all the *actus reus* and *mens rea* elements for theft before considering whether there may be a robbery. As you have to prove theft it follows that you can also use the defences to theft. This means that the **s. 2(1)** defences will apply here too. Thus in **Robinson (1977)** D threatened V with a knife in order to get money he was owed. He believed he had a legal right to the money (even though he knew he had no right to use a knife to get it) so had a defence under **s. 2(1)**. If there is no theft then there can be no robbery.

Task

Look back at the *actus reus* and *mens rea* of theft in Units 30 and 31. Be sure you can explain:

- Appropriation - property - belonging to another
- Dishonesty - intention to permanently deprive

If all these can be proved *and* there is the additional element of force it may be a robbery.

Immediately before or at the time of doing so

The use (or threat) of force must be before or during the theft. This seems to suggest that the use of force once the appropriation has taken place would not be enough to make it robbery. This is not interpreted too strictly by the courts.

Key case

In **Hale (1979)** the Ds entered the victim's house and one went upstairs and stole some items from a jewellery box. The other was downstairs tying up V. The CA declined to quash their convictions for robbery even though the appropriation may have already taken place. The appropriation was seen as a continuing act. Therefore it was open to the jury to conclude that it continued while the victim was tied up.

In **Lockley (1995)** the court confirmed the point in **Hale (1979)** that appropriation was a continuing act. Force on a shopkeeper *after* the D's took some beer could amount to robbery. Remember **Fagan** and continuing acts? No? Then have a look at Unit 14 again.

Examination pointer

When you are looking at a potential case of robbery in an exam question take it step by step. First, consider whether there is appropriation of property belonging to another. Then whether it was dishonestly appropriated with the intention of permanently depriving someone of it. If so, you have theft. Go on to consider if there are any additional elements which may turn the theft into an offence of robbery.

In order to do so

So we can see that the appropriation may continue while D is removing the goods from the premises. If force is used, or threatened, this may amount to robbery. However, the force or the threat of force must be 'in order to' steal. This means it must be applied with the purpose of facilitating the theft. If the jury are satisfied that a defendant stole something, yet the force or threat of it was not applied in order to steal, they cannot convict under **s. 8(1)**. Using force to get away is not 'in order to steal'. It may be theft, but not robbery.

Uses force on any person or puts or seeks to put any person in fear

The word force is not separately defined in the Act. In **Dawson and James (1978)** the CA said that since it was an ordinary word it was for the jury to determine its meaning. In **West (1999)** the judge made the comment in the opening quote and then continued:

> *'What does that mean? What it means, ladies and gentlemen, is: if you are in the supermarket and someone puts their hand into your basket and takes your purse out, a pickpocket, that is theft. It has been stolen from you. If you are outside in the street, and you are approached by someone who held a knife at your throat and then took your purse out of your bag, you will have been robbed, because immediately before or during the course of the theft, you were subject to violence or a threat of violence.'*

The indication here is that violence is needed. It is clear from several cases, though, that the use of force can be small. Snatching a bag from someone's grasp was held to be robbery in **Corcoran v Anderton (1980)**. Similarly, in **Clouden (1987)** wrenching a shopping basket from someone's grasp amounted to robbery.

A second point arose in **Corcoran**. The two Ds had tried to take the handbag by force. It fell from one D's hands and they ran off without it. The court held that the theft was complete when D snatched the handbag from her grasp. This means that a robbery can occur without anything being taken. This isn't as daft as it seems. You can commit theft without taking something. In **Gomez** it was said that taking something from a supermarket shelf was appropriation. If done dishonestly it could be theft even though you haven't left the shop; if done with force it can be robbery.

Example You are in a shop. You put an item in your pocket intending to avoid paying for it. You have appropriated property belonging to the shopkeeper. This would be seen as dishonest in the eyes of 'ordinary' people. You would also be intending to permanently deprive the owner of it. This is theft. If you threaten another shopper to 'keep quiet or else' when you take it, then you have used the threat of force in order to steal. This is robbery. In both cases the crime has been committed even if you drop the item in your hurry to get away.

Note that the force or threat can be on 'any person'. As in my example, it need not be on the victim of the theft. If you wanted to gain entrance to a casino at night to steal the profits then knocking out a security guard would suffice. So might tying up and blindfolding someone whose house overlooks the casino. This would depend on why you did it. If it was to prevent them seeing you and raising the alarm it would be robbery. If it was just to prevent them seeing you and pointing you out at a later date it would not. The difference is that in the first case it is *in order to* steal (without being stopped because the alarm has been raised). In the second it is just to avoid being recognised and doesn't help with the theft.

Task

Look back at theft to remind yourself of all the parts to the *actus reus* and *mens rea*. Apply these to **Clouden**. You should end up by establishing theft. Keep your workings; we'll come back to this.

Food for thought

The use of force can be really minor yet the maximum sentence for robbery is life imprisonment. Consider whether this is just. Prior to the Act the Criminal Law Revision Committee had said that snatching a bag from an unresisting owner would not suffice. **Corcoran** and **Clouden** show that the courts have interpreted the requirement for force very widely. If a person tries to prevent D from taking a bag and there is a struggle then robbery appears an appropriate charge. If, however, there is no resistance then theft would seem to cover it.

Being then and there subjected to force

This means that it must be a threat of immediate force. As with the 'immediately before or at the time' element there is no set time limit. It will be a matter for the jury to decide based on all the circumstances. If the force is used just before or just after (**Hale**) then it may be robbery. However, if D threatens force in a week's time if the security guard doesn't look the other way tonight it is unlikely to be robbery.

Mens rea

First, because robbery requires that a theft took place, the prosecution will need to prove the *mens rea* for the theft. This is dishonesty and intention to permanently deprive. We saw above that this also means D can use the **s. 2** arguments to show lack of *mens rea* in relation to dishonesty. In **Robinson (1977)** D had a defence under **s. 2(1)** because he believed he had a legal right to the money.

Task

Find the notes you made in the last task on **Clouden**. Now add the additional *actus reus* and *mens rea* for robbery. OK? Now you should be able to complete an exam question.

As regards the robbery itself, accidentally using force or causing fear in a victim is unlikely to be robbery. Robbery requires force 'in order to' steal and accidentally using force would not meet this requirement. Thus, the force or threat of it must be intentional or reckless. As we saw in Unit 16, all recklessness is now subjective or **Cunningham** recklessness.

Examination pointer

You may have a scenario which appears to be a robbery because there is evidence of force. Go through all the elements of theft and then **s. 8**. If you then fail to prove robbery on one of the above issues say that although D is unlikely to be convicted of robbery a theft conviction would be possible. The overlap between theft, robbery and burglary means you may need to discuss more than one. Look out for clues as to how (force may make it robbery) and where (if in a building it may be burglary) it happens.

Summary

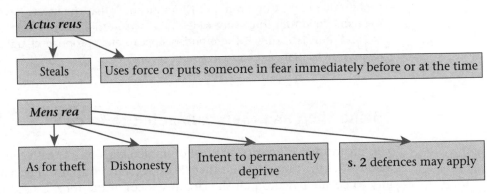

Self-test questions

1 What turns theft into robbery?

2 What are the five elements to theft?

3 How was appropriation treated in **Hale**?

4 What amounted to force in **Corcoran**?

5 What is the *mens rea* for robbery?

For further resources and updates please go to the Companion Website accompanying this book at **www.pearsoned.co.uk/russell**

Burglary

When you invite a person into your house to use the staircase you do not invite him to slide down the bannisters. Scrutton LJ, **R v Jones and Smith (1976)**

By the end of this Unit you should be able to:

- Explain the *actus reus* and *mens rea* of burglary
- Identify the connection with theft and what turns it into burglary
- Explain how the law applies in practice by reference to cases
- Identify possible criticisms

A common view of a burglar is someone sneaking out of a bedroom window late at night with a bag of stolen goodies. This is quite right. Such a person is likely to be a burglar. However there is – as usual – more to the offence than this.

There are several ways to commit burglary. These come under the **Theft Act 1968 s. 9(1)** which has two subsections:

Under **s. 9(1) Theft Act 1968** a person is guilty of burglary if:

'(a) he enters any building or part of a building as a trespasser and with intent to commit any such offence as is mentioned in subsection (2) below; or

(b) having entered any building or part of a building as a trespasser he steals or attempts to steal anything in the building or that part of it or inflicts or attempts to inflict on any person therein any grievous bodily harm.'

Section 9(2) Theft Act 1968 provides:

'The offences referred to in subsection (1)(a) above are offences of stealing anything in the building or part of the building in question, of inflicting on any person therein any grievous bodily harm or raping any woman therein, and of doing unlawful damage to the building or anything therein.'

Actus reus

Much of the *actus reus* is the same for burglary under both (a) and (b). They differ only in the secondary offences, known as the 'ulterior' offences. Under (a) these are theft, grievous bodily harm, rape or criminal damage. D will be guilty without actually doing any of these four things mentioned in **s. 9(2)**. It is enough that the intention to do so is there. In (b) D must commit or attempt either theft or grievous bodily harm, but needn't have intended to do so at the time of entry.

Let's look at the common elements first.

Enters

Both types of burglary require entry as a trespasser. At common law this included entry by any part of D's body or even an instrument used to remove property. This wide definition seems to have been rejected in **Collins (1972)** where the court said entry had to be both effective and substantial.

Key case

In **Collins**, D had had a few drinks. He climbed a ladder to a girl's bedroom and saw her lying naked in bed. He descended, took off his clothes (apart from his socks!), climbed the ladder again and sat on her window sill. She awoke and saw him. The story might have ended there had the girl not also had a few. She thought it was her boyfriend paying a night visit and got up and encouraged him in. They then had sex. At some point she decided that it might not be her boyfriend. She turned on the light to find that she was right. She slapped him and told him to get out. He was charged with burglary under **s. 9(1)(a)**. This meant the prosecution had to prove he entered as a trespasser with intent to rape. He argued that he was outside when the girl asked him in so he didn't enter as a trespasser.

His conviction was quashed because the jury had not been properly directed. The CA held that the jury must be satisfied that entry was both 'effective and substantial'. Edmund Davies LJ said it was not enough that there was trespass at civil law. D had to have known, or at least been reckless as to the fact, that he was trespassing. On these rather unusual facts this was not clear. Had he still been on the ladder when she encouraged him it would not be entry as a trespasser. If he was in the room intending to have sex before this invitation it would be. Sitting on the window sill made it unclear whether he had 'entered' before or after he had been invited. Edmund Davies LJ said, *'The point is a narrow one, as narrow maybe as the window sill which is crucial to this case'*.

Later, in **Brown (1985)** the CA said the word 'substantial' was unnecessary. Entry was proved even if D had not fully entered the building. Here D had the top half of his body inside a broken shop window. He argued that there was no entry and so no *actus reus*. His appeal against conviction was rejected.

The CA again considered the issue of entry in **Ryan (1996)**. Here, D had only his arm and head through a window. Unfortunately for him he got stuck and had to be rescued by the fire brigade! Again D's appeal was on the basis that entry was not proved. Again it was rejected.

Food for thought

Even without the requirement of 'substantial' this type of entry hardly seems to be effective. He wasn't in any position to take anything. Will different juries have different ideas of what amounts to 'effective' entry? Should there be more certainty as to what amounts to 'entry'? It should be noted, though, that the later case was in relation to a residential property. Does this means judges are less sympathetic where a private house is involved rather than a shop or business premises? Consider whether judges are using too much discretion and thus making the law uncertain.

Building or part of a building

Note that **s. 9** refers to part of a building. This means you may have permission to be in a building – and so not be a trespasser – but not to be in a particular part of it. If you enter that part you will be entering 'part of a building' as a trespasser. You may therefore be charged with burglary if the rest of the *actus reus* and *mens rea* can be proved. A customer in a shop can commit burglary by going somewhere where he is not permitted to go. A conviction was obtained in **Walkington (1979)** where D was in a department store and then went behind a counter where he opened a till. The court held that the counter area was a 'part of the building'.

In **Stevens *v* Gourley (1859)** Byles J defined a building as '*a structure of considerable size and intended to be permanent or at least endure for a considerable time*'.

Section 9(4) adds that a building includes a vehicle or vessel that is inhabited. Thus a camper van would be included. It does not have to be inhabited at the time of the burglary.

Food for thought

It is unclear what will amount to a 'building'. Two similar cases had different results. In **B & S *v* Leathley (1979)** a freezer container which had been in the same place for three years and was likely to remain there was found to be a building. In **Norfolk Constabulary *v* Seekings and Gould (1986)** a trailer with electricity and shutters used as a temporary store was not. This seems to be a fine distinction. The main difference seems to be that in the first the wheels had been removed and in the second they were still attached to the chassis. It can be argued that the jury has a difficult job in deciding whether something is a building without a clearer direction from the judge.

As a trespasser

Trespass is going somewhere without, or in excess of, permission. Look back at **Collins**. Note that D must be a trespasser at the time of entry.

Example   Susan is invited to a party. She has an argument with the host and is told to go. On her way out she steals a coat. She can't be convicted of burglary under either subsection because she did not enter as a trespasser. Now consider the difference if she had been told to go and then gone into a bedroom and stolen some jewellery. Now she has entered part of a building (the bedroom) as a trespasser (she no longer has permission to be there) and can be charged with burglary.

As I said above, **s. 9** refers to part of a building so if you have permission to be in one part you can still be a trespasser in another part.

Example   In a pub you are allowed in the bar but not the living quarters. If you went into the living quarters with intent to steal, this would be burglary.

Although permission will usually mean there is no trespass it may still be burglary if D goes beyond that permission. In **R v Jones and Smith (1976)** D had left home but had permission to enter his father's house whenever he liked (his father said at the trial, 'Christopher would not be a trespasser in the house at any time'). He came one day with a friend and stole the television. The CA upheld his conviction for burglary. He had gone beyond the permission granted when he stole the television. As he entered with this in mind he had entered as a trespasser. The opening quote was referred to with approval in this case although it actually came from a civil case. The same could apply to shops where you have permission to be there, but if you enter with intent to steal you have entered as a trespasser.

In **Walkington** he had argued that he had not entered the shop as a trespasser. The court held that the counter area was a 'part of the building' where customers were excluded. He entered this part as a trespasser.

In **Laing (1995)** D was found hiding in the storeroom of a shop after closing time. His conviction was quashed because at the time he entered the shop it could not be proved he was a trespasser.

Food for thought

Compare **Walkington** and **Laing**. Why do you think the court did not treat the storeroom as 'part of a building' in **Laing**? It may be that it was because he had not entered the storeroom with intent to steal. He entered it as a trespasser but not with intent to steal from the storeroom, but from the shop itself.

Another difficulty with the *mens rea* for burglary is that it will be hard to prove what was in D's mind at the time of entry. Not all burglars carry a bag marked 'Swag'!

Examination pointer

Burglary and theft often come up in the same question so look carefully at the given facts. In my example above, you would discuss burglary and conclude Susan could not be convicted. She could be charged with theft so you would go on to explain and apply the law on this.

Mens rea

Both types of burglary require entry as a trespasser. Trespass is a civil law concept but for the criminal law it requires *mens rea*. This is intent or subjective recklessness. You have *mens rea* if you knew or recognised the possibility that you were entering without, or in excess of, permission. This was confirmed in **Collins (1972)**. Edmund Davies LJ said there could be no conviction for burglary '*unless the person entering does so **knowing** that he is a trespasser and nevertheless deliberately enters, or, at the very least, is **reckless** whether or not he is entering the premises of another without the other party's consent*'.

Task

Martin is asked by a householder to fit a kitchen. While working in the house he asks to go to the toilet. Once upstairs he sees the bedroom door open and decides to steal some jewellery. Has he committed burglary and if so which subsection would it come under? Will it make a difference if he doesn't actually take the jewellery?

Once it is proved that D entered a building (or part of one) as a trespasser (knowing this, or being reckless as to it) the *actus reus* and *mens rea* for the ulterior offence(s) must be considered.

Actus reus and *mens rea* of the ulterior offence

In (a) only *mens rea* is needed. D will be guilty even if none of the four things are actually done or attempted. It is enough that the intention to do one of them is there. Again there is the point that this *mens rea* must exist at the time of entry.

Task

Look back at **Collins** again. At what point did he intend to rape her? Did he enter with intent to do so? If the court had found that he did enter as a trespasser do you think the prosecution would have also been able to prove intent for a conviction under **s. 9(1)(a)**?

In (b) D must do or attempt one of the two things (so will need both *actus reus* and *mens rea* for the ulterior offence), but needn't have intended to do so when entering.

Food for thought

Is the law on burglary too complicated? In **s. 9(1)(a)** there must be intent to commit the ulterior offence at the time of entry, but there is no need to actually commit it. For (b) there is no need to prove intent but the ulterior offence must be attempted or committed. There are four ulterior offences in (a) and only two in (b). It also seems odd to many people that you can be convicted of burglary without actually taking anything. Finally, the inclusion of GBH in both subsections and rape in (b) seems inappropriate in a property offence.

Summary of the key issues

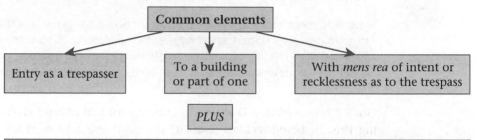

Common elements

Entry as a trespasser

To a building or part of one

With *mens rea* of intent or recklessness as to the trespass

PLUS

At the time of entry D has the *mens rea* of intent to steal, commit GBH, rape or criminal damage for (a) but no further *actus reus* is needed

No intent at the time of entry is needed for (b) but *actus reus* and *mens rea* of theft or GBH (or attempt) is needed

Finally, intent to steal only if there is something worth having is enough; you don't need to intend to steal something specific. The CA in **AG's Reference Nos 1 & 2 1979** considered **Husseyn (1977)** (a theft case) and held that conditional attempt could be enough as long as the indictment related to theft of unspecified items. In **Husseyn** the Ds had broken into a van containing a holdall with sub-aqua equipment in it. Their appeal against conviction for attempted theft was successful. The indictment had stated intent to steal sub-aqua equipment and as they did not know it was there they could not be found to have intended to steal it! In **AG's Reference Nos 1 & 2 1979** the CA did not overrule **Husseyn** but said it only applied where the indictment stated intent to steal something specific.

Example

Dave enters a building intending to steal something only if there is anything of value inside. There isn't anything worth having so Dave leaves empty-handed. This is enough for Dave to be charged with burglary under **s. 9(1)(a)** – as long as the charge is correctly worded. With intent to steal 'some or all of the contents' would suffice.

Burglary is an either way offence, tried in either the magistrates' court or the Crown court, unless there is intent to rape or commit grievous bodily harm in which case it is indictable and can only be tried in the Crown court. The maximum sentence is 10 years or 14 if it is a 'dwelling', e.g. a private house.

Task

Look at the following examples and decide if Paul can be charged with burglary. Look carefully at the *actus reus* and *mens rea* and the differences between burglary under (a) and (b). Ask yourself whether he entered with intent or whether he committed the *actus reus* of an ulterior offence. Then decide which subsection these would come under.

1 Paul comes into your house without permission as he is cold and wants to sleep. He notices a nice clock and takes it.

2 He again enters to sleep and finds a girl in the room; he tries to rape her.

3 He goes to the house intending to steal but once inside gets scared and runs away.

Examination pointer

If you see that a theft has occurred, look for clues which may indicate it is more than theft. If force is used it could be robbery. If it took place in a building it could be burglary. Keep an open mind and discuss all the possibilities – as long as they are sensible and relevant to the question.

Summary

Actus reus				Mens rea
Entry	To a building or part of one	As a trespasser	**S. 9(1)(a) and (b)**	Intent or subjective recklessness

S. 9(1)(a)			S. 9(1)(b)	
Actus reus	**Mens rea**		**Actus reus**	**Mens rea**
No further *actus reus* needed	Intent (to steal, commit GBH, rape or commit criminal damage)		Steals or commits GBH	*Mens rea* for theft or GBH needed
	At the time of entry	← ***mens rea* is needed** → →		At the time of the ulterior offence

Self-test questions

1 What are the three common elements for burglary under both subsections?

2 What is the *mens rea* for the above?

3 What are the four ulterior offences for **s. 9(1)(a)**?

4 What are the two ulterior offences for **s. 9(1)(b)**?

5 At what time does *mens rea* have to exist?

For further resources and updates please go to the Companion Website accompanying this book at **www.pearsoned.co.uk/russell**

Study Block 10 Summary
THEFT, ROBBERY AND BURGLARY

Theft s. 1 Theft Act 1968		
s. 3	*actus reus*	appropriation
s. 4		property
s. 5		belonging to another
s. 2	*mens rea*	dishonesty
s. 6		intent to permanently deprive
Robbery s. 8		theft *plus* force or the threat of it in order to steal
Burglary		entry to a building or part of one as a trespasser
s. 9(1)(a)		with intent to steal, inflict GBH, rape or cause unlawful damage
s. 9(1)(b)		steals or inflicts GBH, or attempts to do so

Task

Add the principle and brief facts to the case (in pencil if it isn't your book!).

Case	Principle	Facts
Gomez		
Woodman		
Ghosh		

Clouden		
Hale		
Collins		
Jones and Smith		

Key criticisms

- Conflicting cases on appropriation have left the law on theft uncertain.
- D can be guilty of theft without actually taking anything.
- The **Ghosh** test is difficult for juries.
- D can be guilty of theft of wild plants and animals if, for example, they are used commercially.
- The distinction between something lost and something abandoned may not be clear.
- The force for robbery can be minor yet the maximum sentence is life imprisonment.
- For burglary what is, and is not, a building remains unclear.
- The burglary offences are unnecessarily complex.

Examination practice

January 2005
Comment on the suggestion that the definition of theft in the Theft Act 1968 has given rise to few problems. *(25 marks)*

Module 6 connections

Morals	Will a jury be able to ignore the moral element if D has acted in a morally acceptable way?	Ghosh
Justice	Justice appeared to have been done in **Lawrence** but then **Morris** confused the issue. **Gomez** restated **Lawrence** but later cases again conflicted. Justice cannot be done if there is uncertainty in the law. For robbery the use of force can be really minor yet the maximum sentence is life imprisonment	Corcoran/ Clouden
Conflicting interests	The subjective element in **s. 2 Theft Act 1968** attempts to balance property rights with D's rights by providing that D may argue a belief even if it is not reasonable	Small
Fault	Theft requires a high level of fault as the *mens rea* is intent	
Creativity	Should there be more certainty as to what amounts to 'entry' for burglary? Are judges using too much discretion to distinguish cases thus making the law uncertain?	Ryan

For further resources and updates please go to the Companion Website accompanying this book at www.pearsoned.co.uk/russell

Study Block 11
DECEPTION OFFENCES, MAKING OFF WITHOUT PAYMENT AND CRIMINAL DAMAGE

Unit 34   Deception offences

Unit 35   Making off without payment

Unit 36   Criminal damage

This Study Block covers the deception offences under two Theft Acts: the **Theft Act 1968** and the **Theft Act 1978**. These are where D either receives property or services due to a deception, or evades liability because of a deception.

It also covers making off without payment under the **Theft Act 1978**. This offence does not require a deception and was added to close the loophole left by the first Act.

Criminal damage is included here as it doesn't need a Study Block all to itself! We will look at the different types of criminal damage, including arson.

Example	I have a meal in a restaurant and persuade the manager to let me leave without paying, saying that I forgot my purse but will pay tomorrow. I have no intention of doing so. I have obtained property (the meal) and services (the serving of the meal) by deception (I lied). If I leave while the waiter is in the kitchen, this would be making off without payment. I haven't deceived anyone, just made off without paying.
	If I kick the door down in my haste to get out; this would be criminal damage. If I set fire to the tablecloth it will be arson.

Note that some of the cases involved a charge under **s. 16** of the **1968 Act**. This was 'obtaining a pecuniary advantage by deception'. This section is now replaced by offences in the **1978 Act** but much of the case law is relevant.

Deception offences

. . . for a deception to take place there must be some person or persons who will have been deceived.

Lord Morris

By the end of this Unit you should be able to:
- Explain the common elements of the 'deception' offences
- Distinguish between the three offences
- Explain how the law applies in practice by reference to cases
- Identify possible criticisms

There are three different deception offences to study:

- Obtaining property by deception **s. 15 Theft Act 1968**
- Obtaining services by deception **s. 1 Theft Act 1978**
- Evading liability by deception **s. 2 Theft Act 1978**

Note the two different Acts which cover these offences. Note also that there is an overlap with theft as 'obtains' and 'appropriates' are similar concepts. In **Gomez** the appropriation occurred after the manager had been deceived into consenting to the transaction. This could have been **s. 15** as the goods were obtained by deception. It was decided in the case that appropriation could occur despite consent. This meant that the conviction came under **s. 1** theft and **s. 15** was not needed.

The common elements

There are three elements common to each of the deception offences. These are:

- a deception;
- the deception must cause the obtaining or evading;
- dishonesty.

We look at these common elements first, then analyse the specific offences.

Deception

This is explained, but not fully defined, in **s. 15(4)**. It is:

> *'any deception (whether deliberate or reckless) by words or conduct as to fact or as to law.'*

The courts have therefore had to further interpret the meaning of deception. As well as by words or conduct, it may be by implication or silence.

In **DPP v Ray (1974)** the HL held that where D orders a meal in a restaurant this is an implied representation that it will be paid for. That representation is treated as continuing until the bill is paid. If D leaves without paying this may now also amount to a **s. 3** offence (see Unit 35). So there would be no need to prove the diner deceived the waiter.

Key case

In **MPC v Charles (1977)** D was convicted when he used his cheque card to back several cheques at a casino. His bank had only authorised the issue of one £30 cheque a day. He was implying he had the bank's authority to use the card. He went beyond that authority by writing a cheque over the amount authorised.

This would also apply where authority to use the card had been withdrawn. Thus in **Lambie (1981)** D was convicted having used her credit card after the issuing bank withdrew its authority to use it.

In **Rai (2000)** D applied for a council grant on behalf of his mother. She died after the council had approved the grant. He did not inform them but had the work done and obtained the grant. This was held by the CA to amount to obtaining services by deception. The reasoning is similar to the 'continuing representation' seen in **DPP v Ray**. Although originally there was no deception he had carried on with the work knowing the circumstances had changed.

Deception has to be of a person. In **DPP v Ray** Lord Morris said 'for a deception to take place there must be some person or persons who will have been deceived.' Deceiving a machine might therefore be theft, but not a deception offence.

The deception must be either deliberate or reckless. The CA in **Staines (1974)** held that reckless meant more than mere carelessness or negligence. In **Goldman (1997)** they held that recklessness was subjective. D must recognise the risk that someone is being deceived and carry on anyway.

'By' deception

The word 'by' needs consideration because it indicates that the deception must cause the obtaining or evading. Thus any deception would have to come first.

Key case

In **Collis-Smith (1971)** D had filled up his car with petrol. He then said that his employer would pay for it. The problem here was twofold. Under contract law ownership passed to him when he put the petrol in the tank and mixed it with his own. This meant it was not 'property belonging to another' for theft under **s. 1**. He lied about his employer paying, which could amount to deception. However, the deception must cause the obtaining and if it comes after the obtaining, as it did here, then it did not cause it. Closing this loophole was one of the reasons the **1978 Act** was passed. This could now be evading liability or making off without payment under **s. 2** or **s. 3** of the **1978 Act**.

Food for thought

It is hard to see a causal connection in **Ray**. The HL seemed to base their decision on the idea that the waiter is lulled into a sense of false security, and thus deceived into leaving the room, giving D the chance to 'do a runner'. Did the waiter only leave the room because of the implied representation though? If not then there is arguably no 'obtaining *by* deception'. What if the waiter had been called over by another customer and D took the opportunity to leg it? The representation by D that the meal would be paid for hasn't caused the obtaining – the other diner has. The courts appear to treat the causation issue somewhat inconsistently.

Dishonesty

'Dishonest' is judged as for theft. This means applying the test in **Ghosh (1982)**. Only if the jury can answer 'yes' to both the following questions is D deemed dishonest:

- Was D dishonest according to the ordinary standards of reasonable and honest people?
- Did D realise that what was done was dishonest by those standards?

So, the common elements for these three deception offences are:

Deception	The deception must cause the obtaining or evading	Dishonesty

Now we'll look at the specific offences.

Obtaining property by deception s. 15(1) Theft Act 1968

'*A person who **by deception dishonestly obtains property belonging to another, with the intention of permanently depriving the other of it** shall on conviction on indictment be liable to imprisonment for a term not exceeding ten years.*'

Obtains

This includes obtaining ownership, possession or control.

Example | I tell you I need your car for an emergency. You kindly lend it to me for the day. I actually just wanted it for a holiday and keep it for a week. I have, by deception (I lied), obtained (got possession of) property (the car) belonging to another (you).

Property belonging to another

This is the same definition as for theft. It can therefore include money and intangible property. In **Preddy (1996)** a problem arose.

Key case

In **Preddy** the Ds made mortgage applications giving false information. The subsequent loans were made by electronic transfer and they were convicted under **s. 15**. Their appeal was allowed on the grounds that the property was not 'property belonging to another'. The credit received in D's bank account was not the same as the property debited from the victim's account.

This problem has now been dealt with by the new **s. 15A** inserted by the **Theft (Amendment) Act 1996**. It adds a new offence of 'obtaining a money transfer by deception'.

Mens rea

In summary:

- The deception must be intentional or reckless – **Goldman (1997)**;
- D must act dishonestly – **Ghosh** test.

The first two have already been covered. The third is the same as for theft, i.e. treating it as your own to dispose of regardless of the rights of the owner.

Obtaining services by deception s. 1(1) Theft Act 1978

'A person who by deception dishonestly obtains services from another is guilty of an offence.'

Obtains a service

This is slightly wider than obtaining in relation to property under **s. 15**. **Section 1(2)** adds that it is an obtaining of services *'where the other is induced to confer a benefit by doing some act, or causing or permitting some act to be done on the understanding that the benefit has been, or will be, paid for'*.

Example

'**Doing**' some act is straightforward. This would include getting someone to give you a haircut, clean your suit or repair your car. You induce them to 'do' something.

'**Causing**' an act to be done would be where the deception is practised on a third party. For example, inducing an employer into telling an employee to cut your hair etc. Here you induce the employer to 'cause' another to do it.

'**Permitting**' an act would include inducing someone into allowing you a service. An example would be inducing the owner of a club to allow you to use the club's facilities. This could also cover self-service situations, such as filling up with petrol. Here you induce someone into 'permitting' something to be done.

In all three cases the act which confers the benefit must be done, caused or permitted as a result of the deception.

The **Theft (Amendment) Act 1996** has affected the law here too. In **Halai (1983)** it had been held that lending money on a mortgage did not amount to a 'service' under **s. 1**. In **Cooke (1997)** the CA ruled that **Halai** should no longer be followed. They confirmed that following **Preddy** a charge under **s. 15** of the 1968 **Act** would fail, but accepted the prosecution's argument that a conviction under **s. 1** of the 1978 **Act** could be substituted. The 1996 **Act** inserts a new **s. 1(3)** into the 1978 **Act** which specifically overrules **Halai**. It provides that it is an obtaining of services where someone is induced to make a loan on the understanding that payments will be made in respect of it (e.g. interest payments).

In **Sofrinou (2003)** D obtained banking and credit card services by deception, then overdrew the accounts and exceeded the credit limit. The CA said the words 'on the understanding that the benefit has been or will be paid for' would exclude free services. However, although free at the outset, the jury could assume the bank would charge interest once the account is overdrawn. **S. 1** applied.

Mens rea

In summary:

- The deception must be intentional or reckless – **Goldman (1997)**;
- D must act dishonestly – **Ghosh** test.

There is no need for intent to permanently deprive.

Task

Look back at the differences in **s. 1** and **s. 15**, then compare the following situations. Would either be obtaining by deception? If so, would it be **s. 1** or **s. 15**?

1 Sam goes to a self-service petrol station and fills up with petrol. He then tells the cashier he has left his wallet at home but that his employer will pay. He gives the cashier the name of a local company. In fact he was sacked last week.

2 Sue goes into the local petrol station and asks the cashier if there is anyone that can help fill her car up as she has broken her arm. She gives the cashier a stolen credit card. The cashier asks one of the guys from the car wash to help out.

Examination pointer

Look for clues, such as the obtaining coming before any deception. A restaurant meal can come under obtaining property (the food) or services (bringing it). If there is no deception discuss **s. 15** and **s. 1** briefly but go on to explain **s. 3** of the 1978 **Act**. (Note this was passed after the **Ray** case.) There may also be liability under **s. 2**.

Evasion of liability by deception s. 2 Theft Act 1978

There are three different offences under **s. 2**. **Section 2(1)** provides there is an offence:

'where a person by any deception':

(a) *'dishonestly **secures the remission of the whole or part of any existing liability to make a payment**, whether his own liability or another's';* or

(b) *'with intent to make permanent default in whole or in part on any existing liability to make a payment, or with intent to let another do so, dishonestly **induces the creditor or any person claiming payment on behalf of the creditor to wait for payment . . . or forgo payment';** or*

(c) *'dishonestly **obtains any exemption from or abatement of liability to make a payment'.***

In what follows I refer to (a), (b) and (c) rather a lot, so flick back to this page whenever you're in doubt.

Securing remission: s. 2(1)(a)

This covers situations where one person deceives another to let them off all or part of an existing debt.

Example	I agree to buy your car. We agree that you will deliver it the next day and I will then come and pay you. When I come to pay I tell you that there was a scratch mark on it and get you to take £50 off the price. I had actually scratched it trying to put it in my garage. I have, by deception (I lied about the scratch), secured the remission (you let me off) of part of the liability (£50).

In **Jackson (1983)** D used a stolen credit card to pay for petrol. The CA held this came under **(a)** as the garage would ask the credit card company for payment. D had therefore secured remission of his liability to pay.

Inducing a creditor to wait or forgo payment: s. 2(1)(b)

For both (a) and (b) there is an existing liability to pay, which D is trying to get out of, so they are similar. However, (b) includes inducing another to *wait for* payment.

Example	I borrow £500 from a colleague. When it is due to be repaid I haven't got the money. I tell her some hard luck story about my poor old mother who needs an urgent operation which can only be done privately. My colleague says, 'Don't worry, pay me later'. I have, by deception (my hard luck story isn't true), induced a creditor (my colleague) to wait for payment (the £500).

In **Turner (1974)** D told his creditors he had no cash and induced them to take a cheque. He knew the cheque would not be honoured. He therefore induced them to wait. Under **s. 2(3)**, if D writes cheques which will not be honoured, this is treated as inducing the creditor to wait.

Key case

In **Holt and Lee (1981)** two Ds made a plan to avoid paying for a meal by telling the waiter they had already paid another member of staff. It wasn't their lucky day – they were overheard by an off-duty policeman who promptly arrested them. They were convicted of an attempt at inducing the restaurant to forgo payment.

Note (b) adds *'with intent to make permanent default'*, so if D intends to pay later there is no offence.

Obtaining an exemption from or abatement of liability: s. 2(1)(c)

This covers situations where D tries to avoid paying an existing *or future debt* or tries to get the debt reduced (abatement means reduction), whereas (a) and (b) only cover *existing* liability. It also arises where D tries to prevent a debt from occurring at all.

Example I pretend to be a student to get reduced travel rates, and buy a season ticket. I have, by deception (pretending to be a student), obtained an abatement (reduced price) of future liability (the full price of the ticket).
Lying on your tax return to avoid paying the full tax due would also come under this offence.

Key case

In **Sibartie (1983)** the CA said the question to ask was whether D's actions came within the 'ordinary meaning' of paragraph (c). By flashing an invalid season ticket at a London Underground inspector D was representing he was the owner of a valid one, and so had obtained an exemption (from the fare due) by deception.

Food for thought

Smith and Hogan, in their textbook *Criminal Law*, argue that a case like **Sibartie** should come under (b). D had induced the inspector to forego payment which was already due. He had not induced the inspector to remit liability but to believe there was no liability. This seems right. It is essentially the same as **Holt**. Someone is induced to forego payment because they believe payment has already been made. These three offences clearly overlap. If judges and academics are unsure where the dividing lines are then the law lacks certainty.

In **Firth (1990)** a hospital consultant was convicted under (c). He had failed to tell the hospital that two patients he had operated on were private patients. He therefore avoided a future liability – being billed by the hospital.

Food for thought

The definition of deception includes 'words or conduct'. It does not say 'silence'. The courts have stretched the meaning of 'conduct' to apparently include silence. This can be seen in **Ray**. The diner didn't *do* anything. Nor did **Firth**.

Mens rea

For all three subsections:

- The deception must be intentional or reckless – **Goldman 1997**
- D must act dishonestly – **Ghosh** test

For (b) there is also intent to make permanent default. This is applied as for **s. 15** intent to permanently deprive.

Examination pointer

Note the overlap between the offences. Pay particular attention to the differences. This will help you to identify which is appropriate. As noted above there may be a problem with the deception not coming before the obtaining. More than one offence will probably need to be explained and applied.

Reforms

Note that the **1978 Act** was passed to fill some of the gaps left by the 1968 one. Thus **Collis-Smith** could now be guilty of evading liability. The **1996 Amendment Act** fills in the gap left by 'services' to include loans and mortgages. This clarifies the confusion following **Halai**.

Consider whether the reforms have gone far enough to make the law satisfactory.

Following a consultation paper in 1999, the **Law Commission** published **Report No. 276** in 2002 on theft and the deception offences. Details of this are on the Commission's website (see p. 500). It highlights some of the remaining difficulties and proposals for further reform.

Summary

Common elements

A deception	Causes the obtaining or evading	Dishonesty
by words or conduct	deception must come first	Ghosh test
of a person	can be a 'continuing representation'	
deliberate or reckless		

Differences

S. 15	S. 1	S. 2(1)(a)	S. 2(1)(b)	S. 2(1)(c)
obtains property	obtains a service, i.e. someone confers a benefit by	secures remission of	induces creditor to wait or forego payment of	obtains exemption from or abatement of
belonging to another	doing an act or		existing liability	
with intent to permanently deprive	causing an act to be done or	existing liability	intent to make permanent default	future liability
	permitting an act to be done			
	on the understanding it is to be paid for			

Self-test questions

1 From which case did the quote at the beginning of this unit come?

2 What are the three common elements of the deception offences?

3 What are the three different ways a service can be obtained?

4 What does **s. 15A** cover and under what Act was it introduced?

5 What is the additional *mens rea* requirement in **s. (2)(1)(b)**?

For further resources and updates please go to the Companion Website accompanying this book at **www.pearsoned.co.uk/russell**

Making off without payment

[making off] *may be an exercise accompanied by the sound of trumpets or a silent stealing away after the folding of tents.*

CA in **Brooks and Brooks (1983)**

By the end of this Unit you should be able to:

- Explain the *actus reus* and *mens rea* of making off
- Explain how the law applies in practice by reference to cases
- Identify possible criticisms in this area of law

The **Theft Act 1978 s. 3** provides:

'*a person who, **knowing that payment on the spot for any goods supplied or service done is required or expected from him, dishonestly makes off without having paid as required or expected and with intent to avoid payment** of the amount due*',

shall be guilty of an offence.

This covers a variety of situations which, for some reason, may fall outside theft and the deceptions. For example, leaving without paying for petrol or a meal. The property doesn't belong to another for theft (because it is now mixed with your own petrol or stomach contents!). If you have not deceived anyone into giving you the goods then the deception offences will also fail. It is for this reason that the **1978 Act** introduced this new offence. There is no need for proof of a deception, nor that the obtaining was caused by any deception.

Let's take the various parts of the *actus reus* and *mens rea* in turn:

- *Actus reus*: Makes off, without having paid as required or expected.

- *Mens rea*: Knowing payment on the spot is required, dishonesty and intent to avoid payment.

Actus reus

Makes off

In **Brooks and Brooks (1983)** the CA held that makes off meant 'depart'. There is no need to run away. They also indicated that the 'spot' was the 'place where payment is required'. This would include a cash desk.

In **McDavitt (1981)** D was not liable under **s. 3** when he refused to pay a restaurant bill after an argument with the manager. The 'spot' was held to be the restaurant itself. He had not yet left the restaurant, so had not made off from the spot.

Compare the following cases.

In **Troughton v MPC (1987)** the CA quashed D's conviction on the basis that payment was not yet 'required on the spot'. D was drunk. He asked a taxi driver to take him home. He couldn't remember exactly where he lived and they had an argument. The taxi driver took him to a police station where he ran off. He had made off, but not from the spot where payment was 'required'.

Another taxi case was **Aziz (1993)**. Here there was another dispute about the fare. When the two passengers refused to pay, the driver started to take them to the police station. They became disruptive and he pulled up. They ran off but D was caught and arrested. He argued that he had not made off from the spot where payment was required. The CA held that the 'spot' could be in the taxi itself or even outside it. There was no need for a specific location. **S. 3** was satisfied.

Food for thought

Are these decisions contradictory on the face of it? Should the 'spot' be more clearly defined? The decision in **Troughton** may be influenced by the fact that as he had not been taken to the agreed destination no payment was legally required. In **Aziz** they had already been taken home.

Without having paid as required

Payment cannot be 'required' if the goods or services supplied are contrary to the law. This could include drugs or stolen goods. It can also cover situations where the payment is not legally enforceable because it isn't yet due, as in **Troughton**.

Mens rea

There are three parts to this:

- D **knows** that payment is required on 'the spot'.
- D is **dishonest**.
- D **intends** to avoid paying.

Knowing payment is required on 'the spot'

If D believes the goods or services are on credit then there may be no offence. Also, if D believed that someone else was paying.

Example You get a taxi back from the office Christmas party. You haven't any money so can't pay when the driver asks for the fare. You thought the taxi journey was on account and a bill would be sent. Alternatively, you believed that your employer was paying for transport home for all staff. In neither case do you 'know payment is required on the spot'. You have not committed an offence.

Food for thought

'From the spot' is part of the *mens rea* (knowing that payment on the spot is required) but has been treated within the *actus reus* in cases such as **McDavitt**. This could cause confusion for a jury. The definition says 'knowing payment on the spot is required D makes off'. This is being interpreted as 'D makes off from *that* spot'.

Dishonesty

This is a matter for the jury. The normal **Ghosh** rules will be applied. Note, however, that D won't be dishonest if there was a genuine reason for not paying.

Example I order a meal in a restaurant. When it eventually arrives I eat a few mouthfuls but it is cold and inedible. I refuse to pay for it and leave. This will not be making off as the *mens rea* is not proved. I have not been dishonest.

Intends to avoid paying

It must be shown that D had no intention of *ever* paying. A temporary intention is not enough.

Key case

In **Allen (1985)** D left his hotel without paying the bill. He argued that he intended to pay as soon as a business deal matured. The HL interpreted s. 3 to mean D intends to avoid paying *permanently*. They held that the question of whether D intended to avoid payment permanently was one for the jury to decide, and quashed his conviction.

Task

Look back at my earlier example of getting a taxi home from the office party. What if I realised the office wouldn't pay but I intended to send the money at the end of the month when I got paid? Explain what I might argue and whether it would relate to *actus reus* or *mens rea*.

Examination pointer

Note the overlap. In a problem question look carefully at the given facts and the timing of any deception. It may be that several offences need discussing. For example, you may see a problem with theft or, for example, the deception not coming before the obtaining. More than one offence may need to be explained and applied.

Summary

Offence	*Actus reus*	Cases	*Mens rea*
S. 3 Theft Act 1978 Making off without payment	Makes off Without paying as required or expected	Brooks Troughton Ghosh Allen	Knowledge that payment on the spot is required Dishonesty Intent to avoid payment permanently

 ## Self-test questions

1 What are the two parts to the *actus reus* under **s. 3**?

2 What are the three parts to the *mens rea* under **s. 3**?

3 Is a deception required?

4 Why was D guilty in **Aziz** but not in **Troughton**?

 For further resources and updates please go to the Companion Website accompanying this book at **www.pearsoned.co.uk/russell**

Criminal damage

> ... it is unnecessary to establish such definite or actual damage as renders the property useless, or prevents it from serving its normal function.
>
> Walters J, **Samuels v Stubbs (1972)**

By the end of this Unit you should be able to:

- Explain the *actus reus* and *mens rea* of the criminal damage offences
- Distinguish between the basic and aggravated offences
- Explain how the law applies in practice by reference to cases
- Identify possible criticisms

The **Criminal Damage Act 1971 s. 1** covers three offences:

- criminal damage s. 1(1)
- criminal damage with intent to endanger life s. 1(2)
- arson s. 1(3)

Arguably there are four offences as arson may also be with intent to endanger life. There is, however, no separate section for this. It would be both **s. 1(2)** and **s. 1(3)**.

Criminal damage

Section 1(1) provides:

> '*A person who **without lawful excuse destroys or damages any property belonging to another intending to destroy or damage any such property or being reckless as to whether any such property would be destroyed** or damaged shall be guilty of an offence.*'

Let's now break the offence down a bit.

Actus reus

Destroys or damages	property	belonging to another	without lawful excuse

Destroys or damages

This covers more than you might think. In **Samuels v Stubbs (1972)** Walters J said it was difficult to lay down any general rules about what would amount to damage. He said much would depend on the particular circumstances, the type of property damaged and how it was affected. He then continued with the opening quote. In **Hardman v Chief Constable of Avon Somerset Constabulary (1986)** members of CND used water-soluble paints on pavements to depict vaporised humans in a protest to mark the 40th anniversary of the dropping of the Hiroshima bomb. This would easily wash away. However, their conviction was upheld as the council had been put to the expense of cleaning the pavements. This can be compared to **R v A (a minor) (1978)** where D spat on a policeman's overcoat and was found not guilty on the grounds that the spittle could be easily removed with a damp cloth.

It would appear to be criminal damage if someone is put to the expense of repairing or cleaning. It will not amount to criminal damage if there is no impairment to usefulness or value. In **Morphitis v Salmon (1990)** a scratch on scaffolding was held not to amount to criminal damage as it did not impair the usefulness or value of the property.

Food for thought

In **Hardman** the drawings would have been washed away by the rain before long. In **Roe v Kingerlee (1986)** a conviction was obtained after D smeared mud on the walls of a police cell. Should the damage be of a more permanent nature in order to find D guilty? Or is the fact that any damage has been caused enough in itself? It could be argued that a wide interpretation helps to prevent unsocial acts such as damaging community garden displays and graffiti.

Property s. 10(1)

The definition is similar to that for theft but there are slight differences. Obviously you cannot damage intangible property, so this is excluded. Wild creatures which have been tamed or are ordinarily kept in captivity are included, but mushrooms, flowers, fruit or foliage of a plant growing wild on any land are not.

Belonging to another

The property must belong to another. As with theft this is wider than just ownership. It includes another having custody or control of property, having a right in property or having a charge on it. It is not an offence to destroy your own property. Also if you *believe* you are destroying your own property you will have a defence. The belief does not have to be justifiable as long as it is honestly held.

In **Smith (1974)** some tenants had damaged floorboards and panels when removing wiring which they had installed with the landlord's permission. However, the wiring had become part of the fixtures of the flat and they had no right to take it. Their conviction was quashed on appeal. The CA held that no offence is committed if a person damages property *'in the honest though mistaken belief that the property is his own, and, provided that the belief is honestly held, it is irrelevant to consider whether or not it is a justifiable belief.'*

Example I break up the dining room furniture to put on the fire because I have run out of firewood. I am not guilty of an offence as the furniture was mine. It turns out that one of the chairs belonged to my lodger. If I did not realise this then I am still not guilty of an offence, as I honestly believed this was also mine.

Without lawful excuse

In addition to the general defences there is a special defence of lawful excuse in s. 5(2)(a) and (b). This does not apply to criminal damage endangering life though. Lawful excuse is where D destroys or damages property in the belief that:

- the person entitled to consent would have consented to the destruction or damage if they had known of it and its circumstances (**s. 5(2)(a)**) or
- it was necessary in order to protect property belonging to himself or another which he believed was in immediate need of protection and he believed the means adopted were reasonable, having regard to all the circumstances (**s. 5(2)(b)**).

Essentially there are two defences here, belief in consent and protection of property. A few cases will help to explain how they work.

Section 5(2)(a)

In **Jaggard v Dickenson (1981)** D was drunk and broke into a house thinking it belonged to a friend. She believed her friend would have consented to the damage caused. In fact it was the house of a stranger and the magistrates held that she could not rely on the defence because she was intoxicated. This was reversed on appeal. It was held that her defence should be based upon her belief and her drunkenness did not invalidate this.

In **DPP v Blake (1993)** a vicar used a marker pen to write a biblical quotation on a wall outside Parliament. He was protesting about the Gulf War and argued the consent defence. In this case he claimed he had God's consent! He failed. The court held that nothing within the meaning of the **Act** covered consent by God.

Section 5(2)(b)

In **DPP v Blake (1993)** the vicar also tried to rely on s. 5(2)(b). He claimed he was protecting the property of the people of the Gulf States. His defence failed on the grounds that the people of the Gulf States were too far away to benefit from his actions, therefore **s. 5(2)(b)** was not applicable.

In **Chamberlain v Lindon (1998)**, however, D successfully relied on **s. 5(2)(b)** when he demolished a neighbour's wall. He believed it blocked his right of access to his own property. He had an honest belief that his property rights needed immediate protection and that the means adopted were reasonable, having regard to all the circumstances.

Food for thought

The decision in **Jaggard** seems at odds with the normal rules on intoxication. Intoxication is not a defence to a basic intent crime such as criminal damage. However, her appeal succeeded and the fact that she may not have made the mistake had she been sober did not invalidate her belief.

Mens rea

The *mens rea* is:

● intention to destroy or damage property belonging to another; or

● recklessness as to whether such property is destroyed or damaged.

Note that recklessness is now subjective recklessness. This comes from **Gemmell and Richards (2003)**. The HL overruled their own decision in **Caldwell (1982)** where they had held that the *mens rea* for criminal damage was objective recklessness. This is no longer good law. The question now would be whether D recognised the risk of damaging or destroying property (and of endangering life for the aggravated offence).

Key case

In **Gemmell and Richards (2003)** two boys aged 11 and 13 set light to some papers outside the back of a shop. Several premises were badly damaged. They were convicted of arson on the basis of **Caldwell** recklessness, i.e. whether the risk of damage was obvious to a reasonable person. Their ages were therefore not taken into account. They appealed. The CA cannot overrule a decision of the HL and their argument under the **Human Rights Act** also failed. They made a further appeal to the HL, which used the **1966 Practice Statement** to overrule their previous decision. The HL held that the **Caldwell** test was wrong and that the *defendant* had to have recognised that there was some kind of risk.

Examination pointer

Criminal damage may well come up with a question on theft or one of the related offences. Look out for things like 'D broke into the house to steal something'. Burglary will be the obvious crime but a discussion of criminal damage in relation to the breaking in can earn extra marks. Unless, that is, the question specifically asks you to discuss only offences under the **Theft Act**. As always, read the question carefully.

Destroying or damaging property with intent to endanger life

This is often referred to as aggravated criminal damage.

Section 1(2) provides that:

'a person who without lawful excuse destroys or damages any property, whether belonging to himself or another:

(a) *intending to destroy or damage any property or being reckless as to whether any property would be destroyed or damaged; and*

(b) *intending* **by the destruction or damage to endanger the life of another** *or being reckless to whether the life of another would be thereby endangered*

shall be guilty of an offence.'

This is similar to criminal damage but with the addition that D intended or was reckless with regard to endangering life. It is a much more serious offence. The maximum sentence is life imprisonment.

Here the damage does not have to be to property belonging to another.

Example I set fire to my house so I can claim on the insurance. This would not be an offence under **s. 1(1)** but if I knew there were people inside I could be convicted under **s. 1(2)**.

Note the words 'intending *by the destruction or damage* to endanger the life of another'. In **Steer (1987)** D was convicted under **s. 1(2)** when he shot at the window of a former business partner. His appeal was successful. The HL held that the danger to life had to come from the destruction or damage of the property. It was not enough that it resulted from the original action (firing shots).

Food for thought

Do you agree with the decision in **Steer**? Do you think firing a gun through someone's window ought to be enough for a conviction? The problem is with the words *'by the destruction or damage'*. The danger was not caused by the broken window but by the shots.

There does not necessarily have to *be* a danger to life. It is enough that D realised that life would be endangered.

Example I cut the brake cable on someone's bike because I have a grudge against the owner. I know that life will be endangered as soon as it is ridden. As it happens the owner has just got a new bike. The old one is taken apart for spares and never ridden. I have not actually endangered life – but I intended to do so. I am guilty of aggravated criminal damage.

Arson

Section 1(3) provides:

'An offence committed under this section by destroying or damaging property by fire shall be charged as arson.'

This is also regarded as a very serious offence. The maximum sentence is life imprisonment. It is criminal damage as above under **s. 1(1)** or **s. 1(2)** but if the damage was caused by fire it 'shall be charged as arson'. Thus there can be arson contrary to **s. 1(1)** and **s. 1(3)** – the basic arson offence – or arson contrary to **s. 1(2)** and **s. 1(3)** – the aggravated offence.

In **MPC *v* Caldwell (1982)** D was convicted of arson when he set fire to a chair in the hotel where he worked. Although the fire was put out before anyone was harmed he had endangered the lives of the residents.

In **Elliot *v* C (a minor) (1983)** a 14-year-old girl with low intelligence was convicted of arson. She had set fire to a neighbour's shed. She had poured white spirit over the floor and set fire to it to get warm. This case was decided on the old test for recklessness. This meant it did not matter that she did not recognise the risk. A reasonable person would have seen the risk and this was enough. Since **Gemmell** the test is subjective recklessness. Under this test she would have had no *mens rea*.

The lawful excuse defence can be used here too. Thus in **Denton (1982)** D set fire to his employer's mill and successfully argued that his employer had consented to this in order to make a fraudulent insurance claim. As with criminal damage it can only be used for the basic offence. If the damage by fire is done with intent to endanger life then lawful excuse cannot be used.

Food for thought

Elliott is a case which can be used to discuss the problems of **Caldwell** recklessness and why it has been abolished.

Task

Look at the summary of the offences, below. Make a note of the differences and add a case example for each. Keep this for revision.

Summary

The basic offence s. 1(1)

Actus reus	*Mens rea*	Defences
damaging or destroying	intent or subjective recklessness	belief in consent
property	as to whether property is damaged or destroyed	belief the property needs protecting
belonging to another		general defences

The aggravated offence s. 1(2)

Actus reus	Mens rea	Defences
damaging or destroying	intent or subjective recklessness	general defences only
property	as to whether property is damaged or destroyed and	
(need not belong to another)	as to endangering life	

Arson s. 1(3)

Actus reus	Mens rea	Defences
damaging or destroying	intent or subjective recklessness	belief in consent
property	as to whether property is damaged or destroyed	belief the property needs protecting
belonging to another		
by fire		general defences

Self-test questions

1 Does damage have to be permanent?

2 What is the *mens rea* of the basic offence?

3 What changed in **Gemmell**?

4 What is the lawful excuse under **s. 5(2)(a)**?

5 Does D's belief have to be reasonable for **s. 5**?

For further resources and updates please go to the Companion Website accompanying this book at **www.pearsoned.co.uk/russell**

DECEPTION OFFENCES, MAKING OFF WITHOUT PAYMENT AND CRIMINAL DAMAGE

Deceptions	
Obtaining property by deception	**s. 15 Theft Act 1968**
Obtaining services by deception	**s. 1 Theft Act 1978**
Evading liability by deception	**s. 2 Theft Act 1978**
Common elements Deception must cause the obtaining Must be intentional or reckless D must act dishonestly	**Main differences** **s. 15** intent to permanently deprive **s. 2(1)(b)** intent to make permanent default **s. 2(1)(c)** includes future liability
Making off without payment	**s. 3 Theft Act 1978**
Actus reus *Mens rea*	Makes off without paying Knowledge, dishonesty, intent to avoid payment permanently
Criminal damage	**s. 1 Criminal Damage Act 1971**
Actus reus *Mens rea*	To damage or destroy property belonging to another Intent or subjective recklessness (**Gemmell**)

Task

Add the principle and brief facts to the case

Case	Principle	Facts
MPC *v* Charles (1977)		
Collis-Smith (1971)		
Preddy (1996)		
Holt and Lee (1981)		
Sibartie (1983)		
McDavitt (1981)		
Allen (1985)		
Hardman (1986)		
Gemmell and Richards (2003)		

Key criticisms

- The courts appear to treat the causation issue somewhat inconsistently – **Ray**.
- Applying the test in **Ghosh** is no easier for the jury here than it is in theft cases.
- The **1996 Amendment Act** clarifies the confusion following **Halai**, but have the reforms made the law satisfactory?
- The **Law Commission Report No. 276** highlights some of the remaining difficulties.
- The considerable overlap between the three deception offences can be confusing.
- The law on deceptions is unnecessarily complicated, in s. **2 Theft Act 1978** particularly.
- The conflicting case law on what amounts to criminal damage is unfair.

Examination practice

AQA January 2003
In your view, how satisfactory is the current law on the deception offences?

(25 marks)

Module 6 connections

Morals	Criminal damage allows a defence of lawful excuse. There may be times when it is morally right to cause damage, e.g. where D believes the owner would consent or where it is necessary to protect other property	s. 5(2) Jaggard/ Chamberlain/Blake
	It is usually unacceptable for intoxication to be a defence; however, it is allowed for criminal damage	Jaggard
	Arguably there was a greater moral argument for acquitting CND than there was in the case of spitting at a policeman	Hardman/A
Justice	It is hard to say justice was done when comparing some of the decisions of the courts	Hardman/A
	Justice for the young boys was achieved by making recklessness subjective for criminal damage; they didn't realise the risk so there was no liability	Gemmell and Richards
Conflicting interests	In anti-war demonstrations and environmental protests the individual's right to protest is balanced against community interests, the individual's right to freedom of speech as against the community interests in having a clean environment	Hardman/Blake
Fault	Intent to make permanent default or not to pay permanently may be very hard to prove. D can say, 'I was going to pay next week when I got my wages'	s. 2(1)(b)/s. 3 Allen
	Do you think the *mens rea* for criminal damage should be subjective or objective recklessness?	Gemmell and Richards
Creativity	The courts have been ahead of Parliament in several cases. Should Parliament make further changes or should the judges continue to do so?	Cooke/Turner
	Do you think the HL was right to overrule itself in relation to the *mens rea* for criminal damage?	Gemmell and Richards

For further resources and updates please go to the Companion Website accompanying this book at www.pearsoned.co.uk/russell

Study Block 12
DEFENCES

Unit 37   Necessity, duress and duress of circumstances

These defences are used where D feels compelled to commit an offence because of a threat of some sort. There is an overlap between them so you should bear this in mind as you read the Unit, you will often have to discuss more than one when applying the law to a problem scenario involving a threat to D.

Example   Harry tells Andy that if Andy doesn't rob a bank he will beat him up. This is duress. If Andy drives into another car because he is being chased by a gang threatening to beat him up, this would be duress of circumstances. Here the threat isn't directly from another person but from the circumstances Andy finds himself in. It could also be seen as necessity but you will see that this defence is rare.

The only defences I have covered in this unit are those which are on the syllabus in Module 5 but not in Module 4. If you are not studying crime in Module 4 you will need to refer to the Units on:

- intoxication (p. 236);
- self-defence, prevention of crime and mistake (p. 242).

All these defences may apply to any of the crimes in Module 5; however, for examination purposes, duress is the *general* defence most often seen. Consent (or rather, belief in it) is also important but has a special meaning in relation to theft (and therefore robbery and burglary) and criminal damage. It is not on the syllabus as a *general* defence for Module 5; however, you should recognise that in a case of burglary, under **s. 9(1)(b)**, consent may have the effect of making grievous bodily harm lawful, so part of the *actus reus* would be missing. The same applies to self-defence. Intoxication is also popular and applies to all the Module 5 offences; in particular, it may remove the *mens rea* of intent in a theft charge even where the intoxicant is taken voluntarily. 'Drunken mistake' has also been allowed for a charge of criminal damage, even though not usually accepted for other crimes.

> **Example** In **Jaggard v Dickenson (1981)** D was drunk and broke into a house thinking it belonged to a friend and believing her friend would have consented to the damage caused – a defence under **s. 5(2) Criminal Damage Act 1971**. It was held that her drunkenness did not invalidate this defence; it was based upon her *belief* that her friend would consent; the reason for the belief didn't matter.

The summary at the end of this Block will also include the Module 4 defences so that you can compare them, and their effect.

Note that you no longer need to discuss defences in essay questions, i.e. there is no requirement for an evaluation of them. However, I have included 'Food for thought' boxes as this is a good area for tying in with Module 6. Defences often relate to issues of fault and morality (some defences excuse, or justify, the commission of a crime, some are limited for ethical reasons) and are taken into account when balancing the conflicting interests of D and the wider community, and are used as a way of achieving justice – and in some cases not doing so.

Necessity, duress and duress of circumstances

Necessity would open a door which no man could shut.

Lord Denning, **Southwark London Borough *v* Williams (1971)**

> **By the end of this Unit you should be able to:**
> - Explain these three defences and the limitations on them
> - Distinguish between these three defences, while noting the overlap between them
> - Explain how the law applies in practice by reference to cases
> - Identify possible criticisms

In each of these three defences D is arguing that there was no alternative to committing the crime. It was 'necessary' due to a threat or to the circumstances. In **Shayler (2001)** the CA suggested that duress and necessity were the same. Both were available to a charge under the **Official Secrets Act 1989**, although the argument that information had been revealed in the public interest was not enough, there had to be an imminent threat to life or limb. There is some difference between the defences. Necessity was used to justify a death in **Re A (Conjoined Twins)** but it is clear that duress cannot apply to murder. However, the dividing line between duress of circumstances and necessity, if any, is very faint and the terms have been used interchangeably by the courts. In fact in **Quayle (2005)**, discussed below, a new term, 'necessity by circumstances', was used.

Duress of threats is where there is a specific threat of harm to D if a particular crime is not committed. **Duress of circumstances** is where there is also a threat of harm. However, here the threat comes not from another person but from the surrounding circumstances. **Necessity** is similar to the latter. The circumstances leave D no alternative but to commit a crime. There is no need for a threat of harm to D, though. It is rarely seen and most cases of necessity now come under duress of circumstances.

Example

Don tells Dave that if he does not rob a bank he will kill his family. Dave can use duress as a defence to a burglary charge.

Don finds that Dave's family are away so instead he says he will set fire to his house if he doesn't rob the bank. Dave can't use the duress defences here as there is no threat of harm. He can't use necessity because there are alternatives – he could go to the police.

Dave is attacked by a violent gang while waiting at the traffic lights. He jumps the red light to get away. Dave can use duress of circumstances to the driving offence. This could also be called necessity.

Necessity

Necessity is rarely a defence in itself, though it may be used to reduce a sentence. Thus, stealing because you are starving is still theft, but your sentence may be less because you had some justification. In **Southwark London Borough v Williams (1971)** homelessness was not accepted as a reason for squatting (trespass). Lord Denning said that if it was, 'no one's house could be safe', and continued with the opening quote. He also said that if hunger could be used as a defence to theft, it would open another door through which 'all kinds of lawlessness and disorder would pass'.

In **Dudley and Stephens (1884)** the Ds had been shipwrecked and after several days in a lifeboat with no food they believed they would die. They killed and ate the cabin boy in order to save their own lives. The defence of necessity was rejected.

Duress of circumstances is really necessity in a modern form, but there are few 'real' cases of necessity. It may be allowed in particular circumstances laid down by statute. An example is **s. 5(2)(b)** of the **Criminal Damage Act 1971**, which allows for it to be a defence where damage is 'necessary' in order to protect property. One of the very few cases where necessity was successfully raised is **Re A (2000)**. A hospital sought a declaration that it would be lawful to operate on Siamese twins in the knowledge that one twin would die. The operation was the only way to save the life of the other twin. Although they may not have been prosecuted, they *could* have been charged with murder. They operated in the knowledge that one twin would die and so intended that consequence, even though they didn't desire it. The CA granted the declaration and confirmed they would have a defence of necessity. They made a distinction between cases of duress by threats or circumstances, and cases of real choice. In the latter, the question is one of justifying a choice between two evils. This is the defence of necessity. It would only succeed where the act *was necessary to avoid an inevitable evil, and the evil inflicted was not disproportionate* to the evil avoided.

Food for thought

It is clear from case law that duress is not a defence to murder. This was stated in **Howe (1987)** and extended to attempted murder in **Gotts (1992)**. **Dudley and Stephens** indicated this rule would also apply to necessity, although there was a special verdict in this case so it does not set a precedent. **Re A** suggests that it is possible that it could apply to murder. This case is seen as unique though, so again is unlikely to set a precedent. There is good reason for the limits on the defence. Nobody should be able to say that one person's life is any more important than another's. The difference between **Dudley** and **Re A** is that in the latter the doctors were not choosing another life over their own.

It could be argued that necessity should apply to more minor crimes, but Lord Denning's comments show the dangers of this. If you can argue that you have some kind of right to commit a crime in certain circumstances, there is a danger that people will not feel safe.

It was confirmed in **Quayle (2005)** that 'necessity' and 'necessity by circumstances' should be decided on a case-by-case basis. There are, however, certain requirements which will apply generally. We will look at duress first, as this is where the rules were established. Then we can look at some cases to illustrate duress of circumstances. Where these have developed, or reconfirmed, the law on duress generally I have included them in the discussion of duress. You should note in particular that the HL reconsidered the whole issue of duress in **Hasan (2005)** (duress of threats), and this was applied by the CA in **Quayle (2005)** (duress of circumstances) with approval.

It is for D to provide evidence of duress, but then the burden of proof is on the prosecution to disprove it. If the defence succeeds then D will be acquitted.

Duress

The original defence of duress occurs where D is forced to commit a crime because of a threat. An example would be 'if you don't steal the money, I will shoot you'. It is sometimes called duress of threats. This is mainly to distinguish it from the more recently developed duress of circumstances.

Key case

The test for establishing the defence was laid down in **Graham (1982)**. D was a homosexual who lived with his wife and another man. He was charged with the murder of his wife. He alleged that the other man had threatened and intimidated him, and argued duress as a defence. The HL upheld his conviction and established the test for duress. It is a two-part question for the jury:

Was the defendant impelled to act as he did because he believed that he had good cause to fear that if he did not so act he would be killed or caused serious injury? If so, have the prosecution made the jury sure that a sober person of reasonable firmness, sharing the characteristics of the defendant, would not have responded that way.

Put more simply:

- Did D believe that there was good cause to fear death or serious injury if the crime was not committed? (subjective)
- Would a sober person of reasonable firmness sharing the same characteristics have responded that way? (objective)

The test is therefore in part subjective and in part objective. However, the first part is not fully subjective because D must have 'good cause to fear'. Unlike self-defence and mistake, where as long as a belief is genuinely held it need not be reasonable, for duress it must be a reasonable belief.

The threat

The threat has to be a serious one. First, it must be a threat of *harm*. In **Valderrama-Vega (1985)** it was said that financial pressure and a threat of disclosing that D was a homosexual was not enough. In **Shayler (2001)** the CA said that duress was only available where the threat was to 'life or serious injury'. Second, it must be *imminent*. The rule was that if D could seek police protection or take evasive action then the defence was unavailable. Thus in **Gill (1963)** the defence failed because although there was a threat of harm if D did not steal a lorry, he had time to escape and seek help. This rule was relaxed in **Hudson and Taylor (1971)**. Two young girls had lied in court because they were told they would be harmed if they testified against the accused. They successfully appealed against their conviction for perjury. The CA rejected the prosecution's argument that the threat wasn't imminent. They said that it was irrelevant that it could not be carried out immediately; it could be carried out on the streets late that night. The CA clearly recognised that the girls may not have received effective police protection from the threats. In **Abdul-Hussain (1999)** the Ds successfully appealed against a hijacking conviction. They believed they would be executed if returned to their own country, which they thought was imminent, and hijacked a plane to escape. The CA accepted duress of circumstances did not need an *immediate* threat, as long as it was *influencing* D at the time the crime was committed.

However, in **Hasan (2005)** Lord Bingham referred to both these cases and disapproved them on this point. He thought the limitation that D must have no chance of evasive action had been 'unduly weakened'. This HL case reaffirms that the threat must be immediate, or at least there should be no possibility of taking evasive action.

Key case

In **Hasan (2005)** D had fallen in with a drug dealer who was known to be violent. He told the dealer about a house where there was a lot of money kept in a safe. The dealer then told him that if he didn't burgle the house his family would be harmed. When charged with burglary he argued duress. Lord Bingham said that the defence was excluded where, due to a 'voluntary association' with criminals, '*he foresaw, or ought reasonably to have foreseen, the risk of being subjected to any compulsion by threats of violence*'. He also said that if the harm threatened was not '*such as he reasonably expects to follow immediately, or almost immediately*' then there was little doubt that D should take evasive action '*whether by going to the police, or in some other way, to avoid committing the crime*'.

In **Hasan (2005)** Lord Bingham restated the essential requirements for duress. These are:

- The threat relied on must be to cause death or serious injury.
- The criminal conduct which it is sought to excuse has been directly caused by the threats.
- The threat must be directed to D or a member of D's family, or to '*a person for whose safety the defendant would reasonably regard himself as responsible*'.
- D may rely on duress only if there was no evasive action that could reasonably have been taken (such as going to the police, disapproving **Hudson and Taylor**).
- The questions for the jury were both objective (did D '*reasonably believe*' there was a threat, approving **Graham**).

● The defence is not available where, as a result of a voluntary association with criminals, D *'ought reasonably to have foreseen'* the risk of violence.

Examination pointer

Look for any evidence of a threat in the given scenario. If there is a threat from a person then duress will be appropriate. You will need to apply each of the rules from **Hasan** to decide whether you think the defence will succeed.

Sober person of reasonable firmness

In **Graham**, D had been drunk as well as threatened but the court said that voluntary intoxication could not be taken into account. The test refers to a *'sober person'*. *'Of reasonable firmness'* means factors such as timidity and susceptibility to threats will not be taken into account. In **Bowen (1996)** D had been charged with obtaining services by deception. He said he only did it after he and his family were threatened. The court refused to take his low IQ into account. However, as well as age and sex the CA did say that pregnancy, a recognised mental illness or serious physical disability could be relevant characteristics because these could affect D's ability to resist.

Food for thought

In **Bowen**, the fact that his very low IQ made D particularly vulnerable to threats was not taken into account. However, his low IQ clearly affected his ability to be 'firm'. This can seem unjust.

Self-induced duress

In **Sharp (1987)** D had been involved in a plan with a gang to commit a robbery; he then tried to withdraw but was threatened. Someone was killed during the robbery and his conviction for manslaughter was upheld. The CA made clear that the defence would fail where D knew that the gang he had joined might put pressure on him to commit an offence. This is self-induced duress as D had a choice in the first place. The key issue is what is known about the gang. In **Shepherd (1987)** the defence succeeded as there was no evidence of any violence prior to the threats. It is now clear that this is an objective test. Even if D didn't know of any violent tendencies, the defence will fail if these would have been obvious to anyone else. This was made clear in **Hasan**, which is an example of self-induced duress. The question is whether D *should* have known, rather than whether D *did* know, that there was a risk of being threatened. The words *'or ought reasonably to have foreseen'* in **Graham** had indicated this.

Duress of circumstances

Duress of circumstances is relatively new. It arose during the 80s in driving offence cases. Recognising that necessity was rarely allowed as a defence, lawyers had started to argue that duress could extend beyond the traditional 'threat by a person' to situations where D has no alternative but to commit a crime. In **Conway (1988)** D was in his car when he was approached by two men. He believed they were going to attack him and he drove recklessly to escape from the perceived threat. The CA accepted the defence and said it was 'convenient' to refer to such a defence as 'duress of circumstances'. In **Martin (1988)** D had driven his son to work while disqualified. He argued that his son might lose his job if he was late and his wife had threatened to commit suicide if he did not take him. The judge said that English law recognised a 'defence of necessity' in extreme circumstances. In such cases, where the threat came from dangers other than a threat from another person, '*it is conveniently called duress of circumstances*'. In the early days it was most commonly used for driving offences. In **DPP v Bell (1992)** D drove while drunk, again to escape from a threatening gang. The defence succeeded because as soon as he was out of danger he stopped in a lay-by. In 2000, the footballer David Beckham was not so lucky. He was being chased by reporters and was charged with speeding. His defence of duress was rejected on the basis that driving at over 75 mph in a 50 limit was not the only option available to him.

It is not confined to driving offences though. In **Pommell (1995)** D was charged with possession of a firearm and successfully argued duress. He said that he had taken the gun from someone who was threatening to use it in a revenge attack. As this was in the early hours of the morning he kept it overnight, intending to take it to the police in the morning. The police had, he said, arrived before he could do so.

Although coming from circumstances rather than a person, in all these cases there was a threat of physical harm, either to D or to another. It will still not apply to the cases that concerned Lord Denning, theft and trespass.

Examination pointer

If there is no evidence in the given scenario of a threat from a person, look for any circumstances that may be threatening, and consider necessity or duress of circumstances. There still needs to be a threat of physical harm, whichever defence is used. Duress of circumstances is more common, so apply the rules from **Hasan**. If there is any evidence that D belongs to a gang, look at how **Hasan** confirmed the rules on self-induced duress seen in **Sharp** and **Shepherd**.

Task

Look at the following situations and decide if I can successfully use a defence of duress:

● I am threatened with being exposed as a cheat and a drunk if I do not steal a packet of smoked salmon from the supermarket. I do so and am charged with theft.

● I am chased by a man who is threatening to hit me. I steal a car to escape. I drive to a nearby house where I have friends. I am charged with theft.

● I am at a party and a bit drunk. As I live 30 miles away I intend to stay overnight. An old enemy turns up and threatens to beat me up. I run outside and see my car in the drive. I get in and drive all the way home. I am charged with driving with excess alcohol.

The overlap

It had seemed that necessity had been replaced by duress of circumstances. However, cases such as **Re A** show that there may still be occasions where only necessity can be used. In most cases, however, there is no difference between the defences except in the words used to describe them.

In **Quayle (2005)** D had argued necessity in defence to a charge of growing cannabis. He argued that it was necessary for medical reasons. He was in pain and it was the only drug that allowed him to sleep without knocking him out. He did not want to take anything that knocked him out as he had children to look after. The CA rejected his appeal. They referred to the *'defence of necessity where the force or compulsion is exerted not by human threats but by extraneous circumstances'*. They relied on **Rodger and Rose (1998)** where the Ds had been suicidal because they were in prison and when caught escaping had argued duress of circumstances. The defence had failed and the earlier cases were distinguished on the basis that the threat was not from an extraneous source, it was the suicidal tendencies of the Ds themselves. The CA in **Quayle** confirmed that the threat could come from circumstances rather than a person but restated that it must come from an external source.

The CA in **Quayle** recognised the overlap between the defences and said that both 'duress of threats and necessity by circumstances' should be confined to cases of threats of physical injury. They did point out, however, that there was no 'overarching principle' which applied to all cases. They referred to the comments of the CA in **Abdul-Hussain**, that in the absence of parliamentary intervention, the law should develop on a case-by-case basis.

Food for thought

Developing the law on a case-by-case basis may be achieving justice but is it at the expense of consistency? The courts have clearly stated that Parliament should address the issue. In **Safi (2003)** (another hijacking case) the CA noted that the courts had 'repeatedly' emphasised the urgent need for legislation on duress. It appears from the detailed discussion in **Hasan** that the HL has decided to try to clarify the law itself.

Task

The courts have called for Parliament to intervene. Read back over this Unit and ask yourself how you would draft a bill on the defence of duress. What features of duress would you keep? Would you add any new conditions? Write these out, adding a few comments on your reasons. Keep this for a discussion for and against the defence. It can be used for an essay on defences or for a discussion of law and justice or fault.

Duress and mistake

Conway shows that D can use the defence even if there is no actual threat. It turned out that the people D thought were going to attack him were plain-clothes policemen. However, he was able to rely on duress even though he was mistaken as to the threat. He was judged on the facts as he honestly believed them to be.

In **Safi (2003)** the judge had suggested there had to *be* a threat but the CA said that this was wrong. They confirmed that the **Graham** test was still the law. Thus both types of duress could (as with self-defence) be used with mistake. However, there is a difference. With duress the mistake must be reasonable. This was implied by the test in **Graham** (did D have '*good cause to fear*'?) and has now been confirmed by the HL in **Hasan**. Lord Bingham said that '*there is no warrant for relaxing the requirement that the belief must be reasonable as well as genuine*'.

Food for thought

Lord Bingham suggested that the stricter requirements for duress were fair because, unlike self-defence and provocation, the victim was totally innocent. This is a fair point. However, it can be argued that the same is true in many cases of self-defence. If D mistakenly believes someone is being attacked and assaults the attacker, as in **Williams (Gladstone)**, then that 'attacker' is as innocent as the victims in cases of duress.

Limits to the availability of the defence of duress

We have seen some of the limitations in the cases discussed. They were restated by the HL in **Hasan (2000)**:

● Duress does not apply to murder – **Howe (1987)**;

● Nor attempted murder – **Gotts (1992)**;

● D may not rely on duress as a result of a voluntary association with others engaged in criminal activity where there was a foreseeable risk of being subjected to threats of violence – **Sharp (1987)**.

Criticisms and reform

The defence has not been without its critics and in its **1978 Report** the Law Commission acknowledged several criticisms of the defence of duress. These included:

● It should not be justifiable to do wrong or cause harm.

● The defence could be used as an excuse to commit a crime.

● It should not fall upon an individual to balance wrongdoing against the avoidance of harm to themselves or to others.

● It could encourage terrorists and kidnappers.

There are some fair points here. However, the Commission proposed that legislation should provide a defence and recommended that:

- Duress should be a general defence applicable to all offences including murder and attempted murder.
- Threats of harm to individuals should be allowed but not threats to property. Self-induced duress should not be allowed.
- The burden of proof should be on the defendant to establish duress.

Food for thought

Many of the Commission's recommendations have been incorporated by case law. The proposal in regard to murder is one that hasn't. It is somewhat contentious. It is arguable that it is not up to D to decide whose life is worth more. In **Hasan (2005)** the HL noted the logic of the Commission's recommendation, but also noted that the recommendation had not been adopted *'no doubt because it is felt that in the case of the gravest crimes no threat to the defendant, however extreme, should excuse commission of the crime'*. One problem is that the defence results in an acquittal. It could be argued that allowing it to be used as a partial defence to murder, reducing murder to manslaughter, would be more satisfactory.

Essentially, the defence needs to be clarified by Parliament, as requested by the courts.

Summary

Defence	Requirements	Limits
Necessity	The evil avoided is greater than the evil done	Case-by-case basis. Could justify a killing (**Re A**)
Duress	Imminent threat of death or serious injury (from a person) D had 'good cause' to believe such a threat (**Graham/Hasan**) A reasonable person would have acted as D did	Not murder or attempted murder (**Howe/Gotts**) Not where D voluntarily associates with those foreseeably posing a risk of threats No evasive action possible (**Hasan**)
Duress of circumstances	Imminent threat of death or serious injury (from circumstances) D had 'good cause' to believe such a threat (**Graham/Hasan**) A reasonable person would have acted as D did	Not murder or attempted murder No evasive action possible (**Hasan**) The threat need not come from a person but must be external to D (**Quayle**)

Self-test questions

1 In which case was the test for duress established?

2 What did **Hasan** confirm in regard to the first part of this test?

3 What defence was used in **Re A** and how does this differ from duress?

4 What point was confirmed in **Quayle** about the source of the threat?

5 Why did **David Beckham** fail when using duress?

 For further resources and updates please go to the Companion Website accompanying this book at **www.pearsoned.co.uk/russell**

Study Block 12 Summary
DEFENCES

Defence	Main points	Which crimes	Effect
Intoxication – involuntary	Must remove *mens rea* – Kingston	All crimes requiring *mens rea*	Acquittal
Intoxication – voluntary	Majewski	Specific intent crimes	Reduces to basic intent crime
		Basic intent crimes	Guilty
Self-defence	Force must be reasonable	All	Acquittal
Mistake	Must be genuine but need not be reasonable	All	Acquittal
Necessity	Limited defence	All	Acquittal
Duress	Direct threat of imminent death or serious injury	Not murder or attempted murder	Acquittal
Duress of circumstances	Threat of imminent death or serious injury by circumstances	Not murder or attempted murder	Acquittal

Task

Add the principle and brief facts to the case.

Case	Principle	Facts
Kingston		
Majewski		
Williams (Gladstone)		
Re A (twins case)		
Graham		

Hasan		
Sharp		
Quayle		
Gotts		

Key criticisms

You no longer need to evaluate these defences but look at the Module 6 connections for how you might relate the problems to the wider concepts.

Examination practice

There is no longer an essay question on defences so for examination practice look at the problem questions at the end of this Part. You will always need to consider the appropriate defences in any application of the law.

Module 6 connections

Morals	The law on duress recognises that D may be morally justified in committing an offence, e.g. for fear of harm	Martin
	Duress is not a defence to murder; killing cannot be morally justified	Howe
Justice	The law on necessity attempts to do justice based on the particular circumstances	Re A
	However, the law on duress excludes D's vulnerabilities, which can be unjust	Bowen
Conflicting interests	The individual's right to be safe from harm has to be balanced against the community interest in being safe from crime	
	The interests of both twins, the doctors and the community had to be balanced	Re A
Fault	The rules on these defences recognise D is less at fault in that although *mens rea* is present, the offence is committed for a reason. The limits on the defence mean this is kept within strict bounds	
Creativity	The *stare decisis* rule says 'treat like cases alike' and deciding whether duress applies on a case-by-case basis can lead to uncertainty.	Quayle
	Should Parliament act to clarify the issue or have the courts succeeded in doing so?	Hasan

January 2005

Alan was out in the town when he saw a watch which seemed to have been left on a bench. Though it bore the name 'Rolex', Alan mistakenly believed it to be a very cheap imitation and, after examining it, he threw it into a waste bin. He then ordered a bottle of wine and a meal in a café, but changed his mind about paying before he got the bill. He told the waiter that he had forgotten his money and was allowed to leave after giving his name and address, both of which were false. As he left the café, he gave £5 to Brad, who said that he was collecting for a well-known charity. In fact, Brad intended to keep the money for himself.

By this time, the bottle of wine that he had drunk was beginning to affect Alan and he ran down the street and snatched a baked potato from a stall, not realising that it was being offered free as part of a promotion. Chris saw the disturbance as Alan ran off and pursued him, believing that Alan had committed some offence. As Chris caught him up, Alan barged him out of the way and continued running with the potato.

(a) Discuss Alan's criminal liability in connection with the 'Rolex' watch *and* his failure to pay at the café, and discuss Brad's criminal liability in connection with the £5 he collected from Alan. *(25 marks)*

(b) Discuss Alan's criminal liability for **property** offences in connection with the baked potato and the further incident with Chris. *(25 marks)*

(c) Comment on the suggestion that the definition of theft in the **Theft Act 1968** has given rise to few problems. *(25 marks)*

Guide

(a) There are several issues here. The more you deal with, the less detail you need.
Alan: theft, in particular the *mens rea* element; evasion of liability and/or making off. Briefly outline the *actus reus* then discuss dishonesty and intent to permanently deprive in more detail. Dishonesty: **s. 2(1)(c)**. Arguably the watch would be claimed so the owner found by handing it in to the police. Emphasise he need not take steps to find the owner, it is his belief that counts, so his belief that it was worthless could mean he thought no one would claim it. Alternatively, use the **Ghosh** test. Intent: he treated the watch as his own to dispose of – **s. 6**.

Not paying for the meal can be **s. 2(1)(b)** of the **1978 Act** (inducing the café to wait for payment) – **Turner**. He must intend permanent default – likely as he gave a false name. Alternatively making off without payment under **s. 3**. Note the deception offences can't be used as the deception came *after* the obtaining.

Brad: theft and/or obtaining property by deception.

He 'appropriated' even though he was given the money – **Gomez/Hinks**. Alternatively argue he had been given it with an obligation to use it for charity – **s. 5(3)**. Either way, his dishonesty (he lied) means he has *actus reus* and *mens rea* of theft. **Gomez** shows the overlap with obtaining property by deception under **s. 15** so you can discuss this instead – or as well.

(b) Alan can be guilty of theft of the potato even if the owner consents or transfers ownership – **Hinks**. He was dishonest if he knew people would view it as dishonest – **Ghosh**.

Alan barging Chris out of the way may make it **s. 8** robbery. Was force sufficient? Probably – **Clouden**. Was it 'before or at the time of' the theft? The theft may be seen as continuing – **Hale**. Use **Hale** to say it *may* also be 'in order to steal'. There is a theft and arguably a robbery. Both are specific intent offences, so discuss intoxication (voluntary) and whether he had the capacity to form the *mens rea* for either offence – **Majewski**.

(c) Both *actus reus* and *mens rea* can be discussed. Again the more you deal with, the less detail you need. You could discuss:

- conflicting cases on appropriation leave the law uncertain
- the liberal interpretation of appropriation in **Gomez** and **Hinks**
- that D can be guilty of theft without actually taking anything
- the complexity of the **Ghosh** test
- the narrowness of the **Lloyd** approach (but the wider approach in later cases make D liable even where there is little evidence of intent to permanently deprive)
- that it is not always clear whether something is lost or abandoned
- the overlap with **s. 15** deception in cases like **Gomez**

Look at the key criticisms and 'Food for thought' boxes for more ideas

DON'T FORGET CASES TO ILLUSTRATE!

Part 4

MODULE 5 TORT

Study Block 13   NEGLIGENCE

Study Block 14   OCCUPIER'S LIABILITY

Study Block 15   NUISANCE, STRICT AND VICARIOUS LIABILITY

Study Block 16   DEFENCES AND REMEDIES

Introduction to Part 4
MODULE 5 TORT

What is a tort?

The word **tort** comes from the French and means a civil wrong. Unlike crime, civil law is based on people's responsibility to each other rather than to society as a whole.

Remember the case of **Donoghue v Stevenson** and the snail in the ginger beer bottle? Study Block 13 on negligence contains some familiar material. It covers *duty*, *breach* and *causation*. However, it also covers two new types of 'harm', *economic* and *psychiatric*, where the rules on duty in the **Donoghue** case are more restrictive.

A word of warning. Please don't be tempted to skip the early Units on the basis that you know them – you don't! Hopefully you have got a good base to build on, but you need a much greater depth to your knowledge at this level. Another reason for looking at these issues again is that when you come to Module 6 you will see that this is based on the material in *all* other modules, including Modules 1, 2 and 3. In particular, the Unit on 'Fault' relates to breach, the fault element in negligence.

Study Block 14 covers liability for harm which occurs on someone else's property, or *occupier's liability*. This is a form of negligence but there are special rules governing liability contained in two Acts of Parliament.

Study Block 15 covers *nuisance*, where someone is causing a nuisance to someone else, e.g. by continually having noisy parties. We also look at *strict liability* under the rule in **Rylands v Fletcher**, so called after a case of that name and where there is no need to prove negligence, and *vicarious liability*, where one person is liable for the negligence of another. This area also ties in with fault for Module 6.

In Study Block 16 we look at two *defences* which apply to all torts, consent and contributory negligence. Finally, the issue of *remedies* will be considered.

Study Block 13
NEGLIGENCE

Unit 38   Duty of care: physical harm

Unit 39   Duty of care: economic loss and negligent misstatement

Unit 40   Duty of care: psychiatric harm

Unit 41   Breach of duty

Unit 42   Causation

In order to be able to claim compensation for harm caused by D's negligence, three things must be proved:

1 D owes C a duty of care.

2 D has breached that duty.

3 D's breach caused the harm.

The rules on duty, breach and causation *all* need to be applied to the facts of a case to prove liability.

You will have studied each of these issues in Module 3, but will need more at this level. Units 38–40 cover duty in relation to three types of harm. First, physical harm, which you have already seen, then two new types of 'harm', economic and psychiatric. Economic harm, or loss, occurs when someone has lost financially due to another's negligence, e.g. by way of a misstatement as in **Caparo v Dickman**. Psychiatric harm is where the harm is mental rather than physical. These two areas are very popular in examination essay questions and you need to know the developments and problems as well as the current law.

Example You may have seen these two cases before.

Caparo v Dickman established the three-part test for proving a duty. Auditors negligently prepared a company's accounts. A purchaser of shares relied on the information and lost money. This was a case of economic loss.

In **Bourhill v Young** a pregnant woman heard a crash and was so traumatised that she later gave birth to a stillborn baby. This was a case involving psychiatric harm.

Both types of loss, or harm, have special rules for proving a duty.

For breach and causation you will need to apply the rules you studied in Module 3 to new torts, and also to negligence cases where the loss is economic or psychiatric. We will recap and expand on both these issues. Again, more is needed at this level, both in relation to evaluation and application. In nuisance and under the rule in **Rylands and Fletcher** the law on causation is now the same as for negligence, so the **Wagon Mound** rules on causation apply to all three torts. Also, a negligence claim may be an alternative route to discussion in an exam question on, for example, occupier's liability or nuisance.

So remember, for all the areas covered in Module 3, you will need a greater understanding of the law and cases. The scenarios will be much more complex and you will need to be able to evaluate the law and consider whether it is satisfactory. Don't be tempted to skip through these early Units too quickly!

Unit 38

Duty of care: physical harm

You must take reasonable care to avoid acts or omissions which you can reasonably foresee would be likely to injure your neighbour.

Lord Atkin, **Donoghue *v* Stevenson (1932)**

> **By the end of this Unit you should be able to:**
> - Explain the rules on how to prove a person is owed a duty of care by another
> - Show how the law has developed by reference to cases
> - Identify problems with the law in order to attempt an evaluation

Here we will look at how to prove a duty of care in relation to physical harm caused by someone's negligence. This is important because if there is no duty, the claim will fail. There will be no need to consider the other two points.

Duty

Whether there is a duty is based on what is known as the 'neighbour principle' from **Donoghue *v* Stevenson (1932)**. This case is famous for establishing liability in negligence and is often referred to as 'the snail in the ginger beer case'. Ask anyone who has ever studied law and they will know it!

Key case

Mrs Donoghue was in a café with her friend. She drank some ginger beer with her ice cream, and later she emptied the rest of the contents into a glass. To her horror a decomposing snail came out. She was ill (whether from drinking the beer or from seeing the snail in its state of decomposition is not clear) and sued the manufacturer. As her friend had paid, there was an important legal issue to consider. Mrs Donoghue was owed no contractual duty because she did not buy the drink herself. The case eventually went to the HL on the issue of whether the manufacturer could owe a duty to a consumer who did not buy the goods. Lord Atkin gave the leading judgment and produced the now famous 'neighbour test'. He said that the biblical requirement that we must 'love our neighbour' became, in law, that we must not injure our neighbour. He said, '*You must take reasonable care to avoid acts or omissions which you can reasonably foresee would be likely to injure your neighbour.*' He then goes on to consider the question 'who then, in law, is my neighbour?' and answers, '*persons who are so closely and directly affected by my act that I ought reasonably to have them in contemplation as being so affected when I am directing my mind to the acts or omissions which are called in question.*'

So a precedent was set. Tort law now protects those without a contract.

Example I am babysitting for someone at work and being paid. I have a contract so there is no problem – I owe a duty under the contract and can be sued if the baby is harmed due to my negligence. However, if I am doing it for free, perhaps for a friend, then there is no contract. Since **Donoghue**, I can be sued in tort, as I owe a duty to anyone affected by my acts or omissions. The baby would be someone I would have in mind when I am contemplating, or thinking about, doing (or omitting to do) whatever is being questioned – my negligent action (or inaction).

The test is essentially one of foreseeability. If the result of your actions is foreseeable harm to someone, you will owe that someone a duty of care.

Task

You may not be able to remember the entire quote so write out Lord Atkin's neighbour test in full, but then put it in your own words so it is clear to you.

Over the next few decades the courts were reluctant to extend the law further. Then, in the 60s, they became more expansive, and a high point was reached in **Anns v Merton LBC (1978)**. I am not repeating the facts here as what followed was a retreat from this case and it was later overruled in **Murphy v Brentwood BC (1990)**. The judges began to use an incremental approach, i.e. not expanding in great leaps but bit by bit, case by case. A line from an Australian case has been quoted with much approval. The case is **Sutherland Shire County v Heyman (1985)** and the Judge, Brennan J, said, *'It is preferable, in my view, that the law should develop novel categories of negligence incrementally and by analogy with established categories.'*

In **Caparo v Dickman (1990)** these words were approved again by the HL. The HL said that there was no general principle which applied to all cases and it was necessary to consider whether imposing a duty was 'just and reasonable' in the circumstances. In many cases, for a duty to arise:

- there must be foreseeability of harm;
- there must be proximity between C and D;
- it must be fair, just and reasonable to impose a duty on D.

Key case

In **Caparo**, C had claimed that the auditors of a company's books owed him a duty of care. They had produced inaccurate accounts and he had lost money by investing in the company. Arguably it was foreseeable that people in his position, who had relied on the accounts, would suffer loss. The HL held, however, that there was no proximity between him and the auditors. The auditors produced the accounts for the company, to comply with the legal requirements to produce annual accounts, not for potential investors. Nor was it fair, just and reasonable to make the auditors liable for losses to unknown investors.

The first two parts of the **Caparo** test are similar to the neighbour test from **Donoghue**. The third is a matter of what is fair in the circumstances of the particular case. In brief:

Caparo	Donoghue	Meaning
It must be foreseeable that someone will be harmed by D's actions	D should have that someone 'in contemplation' when acting	'Someone' is a group, or class, of people, not an individual. Thus a duty was owed to all consumers, not to Mrs Donoghue in particular. It is foreseeable that a consumer will be affected by the act or omission of a manufacturer
There is proximity between C and D	C is D's 'neighbour'	There is some kind of legal connection or relationship between C and D
It is fair, just and reasonable to impose a duty on D	Not specifically mentioned, although it was arguably the attempt to achieve justice that extended the law	A matter of policy, of what is right in the circumstances

The **Caparo** case involved economic loss rather than physical harm, but the three-stage test applies to all types of harm. It is applied more strictly in relation to economic loss and psychiatric harm, and we will look at these important issues in separate Units. In **Caparo** itself, Lord Roskill recognised that *'there is no simple formula or touchstone'* for deciding whether to impose liability. The third part of the test allows for a certain amount of flexibility, based on what is 'fair' in the circumstances.

Food for thought

Do you think that the incremental approach is a good one? Arguably it is leaving a lot to the individual judge on the particular facts of a case leading to uncertainty in the law. The fact that **Caparo** provides a test, but at the same time makes it clear that it may not always apply, is also somewhat problematic. Should there be a clearer set of rules? Would this make the law too rigid? There is always a need for a balance to be struck between certainty and flexibility. People need to know what the law is so that it can be relied on, but at the same time the law may need to adapt to the circumstances.

Let's take a look at the three issues.

Foreseeability

It must be foreseeable that D's act (or omission) will cause harm. Thus in **Donoghue** it can be said to be foreseeable that the manufacturer's act (of allowing a snail to get in the bottle), or omission (the failure to clean the bottles properly), will affect any consumer of the ginger beer.

Despite Lord Atkin's words in **Donoghue** that you should avoid acts or omissions which '*you*' can foresee might injure your neighbour; the test for foreseeability is an objective one. It is what the *reasonable person* foresees, not what D foresees.

Proximity

The concepts of foreseeability and proximity overlap. The more proximate you are to someone, the more foreseeable it is that his or her actions may harm you. In **Bourhill v Young (1943)** a woman heard an accident and the shock caused her to miscarry and lose her baby. She failed in her claim, as she hadn't actually seen the accident. It was not *foreseeable* that she would be harmed; nor was she in close *proximity*. It is not just physical proximity, however, but whether the *relationship* between the parties is proximate enough. In **Donoghue** the relationship was one between a manufacturer and consumers. In **Caparo** there was proximity between the auditors and the company whose accounts they did, but not between the auditors and investors. The latter relationship was not sufficiently close, or 'proximate'.

Fair, just and reasonable to impose a duty

The last point is a matter of public policy. This is perhaps the most difficult of the three. It means that the court looks at what is best for society as a whole. So actions against bodies such as the police, hospitals, rescue services and local councils may fail on this point. Sporting activities also enjoy a limited immunity. Let's look at the type of cases where a duty may be refused, even though harm is foreseeable.

Police

In **Hill v CC for West Yorkshire (1988)**, a consequence of the 'Yorkshire ripper' case, the police were held not to owe a duty to potential victims of a crime after releasing a suspected killer through lack of evidence. When he killed again the mother of the victim sued the police, claiming they owed a duty to her daughter. The HL refused to find a duty, partly on lack of proximity between the police and an unknown member of the public. However, the policy issue also arose. The HL felt that the threat of being sued could make the police less efficient in carrying out their duties. This would not be in the public interest. This immunity for the police is not, however, absolute. There have been several successful claims against the police where there has been a greater degree of proximity between them and C. This shows that all three parts of the test are connected. The more foreseeable something is, and the greater the degree of proximity, the more likely it is that it will be fair, just and reasonable to impose a duty. In **Reeves v MPC (1999)** the police were held to owe a duty to a prisoner who committed suicide while in their care, and whom they knew to be a suicide risk. The police had left the door flap open and he used it to hang himself. An important factor in **Reeves** was that the police *knew* that he was a suicide risk. In another suicide case, **Orange v CC of West Yorkshire Police (2001)**, a similar claim failed. In this case the man who hanged himself while in custody, after being arrested while drunk, was *not* a known suicide risk.

Example	**Reeves** can be used to illustrate all three issues. Harm was *foreseeable* because the police knew that he was a suicide risk. There was *proximity* between C and the police because he was in one of the police cells. In such circumstances it seems *fair, just and reasonable* to impose a duty on the police to the group of people – prisoners – who are in their care. There were no policy reasons to exclude a duty as it was to a limited, and known, group.

A rather unusual claim was made against the police in **Vellino v CC of Greater Manchester (2001)**. D was severely injured while trying to escape from the police and sued them for not preventing this. He argued they were under a duty not to negligently let him escape, had breached the duty by just standing by while he jumped from a window, and that the injuries were a foreseeable result. The CA held that in a case where the prisoner was escaping from custody, the police would not owe a duty because the prisoner was now no longer in the control of the police.

Councils

There are a lot of case examples to choose from in relation to local councils. Here are a couple. In **Gorringe v Calderdale MBC (2004)** C had been driving up a hill. Nearing the top she suddenly saw a bus coming towards her and she was injured when she hit it. She argued that there should have been a warning sign of some sort. The HL found that there was no duty to provide road signs. In **Sandhar v Department of Transport (2004)** C's husband had been killed when he skidded on ice on the road. The council had a policy in place in regard to salting the roads, but had not carried it out on this particular road. The court held that the council did not owe a duty to all road users to ensure that all roads were kept free of ice.

Food for thought

In deciding whether imposing a duty is 'fair, just and reasonable' the courts are presumably taking into account how far councils with limited budgets should be expected to use their funds in a particular way. The money would have to come from another area. The courts are balancing the rights of people harmed to compensation, and the burden to the council – and therefore to local residents – of imposing too strict a duty. How far do you think the court should decide such matters? Arguably, this is a job better suited to an elected government.

Sports

In **Watson v British Boxing Board (2000)** the boxer Michael Watson suffered head injuries during a fight against Chris Eubank. He sued the Board on the basis that had proper medical treatment been given at the ringside he would not have suffered brain damage. The CA found that it was 'just and reasonable' to impose a duty on the Board to ensure adequate medical facilities were available, and upheld his claim. A similar decision was made in **Vowles v Evans (2003)** where a player was injured in an amateur rugby match when a scrum collapsed. Without going into the finer details of the rules of rugby, the essence was that the scrum collapsed due to the referee not applying the rules properly, and the player sued. Allowing his claim, the judge said that the rapport between referee and players is crucial to a good game of rugby, and would not be lessened by the knowledge that the referee owed a duty of care for the players' safety. (Unlike **Hill** where it was thought police efficiency *would* be lessened by such knowledge.) Applying **Caparo**, the CA held that as a matter of policy it is 'just and reasonable' that the law should impose a duty to take reasonable care for the players' safety. This could be achieved by the sensible and appropriate application of the laws of the game.

Task

Read the **Donoghue** case and answer the following questions. The last one relates to breach of duty which we will look at next.

- Why couldn't Mrs D sue the shopkeeper?
- Whom did she sue and what did the HL decide?
- In what way do you think the manufacturers were negligent?

Omissions

In **Donoghue**, Lord Atkin referred to *'acts or omissions'*. This means D can be liable for *not* doing something, as well as doing something negligently. There may be liability for an omission when there is a particularly close relationship, such as that between an employer and employee, or where there is a high degree of control by one person over another. There will be a duty to take care of that person's safety, and failure to do so may result in liability, e.g. not preventing a suicide in **Reeves**.

Examination pointer

Note the words of Brennan J. He said that the courts should develop novel categories of negligence incrementally and by analogy with established categories. This means that you only need to use the three-part test where it is a new situation, one which has not been to court before. For example, it has already been established that a manufacturer owes a duty to a consumer so this is not a 'novel' situation. An examiner may use a scenario where there is a clear duty because you are expected to focus on another issue, like breach or causation.

Summary

Donoghue – the neighbour test on foreseeability

Caparo – the three-part test

Foreseeability

Proximity

Is it fair, just and reasonable to impose a duty?

Is there immunity for, e.g., the police or a local council?

 ## Self-test questions

1 What did Brennan J say in **Sutherland Shire County**?

2 What is the three-part **Caparo** test?

3 Who might be immune from owing a duty?

4 Why was no duty owed in **Bourhill v Young**?

5 Why was no duty owed in **Caparo**?

 For further resources and updates please go to the Companion Website accompanying this book at **www.pearsoned.co.uk/russell**

Duty of care: economic loss and negligent misstatement

... liability can, and in my opinion should, be founded squarely on the principle established in Hedley Byrne itself.

Lord Goff, **Henderson v Merrett Syndicates (1995)**

By the end of this Unit you should be able to:

- Explain the special rules for proving a duty of care in cases of economic loss by misstatements and by acts
- Show how the law has developed by reference to cases
- Identify problems with the law in order to attempt an evaluation

---

Where the loss is financial rather than physical, liability is more limited. This is based on policy and what is known as the 'floodgates' argument. In **Ultramares v Touche (1931)** Cardozo CJ said that allowing claims for pure economic loss would lead to liability *'in an indeterminate amount, for an indefinite time and to an indeterminate class'* – it would open the 'floodgates' to claims. A distinction is made between economic loss and *pure* economic loss. A great many claims involve economic loss of some sort, e.g. loss of earnings would be a result of many physical injuries and is included in the claim for damages for that injury. However, where there is no physical damage, either to person or property, any such claim would usually fail because the loss is *only* economic.

Example   You are walking to work when you see someone screaming that her husband has been hit by a car. You stop to help. As a result, you are late for a meeting, which means you lose an important contract. You also lose a day's pay. The husband can claim for his injuries and for loss of earnings while off work. The wife may have a claim for psychiatric harm, which will also include any loss of earnings. However, *your* loss of earnings was not a result of either physical or psychiatric harm so you cannot claim. In all three cases there is economic loss (earnings). Only in the last is it *pure* economic loss and so not recoverable.

The law also makes a distinction between economic loss caused by negligent statements (or, more correctly, misstatements), and economic loss caused by negligent acts. In this Unit we will look at the rules for finding a duty in respect of negligent misstatements, and see that there is no duty in respect of negligent acts.

Negligent misstatements

The law has developed over the years and since 1963 the rule that no negligence claim involving pure economic loss could succeed has been eased in cases where the loss is a result of a negligent statement rather than a negligent act.

Key case

The leading case is **Hedley Byrne v Heller (1963)** where the HL approved a dissenting judgment by Denning LJ in **Candler Crane v Christmas (1951)**. Lord Denning had argued that accountants owed a duty not only to their employer, but also to anyone to whom they showed the accounts. This would include people that they knew their employer would show them to but not '*strangers of whom they have heard nothing and to whom their employer without their knowledge may choose to show the accounts*'. This was accepted and developed in **Hedley**. A bank gave a credit reference in which they negligently stated that their client was sound. The Cs relied on this and consequently suffered heavy losses when the client went into liquidation. On the facts the claim failed due to a disclaimer. However, the *principle* was established that there could be liability in tort for such losses if there was a 'special relationship' between C and D.

The neighbour principle from **Donoghue v Stevenson**, used for cases of physical harm, was held to be too wide. Lord Reid said statements had to be treated differently for the following reasons:

- words can spread further than acts;
- people in a social situation may make statements less carefully than they would in a business one.

Essentially a 'special relationship' means that:

- a special skill is possessed by D, who makes the statement;
- C reasonably relies on D's statement;
- D knows that C is 'highly likely' to rely on the statement.

There is an overlap between these three points. The more special someone's skill is, the more reasonable it is to rely on it. This is best illustrated by cases.

Examination pointer

Cases are always important when dealing with a problem question, but a sound knowledge of them is also needed for an essay so that you can show how the law has developed.

Special skill

Mutual Life and Citizen's Assurance Co. v Evatt (1971) and **Esso Petroleum v Marden (1976)** illustrate the 'special skill' aspect. In the first case the claim failed because D was in the insurance business and the advice was in respect of invest-ments. The majority (3–2) held that only if they were in the business of giving that type of advice would a duty arise. The minority thought a duty could arise when D knew the statement would be reasonably relied on, even if they were not in that particular line of business.

The minority view was applied in **Esso**. Esso gave a negligent estimate of the potential turnover of a garage. This was not within their area of expertise, but the court held that they were liable to the buyer. They knew that the statement would be relied on and they had implied that they had expertise. It was also reas-onable for the Cs to rely on it. This shows how 'skill', 'knowledge' and 'reason-able reliance' overlap.

Knowledge

In **JEB Fasteners Ltd *v* Mark Bloom (1983)** auditors prepared company accounts knowing the company needed finance. They knew that anyone considering a takeover would rely on the accounts. They were thus liable. Note that the court did not require that they should be able to identify a particular individual who would rely on them. It was enough that they knew *someone* would rely on them.

Key case

Remember **Caparo plc *v* Dickman (1990)**, which established the three-part test for proving a duty? This was a 'negligent misstatement' case. Auditors negligently prepared a company's accounts. They were held not liable to a purchaser of shares who had relied on them. This case shows how the 'knowledge' requirement can significantly limit cases. Because the auditors prepared the accounts for the com-pany, not potential investors, they could not know Caparo, as potential investors, would rely on them.

In **Smith *v* Bush (1989)** the HL held a surveyor owed a duty to a house buyer even though he prepared the survey for the building society lending them money. He owed a duty to the third party buyers because it was quite obvious that they would rely on his survey. There were *obiter dicta* in **Smith** which suggest a com-mercial buyer, however, might fail. Because it is normal practice in commercial deals to have your own survey done, a surveyor for the lender would not 'know' the buyer would rely on their survey – they would expect them to have a survey done for themselves. The court felt there would only be a duty if it was '*highly likely*' C would rely on the statement.

Here, as in **Hedley**, there was a disclaimer but by this time further protection could be found in the **Unfair Contracts Terms Act 1977**. This Act prohibits unreasonable exclusions of liability.

In **Spring *v* Guardian Assurance plc (1993)** the HL held that an employer owed a duty to an employee in respect of a negligent reference, as they knew it would be relied on by a potential employer. In this case the advice was not given *to* C but was *about* C. This further extends the duty owed to third parties.

Task

Compare **Caparo** and **JEB**. They aren't too different, so why was a duty found in one and not the other?

Reasonable reliance

Lord Reid said in **Hedley** that there would be no duty of care for statements made on a social occasion. This seems fair. It would not be 'reasonable' to rely on a piece of information passed on in a drunken moment at the Christmas party! It isn't an absolute rule though. For example, in **Chaudhry v Prabhakar (1989)** a friend who negligently gave advice on buying a car was held to owe a duty to C. He had knowledge of such matters and she had reasonably relied on that knowledge.

Food for thought

Do you think a duty should have been found in **Chaudhry**? Will it make people reluctant to help out a friend?

In **Caparo** the purpose of the information was relevant. It is not likely to be found reasonable to rely on information intended for someone else for a different purpose. However, in **Ross v Caunters (1980)** a solicitor was found liable to a third party, the beneficiary under his client's will, when he acted negligently and this resulted in the beneficiary losing financially. This was a major extension of the law at the time, because it appeared to relate to negligent *acts* rather than *statements*. However, the HL found a solicitor owed a duty to a third party in **White v Jones (1995)** (see below), based on an *'assumption of responsibility'* for his professional advice.

Assumption of responsibility

The principle of 'assumption of responsibility' was rooted in **Hedley Byrne** but more emphasis was put on it during the nineties. In **Henderson v Merrett Syndicates (1995)** the HL held that syndicate managers could owe their members (underwriters of insurance policies) a duty in tort as well as contract. That duty was to exercise reasonable skill and care. Lord Goff made the remark in the opening quote and added that where someone assumed responsibility for professional services, this would be enough to impose a duty.

Key case

In **White v Jones (1995)** two daughters had been cut out of their father's will. Before he died he changed his mind and instructed his solicitor to amend his will. Despite a reminder this was never done and the daughters did not receive their inheritance. The HL found the solicitors liable to the daughters for their losses. The emphasis was on the fact that the solicitor, as a professional, had 'assumed

▶

responsibility' for his work and thus was under a duty not to do it negligently. It is reasonable for beneficiaries of wills to rely on solicitors doing their jobs properly.

The majority based their decision on achieving 'practical justice' and appear to be filling in a gap in the law in order to allow a third party beneficiary (who has no contract with the solicitor and so cannot sue in contract law) to claim for the loss of their inheritance. (This is a good example of judicial creativity.)

The idea of 'assumption of responsibility' is related to the 'fair, just and reasonable' requirement. In **Phelps v Hillingdon BC (2001)** the CA held that an educational psychologist had not assumed responsibility for C when he failed to diagnose her dyslexia in a report made for the education authority. It was therefore not 'fair, just and reasonable' to impose a duty. The HL reversed this decision on the basis that a professional asked to work with a specific child could be liable to her for his lack of care and skill in the exercise of that profession. Similarly in **Carty v Croydon LBC (2005)** C sued the council for damages for failing to assess his special educational needs properly and failing to provide him with a suitable education. The CA held that an education officer was a professional and so there could be a duty if he had 'assumed responsibility' towards a child. Dyson LJ said that this would be based on the normal **Caparo** three-part test of foreseeability, proximity and whether it was fair, just and reasonable to impose a duty.

Key case

In **Customs and Excise Commissioners v Barclays Bank (2004)** a bank allowed money to be transferred out of two accounts, which had been frozen by Customs and Excise. This meant that the money owed to Customs by the companies involved could not be paid in full, so the Customs and Excise Commissioners sued the bank for the balance. The trial judge found that the bank did not owe a duty to the third party (Customs and Excise), mainly based on the lack of any 'assumption of responsibility'. In the CA, Longmore LJ summarised the position. He said that the modern law derived from four cases: **Caparo**, **Henderson**, **White** and **Phelps**. In cases of economic loss it was appropriate to use each of the following tests:

1 The threefold **Caparo** test:
   (i)   foreseeability
   (ii) proximity
   (iii) whether it is fair, just and reasonable to impose a duty;
2 The 'assumption of responsibility' test (**White v Jones**);
3 The 'incremental' test (liability is not extended in a giant leap but in short steps).

He said that the tests merged into each other, and that although an 'assumption of responsibility' may sometimes be enough for a duty to exist, it was not always a *necessary* ingredient. The CA went on to apply all these tests, and found that the bank owed a duty to Customs and Excise.

Summary of negligent misstatement

The requirements for proving a duty of care for a negligent misstatement are foreseeability, proximity and whether it is fair, just and reasonable to impose a duty. Proximity is essentially a matter of finding a special relationship, and this involves:

- a special skill is possessed by D;
- C reasonably relying on the statement;
- D knowing that C is 'highly likely' to rely on the statement.

It may also be necessary to consider the 'assumption of responsibility' and that any extension of liability should be incremental.

Economic loss by acts

The question of whether economic loss could be claimed in respect of negligent acts was answered in the negative in **Spartan Steel and Alloys Ltd v Martin & Co. (1973)** by the CA.

Key case

In **Spartan Steel** the Ds negligently severed a power cable to C's factory and caused damage to steel in production. The Cs were able to claim for the physical damage to the steel and for the consequential loss of profit on that steel, but not for further loss of profit due to other, undamaged machines lying idle. This last sum was pure economic loss because it did not stem from any physical damage.

There is a case where a claim for pure economic loss has been successful, but this was where there was an exceptionally close proximity between C and D. In **Junior Books v Veitchi (1983)** a subcontractor was held liable to the owner of the premises he was working in and who had ordered the work (through the main contractor). This was almost a contractual relationship and so it sets no precedent for cases where the degree of proximity is less than this.

The rule against recovery for economic loss was reinforced by the HL in **Murphy v Brentwood DC (1990)**. The Council's building inspector approved plans which meant C's property was poorly constructed and in a dangerous state. This led to a drop in its value. Reversing the decision of the CA, the HL held there was no duty. The judges appeared to have differing reasons for their decision but the result is that if there is a defect but it has not yet caused any damage, there is no duty. Of course, if the defect actually leads to damage then the usual rules for physical harm would apply.

Example A property is built according to a set of plans that were negligently prepared. The balcony is unstable, thus making the property worth less than it should be. This is a defect but there is no damage yet. The owners cannot claim as their loss is purely economic – i.e. a lower value. However, if the balcony falls off then the house is now physically damaged and a claim can be made – make sense?

Food for thought

It has been made clear that you cannot claim for economic loss caused by a negligent act but there is little difference between the solicitor's negligence in **White v Jones** and that of the building inspector approving the plans in **Murphy**. It could be argued that a duty could be imposed whatever the type of loss as long as the **Caparo** test is satisfied.

Examination pointer

Note that proving a duty is just the first step in a negligence case. In order to win, C will still have to prove that the duty was breached, and that the breach caused the loss suffered.

Summary

Summary of misstatements
Hedley Byrne v Heller (1963) – a bank gave a credit reference in which they negligently stated its client was sound. Although the neighbour principle was held to be too wide, the HL accepted there could be a duty of care in appropriate circumstances for economic loss caused by a negligent statement. There has to be a 'special relationship' between D and C. This means: D has a special skill C reasonably relies on D's statement D knows that C is 'highly likely' to rely on the statement
Mutual Life and Citizen's Assurance Co. v Evatt (1971) – the Privy Council held that only if the defendants were in the business of giving that *type* of advice would a duty arise. The minority thought a duty could arise when D *knew the statement would be reasonably relied on*.
Esso Petroleum v Marden (1976) – Esso gave a negligent estimate of the potential turnover of a garage. This was not within their area of expertise but the court held that Esso was liable as they *knew* the statement would be relied on. It was also *reasonable to rely* on it.
JEB Fasteners Ltd v Mark Bloom (1983) – auditors prepared company accounts *knowing* the company needed finance and that anyone considering a takeover would rely on the accounts. They were thus liable.
Caparo v Dickman (1990) – the auditors prepared the accounts for the company, *not* potential investors so they could not *know* Caparo would rely on them. Thus it was not 'fair, just and reasonable' to impose a duty.
Smith v Bush (1989) – a surveyor owed a duty to a house buyer even if he prepared the survey for the building society, as he *knew* that the buyer would rely on his survey.

Summary of misstatements (*continued*)
Chaudhry *v* Prabhakar (1989) – a friend who negligently gave advice on buying a car owed a duty to C as he had knowledge of such matters, so it was *reasonable* for her to rely on it.
Spring *v* Guardian Assurance plc (1993) – an employer owed a duty to an employee in respect of a negligent reference as they *knew* it would be relied on.
White *v* Jones (1995) – a solicitor, as a professional, had '*assumed responsibility*' for his work and thus was under a duty not to do it negligently.
Phelps *v* Hillingdon BC (2001) – a professional asked to work with a specific child could be liable to her for his lack of care and skill in the exercise of that profession.

Summary of acts
Spartan Steel and Alloys Ltd *v* Martin & Co. (1973) – C could claim for the physical damage to the steel and for the *consequential* loss of profit on that steel but not for further loss of profit due to other, undamaged machines lying idle, which was *pure* economic loss.
Murphy *v* Brentwood DC (1990) – if no damage has yet been done, C cannot claim for the fact that the property is worth less than it should be because there is an inherent defect due to negligent building inspections.

Finally, don't forget that in all cases, even if a duty of care is proved, in order to win the case C will still have to prove that the duty was breached, and that the breach caused the loss suffered.

Self-test questions

1 What constitutes a special relationship?

2 Why did the claim fail in the **Mutual Life** case?

3 **Smith *v* Bush** shows a surveyor for a building society can owe a duty to a buyer. When might there not be such a duty?

4 On what was the emphasis in **White *v* Jones**?

5 How did Longmore LJ summarise the position in **Customs and Excise Commissioners *v* Barclays Bank**?

For further resources and updates please go to the Companion Website accompanying this book at **www.pearsoned.co.uk/russell**

Duty of care: psychiatric harm

In cases involving nervous shock, it is essential to distinguish between the primary victim and secondary victims. In claims by secondary victims the law insists on certain control mechanisms, in order, as a matter of policy, to limit the number of potential claimants.

Lord Lloyd, **Page** *v* **Smith (1995)**

By the end of this Unit you should be able to:

- Explain the rules for proving a duty of care in cases of psychiatric harm
- Show how the law has developed by reference to cases
- Identify problems with the law in order to attempt an evaluation

What is meant by psychiatric harm?

Also called 'nervous shock', psychiatric harm includes such things as post-traumatic stress, clinical depression and personality change. It occurs when someone has suffered harm due to another's negligence, but that harm is psychiatric rather than physical. The courts tend to limit liability in such cases, mainly because of what is called the 'floodgates' argument. This means that because the number of potential Cs could be vast, it could open the 'floodgates' to claims. The opening quote relates to this.

Example   A drunk driver ploughs into a queue of people at a bus stop. Many are killed or injured. Any of these people can claim in the normal way. The driver will owe them a duty based on foreseeability, proximity and whether it is fair, just and reasonable to impose a duty (**Caparo**). However, hundreds of other people may have seen the accident. For them, the rules are stricter.

Examination pointer

For problem questions the current law and a few example cases will be needed. The cases you select will depend on the scenario you are given. Essay questions on this area are common and a knowledge of how the law has developed is important for these. The diagrams at the end of the Unit will provide a revision guide on what you could include in each type of question.

The current law will be better understood in the light of its development, so we'll look at that first.

Development

A claim in negligence for psychiatric harm requires the usual proof of duty, breach and causation. It is only the rules on duty that change, depending on the type of harm. Foreseeability and proximity (**Caparo**) are still required (see **King** and **Bourhill** below), but subject to a stricter test.

The first successful claim for nervous shock was **Dulieu *v* White (1901)**. Here a person suffered shock when a van and horses drove into the pub where she was working (yes, horses – but note the date). It was held that the driver owed her a duty of care. The principle was established that in order to succeed C must be in fear for his or her own safety.

In **Hambrook *v* Stokes (1925)** a mother was successful in her claim when she suffered shock after seeing a runaway lorry careering towards her children. Although they were not harmed and she was not in danger herself the court recognised that the close relationship could bring her within the class of people to whom a duty was owed. She had also seen the incident herself. The principle here is that even if you are not in danger yourself, a particularly close relationship to someone who is may be enough *if* you see the incident with your own eyes.

In **Bourhill *v* Young (1943)** a pregnant woman heard a crash and was so traumatised that she later gave birth to a stillborn baby. The court rejected her claim against the driver because she was some distance away and safe herself. No duty is owed where C was not in proximity to any foreseeable danger, as here.

In **King *v* Phillips (1952)** a mother suffered shock when she (wrongly) believed that her son had been run over by a taxi. She failed in her claim against the driver. The court held that injury *by shock* had to be foreseeable.

Key case

In **McLoughlin *v* O'Brien (1982)**, the first case to reach the HL since **Bourhill**, a test for dealing with such cases was established. Mrs McLoughlin was told about an accident in which her husband and children had been seriously injured; one child had, in fact, died. She went straight to the hospital where she saw them before they had been attended to. She suffered 'nervous shock' as a result. She sued the person who negligently caused the accident. In allowing her claim the HL held that there were three matters to consider in claims for nervous shock:

● the relationship between C and the victim
● the proximity of C to the accident
● the means by which the shock was caused

The HL confirmed the test in the next case.

Key case

In **Alcock v CC of South Yorkshire (1991)** many people had been injured or killed in the Hillsborough football stadium disaster. There were also many claims from people who had been at the ground or had watched the news on television and knew that their loved ones were at the stadium. The HL confirmed that the above test applied to these people, but said the first point extended to those with *'close ties of love and affection'*. There must also be a *sudden shock* and the shock must cause a *recognisable psychiatric illness* (mere grief is not enough). It was also said that those watching the events on television could not succeed. There were, however, *obiter dicta* to the effect that a live broadcast may be different. A hypothetical example was given of seeing live television pictures of a hot-air balloon catching fire knowing that your children were in it.

Task

Write a brief comparison of **Hambrook v Stokes** and **King v Phillips** to show why one succeeded and the other didn't.

Before looking at *how* the test applies, we need to consider to *whom* it applies. An important distinction is made in **Page v Smith (1995)** between primary and secondary victims.

Primary and secondary victims

Key case

In **Page v Smith**, C was a passenger involved in a car accident and, although he was not physically hurt, his ME condition, which had been in remission, recurred. The HL drew a distinction between primary and secondary victims. A primary victim is someone who is directly affected and in danger of harm. A secondary victim is not directly affected, but a passive witness to the events. In all cases, *some* harm must be foreseeable, whether physical or psychiatric. However, in the case of secondary victims, only foreseeability of *psychiatric* harm, in a *'person of normal fortitude'*, will suffice. The HL held that here the C was a primary victim, so there was no need to prove that psychiatric harm was foreseeable. In the opening quote Lord Lloyd refers to secondary victims; he then goes on to say that the control mechanisms have no place where the C is a primary victim.

This case is also an example of the 'thin skull rule' – that you must take your victim as you find them. Under the thin skull rule some harm must be foreseeable, but if it is, then the fact that the C suffered greater harm due to a pre-existing weakness will not cause the claim to fail.

Task

Compare this case to the next one. Can you identify the difference between the passenger in **Page** and the police in **White**?

In a further case involving the Hillsborough disaster, **White *v* CC of South Yorkshire (1999)**, police assisting at the scene claimed compensation. The HL clarified the position on rescuers and restated the test for secondary victims.

Key case

In **White** the CA had suggested that as the police were rescuers there was no need to prove close ties to the victims. The HL reversed the decision, and held that they could only succeed if their own safety were at risk. Lord Hoffmann restated the control mechanisms for secondary victims:

- C must have **close ties of love and affection** with the victim. Such ties may be presumed in some cases (e.g. spouses, parent and child) but must otherwise be established by evidence.
- C must have been **present at the accident or its immediate aftermath**.
- The psychiatric harm must have been caused by **direct perception of the accident** or its immediate aftermath, and not upon hearing about it from someone else.

In **Donachie *v* Chief Constable of Greater Manchester (2004)** the issue arose again. A policeman was instructed to attach a tag to the car of suspected criminals. It was parked near a pub where the suspects were drinking. His colleagues kept watch from the tracker van in case they left the pub. He attached the device but it did not work. He made several trips to retrieve and then reattach it until it finally gave a signal. He became increasingly frightened of being caught by the suspects. Unknown to his employers, he had hypertension and suffered psychiatric harm that led to a stroke. The judge found they had been negligent as there was a history of problems with the tagging devices. The issue was which type of victim C was. The judge classed him as a secondary victim. He therefore had to prove *psychiatric* harm was foreseeable. As his employers did not know of his existing condition then the stroke was not foreseeable and they were not liable. On appeal C argued that he was a primary victim because there was a danger of being assaulted by the suspects. The CA agreed and allowed the appeal.

Although the primary/secondary distinction was specifically made in **Page**, examples of it can be seen in earlier cases.

Rescuers

In **Chadwick *v* BTC (1967)** a rescuer at a train crash was successful in a claim for nervous shock after assisting for several hours. He can be seen as a 'primary' victim because he was in danger at the time. Compare this case to **McFarlane v Caledonia Ltd (1993)**. A person on a support ship which rescued people from a fire on an oil rig was classed as a 'bystander', not a 'rescuer', because he was not in danger. He therefore had to satisfy the test for secondary victims. As the ship had not got into close proximity to the disaster, and he had no close relationship with the victims, his claim failed. The court also repeated the point that C must be compared to a *'person of ordinary fortitude and phlegm'*.

In **Greatorex v Greatorex (2000)** the slightly unusual question that arose was whether D owed a duty to a rescuer who was also his father. D was injured in a road accident as a result of his own negligence. His father was a fireman who assisted in the rescue and as a result suffered nervous shock. He brought an action against his son. It was held that D did not owe his father a duty of care for policy reasons. It would be *'undesirable and detrimental to family life and relationships'* for members of a family to sue each other. It was made clear that, following **White**, where there is no personal risk, a rescuer is a secondary victim and so has to satisfy the **McLoughlin/Alcock** control mechanisms.

Examination pointer

The **McLoughlin/Alcock** control mechanisms confirmed in **White** will be needed for a problem question. Reference to the primary/secondary distinction in **Page** will also be needed. Watch carefully for the type of harm suffered and whether C is in any danger. For primary victims the usual rules (**Caparo**) apply. For secondary victims apply the mechanisms. You may also need to refer to the role of rescuers.

Task

Before reading on, look at the cases again and consider how the control mechanisms have been applied. See if you can spot any inconsistencies or difficulties yourself. Jot down your thoughts.

The control mechanisms

Let's run through the control mechanisms, and look at any difficulties which arise.

Close ties of love and affection

C must have close ties of love and affection with the victim. Such ties may be presumed in the case of spouses, or parent and child (**McLoughlin**) but must otherwise be established by evidence (**Alcock**). As regards rescuers, if in danger themselves they would be primary victims and so the normal rules on duty would apply (**White**). If not, they will be secondary victims and have to prove 'close ties' to the victim (**McFarlane**).

Food for thought

Extending the relationship from the immediate family to those with close ties seems fair. A loving relationship with a partner may be much closer than one between a husband and wife who have grown apart. The problem is how you prove 'close ties'. It is presumed in cases of spouse and parents but what about brothers, uncles, grandparents and friends – all of whom failed in **Alcock**? The Law Commission proposes that the 'close ties' requirement should be kept, albeit with some extension of the presumptions.

Immediate aftermath

C must have been present at the accident or its 'immediate aftermath'. In **McLoughlin** the mother heard about the accident an hour or so after it happened and went straight to the hospital. In **Alcock** a lapse of eight or nine hours before going to the mortuary caused several claims to fail. In **Taylorson v Shieldness (1994)** the parents of a child who was seriously injured in an accident did not get to the hospital in time to see him properly before he was operated on. They stayed with him during the next two days until he died. The CA refused to extend the 'immediate aftermath' of the accident to the death two days later. In **Atkinson v Seghal (2003)** a mother arrived at the scene of a road accident to be told her daughter had been killed. The body had already been removed and she went to the mortuary. She then suffered a psychiatric illness. The trial court held that the visit to the mortuary was not within the immediate aftermath. The CA reversed this decision and held that the aftermath extended to the mortuary visit.

Food for thought

So, what is the 'immediate aftermath'? Do we measure this in minutes, hours or days? These decisions raise some serious questions about the state of the law. Reporting in the *New Law Journal* in 1995 Andrew Ritchie says: '*It would appear that unless the victim is seen in hospital, covered in blood, success may be tricky. In my opinion this is not an admirable distinction to make*'.

How shock was caused

The means by which the shock was caused has generally been restricted to first-hand knowledge and would not include being told by a third party, nor to seeing events on television (**Alcock**). In **Atkinson v Seghal** the trial court had held that the shock was caused by the news of the death, not the visit to the mortuary. The CA held that the illness was caused in part by the visit to the mortuary and not just by being told of the death by the police at the scene (which would be via a third party and so would not have been enough).

Food for thought

Arguably, this has not been entirely consistent. In **McLoughlin** she was told by a third party (although she then did see the resulting injuries). Also, there were *obiter dicta* in **Alcock** to the effect that there could be occasions where seeing events on television would be enough – such as a live broadcast.

Anything else?

The HL in **Alcock** also made clear that there must be a *sudden shock* and that the shock must cause a *recognisable psychiatric illness*. Medical evidence will be needed. The HL also said that *mere grief is not enough*.

In **North Glamorgan NHST v Walters (2003)** a mother suffered psychiatric illness after sitting with her 10-month old baby as his condition deteriorated following the (admitted) negligence of the hospital. After 36 hours, his life support system was turned off. There were various reasons behind the CA's decision, but one issue was whether the 'sudden shock' requirement in **Alcock** had been satisfied. Apparently so. She won her claim for psychiatric harm caused by the hospital's negligence.

In **Vernon v Bosley (1997)** compensation was awarded to a father who saw his daughters' bodies retrieved from a car which had gone into the river. The court held that the 'abnormal' grief he suffered from seeing the immediate aftermath of the accident could not be distinguished from the 'normal grief' to be expected. He could therefore claim for both.

Food for thought

The implication in **Alcock** was that 'sudden shock' would not include any illness caused by, for example, long-term caring for a terminally ill relative. However, **Walters** shows that this requirement may have been relaxed. It remains to be seen whether the courts will continue this trend or treat each case on its own facts.

Second, it has been made clear that 'normal grief' is not enough. However, the father succeeded in **Vernon v Bosley** because the 'abnormal' grief could not be distinguished from the 'normal grief' to be expected. It may be hard to decide what is 'normal' because what is normal in one person may be abnormal in another.

A general criticism is that if the law is unclear, it is impossible for people to know what it is. It is also hard for a lawyer to advise a client as to how a case is likely to be decided. This means fewer cases can be settled out of court by negotiation.

Law Commission proposals for reform

The Law Commission has examined the law on this area (*Consultation Paper No. 137, Liability for Psychiatric Illness,* 1995) and this was followed by a Report

(*Law Commission No. 249,* **March 1998**), which recommends the removal of the requirements of proximity to the accident and the limits on the means of hearing about it. However, the Commission suggests that the 'close ties' aspect should be retained, but extended to other relationships regarding the presumptions (parents, children, spouses). The courts have shown a reluctance to expand the law any further and have indicated that it is up to Parliament to address the matter. Whether or not the Law Commission's proposals are acted upon is not certain – the law is still developing in this area. Watch out for changes.

Summary

Developing principles	Case example
C must be in fear for their own safety to succeed	**Dulieu *v* White (1901)**
No duty owed unless C was in foreseeable danger and in proximity to the accident	**Bourhill *v* Young (1943)**
Established the three matters to consider in nervous shock claims	**McLoughlin *v* O'Brien (1982)**
Confirmed the **McLoughlin** test but added 'close ties of love and affection' and that there must be a 'sudden shock' which caused a recognisable psychiatric illness	**Alcock *v* CC of South Yorkshire (1991)**
Distinction between primary and secondary victims drawn	**Page *v* Smith (1995)**
Reconfirmed the test but said that rescuers had to meet the test for secondary victims unless in danger themselves	**White *v* CC of South Yorkshire (1999)**

Summary diagram as a guide for a problem question

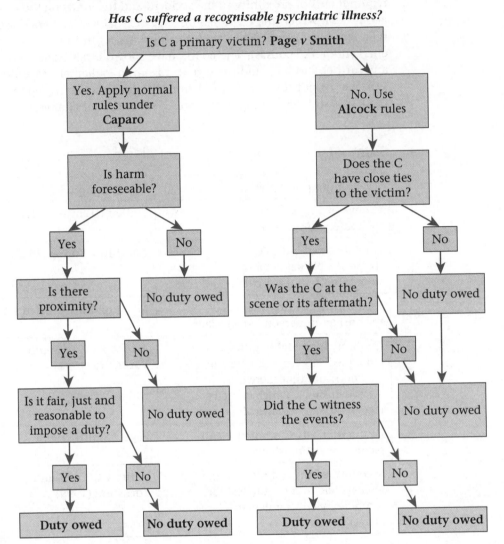

Has C suffered a recognisable psychiatric illness?

Is C a primary victim? **Page v Smith**

Yes. Apply normal rules under **Caparo**

No. Use **Alcock** rules

Is harm foreseeable?

Does the C have close ties to the victim?

Yes — No

Yes — No

Is there proximity?

No duty owed

Was the C at the scene or its aftermath?

No duty owed

Yes — No

Yes — No

Is it fair, just and reasonable to impose a duty?

No duty owed

Did the C witness the events?

No duty owed

Yes — No

Yes — No

Duty owed

No duty owed

Duty owed

No duty owed

Self-test questions

1 Which case highlighted the distinction between primary and secondary victims? Explain these two terms.

2 In which case (in the HL) was the first successful claim for nervous shock by a secondary victim?

3 In that case what did the Lords say needed to be looked at in such claims?

4 What was added in **Alcock**?

5 What reforms does the Law Commission suggest?

Breach of duty

We must not look at the 1947 accident with 1954 spectacles.

Denning LJ, **Roe *v* Ministry of Health (1954)**

> **By the end of this Unit you should be able to:**
> - Identify the standard expected of people in assessing whether there is a breach
> - Explain what factors are considered in assessing this standard
> - Recognise that it is an objective test, but also identify the subjective element
> - Show how the law is applied by reference to cases

A breach of duty occurs when D has not taken care, i.e. has been negligent. There is no clear standard by which a person's conduct is measured, it is an objective one, based on what is 'reasonable'. The courts will consider what a reasonable person would have done given the same circumstances. In **Blyth *v* Birmingham Waterworks Co. (1856)** Baron Alderson said:

> *'Negligence is the omission to do something which a reasonable man . . . would do, or doing something which a prudent and reasonable man would not do.'*

So what would a 'reasonable man' do? Well, for a start we should say 'reasonable person' now, although the courts often still refer to the reasonable man. Old habits die hard. The courts will consider several factors in deciding what is reasonable.

How to assess what is 'reasonable'

You should know the main factors which the court will take into account, with a case on each.

The degree of risk

The greater the risk of harm, the greater is the obligation on D to take precautions. No breach will have occurred if the risk was impossible to foresee. In **Fardon *v* Harcourt-Rivington (1932)** D's car was parked on a street with a dog inside. As C walked past the dog jumped up and broke the window and some glass went in C's eye. The HL held there was no duty to guard against *'fantastic possibilities'*.

In **Roe v Ministry of Health (1954)** contamination of an anaesthetic left C paralysed. Medical knowledge at the time was not such that this could have been expected; in fact it was this event that alerted the medical profession to the problem. There was no known, or foreseeable, risk, so the Ministry of Health was not liable. The court will not use hindsight to assess this; the question is whether the risk of harm was foreseeable *at the time*. This was seen again in **Maguire v Harland & Wolff plc (2005)**. C's husband was exposed to asbestos dust at work, but he did not become ill, *she* did. She claimed damages on the basis that she was exposed to the dust he brought home. The judge found in her favour, saying that it was reasonably foreseeable that there was a serious risk to her health. The CA allowed D's appeal. At the time of C's exposure the risks of secondary exposure were unknown. The injury to a member of C's family was therefore not foreseeable.

If the risk is foreseeable, but small, the other factors will be relevant in deciding whether D had done enough. In **Bolton v Stone (1951)** a woman was hit by a cricket ball while walking near a cricket ground. The cricket club had taken precautions by erecting a 17-foot fence and the ball had gone over it only a matter of five or six times in some 35 years. There was thus a foreseeable, but only very small, risk of a ball going over and, balanced against the other factors, the club had done all that was expected of it.

The seriousness of the potential harm

A higher standard of care may be required where, although the *risk* is small, the *consequences* may be serious. This can be seen in **Paris v Stepney BC (1951)** where C was a worker who was already blind in one eye. While doing some welding he was injured in the other eye. His job only involved a slight risk of injury, but the HL held that although a failure to provide goggles would not always make the council liable to their employees, in this case the seriousness of the harm that *could* occur was very great. There was therefore a duty to take greater care.

Examination pointer

The *Paris* case shows that a greater duty is owed to those suffering under a disability. This would also apply to children or the elderly, so look for clues in the scenario. What may be doing enough in respect of a fully able person may not be so in other cases. Note also that it is potential harm that is looked at. Don't be tempted to say that there is a breach because the harm actually suffered is very great. It is what harm might occur that is relevant, not what has occurred.

Whether the risk was justifiable

The taking of a risk may be justifiable in certain circumstances. A risk which is of some benefit to society, for example, may be deemed acceptable even though it could be foreseen. Thus in **Watt v Hertfordshire CC (1954)** a fireman was injured when a heavy car jack fell on him. The vehicle he was in was not adapted to carry such equipment, but it was held that this was an acceptable risk in the circumstances because they were on their way to rescue a woman trapped under a car.

The expense and practicality of taking precautions

D may argue that avoiding a risk altogether would be too costly. The courts are unlikely to accept risk-taking based *solely* on the cost of avoidance, but it may tip the balance when considering the other factors. In **Latimer v AEC (1952)** the HL found a factory owner not liable for the injury to an employee who slipped on a wet floor. It was wet due to exceptional rain and flooding, and the owners had put down sand and taken other precautions. On the facts they had done enough. Shutting the factory would not only have been costly, but also impractical.

Example | If everyone drove at 5 mph there would be fewer road accidents, but no one would expect the government to rule that such precautions should be taken. That would be impractical. In **Bolton v Stone**, the cricket club had already built a high fence – arguably, it would be impractical to do more than they had done, as in **Latimer**. By comparison, in **Paris v Stepney BC** it would have been neither costly nor impractical to provide goggles.

Examination pointer

These four factors are balanced against each other when the courts are deciding whether D breached the standard of care expected of the reasonable person. Look for particular clues but be prepared to discuss all four if necessary.

Let's try this using **Bolton v Stone (1951)**.

The potential harm would be serious as cricket balls are very hard and could kill. However, this is balanced against the low degree of risk (it had rarely happened) and the precautions the cricket club had taken (erecting a high fence). It is also arguable that it was justifiable due to the social benefit of the game of cricket. On balance, the club had done all that was expected of it.

Objective standard?

The standard expected is said to be objective. It is based on what the reasonable person would do. A striking illustration of this is **Nettleship v Weston (1971)**. Here a learner driver was liable for injuries to her driving instructor due to her negligent driving. The CA said that a learner driver should show the skill of an ordinary, competent driver.

However, the standard is also measured by reference to the particular circumstances. This makes it slightly more subjective. A child would be expected to reach the standard of a child of similar age, not an adult. In **Mullin v Richards (1998)** a schoolgirl of 15 was injured during a play-fight using plastic rulers as swords. The CA found the other girl not to be liable in negligence. An adult may have seen the risk; a child would not.

Where D acts in a professional capacity the standard expected is that of a person in that line of work. In **Bolam v Friern HMC (1957)** it was accepted that if a doctor acted in accordance with '*a practice accepted as proper by a reasonable body of medical men*' there would be no breach. This was tempered somewhat in **Bolitho v City & Hackney HA (1998)** where it was added that the medical opinion must have some logical basis. Thus a doctor must show the skill that normal medical opinion would expect of a doctor, not just any 'reasonable person'.

Note that the 'balancing factors' are still relevant in cases where there is a subjective element such as age or professional competence. In **McDonnell v Holwerda (2005)** the question was whether a GP had fallen below the standard expected of a reasonably competent GP by not recognising the possibility of meningitis in a child, following an examination. The court held that she had not fallen below the standard expected on the first occasion that she assessed the child. However, the GP had seen the child on a second occasion and, as the degree of risk was high due to the fact that the meningitis infection spreads so quickly, the standard expected was higher. She had fallen below this standard because she had not carried out a full enough investigation.

Food for thought

In **Nettleship** it was said that a learner should show the skill of a competent driver. Is this fair to learners? We all have to start somewhere and it does not allow for a lower standard for those attempting to gain experience. Arguably, in a driving case this is OK, because everyone must have insurance. It won't be D paying, but an insurance company, which can best bear the cost. In other cases it may be less justifiable.

There are plenty of cases on breach. For more examples look back at the 'duty' cases. We saw in **Vowles v Evans (2002)** that a referee in an amateur rugby match owed a duty of care for the players' safety. By allowing an inexperienced player to play in a scrum position for which he was not trained the referee hadn't reached the standard expected, and so was in breach of duty.

Examination pointer

It is clear from the cases that the standard expected will always depend on the particular circumstances. You will not be expected to make an absolute decision on breach. Look at the facts for clues, e.g. mention of D's profession or age. Then apply the factors as appropriate and conclude as to what you think is most likely.

Task

Choose any three cases seen so far and consider which factors may have been relevant in deciding whether there was breach of a duty of care. See how many of them you can apply, as I did with **Bolton v Stone** above.

Summary

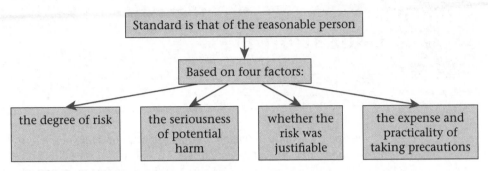

Standard is that of the reasonable person

↓

Based on four factors:

| the degree of risk | the seriousness of potential harm | whether the risk was justifiable | the expense and practicality of taking precautions |

Task

Draw up the summary into a diagram, adding a case on each, and keep it for revision.

Self-test questions

1 In which case was the objective standard explained, and by whom?

2 State the four factors which the court may consider when deciding what is reasonable.

3 Give a case example for each of the above.

4 What standard is expected of a professional? A child?

5 Why had the employer not breached their duty in **Maguire v Harland & Wolff plc (2005)**?

For further resources and updates please go to the Companion Website accompanying this book at **www.pearsoned.co.uk/russell**

Causation

... children's ingenuity in finding unexpected ways of doing mischief to themselves and others should never be underestimated.

Lord Hoffmann, **Jolley *v* Sutton LBC (2000)**

> **By the end of this Unit you should be able to:**
> - Explain the rules on both factual and legal causation
> - Show how the law applies by reference to cases
> - Identify problems with the law in order to attempt an evaluation

The third matter that must be proved is causation. C not only has to prove that damage occurred, but must also prove D was the cause of that damage, both in fact and in law. Damage must be factually caused by D's breach and be reasonably foreseeable.

Causation in fact: the 'but for' test

The question here is whether D's breach in fact caused the damage. The courts apply the 'but for' test. This asks, 'But for D's negligence would the harm have occurred?' If the answer is 'no' then D is liable. However, if the damage would have happened regardless of the negligent act or omission, D will not be liable for it.

Key case

The leading case is **Barnett *v* Chelsea & Kensington HMC (1968)** where a man suffering from vomiting and pain called at a hospital but was sent home without being treated. He later died of arsenic poisoning and his widow sued the hospital management committee. The hospital clearly owed a duty to patients, and was found to be negligent, but they were not found liable because he would have died regardless of whether he was treated. Here the answer to 'But for D's negligence would the harm have occurred?' was 'Yes, it would', so D was not liable. Both duty and breach were proved, but the claim failed on the third issue, that of causation.

Successive and multiple causes

In cases where there is more than one possible cause a claim could fail if causation could not be proved in respect of any particular D. In **Fairchild *v* Glenhaven**

Funeral Services Ltd (2002) the HL made clear that the 'but for' test is *necessary* but not always *conclusive*, and modified the rules.

Key case

The facts of **Fairchild** were that C became ill after exposure to asbestos dust in the course of successive employments. The CA had held that he could not recover damages from any of the employers, since he could not establish which period of employment had caused his illness. This seemed unfair to C, because each of the employers could be shown to be in breach of duty. It just wasn't clear which particular breach was the cause of the illness. The HL reversed the CA's decision and held that if C could show that D had *'materially increased the risk'* of harm then the causation test could be satisfied. The HL said that the causation rules might be modified on policy grounds *'in special circumstances'*.

Despite the comment about 'special circumstances' in **Fairchild**, this principle was extended to a different type of case in **Chester v Afshar (2004)**. Here C had back problems and needed an operation. She was not told that there was a small risk of nerve damage. She had the operation and suffered such damage. The surgeon had breached his duty by not warning her, but had this caused the nerve damage? The answer to the question 'But for the lack of warning would the harm have occurred?' may well have been 'Yes'. It might have happened anyway. However, the HL allowed her claim on the basis that although there was evidence that after taking further advice she *might* still have had the operation, she would have not had it *at that time*. The lack of warning had therefore caused the damage. These cases show that if there was a *possibility* that D's breach caused the harm, rather than a *probability*, causation may still be proved.

Loss of chance

The HL refused to extend this idea of 'possible' rather than 'probable' causes to allow compensation for *loss of chance* in **Gregg v Scott (2005)**. Here a doctor negligently misdiagnosed C's cancer. If treated earlier the cancer might not have spread. It was shown that he had previously had a 45 per cent chance of surviving 10 years. This had fallen to 25 per cent. The judge held that even though there was a reduced chance, the chance of survival was still under 50 per cent. The late diagnosis had not made sufficient difference to the result. On appeal the HL accepted that there *could* be a claim for a loss of chance *'when overall fairness so requires'*. However, they held that a complete adoption of 'possible' rather than 'probable' causation was too great a change in the law and should be left to Parliament.

Food for thought

Do you agree with the decisions in **Fairchild** and **Chester**? Is this too generous to C or a fair compromise?

Even if D's act was found to be the factual cause of the harm, there is still one more hurdle for C to get over. The harm must not be 'too remote' from D's act.

Causation in law: remoteness of damage

The test here is one of foreseeability. If the loss or damage is not foreseeable it is said to be 'too remote' from the breach. This was established in **The Wagon Mound (1961)**, which replaced the wider test in **Re Polemis (1921)** that you were liable for *all* the direct consequences of your actions. The later test asks whether it was *foreseeable* that the damage would occur. D is only liable for the foreseeable consequences of any breach of duty.

The full name of **The Wagon Mound** is **Overseas Tankship (UK) Ltd v Morts Dock & Engineering Co. (1961)**, but it is commonly called **The Wagon Mound**.

Key case

In **The Wagon Mound** oil was negligently spilt by the Ds. This oil caused a fire that damaged C's wharf two days later. The Ds were not liable because it was not believed that this type of oil could catch fire on water. The damage to the dock by *oil* was foreseeable, so C could claim for this, but not damage caused by the later *fire*. That damage was too 'remote' from the Ds' act, because it was not foreseeable.

Intervening act

Sometimes something happens between D's negligent act and C's injury. This is referred to by the Latin tag '*novus actus interveniens*' or in modern parlance, 'new act intervening'. Such an act may sometimes break the chain of causation between D's act or omission and the harm to C. In **Smith v Littlewoods (1987)** an owner of a disused cinema had left his property unsecured and vandals broke in. They caused a fire which spread to a neighbour's property. The neighbour sued the cinema owner. The claim failed. D successfully argued that the act of the vandals had broken the chain between the omission (not locking up properly) and the damage. An example of the argument failing can be seen in a case we looked at earlier, **Reeves v MPC**. The police argued that the prisoner's suicide was an intervening act, which broke the chain of causation. The HL did not accept this.

Type of damage

If the *type* of damage is foreseeable then the fact that it occurred in an unforeseeable way, or that the consequences were more extensive than could be foreseen, will not affect liability. In **Hughes v Lord Advocate (1963)** a child knocked over a paraffin lamp which caused an explosion. He was very badly burnt. The court found that the *type* of injury was foreseeable (burns) even though the way this had occurred (an explosion) was not. D was liable.

The principles of both **The Wagon Mound** and **Hughes** were confirmed by the HL in **Jolley v Sutton LBC (2000)**.

Key case

In **Jolley** a 14-year-old boy was badly injured when working with a friend on an abandoned and derelict boat on council land. The CA had held that the council were not liable. While it may be foreseeable that children might *play* on such a boat it was not foreseeable that they would attempt to *repair* it. The HL reversed the decision and made the point in the opening quote that the ingenuity of children should not be underestimated. It was foreseeable that they would meddle with the boat in some way – it did not matter that they had been repairing it rather than playing on it.

Food for thought

The **Hughes** test seems much wider than **The Wagon Mound**. It suggests that the harm itself does not necessarily have to be foreseeable. It would appear, at least in the case of children, that the wider principle is correct because it was approved by the HL in **Jolley**.

Further support for this view can be seen in **Gabriel v Kirklees Metropolitan Council (2004)**. Although it was not a claim by a child, it involved children 'doing the unexpected'. C had been walking past a building site and was injured by material thrown by children playing there. A claim was made against the council that owned the site, which was in a residential area. The council admitted that at the time it was unfenced. The main issue was therefore whether this breach of duty had caused the harm to C. The judge dismissed the claim on the grounds that harm was not foreseeable. The CA noted that the judge had relied on **The Wagon Mound** test in regard to foreseeability of harm but had not referred to **Jolley v Sutton LBC (2000)** on the issue of *'children's ingenuity in finding unexpected ways of doing mischief'*. The CA said that the judge ought to have asked the following:

- whether it was reasonably foreseeable that children would go on to the site;
- whether it was reasonably foreseeable that the children would play there;
- whether it was reasonably foreseeable that, in playing there, they would throw whatever came to hand; and
- whether in playing with the material on the site it was reasonably foreseeable that they might cause injury to those passing by.

The CA ordered a new trial before a different judge.

Overlap

Note the overlap between foreseeability and intervening act. An intervening act will only break the chain of causation if it was unforeseeable itself.

Example In **Reeves**, the prisoner was on suicide watch so suicide was foreseeable and didn't break the chain. If the police had left the door flap open and a mouse had crawled in through the hole and then bitten the prisoner who happened to suffer a rare allergy to mouse bites and died, this would be an unforeseeable event and so would be likely to break the chain between the negligence of the police and the death.

Examination pointer

Gabriel v Kirklees shows that it may be important to refer to **Jolley**, not just **The Wagon Mound** test, if the scenario involves children. Use **The Wagon Mound** as setting the test, but go on to mention the points made in **Gabriel**.

Task

Use two cases that you remember from looking at duty or breach. Use the 'but for' test to apply causation *in fact*. Then add the rules from **The Wagon Mound** and **Jolley** to see if D *legally* caused the harm.

The thin skull rule

There is another apparent exception to the foreseeability test. It is a common law rule that D must take the victim as he or she is found. This means that if a particular disability in the victim means they are likely to suffer more serious harm, or die, D is still liable, even though a person without that disability would not have been so seriously harmed. An example is **Smith v Leech Brain (1962)** where D's negligence caused a small burn, which activated a latent cancer from which C died. His wife sued his employer and the court held that C's particular vulnerability (the pre-existing cancer) did not affect liability. C's wife did not have to prove that cancer was foreseeable, only that some harm was, even though it was of a different type. It is called the 'thin' or 'eggshell' skull rule because the essence of the rule is that if there is something which makes V more vulnerable than other people this will not affect D's liability.

Example Jake is riding his bike too fast and knocks over a man who has a very thin skull. Most people would have only suffered a few knocks and bruises, but this man dies because as he fell his skull broke open. Jake can be liable for the death, not just the foreseeable injuries, under the 'thin skull' rule.

Summary

When applying the law ask the following questions:
Would the harm have occurred 'but for' D's act or omission?
Is there more than one cause? If so, the test may be modified.
Was the harm foreseeable or was it too remote?
Was this *type* of harm foreseeable?
Does the thin skull rule apply?

Task

Draw up a diagram as a guide for a problem question based on the summary of the principles. Add a case for each issue, briefly explaining the facts as far as they relate to the principle.

Self-test questions

1 What is the 'but for' test and from which case did it come?

2 Which case established the rule on foreseeability?

3 What did **Hughes** add to this?

4 Can you explain the 'thin skull rule'?

5 What was the point made in **Jolley** (in the HL) in regard to children?

For further resources and updates please go to the Companion Website accompanying this book at **www.pearsoned.co.uk/russell**

Study Block 13 Summary
NEGLIGENCE

Summary of duty for all types of loss

Type of harm/loss			
Physical (to person or property)	**Psychiatric**	**Economic**	
		By statement	By act
⬇	⬇	⬇	⬇
Duty based on **Donoghue/Caparo** test	Duty based on **Alcock** test	Duty based on **Hedley** test, **Caparo** test and assumption of responsibility	No duty
Go on to prove breach and causation	Go on to prove breach and causation	Go on to prove breach and causation	No claim

Task

Look up the tests mentioned above. Draw a diagram adding the tests for each type of harm or damage. Keep this for revision.

Breach of duty

Standard is that of the reasonable person, an objective test. Note, though, the subjective element:

> **Bolitho v City & Hackney HA (1998)** – professionals
> **Nettleship v Weston (1971)** – learners
> **Mullin v Richards (1998)** – children

Look at the four factors:

- the degree of risk – **Maguire *v* Harland & Wolff plc (2005)**
- the seriousness of potential harm – **Paris *v* Stepney BC (1951)**
- whether the risk was justifiable – **Watt *v* Hertfordshire CC (1954)**
- the expense and practicality of taking precautions – **Latimer *v* AEC (1952)**

Damage caused by the breach

- Would the harm have occurred 'but for' D's act or omission? **Barnett *v* Chelsea & Kensington HMC** but note also **Fairchild *v* Glenhaven Funeral Services Ltd**
- Was the harm foreseeable or was it too remote? **The Wagon Mound**
- Was this type of harm foreseeable? **Hughes *v* Lord Advocate**
- Does the thin skull rule apply? **Smith *v* Leech Brain**

Note that foreseeability comes into all three areas, but becomes more specific at each stage.

Duty	Was it foreseeable that C *could be* harmed by D's actions? **Donoghue**
Breach	Was the *risk* of harm foreseeable? **Roe**
Damage	Was this *type* of harm foreseeable? **The Wagon Mound/Hughes**

Key criticisms

- Is the **Caparo** test sufficiently clear?
- Should a distinction be made between economic loss by actions and by statements?
- Should children be able to sue the council for failing to, e.g., diagnose dyslexia? Would the money be better used in employing more (and better) psychologists?
- It may be difficult to prove 'close ties' in psychiatric harm cases.
- The 'immediate aftermath' is hard to measure.
- The law has not been entirely consistent on these issues.
- Psychiatric harm has many problems; look back at the 'Food for thought' sections for more.
- Learners are treated in the same way as experienced drivers – **Nettleship**.
- The thin skull rule can be seen as unfair to D who will be liable for unforeseen harm – **Smith *v* Leech Brain**.
- On a positive note, the harm must now be foreseeable, which is fairer than the old rule that D was liable for all direct consequences – **The Wagon Mound**.

Task

Add the rules on breach and causation to your diagram on the duty rules.

Examination practice

January 2005
How far would you agree that rules in the English law of tort ensure that a claimant may be properly compensated for pure economic loss caused by the negligence of another? *(25 marks)*

January 2005*
How far would you agree that rules in the English law of tort ensure that a claimant may be properly compensated for psychiatric injury caused by the negligence of another? *(25 marks)*

Module 6 connections

Morals	The neighbour principle developed from morality and the Bible	**Donoghue v Stevenson**
	It is morally undesirable for members of a family to sue each other	**Greatorex**
	Should the law be involved in arrangements between friends?	**Chaudhry**
	Is the thin skull rule morally defensible?	**Smith v Leech Brain**
Justice	The neighbour principle does justice to the consumer	**Donoghue**
	Is it just that learners are fully liable for their negligence?	**Nettleship**
Conflicting interests	The rights of the police to compensation was balanced against the fact that many relatives had been unable to succeed, so they failed in their claim	**White v CC of South Yorkshire**
	Whether the risk was justifiable means the risk of harm is balanced against the wider community interests	**Watt v Hertfordshire CC**
	The expense and practicality of taking precautions is also balanced against the wider community interests	**Latimer v AEC**
Fault	The fault element in negligence is breach of duty, so any of these cases can be discussed. Note that, e.g., a learner can be said to be less at fault than a qualified driver but is still in breach	**Nettleship**
Creativity	**Donoghue v Stevenson** established that a manufacturer owes a duty to a consumer, later developed to other relationships	
	Hedley Byrne established that there could be liability in tort for economic loss if there was a 'special relationship' between C and D	
	White v Jones filled in a gap in the law in order to allow a third party beneficiary to claim for the loss, but the courts have shown a reluctance to expand the law any further on psychiatric harm and have indicated that it is up to Parliament to address the matter	
	The HL said a complete adoption of 'possible' rather than 'probable' causation was too great a change in the law and should be left to Parliament	**Gregg v Scott**

Study Block 14
OCCUPIER'S LIABILITY

Unit 43   Occupier's liability 1: lawful visitors
Unit 44   Occupier's liability 2: non-visitors

This Study Block covers liability for harm which occurs on someone else's property. There are two Acts which govern this, the **Occupier's Liability Act 1957** and the **Occupier's Liability Act 1984**. The first deals with people who have permission to be on the property and the second with those who don't.

What is meant by occupier's liability?

An occupier of property can be liable for harm that occurs to someone who is on that property. The occupier, who is the person in control of the property, owes a duty to keep people on it safe from harm. This duty arises merely by the fact of having *control* of the property on which the harm occurred. The first Unit of this Study Block looks at the **Occupier's Liability Act 1957** and lawful visitors. Originally this was included in the tort of negligence at common law, but it is now governed by statute. This means that although you may have a claim in negligence wherever the harm occurred, there may be an alternative action if it occurred on someone else's property.

Example   The council is building a new block of flats on their land. The builders have dug a large hole and gone to lunch. Fred falls into it while delivering to the site and is injured. The council will owe Fred a duty, despite not being present at the time. The council has control of the site and will owe a duty to anyone visiting it. The builders may also owe Fred a duty, but the council may be better able to meet Fred's claim. Fred can sue in negligence or under the **OLA 1957**. The latter may be better as he will not have to prove negligence by the council.

If Fred had not been delivering, but had been trespassing on the site, he will not be a lawful visitor. In this case he will have to use the **Occupier's Liability Act 1984**. The liability is more limited under this Act, and we cover the special rules on this in Unit 44.

Unit 43

Occupier's liability 1: lawful visitors

. . . the responsibility for the safety of little children must rest primarily upon the parents.

Devlin J, **Phipps v Rochester Corporation (1955)**

By the end of this Unit you should be able to:

- Explain the special rules involving cases where harm was caused on someone's property
- Show how case law and statute law apply to visitors
- Identify problems with the law in order to attempt an evaluation

The **Occupier's Liability Act 1957 (OLA 1957)** provides that an occupier of property owes a duty to lawful visitors to ensure their safety. The Act covers not only those people expressly invited, but also those who may have implied consent, or a right, to be on the property.

Task

Other than invited friends, the window cleaner might be classed as a lawful visitor. Make a list of five other people you think might be included.

We will now consider what the *duty* is, who the *occupier* may be, and who will be classed as a *lawful visitor*.

The duty

Under **s. 2(2)** the duty on an occupier is to:

> *'take such care as in all the circumstances of the case is reasonable to see that the visitor will be reasonably safe in using the premises for the purposes for which he is invited to be there.'*

Although **s. 1(1)** refers to *'dangers due to the state of the premises or to things done or omitted to be done on them'*, it is clear from **s. 2** that the duty is to keep the *visitor* safe, not necessarily the premises.

Example My shed is falling down and unsafe. I cordon it off and put up a large sign saying 'DANGER'. Although my **premises** are not safe, the fact that it is cordoned off and clearly marked will probably mean any **visitors** will be safe.

The occupier

The occupier is the person *in control* of the premises. This was established in **Wheat v Lacon (1966)**. C had fallen downstairs while staying at a pub. There was evidence to show that someone had removed a light bulb. The HL held that a duty was owed by the brewery who owned the pub, as well as the licensees who let the room to C. Lord Denning described the occupier as a person who had '*a sufficient degree of control over the premises*'. Although it was found the brewers had not *breached* their duty, the principle is that there can be more than one occupier.

Lawful visitors

Who did you think might be a lawful visitor in the task on page 376? Many people have implied consent to enter, e.g. when making deliveries or reading the meter, professionals you have called in such as a doctor, plumber or electrician, as well as those who may have a right to be there such as the police – with a warrant – and firefighters attending a call-out.

Examination pointer

The **OLA 1957** makes provision for particular situations. It is important to know these as exam questions often include a particular issue which you will be expected to pick up on. Let's take a look.

Children s. 2(3)(a)

This section provides that:

> '*an occupier must be prepared for children to be less careful than adults. If an occupier allows a child to enter the premises then the premises must be reasonably safe for a child of that age.*'

Not only is the degree of care higher in respect of children, but also age may be relevant in deciding whether someone is a visitor or a trespasser. Cases before the **Acts** are still relevant on both these issues. In **Glasgow Corporation v Taylor (1922)**, there was no warning or fence in front of a shrub containing poisonous berries in a public park owned by the corporation. A child died after picking and eating some. The council would probably not have breached its duty in the case of an adult, as an adult would probably have been treated as a trespasser on the basis that there was no right to take the berries. However, in respect of a 7-year-old, who would be fascinated by the bright berries, it *was* liable.

In **Phipps v Rochester Corporation (1955)** it was said that an occupier could expect very young children to be in the care of an adult. This meant the council had not breached its duty when a 5-year-old C was injured on their land. He was with his 7-year-old sister, but no adult or responsible older person was present. Devlin J also made clear that different considerations would apply *'to public parks or to recognised playing grounds where parents allow their children to go unaccompanied in the reasonable belief that they are safe'*.

Examination pointer

You should take special care if the scenario involves a child. Although D has to take greater care in respect of children, if the child is very young, D can argue that the parents should have been responsible (**Phipps**). Also, in **Glasgow Corporation v Taylor** the court said that such attractions can be 'fascinating but fatal' to children. This is referred to as an allurement. It means that a child who is attracted by something on D's land is being allured and thus, in a sense, invited, even if it isn't open to the public. Look out for clues such as 'a pile of sand', 'fireworks', 'a pond' etc., which might be attractive to a child. An implied invitation can make someone a lawful visitor and so come within the **OLA 1957**, rather than the **OLA 1984**. If in any doubt discuss both and explain why you are doing so. Note, though, that the duty to trespassers is more limited, so bringing an action under the **OLA 1957** may be better.

Task

Write a brief comparison of **Glasgow** and **Phipps** to show why one claim succeeded and the other didn't.

In **Jolley v Sutton LBC (1998)** the CA held that the council was not liable when a boat left abandoned and rotting on council land fell on a 14-year-old boy. He and a friend had been trying to repair it and had propped the boat up to work underneath it. The decision of the CA was based on the fact that, although the boat was both potentially dangerous and attractive, the injury was not foreseeable. There were indications that the decision may have been different if the boys had been playing rather than working. This distinction was not accepted by the HL, which reversed the decision.

Key case

In **Jolley v Sutton LBC (2000)** the HL found that there was a foreseeable risk of children meddling with the boat and injuring themselves. That they were working on it rather than playing on it was not important. There was a *foreseeable risk of some harm occurring*. Lord Hoffmann said that the ingenuity of children in finding unexpected ways of doing mischief to themselves should not be underestimated. The boy's injury was within the **Wagon Mound** test, i.e. the injury was *not too remote* from the danger (of a rotting boat).

Food for thought

Read the cases and form your own opinion on how far an occupier should be responsible for the safety of children. This is a popular area for problem questions, but could also come into an essay. Consider whether parents should have responsibility for very young children, but also how to decide at what age this moves to the occupier. The extent of the duty under the common law and the Act is the same, so cases prior to the Act can be cited in support of an answer.

Professionals s. 2(3)(b)

The duty of care for professional people is more limited in that they are expected to take their own precautions against risks that are incidental to their area of expertise. This section provides that:

> *'An occupier may expect that a person, in the exercise of his calling, will appreciate and guard against any special risks ordinarily incidental to it.'*

Example
> You need to get your house rewired and call a qualified electrician to come and do it. The electrician gets a bad shock from a bare wire and is off work for several days. He is unlikely to win a claim for compensation as he should have appreciated this type of risk.

In **Roles v Nathan (1963)** two chimney sweeps were not protected by the Act as they should have recognised the danger of carbon monoxide gas escaping from a boiler chimney. Similarly, in **General Cleaning Contractors v Christmas (1953)** a window cleaner was injured when he fell off a building after a defective window closed on his hand. He failed in his claim (under common law) as he was expected to guard against that type of risk. It should be noted, however, that this does not mean that D is never liable to a professional doing his job, as the next case shows.

Key case

In **Ogwo v Taylor (1988)** D had negligently started a fire when using a blowtorch. C was a fireman who was injured trying to put it out. It was held that he was owed a duty as he was only there in the exercise of his calling because of D's negligence. Note that he had taken normal precautions, i.e. he had *'guarded against the normal risks'*. Had he not done so, e.g. if he had not worn protective clothing or had taken unnecessary risks, it is unlikely that there would have been liability.

Independent contractors s. 2(4)(b)

The occupier is not usually liable for harm caused by independent contractors if:

> *'in all the circumstances he had acted reasonably in entrusting the work to an independent contractor and had taken such steps (if any) as he reasonably ought in order to satisfy himself that the contractor was competent and the work had been properly done.'*

Thus, if the occupiers did not take care in selection, or did not check on the work, then they may be liable. Much will depend on what type of work the contractor is doing. In **Haseldine v Daw (1941)** the occupier had discharged his duty by giving the job to a competent lift engineer, as he could not be expected to have the expertise to check such specialist work himself. In **Woodward v Mayor of Hastings (1945)** a pupil was injured slipping on an icy step, which a cleaner had left in a dangerous state. The occupier was liable for the cleaner's negligence in this case because he should have checked that the snow had been properly cleared from the steps. Note:

- s. 2(3)(b) relates to liability *to* contractors and other professionals
- s. 2(4)(b) relates to liability *for* contractors whose negligence harms someone else

Example

I have a very large tree in my garden, which is rotten. I get a tree surgeon in to remove it but while he is doing so a branch breaks and he falls. Unfortunately he lands on my neighbour's son, Jim, who is playing in the garden with my kids. Both the contractor and Jim are injured. I am unlikely to be liable *to* the contractor. A branch breaking is likely to be seen as incidental to the job and he should have appreciated and guarded against such a risk, s. 2(3)(b).

I also wouldn't owe a duty to Jim *for* the contractor's negligence (in working while children are nearby) if I had chosen a reputable tree surgeon. However, if he was just a mate from the pub, I may be liable *for* his negligence because I did not act reasonably in selecting him, s. 2(4)(b).

The CA considered the issue of liability for independent contractors in **Gwilliam v West Hertfordshire Hospitals NHS Trust (2002)**. C was injured when using a 'splat-wall' (if you've never heard of one it is where people bounce from a trampoline and stick – by wearing a Velcro suit – to a wall) at a fund-raising fair in the hospital grounds. It had been set up negligently by a contractor, and, as their insurance had expired, C claimed against the hospital. As the occupier, the hospital owed C a duty of care under **s. 2(1)** to take reasonable steps to ensure that a contractor had public liability insurance. The hospital had specifically requested, and paid for, such insurance and the CA held that it would be unreasonable to expect them to check the terms of the actual policy. The duty had been fulfilled so the claim failed.

Task

Compare the **Woodward** case to **Gwilliam**. Can you identify the difference? Now look at the next one. Why was a duty owed by the cricket club but not by the hospital?

In **Bottomley v Todmorden Cricket Club (2003)** a cricket club hired an un-insured stunt team to perform firework displays on its land. An amateur helper was injured because of the team's negligence, and sued the club. The CA held that an occupier had a duty to take reasonable care in selecting a suitable contractor to carry on a dangerous activity over his land. This would include checking that insurance was in place. As they had not done so they were liable for the injuries sustained.

Note that if the person who is negligent is the occupier's *employee* rather than a *contractor*, the occupier may be vicariously liable for that person's negligence (see Unit 47).

Warnings s. 2(4)(a)

The occupier can discharge liability by placing warning signs, but these must be sufficient to keep the visitor safe. The **Act** provides that such a warning is not enough '*unless in all the circumstances it was enough to enable the visitor to be reasonably safe*'. So the circumstances will need looking at. If you open your premises to children you would need to have clearer warnings than for adults. You would also be expected to consider the disabled; for example, a written notice would not be sufficient to keep a blind person safe. If the danger is obvious a warning may not be needed. In **Cotton v Derbyshire Dales DC (1994)** C was injured after slipping on a cliff path. The words of Lord Shaw in **Glasgow Corporation v Taylor**, that a duty to make premises reasonably safe '*does not include an obligation of protection against dangers which are themselves obvious*' were cited with approval in the CA. In **Staples v West Dorset CC (1995)** a walker slipped on a coastal path while taking a photograph. The trial judge had held the council had failed in its duty by not erecting a notice warning that the surface was slippery. The CA reversed the decision and held that they were not liable as the danger was obvious.

Key case

In **Darby v National Trust (2001)** a man had drowned while swimming in a pond on National Trust property. His widow sued them under the **OLA 1957** on the basis that they should have had signs warning of the danger. The CA held that the danger of drowning was an obvious risk and so there was no need to erect warning signs.

Several other cases involving swimming accidents and 'obvious dangers' were brought under the **OLA 1984**, because C was trespassing at the time. These are discussed in the next Unit.

Examination pointer

If C is harmed while lawfully on someone's property then you should consider a claim under the **OLA 1957**. However, you may need to look at negligence as an alternative. This is because there is some doubt as to whether the **Act** or common law rules of negligence apply when harm is caused by an activity on the property rather than occupancy of the property. In **Ogwo v Taylor (1988)** the fireman claimed under both common law negligence and the **OLA 1957**, the first regarding the activity of starting the fire, the second regarding D's occupancy of the house. The HL held that the duty owed was the same, but they did not address the issue of which type of action was appropriate. If in doubt, discuss both.

Food for thought

Where harm is caused by an *activity* on the property rather than *occupancy* of the property it is unclear whether the **Act** or common law rules apply. The CA in **Bottomley** said that an occupier had an 'activity duty' in respect of activities permitted or encouraged on the land, and an 'occupancy duty' for the state of the premises. This case shows that both *can* come under the **Act** but, as in **Ogwo**, did not make it clear when. Is it satisfactory that such doubt exists? If I invite you on to my land, should it make any difference if you are injured by something *done* on my property (an activity) or by the mere fact that I *control* the premises (my occupancy)? **Section 1(1)** implies that both come under the **Act**.

Breach of duty and causation

Once duty has been addressed you will still have to prove breach of duty *and* causation. Breach will depend on 'all the circumstances', including C's age and any warning signs. The normal negligence rules apply, such as degree of risk and expense and practicality of taking precautions. Thus, in **Jolley** the HL held that the risk was foreseeable and would take little expense to avoid. In not removing the boat the council had therefore not reached the expected standard, so had breached its duty.

As regards causation, the normal 'but for' and 'remoteness of damage' tests will apply (see Unit 42). This was confirmed in **Jolley**.

Task

Pete the plumber comes to mend Tim's water tank in the loft. While there he falls through some rotten planking and is injured. Eddie, a qualified electrician, has also been called in to repair some faulty wiring. While doing so, he is electrocuted. Is Tim liable for either injury? Why/why not?

Exclusions s. 2(1)

An occupier can limit or exclude liability *'in so far as he is free to'*. Exclusion notices are subject to the **Unfair Contract Terms Act 1977 (UCTA)**. **Section 2(1)** prohibits any attempt at excluding liability for death or personal injury caused by negligence. Excluding liability for damage to property is allowed, but it must be reasonable. **UCTA** applies to business dealings, but not to private occupiers. One problem that arose was that if an occupier could not exclude *liability*, then they were better off excluding *visitors* – no more school trips! An amendment was therefore added by the **OLA 1984**. If the visit is for educational or recreational purposes then this doesn't come within 'business' – unless the occupier runs such a business.

Example You own an orchard. If you charge the public to come in to pick the apples, you are running a business and **UCTA** applies. You are unable to exclude liability for injury by negligence, and any other exclusion, for example in respect of damage to cars, has to be reasonable. If you allow the public free access for recreational purposes, e.g. to park and picnic there, then you are able to exclude liability as you come within the exceptions.

Task

Walk around your school, college or work premises. Can you find any warning signs or signs that attempt to exclude liability? Look around the locality too. There are usually signs in railway stations warning of the danger of slippery floors. Getting too close to the edge of the platform is dangerous but would a warning be needed or is it an obvious risk?

Defences

Finally, as with negligence, you will need to consider defences. Apart from warnings (which **discharge** liability) and exclusion notices (which **avoid** liability), the defences of contributory negligence and consent may apply. Contributory negligence is implied in **s. 2(3)** of the **Act**, which says the courts may take into account the degree of care the visitor can be expected to show for their own safety. Consent is dealt with specifically – **s. 2(5)** states: '*The common duty of care does not impose on an occupier any obligation willingly accepted as his by the visitor.*'

Both defences are discussed in Unit 48.

Summary

The duty	to see that the visitor will be reasonably safe	s. 2(2)
Occupier	the person in control of the premises	**Wheat v Lacon**
Children	an occupier should be prepared for children to be less careful	s. 2(3)(a) **Jolley**
Professionals	are expected to take their own precautions against risks related to their trade	s. 2(3)(b) **Roles v Nathan**
Warnings	must be enough to ensure the visitor is reasonably safe if the danger is obvious, a warning is less likely to be needed	s. 2(4)(a) **Darby v National Trust**
Exclusions	can limit or exclude liability 'in so far as he is free to'. Thus any such attempt is subject to **UCTA 1977**	s. 2(1)
Contributory negligence	damages may be reduced if C fails to take reasonable care for their own safety	s. 2(3)
Consent	not liable in respect of risks willingly accepted	s. 2(5)

Self-test questions

1 What test is used to find who the occupier is?

2 What is the extent of the occupier's duty under **s. 2(2)**?

3 What is an 'allurement' and what effect does it have?

4 When may an occupier owe a duty for work done by an independent contractor?

5 Which cases will support your answers to each of the above questions?

 For further resources and updates please go to the Companion Website accompanying this book at **www.pearsoned.co.uk/russell**

Unit 44 Occupier's liability 2: non-visitors

If the risk of serious injury is so slight and remote that it is highly unlikely ever to materialise, it may well be that it is not reasonable to expect the occupier to take any steps to protect anyone against it.

Lord Hobhouse, **Tomlinson *v* Congleton Borough Council (2003)**

By the end of this Unit you should be able to:

● Explain the occupier's duty in cases where the harm was caused to someone not lawfully on the property

● Show how the law has developed by reference to appropriate cases

● Identify problems with the law in order to attempt an evaluation

What is meant by occupier's liability for non-visitors?

The **Occupier's Liability Act (OLA) 1984** deals with cases where harm is caused to someone not lawfully on the occupier's property. Usually this will mean trespassers but the word non-visitor is used because there are a few other people exercising certain rights who are covered by this Act rather than the **1957** one. In particular, the **Countryside and Rights of Way Act 2000** has increased access rights to land and amended the **OLA 1984**. An occupier of land owes the more limited duty under the later Act to people exercising access rights, but not in respect of 'natural features', nor ponds, ditches and rivers.

Note that you can be a lawful visitor and a non-visitor in different parts of the same building. For example, you are a visitor in a pub but would be a trespasser in the living area, which is normally marked private. Similarly if you get a plumber in to mend the kitchen sink he would become a trespasser if he went into your bedroom.

Examination pointer

You should look at the alternatives. If the harm occurred on someone's property then consider a claim under the **OLA**. Look for clues as to whether C is a lawful visitor or a trespasser to decide which Act to discuss. You may need both. Don't forget the **Glasgow** case suggests that an allurement may bring a child trespasser within the **OLA 1957**. This could help if, for example, the claim is for damage to property, which is not covered under the **OLA 1984**. You can use the cases involving children from the previous Unit, even if you are discussing the **OLA 1984**.

The **OLA 1984** followed a case where two boys were injured playing on a railway track. This case is important as it led to a change in the law.

Key case

The case is **British Railways Board _v_ Herrington (1972)**. The boys could not sue under the **OLA 1957** as they should not have got through the fence onto BR's land so were not lawful visitors. The HL held BR owed them a _'common duty of humanity'_ because they knew of the danger, i.e. that the fence had many gaps in it, knew that children had been getting in, and had done nothing to prevent trespassers entering.

The duty s. 1(3)

Parliament then passed the **OLA 1984**. A person can sue under this **Act** even if they are a 'non-visitor'; however, it is more limited than the **OLA 1957**. There is no liability for damage to property, and a duty may only arise under **s. 1(3)** if:

- D is aware of the danger or has reasonable grounds to believe it exists.
- D knows or has reasonable grounds to believe a 'non-visitor' is in, or may come into, the vicinity of the danger.
- The risk is one against which, in all the circumstances of the case, D may reasonably be expected to offer protection.

If these points are satisfied then the actual duty is similar to that under the **OLA 1957**, i.e., to:

> _'take such care as in all the circumstances of the case is reasonable to see that . . . (the non-visitor) . . . does not suffer injury on the premises by reason of the danger concerned.'_

Example Bodgem Builders Ltd are building a house on a site next to a children's playground. They finish at 5 p.m. and leave the site unlocked. A child goes on to the site and falls into a large hole, injuring herself. Applying **s. 1(3)** we can say that:

- Bodgem know of the danger of having an open building site.
- They have reasonable grounds to believe a non-visitor will come on to the site, as they know there is a playground next door.
- In these circumstances it is reasonable to expect them to protect against the risk by locking up.

Examination pointer

The occupier need not know of the danger or the trespasser, but there would need to be some evidence for there to be 'reasonable grounds'. In a problem scenario, you should look for clues such as 'several times' or 'X knew that . . .' Also, reference to something like a playground, as in my example, would give D 'reasonable grounds' to believe a child might enter the site. Also look at the ages given, if any. In my example, you could use **Glasgow Corporation** to suggest that Bodgem may be liable, as they should take greater care in respect of children. If told the child is very young, use **Phipps** to say Bodgem may avoid liability as the parents should be responsible. However, then note it was suggested in **Phipps** that this may not apply to a playground, where it is more reasonable to expect children to be alone. Finally, consider 'allurements' as these may imply an invitation and thus the **1957 Act** - **Jolley**.

Warnings s. 1(5)

The occupier can discharge the duty by taking proper care or by putting up warning signs, but as for the **OLA 1957** these must be adequate to protect C. **Section 1(5)** provides that the occupier must take '*such steps as are reasonable in all the circumstances of the case to give warning of the danger*' so will again depend on the particular circumstances of the case. If children could gain access you would need a clearer warning than for adults. However, if the danger is obvious there may be no duty to provide a warning at all. In **Ratcliff v McConnell (1999)** a student was seriously injured diving into a swimming pool at his college. It was closed (and locked) for the winter and he had climbed in at night. He had been drinking but the evidence was that he knew what he was doing. The court found that the risk of hitting his head on the bottom would be obvious to anyone, so the occupier was not liable.

In **Donoghue v Folkestone Properties (2003)** a trespasser went swimming in a harbour late one evening in midwinter, and was injured by an underwater obstacle. At first instance the court found a duty was owed, but the CA allowed D's appeal. Although D knew of the obstruction, and may have known that someone was in the habit of swimming in the harbour during the summer, there were no reasonable grounds for knowing that he or anyone else would come into the vicinity of the danger late at night in midwinter. These cases seem clear; however, between them came **Tomlinson v Congleton Borough Council (2002)**. The facts were very similar. An 18-year-old dived into a lake and sustained injury. There were notices prohibiting swimming and at first instance the judge found the risks to be 'obvious' and so dismissed his claim. The CA reversed the decision. Applying **s. 1(3)** they found the Ds to be aware of the fact that people could be in the vicinity of a risk, and the risk was one they might reasonably be expected to offer some protection against. The appeal to the HL is important.

Key case

In **Tomlinson v Congleton Borough Council (2003)** the HL reversed the CA decision. Lord Hobhouse expressed '*complete agreement with*' **Donoghue v Folkestone** and made the opening comment, adding, '*The law does not require disproportionate or unreasonable responses*'.

The HL found that there was no duty to C where the injury derives from the dangerous nature of a voluntary activity rather than the state of the premises. Lord Hoffman stated *obiter* that even if a duty had been owed, that duty would *not* have required the council to take steps to prevent C from diving or warning him against dangers which were '*perfectly obvious*'.

Food for thought

It is always worth noting any conflict between the CA and HL because disagreement at this level is something that can be criticised as making the law uncertain. The CA had significantly increased the chance of an occupier being liable to a trespasser, and seemed to give a trespasser more protection than a visitor – see **Darby v NT** (p. 381) – so the HL view is probably to be preferred.

Also, it may not always be clear what amounts to an 'obvious' danger, especially if C is a child, and this can lead to inconsistent decisions.

Task

In **Tomlinson v Congleton (2003)** the HL reversed the CA's decision, allowing the appeal. Write a few sentences on which court you agree with and why.

Defences

Consent is dealt with in **s. 1(6)**, which states that no duty is owed to any person *'in respect of risks willingly accepted'*. Contributory negligence may also apply. These overlap with the idea of warnings in that the bigger the warning, the more likely the risk is 'willingly accepted', or that C was contributorily negligent.

These defences are discussed in Unit 48. As in negligence, they are less likely to succeed against children.

Examination pointer

Look for clues that something is forbidden. Doing something without permission is equal to being somewhere without permission, so makes D a trespasser. **Tomlinson** came under the **OLA 1984** because he ignored the 'No Swimming' signs, thus becoming a trespasser. Look carefully at any warning. Is it adequate to keep people safe? If children are involved will it keep them safe? If a warning is not adequate then it may actually make it more likely that the claim will succeed, as it shows the occupier knew of the danger. Clues like 'swimming at night', in a 'deep lake' or a 'busy harbour' should direct you to the 'obvious risk' issue, that D may avoid liability even without a warning sign. Note warnings and **s. 1(3)** overlap. An 'obvious' danger is not one it would be reasonable to expect D to protect against. Finally, consider whether the defences apply.

Food for thought

Do you think D should be liable to trespassers at all? It can be argued that there should be no liability to those who should not be on your property in the first place. However, the **Act** is aimed at cases like **Herrington** where the children were trespassing and so would not have been owed a duty under the **OLA 1957**.

Task

Paul has a very deep swimming pool in his garden. The neighbours' kids sometimes sneak in at night so he puts up a high fence and a big sign saying 'KEEP OUT'. He knows you are studying law so he asks you if this will protect him from being sued if one of them is injured. What will you tell him?

After a few years Paul's fence has several gaps in it which he keeps meaning to fix. The neighbours' son climbs through a gap in the fence and drowns. Paul is surprised at being sued and asks you why. How will you explain why your advice might be different now?

Breach of duty and causation

Whether the duty is breached will depend on the facts of the case, including the age of the C and any warning signs. The usual factors looked at in assessing the standard of care at common law will also apply. In **Tomlinson**, Lord Hoffman said that what amounted to reasonable care depended not only on the likelihood of harm or the seriousness of potential injury, but also on the social value of the activity and the cost of preventative measures.

The law on both factual and legal causation is also as for negligence.

Task

Read back over the last two Units and make a flow chart showing how to prove liability under both OLAs. Add a case in support of each point. Keep this to refer to when practising answering a problem question. Many of the cases, especially those involving children, are relevant to both areas.

Summary

The duty s. 1(3)

For a duty to be owed:
(The occupier) must be aware of the danger or have reasonable grounds to believe it exists
(The occupier) must know or have reasonable grounds to believe a 'non-visitor' is in, or may come into, the area
The risk is one against which it is reasonably expected to offer protection
The occupier must *'take such care as in all the circumstances of the case is reasonable to see that . . . (the non-visitor) . . . does not suffer injury on the premises by reason of the danger concerned'* – s. 1(4)

Avoiding the duty
The occupier must take *'such steps as are reasonable in all the circumstances of the case to give warning of the danger'* – **s. 1(5)**
If the danger is obvious then a warning is less likely to be needed – **Ratcliff/Tomlinson**
Apart from warnings and exclusion notices which either discharge or avoid liability, the usual defences of **contributory negligence** and **consent** will apply
There is no liability for damage to property

Self-test questions

1 What case led to the **OLA 1984**?

2 What are the three points for proving the occupiers duty? (**s. 1(3)**)

3 Why was there no liability in **Ratcliffe**?

4 What did the CA and HL disagree about in **Tomlinson**?

5 On what basis do cases involving child trespassers sometimes come under the **OLA 1957**?

For further resources and updates please go to the Companion Website accompanying this book at www.pearsoned.co.uk/russell

Is D an occupier?	Control test: **Wheat *v* Lacon**	
Is C a lawful visitor?		
Yes ←		→ *No*
OLA 1957	**OLA 1984**	
What is the *duty*?	What is the *duty*?	
S. 2(2): to keep V *reasonably safe* for the purposes of the visit	**S. 1(3)**: the three points	
Covers injury and damage to property	Does not cover damage to property	
OLA 1957 and OLA 1984		
Is there a *breach of duty*? – D must take reasonable care in all the circumstances of the case (apply the ordinary standard/factors for breach)	**Jolly**	
Children – greater duty Consider age and parental responsibility	**S. 2(3)(a)** **Glasgow/Phipps**	
Is there an allurement?	**Glasgow/Jolly**	
Contractors – lesser duty – they should guard against risks incidental to their calling	**Roles *v* Nathan**	
Is an independent contractor negligent? Occupier may be liable if work not checked but not if too technical	**S. 2(4)(b)** **Woodward Haseldine**	
Did breach *cause the harm*? – 'but for' test + foreseeability/remoteness	**Barnett** **Wagon Mound/Jolly**	
Can D *avoid* liability?	**OLA 1957**	**OLA 1984**
Warning signs – must be adequate, but not needed for 'obvious' dangers	**Darby *v* National Trust** – **S. 2(4)(a)**	**Tomlinson S. 1(5)**
Exclusion notices subject to UCTA	**S. 2(1)**	Not explicitly mentioned in **OLA 1984**
Contributory negligence	**S. 2(3)**	Not explicitly mentioned in **OLA 1984** but likely to apply
Consent	**S. 2(5)**	**S. 1(6)**

Negligence and occupier's liability overlap:

- For negligence discuss the **Caparo** test
- If the harm occurred on someone else's property discuss **OLA**
- For both you need to prove breach and damage as well as the duty

Task

Add the principle and brief facts to the cases.

Case	Principle	Facts
Glasgow Corporation *v* Taylor		
Phipps *v* Rochester Corporation		
Jolley *v* Sutton LBC		
General Cleaning Contractors *v* Christmas		
Ogwo *v* Taylor		
Bottomley *v* Todmorden Cricket Club		
Cotton *v* Derbyshire Dales DC		

Key criticisms

- It is not clear at what age a child becomes the occupier's responsibility rather than the parent's.
- It may be difficult for an occupier to know whether the property contains an allurement; what is alluring to a child may be quite uninteresting to an adult.
- It may not always be clear what dangers are 'obvious' so that no warning is necessary.
- The HL overruling the CA in **Tomlinson** shows conflict in the higher courts, and thus uncertainty in the law.
- How far should you be liable for trespassers? It seems fair where children are concerned but less so for adults; on the other hand, it can be said it makes people take greater care for safety generally.
- It is not clear whether **UCTA** applies to **OLA 1984**; if not, it means trespassers have more rights than visitors as D will not be able to exclude liability.

Examination practice

This area comes into problem questions rather than essays – at least that is the case so far, but there are no guarantees! The 'Food for thought' sections, together with the key criticisms above, should give you sufficient guidance to prepare for a possible essay question.

Module 6 connections

Morals	The original duty to trespassers was stated to be one of 'common humanity', indicating that there may be a moral duty to take care which in some cases should be made into a legal duty	**BRB *v* Herrington**
Justice	Justice for the boys and their families was achieved by bringing them within the common law and avoiding the harshness of the rule that no duty was owed to a trespasser even if D had been negligent	**BRB *v* Herrington**
	The fact that D should take care in selecting a contractor, but is not expected to check on specialist work, attempts to achieve justice for both D and C	**Haseldine *v* Daw**
Conflicting interests	Parents are expected to take responsibility for very young children, balancing the need to protect children against imposing too harsh a duty on the occupier	**Phipps**
	The creation of the **1984 Act** was an attempt to balance the interests of a trespasser (especially a child) against D's property and privacy rights. The duty is more limited and also C cannot claim for damage to property	
Fault	As with negligence, the fault element in occupier's liability lies in the breach. Where an occupier had taken due care, or put up adequate warnings, there will be no fault, and thus no liability	**Tomlinson *v* Congleton**
	The defence of contributory negligence takes into account any fault on the part of C	
Creativity	**BRB *v* Herrington** set a precedent which was later followed by statutory reform	
	The HL overruled the CA in relation to whether a duty was owed to a teenage trespasser diving into a lake and suffering injury	**Tomlinson**

For further resources and updates please go to the Companion Website accompanying this book at www.pearsoned.co.uk/russell

Study Block 15
NUISANCE, STRICT AND VICARIOUS LIABILITY

Unit 45   Nuisance

Unit 46   Rylands *v* Fletcher

Unit 47   Vicarious liability

Nuisance is exactly that – one person causes a nuisance to another by, for example, noise, smells, pollution or other irritants. Those who suffer can sue in the tort of nuisance. The rule in **Rylands *v* Fletcher** is similar but more often deals with physical damage to property caused by something on neighbouring land. Nuisance helps those affected by long-term problems, whereas **Rylands** can be used for one-off matters, such as a burst pipe which floods adjoining land. Liability in **Rylands** is called *strict* because it does not require C to prove D is at fault, or negligent.

> **Example**   Tina has a firework party every night. Her neighbours are fed up with the noise and one day a firework lands in their garden and sets fire to a shed. They can sue in nuisance in respect of the noise and under the rule in **Rylands *v* Fletcher** for the damage to the shed. If Tina has been negligent in the way she set up the firework display an action in negligence is also possible. Under **Rylands** the neighbours won't have to prove Tina was negligent, just that the firework caused the damage, so this would be better for them.

Although liability is strict, it is not absolute, and there are special defences to this tort to study. We will also consider other provisions in relation to dangerous products. There is an overlap between nuisance and **Rylands *v* Fletcher**, and also with negligence. Many claims are started in all three torts, so there is a comparison chart at the end of this Study Block.

Vicarious liability is where one person is liable for the wrong of another. This can apply to most torts. It occurs in employment cases, where an employer is sued even though it was a member of staff who caused the damage. An employer is usually in a better position to pay and, to a certain extent, has control over employees.

> **Example**   Bill, a delivery driver, crashes into your car. Instead of suing Bill, who may not have much money, you can sue his employer. The employer will be *vicariously liable* for Bill's negligence.

Nuisance

... the answer to the issue falls to be found by applying the concepts of reasonableness between neighbours and reasonable foreseeability.

Lord Cooke on how to prove nuisance,
Delaware Mansions Ltd v Westminster City Council (2001)

By the end of this Unit you should be able to:

- Explain the rules relating to both public and private nuisance
- Show how the law has developed by reference to appropriate cases and how nuisance connects with other torts
- Identify problems with the law in order to attempt an evaluation

---

What is nuisance?

Nuisance relates to quality of life. Examples include noise, smells, pollution and overhanging tree branches. Nuisance cases usually involve inconvenience rather than physical harm, but can include physical damage to property, and in some cases personal injury. There are three types: statutory, public and private. The last of these overlaps with negligence and an action may be brought in both torts, as Mrs Stone did in **Bolton v Stone** (see p. 362).

Statutory nuisance

There are now many statutes dealing with pollution and other matters which affect the environment and public health. Some deal with specific problems which occur between neighbours, such as noise and high hedges (the **Anti-Social Behaviour Act 2003** covers both of these). Most public nuisance is now covered by statute, but private nuisance cases still abound.

Examination pointer

Watch for the overlap between nuisance and other torts. Not only is there an overlap with negligence, as in **Bolton v Stone**, but also with occupier's liability and **Rylands v Fletcher** (see Unit 46). Look carefully at the facts of a given scenario, especially whether either C or D, or both, have an interest in land. You may need to discuss more than one possible claim. At the end of the Study Block is a comparison chart.

Public nuisance

Public nuisance was defined by Romer LJ in **AG v PYA Quarries (1957)** as one which *'materially affects the reasonable comfort and convenience of life of a class of Her Majesty's subjects'*.

It is thus a nuisance which affects the public or a section of the public. Public nuisance is a crime, prosecuted by the Attorney General, but if an individual suffers 'special damage' there is a remedy in tort.

In **Castle v St Augustine's Links** golf balls were frequently hit on to a nearby road. The siting of the hole so near to the road was a public nuisance. It affected road users who are a *'class'* of people. A taxi driver who was injured when a golf ball broke his windscreen was able to sue in tort as he suffered *'special damage'*. Nuisance is similar to negligence but something must usually happen often in order to be deemed a nuisance; thus the claim failed in **Bolton v Stone**.

Task

Compare **Bolton v Stone** to **Castle v St Augustine's Links**. Make a note of the differences and why the latter claim succeeded whereas the first failed.

Common law public nuisance will be rare following the HL decisions in **Goldstein** and **Rimmington (2005)**.

Key cases

In **Goldstein** a Jewish food merchant paid an outstanding debt by post and added some salt to the envelope as a joke (don't ask!). Unfortunately this was around the time of the anthrax scare in the States and when some of it leaked it caused a major scare and mass evacuation at the sorting office. Clearly no one got the joke and poor Mr Goldstein was convicted of public nuisance. In **Rimmington** a man had sent racist letters to several individuals and was also convicted of public nuisance. The HL allowed both appeals. The first on the basis that Mr Goldstein had no idea of the consequences of his joke (no *mens rea*); the second because the mail was sent to several people, but they were not a 'class'. The HL said that now statutory nuisance covered most areas, common law nuisance *'will be relatively rare'*. Lord Bingham said there may be a case for abolishing it but *'the courts have no power to create new offences, so they have no power to abolish existing offences. That is a task for Parliament'*.

Private nuisance

Traditionally this is defined as *unreasonable interference with a person's use or enjoyment of land*. It is sometimes described as *unlawful* interference, but essentially it becomes unlawful only if it is found to be unreasonable.

> **Example**
>
> It is your birthday and you have a very noisy party which goes on all night. The neighbours complain that they cannot sleep. They may call this a 'nuisance', but it is unlikely to be found unreasonable, as it is only a one-off. It is therefore not unlawful and they cannot sue. However, if you have a party every night, they *can* sue and ask the court to stop you doing this and/or claim compensation for their sleepless nights.

Although traditionally interference was indirect and usually related to a person's use or enjoyment of land there are signs that direct interference is now included in nuisance. In **Hunter v Canary Wharf (1997)** Lord Lloyd said that private nuisance was of three kinds:

1 encroachment;

2 direct physical injury to a neighbour's land; and

3 interference with a neighbour's quiet enjoyment of land.

These three forms of nuisance overlap.

> **Example**
>
> I have a big tree in my garden. Some branches overhang my neighbour's garden. The roots also grow under my fence on to her land. The branches and the roots *encroach* on her land. The roots also cause *damage* to her lawn. This is direct physical injury to the land. The shade from the branches prevents her sunbathing. This affects her *enjoyment* of the land.

What is unreasonable?

Some types of interference are unlikely to amount to nuisance. In **Hunter** it was held that interference with television reception caused by a tower block was not actionable. This was based on the fact that it was similar to the blocking of a view, which had long been held not to give rise to such an action. In **Network Rail v Morris (2004)** a rail company had installed a new signalling system. C owned a recording studio nearby and complained of electromagnetic interference. His nuisance claim succeeded at first instance, but the CA did not consider that such interference should amount to nuisance and allowed the rail company's appeal.

Food for thought

It seems strange that interference with television reception is not actionable. This is something that affects people's everyday lives. It certainly affects the 'use and enjoyment' of a property. For many people not being able to watch television would be a major problem. The **Network Rail** case seems to confirm the view in **Hunter** that the law of nuisance does not protect such amenities.

The courts will look at, and balance, the following factors in deciding if interference is unreasonable.

Frequency and duration

A 'one-off' or temporary act is not generally enough. A claim is only likely to succeed where something happens frequently. Thus in **Bolton v Stone**, where the cricket ball went over only six times in 35 years, it was not deemed to be a nuisance. Such an infrequent act *could* amount to negligence (but it wasn't negligent on the facts as the club had taken sufficient care). Building works *could* be a nuisance but this is unlikely as they are only temporary. If they occurred at night an action in nuisance might succeed.

In **Miller v Jackson (1977)** a cricket club had played cricket on a site near C's house for some 70 years before she moved in. Balls from the ground landed in her garden several times a year and she succeeded in an action in nuisance.

State of affairs

An apparent exception to the need for frequency is where something constitutes a continuing 'state of affairs'. An illustration is **Spicer v Smee (1946)**. Here D's faulty wiring led to a fire which damaged C's property. Although this seemed to be a one-off, the claim in nuisance succeeded on the basis that the faulty wiring amounted to a continuing 'state of affairs'. In **Castle v St Augustine's Links** (above) the siting of the hole on the golf course was considered to be a 'state of affairs'.

Locality

Where the nuisance happens will be a relevant factor in assessing reasonableness. In **Sturges v Bridgman (1879)** Thesiger LJ said, '*what may be a nuisance in Belgrave Square may not be so in Bermondsey.*' This means that much will depend on the type of area. The remark is hardly politically correct, but the point is valid. Noise or smells in a quiet garden suburb may constitute a nuisance, whereas the same noise or smells elsewhere may not. It is perhaps better to say that what may be a nuisance in a residential area may not be in an industrial estate.

An important distinction between physical damage and discomfort was made in **St Helen's Smelting Co. v Tipping (1865)**. Here C lived in a manufacturing area, and fumes from D's copper works caused damage to his garden plants. The action for an injunction succeeded. The HL held that where material damage had been suffered, *the locality was not relevant.*

Usefulness

If something is for the public benefit it is less likely to be a nuisance – this is the 'utility' argument. It is unlikely to suffice alone and the other factors, such as locality, will be balanced against the usefulness. Thus in **Adams v Ursell (1913)** smells from a fish and chip shop amounted to a nuisance. Although providing a service, it was opened in a residential area.

Task

Compare **Bolton v Stone** to **Miller v Jackson** and consider why the latter claim succeeded and the first failed.

Sensitivity

If C (or what is harmed) is particularly sensitive, then an action is unlikely to succeed. In **Robinson v Kilvert (1889)** heat from a neighbour's boiler damaged special paper stored above. Normal paper would not have been affected and so the claim failed. However, if normal paper *would* have been affected then the claim could succeed and include sensitive items. Thus in **McKinnon Industries v Walker (1951)** C was able to obtain damages in respect of damage to some delicate orchids because it could be shown that normal plants would have been damaged. In **Network Rail v Morris (2004)**, above, the CA noted that no one else had complained of interference. The claim would therefore probably have failed on the sensitivity issue even if it had been accepted that electronic interference was actionable.

Malice

Malice and motive are rarely relevant in law. *Why* you do something is usually unimportant; it is whether what you do amounts to an illegal act that matters. However, if one person acts out of spite it could tip the balance when considering 'unreasonableness'. In **Christie v Davey (1893)** two neighbours caused a nuisance to each other, one by giving piano lessons, the other by retaliating during these lessons by banging tin trays together and whistling. The latter was found liable in nuisance because his behaviour was unreasonable.

Task

Look - and listen - around your neighbourhood. Is there something happening that you think might be a nuisance? Apply the above tests and see if, on balance, it would amount to a nuisance in law. Don't rush off and sue anyone though!

Claimants: who can sue?

As nuisance is an interference with the use of land, it has long been accepted that this tort is there to protect such interests. It is therefore not available to those who have no proprietary interest in land. This was established in **Malone v Laskey (1907)**. In **Miller v Jackson (1977)** Lord Denning said that:

> *'the very essence of private nuisance is the unreasonable use by a man of his land to the detriment of his neighbour.'*

Proprietary means a legal interest in the land or property. This would include an owner or tenant but not a lodger. Arguments have arisen over whether members of the household who do not have a proprietary interest can claim in nuisance. In **Khorasandjan v Bush (1993)** the HL adopted a more sympathetic view of what amounted to an interest in land. They found in favour of the daughter of the house, who had no legal interest in the property. The claim was for an injunction to prevent nuisance telephone calls from her ex-boyfriend. The decision can be seen as a way of providing a remedy when there appeared to be no alternative action. As this situation has now been dealt with by the **Protection of Harassment Act 1997**, there is no longer a need for a common law remedy. The case has now been overruled by **Hunter v Canary Wharf (1997)**, which reconfirmed **Malone**.

Examination pointer

An individual who is especially affected can sue in **public** nuisance **without** an interest in land. In **private** nuisance C **must** have such an interest. This may be important in considering how to address an exam scenario. Watch out for clues like 'C was staying with friends' or 'her boyfriend was staying over'. You may need to explain why there can't be an action in private nuisance, and go on to discuss public nuisance.

Defendants: who can be sued?

In most cases D is the 'creator' of the nuisance. This usually means the owner or occupier of the property from which the nuisance comes, but can include someone who created the nuisance even if no longer in occupation. There may also be liability if you *know* about a nuisance you did not personally create, but you continue, or 'adopt' it. This can include acts of a third party or natural hazards. The following three cases illustrate the courts' approach to this issue.

Key cases

In **Sedleigh Denfield v O'Callaghan (1940)** D was liable for the flooding of C's land. A blocked pipe, laid along his property by the local authority, caused the flooding. However, he *knew* of its existence and had *used* it, thus he had *'adopted'* the nuisance.

In **Tetley v Chitty (1986)** C brought an action against the council in relation to disturbance from a go-kart track. A club, which leased the land from the council, ran the track. The council were found liable on the basis that the 'interference' was a necessary consequence of operating this activity on the council's land. In effect they had implied *knowledge* of it. An injunction was granted to stop the activity.

In **Goldman v Hargrave (1967)** lightening struck a tree on D's land and it caught fire. He cut it down and left it to burn. Fire spread to C's land when a strong wind rekindled it a few days later. He was found liable for the damage caused as he *knew* about the risk and so had a duty to do something about it. The decision was much influenced by the case of **Sedleigh**, above.

In cases where D has 'adopted', rather than 'created', the nuisance the test for what is reasonable is subjective rather than objective, i.e. it is what *this particular* D should have done, not what *the average* person would do. In **Leakey v National Trust (1980)**, due to natural causes, part of a mound on the Trust's property slid down a hill on to neighbouring land. It was held that they were liable for the damage caused because they knew of the risk. Megaw LJ said that:

> *'D's duty is to do that which is reasonable for him to do. . . . having regard, among other things, where a serious expenditure of money is required to eliminate or reduce the danger, to his means.'*

Foreseeability is also a key factor. In **Holbeck Hall Hotel v Scarborough Borough Council (2001)** a hotel collapsed due to erosion on neighbouring land owned by the council. The court held that liability would depend on the resources of the council and the expense of any remedial work. Also, the destruction of the hotel was not foreseeable. The claim failed. In **Rees v Skerrett (2001)** D knocked down his own property, thus exposing his neighbour's wall to the elements. Here the damage to the neighbour's wall was foreseeable, and failure to take reasonable remedial action was actionable.

Examination pointer

For a problem question you will need to define nuisance and then look at any of the relevant factors to decide on 'unreasonableness'. Don't forget to consider who can sue and who can be sued.

Food for thought

Consider the following questions.

- Should C have an interest in land or should it be enough that they live in the affected property? Compare **Khorasandjan v Bush** with **Hunter v Canary Wharf**.

- Should a person be liable for natural dangers? Compare **Holbeck Hall Hotel v Scarborough BC** with **Rees v Skerrett**.

- Should a person be liable for the actions of a third party as in **Sedleigh Denfield** and **Tetley v Chitty**?

- Should D's resources be taken into account? It seems fair in certain cases that you should only be expected to do what you can reasonably afford to do, but is this fair to C? Should a claimant living next to a pop star have a different right to one living next to a person with limited means?

As always there is no right answer to these questions so feel free to explore your own ideas. Don't forget, though, to use cases to support any argument you make.

Causation

As with negligence, it must be proved that D's nuisance caused the harm suffered. This means applying the **Wagon Mound** test for remoteness of damage. This was confirmed in **Cambridge Water Co. Ltd *v* Eastern Counties Leather plc (1994)**. A claim was brought in three different torts: negligence, nuisance and **Rylands *v* Fletcher**. C had suffered damage due to contamination by chemicals leaking from D's property. At the time it was not realised that these chemicals were present and also it was only later, when a European Directive provided for stricter rules, that it was recognised that their presence could cause harm to C's water facility. The HL held that for all three torts the **Wagon Mound** test applies. D is not liable for unforeseeable damage.

Defences

There are two main defences to an action in nuisance.

Statutory authority

This means authorised by an Act of Parliament. In **Allen *v* Gulf Oil (1981)** an Act of Parliament authorised the building of an oil refinery. The court held that it would be inconceivable that it would authorise the building but not the running of it. There was implied authorisation for the latter so Gulf Oil could not be liable in nuisance for noise from the refinery. The defence succeeded.

Planning permission is unlikely to amount to statutory authority but may have an effect. If it changes the character of the neighbourhood, the courts look at the locality factor *after* it has changed. In **Gillingham Borough Council *v* Medway Docks (1993)** a local authority brought a claim against the docks for public nuisance. Although the court held that planning permission did not equate to statutory authority, it had meant that the area had become a busy commercial dock. Thus there was no nuisance. If the permission does not have the effect of altering the character of the neighbourhood, it is unlikely to be accepted as a defence. Thus in **Wheeler *v* Saunders (1995)** planning permission was granted to erect pig houses but it was held that the smells from the pigs could constitute a nuisance.

A statutory scheme may also exclude an action in nuisance. In **Marcic *v* Thames Water Utilities Ltd (2003)** D's garden was subject to flooding after heavy rain, due to water overflowing from the sewerage system. The CA had relied on **Goldman *v* Hargrave (1967)** and **Leakey *v* National Trust (1980)** and found the sewerage company liable. However, the HL allowed the appeal on the basis that the **Water Industry Act 1991** made provision for enforcement by an independent regulator whose decisions were subject to judicial review by the courts. To allow a common law right would effectively supplant this regulatory role, which D had chosen not to use. Although not strictly used as a defence, because there was a statutory scheme he could not rely on the common law.

Prescription

The defence of prescription applies where a nuisance has continued for 20 years without complaint. Once 20 years has passed D has a right to continue the activity. It is important to note that time starts from when the nuisance starts. In **Sturges v Bridgman**, a doctor built consulting rooms near to D's workshop and then claimed the noise from the workshop was a nuisance. D could not claim prescription because the *nuisance* had not been going on for 20 years. It didn't start until the doctor built his consulting rooms. D cannot argue that C 'came to the nuisance'.

Food for thought

The effect of **Sturges** is that C can effectively 'self-inflict' the nuisance. This can seem unfair. For example, I build a nice Gazebo at the end of my (very long) garden. Should I be able to sue my neighbour if I am now disturbed by the noise he makes with his car repair workshop, which he has been running for generations?

Consent and contributory negligence apply but are general defences, so see 'Defences' Unit 48. Act of God or act of a stranger may also apply – see 'Rylands' Unit 46.

Remedies

Damages may be appropriate if actual harm has occurred – as in negligence. The same rules will therefore apply. However, there are two remedies that are particularly relevant to nuisance.

Injunction

The most effective remedy for a claim in nuisance is an injunction. This is a court order to stop it. The rules on granting an injunction were laid down in **Shelfer v City of London Electric Lighting Co. (1895)**. The court held that an injunction should be the remedy unless there are exceptional circumstances. The principle is that D should not be able to 'buy' the right to commit a nuisance by paying money to C. Damages should only be awarded as an alternative if an injunction would be oppressive and the injury to C's rights were small and capable of being compensated by an award of money. This happened in **Miller v Jackson**. No injunction was granted but damages were awarded instead. It may depend on what constitutes the nuisance. In **Tetley v Chitty** an injunction *was* granted.

Food for thought

In **Tetley _v_ Chitty**, the council were liable for the disturbance from the go-kart track run by their tenants. An injunction was granted to restrain the activity. No such injunction was granted in **Miller _v_ Jackson**. Is go-karting less socially useful than cricket?

Abatement

Abatement is a 'self-help' remedy to stop the nuisance. An example would be chopping off overhanging branches from your neighbour's tree. However, this can only apply if it can be done without trespass. This means you should either do it from your own side of the fence or ask permission to enter your neighbour's garden. The following case shows that you can also claim damages to prevent a nuisance continuing.

Key case

In **Delaware Mansions Ltd _v_ Westminster City Council (2001)** a local authority owned a tree, the roots of which caused damage to some nearby flats. C undertook some work to remedy the problem and then claimed against the authority to recover the costs. The HL held that where there is a continuing nuisance of which D knew, or ought to have known, an owner who had spent money in an attempt to remedy the problem may recover reasonable expenditure. The tree was close to the property, so a real risk of damage was foreseeable. The authority had plenty of notice before the work was done and was therefore liable to pay the costs.

Overlap

In **Delaware Mansions** the HL treated the labels 'nuisance' or 'negligence' as of no real significance. They looked at the concepts of reasonableness between 'neighbours' and reasonable foreseeability. Reference was made to the **Wagon Mound (1966)** where the judgments were based on what a reasonable person would have done in the circumstances. Many cases involve a claim in both torts.

Summary

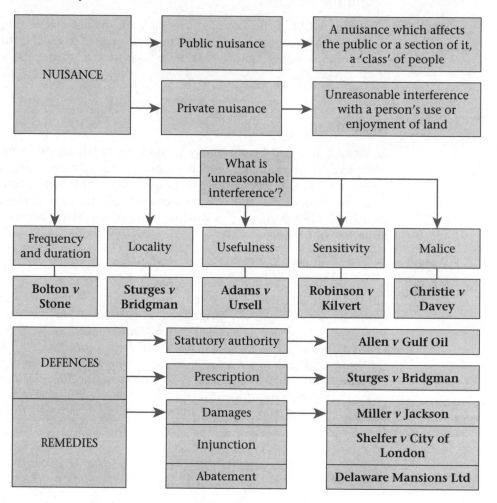

 Self-test questions

1 What did the HL decide in **Goldstein** and **Rimmington 2005**?

2 *State three factors which help the court to decide on whether something is unreasonable?*

3 When might a one-off occurrence amount to a nuisance?

4 Who can sue and which case re-established this?

5 When are D's own resources relevant?

 For further resources and updates please go to the Companion Website accompanying this book at **www.pearsoned.co.uk/russell**

Rylands *v* Fletcher

. . . the person who, for his own purposes, brings on his land and collects and keeps there anything likely to do mischief if it escapes, must keep it in at his peril.

Blackburn J, **Rylands *v* Fletcher (1868)**

By the end of this Unit you should be able to:

- Explain how the constituent parts of the 'rule in **Rylands *v* Fletcher**' apply
- Show how the law has developed by reference to cases
- Identify problems with the law in order to attempt an evaluation

The rule in Rylands *v* Fletcher

This is a tort in its own right, named after the case in which it was first established, **Rylands *v* Fletcher (1868)**. The facts of the case were that a landowner employed a contractor to build a reservoir on his land. The contractors discovered some disused mine shafts but they appeared to be filled in so they didn't seal them. When the reservoir was filled water flooded through these shafts and caused damage to C's mine. He sued for compensation but the court held that there was no case. He then took the matter to the Court of Exchequer Chamber, where Blackburn J said:

> *'. . . the person who, for his own purposes, brings on his land and collects and keeps there anything likely to do mischief if it escapes, must keep it in at his peril; and if he does not do so, is prima facie answerable for all the damage which is the natural consequence of its escape.'*

He added that to be liable D must have brought on to the property something that was *'not naturally there'*. The case then went to the HL where Lord Cairns LC quoted the words of Blackburn J with approval and developed 'not naturally there' to *'putting the land to a non-natural use'*.

Examination pointer

Note carefully the various constituent parts ('brings on to land', 'do mischief', 'escapes' and so on). You will need to apply each of them to a given scenario in a problem question on this area. It is also an area which has a number of problems and is therefore a suitable topic for an essay.

Food for thought

In its report on *Civil Liability for Dangerous Things and Activities* 1970 (No. 32), the Law Commission described the state of the law in this area as *'complex, uncertain and inconsistent in principle'*. As you read the cases try to form your own opinion on this.

Brings on to land

This requires that whatever causes the harm was not *naturally* on the land. In **Rylands** the water was not naturally on the land but *brought on to it* to fill the reservoir (compare this to, for example, a heavy rainfall or a river). In **Giles v Walker (1890)** D ploughed up a field and thistles grew on it; thistledown escaped on to a neighbour's land and seeded itself. D was not liable as he did not *bring on* the thistles, they were *naturally* there. The **Rylands** requirement that D must have brought on something 'not naturally there' was referred to in the HL as 'non-natural user'; this suggests an unusual activity on the land or a special use of it. Many cases fail on this point.

Non-natural user

This is interpreted narrowly. In **Rickards v Lothian (1913)** C claimed for damage done to his stock by flooding from D's basin on a higher floor in the office block. The 'non-natural' requirement was narrowly interpreted to mean *abnormal*. Water in the washbasin was found to be natural, even though it was arguably 'brought on', and not there by nature but by plumbing. In **Read v Lyons (1947)** the HL held that the manufacture of high-explosive shells in wartime was *natural* use (although on the facts the case was decided on the issue of 'escape', discussed below). They said one must look at all the circumstances, and these will include time, place and normal practice.

This was confirmed in **Mason v Levy Autoparts (1967)**. Here, D kept large quantities of petrol, paint and other combustible materials. They ignited and the fire spread to C's premises. In deciding that this was *non-natural user* the court held that the relevant matters to consider were:

- the quantities of combustible material;
- the way in which it was stored;
- the character of the neighbourhood.

Food for thought

There is an overlap between *non-natural* use and *negligent* use. The factors looked at in **Mason** would, as the judge recognised, also be relevant to a finding of negligence. If this is the case is the rule really necessary?

In 2004, the HL had a chance to reconsider the rule.

Key case

Transco Plc *v* Stockport BC (2004) again involved an accumulation of water which escaped from D's property. This caused subsidence, which threatened C's property. On the facts the HL decided that the use was natural and D was not liable. The HL did, however, attempt to clarify the rule, and restated that there must be **an escape** and a **non-natural use of land**. Also that a claim for death or personal injury was outside the rule, because it does not relate to any right in land.

Lord Hoffman said:

'there is a broad and ill-defined exception for 'natural' uses of land. It is perhaps not surprising that counsel could not find a reported case since the Second World War in which anyone had succeeded in a claim under the rule. It is hard to escape the conclusion that the intellectual effort devoted to the rule by judges and writers over many years has brought forth a mouse.'

Lord Bingham felt that it should be restated:

'so as to achieve as much certainty and clarity as is attainable, recognising that new factual situations are bound to arise posing difficult questions on the boundary of the rule, wherever that is drawn.'

Food for thought

In **Transco**, Lord Hoffman recognised that what was natural was 'ill-defined', the HL did not agree on what it *did* amount to, so this remains a difficulty. Do you think the law should be more clear-cut? Lord Bingham recognised the need to be able to apply it to new situations, so perhaps if it were *too* clearly defined it would be inflexible.

On the plus side, the HL did restate the rule in somewhat clearer terms and noted that most of the confusion had come from later cases rather than **Rylands** itself. Perhaps the mouse will roar yet!

In **LMS International Ltd *v* Styrene Packaging & Insulation Ltd (2005)** the court approved **Transco** and restated the criteria:

- D must have brought on something **likely to do mischief**.
- D's actions must arise from a **non-natural use** of land.
- The damage must be **foreseeable**.

In applying these to a case of a fire spreading from a factory to neighbouring land, the court found D liable. Flammable material was stored near to machinery which got very hot. Storage was therefore *non-natural* and it was *foreseeable* it could catch fire.

Examination pointer

If D did not bring on the thing that escaped, or it is found to be natural, there may still be an action in nuisance, so you should be prepared to discuss this as an alternative. Nuisance may be easier to prove because it only requires use to be 'unreasonable' rather than 'unnatural'.

Likely to cause mischief - must it be dangerous?

The 'mischief' requirement would indicate that whatever is brought on to the land must be dangerous in some way. However, it need only be dangerous ('likely to cause mischief') *if it escapes*. This means quite ordinary things could be included, such as water, gas, fire, animals, etc.

Example | Mary has a little lamb. She lives next to a garden centre. The lamb is not 'dangerous', but if it gets into the garden centre it could *cause mischief*. Mary could be sued under the rule in **Rylands** if it escapes and causes damage.

If it escapes

The thing that is brought on to the land must cause damage *off* the land. Thus the claim failed in **Read v Lyons**. The explosion which injured C occurred at the factory making the shells, so there was no 'escape'.

Examination pointer

In a problem scenario involving someone's land look at whether there is an 'escape'. If not, consider occupier's liability as an alternative.

In **Crown River Cruises Ltd v Kimbolton Fireworks Ltd (1996)** the court held that it was possible to include 'accumulations' on a boat. Here, fireworks from a display on a boat had caused damage to a nearby barge. An action was brought in negligence, nuisance and under the rule in **Rylands**. The decision was based on liability in nuisance, but the point was made that the escape does not need to be from *land*.

Earlier cases had conflicted on whether a person without an interest in land could sue, and whether personal injury could be claimed. In **Crown** the owners of a barge were able to sue (although possibly on the basis that the boats were permanently moored and so *equated* to land) and a claim for personal injury was allowed in **Hale v Jennings (1938)**, where a stallholder at a fair suffered injury when a 'chair-o-plane' *escaped* from D's ride. However, according to the HL in **Transco** the answer is 'no' to both these questions.

Another case brought in negligence, nuisance and under the rule in **Rylands** is **Cambridge Water Co. v Eastern Counties Leather (1994)**. It is important in relation to causation.

Key case

In **Cambridge** D used chemicals in the process of manufacturing leather. Some spillages leaked into the soil and eventually found their way into C's waterworks where water was extracted for public consumption. Due to a European Directive, issued after the spillages occurred, the water could not be used for drinking, so the company sued for their loss. Although the chemicals *could* amount to non-natural use, D was found not liable. The court held that the **Wagon Mound** test of foreseeability applied to both nuisance and **Rylands**. This meant D was not liable if damage could not have been foreseen, as was the case here. The HL saw no need to develop the law because environmental protection was something that Parliament was already looking at.

Is liability strict?

Rylands *v* Fletcher is called a strict liability tort because D will be liable even if not at fault. In the HL, Lord Cranworth said, '*If it does escape, and cause damage, he is responsible, however careful he may have been, and whatever precautions he may have taken*'. This means that C need not prove negligence by D, merely that something has escaped and caused damage.

Example Mary takes great care of her lamb. She trains it properly and keeps it tied up very firmly when in the garden. She also builds a wall to make sure it can't escape. Despite all these precautions the lamb manages to get out and tramples the plants in the garden centre next door. Although Mary was careful she is liable for the *mischief* caused by the *escape*. This is because liability is strict so the garden centre does not have to prove that she is at fault. They can prove all the **Rylands** elements and also causation, as it is *foreseeable* that damage to the plants could occur, so it is not too remote.

Task

Using this, or an example of your own, go through each of the **Rylands** elements and apply them, adding a case where possible.

Although liability is strict in that if damage *is* foreseeable then D is liable regardless of the amount of care taken, **Cambridge Water** limits this by saying if the damage is *not* foreseeable D will avoid liability.

It is also possible for D to avoid liability by using a defence. Let's take a brief look at these. There are several so you won't need a lot of detail.

Defences

- **Statutory authority**: It was confirmed in **Transco** that where something is permitted under an Act of Parliament this may be a defence to an 'escape'.

- An act of God or a stranger effectively breaks the chain of causation:
  - **act of a stranger**: an unforeseeable act by someone else means D may avoid liability. In **Rickards v Lothian** D was not liable because an unknown person had blocked up the basin and overflow pipe, causing the flooding. However, in **Hale v Jennings** the defence failed as it was foreseeable that a passenger might tamper with the chair.
  - **act of God**: this is used where D has no control over some force of nature. In **Nichols v Marsland (1876)** C created artificial lakes on her land, but it was an exceptionally heavy rainfall which caused them to flood and damage neighbouring land. She was not liable.
- **Default of claimant**: Blackburn J continued his comments in **Rylands** with the words '*He can excuse himself by showing that the escape was owing to the plaintiff's default*'. This means that if C has done something, or *failed to do something*, which causes the damage, D will not be liable.
- **Contributory negligence**: If C is partly to blame for the damage the amount of compensation may be reduced in relation to C's 'contribution'.
- **Consent**: If C consents to the accumulation by D, then D will not be liable for damage caused by its escape. (Note: Both contributory negligence and consent are dealt with in Unit 48 as they apply to other torts.)
- **Common benefit**: If the accumulation benefits C as well as D then there is unlikely to be liability.

Example
Harry and Tom are neighbours. They are worried about a spate of burglaries in the area. They decide to get a guard dog and Harry has the most space. The dog is kept in the garden during the day. Tom has a very old and decrepit fence and the dog gets through and causes a lot of damage to his plants. If Tom sues he will argue that Harry *brought on* the dog and that it *escaped* and did *mischief*. Harry can argue that Tom *consented* to him 'bringing on' the dog. He can also argue *contributory negligence* in that Tom was partly to blame by not mending his fence. Then, even if found liable, Harry would pay less compensation. It may even amount to Tom's '*default*' so Harry avoids liability altogether. Finally, Harry can argue that the dog was of *common benefit* to them both. Harry should be OK.

Task

Write out how the rule works and then comment on whether it is needed. In **Transco**, Lord Bingham recognised there were arguments both for extending and abolishing the rule, but said he favoured retaining it. There will be opinions on both sides of the argument so don't look for a 'correct' view. Form an opinion based on your own understanding of the rule and how it applies.

Summary

Summary of the application
D brings on to land   ● something non-natural;   ● and likely to do mischief;   ● which escapes on to other land;   ● and causes foreseeable damage;   ● to property belonging to C.

Task

Find a case to support each of the issues in the summary and make a chart for your file. Note, though, that in an exam you can now use **Transco** for most of these if time is short.

It is argued that **Rylands** is unnecessary as there are many Acts covering hazardous activities involving nuclear power, fire and chemicals, as well as the **Consumer Protection Act 1987**, which covers dangerous products causing damage (as in **Donoghue**). However, in **Transco** this was a reason the HL gave for *not* abolishing it. They felt that Parliament had covered areas to which **Rylands** *didn't* apply, so if it was abolished it would leave gaps in the law.

Summary of the difficulties
Overlap with nuisance and negligence means it is arguably unnecessary – **Crown**
Courts are reluctant to develop it – **Cambridge Water**
But are also reluctant to abolish it – **Transco**
There are so many defences that it is very unlikely to succeed

Self-test questions

1 What were the facts in **Rylands**?

2 Why, on similar facts, was D not liable in **Transco**?

3 Explain three of the defences.

4 What was the importance of **Cambridge Water**?

5 State three difficulties with this area of law.

For further resources and updates please go to the Companion Website accompanying this book at www.pearsoned.co.uk/russell

Vicarious liability

Vicarious liability is a species of strict liability ... an employer who is not personally at fault is made legally answerable for the fault of his employee.

Lord Millett, **Lister v Helsey Hall (2001)**

By the end of this Unit you should be able to:
- Explain how far one person can be liable for the actions of another
- Show how the law applies to particular situations by reference to cases
- Identify problems with the law in order to attempt an evaluation

What is vicarious liability?

Vicarious liability essentially means liability for someone else. It applies to all torts. Most commonly, it applies in employment situations, where an employer is liable for the torts of an employee. This means that the employer rather than the employee can be sued. The person committing the tort, e.g. being negligent or causing a nuisance, is called a **tortfeasor**. Examples we have already seen include **Phelps v Hillingdon BC (2001)** and **Carty v Croydon LBC (2005)**, where the council were vicariously liable for the negligence of a psychologist and an education officer respectively (see p. 348). Also **Woodward v Mayor of Hastings (1945)**, where a school was liable for a cleaner's negligence (see p. 380).

Why is it needed?

There are several arguments for making an employer liable for the actions of employees. The main one is purely a matter of who can best bear the cost. The economic reality of the situation is that an employer is normally in a better position to pay compensation. This may be because the employer is wealthier than the employee, and because the employer is usually insured. If it was not for the fact that an employer can be sued, in many cases C may not be compensated at all.

Food for thought

The main argument against this type of liability is that an employer will be liable even if not at fault. On the other hand, it can be said to be fair because an employer has a certain amount of control over what an employee does.

Task

As you read this Unit make a few notes on the cases, adding a comment of your own as to whether you agree with the decision. When you get to the recent cases, note what has changed over the years.

There are two essentials to showing that the employer is liable:

- that the tortfeasor is *an employee* (rather than an independent contractor);
- that the tortfeasor is acting *in the course of employment* (rather than on a '*frolic of his own*').

Note the word *tortfeasor*. If the employee has not committed a tort, e.g. has not been negligent, *no one* will be liable.

Examination pointer

It is a common mistake to discuss only vicarious liability and nothing more. However, C will have to prove that the employee has committed a tort. This will require applying the usual rules for that particular tort. Thus if the case is one of negligence, there will be no liability if the employee has reached the standard expected of the reasonable person. This will involve looking at the usual factors such as degree of risk and cost of precautions.

Example   Julie is stacking shelves in Tesco and drops a bottle of oil. She puts a warning sign in front of it and immediately goes to get a cloth to clear it up. Beth is shopping but doesn't notice it; she slips and injures herself. Tesco is unlikely to be vicariously liable because Julie has not been negligent. However, if Julie had left the spillage and gone for her tea break, Beth is likely to succeed in proving Julie was negligent. There is quite a high likelihood of someone slipping and the cost of putting out a warning or taking other precautions is very low. Beth can sue Tesco on the basis of *vicarious liability* for Julie's *negligence*. If she wins, she is more likely to be able to get the money from the supermarket than a shelf-stacker, who will be on limited wages. Also note that an employer can be both vicariously and primarily liable, e.g. for having poorly trained staff. In both cases, Beth will sue Tesco, but in the first, she must prove Julie was negligent, in the second that Tesco was.

It is important to distinguish between an *employee* and an *independent contractor*, for whom an employer is **not** liable.

Status: test for an employee

Where people are employed on a casual basis, it may not always be clear whether they are employees or contractors. There have been various tests produced over the years to decide on this issue. Early tests centred on the amount of *control* the employer had over the work done, and how far the work was an *integral* part of the business concerned. Then in **Ready Mixed Concrete *v* Minister Of Pensions (1968)** the 'multiple', or 'composite', test was established. This looks at several factors to assess the *economic reality* of the situation. These include:

- whether the work is done in return for a wage;
- whether the employee agrees that the employer controls the work done;
- who pays National Insurance;
- who supplies equipment;
- who takes the financial risks.

However, even this test is not conclusive, merely a starting point. In **Hall *v* Lorimer (1994)** the CA said that individual circumstances will affect the employment status, so no single test will be absolute. In **Dacas *v* Brooke Street Bureau (2004)** it was confirmed that it was important to look at the overall circumstances in each case, but lack of a mutual obligation to provide or accept work, and lack of control over the work done, were factors in deciding that an agency worker was not an employee.

Where an employee is 'lent' to another employer it may be hard to decide which employer to sue. Here the control test may be most appropriate. In **Mersey Docks Harbour Board *v* Coggins and Griffiths (Liverpool) Ltd (1947)** the HL said that where a crane driver and his crane had been lent to the Harbour Board, the original employer was liable when the driver ran someone over. It was this employer who controlled the method of performance (the way he drove the crane). An important development came in **Viasystems (Tyneside) Ltd *v* Thermal Transfer (Northern) Ltd (2005)**. The CA held that the long-standing assumption that 'dual vicarious liability' was not permissible was not justified. In cases where the main question is one of control, *both* employers could be sufficiently in control to share liability for the employee's negligence.

Examination pointer

As the tests are not fully conclusive, you will not be expected to be too definite about the employment status. Look for clues and use the **Ready Mixed Concrete** points to guide you, then point out that the courts have made clear that all factors affecting the employment will be relevant. Note that liability can now be imposed on more than one employer - **Viasystems**.

In the course of employment

Traditionally, acting 'in the course of employment' would include not only acts expressly authorised by an employer, but also authorised acts done in a wrongful way, even if specifically prohibited. A comparison of the following two cases illustrates this.

Limpus v London General Omnibus Company (1862)	A bus driver was forbidden to race other buses but he did so and his employer was found liable for the resulting damage. This is a *wrongful* way (racing) of doing something *authorised* (driving)
Beard v LGOC (1900)	A conductor drove a bus and injured someone. Here the employer was not liable because driving was not within the scope of his job as a conductor; it was not *authorised*

An employer may avoid liability if the employee is on what judges call 'a frolic of his own'. Again, a comparison will illustrate this.

Twine v Bean's Express (1946)	The driver had been told not to give lifts and had done so. The employer was not liable to a hitchhiker for the driver's negligent driving as it was outside the scope of employment and a 'frolic of his own'
Rose v Plenty (1976)	Despite there being a strict order not to carry children, the employer was liable for a boy's injuries incurred while on a milk float. Here the boy was actually assisting in the deliveries and this brought it within the scope of employment

New definition

The 'authorised acts' approach caused difficulty in **Lister v Helsey Hall (2001)**.

Key case

In **Lister**, unknown to the employer, a warden sexually abused boarders at a school for children with behavioural difficulties. The children sued, alleging the school was vicariously liable. The CA held that the assaults could not be seen as 'authorised acts' so the school was not liable. In allowing the appeal the HL used a different approach. Rather than asking whether the act was *authorised* it was better to concentrate on the *closeness of the connection* between the nature of the employment and the tort. Sexual abuse against pupils, committed by a warden of a boarding house, was sufficiently connected with the work he was employed to do to be within the course of his employment. The HL overruled **Trotman v North Yorkshire CC (1999)** where the employers had been found not to be vicariously liable for a sexual assault by a teacher during a residential school trip.

The principle that comes from **Lister** is that the test is now based on whether the tort has a '*close connection with the employment*'. Lord Millet said it would be '*stretching language to breaking point*' to describe the warden's actions as '*merely a wrongful and unauthorised*' method of performance. He also made the defining comments in this Unit's opening quotation. Many of the older cases would be included in this new definition, but the decision itself is not without its critics.

Food for thought

There are strong and conflicting arguments as to whether **Trotman** or **Lister** is to be preferred. Bill Thomas, in *The Legal Executive* (July 2001), argues that the **Lister** case is *'illogical'* and refers to **Trotman** (which it overruled) as a *'bastion of old-fashioned common sense'*. Terry Kynaston, a practitioner dealing with child abuse cases, replies in October in the same journal. He argues that the House is to be congratulated on its *'fair and open-minded approach to a complex issue whilst also adhering to legal principle'*. Both have valid points. You should make up your own mind as to whether an employer should be liable for assaults by employees whose duties include protecting those in their care.

Other types of assault are treated in a similar way. In **Mattis v Pollock (2003)** a club doorman stabbed and seriously injured a man outside the club. The evidence was that he had gone home to get the knife. The injured man claimed that the club owner was vicariously liable. The trial judge referred to **Lister**, but felt that there was not a sufficiently close connection between the employment (as a doorman) and the attack. The CA disagreed and said that as a doorman he was expected to use physical force in his work, and that the stabbing was connected to an earlier argument in the club. The club was vicariously liable.

Task

Jack is a bouncer in a club. One night he sees Frank, against whom he has an old grudge for stealing his girlfriend. When Frank leaves, Jack follows him up the road and attacks him. Do you think the club owner will be liable? Will **Mattis** be followed or distinguished?

Examination pointer

When answering an essay question you may need to consider why vicarious liability should be imposed, e.g. because an employer may be better able to meet a claim. Most employers will be insured and can include such costs when calculating price structures. You could also discuss how far an employer should be liable for assaults. This is a little more controversial and there is no right answer. Use the recent cases to support your own opinion.

Summary

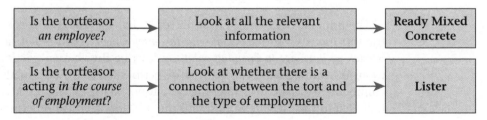

| Is the tortfeasor *an employee*? | → | Look at all the relevant information | → | **Ready Mixed Concrete** |
| Is the tortfeasor acting *in the course of employment*? | → | Look at whether there is a connection between the tort and the type of employment | → | **Lister** |

Self-test questions

1 Why was the employer liable in one case against the London bus company but not the other?

2 What are the names of these two cases, and which is which?

3 Which case was overruled by the HL in **Lister** and what is the new test for establishing whether an employee is within the scope of employment?

4 Give two reasons why you think that vicarious liability *should* be imposed.

5 Give two reasons why you think that vicarious liability *should not* be imposed.

 For further resources and updates please go to the Companion Website accompanying this book at **www.pearsoned.co.uk/russell**

Comparison of nuisance and Rylands

Nuisance			Rylands *v* Fletcher
public	**private**		
a crime, but also a tort if C suffers special damage; now rare – **Goldstein** and **Rimmington** (2005)	a tort		a tort
affects a class of people	affects C's enjoyment		something likely to do mischief escapes and causes damage
C need not have an interest in land	C must have an interest in land		C must have an interest in land
needs to occur more than once			can be a one-off
D must act unreasonably			D need not be at fault, but use of land must be 'non-natural'
Causation: **Wagon Mound** test applies to all – **Cambridge Water**			
defences are contributory negligence and consent *plus* statutory authority act of God act of a stranger prescription			**defences** are contributory negligence and consent *plus* statutory authority act of God act of a stranger default of claimant common benefit

Task

Look up the tests mentioned above. Draw your own diagram adding a case for each point, and the factors affecting liability. Keep this for revision.

Summary of vicarious liability

Is D an employee?	No single test – **Ready Mixed Concrete**
Dual vicarious liability possible	**Viasystems**
Is D in the course of employment?	Is there a connection? – **Lister**
Or on a 'frolic'?	**Twine**
If D is an independent contractor consider **Occupier's Liability Act 1957**	Occupier may be liable if work not checked s. 2(4)(b) – **Woodward**

Key criticisms

- The effect of **Sturges** is that C can effectively 'self-inflict' the nuisance.
- A person can be liable for the actions of a third party as in **Sedleigh Denfield**.
- Interference with television reception and electromagnetic interference is not actionable – **Hunter/Network Rail**.
- The overlap with nuisance and negligence means **Rylands** is arguably unnecessary – **Crown**.
- Courts are reluctant to develop **Rylands** – **Cambridge Water** – but are also reluctant to abolish it – **Transco**.
- There are so many defences and limits that a **Rylands** action rarely succeeds.
- Vicarious liability means D is liable even if not at fault.
- The decision on vicarious liability in **Lister** arguably goes too far.

Examination practice

June 2005
Critically analyse the rules on vicarious liability, and explain why it should be imposed.

(25 marks)

Module 6 connections

Morals	Should the law be involved in disputes between neighbours?	
	Should an employer be liable for the immoral acts of an employee?	**Lister**
Justice	Is it just that the doctor should get an injunction against the confectioner in **Sturges** when it wasn't a nuisance until he built his consulting rooms nearer to it?	**Sturges**
	Both employers could be sufficiently in control to share vicarious liability, which achieves justice	**Viasystems**
Conflicting interests	Any nuisance case can be discussed as the whole area is based on the conflicting interests of C and D. Similarly with **Rylands**	
	Viasystems can be discussed here too as the interests of both 'employers' as well as C are balanced	
Fault	**Rylands** is a strict liability, or 'no fault', tort.	
	Vicarious liability can be discussed, as the employer, even though not at fault, is being sued for compensation. Much of the answer to the above exam question could be used in a Module 6 essay	**Lister**
	Defences such as 'act of God' remove fault	**Nichols *v* Marsland**
Creativity	**Rylands** and the refusal by the courts to be more creative can be discussed	**Cambridge Water** and **Transco**
	Is the decision on vicarious liability in **Lister** *too* creative?	
	The HL has said it was for Parliament to abolish public nuisance, but has limited the cases where it would apply	**Goldstein** and **Rimmington**

 For further resources and updates please go to the Companion Website accompanying this book at www.pearsoned.co.uk/russell

Study Block 16
DEFENCES AND REMEDIES

Unit 48 Contributory negligence and consent

Unit 49 Remedies

The final step before C gets any compensation is to see if D has a defence. We have looked at some of the defences which apply to specific torts. Here we look at two defences which apply to *all* torts. It may be that C was partly to blame for the harm suffered, or consented to the action. We will look at these two issues here. Then the issue of remedies will be looked at. Once C has proved duty, breach and damage and any defence by D has been considered, then the question will be what remedy will be most appropriate. The most usual remedy in tort is financial compensation, called *damages*. A second remedy, particularly appropriate in cases like nuisance or **Rylands *v* Fletcher**, is an *injunction* to stop the activity.

Example John is injured when diving into his local swimming pool. He sues the council, which owns it. The council can argue that John *consented* to the risk of injury. The effect would be that the council is not liable. The council can also use the defence of *contributory negligence*; this leads to a reduction in the amount the council has to pay. John's *damages*, or compensation, will be reduced according to the amount he is seen to be at fault himself. If the swimming pool was causing a nuisance, perhaps because of noise if it is open late at night, then local residents might want to apply for an *injunction* to stop this happening.

Contributory negligence and consent

The accident is caused by bad driving. The damage is caused in part by the bad driving of the defendant and in part by the failure of C to wear a seat belt.

Lord Denning, **Froom v Butcher (1976)**

By the end of this Unit you should be able to:

- Explain how to prove the two defences
- Show how the law has developed by reference to cases and Acts of Parliament
- Show how the defences apply in particular situations by reference to cases

We will look at the two defences separately but note that they often overlap. If C's own negligence *contributes* to the injury it can sometimes also be said that there is *consent* to the injury.

Example I accept an offer to go water-skiing with a powerboat driver who I know is drunk. He loses control and I am injured. I can claim compensation. He owes *a duty* to passengers in his boat, has *breached* it by driving while drunk and this *caused* my injury. He can argue that I *contributed* to my injury by getting in the boat knowing he was drunk. He can also argue that I *consented* to the risk of harm by doing so.

Contributory negligence

The main defence used in tort claims is *contributory negligence*. It is not a full defence but can reduce the amount D has to pay to C in compensation. It is called *contributory* negligence because it is based on C being partly to blame by 'contributing' to the harm caused. In **Jones v Livox Quarries (1952)** C was riding on the tow bar of a vehicle when he was injured. He had exposed himself to the risk of harm and so was partly responsible for his own injuries.

Effect

The effect of successfully using this defence is that if C is shown to have 'contributed' to the harm then the amount of compensation (*damages*) will be apportioned by the court. This is governed by the **Law Reform (Contributory Negligence) Act 1945.**

Section 1(1) of the Act allows the court to use its discretion to reduce the damages awarded *'to such extent as the court thinks just and equitable having regard to the claimant's share in the responsibility for the damage'*.

There are two ways C can 'contribute':

- by contributing to the amount of damage or loss suffered;
- by contributing to the accident itself.

To the damage/loss

In **Froom v Butcher (1976)** a passenger had contributed to his injury by not wearing a seat belt. The court held that damages should be reduced as he had been partly to blame for the amount of harm that occurred. Lord Denning said, *'The accident is caused by bad driving. The damage is caused in part by the bad driving of the defendant and in part by the failure of C to wear a seat belt'*. In this case he had not contributed to the accident, but had contributed to the amount of harm he suffered.

To the accident itself

In **Sayers v Harlow (1958)** C got stuck in a public lavatory, she didn't want to wait too long to be rescued so tried to climb out. She was held to be 25 per cent contributorily negligent in putting her weight on the toilet-roll holder when attempting to climb out of the cubicle. Had she not done so she would not have been harmed at all.

In **Scutts v Keyse (2001)** C was hit by a police car responding to an emergency. The trial judge found that the police constable had been negligent in driving too fast, but reduced damages due to contributory negligence by C who had not kept a look out despite the fact that the siren was on. The CA allowed the appeal by the police. The CA felt that, although the driver must take reasonable care, even in an emergency, he was entitled to assume other road users would not ignore the siren. This shows that D may prefer not to rely on the defence, which can only reduce the amount of compensation, and may be better trying to show that there was no breach, as here.

. Whichever way C contributes, the court will consider all the circumstances of the situation. The question will be whether C's action is reasonable *in the circumstances*. This includes factors such as C's age, whether it was an emergency or rescue situation, etc. The less reasonable C's act then the more likely damages will be reduced by a larger amount. Children are less likely to be found to be contributorily negligent. In **Yachuk v Oliver Blais Ltd (1949)** a 9-year-old boy was found not to be contributorily negligent after he bought petrol at a garage and burnt himself. The court held that the child was not expected to see the danger involved in asking for petrol, so the garage which sold it to him was fully liable for the injuries caused by the burns. He should be judged by the standard expected of a 9-year-old child, not an adult. This can be compared to **Gannon v Rotherham MBC (1991)** where the court held that a 14-year-old ought to recognise the danger of diving into the shallow end of a pool so he was found to have contributed to his injuries.

Food for thought

Consider how fair the defence is. Until the Act a claim would fail altogether if C was shown to be partly to blame. This is one area where it can be argued that the law has improved. If C is partly at fault, there is a good argument that the compensation should be reduced accordingly. The Act allows the judge to have *'regard to the claimant's share in the responsibility for the damage'*. This means that the circumstances can be taken into account and allowance made for factors such as C's age. On the other hand, it means that D may pay more or less depending on unknown factors like this.

Examination pointer

Look out for clues such as C's age. A young child is less likely to be found to have contributed, as in **Yachuk**. The older the child, the more likely the court will apportion the amount of compensation, as in **Gannon**.

Breaking the chain of causation

If C's action is extremely unreasonable it may break the *chain of causation* altogether. Although not strictly a 'defence', it should be discussed either when looking at the causation issue or when looking at the defence of contributory negligence. The effect here is that it removes D's liability altogether. If the damage is not foreseeable, it is too remote and D may avoid liability. A 'contribution' by C which is unreasonable is quite likely to be unforeseeable and so break the chain of causation. This is called *novus actus interveniens*, or 'new act intervening'.

Consent

The Latin expression for the defence of consent is **volenti non fit injuria**. It means that if C voluntarily accepts a risk of harm, any claim for injury will fail. Both terms are still used by the courts but consent is more common these days. For the defence to succeed there must be 'true' consent and this involves two things:

- knowledge of a risk of harm;
- real consent to that risk.

This means just *knowing* of a risk is not enough in itself; C must have voluntarily accepted the risk *of harm*. Much will again depend on the particular circumstances. The courts are reluctant to find consent in cases involving employees and rescuers because there is no *true* consent. In the first case because an employee may consent to a risk of harm only in order to keep a job, and in the second because a rescuer may be acting under a moral obligation to take a risk to save another.

An example of an employment situation can be seen in **Smith v Baker (1891)**. Here an employee was told to work under a crane which was moving large stones.

He was injured when a stone fell on him. The court held that there was no true consent; he consented only in order to keep his job. The employer's defence failed and he had to pay compensation.

The following cases illustrate the courts' approach to rescuers.

In **Haynes v Harwood (1935)** a policeman was injured when he attempted to stop some horses which had bolted and which were putting others in danger. He was not found to have truly consented because he was under an obligation to act. This can be compared to **Cutler v United Dairies (1933)** where, in similar circumstances, a horse had bolted but was posing no danger to others, having ended up in a field. In this case the 'rescuer' was held to have consented to the risk of harm and so failed in his claim for compensation when he was injured. In **Chadwick v BTC (1967)** (see p. 355), a rescuer at a train crash was found not to have consented to the risk of harm.

Other relevant factors would include the type of risk and how obvious it is. In **Morris v Murray (1990)** C consented to going in a plane with a very drunk pilot. This was a defence to his claim for damages because the risk of harm was obvious. Compare this to **Dann v Hamilton (1939)** where a passenger was not found to have consented to the risk of harm in getting in a car with a driver who had been drinking because he was not obviously drunk.

Road Traffic Act 1988

Note that it is now impossible for a driver to use consent as a defence in relation to harm to a passenger. This is stated in **s. 149** of the **Road Traffic Act 1988**. However, contributory negligence is still a possible defence in these circumstances.

Examination pointer

Watch for cases where the **Road Traffic Act 1988** applies. Mention that the defence of consent will fail due to this but then go on to discuss contributory negligence as an alternative. Also note that the Act only applies to road transport; in cases like **Morris** the defence can still be argued.

Implied consent

There is *implied consent* in certain situations. This is commonly seen in sports, where participants are deemed to have consented to the risk of some harm, especially in contact sports like boxing and rugby. It will generally only apply where the harm occurs within the rules of a game. Thus in **Condon v Basi (1985)** the defence failed. A rough tackle broke a footballer's leg and he sued the other player. As the tackle was found by the referee to be foul play, the injured player had not consented to it. The CA said the test was whether a player had taken reasonable care in the circumstances. In **Woolridge v Sumner (1963)** a photographer at a race who was injured by a horse failed in his claim against the organisers of the event.

Food for thought

In **Woolridge**, Diplock LJ said, '*a person attending a game or competition takes the risk of any damage caused to him by any act of a participant done in the course of and for the purposes of the game or competition*'. How far spectators at sporting events may be shown to have consented is somewhat unclear. There is an overlap here between consent and breach of duty. The court was of the opinion that the organisers had not been negligent and Diplock LJ continued by saying, '*unless the participant's conduct is such as to evince a reckless disregard of the spectator's safety*'. This indicates that there was no breach of duty, rather than that the spectator had consented to harm.

Drunks

If C is drunk there may be a successful plea of consent to a claim against D, or, if consent fails, there may still be a possibility of using contributory negligence. In **Ratcliff v McConnell (1999)** a 19-year-old student was seriously injured diving into a swimming pool at his college. He had been drinking but the evidence was that he knew what he was doing. The court found that the risk of hitting his head on the bottom was obvious so the defence of consent succeeded. In **Barrett v MOD (1995)** the defence of contributory negligence succeeded. D's employer had been negligent in not looking after him when he passed out through drink. However, damages were reduced by two-thirds because C had been drinking heavily so was partly to blame for his own death.

Examination pointer

Note that if D can show C consented, the effect is that D is not liable. This is also the case if the chain of causation is broken. However, contributory negligence merely leads to a reduction in the amount D has to pay. Show that you understand the effect of using these defences by pointing this out in your answer. In many cases you will need to discuss both defences.

Example Both these defences, and the chain of causation argument, were seen in **Reeves v MPC (1999)** (see p. 340). D's argument that C *consented* to his own suicide failed, as did the argument that C's actions broke the *chain of causation* between the breach of duty and the suicide. However, *contributory negligence* was accepted and damages apportioned fifty-fifty between his estate and the police.

Task

Explain whether contributory negligence or consent, or both, was used in each of the following cases and what the effect was (reduction in damages, no liability, full liability).

Jones v Livox Quarries (1952)	
Sayers v Harlow (1958)	
Barrett v MOD (1995)	
Yachuk v Oliver Blais Ltd (1949)	
Smith v Baker (1891)	
Gannon v Rotherham MBC (1991)	
Morris v Murray (1990)	
Condon v Basi (1985)	
Froom v Butcher (1976)	

Summary

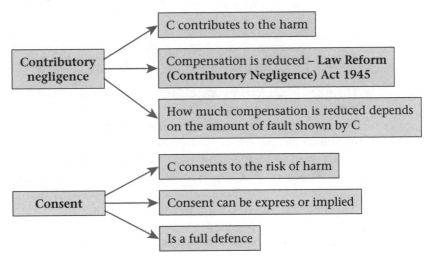

 Self-test questions

1 What does s. 1(1) of the **Law Reform (Contributory Negligence) Act 1945** provide?

2 What were the facts of **Sayers v Harlow (1958)**?

3 Compare **Yachuk v Oliver Blais Ltd (1949)** to **Gannon v Rotherham MBC (1991)**. In which did the defence of contributory negligence succeed and why?

4 Why is the defence of consent likely to fail in rescue cases? Give an example.

5 In what other cases is it likely to fail, and why?

 For further resources and updates please go to the Companion Website accompanying this book at **www.pearsoned.co.uk/russell**

Unit 49 — Remedies

I just want to be allowed to live in peace. Have we got to wait until someone is killed before anything is done?

Miller *v* Jackson (1977)

By the end of this Unit you should be able to:

● Explain the monetary remedy of damages
● Explain the alternative remedy of injunction

Damages

The most usual remedy in tort is an award of money, i.e. compensation for any loss. This is called *damages*. It is intended to compensate C rather than punish D. The idea is that C should be returned (as far as this is possible) to the position he/she would have been in but for the tort. C can only claim in respect of loss which was foreseeable. This was confirmed in **The Wagon Mound (1961)**.

An award of damages is usually a once-and-for-all payment but structured settlements are becoming more popular. This is particularly appropriate for long-term loss, e.g. where C is unable to work again. Under a structured settlement, D provides periodic payments through an annuity.

There are two types of damages, special and general.

Special damages

Loss of earnings and expenses are reasonably straightforward and can usually be agreed between the parties. Special damages cover *pecuniary* loss, i.e. financial losses. They are easy to quantify as payslips and receipts can be produced to cover loss of earnings and things like damage to a car or other belongings, transport costs, medical expenses etc.

Loss of *future* earnings is calculated by taking the current earnings and multiplying it by a figure (called the multiplier) representing the number of likely working years but reduced to account for investment income and the possibility of reduced employment for other reasons. No allowance is made for inflation or tax.

Loss of earnings *capacity* may be awarded. This was stated in **Smith *v* Manchester Corporation (1974)** where C was able to claim because she had a reduced chance of getting a job.

General damages

This covers what is called *non-pecuniary* loss. It is any loss which does not have a quantifiable monetary value, which will be assessed by the court.

This includes:

- pain and suffering
- the injury itself
- loss of amenity

Pain and suffering – an amount based on the pain caused by the injury and any particular suffering. Matters such as distress at disfigurement and a reduced life expectancy may be included in suffering. No award for pain is awarded if the claimant is unconscious or cannot feel.

The injury itself – there are set amounts for the loss of particular limbs, an eye etc.

Loss of amenity – this relates to a reduction in C's *quality* of life. Compensation may be increased if the injury affected a special interest or hobby.

> **Example** My hobby is cycling and due to someone's negligence I am badly injured. I have to have a leg amputated. In addition to any claim for compensation for loss of earnings and expenses, I can claim for the *pain and suffering* caused by the injury and a set amount for the *injury itself*, the loss of a leg. I can claim a further amount to compensate me for not being able to carry on with my hobby – this would come under *loss of amenity*.

The court will assess these general damages by reference to information supplied by the **Judicial Studies Board** based on other *recent* cases.

Injunction

Another remedy is an injunction. This is a court order used to prevent D carrying out some type of act. It is most commonly used in nuisance cases.

> **Example** Tim has started a pop group and they practise at home every night. Alan is a neighbour who cannot sleep. Alan doesn't really want compensation; that won't help him to sleep. He could sue Tim in nuisance and if he wins he should apply to the court for an injunction.

An injunction may be total or partial. In my example, the first would stop Tim practising at home, the second would stop him doing so at certain times, after midnight for example.

In **Tetley *v* Chitty (1986)** a *total injunction* was granted to stop the go-kart racing altogether. In **Kennaway *v* Thompson (1981)** a *partial injunction* was granted to stop the noise on a lake caused by speedboat racing, but it was limited to particular times.

An injunction is a *discretionary* remedy. This means it is granted at the court's discretion. Even if C wins the case, the court may decide not to grant an injunction. This is different to damages, which are granted as a right if C wins. Therefore, sometimes the court will award damages rather than an injunction, even in nuisance cases. This stems from the case of **Shelfer *v* City of London Electric Lighting Co. (1895)**. In this case it was said that the court could award damages rather than an injunction where the harm to C was minor and an injunction would be oppressive to D. This can be seen in **Miller *v* Jackson** (see p. 399). Mrs Miller claimed an injunction and the opening quote is what she said to the judge. The CA felt that the public interest outweighed hers and refused it. They would not order the club to stop playing cricket, but awarded damages to compensate Mrs Miller for the inconvenience of having cricket balls landing in the garden.

Task

Look back at the unit on nuisance. Choose three cases and decide how an injunction could help C in each of them.

Summary

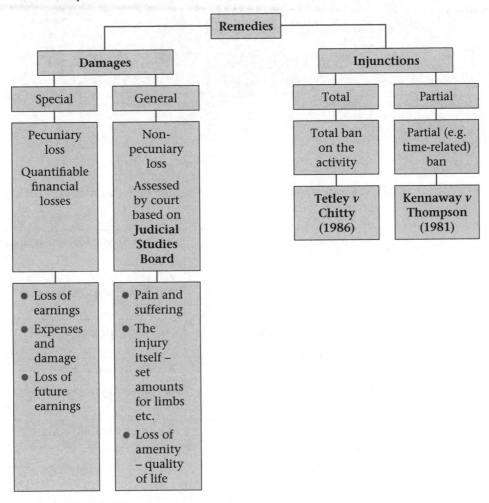

 ## Self-test questions

1 Can you explain the difference between special and general damages?

2 Can you explain the difference between pecuniary and non-pecuniary loss?

3 What is an injunction and when is it an appropriate remedy?

 For further resources and updates please go to the Companion Website accompanying this book at **www.pearsoned.co.uk/russell**

Before looking at whether D has a defence to a claim and what remedy is most appropriate, C has to prove:

Duty of care	**Donoghue *v* Stevenson/Caparo *v* Dickman** • Proximity • Foreseeability • It is fair, just and reasonable to impose a duty
Duty is restricted in cases of **nervous shock**	**McLoughlin/Alcock**
and **economic loss**	**Hedley Byrne/White *v* Jones**
Occupier's liability: Duty to a visitor	**Occupier's Liability Act 1957**
Occupier's liability: Duty to a non-visitor	**Occupier's Liability Act 1984**
Breach of duty	The courts will consider: • The degree of risk • The seriousness of the potential harm • Whether the risk was justifiable • The expense and practicality of taking precautions These factors are balanced against each other when the courts are deciding whether D breached the standard of care to be expected Where D acts in a professional capacity the skill expected is that of the profession – **Bolam/Bolitho**
Damage caused by that breach:	
Causation in fact	Apply the 'but for' test – **Barnett *v* Chelsea and Kensington HMC**
Causation in law – **remoteness of damage**	The test here is one of foreseeability – **Wagon Mound**

If the case is one of **nuisance** or **Rylands _v_ Fletcher**, apply the special rules. See Summary on page 420.

Does D have a defence?	
Contributory negligence	C has _contributed_ to the harm – **Jones _v_ Livox Quarries (1952)** Governed by the **Law Reform (Contributory Negligence) Act 1945**
Consent	C has _consented_ to the risk of harm – **Smith _v_ Baker (1891)** Must be true consent – **Smith _v_ Baker (1891)/Chadwick _v_ BTC (1967)** Can be implied, e.g. in sports – **Woolridge _v_ Sumner (1963)**
If the case is one of **nuisance** or **Rylands _v_ Fletcher** you may also need to look at the special defences.	

Note the effect of the defences:

What the claimant does	The effect for the defendant
C _broke the chain of causation_ Not strictly a defence but has the same effect as one	D avoids liability altogether
C _consents_ to the harm	D avoids liability altogether
C is _contributorily_ negligent	D is liable but damages are reduced by the court in proportion to C's contribution to the harm caused

And finally what remedy will C be awarded?

- _Damages_ is the most usual remedy.
- _An injunction_ may be sought instead of (or as well as) damages, but this is discretionary and so the court may refuse it.

Task

Add the principle and brief facts to each of the cases.

Authority	Principle	Facts or effect
Sayers v Harlow UDC (1958)		
Froom v Butcher (1976)		
Gannon v Rotherham MBC (1991)		
Woolridge v Sumner (1963)		
Condon v Basi (1985)		

Examination practice

There is rarely an essay question on this area alone so look at the exam practice at the end of Part 4. A good answer to a problem scenario will always be rounded off with a conclusion as to liability. Consider whether a defence is available to D and then mention what remedy will be appropriate.

Module 6 connections

Morals	Compensation is intended to compensate C rather than punish D, who may not always be morally to blame, especially in cases of strict liability	
Justice	The courts will find there is no true consent where an employee consents to the risk of harm only in order to keep the job; this achieves justice for C and protects employees in general	**Smith v Baker**
	An injunction is a *discretionary* remedy so will only be awarded if it is just in the circumstances	**Shelfer v City of London Electric Lighting**
Conflicting interests	Contributory negligence balances both the interests of C and D by reducing C's damages appropriately	**Reeves**
	The public interest may outweigh C's and so an injunction to stop an activity which has a public benefit may be refused	**Miller v Jackson**
Fault	The defence of contributory negligence recognises that where C is also at fault damages should be reduced	**Barrett v MOD (1995)**
Creativity	There has been little need for creativity in this area, the **Law Reform (Contributory Negligence) Act** allows the court to use its discretion and the other areas are not controversial	

Examination Practice for Part 4
MODULE 5 TORT

Lister Properties engaged Martin to advise on substantial renovation of a newly acquired derelict building. Part of the upper floor collapsed while Martin was carrying out an inspection, and he fell through it and broke his leg. Lister Properties then boarded up doors and windows pending further works. However, during school holidays, children managed to break in and, after three days of playing in the building with her friends, Nabeela (aged 11) fell from an upper floor and became trapped in debris.

She suffered serious back and leg injuries, and her screams were heard by Oliver, a police officer who was walking past the building. As soon as he saw her, he telephoned for an ambulance and then tried to remove rubble from her and to comfort her. Meanwhile, other children had run to tell Nabeela's aunt, Pat, who lived close by. Pat arrived just in time to see paramedics sedating Nabeela and putting her into the ambulance. Both Oliver and Pat found it very difficult to recover from the experience and both were away from work for prolonged periods of time with anxiety and depression.

(a) Discuss the rights *and* remedies available to **Martin** and to **Nabeela** against Lister Properties.

(25 marks)

(b) Discuss the rights available to **Oliver** and to **Pat** against Lister Properties.

(25 marks)

(c) How far would you agree that rules in the English law of tort ensure that a claimant may be properly compensated for psychiatric injury caused by the negligence of another?

(25 marks)

Guide

(a) Martin: OLA 1957, duty to independent contractors; he is in the exercise of his calling – s. 2(3)(b) and **Roles *v* Nathan**. Breach of duty is less likely in these circumstances.

You are specifically asked about remedies. Even if you decide there is no duty or breach you need to deal with this. *If* there is a duty which is breached Martin can claim damages for foreseeable harm – **Wagon Mound**. He should be returned (as far as this is possible) to the position he would have been in but for the tort. Damages is intended to compensate Martin, not punish Lister.

Nabeela: OLA 1984 and s. 2(3)(a) OLA 1957 regarding children.

Apply the three parts to the duty under the **1984 Act**. Lister knows of the danger and 'three days' and 'school holidays' indicates they may know, or at least have reasonable grounds to believe, children are playing there. Breach is likely unless boarding it up is deemed sufficient to keep children safe. Arguably the building is an allurement, so the **1957 Act** can be discussed *as well*, but not instead of the **1984 Act**. Anyway **s. 2(3)(a)** and cases on children apply to both – an occupier must be prepared for children to be less careful than adults plus the ingenuity of children should not be underestimated – **Jolley**. Nabeela is more likely to be successful. Her injuries are serious but probably foreseeable – **Wagon Mound** – as 'substantial' renovations are taking place. Again she is compensated by being returned to the position she would have been in. Defence of contributory negligence could reduce her damages if successful, but this is less likely in the case of children – **Yachuk**. It is unlikely she consented to the risk of harm so this defence would fail.

N.B. It would be possible to treat the case as one of negligence, but occupier's liability is more appropriate.

(b) The issue is psychiatric harm and the special rules for proving a duty.

Oliver: explain the distinction between primary and secondary victims – **Page**.

Rescuers can be either; if within the danger zone they will be primary so the ordinary rules of negligence will apply. Arguably there is a possibility of a further collapse. However, police failed in **White** so discuss this on the role of rescuers.

Pat: is a secondary victim so apply **Alcock/White**. She is not a parent so needs to prove close ties of love and affection. How the shock was caused – usually restricted to first-hand knowledge so was being told by a third party enough? Did she see the event? No, but saw the immediate aftermath – **McLoughlin**. Is there a 'sudden shock' which caused a recognisable psychiatric illness? – **Alcock**. Is anxiety and depression enough?

She will need medical evidence.

Pat may succeed, but Oliver will only do so if a primary victim.

(c) there are many problems and this is a popular area for exams so it is covered in detail in the Unit itself and the Study Block summary. You could discuss:

- the law on several of the issues has not been entirely consistent;
- it may be hard to measure the 'immediate aftermath';
- the 'close ties' requirement seems fair but may be hard to prove;
- how far away do you have to be to be a 'bystander' not a 'rescuer';
- medical evidence is difficult in psychiatric cases and may be conflicting;
- the law is uncertain and requires a fully debated Act of Parliament.

Look at the key criticisms and 'Food for thought' boxes for more ideas
DON'T FORGET CASES TO ILLUSTRATE!

Part 5

MODULE 6 CONCEPTS OF LAW

Study Block 17   CONCEPTS OF LAW

Introduction to Part 5
MODULE 6 CONCEPTS

This Part is shorter because it is *synoptic*. This means it connects to the other Modules you have studied, not just the substantive law, but the institutions and procedures. You will be expected to show your understanding of these by relating them to the more theoretical concepts found here. For example, how far the law involves issues of *morality*, how far it achieves *justice* and how far it must be proved that a person is at *fault* before liability will be imposed. For judicial *creativity* you will need to refer in particular to your Module 1 notes on precedent and statutory interpretation. I have repeated the rules in outline, but mainly concentrated on *how* and *whether* they allow creativity. For *conflicting interests* we look at how the law can be used as a 'tool' to engineer a particular balance between the various competing interests within society. You can use any cases you know to illustrate these concepts. Mine are just a few examples, where possible taken from the other Units so they will be familiar.

Unit 50   Law and morals

Unit 51   Law and justice

Unit 52   Balancing conflicting interests

Unit 53   Fault

Unit 54   Judicial creativity

As I said in the introduction, this area is synoptic, so all these Units are related to the law you have learnt throughout your studies. The theory of law is called *jurisprudence*, and is a compulsory part of most law degrees. The academics and judges who have written about these concepts will have tackled several of them so will appear in more than one Unit, as will some of the cases. The main thing when it comes to the examination is to have a clear focus and keep your answer centred on the specific question asked – be relevant.

Note the overlap not only with other Units but also *between* these Units. There is a summary at the end to illustrate this, but here is a brief example.

Example   **R v R (1991)** involved a man accused of raping his wife. This is a **moral** issue, and it is questionable whether judges or Parliament should decide on whether this type of immoral act is against the law. In deciding that it was rape, the judges were **creative**; this had not been against the law within marriage before. Presumably they felt they achieved **justice** for the wife but had to **balance the conflicting interests** of D (not to be guilty of what had previously been a legal act) against those of his wife (to have the law's protection) and the wider community (harmful activities affect society as a whole). The fact that the act was accompanied by violence showed a greater degree of **fault**, which may have tipped the balance against D.

Examination pointer

As you may only have studied one area, the questions will allow you to use **either** civil **or** criminal law, and sometimes both. Whether you choose one area or discuss both, the marks will be the same. Whichever approach you take, make sure you answer the particular question.

Law and morals

*. . . there remains an area of private morality and immorality that is not the law's
business.*

The Wolfenden Report, **1957**

By the end of this Unit you should be able to:

- Distinguish between law and morals and recognise and illustrate the diversity of moral views
- Identify opposing academic and judicial views on the relationship between law and morals
- Explain how the law may be used to promote or enforce morality
- Produce an argument for or against the law promoting/enforcing morality, using case examples

There is no strict definition of what amounts to 'morality'. A common view is that it is a body of rules which govern a group's behaviour. This sounds a bit like law too, so what is the difference? Well, to some people there isn't one, but to others the two concepts are separate. We will look at some of the different views in this Unit, but first an example.

Example

A common example used is that of a person walking past someone who is drowning and taking no action. Asked whether it is a crime not to try to save them, many students answer 'yes', but in the UK the answer is 'no'. There is usually no criminal liability for a failure to act, an omission. You might say, 'Well, you *should* try to save them.' This is a **moral** issue. You may have a **moral** duty to act but you have no **legal** duty to do so. As our law stands, it is left to the individual. This is what law and morals is all about: the question of how far the law *is*, and *should be*, imposing rules and how far any action should be left to individual choice.

Task

Tick the boxes to show what you think. If possible, ask a friend to do this too. See if you agree.

Action	Is it illegal?		Is it immoral?	
	Yes	**No**	**Yes**	**No**
Murder				
Smoking in public				
Cheating in examinations				
Speeding				
Swearing in public				
Shoplifting				
Adultery				
Lying				
Parking on a double yellow line				

There is a significant overlap between morality and law. Crimes such as murder, theft and rape are generally held to be immoral as well as illegal. Not all crimes are seen as immoral. For example, traffic offences. However, even parking on a yellow line is arguably immoral if you are blocking an emergency exit. Adultery, swearing and cheating are not illegal but may be viewed as immoral. Lying may be immoral, but is not usually illegal – unless you lie in court. Shoplifting is theft, but some would argue it isn't morally wrong to take a bone from a butcher's shop to feed a starving dog. Smoking is probably going to be banned in all public places. Many argue the law should not interfere, that it is a matter of individual choice. Others argue that smoking can harm others, so should be illegal. Similar debates arose over the banning of fox hunting.

Diversity of moral views

There is no single moral standard to apply. What some people see as immoral, others don't. What is regarded as immoral in one society, or in one time, may not be so in another. We live in a plural society with diverse views; there is no 'shared morality'. Adultery and abortion are examples. These are legal but some believe them to be immoral, and in some countries they are crimes. Even giving advice on contraception in order to avoid an unwanted pregnancy has been the subject of legal challenge. In **Gillick v West Norfolk and Wisbech AHA (1986)** a mother challenged her daughter's doctor for prescribing contraceptives. She lost at first instance, won in the CA and lost again in the HL by a majority of 3–2. No shared morality here either. The case became famous and led to children having greater rights to make their own decisions on such matters as medical treatment, as long as they are what is now called 'Gillick competent'.

Also times change; for example, advances in medical technology led to the setting up of the **Warnock Committee**. This looked at several issues involving in vitro fertilisation (IVF), including the use of embryos in medical research. It reported in 1984 and many of its findings were included in the **Human Fertilisation and Embryology Act 1990**. There is still much debate on the subject and opinion is divided, for example, on IVF technology and the creation of 'designer babies', discussed below.

Both law and morals involve rules. The courts enforce the law, but not social rules. However, if the morality is shared then most people will obey the rules. The question is should moral issues be a matter for society alone, or should the law reflect or even promote morality? The problem with making social rules into legal ones is the conflict of opinion about most moral issues. If morality is not shared then *whose* values should be promoted or enforced? The difficulties were recognised at the time of the Committee report. Mary Warnock, the academic who chaired the committee, made this point:

> *'I do not believe there is a neat way of marking off moral issues from all others; some people, at some time, may regard things as matters of moral right and moral wrong, which at another time or in another place are thought to be matters of taste, or of no importance at all.'*

Task

Social rules can be enforced by society's disapproval of any breach of the rules. Jumping the queue at the supermarket checkout to get your shopping home earlier isn't illegal but few of us do it.

Legal rules are enforced by the police and the courts. Jumping the lights to get your shopping home earlier *is* illegal.

Imagine you are with a group of people stranded on a desert island. You need to make some rules to govern behaviour. Make a list of six rules you think are important. Now go on to decide if they should have the force of law. How will they be enforced?

Examination pointer

Read the question carefully. You may be asked how far the law promotes moral values; if so, discuss laws which actively seek to make society behave in a certain way. Examples would be laws banning smoking and fox hunting. These laws aim to promote morality by providing new rules. If asked how far the law enforces moral values then emphasise laws which reflect society's views. A case example is **R v R (1991)** where the HL abolished the rule that a man could not be guilty of raping his wife. Previously this was not rape as the woman was deemed to have consented to sex by virtue of marriage. However, society no longer regarded woman as the property of their husbands and in their judgment the Law Lords reflected this view.

In 2004 a Russian newspaper carried a report that Moscow city authorities were considering a ban on kissing and embracing on the underground. The *Stolichnaya*

Vechernaya said the ban, aimed at raising public morality, could even extend to a husband embracing his wife. This may be a Russian case but it is a clear example of a government promoting moral values via the law.

The relationship between law and morals

The relationship between law and morality is complex and questions arise as to whether one is shaped by the other. If so, which shapes which – and which *should* shape which? Does the law decide what is 'moral' or does society's view of morality shape the law?

Food for thought

Should the law reflect and reinforce morality? This depends on your view of law and the purposes it serves in society. Whether judges (rather than Parliament) should develop the law to enforce morality is another question. It is argued that judges are appointed rather than elected and not accountable to the people, so should not attempt to impose their views on others. On the other hand, it can be argued that they are independent, more objective and don't have to give way to popular fashion or the current mood of society in order to keep the electorate happy. Development of the law can involve judges in questions of morality. This is arguably the role of Parliament where the issues can be fully debated. In the 'designer baby' case, the pressure group CORE said the decision was *'certainly a defeat for parliamentary democracy.'*

These issues also relate to 'Judicial creativity' and 'Law and justice'. Consider whether, and how far, the courts should be 'making' law. Should the HL have decided as it did in **R v R (1991)**? The result may seem (to you?) just and it is clear that women's role in society has changed over the years, but at the time it wasn't a crime, so we have to consider how far justice for the husband was achieved.

One major report about the law and how far it should reflect morality is the **Wolfenden Committee Report 1957** on homosexuality and prostitution. This said the purposes of the criminal law are:

'. . . to preserve public order and decency, to protect the citizen from what is offensive and injurious and to provide sufficient safeguards against exploitation and corruption of others especially the vulnerable . . . The law should not intervene in the private lives of citizens or seek to enforce any particular pattern of behaviour further than necessary to carry out the above purposes.'

The Committee recommended that prostitution and homosexual acts between consenting adult males in private should no longer be criminal offences. However, activities associated with prostitution, which could cause offence to others (such as soliciting in the street) were still to be regulated by the law.

The **Wolfenden Report** became the subject of a major legal debate between **Lord Devlin**, a judge who took the view that law and morality are inextricably linked, and **Professor Hart**, an academic who argued that there is no widely shared morality (see also the Unit on Justice).

View 1 - law and morality are separate

Hart argued that using the law to enforce morality was unnecessary, undesirable and morally unacceptable.

- *Unnecessary* because society would not otherwise disintegrate.
- *Undesirable* because it would freeze morality at that time.
- *Unacceptable* because it would restrict the freedom of the individual.

Hart was heavily influenced by John Stuart Mill, and he approved of the Committee's approach to liberalising the laws.

View 2 - law and morality are linked

Lord **Devlin** was vehemently against it. He argued that immoral acts, even in private, could weaken the fabric of society and that society should punish an act thought grossly offensive and immoral by the standards of the 'right-minded person'. This begs the questions – how do we identify the content of this morality and who are these right-minded people?

The philosopher's view

The philosopher **John Stuart Mill (1806–1873)**, of whom more in the next Unit on 'Law and justice', would have agreed with the Committee. His view was that the law should leave people to make their own choices, so long as they do not harm others. Many lawyers and judges have been influenced by this view. It can be argued, however, that there are very few actions that have no effect on others. Look back to the smoking argument. Would Mill have banned smoking or not?

Two older cases illustrate support for Lord Devlin's view. In **Shaw v DPP (1961)** arguments for upholding a conviction for *'conspiring to corrupt public morals'* (by publishing a directory of prostitutes) rested on the need to *'conserve the moral welfare of the state'*. As we noted above, it can be argued that judges are not the right people to decide such issues. If these questions are not to be left to individual choice, should it be for Parliament alone to lay down the law?

The Committee recognised that one of the functions of the law is to provide safeguards against the exploitation and corruption of others. In the case of **Knuller v DPP (1973) HL** the court convicted the Ds for publishing advertisements for homosexuals. Although the **Sexual Offences Act 1967** had made homosexuality legal following the Wolfenden Report, Lord Reid said, *'if people choose to corrupt themselves in this way that is their affair and the law will not interfere. But no licence is given to others to encourage this practice.'*

Support for Lord Devlin is not confined to older cases, though.

The Brown Case - opposing views in the Lords

In **Brown (1994)** the HL held that, where the Ds had committed homosexual sadomasochistic acts, resulting in injuries, public policy demanded that these acts be treated as unlawful even though they occurred in private and the participants had consented. There was not only disagreement in the decision (a 3–2 majority), but also in the reasoning behind it. However, the morality issue was present in several of the speeches. Lord Templeman said, '*Society is entitled and bound to protect itself against a cult of violence. Pleasure derived from the infliction of pain is an evil thing.*' Lord Lowry said such activities were not '*conducive to the welfare of society*'. Lord Mustill, dissenting, took the view that although the acts were immoral that did not make them unlawful and the conviction should be quashed. Lord Slynn, also dissenting, said it was not for the courts to protect people from themselves. (*N.B. The European Court of Human Rights upheld the majority view in* **Brown**.)

Task

What would Mill's view have been had he been a judge in this case?

Professor Hart would agree with Lords Mustill and Slynn – that law and morality were not inextricably linked. The fact that the decision was influenced by the judges' views of what was morally acceptable can be seen by comparing it to **R v Wilson (1996)** where the D was acquitted after branding his initials on his wife's buttocks.

Food for thought

Do you think the courts should be involved in such moral issues? In **R v Gibson (1991)** an artist exhibited earrings made from freeze-dried foetuses. He was convicted of the common law offence of outraging public decency. Society may be 'outraged' but has it been harmed? Mill would probably argue that the law should not interfere.

'Designer' babies

There is much argument about whether or not people should be able to choose the genetic make-up of their babies. Many argue that this should not be done for social reasons, e.g. to balance the number of boys and girls in a family. However, where there are medical reasons the issue is more complex. This moral question also raises legal issues. It was the subject of **Quintavalle v Human Fertilisation and Embryology Authoity (2005)**. A couple had been granted the right by the Authority to use 'tissue typing' to select an embryo that would be a match for their son who was seriously ill and needed a transplant. This would mean an embryo that was not a match would be discarded. The pressure group CORE (Comment of Reprographic Ethics) challenged the Authority's right to do so under the **Human Embryology and Fertilisation Act 1990**. They argued that it could lead to people being able to have embryos tested (and discarded) for other characteristics, such as sex or hair colour – hence the term 'designer babies'. The HL, while recognising the case raised '*profound ethical questions*', ruled that the **Act** could be interpreted as allowing selection. In August 2005 the government issued a consultation paper to assess public opinion on these issues. I am sure there will be a wide divergence of views.

Legal enforcement of morality

Here are a few examples, but use your own too. You will produce a better discussion if you use cases you know well.

Note that your argument is not about right and wrong, but whether the matter should be classed as a legal issue or a matter of personal choice.

Crime

Brown is an obvious example of enforcing morality. Devlin would agree with the decision in **Brown**, and argue that the law needed to step in to protect society against evil. Hart and Mill would say it is not the law's place to enforce moral values. **Wilson** can be used in comparison; did the judges decide differently on moral grounds? You can use cases on murder and manslaughter to support your discussion about the right to life – and death. Although killing is seen as both immoral and illegal, there are situations where there may be a moral case for killing, as in Diane Pretty's case. In **Bland** and **Re A** doctors had to make a moral decision but needed the court to confirm there would be no legal repercussions. Failing to save a life may be immoral but not usually illegal, but in cases such as **Stone and Dobinson** and **Gibbins and Proctor** there was a duty to act and so criminal liability arose.

Defences provide examples of how the law reflects morality. The rules on insanity and automatism recognise the law should not punish someone who does not know they are doing wrong. The limitations on the intoxication defence reflects society's view that drinking should not excuse criminal activity. The defence of consent has been discussed above. Note that it was refused in **Brown** but allowed in **Aitken** and **Gibson**.

Theft can be related to the argument that stealing from the rich and giving to the poor is not immoral, although it is certainly illegal. Similarly in cases of criminal damage and GM crops, protesters have argued that such crops are harmful to the environment and so argue a moral right to damage them. In **DPP v Blake (1993)** a vicar claimed, unsuccessfully, that he had God's consent to cause criminal damage.

Contract

Although contract is an area with fewer moral issues, there are still examples to be found. Contract is based on the exchange of promises and the law will impose sanctions on those who break their promises. Generally, though, the courts are reluctant to interfere in the making of contracts based on 'freedom of contract'. This is in accord with Mill's argument that the law should not interfere unless harm will result. This can include economic harm so you could discuss the way both Parliament and the courts *will* interfere to protect the weaker party in consumer contracts, e.g. by imposing terms (**Sale of Goods Act/The Moorcock**) and by limiting the ability of a business to exclude liability (**UCTA**). The courts will also interfere where an agreement is the result of duress or fraud.

Tort

Donoghue shows the courts are prepared to develop the law to protect the consumer. A moral link can be seen in the biblical idea of 'love thy neighbour' which Lord Atkin developed to 'do not harm your neighbour'. In **White** the police were unable to succeed in a claim for psychiatric harm, in part because it would be immoral to allow their claims but not those of some of the victims' families. In **Greatorex** the court thought it undesirable to allow members of a family to sue each other. In **BRB *v* Herrington** the HL held BR owed a 'common duty of humanity' to a child trespasser.

Food for thought

A few more ideas for discussion:

- **Drinking:** should the law tell us when we can drink, and where? Some councils ban drinking on the street and other public places, some don't. Should it be all or nothing?
- **Smacking:** under the **Children Act 2004** smacking is no longer lawful if it causes bruising or cuts, but is otherwise legal.
- **Smoking:** should the law ban smoking in public? If so, should it be total? In December 2005 the Select Committee on Health criticised the government for exempting private clubs and bars which do not sell food. In February 2006 Parliament voted against this exemption, so now the ban will apply to all.
- **Praying:** daily collective worship is a legal requirement in schools – should the law be involved in what is essentially a purely moral issue?
- **Gay 'marriages':** there is much less debate about homosexuality itself these days and more about whether gay couples should have equal rights to married couples. Since December 2005, some legal rights, e.g. involving pensions and inheritance tax, are available to gay couples who formalise their relationship under the **Civil Partnership Act 2004**.

There are many other possibilities. Look in the newspapers or watch the news and see what interests you.

Examination pointer

Read the question carefully for specifics. In a more general question use cases and Acts to show the relationship between law and morals – or, if you prefer, to show there isn't one. There is no right answer to such questions, so form your own opinion. However, a word of warning – avoid using this area to voice personal views too strongly, and ALWAYS support what you say with examples and academic discussion.

Summary

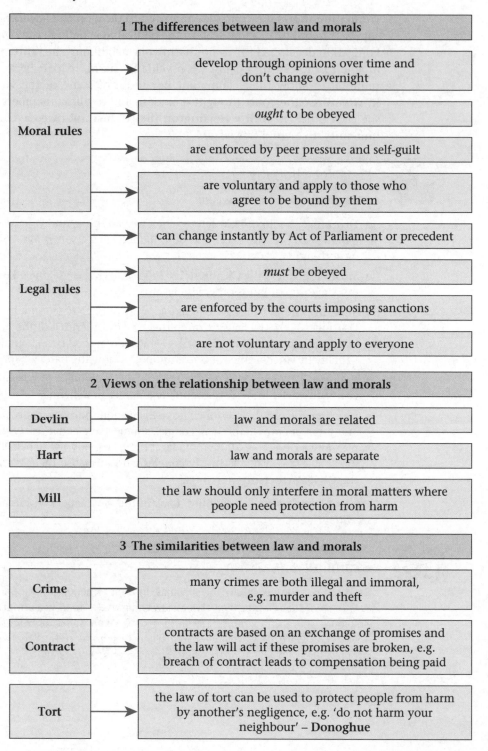

1 The differences between law and morals

Moral rules
- develop through opinions over time and don't change overnight
- *ought* to be obeyed
- are enforced by peer pressure and self-guilt
- are voluntary and apply to those who agree to be bound by them

Legal rules
- can change instantly by Act of Parliament or precedent
- *must* be obeyed
- are enforced by the courts imposing sanctions
- are not voluntary and apply to everyone

2 Views on the relationship between law and morals

Devlin	law and morals are related
Hart	law and morals are separate
Mill	the law should only interfere in moral matters where people need protection from harm

3 The similarities between law and morals

Crime	many crimes are both illegal and immoral, e.g. murder and theft
Contract	contracts are based on an exchange of promises and the law will act if these promises are broken, e.g. breach of contract leads to compensation being paid
Tort	the law of tort can be used to protect people from harm by another's negligence, e.g. 'do not harm your neighbour' – **Donoghue**

Self-test questions

1 Summarise the opposing views held by the Law Lords in **Brown**.

2 What is the basic distinction between **Hart** and **Devlin**'s views?

3 What was the outcome of **Quintavalle**?

4 What is the **Wolfenden Report** about?

5 Make a list of three arguments that support *your* views in this area.

For further resources and updates please go to the Companion Website accompanying this book at **www.pearsoned.co.uk/russell**

Law and justice

Everyone seems to have a view of the proper outcome. I am very well aware of the inevitability that our answer will be applauded by some but that as many will be offended by it.

Ward LJ, **Re A (2000)**

By the end of this Unit you should be able to:

- Explain some of the different theories about what is meant by the term 'justice'
- Evaluate the role of both formal and substantive justice in the legal system
- Illustrate your evaluation by reference to cases and examples

---

The meaning of justice

Many people see law and justice as the same thing but this is not necessarily the case. It is quite possible to have unjust laws. It is also possible to have unjust outcomes from just laws. That said, in liberal democracies at least, it is the primary aim of any legal system to deliver justice. Unjust laws are likely to be challenged and may become unenforceable. An example is the poll tax in the 80s. It was widely thought that the tax was unfair and enough people, from many different social groups, demonstrated against it to force a change in the law.

So what is justice? A simple notion of justice is that of fairness – treating everyone equally. When you hear someone say 'But that's not fair!' it usually means 'You aren't treating everyone the same.' However, justice can mean different things to different people. There are several theories on the subject. You should be able to discuss some of them.

Examination pointer

Don't try to learn all the theories outlined here. You won't have time to discuss many of them, so use ones that make sense to you. Your essay will be more confident and it will be easier for you to use examples. Two or three theories well illustrated with examples will earn more marks than a recitation of several theories without developing any of them.

Many books have been written by, and about, the people putting forward different theories. It is a good idea to try to read someone first-hand if possible. You will get a much better feel for what they mean than you will by merely reading *about* them. It is only possible here to give an outline of the main ones.

Theories of justice

Natural Law

The Natural Law theory regards law as coming from a higher source. Laws are based on moral rules. The origins of Natural Law theories lie with **Aristotle** and **St Thomas Aquinas**.

Aristotle (384–322 BCE) said that moral rules come from Nature. We have 'natural' rights. He argued that the basis of justice is fairness, and that this takes two forms:

1 *Distributive justice* – the law acts to distribute benefits and burdens fairly throughout society. This can occur through various laws governing property rights, e.g. in the law of theft and contract.

2 *Corrective justice* – the law acts to correct attempts by individuals to disturb this fair distribution. In crime, confiscation, compensation and restitution are corrective sentences. In contract and tort, D pays compensation to C to correct any wrongdoing.

Example
Football is played by equal numbers on both sides, using the same pitch, the same ball and the same-sized goals. If one team's goal were smaller than the other's, that would be a breach of *distributive justice* – it wouldn't be treating the teams fairly. When a player breaks the rules, the referee (another word for 'judge', of course) may award a penalty, a free kick, send the offending player off the pitch or whatever. In this case, the referee is using *corrective justice* – trying to compensate one team for the offence of the other.

Saint Thomas Aquinas (1227–1274) said that moral rules come from God. We have 'God-given' rights. He suggested that any law which went against morality would not be just. If a law is not a just law, we need not obey it. This is because it is not a 'true' law. However, he also said that such a law should be obeyed if *not* obeying it would disrupt society. This is because that would not be in accordance with God's will either.

Many countries have a constitution which sets out certain rights. These are seen as a higher form of law. If a law were passed which conflicted with constitutional rights, it could be subject to challenge. Britain does not have a written constitution. However, the **Human Rights Act 1998** has provided that the 'natural' rights set out in the **European Convention on Human Rights** are now part of domestic law.

Positivism

Positivists have tried to find a more scientific way of describing law, without reference to morality. For positivists, law *may* be based on ideas of morality or justice, but these are not *necessary*. The validity of law is not affected by whether it is morally acceptable. Most positivist theories attempt to explain what law *is* rather than what it *ought* to be. Although this means that a law is valid even if it is unjust or immoral, it does not mean it has to be followed blindly. Most positivists acknowledge that there may be times when a law should not be obeyed. What they *do* say is that even though it is unjust, it is still *law*.

Two important positivists are **Kelsen** and **Hart**.

Kelsen (1881–1973) felt it was impossible to define justice. He tried to provide a science of law which excluded any political or moral content. He based his theory on a set of 'legal norms'. He saw law as a form of social control. The legal norm imposes duties or confers powers on officials to apply sanctions. This can be seen in sentencing and remedies.

Hart (1907–1992) distinguishes between 'procedural justice' and 'substantive justice'. The first he calls 'justice *according* to law' and this involves questions of whether the *legal process* is just. The second he calls 'justice *of* the law' and this looks at whether the *law itself* is just. To Hart, the law is based purely on rules and separate from issues of morality.

Food for thought

Parliamentary supremacy in the English legal system means that Parliament can make any law it likes. If it made an immoral law, should we obey it?

Positivism is clearly opposed to Natural Law theories. For a positivist a bad law would still be valid and have to be obeyed. A Natural Law theorist would disagree. Nazi law is often used as an example. Positivists might say laws discriminating against Jewish people should be obeyed. Natural Law theorists would argue that law must follow some 'higher natural law' and if it did not it would not be 'true' law. The segregation of African Americans in the USA and the apartheid laws of South Africa are other examples.

Utilitarianism

Utilitarianism looks at the *consequences* of a law, and asks whether it benefits more people than it harms. If a law 'maximises happiness', i.e. increases the total happiness or welfare of a society, it is just. Utilitarianism is often simplified as 'the greatest good for the greatest number'. However, utility is not concerned with *equal* distribution of happiness, but with *total* happiness. It can therefore lead to injustice because if there are a few *very* happy people, then total happiness may be greater even if there are lots of slightly unhappy people. Utilitarianism focuses on the needs of society rather than the individual. It is in conflict with individual rights and freedoms and is criticised by libertarians, who see the rights of the individual as all-important.

Jeremy Bentham (1748–1832) was a Utilitarian. He had little time for individual rights in the sense of natural rights, which he referred to as '*nonsense on stilts*'. His Utilitarian theory was an attack on the Natural Law theory. He tried to produce a more scientific approach to justice. He suggested that law should be evaluated by reference to the principle of utility, and not by reference to a '*misguided belief*' in Natural Law and natural rights.

Example	A law is passed which bans smoking in public. A Utilitarian would argue that the rights of the majority to protection from health risks outweigh the rights of the individual to smoke. This law would therefore be just. Some years ago, when more people smoked, a Utilitarian might argue against such a law.

Food for thought

The introduction of the **Human Rights Act 1998** increases the rights of individuals. Is this against the Utilitarian theory? Maybe not. It can be argued that society itself benefits from certain rights being enshrined in law.

Anti-terrorism laws are arguably for the greater good of society. A Utilitarian could argue that the ends justify the means. An alternative argument would be that society itself is diminished by going against the rule of law. These laws could be seen as against 'natural' law as they conflict with the rule that no one should be imprisoned without a fair trial.

John Stuart Mill (1806–1883) was a leading Utilitarian and is still influential today. Mill was also a libertarian and attempted to unite the ideas of Utilitarianism and individual rights. He had a minimalist approach to law, arguing that people should have the right to act unless exercising that right harmed others. Only then should the law interfere to restrict those rights.

Task

Would Mill have agreed with:

● the law against drinking and driving?

● the law making the use of seat belts compulsory?

Note that Utilitarianism and positivism overlap.

● Positivism *separates* legal rules (law) from social rules (morals).
● Utilitarianism focuses on the *consequences* of the rules.

Economic theories

Many economic theories are modern alternatives to Utilitarianism. Traditionally, Utilitarianism looks at maximising happiness. Economic theories try to measure this in terms of material wealth. Three important economic theorists are Karl **Marx**, John **Rawls** and Robert **Nozick**.

Marx (1818–1883) believed that the law only served the ruling classes, those who '*own the means of production*'. He wanted to see distributive justice (remember Aristotle?): '*from each according to his ability, to each according to his needs*' and thought the state should intervene to redistribute wealth. Marx did *not* support *equal* distribution, but distribution according to ability and need. He did not focus on individual rights as he saw these as reducing the power of people to work together for change.

Rawls (1921–2002) argued that Utilitarianism was flawed because it failed to take account of the *'separateness of persons'*. His theory is based on what rules a group of individuals would choose in order to make their society just – what earlier writers had called a 'social contract'. Rawls added a new ingredient called the 'veil of ignorance'. This means that the individuals making the rules would not know who they were and so could not be influenced by self-interest. If people do not know whether they are rich or poor, young or old, male or female, Jews or Christians, able or disabled etc. then they will agree only to rules which would protect them *whatever* the circumstances. Such rules would therefore achieve justice. This theory of justice is Egalitarian, based on equality.

Nozick (1938–2002) argues that for a just society there should be minimal interference in people's lives by law and state. Although he too rejected the Utilitarian argument, he did not agree with **Rawls** that wealth should be redistributed. He argued that if people come by something fairly, then the law should not attempt any redistribution because that would interfere with people's rights to their property. *How* goods or wealth were distributed within society would be just, as long as everyone *received* their property in a just manner.

Food for thought

In September 2005 a woman threatened to take her local Health Trust to court for not supplying a new drug (Herceptin) shown to reduce the risk of recurrence of breast cancer. It cost £20,000 per year and was not yet available on the NHS. Following this, the Minister for Health said that it would be available on the NHS for new patients.

- Should all Trusts be made to supply it?
- Should the Trust make the decision on a case-by-case basis, depending on available funds?
- Should the money be used to treat several other patients with more minor problems?

Hospitals and doctors with limited resources face these difficult economic issues every day.

Task

What is the theory?

We believe that law is separate from morality. We base our understanding of the law on rules to be obeyed - what some call legal norms. A law may be unjust but it is still a law.	Our theory is described as
We are concerned to maximise happiness. Some of us reject individual rights but others believe that the law should only interfere if someone exercising a right harms others.	Our theory is described as
We believe law is closely linked to morality and that moral rules come from a higher authority than the law. Unjust law is not true law.	Our theory is described as

How far does the law achieve justice?

Refer to all areas of the law you have studied for ideas on the extent to which substantive legal rules, institutions and processes achieve justice. Ask yourself the following questions.

- Is the legal system just?
- Is a particular law just?

Here are a few starting points.

Procedural justice – legal institutions and process

Justice requires that there is a system of independent tribunals for the administration of law and the resolution of disputes. (What Hart called 'justice *according to law*'.) This would include trial by jury, appointment and independence of judges, financing of court cases, sentencing, remedies and so on.
    You could discuss:

- Reforms under the **Access to Justice Act 1999** – improving access to advice and representation.
- The **appeals system** and **juries** to provide greater protection for D.
- The **Criminal Cases Review Commission**. This was set up in 1995 with the sole purpose of correcting injustice (see **Kennedy (2005)** p. 182) and its establishment is a clear acknowledgement by the state that injustices do occur. In February 2005, for example, the Prime Minister issued a public apology to victims of what he called 'state injustice' such as the 'Guildford Four'.
- **Precedent** is based on treating like cases alike, which is fair, and other rules of precedent can be used to avoid injustice, e.g.:
  - Crime: The use of the 1966 Practice Statement in **Gemmell** to *overrule* **Caldwell**.
  - Contract: **Merritt** *distinguishing* **Balfour**.
  - Tort: *Setting a precedent* in **Donoghue**.

Remedies and sentencing

Remember Aristotle's '*corrective justice*'? Civil remedies aim to achieve justice by ensuring D compensates C for any wrongdoing. In sentencing, the aim is to achieve a just balance between the interests of society (deterrence and retribution) and the defendant (rehabilitation). Mitigating and aggravating factors can influence the judge to do what is just in the circumstances.

Substantive justice – the legal rules

How far does the law achieve justice in crime, contract and tort? (This is Hart's 'justice *of* the law'.) Here are a few ideas.

Crime

There is plenty to discuss here. The rules relating to *mens rea*, especially for murder, are problematic. The attempt to achieve justice has left the law uncertain and arguably unjust. Crimes of strict liability allow a criminal conviction without proof of *mens rea*. This seems unjust so if the Act is silent the courts will presume *mens rea* is needed, as in **Sweet v Parsley**. In **Gemmell and Richards** the HL used the **1966 Practice Statement** to overrule their earlier decision on recklessness in order to achieve justice.

The problems of the law on manslaughter can be considered – in particular, the calls for reform in order to achieve justice following several rail disasters (see below on Hatfield).

The defence of necessity is rare, but is based on the Utilitarian concept of the greater good. In **Re A (conjoined twins) (2000)** the operation to separate conjoined twins (Mary and Jodie) would lead to the death of Mary. Without the operation both twins would die, so it could be argued that her death was justified to bring about the 'greater good' of life for Jodie. The operation was allowed. The opening quote came from this case, recognising that justice means different things to different people.

Theft is a crime whatever is stolen, so if a mother steals milk for her baby she is still guilty of theft. Some people may think the law is unjust, although everyone is being treated equally. However, if each case is decided on its own facts it creates uncertainty. Justice may be achieved during the sentencing stage, rather than by deciding it is not theft.

In **Brown (1994)**, on consent to harm, Lord Lowry said sadomasochism was *'not conducive to the welfare of society'*, so a Utilitarian might agree with the verdict. The rights of the individuals to consent to harm were outweighed by the effect on society. What do you think Mill would have thought of that?

Contract

The law tries to achieve a balance between allowing people freedom to make agreements in their own way and protecting the individual against those with more power, who may try to exploit this freedom. The **Unfair Contract Terms Act** limits a business's right to exclude liability. Terms are implied into contracts by both statutes and the courts (e.g. **Sale of Goods Act, The Moorcock**).

Innominate terms, as seen in **Hong Kong Fir**, are an attempt to achieve justice by focusing on the result of a breach, rather than on the term itself.

In deciding whether something is a term or a representation, the courts will take into account any specialist knowledge in order to do justice to both parties (**Oscar Chess Ltd**).

Judges are reluctant to find a contract void for mistake because if the contract is void the effect on a third party may be unjust. Equity is based on fairness and can be seen as a higher source of law. Thus, equitable remedies, such as rescission, will only be granted if injustice won't be caused. In **Phillips v Brooks** it was refused in order to protect the rights of the third party buyer. Similarly, specific performance will not be granted if this would be unfair, thus in **Watkin v Watson-Smith (1986)** the court refused an order to perform the sale after the seller had offered his bungalow at £2,950 instead of £29,500, by mistake.

Tort

In **Hill v Chief Constable of West Yorkshire (1989)** the police owed no duty of care because it could detract from their overall effectiveness. The individual's right (to damages) was outweighed by the benefit to the public. This is a Utilitarian argument.

In **Miller v Jackson** the utility argument can also be seen. The public benefit of cricket outweighed the individual nuisance and no injunction was granted.

Rylands v Fletcher is a tort of strict liability, which makes a person liable without proof of fault. This can be seen as unjust.

In **Donoghue v Stephenson** a precedent was set to achieve justice for the consumer. Did the manufacturer get justice?

The decision that a learner driver is expected to reach the standard of a competent driver could be seen as unjust in **Nettleship v Weston**. However, the driver was best able to bear the cost, through her insurance company.

The defence of contributory negligence allows the court to apportion liability in a way that seeks to achieve justice. Use any cases on this defence to discuss this. In addition, on defences, in **Smith v Baker** the court protected the weaker party by finding there was no true consent.

Current affairs

The consultation document on corporate killing reflects public concern that justice is not being done. The Hatfield rail crash in October 2000 caused four deaths and over 100 injuries. At the trial of Balfour Beatty in October 2005, charges of manslaughter were dismissed but the company was fined £10 million for extremely poor safety procedures.

On the same day that this trial was reported in the newspaper there was a report of a case of stock market abuse. Two directors of a company had supplied false information to the market. They were both given jail sentences. A week later the manager of Darlington Football Club was jailed for three years for cheating the taxman. People may find it hard to see justice here.

Examination pointer

Read the question carefully. You may be asked for a general discussion and/or to consider a specific question, e.g. 'How far does the law promote justice?' Parliament can attempt to promote justice by making particular rules. In contract, various Acts give protection to consumers. In tort, the **Occupier's Liability Act 1984** protects people even though they may have no right to be on someone's land. It was the attempt to do justice in **BRB v Herrington** that led to this Act being passed. This shows that case law can also promote justice.

Sentencing and remedies can also promote justice, e.g. by deterrence and by making people act more carefully in future.

Not only do the theorists differ in their ideas of justice, so do most ordinary people. In a televised report of a court case you often see pictures of families and friends of the victim, and the accused, demanding 'justice'. Whatever the outcome of the case, they are unlikely all to think that they got it.

Food for thought

What do you think the families and friends actually mean by justice in these cases? Look out for stories in the press. As you read, ask yourself whether 'justice' has been achieved. Then consider whether any of the above theorists would have agreed. Finally, ask the all-important question, 'justice for whom?' Write some notes on this to keep for revision.

Examination pointer

Examiners are looking for independence of thought so you need to develop your own ideas. Use some of the examples but don't just cite them. Pick out a few and see how well you can explain them. Include references to some of the theories and add cases to illustrate. Try to add something current that involves a question of promoting or achieving justice.

Summary

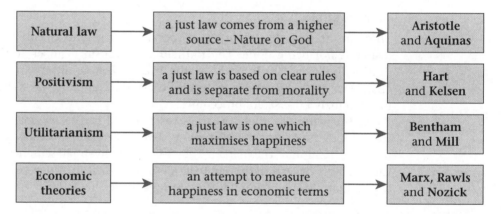

Self-test questions

1 What is the Utilitarian theory based on?

2 What do positivists attempt to separate?

3 What did Mill add to Utilitarianism?

4 Where does Natural Law come from?

5 Apply one of these theories to any case of your choice.

For further resources and updates please go to the Companion Website accompanying this book at **www.pearsoned.co.uk/russell**

Balancing conflicting interests

There is a contest here between the interest of the public at large and the interest of a private individual.

Lord Denning MR, **Miller v Jackson (1977)**

By the end of this unit you should be able to:

- Identify the competing interests in society
- Explain how the law attempts to achieve a fair balance between such interests
- Use cases and examples to show how the law is used to 'engineer' this balance

---

This Unit will identify and illustrate how competing interests are weighed up and balanced during the making and application of the law.

Examination pointer

Try to discuss interests outside the obvious claimant/defendant or claimant/victim roles. These are certainly valid examples but there are many wider issues. A common point made in examiners' reports is that students often fail to refer to the wider impact on society.

Identification of different interests: public and private interests

Interests conflict in all areas of public and private life – from deciding which TV programme to watch to drafting anti-terrorism legislation. There is a need to balance individual interests against each other, and also against those of society. Private interests may be subordinated to those of the community – the Utilitarian theory of maximising happiness can be seen in this.

When looking at the legal process, cases and legislation ask yourself the following questions:

- What are the interests that might conflict here?
- What is an appropriate balance between those interests?

- Has this particular case/Act/process achieved that balance?
- *How* has the law 'engineered' the balance?

Examination pointer

There is a clear overlap with justice. Theories of justice attempt to define justice. Balancing conflicting interests is an attempt to achieve justice. You can therefore mention one or two theories from 'Law and justice'. A Utilitarian, like Bentham, might say justice is best achieved by balancing the interests to ensure the greatest good for the greatest number. A Marxist would want to ensure that individuals receive what they need while contributing what they can. Aristotle would suggest a redistribution in proportion to people's claims to benefits to balance the interests. As an Egalitarian, Rawls would want any redistribution to be equal. Nozick would claim that any state-initiated redistribution was unjust.

Task

Remind yourself of Aristotle's theory of distributive justice in the Unit on 'Law and justice'. How could you use this theory to support the decision of the court in **Miller v Jackson** not to award an injunction?

Bentham saw the law as balancing interests to achieve maximum happiness, 'the greatest good'. He influenced the work of **Jhering**. Jhering (1818–1892), another Utilitarian, emphasised the needs of society when balancing interests. He saw law as a form of social engineering, ordering the way society behaved. Whether the law was just was measured by how far it achieved a proper balance in resolving the conflict in society between people's social interests and people's individual interests. Jhering's work was in turn relied on by one of the main writers on the subject of conflicting interests – the American academic lawyer Roscoe Pound.

Roscoe Pound

Roscoe Pound (1870–1964) regarded law as an engineering tool, a form of social control. He studied law's position in society and how it could be used to 'engineer' a balance between the different interests within society. He developed the theory of 'social engineering'. Where interests are in conflict, the law will try to engineer a balance which will achieve social cohesion. The purpose of law is to satisfy as many interests as possible. The maximum number of wants satisfied with the minimum amount of friction and waste. Where interests conflicted they had to be weighed, or balanced, against each other with the aim of satisfying as many as possible. Pound developed Jhering's theory of using the law to achieve a balance, but argued that interests could only be balanced on the same level. Thus, social interests should not be balanced against individual interests, only other social interests, and vice versa. An example would be the recent debate on smoking in public. In Pound's view, the individual interests of those who want a ban (avoiding passive smoking) can be balanced against the interests of those who don't (freedom of choice), as they are on the same level, but not against the wider social interests. Alternatively, the social benefits (lots of tax on cigarettes which helps pay for other social benefits) and burdens (health problems, burden on the NHS) can be balanced against each other, but these shouldn't be balanced against the individual's interests.

Parliament voted for a smoking ban in February 2006 so, in effect, the law is being used to 'engineer' the way society behaves – to stop people smoking. Both social and individual interests were taken into account during the debate. Neither Parliament nor the courts has always followed Pound's theory in so far as balancing interests only on the same level is concerned. However, the idea of the law acting to resolve conflict, and 'engineering' a balance between competing interests, is seen in many areas. You should be able to discuss some of these.

The tools

The 'engineering tools' used to try to balance the interests are:

- the substantive law
- the legal process
- sanctions and remedies

As you look at the examples in each of these, ask yourself the questions at the beginning of this Unit.

The substantive law

Whichever area of law you are studying, you'll find plenty of cases to choose from. Here are a few ideas. I have not included the full facts as these can be found elsewhere.

Crime

The public interest is taken into account when making and applying the law; this is seen particularly clearly in relation to defences. The interests of the individuals involved are also taken into account. Consider the competing interests in the example below.

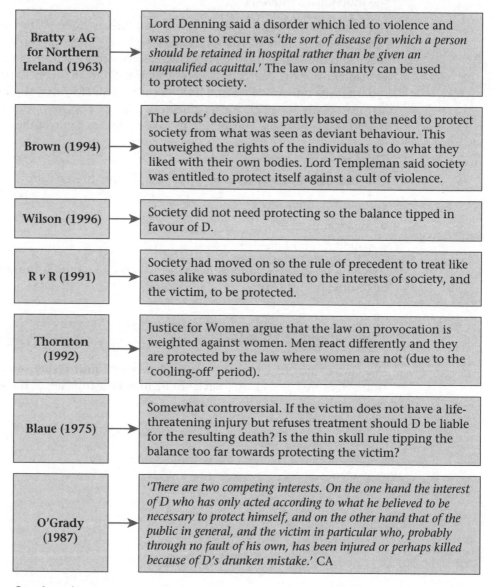

Bratty v AG for Northern Ireland (1963)	Lord Denning said a disorder which led to violence and was prone to recur was *'the sort of disease for which a person should be retained in hospital rather than be given an unqualified acquittal.'* The law on insanity can be used to protect society.
Brown (1994)	The Lords' decision was partly based on the need to protect society from what was seen as deviant behaviour. This outweighed the rights of the individuals to do what they liked with their own bodies. Lord Templeman said society was entitled to protect itself against a cult of violence.
Wilson (1996)	Society did not need protecting so the balance tipped in favour of D.
R v R (1991)	Society had moved on so the rule of precedent to treat like cases alike was subordinated to the interests of society, and the victim, to be protected.
Thornton (1992)	Justice for Women argue that the law on provocation is weighted against women. Men react differently and they are protected by the law where women are not (due to the 'cooling-off' period).
Blaue (1975)	Somewhat controversial. If the victim does not have a life-threatening injury but refuses treatment should D be liable for the resulting death? Is the thin skull rule tipping the balance too far towards protecting the victim?
O'Grady (1987)	*'There are two competing interests. On the one hand the interest of D who has only acted according to what he believed to be necessary to protect himself, and on the other hand that of the public in general, and the victim in particular who, probably through no fault of his own, has been injured or perhaps killed because of D's drunken mistake.'* CA

Contract

Contract law is based on the idea of agreement. In general the courts are reluctant to interfere in order to engineer a balance of interests, preferring to allow the parties freedom to contract as they wish. However, there are times when a person's interests may need protecting, particularly where one party is in a weaker position than the other. Consider the competing interests in the examples that follow on page 467.

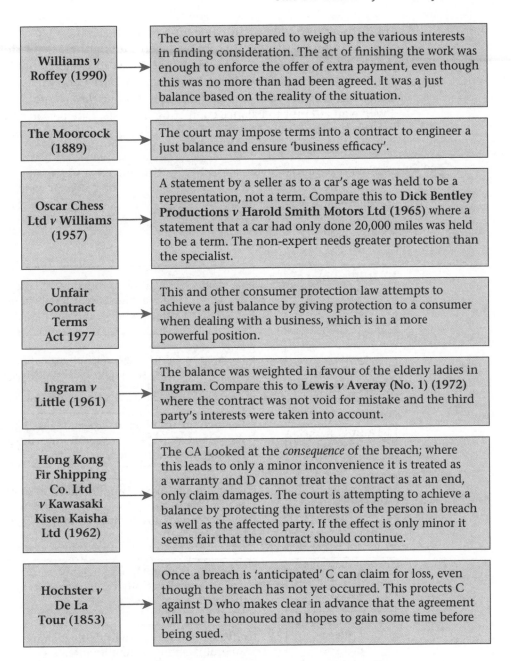

Williams v Roffey (1990)	The court was prepared to weigh up the various interests in finding consideration. The act of finishing the work was enough to enforce the offer of extra payment, even though this was no more than had been agreed. It was a just balance based on the reality of the situation.
The Moorcock (1889)	The court may impose terms into a contract to engineer a just balance and ensure 'business efficacy'.
Oscar Chess Ltd v Williams (1957)	A statement by a seller as to a car's age was held to be a representation, not a term. Compare this to **Dick Bentley Productions v Harold Smith Motors Ltd (1965)** where a statement that a car had only done 20,000 miles was held to be a term. The non-expert needs greater protection than the specialist.
Unfair Contract Terms Act 1977	This and other consumer protection law attempts to achieve a just balance by giving protection to a consumer when dealing with a business, which is in a more powerful position.
Ingram v Little (1961)	The balance was weighted in favour of the elderly ladies in **Ingram**. Compare this to **Lewis v Averay (No. 1) (1972)** where the contract was not void for mistake and the third party's interests were taken into account.
Hong Kong Fir Shipping Co. Ltd v Kawasaki Kisen Kaisha Ltd (1962)	The CA Looked at the *consequence* of the breach; where this leads to only a minor inconvenience it is treated as a warranty and D cannot treat the contract as at an end, only claim damages. The court is attempting to achieve a balance by protecting the interests of the person in breach as well as the affected party. If the effect is only minor it seems fair that the contract should continue.
Hochster v De La Tour (1853)	Once a breach is 'anticipated' C can claim for loss, even though the breach has not yet occurred. This protects C against D who makes clear in advance that the agreement will not be honoured and hopes to gain some time before being sued.

Tort

Tort provides plenty of examples. In **proving a duty of care** in negligence the courts will ask whether it is fair, just and reasonable to impose a duty on policy grounds. This involves balancing the right of C to compensation not only against the cost to D, but also the wider community interests. This is particularly evident in cases involving the police, rescue services, hospitals and schools where compensation would usually come from public funds (i.e. taxpayers). Various factors are balanced against each other when proving **breach of duty**, including any benefit to society. A particularly good area to explore conflicting interests is the tort of **nuisance**. In **Hunter v Canary Wharf (1997)** nuisance was said to involve '*striking a balance between the interests of neighbours*', so all nuisance cases involve an attempt to balance competing interests. One person's freedom can be another's misery. Consider the competing interests in the examples listed below.

Example   I work late in a nightclub and when I get home I want to relax and enjoy some music. This is fine if I live in a detached house miles from anyone, but I live in a terrace with neighbours on either side. My right to play music at 3 a.m. has to be balanced against the neighbours' right to a good night's sleep.

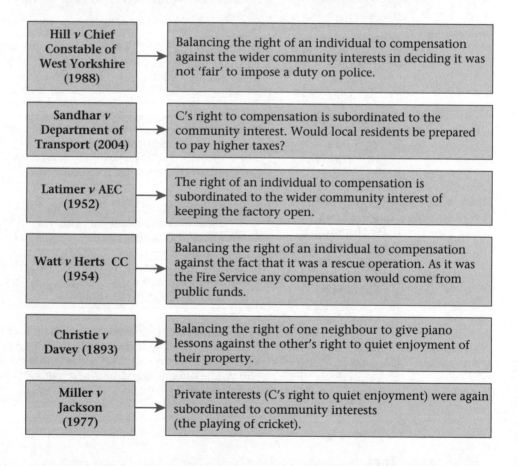

Hill v Chief Constable of West Yorkshire (1988)	Balancing the right of an individual to compensation against the wider community interests in deciding it was not 'fair' to impose a duty on police.
Sandhar v Department of Transport (2004)	C's right to compensation is subordinated to the community interest. Would local residents be prepared to pay higher taxes?
Latimer v AEC (1952)	The right of an individual to compensation is subordinated to the wider community interest of keeping the factory open.
Watt v Herts CC (1954)	Balancing the right of an individual to compensation against the fact that it was a rescue operation. As it was the Fire Service any compensation would come from public funds.
Christie v Davey (1893)	Balancing the right of one neighbour to give piano lessons against the other's right to quiet enjoyment of their property.
Miller v Jackson (1977)	Private interests (C's right to quiet enjoyment) were again subordinated to community interests (the playing of cricket).

Task

Choose a case on your area of study, or use one of my examples. Write a note of the facts and the judgment. Then add a paragraph on how, and whether, you think that the court achieved an appropriate balance between the competing interests.

Food for thought

It can be argued that if a decision is made on the basis of doing right in the particular circumstances, rather than always doing the same regardless of the circumstances, then consistency may be lost. Consider whether the law is achieving justice at the expense of certainty when balancing competing interests.

The legal process

Conflicting interests will be seen at various stages during the law-making process. The government has to balance these when formulating policy. Take, for example, the anti-terrorism laws allowing for custody without charge or trial. The Prime Minister, Tony Blair, said he had to *'weigh the wrong which is being done to a tradition in history of the primacy of law versus the wrong that would be done were any of these terrorist organisations to succeed in their ambitions.'* The Law Society said, *'We recognise the government has a difficult balancing act. But it is essential that emergency terror legislation protects the country without compromising the government's duty to uphold fairness and justice.'* At the next stage, the **Human Rights Act 1998** affects the balance between the potentially conflicting interests of the state and the people. This Act ensures human rights are taken into account when the policy is drafted into a Bill. Also, the Green and White consultation papers allow for different interest groups to be consulted. The resulting law may well reflect their interests. During the process of the Bill becoming an Act, various bodies will be lobbying Members of Parliament to vote in their interests. Finally, judges have to interpret and apply the Act once it becomes law. The **Human Rights Act** has an influence on the balance here too because judges must take human rights into account when interpreting laws. Here are some other examples from the legal process.

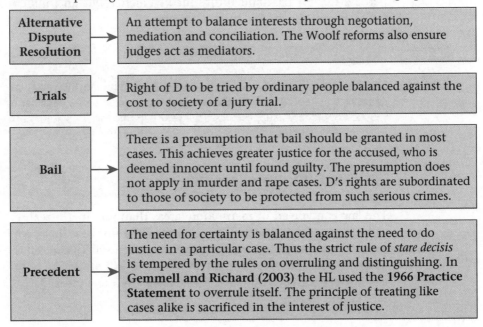

Alternative Dispute Resolution	An attempt to balance interests through negotiation, mediation and conciliation. The Woolf reforms also ensure judges act as mediators.
Trials	Right of D to be tried by ordinary people balanced against the cost to society of a jury trial.
Bail	There is a presumption that bail should be granted in most cases. This achieves greater justice for the accused, who is deemed innocent until found guilty. The presumption does not apply in murder and rape cases. D's rights are subordinated to those of society to be protected from such serious crimes.
Precedent	The need for certainty is balanced against the need to do justice in a particular case. Thus the strict rule of *stare decisis* is tempered by the rules on overruling and distinguishing. In **Gemmell and Richard (2003)** the HL used the **1966 Practice Statement** to overrule itself. The principle of treating like cases alike is sacrificed in the interest of justice.

Sanctions and remedies

These will be relevant when considering *how* a balance is achieved. The public interest is often seen in sentencing (sanctions) policy. When deciding on appropriate remedies the judge will try to engineer what Pound called '*the maximum number of wants with the minimum amount of friction and waste*'.

Sentencing

A deterrent sentence may sacrifice the interests of the particular D to those of society. For example, a custodial sentence may be given where the offence does not really warrant one. It is used to stop reoffending and deter others from offending, thus protecting society. A crime against children or the elderly often leads to a public demand for a harsher sentence; here the community interest may outweigh D's. V's interests are also weighed in the balance, especially now that courts will take into account a Victim Impact Statement, showing the effect of the crime on V.

Remedies

When deciding on appropriate remedies, especially equitable ones, the judge must balance the competing rights of the individual parties in an attempt to find a just solution. The community interest may affect the balance. The law acts as mediator, and the judge will attempt to achieve a compromise which will most satisfy all interests. Look at **Miller *v* Jackson**. The court allowed her claim but refused to grant an injunction to stop the cricket. She received damages to compensate her for past and future inconvenience but an injunction was refused, which meant the cricket could continue.

Task

Choose three procedures. Write down the competing interests involved and how the law engineered a balance between these interests. Now consider which theories of justice would most support this balance. Keep this for revision of both areas.

Current affairs examples

The law is involved in many more areas than you might realise, and the papers carry stories every day that can be used. It is unlikely that people will agree on issues like fox hunting, smoking and whether a school can tell the children what to eat or what not to watch on TV, so there will always be a lot of debate when the law gets involved in such areas. Here are a few ideas. Also see the Units on Morals and Justice.

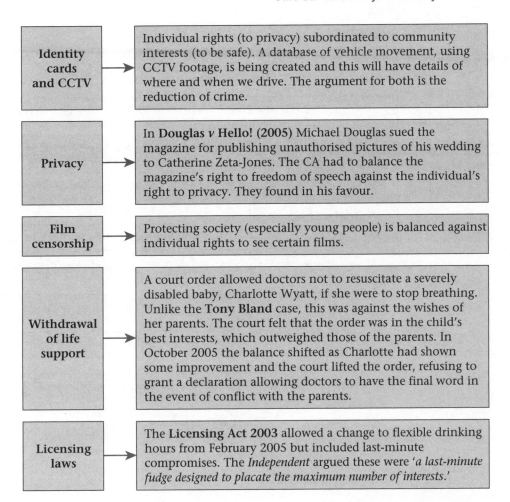

Identity cards and CCTV	Individual rights (to privacy) subordinated to community interests (to be safe). A database of vehicle movement, using CCTV footage, is being created and this will have details of where and when we drive. The argument for both is the reduction of crime.
Privacy	In **Douglas v Hello!** (2005) Michael Douglas sued the magazine for publishing unauthorised pictures of his wedding to Catherine Zeta-Jones. The CA had to balance the magazine's right to freedom of speech against the individual's right to privacy. They found in his favour.
Film censorship	Protecting society (especially young people) is balanced against individual rights to see certain films.
Withdrawal of life support	A court order allowed doctors not to resuscitate a severely disabled baby, Charlotte Wyatt, if she were to stop breathing. Unlike the **Tony Bland** case, this was against the wishes of her parents. The court felt that the order was in the child's best interests, which outweighed those of the parents. In October 2005 the balance shifted as Charlotte had shown some improvement and the court lifted the order, refusing to grant a declaration allowing doctors to have the final word in the event of conflict with the parents.
Licensing laws	The **Licensing Act 2003** allowed a change to flexible drinking hours from February 2005 but included last-minute compromises. The *Independent* argued these were '*a last-minute fudge designed to placate the maximum number of interests.*'

Food for thought

It is not always clear what an appropriate balance *is*. Look at the notes you made for the tasks. Did the laws you chose achieve an appropriate balance? Was justice achieved? For everyone or just one of the people involved? These are difficult issues and it is unlikely the law will always get it right. It is often the case in life that if you try to please everybody you end up pleasing nobody; the law is no different.

Task

Would it be acceptable to torture a suspected bomber to get the location of a bomb which could kill hundreds of people? Apply the Utilitarian theory of justice. Now go on to consider whether it is in the interests of society and whether this outweighs those of the individual? Is society itself degraded by such treatment?

Don't panic, there is no 'right answer' here. Just jot down your thoughts.

Summary

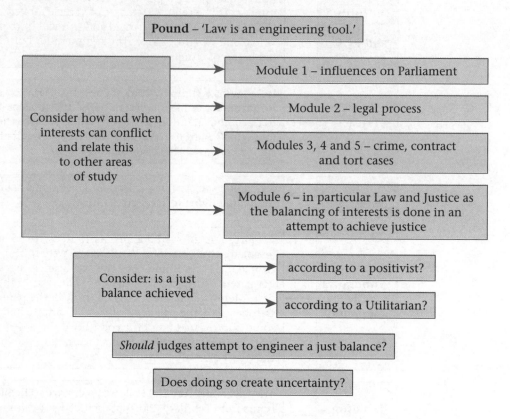

Pound – 'Law is an engineering tool.'

Consider how and when interests can conflict and relate this to other areas of study

Module 1 – influences on Parliament

Module 2 – legal process

Modules 3, 4 and 5 – crime, contract and tort cases

Module 6 – in particular Law and Justice as the balancing of interests is done in an attempt to achieve justice

Consider: is a just balance achieved

according to a positivist?

according to a Utilitarian?

Should judges attempt to engineer a just balance?

Does doing so create uncertainty?

Self-test questions

1 What does Pound mean by saying that law is an engineering tool?

2 Give one example from **either** tort, contract **or** crime **and** one from the legal process where you can explain the competing interests.

3 What effect does the **Human Rights Act** have on court cases?

4 How would a Utilitarian engineer the balance between conflicting interests?

5 What happened in **Miller *v* Jackson**?

For further resources and updates please go to the Companion Website accompanying this book at **www.pearsoned.co.uk/russell**

Fault

Vicarious liability is a species of strict liability . . . an employer who is not personally at fault is made legally answerable for the fault of his employee.

Lord Millett, **Lister v Helsey Hall (2001)**

By the end of this Unit you should be able to:
- Explain the meaning and importance of fault in criminal liability
- Explain the meaning and importance of fault in civil liability
- Evaluate the role of fault and compare this to strict liability in criminal and/or civil law

What is fault?

Fault implies a sense of blameworthiness. If you are accused of doing something you might say, 'But it wasn't my fault'. You will usually mean that you are not to blame for it. The concept of fault is seen in both criminal and civil law. It is particularly important in crime as this requires proof of *mens rea* in most cases, or D will be found not guilty. However, there is also an element of fault in contract and tort, in that both require a breach by D before a court will provide a remedy.

Examination pointer

Although liability is usually based on 'fault', there are exceptions, and any question on fault is likely to want you to discuss not only the concept and its importance, but also whether it is right to impose liability without proof of fault.

We will look at the importance of fault and then at instances of strict liability in the different areas of law.

The importance of fault in criminal law

Fault is very important in criminal cases. Most crimes require *mens rea*, so even if D has carried out a criminal act, there will be no liability unless it happened with *mens rea*. There are different levels of *mens rea*, or fault. Intent is the highest, then subjective recklessness and gross negligence.

Intent is the *mens rea* for murder, theft and some deception offences. The property offences require a high level of fault, not only proof of intent but also dishonesty or deception. In **Madeley**, D was not guilty of theft as he was able to show he was suffering from stress and merely forgot to pay for the goods. However, in the most serious crime, murder, D may be guilty even if there is only intent to seriously injure – **DPP *v* Smith (1960)**.

Subjective recklessness involves finding that D recognised the risk of the consequence, but went ahead anyway. Thus, in **Cunningham** the prosecution failed to prove that D was aware his actions might cause harm, so he was not guilty.

At one time there was also objective recklessness. When the HL, in **Gemmell and Richards**, overruled **Caldwell** and abolished objective recklessness, they recognised the injustice of finding D guilty where there was no real fault, i.e. where D did not recognise a risk of the consequence. **Elliott** is an example of this injustice.

Gross negligence is the fault element for manslaughter. Whether D's conduct was sufficiently grossly negligent for criminal (rather than civil) liability is for the jury to decide. This was stated in **Adomako** and confirmed in **Misra**. This may be difficult, and different juries may come to different decisions on how much 'fault' D has shown. Problems also arise in corporate manslaughter cases due to the difficulty in finding the '*controlling mind*'. It is hard to prove *mens rea* in respect of a company. Also, an employee could be guilty when it is really the company that is at fault.

> **Example** A company employs a train driver and insists the driver works for long hours without a break. An accident is caused because the driver is tired, and he is charged with manslaughter. Who is really at fault, the driver or the company?

Although *mens rea* is the main fault element in criminal law, *actus reus* also relates to fault. The rule is that D's actions must be voluntary, thus there was no conviction in **Leicester *v* Pearson** because D was pushed on to the crossing by another car.

Food for thought

State of affairs crimes such as **Winzar** mean D can be liable without being at fault, or even acting voluntarily. This seems unfair. Similarly, there can be a duty to act in some circumstances, so that D can be liable for *failing* to do something. Use case examples on omissions to discuss how far D should be liable in such cases. For example, in **Pittwood** the gatekeeper failed to close the gate and was guilty of manslaughter. Should you be liable for forgetfulness? Arguably yes, if the result of your forgetfulness can have serious results, but *mens rea* is what is intended or foreseen, and not usually a matter of hindsight.

Causation also has a connection with fault. Although part of the *actus reus*, not the *mens rea*, there will be no liability if D did not cause the result. Thus, for example, if the victim or a third party does something that breaks the chain of causation there is no liability. D may be at fault in respect of a lesser crime, but not the one that resulted. This is often seen in unlawful act manslaughter where, for example, D is committing a burglary or an assault and death results. In **Watson**, D was not guilty of manslaughter as it could not be proved that the act of burglary caused the heart attack. The burglary was D's 'fault', but not the death.

Task

Using three cases you know, explain the fault element and how this affected whether or not D was found guilty of an offence.

The fault element can be removed or mitigated by the defences. Defences such as diminished responsibility and insanity show a reduced level of fault in that D is not fully responsible. Automatism shows no fault at all as D has no control over the act committed. This total lack of fault is reflected in the result. A successful plea of automatism means an acquittal. Duress and self-defence show a reduced level of fault, although they *excuse* rather than remove it, as you are not saying *'I did it but it wasn't my fault'* but *'I did it but had good reason to do so'*. Intoxication may remove fault if D is *involuntarily* intoxicated and can't form an intent. Voluntary intoxication reduces the level of fault if the *mens rea* is intent, but won't succeed if it includes recklessness, because D is seen to be reckless, and thus at fault, in getting drunk (**Majewski**).

The **Homicide Act** defences recognise that D is not fully blameworthy in some circumstances. They reduce murder to manslaughter, thus allowing the judge to take into account the fault element when sentencing. Which brings us to the last point.

At the final stage of a criminal case the sentence given will reflect the level of fault. Mitigating and aggravating factors are also taken into account. One problem is the mandatory life sentence for murder, which means the judge cannot take into account any lack of moral fault, e.g. in euthanasia cases.

Food for thought

- Should intent to commit serious harm be enough for murder?
- How much real fault is there in cases involving omissions?
- The degree of fault in murder cases may be very different, but the result is the same – a life sentence. Compare the level of fault in a vicious murder to that in euthanasia cases.
- Unlawful act manslaughter only requires that D has *mens rea* for the act, not for the death. This seems a lower level of fault than such a serious crime warrants.

There are some crimes that do not require *mens rea* in any form. Liability without fault is called *strict* liability. You studied this in Module 3. You may have to consider how far someone *should* be criminally liable without proof of fault, and as always there are arguments on both sides. A quick recap.

Liability without fault in criminal law

Strict liability often applies to regulatory offences, i.e. offences that are not truly criminal in nature, such as traffic offences. Also offences covering areas of social concern or public health, such as the sale of food and alcohol, pollution and protection of the environment, are often strict liability offences.

Example

In **Meah v Roberts (1977)** two children were served lemonade which had caustic soda in it. D was not responsible for it being there, but was found guilty under the **Food and Drug Act 1955**, even though not at fault herself.

In **Harrow LBC v Shah (1999)** it was held that the offence of selling a lottery ticket to a person under 16 was one of strict liability. In 'real' crimes there is more controversy, as seen in **Sweet v Parsley (1970)**. A woman let rooms to students and the police raided the premises and found cannabis. She was charged with being *'concerned in the management of premises used for the purpose of smoking cannabis'* under the **Dangerous Drugs Act 1965**. She was found guilty even though not at fault – she was completely unaware of the cannabis smoking. The HL eventually acquitted her and established the rule that strict liability could only be imposed where the Act specifically made the offence one of strict liability. In all other cases a need for *mens rea* would be presumed. In **B v DPP (2000)** the HL reversed a conviction of inciting a child of 14 to indecency on the basis of this principle, saying it was particularly strong in serious offences, D having argued he was not at fault as he believed the child was older.

Should there be liability without fault in criminal cases?

Although there are several arguments for strict liability, the arguments against are convincing.

Arguments against:

- It is unfair to convict D of a criminal offence if not at fault.
- It leads to the punishment of people who have taken all possible precautions.
- It also means such people have a criminal record.
- Imposing a requirement of negligence would be fairer to D, but is a low level of fault so would still protect the public.

Arguments for:

- It makes people more careful.
- It protects the public.
- Most such offences are minor and carry no social stigma.

- Proving *mens rea* is hard in many minor offences, e.g. trying to prove someone *knew* they had parked on a yellow line in the snow, so time and money is saved.
- The judge can address the issue of fault when sentencing.

Examination pointer

Use cases you are familiar with from whatever area of law you have studied to illustrate an answer. Some of the ideas here could also be considered in a discussion of law and justice so make a note of those where you feel justice has not been achieved.

The importance of fault in civil law

Fault is also an element of many areas of civil law. It is seen in contract but is particularly important in tort. The word negligence itself implies someone is at fault.

Contract law

Fault is, perhaps, less important in contract cases. The fact of breach is enough and there is no need, for example, to prove negligence. However, the party in breach is seen as the one at fault, and so damages are awarded to the other party. Any breach cases can be used to illustrate the concept.

Task

Look at the Unit on breach and find three cases. Note the element of fault and how far this was reflected in the remedy.

Misrepresentation usually relies on proving fraud or negligence. Fraud is a higher level of fault. In **Derry *v* Peek (1889)** it was described as where a false statement was made *knowingly*, without belief in its truth, or *recklessly*, careless as to whether it is true or false. Negligence is lower in that a statement is honestly made, as in **Howard Marine and Dredging Ltd**, but D was at fault, or negligent, in not checking the information.

Food for thought

Since the **Misrepresentation** Act an action for innocent misrepresentation is possible. Here there is no fault. Do you think this is fair to D?

Mistake cases often involve fraud. These can lead to injustice as the wronged party often has no remedy, even though there is a high degree of fault, because there is a third party involved, as in **Phillips *v* Brooks**.

The law on frustration reflects the fact that where parties to a contract are *not* at fault in ending it, neither can enforce it. In **Davis Contractors** Lord Radcliffe said, '*frustration occurs whenever the law recognises that, without default of either party, a contractual obligation has become incapable of being performed*'. So only where neither party could foresee an event can that event frustrate a contract, if one party could foresee it, or is at fault, the contract will not be frustrated, e.g. **Super Servant II**.

The rules on '*non est factum*' mean that if C is at fault, or negligent, when signing a document, they will not be able to claim.

Contract remedies will reflect the degree of fault by the party in breach. Damages are only awarded for foreseeable loss, as established in **Hadley**. Also, rescission is a discretionary remedy, and will not be awarded to a party that is at fault.

Tort law

Tort is usually based on proving D has been negligent, i.e. has breached a duty at common law or under the **Occupier's Liability Act**, or has interfered unreasonably with someone's enjoyment (nuisance). In other words, D is *at fault*.

You can use any breach of duty cases to discuss the importance of proving fault. Note that D is judged by the standard expected of the reasonable person, not D's own standards. However, it is recognised that in the case of children age is relevant and they should have a higher degree of fault before being found negligent, as in **Mullin v Richards**. Discuss the factors the courts consider when deciding if the standard has been reached, e.g. if there is only a low risk of something happening and precautions have been taken to avoid the risk, D is less likely to be found at fault, as in **Bolton v Stone**.

Food for thought

In **Nettleship v Weston** it was said that a learner driver should show the skill of an ordinary, competent driver. Do you think a learner driver is showing the same degree of fault as an experienced 'competent driver' would be when driving negligently?

Task

Look at the Unit on breach of duty and find three cases. Note the element of fault and how it affected liability.

In nuisance cases it must be shown that D's act was unreasonable. This is a lesser degree of fault than negligence. In **Adams v Ursell** smells from D's fish and chip shop were unreasonable even though he was providing a service, and arguably not doing anything wrong. A higher level of fault was seen in **Christie v Davey**. D was liable in nuisance because his behaviour was malicious and more clearly unreasonable.

Although we saw it in tort, public nuisance is also a crime and so requires *mens rea*. This was confirmed in **Goldstein**, so D was not guilty as he did not *know* that his joke would cause such problems.

Tort defences may be used to argue either a total lack of fault, or reduced fault.

Example | You come home very late one night and are told you cannot go out in the evening for a week as a punishment. The reason you are late is that a bolt of lightning hit the bus you were in, causing severe delays. You would argue that this was an act of God, so you should not be punished.

This special defence of act of God shows that if D is not at fault in any way, there is no liability. It not only applies in nuisance, but also in **Rylands**, which is a tort of strict liability. Thus liability may be strict, but is not absolute. Other defences recognise that D may not have been solely at fault. In contributory negligence, damages are reduced to reflect the amount that C is at fault, as in **Gannon v Rotherham MBC**.

Remedies are intended to compensate C rather than punish D, so do not necessarily reflect the degree of fault, just the amount of damage. However, D is only liable for *foreseeable* damage, as per **The Wagon Mound**, so fault is relevant here. The more foreseeable something is, the more at fault you are for not avoiding it.

Liability without fault in civil law

We'll take a look at some examples of 'no-fault' liability in contract and tort, and then consider how far liability without fault *should* be imposed.

Contract

The rules on revocation and acceptance mean a contract can be formed unknowingly and so can be breached without any fault. In particular the postal rule can be discussed. Acceptance by post is complete as soon as it is posted even if it doesn't arrive, as confirmed in **Household Insurance v Grant**. This means the other may believe that the offer has not been accepted.

Example | Geoff offers to sell his car to Paul. Paul writes to accept but Geoff doesn't get the letter. Thinking Paul doesn't want the car Geoff revokes his offer, and sells it to someone else. Paul can sue for breach of contract, but it can hardly be said that Geoff is at fault. The argument for this rule is that Geoff could exclude it by saying that acceptance must be in a particular form, or must reach him.

The implied terms under the **Sale of Goods Act** impose liability without fault. Thus, in **Godley v Perry** the seller could be sued for the catapult not being of satisfactory quality, even though not personally at fault. On the other hand, **s. 14** will not apply if the defects were brought to the buyer's attention, or the goods were examined and the defect should have been noticed. This recognises that if C is at fault, D should not be liable.

Innominate terms look at the effect of the breach on C, rather than the degree of fault by D. This means that whatever the level of fault, if the consequences are serious C can rescind the contract as well as claim damages.

Tort

The main area of strict liability in tort is **Rylands *v* Fletcher**. There is no need to prove fault, i.e. C need not prove negligence, merely that something has escaped and caused damage. However, a small degree of fault has entered the law here. Although liability is strict in that if damage *is* foreseeable then D is liable regardless of the amount of care taken, in **Cambridge Water Co.** the HL added that if the damage is *not* foreseeable, D will avoid liability.

The other area of strict liability in tort is vicarious liability. As seen in the opening quote, it is not necessary to prove an employer is at fault in any way. In fact, if the employer *is* at fault there will be primary, rather than vicarious liability. Fault is still an important element, as C must prove the negligence (breach) by the employee; however, it is the employer who is sued, not the person at fault. This applies even to acts which seem well outside the scope of employment, such as sexual activities, as seen in **Lister**.

Should there be liability without fault in civil law?

So why do the courts impose liability on someone who appears blameless? There is little controversy in contract law on this issue (there had been in cases where the contract was impossible to perform, until the courts created the doctrine of frustration in **Taylor *v* Caldwell**), but how far fault should be proved in tort cases has been discussed at length. The question was the subject of the **Pearson Commission Report** in 1978, and this is a good base for a discussion of the idea of fault-based liability as opposed to strict liability.

The Commission was set up because it was recognised that there are many problems for people who have suffered damage. Fault can be hard to prove and many victims are left without compensation for their injuries. One of the main arguments for the introduction of a no-fault compensation scheme is that the tort system is too irrational in providing different levels of remedy for the same type of accident, and sometimes no remedy at all.

For all its faults, the Commission felt the tort system should be retained, but supplemented by a more widespread system of social security, e.g. a no-fault compensation scheme was suggested whereby road accident victims could be compensated from a fund administered by the state and funded by about a penny on a gallon of petrol. Tort would remain as an alternative. The Commission also recommended a no-fault scheme for product liability, ultra-hazardous activities and authorised vaccines. The first is now covered by the **Consumer Protection Act** and the last by the **Vaccine Damage Payments Act 1979**, but the recommendation that strict liability should be imposed on 'ultra-hazardous' activities was not implemented – although there are one or two Acts dealing with particular areas such as oil pollution and nuclear installations. Such activities are partly covered by the rule in **Rylands *v* Fletcher**, but many would prefer them to be governed by statute, as **Rylands** is seen as unpredictable. In **Cambridge Water** and **Transco**, the HL, although declining to abolish the rule, also declined to extend the scope of strict liability further, indicating that it was for Parliament to legislate. Legislation would be able to provide that insurance is compulsory for people dealing in dangerous materials or activities.

There was some expectation that a no-fault scheme for medical accidents would be put forward but only a further investigation of the no-fault system operating in New Zealand was suggested, and nothing was done in this area. The problems continued to be the subject of much debate. The **NHS Redress Bill**, published in October 2005, may help. This will allow for compensation up to £20,000 to be paid without the need for a court action, although the right to sue will still be available. The Health minister said, '*We need to move away from the current way of responding to clinical negligence, which is characterised by variations in outcome, long and complicated processes and legal costs that often exceed the amount paid out.*' The Bill will put the emphasis on getting it right rather than apportioning blame. Staff will be encouraged to report errors and mistakes so there will be less confrontation. It is expected to come into force in 2007/8.

Arguments for a no-fault system

- Everyone is compensated.
- Insurance is available to protect D.
- It makes people careful.
- The benefit to society of many hazardous activities (e.g. in industry or medicine) means society, not the individual, should bear the cost.
- It limits the number of court cases, so courts are not overloaded.
- The fault system can be unfair as sometimes C is fully compensated but sometimes gets nothing.
- Proving fault is time-consuming and costly.
- The adversarial nature of court proceedings means it may make a relationship worse, e.g. in employment cases.

Arguments for a fault system

- The wrongdoer pays.
- C is fully compensated.
- A no-fault system may not make D more careful.
- 'No win, no fee' helps C to claim without the worry of solicitor's fees.

Task

You will need to develop these arguments so pick a few that make sense and expand on them. If possible use a case to illustrate.

Examination pointer

Whatever area you are studying be sure to relate your cases to the specific question. You will need to do more than explain fault and/or strict liability. Consider how important fault is in proving liability. Use cases to support what you say, perhaps some where you feel the outcome was unjust because D had a low level of fault.

Summary

Note the importance of fault in proving liability and the cases where no fault is required.

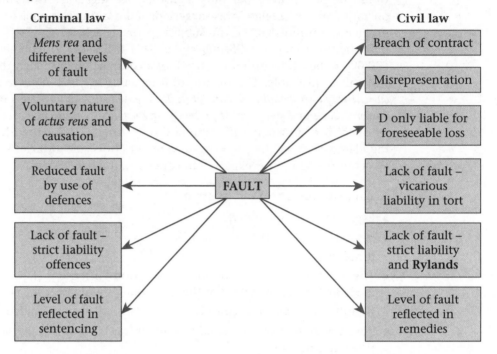

Criminal law

- *Mens rea* and different levels of fault
- Voluntary nature of *actus reus* and causation
- Reduced fault by use of defences
- Lack of fault – strict liability offences
- Level of fault reflected in sentencing

FAULT

Civil law

- Breach of contract
- Misrepresentation
- D only liable for foreseeable loss
- Lack of fault – vicarious liability in tort
- Lack of fault – strict liability and **Rylands**
- Level of fault reflected in remedies

 Self-test questions

1 Explain how fault is proved in either civil or criminal law.

2 How may a defence reflect the degree of fault involved?

3 Explain two cases where there was no liability because fault could not be proved.

4 Use two cases to support an argument for imposing/not imposing strict liability.

5 How did **Cambridge Water** add a degree of fault to the strict liability rule under Rylands?

For further resources and updates please go to the Companion Website accompanying this book at **www.pearsoned.co.uk/russell**

Judicial creativity

A live system of law will always have regard to changing circumstances.

Lord Keith, **R v R (1991)**

By the end of this Unit you should be able to:

- Explain how and whether judges may be creative when applying the rules of precedent
- Explain how and whether judges may be creative when interpreting statutes
- Identify some of the arguments on how far judges do and should make or develop the law, giving case examples

When reading this Unit keep the following issues in mind. There are several questions, and answers, even in respected academic circles, will differ.

- Do judges make law?
- How do judges make law?
- Should judges make law?
- What is the balance between the roles of Parliament and the courts in making law?

Do judges make law?

Whether developing case law or interpreting statutes, judges have a certain amount of discretion. Arguably this is 'making' law, but opinions differ.

We have met Hart before. Hart would accept judges make new law and that this is necessary where there are no existing rules to cover the situation. Another academic, with whom Hart had much debate, is Dworkin. He says judges don't make law but *find* it by using existing legal principles and applying these to different situations.

Example   Hart could see **Donoghue v Stevenson** as *making* a new law (that a manufacturer is liable to the consumer for defective products), which filled in the gap in the existing law. Dworkin could see it as *finding* an existing principle (that people had a duty not to harm others), and extending this to a new situation. There is a fine line and no right answer. You must make up your own mind.

Not only academics, but also judges themselves differ on the issue. Here are a few quotes.

In the **Times Law Awards** ceremony 1997, Lord Mackay (the then Lord Chancellor) said, '*The duty of the judge is to apply the law as he finds it, not to seek to rectify perceived inadequacies by the use of creative interpretation*'. He also said where there is a gap in the law judges are required to take account of precedent but '*where this is unclear he must decide the best way to proceed and the result may be a decision which is in some way innovative . . . but the fundamental principles were always part of the law*'. Thus, he believes (along with Dworkin) that judges find law by applying already existing principles.

Similarly, Lord Diplock in **Dupont Steels Ltd *v* Sirs (1980)** said, '*Parliament makes the laws, the judiciary interpret them*'.

Lord Denning would side with Hart; in **Re Sigsworth** he said, '*we fill in the gaps*'.

Austin (a pupil of Jeremy Bentham, see p. 456) was also clearly in favour of judicial law-making. He said, '*I cannot understand how any person can suppose . . . that society could have gone on if judges had not legislated.*'

Examination pointer

So, opinions differ on whether judges 'make' or 'find' law. You can offer your own, as long as you back it up with cases and examples. Look carefully at the question as you could be asked whether judges should make law. Opinions differ on this question too. We'll take a look after seeing how they may be creative. Reading case reports is a good idea, as you will see how the judges discussed these issues.

How do judges make law?

Both case law and the rules of precedent, and statute law and the rules on **statutory interpretation**, involve a certain amount of discretion. The greater the discretion, the more arguable it is that judges are making law.

Some cases involve *both* precedent and statutory interpretation, so the examples are after both sets of rules.

Task

Look back at Module 1 and look up precedent and interpretation of statute in the Glossary. Draw a diagram showing the main rules of precedent and how these may be avoided. Then add the different approaches to interpretation, with a case on each. Keep this as a base on which to build some ideas about how far judges are being creative - or not - and to refer to as you read this Unit.

OK, got your diagram handy? Let's take a look at how these rules may allow creativity.

Creativity and the rules of precedent

Although the strict rule of precedent is *stare decisis*, or follow what went before and treat like cases alike, there are many ways to avoid it which allow for creativity. Overruling earlier cases by a higher court or use of the **1966 Practice Statement** by the HL are obvious examples you can use to support a 'creativity' argument. The **Practice Statement** allows the HL to overrule its own earlier decisions if '*it appears right to do so*'. This gives a wide discretion and allows an old law to be changed and a new one created. The **Young** rules allow the CA to overrule its own earlier decisions in certain circumstances, but these are limited so allow little real creativity. Lord Denning wanted the use of the **Practice Statement** to extend to the CA, but he was criticised by many other judges for this view. Distinguishing can also be creative. A case may be distinguished where material facts are different, and which facts are material may depend on the judge's view. Professor Goodhard said, '*It is by his choice of material facts that the judge creates law*'. Finally, the *ratio decidendi* can be difficult to find, especially if the judgment is complex or the reasoning obscure. In the appellate courts' decisions are based on the majority view, so there are several judgments and the reasons for the decision may differ. Judges may agree what the decision *is* but not *why*, thus producing conflicting *ratios*. This allows the later judge to choose which to follow. In **Brown** it can be argued the *ratio* was either that a person cannot consent to **serious harm** or that a person cannot consent to **intentional** harm.

Creativity and statutory interpretation

The **literal rule** means the words of an Act are followed strictly, so cases where this is used can support an argument that judges are *not* creative. The **golden rule** only applies if the **literal rule** leads to absurdity, so allows little creativity. The **purposive approach** (developing the **mischief rule**) is more creative. This looks at the intention of Parliament and why it passed the Act in the first place. Although this appears to uphold parliamentary sovereignty and the 'finding' law view, it is arguable that judges are putting their own values on what they think Parliament intended. This is particularly true when interpreting an old Act. How can a judge know what Members of Parliament were thinking, for example, when the **Offences Against the Person Act 1861** was passed nearly 150 years ago? It is difficult even though judges are now allowed to consult Hansard, which reports the debates in Parliament during the passing of the Act. The more purposive approach, favoured by judges like Lord Denning, is an extension of the mischief rule and can mitigate the harshness of the literal rule. In **Pepper *v* Hart** Lord Griffiths said, '*the days have long passed when the courts adopted a strict constructionist view of interpretation*' and preferred the purposive approach, which seeks to give effect to the purpose of legislation. The case was itself creative, allowing, for the first time, the use of Hansard to find that purpose. The purposive approach was seen in **Quintavalle** (see p. 449) where the statute was interpreted to allow for tissue typing.

Examination pointer

You can answer a question on creativity by reference to precedent or statutory interpretation, or both. Read the question carefully to make sure you are not being directed to one or the other, though. Also note that at this level you need to discuss both the rules and the ways to avoid them, using cases and quotes to relate your discussion to the specific question.

Judges must now consider the **Human Rights Act** when interpreting statutes and this could lead to a more creative decision where the previous law infringed someone's rights, as in **Douglas *v* Hello**! which arguably created a privacy law.

Task

Before going on, make a note of three cases where you feel the judges have been creative (or not) in using the rules outlined above.

Here are a few examples. I am sure you'll think of plenty more.

Crime

- **Brown** on sadomasochism is arguably creative. The question was whether consensual injuries could amount to a crime under the **Offences Against the Person Act** or common law. The **Act** did not deal with consent, and at common law cases conflicted on whether it was a defence to serious injuries. This decision distinguishes earlier cases based on the amount of harm that occurred. However, even the judges themselves were unclear on the reason for their decisions. The case was decided on a 3–2 majority. Lord Slynn thought the precedents cited were not conclusive and said it is '*a matter of policy for the legislature to decide*'. Lord Mustill also thought it was a matter for Parliament. He said if the level of harm amounted to assault regardless of consent then deciding whether private sexual activities should be exempt was '*a task which the courts are not suited to perform*'. The other three judges thought the courts *should* intervene to protect society as a whole, Lord Templeman saying that pleasure derived from pain was evil.

- In **R *v* R** the HL used the Practice Statement and held that a man could be guilty of raping his wife. Until this case it was not rape, as a wife was deemed to consent to intercourse by marrying.

- In **Gemmell and Richards** the HL used the Practice Statement to overrule the decision in **Caldwell** and made a new rule that all recklessness is now subjective.

- **Camplin** overruled **Bedder** when interpreting the **Homicide Act** and set a precedent. **Smith** was creative but shows judges are divided, and in **Holley** the Privy Council rejected **Smith**. Although Privy Council decisions are not *strictly binding*, as they are made by Law Lords this decision is highly *persuasive*. The desire for Parliament to produce a clearer test for provocation is apparent in the judgments, showing a reluctance for further judicial development.

Contract

There is perhaps less creativity in contract, as judges are reluctant to intervene in the rights of people to be free to make their own contracts. This is one of the reasons there are so many old cases in contract; they have remained undisturbed over the years. However, there are still many examples to be found.

- **Taylor *v* Caldwell** set a precedent in establishing the doctrine of frustration.
- **Adams *v* Linsell** established the postal rule (though many argue it is time the judges got creative again and abolished it!).
- **Merritt** distinguished **Balfour** on the presumption that in social arrangements the parties do not intend to be legally bound.
- **Williams *v* Roffey** distinguished earlier cases such as **Stilk** so that consideration could be 'found' even though there was little evidence of it.
- **The Moorcock** introduced the idea that courts could intervene in order to give 'business efficacy' to contracts.
- **Solle *v* Butcher** created the rule which allowed equity to provide a remedy for mistake even though the contract was not void at common law. The CA in **Great Peace** rejected this and said it was for Parliament to amend the law.
- **Fisher *v* Bell** could be used to show how *lack* of creativity on the part of judges can lead to an Act being ineffective. Use of the purposive approach could have resulted in a conviction.
- Also in **Dunnachie *v* Hull CC (2004)** the HL followed **Addis *v* Gramophone Co. Ltd** and refused to allow damages for non-pecuniary loss, such as hurt feelings, in unfair dismissal cases.

Tort

- As we discussed earlier, **Donoghue** set a precedent but it could be argued that the principle of not harming others already existed.
- In **McLoughlin *v* O'Brien** the law on nervous shock was developed by the HL, but in **Alcock** Lord Oliver indicated that further developments should be left to Parliament.
- **BRB *v* Herrington** was an early use of the Practice Statement by the HL which overruled the case of **Addie *v* Dumbreck** and allowed child trespassers to sue an occupier in negligence. This then led to the passing of the **Occupier's Liability Act 1984**, showing that the courts can also persuade Parliament to create law.
- In **Goldstein** and **Rimmington (2005)**, on public nuisance, Lord Bingham said, '*the courts have no power to create new offences, so they have no power to abolish existing offences. That is a task for Parliament*'.
- **Rylands *v* Fletcher** was introduced by analogy with the law on damage by fire and animals, so although apparently creating a new law, it was arguably only extending existing principles to other 'dangerous' things.
- You can use **Cambridge Water** to highlight judicial reluctance in developing the law in this area. Lord Goff said, '*it is more appropriate for strict liability in*

respect of operations of high risk to be imposed by Parliament than by the courts'. **Transco** also shows such reluctance.

● In **Lister** the HL overruled **Trotman** on vicarious liability for the sexual acts of an employee. Is this too creative?

When looking at the examples think about whether judges *should* be creative, and the different roles of Parliament and the courts. Let's look at these.

Should judges make law?

The main argument for judges being creative is that rules are rarely absolute. They cannot provide for all that the future may bring. Hart says because rules are indeterminate, i.e. they have an 'open texture', judges must 'fill in the gaps', a point Lord Denning has made several times. If a new situation arises, such as text-messaging scams or Internet abuse, a judge has to decide the matter and can hardly say 'the rules have run out so I can't make a judgment'. The judge uses the tools available, the rules on precedent and interpretation, to come to a decision. Again, opinions differ and the idea of 'filling in the gaps' is restricted. Lord Diplock, in **Duport Steels Ltd v Sirs (1980)**, argues that this approach can only be used if there is ambiguity in the law, i.e. if the literal rule can't be used. As we saw, Lord Mackay said the duty of the judge is *'to apply the law as he finds it, not to seek to rectify perceived inadequacies by the use of creative interpretation'.*

Not only does technology change, so do social values. For example, in **R v R** it was felt no longer acceptable to allow marital immunity against a charge of rape. Lord Keith made the opening comment. However, he agreed with Lord Lane's comment in the CA that *'This is not the creation of a new offence, it is the removal of a common law fiction which has become anachronistic and offensive'.* An argument against judges being creative is that the law should not be used to enforce morality. Again, in **Brown**, some judges seemed to base their decision on what was morally right. Arguably, this is not a good basis for finding criminal behaviour, and it is for Parliament to decide on such matters.

Food for thought

Should society lead and the law follow or the other way round? For example, in relation to homosexuality and prostitution, as society changes and becomes more tolerant the law is eventually changed to reflect this. It can be argued this should be left to Parliament but, as we have seen, enacting law is a lengthy process and the courts can develop the common law to meet changing conditions quicker. Developing technology leads to new problems; case law responds to such changes as they occur.

A strong argument against creativity is that if a judge makes law it applies retrospectively, at least to the parties in court. In both **Brown** and **R v R** it would be difficult to find a law stating the behaviour was a crime at the time D acted. That someone can be guilty of a crime which appears not to have existed at the time it was committed is arguably unjust. When Parliament makes a law it only applies to the future, i.e. it is forbidden to do this *from now on*. This brings us to the differing roles of Parliament and the courts.

The balance between the roles of Parliament and the courts

Parliament is elected. Members of Parliament are our representatives and so can be said to make laws on our behalf, to protect society as a whole. Most people accept Parliament's *right* to make law, even if not agreeing with a particular law. Judges are not elected and people may find it harder to accept their role in law-making, especially if this involves a matter of policy. In **McLoughlin *v* O'Brien**, Lord Scarman said, '*the objective of judges is the formulation of principles, policy is the prerogative of Parliament*'. He felt any creativity had to be based on legal principle and not policy. Policy is concerned with what is right for society as a whole, a collective goal. The government formulates a policy, e.g. to ban smoking in public, produces a Bill aimed at fulfilling that policy, and puts it before Parliament for debating and voting on. Many think policy should *only* be a matter for government and Parliament. However, judges are clearly involved in policy decisions and often take the wider community interests into account, e.g. **Hill *v* CC of West Yorkshire** and the 'fair, just and reasonable' issue in relation to proving a duty of care.

Food for thought

There are sound arguments on both sides. The need for certainty and consistency supports always following the letter of the law, using the strict rule of precedent and the literal rule where possible. However, justice in a particular case may indicate a need to be creative. As will changing technology and social values. One problem is that in precedent the later judge finds the *ratio* and decides which facts are material, and in statutory interpretation the judge chooses which rule to use. This means different judges may come to different decisions on the same set of facts.

The fact that judges are not elected and Parliament is supreme supports the view that it is not the job of a judge to make law. This may be why judges often try to give the appearance of 'finding' law, even when it can be said that they are 'making' it. Some explicitly recognise it is not their job, as we saw by Lord Goff's comment in **Cambridge Water**.

Task

Read through the different opinions and draw up a list of arguments for and against creativity, using the quotes. This will help you produce your own argument and can be referred to for essay material.

Summary

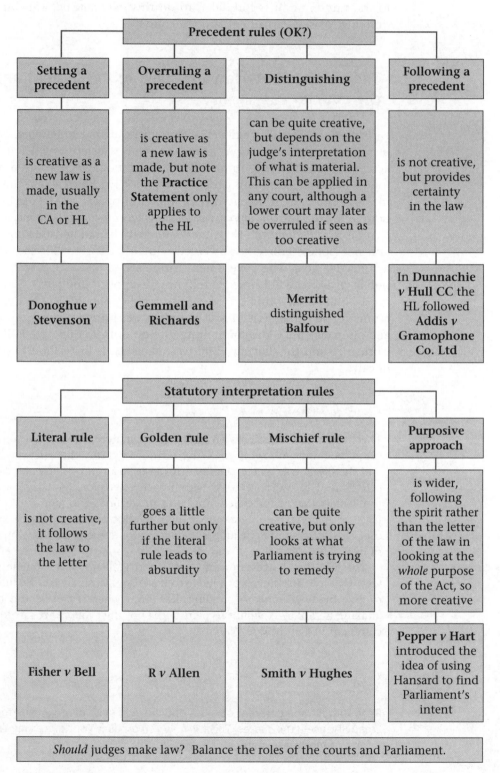

Precedent rules (OK?)			
Setting a precedent	**Overruling a precedent**	**Distinguishing**	**Following a precedent**
is creative as a new law is made, usually in the CA or HL	is creative as a new law is made, but note the **Practice Statement** only applies to the HL	can be quite creative, but depends on the judge's interpretation of what is material. This can be applied in any court, although a lower court may later be overruled if seen as too creative	is not creative, but provides certainty in the law
Donoghue v Stevenson	**Gemmell and Richards**	**Merritt** distinguished **Balfour**	In **Dunnachie v Hull CC** the HL followed **Addis v Gramophone Co. Ltd**

Statutory interpretation rules			
Literal rule	**Golden rule**	**Mischief rule**	**Purposive approach**
is not creative, it follows the law to the letter	goes a little further but only if the literal rule leads to absurdity	can be quite creative, but only looks at what Parliament is trying to remedy	is wider, following the spirit rather than the letter of the law in looking at the *whole* purpose of the Act, so more creative
Fisher v Bell	**R v Allen**	**Smith v Hughes**	**Pepper v Hart** introduced the idea of using Hansard to find Parliament's intent

Should judges make law? Balance the roles of the courts and Parliament.

Self-test questions

1 Why might a judge need to be creative?

2 Give two arguments against judicial creativity.

3 Why does Hart say judges must 'fill in the gaps'?

4 Who else said this?

5 Who argues that judges are merely applying existing principles and not making law?

 For further resources and updates please go to the Companion Website accompanying this book at **www.pearsoned.co.uk/russell**

This shows the overlap between the concepts. For a summary of each refer to the individual Unit summaries.

A criminal example of the overlap

Should the law be used to enforce morality? Students *ought* to do their homework but there is no enforceable law that says they *must*. People *ought* not to hurt each other but should there be a law that says they *must* not do so even consensually?	**Morals** *Ought and must*			**Creativity** *Hart and Dworkin*	Is this a new law (that there can be no consent to intentional harm) or was it based on existing principles (do not harm others)?

R *v* Brown (1994)

Justice *Utilitarianism and Natural Law*	**Conflicting interests** *Has an appropriate balance been achieved? Policy arguments*	**Fault** *Mens rea and defences*
Was justice done? Is the greatest good achieved by making such activities illegal? (Utilitarianism) Is there a higher law that requires people not to harm each other? (Natural Law)	Interests of the individual (to do as you like with your own body) may be subordinated to the interests of society (to protect itself against deviant behaviour)	Criminal liability is normally fault based. Here the Ds intended harm but does/should consent negate fault?

A civil example of the overlap

Love thy neighbour became do not harm your neighbour. People *ought* not to do things that may harm their neighbour. Following the case the law now says they *must* not do so	**Morals** *Ought and must*	**Creativity** *Hart and Dworkin*	Is this a new law (that a manufacturer owes a duty of care to a consumer) or was it based on existing principles (do not harm others)?

Donoghue v Stevenson (1932)

Justice *Utilitarianism and Natural Law*	**Conflicting interests** *Has an appropriate balance been achieved? Policy arguments*	**Fault** *The claimant must usually prove fault*
Was justice done? Maximise happiness – is the greatest good achieved by protecting the consumer? (Utilitarianism) Is there a higher law that requires people not to harm each other? (Natural Law)	Interests of the consumer (not to be harmed) outweighed the interests of the manufacturer (to produce goods in the way they wish). There is no policy reason not to impose a duty	C must prove negligence (breach). Following the **Consumer Protection Act** this is no longer needed in a situation like Mrs Donoghue's. It is now a tort of strict liability. Does this make manufacturers more careful?

Task

As a final task, choose a case of your own and make a note of how you would relate each of the different concepts to it; if you can't relate all of them, don't worry, not all cases involve, for example, a question of morals. Keep this for revision.

Examination practice

June 2003
Explain the meaning of 'fault' and assess its importance in the imposition of liability in English law. (*30 marks*)

January 2003
Discuss how, and to what extent, judges succeed in displaying creativity when interpreting and developing common law rules and statutory rules. (*30 marks*)

There will never be a 'right' answer to such abstract concepts, so rather than a guide I have added two answers to very similar questions from an A-level student. These were done for homework, not in exam conditions, so you would not be able to cover this much; in particular, you can reduce the facts of cases. Pick out some of the cases you know and the parts that make most sense to you, then develop your own answer. Both answers cover the law very well indeed, certainly in the top-mark band. I have added a very brief comment at the end in relation to the specific questions above.

Example answers

STUDENT ESSAY
Laura Mansbridge

'It is a principle of fundamental importance in English law that there should be no liability without fault.'

Consider how far fault is an essential requirement of liability in English law, and discuss the suggestion that fault should be an essential requirement.

Fault itself provides that an act does not make a person guilty of a crime unless his mind is also guilty. For someone to be deemed at fault, the *actus reus* (physical element) must be voluntarily or freely willed. This is because there have been instances where the *actus reus* was involuntary and the defendant was therefore not at fault nor liable. A case example of such an instant is the case of **Hill *v* Baxter (1958)** where the defendant was stung by a swarm of bees whilst driving, and lost control of his car. Such involuntary responses are known as reflex actions and cannot be helped.

However, an exception to this rule is state of affairs cases. In such cases, the defendant need not have formed the required *mens rea* (mental element), but will still be found liable. A case example is **R *v* Winzar (1983)** in which the defendant had been admitted to hospital, was found to be drunk and told to leave. Later he was found in a corridor of the hospital and the police were called to remove him. They took him outside onto the highway and then charged him with 'being found drunk in a public highway'. The defendant appealed but the Divisional Court upheld the conviction, stating that there was no need for the court to have any regard as to how he came to be there; the fact that he was there was enough.

When it comes to omissions, there is generally no liability to act even if the defendant is morally at fault. However, an exception to this has been created where the law has imposed a duty to act. For example, in the case of **R *v* Miller (1983)** where the defendant (a squatter) fell asleep on a mattress smoking a cigarette. The defendant was awoken by the flames, but instead of putting the fire out, he got up and went into another room and went back to sleep. As a result, the house was substantially damaged by fire, and the defendant was convicted of criminal damage. The House of Lords held that once the defendant awoke and realised what had happened, he came under a responsibility to limit the harmful effects of the fire. The defendant's failure to discharge this responsibility provided the basis for the imposition of liability.

Causation must be established for result crimes, as they determine fault and therefore liability. There are two types of causation; in fact and in law. Causation in fact is established if 'but for' the defendants actions the resultant consequences would not have occurred. For example, in the case of **R v White (1910)** the defendant intended to poison his mother by putting cyanide in her drink. She, however, actually died of a heart attack. Therefore, the defendant was acquitted of murder and convicted of an attempt to murder. Although the consequence that the defendant intended occurred, he did not cause it to occur. Causation in law must prove that the defendant was the 'operating and substantial' cause of the resultant consequences. In **R v Smith (1959)** the defendant (a solider) stabbed the victim (a fellow solider), resulting in the victim's death. On being charged with murder, the defendant argued that the chain of causation between the stabbing and the death had been broken by the way in which the victim had been treated. The victim had been dropped twice whilst being carried to the medical station; the medical officer, who was dealing with a series of emergencies, did not realise the serious extent of the wounds; and the treatment he gave him was 'thoroughly bad and might well have affected his chances of recovery'.

However, the court held that the defendant's stabbing was the 'operating and substantial cause' of the victim's death because the victim clearly died from loss of blood caused by the stab wounds inflicted by the defendant.

Criminal liability can sometimes depend on a chance result rather than on the defendant's level of fault. For example, in the case of **R v Blaue (1975)** the defendant stabbed the victim (a Jehovah's Witness) 13 times. The victim refused a blood transfusion on religious grounds and died from her wounds. The defendant was convicted of manslaughter and appealed because the victim had refused treatment and therefore broken the chain of causation. It was held that the defendant had to take his victim as he found her, meaning not just her physical condition, but also her religious beliefs. The question for decision was what caused the death. The answer was the stab wound. The same can be said about the case of **R v White (1910)**, whereby the defendant was only excused because his mother died of a heart attack before she had chance to drink his poison.

Mens rea must be established for most offences and shows blameworthiness. There are three types of *mens rea*, decreasing in the level of fault required.

Firstly, intention, which can either be direct (where the defendant desires the consequences of their actions, so is at fault and therefore liable) or oblique (where the defendant foresees the consequences of their actions as virtually certain and continues anyway).

Secondly, recklessness, which can be subjective (defendant must have realised that there was a risk, as in the case of **R v Cunningham (1957)**) or objective (defendant is compared to a reasonable person, as in the case of **MPC v Caldwell (1982)**). Objective recklessness requires less fault than subjective recklessness, which was shown in the case of **Elliott v C (a minor) (1983)**. In this case the defendant was only 14 and of low intelligence. She stayed out all night without sleep and entered a garden shed, which she set fire to. The Divisional Court reluctantly upheld her conviction for aggravated criminal damage, because the court was bound by the precedent set in **MPC v Caldwell (1982)**.

Lastly, negligence which is falling below the standard of the ordinary and reasonable person. The threshold for negligence ranges all the way to involuntary manslaughter. This was seen in the case of **R v Adomako (1994)**, where the defendant (an anaesthetist) had been left in charge but failed to notice that a tube leading from the patient to the ventilator had become disconnected. Unfortunately, he took the wrong action, which ultimately led to the patient's death. The defendant was convicted but appealed on the grounds that the *mens rea* should have been recklessness. However, the Court of Appeal was satisfied that a duty of care had been owed and that duty was breached.

However, some crimes do not require a form *mens rea* for every part of the *actus reus*, for example strict liability offences. In the case of **R v Prince (1875)** the defendant was found guilty of taking an unmarried girl under the age of 16 out of the possession and against the will of her parents, even though she looked older than her 13 years and told Prince that she was 18. The court stressed that the relevant section did not contain the words 'knowingly' or 'maliciously', so liability arose when Prince merely committed the act.

There can also be instances where fault does exist but liability can be extinguished by a complete defence, for example self-defence where a killing will be lawful if reasonable force was used to defend oneself. A case example is **R v Beckford (1988)** in which a policeman shot a man who had been terrorising his family. Similarly, the defence of insanity under the M'Naghten Rules states that if the defendant suffers from a defect of reason, from disease of the mind, as not to know the nature and quality of the act he was doing, or if s/he did know it, that s/he did not know what s/he was doing was wrong. Proving either of these defences results in an acquittal.

Alternatively, liability can be reduced because of extenuating circumstances, which reflect a lower level of fault; for example, the Homicide Act 1957 creates two partial defences to murder: provocation and diminished responsibility. Proving either of these defences results in a reduced charge of voluntary manslaughter, which generally carries a lower prison sentence.

Finally, fault is relevant to the sentencing process whether the defendant pleads guilty or is found guilty. Firstly, the courts will consider aggravating factors, such as committing burglary with a firearm or imitation firearm, which might increase the defendant's sentence. It will also consider mitigating factors, which might decrease the sentence. Secondly, there can be a discount for an early guilty plea if the defendant admits s/he is at fault. Thirdly, tariff sentencing reflects the defendant's blameworthiness. Fourthly, minimal sentences (in some circumstances) were introduced by the Crime (Sentences) Act 1997, although many judges are opposed to the Act because it fetters their discretion.

Unlike the statement suggests, it does seem that there sometimes is liability without fault, for example in state of affairs cases, where the defendant might not have voluntarily committed an act but will still be liable for it. Conversely, in omissions, there is generally no liability to act even if the defendant is morally at fault. Therefore, fault and liability do not always go hand in hand when it comes to English law. Arguably, fault should be an essential requirement in establishing liability, as it seems unfair to blame someone for something that they didn't mean to do (**R v Winzar (1983)**). Having said that, it also seems unjust to allow someone to get away with murdering someone, for example, just because they suffered from a defect of reason (**M'Naghten (1843)**).

STUDENT ESSAY
Laura Mansbridge

Write a critical analysis of the role of judges in interpreting and developing *both* the common law *and* statutory rules.

Many theorists have argued over whether or not judges make and develop the law, or whether they just interpret what is already there. For example in the case of **R v R (1991)** the House of Lords held for the first time that a man could be guilty of rape even though it was his wife. Up until this case, it was thought a wife could not cry rape as she had consented to intercourse by marrying. Professor Hart would say that the judges made new law by removing the marital immunity and that this was acceptable where there were no existing rules to cover the situation. However, Ronald Dworkin would say that the judges relied on existing principles, e.g. he looked at development of women's role over time and found she was no longer looked on as a thing belonging to the man, therefore the law could protect a wife where there was violence as there is an existing principle of law that assault is wrong.

The doctrine of precedent was set up to maintain consistency in the courts and means that judges have to follow previously established legal principles laid down in previous cases with similar facts. The main rule of the doctrine of precedent is *stare decisis*, which means that judges must 'treat like cases alike'. For such precedent to work, it was necessary to create a court hierarchy which bound the lower courts to the decisions of the higher courts. For example, the Crown Court is bound by the decision of the Court of Appeal. As well as each court being bound by its own previous decisions too.

The binding element of the case is known as the *ratio decidendi* which means, 'the reason for the decision' and judges are supposed to follow the reasons to decide any future cases that are alike. The other parts of the judgment are known as *obiter dicta* which are things said 'by the way'. These do not affect the decision but may create persuasive precedent.

An example of the doctrine of precedent in action can been seen in the case of **Donoghue v Stevenson (1932)** where the claimant became ill after drinking ginger beer that had a decomposed snail in it. However, because her friend had bought the beer, she couldn't sue the seller of the beer, so she sued the manufacturer. The House of Lords made precedent by holding that a manufacturer owes a duty of care to the ultimate consumer. This became accepted as the *ratio decidendi*. Also, an important principle was included in the *obiter dicta* which has since become accepted law and is known as the 'neighbour principle'. The same principle was then used in the case of **Grant v Australian Knitting Mills (1936)** in which the claimant bought some underwear but the material contained a chemical which caused dermatitis. The claimant won the case based on the precedent set by **Donoghue v Stevenson (1932)**.

However, judges can avoid following precedent. In 1966 the Practice Statement was created so that the House of Lords had the freedom to depart from their previous decisions when they felt it was right to do so. An example of this was in the case of **R v Howe (1987)** when the House of Lords declined to follow the decision in **Lynch v DPP for N. Ireland (1975)** where they had held that duress was available as a defence to accomplices to murder. Also, the Court of Appeal held in the case of **Young v Bristol Aeroplane (1944)** that there were circumstances in which they would be able to ignore a previous decision. These included when the previous decision had been made by mistake.

Also, in the previously mentioned case of **Donoghue v Stevenson (1932)** it was possible for judges to create their own precedent if there wasn't anything to follow.

Furthermore, any judge can distinguish a precedent on the grounds that the material facts of the previous case are different to the current case. For example, in **R v Jordan (1956)** the defendant stabbed the victim who was admitted to hospital and died eight days later. The Court of Appeal held that the victim had been given an antibiotic to which he was allergic and large amounts of intravenous liquid; and this treatment, according to the evidence, was 'palpably wrong' and that the immediate cause of death was pneumonia. They also said that the stab wound was merely the setting within which another cause of death operated, and quashed the conviction. However, **Jordan** was distinguished by the Court of Appeal in **R v Smith (1959)** in which the defendant stabbed the victim twice, resulting in the victim being taken to the medical station where he died. The defendant argued that the chain of causation between the stabbing and the death had been broken by the fact that the victim had been dropped twice and he had received poor medical treatment. The defendant was convicted of murder and appealed unsuccessfully. The court held that the defendant's stabbing was the 'operating and substantial cause' of the victim's death.

Statutory interpretation is the process by which judges are asked to decide the precise meaning of the words in an Act of Parliament. However, there are a number of factors that may cause doubt, for example the statute might contain ambiguous words, or there might have been significant developments in society that the statute has not foreseen. Therefore judges have developed general methods of statutory interpretation in order to avoid confusion and obscure results. These methods come in the form of various rules and approaches that a judge can follow.

The literal rule means that judges use dictionary definitions to determine what the words in the statute actually mean. A case example of the use of the literal rule is **Fisher v Bell (1961)** where the defendant, a shopkeeper, was prosecuted for displaying an illegal flick-knife for sale. Because it is an offence to offer such an item for sale (under the **Restriction of Offensive Weapons Act 1951**) he was convicted. On appeal, however, it was held that, under the literal rule, 'offer for sale' has a technical meaning in law, and a shop window display is an invitation to treat, not an offer in contractual terms. The conviction was therefore quashed.

The golden rule allows the judge to adopt an interpretation which tries to avoid an absurd result if the statute includes ambiguous words. In the case of **R v Allen (1872)** the defendant was married and then married again. It is an offence for a married person to 'marry' again unless they are widowed or divorced. When caught, the defendant argued that he did not commit this offence as the law regarded his second marriage as invalid. Through the use of the golden rule, the court held that the word 'marry' should be replaced with 'going through a ceremony of marriage' and so the defendant was guilty.

The mischief rule involves the court trying to discover what was missing in the law before the statute was created, and what that statute was designed to remedy. For example, in **Smith v Hughes (1960)** six women were charged with soliciting 'in a street or public place for the purpose of prostitution'. However, one woman had been on a balcony and the others were behind the windows of ground floor rooms. The court held they were guilty because the statute had aimed to stop people being molested or solicited by prostitutes.

The most modern approach to statutory interpretation is the purposive approach, which is similar to the mischief rule, but emphasises the need to discover what Parliament intended to remedy rather than what the previous law was missing. This was seen in the case of **R v Registrar General ex parte Smith (1990)**. This case was concerned with **s. 51** of the **Adoption Act 1976**, which enables a person to obtain details of their birth certificate when reaching 18 years of age. On a literal view of the law, the Registrar-General had to comply and supply the information. However, in doing so, he would put at risk the life of the applicant's natural mother because the applicant was in a Mental Hospital having murdered twice. Despite the plain language of the Act, the court applied a purposive approach saying that 'Parliament could not have intended to promote serious crime'.

It is highly debatable as to whether or not judges actually make and develop the law, and it is also debatable as to whether or not they should. In the case of **R v Brown (1993)** (sadomasochism) consensual assault didn't amount to a crime under the **Offences Against the Person Act 1861** or common law. The Act did not deal with consent and in common law, consent was a defence to common assault. However, the defendants were found guilty and the judges seemed to base their decision on what was morally right. Arguably, such a decision should be up to Parliament as it could potentially affect the public as a whole. However, creating statutes is a lengthy process and the courts can develop the common law to meet changing conditions more quickly.

It is also arguable that some statutes are out of date or very rushed (such as the **Dangerous Dogs Act 1991**) and the judges' interpretation is the only way to ensure that the law is applied fairly and justly. However, the overriding of precedent can also make the law seem inconsistent and unfair.

Some theorists have argued the point that judges are appointed by the Lord Chancellor, but the members of Parliament are voted for directly by the public, therefore only Parliament should decide the law. Conversely other theorists believe that common law itself is more in touch with the 'here and now' than statute law, as it can adapt to accommodate the changes in society. This is shown in the case of **R v R (1991)** where the development of the woman's role over time means that she is no longer looked upon as a thing belonging to a man and is therefore able to be raped by her husband. This case seems to have been decided fairly in today's society and seems extremely important that the law keeps up with the changes in whatever ways it can and as fast as it can.

Comments

Fault

For the actual exam question I would put the explanation of fault and *mens rea* before *actus reus* as it specifically asked for an explanation of fault. If you have studied civil law you may want to reduce the crime examples and add some civil ones. The conclusion is excellent. It nicely sums up what she has said and directs the examiner to the original quote in the question. This is always a good idea, it reminds the examiner that you are answering the question set.

N.B. *Laura made a small error in relation to insanity: this does not result in an acquittal but one of the four orders, thus a judge can take into account the level of fault when deciding which is appropriate. Errors like this would not lose marks, just be ignored.*

Creativity

Again the actual exam question asked for an explanation of the rules ('*how*'), so I would put these a little earlier. This is a second-year paper so don't be tempted to go into vast detail just because it was your favourite area last year. Be brief on the rules of precedent and statutory interpretation, concentrate on *analysing* them to show how far they allow for creativity, or not.

N.B. *A small typing mistake: the second to last paragraph should read 'the overriding* **rule** *of precedent . . .'*

Further reading

Hart, *The Concept of Law* (Oxford, 1994).
Dworkin, *Law's Empire* (Fontana paperbacks, 1986).
Lloyd and Freeman, *Introduction to Jurisprudence* (Sweet & Maxwell, latest edition).

For further resources and updates please go to the Companion Website accompanying this book at **www.pearsoned.co.uk/russell**

Websites

Use free internet sites to keep up to date with any new developments. The Law Commission site is well worth a visit. It will show you any proposed reforms on various areas of law. Many files require Adobe to view, but this can be downloaded free from: www.adobe.com/products/acrobat/readstep2.html

General

www.cjsonline.gov.uk/
Government site on the Criminal Justice System.

www.dca.gov.uk/
Department for Constitutional Affairs. Lots of information on the law and justice. The Department's responsibilities include running the courts and improving the justice system.

www.lawcom.gov.uk/
The website of the Law Commission with copies of their reports and law under review, e.g. Consultation Paper 177 on reform of the Homicide Act.

www.lawreports.co.uk/
Free site for summaries of official case reports from the Incorporated Council of Law Reporting. Once you have found a case you can go to the HL site for more information.

Educational

www.lawteacher.net/
A very useful website containing lecture notes, cases and statutes used on A-level ILEx Part II courses.

www.aqa.org.uk
The examination board website with past papers, mark schemes, exam reports and timetables.

www.stbrn.ac.uk/other/depts/law/index.htm
A course compiled for a sixth form college law team by John Deft.

www.leeds.ac.uk/law/hamlyn/toc.htm
Useful website provided by Leeds University, covering the legal system.

www.parliament.uk/index.cfm
Parliament home page.

www.parliament.uk/bills
For what bills are going through Parliament.

www.parliament.uk/judicial_work/judicial_work.cfm
House of Lords site, for cases click on 'judgments'.

Specific documents included in text

(Note that sometimes links get broken or addresses change so if you have any problems go to the home page which is the part of the address before the /)

www.cps.gov.uk/index.html
The Crown Prosecution Service site has the **Joint Charging Standards** – go to legal guidance and then 'offences against the person' but there is more on the site so have a browse.

www.cps.gov.uk/legal/section5/chapter_d.html
For self-defence guidelines.

Glossary

Actus reus A phrase referring to elements of the definition of an offence (save those which concern the condition of the mind of the accused), e.g. D's outward conduct, its results and surrounding circumstances. Thus, the *actus reus* of false imprisonment is X's unlawful restraint of Y. May be merely a specified state of affairs, e.g., a 'situation' offence: see, e.g., Road Traffic Act 1988, s. 4(2). Should any element of the *actus reus* not be present, the offence has not been committed. See, e.g., *Haughton v Smith* [1975] AC 476 ('It is not the *actus* which is *reus*, but the man and his mind respectively': *per* Lord Hailsham).

Caveat emptor Let the buyer beware. In general, the buyer is expected to look to his own interests.

Force majeure A superior force. An event that can generally be neither anticipated nor controlled, e.g., an industrial strike which leads to loss of profits. See *André et Cie v Tradax* [1983] 1 Lloyd's Rep 254; *McNicholl v Ministry of Agriculture* [1988] ECR (circumstances must be abnormal and unforeseeable, so that the consequences could not have been avoided through the exercise of all due care).

Interpretation of statutes Where a statute's words are not clear or not certain, the courts may be called upon to interpret them. ('The fundamental object of statutory construction in every case is to ascertain the legislative intention . . . The rules of interpretation are no more than the rules of common sense, designed to achieve this object': *per* Mason J in *Cooper Brookes Ltd v FCT* (1981) 35 ALR 151.) In this they are guided by rules, such as: (1) Literal rule (q.v.) – words of a statute in their original sense will prevail unless they would produce unintended consequences: *Corocraft v Pan Am Airways* [1969] 1 All ER 82. (2) Golden rule (q.v.) – manifest absurdity resulting from interpretation to be avoided: *Becke v Smith* (1836) 2 M & W 191. (3) Statute must be read as a whole. (4) There is a presumption against altering the law or ousting the courts' jurisdiction. (5) The court must adopt an interpretation which will correct the mischief which the statute was passed to remedy: *Heydon's Case* (1584) 3 Co Rep 7a. For conflicts between international obligations and specific statutory provisions, see *Cheney v Conn* [1968] 1 All ER 779. See Lord Scarman's Interpretation of Legislation Bill, introduced into the House of Lords in 1981; *Inco Europe Ltd v First Choice Distribution* [2000] 1 WLR 586; *Mock v Pensions Ombudsman* (2000) *The Times*, 7 April.

Invitation to treat An offer to receive an offer. 'According to the ordinary law of contract the display of an article with a price on it in the shop window is merely an invitation to treat. It is in no sense an offer for sale, the acceptance of which constitutes a contract': *per* Lord Parker in *Fisher v Bell* [1961] 1 QB 394. See *Pharmaceutical Society v Boots* [1953] 1 All ER 482.

Mens rea Translated as 'guilty mind' or 'wicked mind'. More accurately, 'criminal intention, or an intention to do the act which is made penal by statute or by the common law': *Allard* v *Selfridge Ltd* [1925] 1 KB 129. The so-called 'fault element' of an offence. May also include recklessness relating to the circumstances and consequences of an act which comprise the *actus reus*. In general, there must be a coincidence of time of *actus reus* and *mens rea*: see, e.g., *Fagan* v *MPC* [1969] 1 QB 439 (*actus reus* as a continuing act).

Novus actus interveniens New intervening act. General defence in an action in tort (q.v.). When the act of a third person intervenes between the original act or omission and the damage, that act or omission is considered as the direct cause of the damage if the act of the third person could have been expected in the particular circumstances: *Scott* v *Shepherd* (1733) 2 Wm Bl 892. See *R* v *Pagett* (1983) 76 Cr App R 279.

Obiter dictum (plural obiter dicta) Something said by the way. Refers to: a statement of the law by the judge based on facts which were not present, or not material, in a case (see, e.g., the judgment of Denning J in *Central London Property Trust Ltd* v *High Trees House Ltd* [1947] KB 30); a statement of law based on facts as found, but not forming the basis of the decision (e.g., a statement upon which a dissenting judgment is based). It will be of persuasive authority only, and its worth will reflect the seniority of the judge and their position.

Plaintiff One who brings a claim into court. Known now, under CPR, r 2.3.(1), as 'claimant'.

Precedent Judgment or decision cited so as to justify a decision in a later, apparently similar, case. 'The process by which forms of conduct are stamped in the judicial mint as law, and thereafter circulate freely as part of the coinage of the realm': Cardozo CJ, *The Growth of Law* (1924). An *authoritative precedent* is generally binding and must be followed. A *persuasive precedent* (based, e.g., on *obiter dicta*) need not necessarily be followed. A *declaratory precedent* merely applies an existing rule of law. An *original precedent* creates and applies a new rule of law. Decisions on questions of fact must not be cited as precedents: *Qualcast Ltd* v *Haynes* [1959] AC 743. 2. Precedent as applied to the hierarchy of courts (the so-called 'vertical dimension of precedent') is as follows: *House of Lords* – generally bound by previous decisions (see *London Street Tramways Co* v *LCC* [1898] AC 375) but will depart from such decisions where it appears right to do so (see *R* v *Shivpuri* [1987] AC 1); *Court of Appeal (Civil Division)* – bound by previous decisions, except where given *per incuriam* (q.v.) or where inconsistent with a subsequent House of Lords decision; *Court of Appeal (Criminal Division)* – apparently bound by previous decisions; *High Court and Crown Court* – bound by decisions of superior courts; *county courts and magistrates' courts* – bound by decisions of superior courts. See *Young* v *Bristol Aeroplane Co Ltd* [1944] KB 718; *Davis* v *Johnson* [1978] 1 All ER 1132. See also Human Rights Act 1998, s. 2, under which, in determining questions concerning a right under the Convention, a court is obliged to 'take into account' judgments, decisions, declarations of the European Court of Human Rights (q.v.) and decisions of the European Commission of Human Rights. UK courts must treat rulings of the European Court of Justice concerning the interpretation of EU Treaties and the validity of acts of EU institutions as binding: European Communities Act 1972, s. 3(1).

Prima facie Of first appearance; on the face of it. Based on a first impression. A *prima facie* case is one in which the evidence in favour of a party is sufficient to call for an answer from his opponent.

Quantum meruit   As much as he has deserved (i.e., earned). On breach of contract the party injured may be entitled to claim for work done and services performed. See *Planché* v *Colbourn*.

Revocation   An act by which one annuls something he has done.

Ratio decidendi   The reason for a judicial decision. Usually a statement of law applied to the problems of a particular case. In essence, the principle upon which a case is decided. (Goodhart suggests that this principle is to be found by taking account of the facts treated by the judge as material, and his decision as based on them: (1930) 40 Yale LJ 161.)

Res extincta   The subject matter of an agreement which is, in fact, non-existent. In such a case no contract ensues. See, e.g., *Couturier* v *Hastie* (1856) 5 HL Cas 673.

Stare decisis   To stand by decided matters. (*Stare decisis et non quieta movere* – to stand by precedent and not to disturb settled points.) Doctrine according to which previous judicial decisions must be followed. *See* PRECEDENT.

Statutory interpretation   See Interpretation of statutes.

Tort   (*Tortus* – twisted, distorted.) A civil wrong independent of contract. Liability in tort arises from breach of a duty primarily fixed by law which is towards others generally, breach of which is redressable by a claim for unliquidated damages affording some measure of compensation.

Tortfeasor   One who commits a tort.

Volenti non fit injuria   That to which a person consents cannot be considered an injury. Term referring to the harm suffered with the plaintiff's freely given assent and with their prior knowledge of the risk involved, and, hence, a general defence in tort. Knowledge is not assent, but merely evidence of assent: *Dann* v *Hamilton* [1939] 1 KB 509. A person does not necessarily assent to a situation because they have knowledge of its potential danger: *Baker* v *James* [1921] 2 KB 674. 'Knowledge of the risk of injury is not enough. Nor is a willingness to take the risk of injury. Nothing will suffice short of an agreement to waive any claim for negligence': *Nettleship* v *Weston* [1971] 3 All ER 581.

Index

abatement of liability by deception, obtaining an exemption from, 298–9, 300
acceptance, 3, 5, 15–20
  communication, 16–18
    electronic, 18, 19
    instantaneous, 17–18, 19
    receipt of 17
  Internet 18
  offer 10, 12–13, 15–16, 120, 479
  performance, 16–17
  postal rule 18–19, 479, 487
  standard forms, 16
acts of God, 412, 479
actual bodily harm, assault occasioning, 199, 203–7, 210, 213
  actus reus, 203, 204, 206, 207
  battery, 204, 206
  causation, 204
  intention, 205, 206
  mens rea, 204, 205–6, 207
  psychiatry injury, 205
  recklessness, 205, 206
  silent phone calls, 204, 205
actus reus, 127, 128–38, 253–4. *See also under particular offences*
  acts or omissions, 129
  automatism, 233
  causation, 134–6
  circumstances, conduct in certain 132
  conduct, 128–32
  continuing acts 129, 131, 146
  contractual duty to act 130
  dangerous situation, creating a, 131
  fault, 474–5, 498
  intoxication, 239
  mens rea, 139, 146–7, 193
  mistake, 245
  omissions, 129–31
  responsibility, relationship of 130

  result crimes 133
  state of affairs, 129, 131
  voluntary conduct 128–9
advertisements, 7, 8, 31
aggravating factors, sentencing and, 475
agreement, discharge of contract by, 87–8
alternative dispute resolution, 469
arson, 305, 309–10
assault, 195, 196–9, 215 *see also* actual bodily harm, assault occasioning
  actus reus, 197–8, 202, 206
  battery, 200, 221, 223
  immediate and unlawful violence, 199
  intention, 200
  mens rea, 200, 202, 207
  recklessness, 200
  silent telephone calls, 198
  threat of violence, 197–8
  vicarious liability, 417–18, 422, 488
  words or gestures, 198, 199, 200
assisted suicide, 129, 171, 221
auctions, 9
automatism, 219, 233–5, 237, 450
  actus reus, 233
  external factors, 234, 238
  fault, 474
  hypoglycaemia, 230, 231, 234–5, 252
  intoxication, 234–5
  mens rea, 233
  involuntary acts, 233–4
  self-induced, 235, 238

bail, 469
balancing conflicting interests, 443, 463–72, 492, 493
  contract, 466–7
  crime, 466
  Jhering, Rudolf von, 464
  justice, overlap with, 464

balancing conflicting interests (*continued*)
  legal process, 469
  nuisance, 468
  Pound, Roscoe, 464–5, 472
  public and private interests, 463–5
  sanctions and remedies, 470
  sentencing, 470
  social engineering, 464–5, 472
  terrorism, 469, 471–2
  tort, 467–8
  torture, 471–2
battered woman's syndrome, 159–62, 168
battery, 195, 196–7, 200–2, 215
  actus reus, 200–1
  assault, 200, 204, 206
  consent, 201, 221, 223
  direct or indirect force, 201–2
  intention, 202
  mens rea, 201, 202
  omissions, 201
  recklessness, 202
  self-defence, 201
  touching, 200
  unlawful force, 201
battle of the forms, 16
borrowing, 270
breach of contract, 103–8
  actual breach, 103
  anticipatory breach, 104–5, 467
  conditions, 37, 46–9, 86, 115
  continuing with contract, 104–5
  damages, 107, 478
  fault, 477–8
  frustration, 104
  fundamental breach, 62, 106–7
  implied terms, 37, 44
  improper performance, 103
  innominate terms, 37, 47–8, 106–7
  mistake, 106
  non-performance, 103, 105
  repudiation, 104, 105–6
  rescission, 105–7, 478
  warranties, 37, 46–9, 86, 107, 115, 467
breach of duty, 335–6, 361–5, 372–3
  foreseeability, 362
  justifiable, whether risk was, 362
  occupiers' liability, 382, 389, 391
  precautions, expense and practicality of
    taking, 363

  public interest, 467–8
  reasonableness, 361–2, 364, 372–3
  risk, degree of, 361–2
  seriousness of potential harm, 362
  standard of care, 363–4, 372–3
burglary, 259, 281–9
  actus reus, 281–2, 284, 285–7
  attempts, 286
  buildings or parts of buildings, 283–7
  enters, meaning of, 282
  mens rea, 281, 284, 285–7
  recklessness, 284–5
  trespass, 282, 283–4, 286–7

causation
  actus reus, 134–6
  actual bodily harm, assault occasioning,
    204
  but for test, 134, 366–70
  damages, 110
  factual, 133–4, 150–1
  foreseeability, 134–6, 368–71
  intervening acts, 134–7, 368–70, 426,
    474–5
  legal, 134–6, 150
  loss of a chance, 367–8
  manslaughter, 133, 180–2
  murder, 133, 149–52
  negligence, 335–6, 366–71, 372
  nuisance, 403, 420
  occupiers' liability, 382, 389
  remoteness, 368–70
  Rylands v *Fletcher*, 412
  successive and multiple causes, 366–7
censorship, 471
children
  age of criminal responsibility, 220
  occupiers' liability, 377–9, 385–9, 391–3,
    437–8, 451, 478, 487
civil partnerships, 451
codification of criminal law, 216
commercial agreements, 31
conditions
  breach, 37, 46–9, 86, 115
  performance, discharge by, 91
  rescission, 46–9, 86
  warranties, 47
conflicting interests. *See* balancing conflicting
    interests

consent, 221–7, 315. *See also volenti non fit injuria*
  assault and battery, 201, 221, 223
  criminal damage, 307, 315–16
  grievous bodily harm and wounding, 209
  horseplay, 223
  lawful chastisement, 223
  private or public actions, 222
  rape, 346–7
  recklessness, 224, 225
  Rylands v *Fletcher*, 412
  sado-masochistic behaviour, 222
  sex, 224–5, 252
  sports and games, 222, 223
  surgery, 223–4
consideration, 3–4, 5, 21–8, 467, 487
  adequate, 23, 120
  definition, 21
  early payments, 26–7
  executed and executory, 22–3, 88
  existing obligations, more than, 24–6
  instalments, payment in, 26–7
  offer, 6
  open, promise to keep offer, 28
  part-payment of debts, 26–8
  past, must not be in the, 22–3
  penalty clauses, 25–6
  Pinnel's case, rule in, 26–7, 88
  privity of contract, 24
  promise, moving from the, 23–4
  sufficient, 23–7, 88, 120
  third parties, duty to, 26
constructive or unlawful act manslaughter, 177, 178–83, 185–8, 192
  actus reus, 178, 183, 191, 193
  causation, 180–2
  dangerous acts, 179–82
  drugs to someone, administering, 181–2
  fault, 475
  intention, 182
  intervening acts, 181–2
  mens rea, 182–3, 191, 193
  omissions, 178, 181
  recklessness, 182
contra proferentem rule, 53
contract *see also* acceptance, breach of contract, consideration, offer, terms
  balancing conflicting interests and, 466–7
  collateral contracts, 41
  discharge, 85, 87–8

  fault and, 477–8, 480
  justice and, 460
  misrepresentation, 4, 61, 74–80, 121, 467
  mistake, 4, 61–71, 106, 460, 467, 477–8, 487
  morality and, 450, 452
  performance, discharge by, 88–93
  severable or divisible, 89–90
  simple and specialty contracts, 3
  statutory interpretation, 487
  theft, 261–4, 269–70
contributory negligence, 424–6, 461
  damages, reduction in, 424–6, 428, 429
  intoxication, 428
  occupiers' liability, 388, 390, 391, 393
  reasonableness, 425
  Rylands v *Fletcher*, 412
corporate killing, 189–90, 192, 460, 461, 474
corrective justice, 455, 459
corrupt public morals, conspiracy to, 448
credit card services, 296, 297
crime. *See also* particular crimes (e.g. assault)
  age of criminal responsibility, 220
  balancing conflicting interests, 466
  codification, 216
  fault, 473–7, 482
  jury trials, 469
  justice and law, 460
  mistake, 245–8
  morality and the law, 443–4, 450, 452
  public interest, 466
  statutory interpretation, 486
Criminal Cases Review Commission, 459
criminal damage, 305–11, 450
  actus reus, 305–8, 310, 311
  belonging to another, property, 306–7
  consent, 307, 315–16
  destroys or damages, 305–6
  intoxication, 307, 308
  lawful excuse, without, 246, 307–8
  life, destroying or damaging property with intent to endanger, 308–9, 311
  mens rea, 308, 310, 311
  mistake, 246, 306–7, 315
  necessity, 318
  property, meaning of, 306, 310
  protection of property, 307, 310
  recklessness, 308, 310
custom, 43

damages, 85, 109–15, 423, 430–1
  amenity, loss of, 431
  breach of contract, 107, 478
  causation, 110
  consequential loss, 114
  contributory negligence, 424–6, 428, 429
  discharge of contract, 85
  distress, discomfort and disappointment,
    113–14
  expectation loss, 109–10
  expenses, 430
  foreseeability, 111–13, 121, 430, 437
  general damages, 431, 433
  injunctions, 432, 470
  liquidated damages, 114–15
  loss of earnings, 113, 430, 431
  loss of opportunity, 114
  loss of profits, 111, 114
  market price rule, 112–14
  medical negligence, 481
  misrepresentation, 76, 77–9, 121, 477
  mitigation, 113
  no-fault compensation, 480–1
  non-pecuniary loss, 113–14
  nuisance, 404, 432
  pain and suffering, 431
  penalty clauses, 114–15
  performance, discharge by, 91
  public interest, 468
  purpose of, 109
  quantification, 112–14
  quantum meruit, 115
  reliance loss, 110
  remoteness, 110–12
  reputation, loss of, 113
  rescission, 77, 78
  special damages, 430, 433
  structured settlements, 430
  warranties, 46–8, 86, 107, 487
deception offences, 292–300 see also making of
    without payment
  abatement of liability, obtaining an
    exemption from, 298–9, 300
  appropriation, 292, 330
  credit card services, 296, 297
  dishonesty, 294, 296, 299, 329
  evasion of liability by deception, 293, 297–8,
    329
  mens rea, 295, 296, 329

money transfer by deception, obtaining, 295
overdrafts, 296
property by deception, obtaining, 294–5, 296,
  300
recklessness, 293, 295, 296, 299
reform, 299
remission of existing liability, securing, 297,
  300
services by deception, obtaining, 295–6, 299,
  300
silence or implication, 293, 299
theft, 263–4
wait or forgo payment, inducing a creditor,
  297–8, 300
defences, 219–20, 411–12, 420 see also specific
    defences (e.g. consent, insanity)
diminished responsibility, 157, 165–9, 172, 173
  abnormality of mind, 165–8
  battered woman's syndrome, 168
  burden of proof, 168
  fault, 475
  insanity, 232
  intoxication, 166–7
  provocation 165–6, 169
  self-defence, 168
  sentencing, 168–9
  substantial impairment of mental
    responsibility, 167–8
distributive justice, 455, 464
duress, 319–26
  circumstances, by, 317, 318, 319, 321–3, 325
  death or serious injury, threats of, 319–20
  evasive action, 320
  intoxication, 321, 322
  mistake, 324
  murder, 317, 318, 323–5
  reform, 324–5
  self-induced, 321, 325
  sober person of reasonable firmness test, 319,
    321
  threats, 317, 319–25
  voluntary association with criminals, 321,
    324
Dutch courage rule, 239
duty of care 335–43 see also breach of duty
  fair, just and reasonable test, 338, 340–2, 489
  foreseeability, 337–40, 343
  immunity, 340–1, 343
  neighbour principle, 337–9, 343, 372, 451

duty of care 335–43 *see also* breach of duty
(*continued*)
  omissions, 342
  physical harm, 337–43
  police, immunity of, 340–1, 461, 468
  proximity, 339, 340, 343
  sport, 42

economic loss, 335–6, 344, 349–50
  consequential loss, 349, 351
  floodgates argument, 344
  negligent misstatements, 344–8, 372
  proximity, 349
  pure, 344, 349
economic theories, justice and, 457–8, 462
employment. *See* vicarious liability
equitable remedies, 115–16
evasion of liability by deception, 293, 297–8,
    329
exclusion clauses, 51–7, 450
  ambiguity, 53
  common law rules, 51
  contra proferentem rule, 53
  contractual document, whether clause is in,
    52
  course of dealing, 53
  definition, 38
  main purpose rule, 53–4
  misrepresentation, 79
  negligent misstatements, 346
  notice, 52–3
  occupiers' liability, 382–3, 391–2
  reasonableness, 79
  signing, 52
  tickets, 52
  unfair contract terms, 38, 54–6, 79, 382–3,
    391–2, 450, 460, 467
express terms, 37, 39–41
  collateral contracts, 41
  importance, 40
  intention, 39
  representations, 39–40, 121
  special knowledge, 40
  timing, 49

fault, 443, 473–82, 493–6
  actus reus, 474–5, 498
  automatism, 474
  causation, 474–5

civil law, 477–8, 482
constructive or unlawful act manslaughter,
  475
contract, 107, 477–8, 480
corporate manslaughter, controlling mind in,
  474
criminal law, 473–7, 482
diminished responsibility, 475
foreseeability, 479
frustration, 477–8
gross negligence manslaughter, 474
implied terms, 479
innominate or intermediate terms, 479
insanity, 475
intoxication, 475
mens rea, 473–7, 492, 498
misrepresentation, 477
mistake, 477
nuisance, 478
occupiers' liability, 478
Pearson Commission, no-fault compensation
  and, 480–1
recklessness, 474
Rylands v *Fletcher*, 479, 480
sentencing, mitigating and aggravating factors
  and, 475
state of affairs crimes, 474
strict liability, 475–7, 479–81
tort, 478–9, 480
vicarious liability, 480
floodgates argument, 344, 352
force majeure, 98
foreseeability
  breach of duty, 362
  causation, 134–6, 368–71
  damages, 111–13, 121, 430, 437
  duty of care, 337–40, 343
  fault, 479
  frustration, 98, 478
  murder, 151–2
  negligent misstatements, 238–9
  nuisance, 402, 405
  occupiers' liability, 378, 382, 391
  psychiatric injury, 352–4, 359
  Rylands v *Fletcher*, 409, 411, 413, 480
  thin skull rule, 370
formation of contract. *See also* acceptance,
    consideration, intention to create legal
    relations, offer

frustration, 94–102, 487
  advance payments, recovery of, 99–100
  anticipatory breach, 104
  expenses, 100
  fault, 477–8
  force majeure, 98
  foreseeability, 98, 478
  illegality, 97
  implied terms, 98
  impossibility, 85, 94–6
  personal services, 95
  radically different, where performance will be, 95–7
  self-induced frustration, 97–8
  termination, 94–5
  war, outbreak of, 97

grievous bodily harm and wounding, 208–13, 215
  actus reus, 208–11, 213
  causing or inflicting, 209–11
  consent, 209
  intention, 212
  malice, 208, 211
  mens rea, 211–13
  psychiatric harm, 210
  recklessness, 211, 212
  unlawfully inflicting, 209
gross carelessness, killing by, 189, 192
gross negligence manslaughter, 177, 183, 184–91
  actus reus, 184
  breach of duty, 187–8
  conduct amounting to, 188–9
  dangerous acts, 186–7
  fault, 474
  mens rea, 139, 186
  recklessness 183, 185–6

harassment, 210
honour clauses, 31
Human Rights Act 1998, 455, 457, 469, 486

identity cards, 471
immunity, 340–1, 343, 461, 468
implied terms, 37, 41–4
  breach, 37, 44
  business efficacy, 43–4, 487
  buyer beware, 43

courts, terms implied by, 43–4, 467
custom, 43
description, 41, 42
exclusion clauses, 54
fault, 479
fitness for purpose, 41, 42
frustration, 98
officious bystander test, 44
package holidays, 37
sale of goods, contracts for the, 41–2, 479
sample, sale by, 42–3
satisfactory quality, 41–2
statute, implied by, 41–2
title, 41, 42
unfair contract terms, 54
independent contractors, 379–81, 391, 393, 415–16, 421, 437
injunctions, 423, 431–2
  damages, 432, 470
  nuisance, 404–5, 422, 432, 461
  personal services, 115
  total or partial, 431–2, 433
innominate or intermediate terms, 37, 46, 460
  breach, 37, 47–8, 106–7
  fault, 479
  rescission, 106–7
insanity, 228–33, 235, 252, 450, 466
  defect of reason, 229, 231, 238
  diminished responsibility, 232
  disease of the mind, 229–30
  fault, 475
  intoxication, 233, 238–9
  M'Naughten's Rules, 229, 233
  nature and quality of act, does not know, 232
  reform, 233
  wrong, does not appreciate act was wrong, 232
intention
  assault and battery, 200–2, 205, 206
  direct, 140
  express terms, 39
  grievous bodily harm and wounding, 212
  intoxication, 237, 238
  manslaughter, 181–2
  mens rea, 129–44, 151
  murder, 140–2
  oblique, 140–2, 151

intention (*continued*)
  theft, 139–40, 273–5
  virtual certainty, where consequence is a,
      140–3, 151–2
intention to create legal relations, 5, 29–32, 120
  advertisements, 31
  commercial agreements, 31
  honour clauses, 31
  social and domestic agreements, 29–30, 120,
      487
Internet, 18
interpretation. *See* statutory interpretation
intervening acts
  causation, 134–7, 368–70, 426, 474–5
  volenti non fit injuria, 428
intoxication, 236–41, 450
  actus reus, 239
  automatism, 234–5
  contributory negligence, 428
  criminal damage, 307, 308
  diminished responsibility, 166–7
  duress, 321, 322
  Dutch courage rule, 239
  fault, 475
  insanity, 233, 238–9
  intention, 237, 238
  involuntary, 237, 241, 475
  mens rea, 237, 238–9, 252
  mistakes, 239–40, 247–8, 252, 315
  provocation, 161–2
  public policy, 240–1, 247
  recklessness, 236, 237, 239
  spiked drinks, 237
  voluntary, 237–8, 241, 475
invitation to treat, 7, 8
involuntary manslaughter, 157
  gross carelessness, killing by, 189, 192
  reckless killing, 189, 192
  see also constructive or unlawful act
      manslaughter, and gross negligence
      manslaughter

Joint Charging Standards, 195, 196–7, 205
judicial creativity, 483–91
  Dworkin, Ronald, 483, 492, 403
  Hart, HLA, 483, 492, 493
  parliament and courts, relationship between,
      489
  precedent, 484–7, 488–90, 494, 496–9

retrospectivity, 488–9
statutory interpretation, 483–8, 494, 496–9
justice, law and, 454–62
  Aquinas, Thomas, 455
  Aristotle, 455, 459, 464
  balancing conflicting interests, 464
  Bentham, Jeremy, 456–7, 464
  contract, 460
  corrective justice, 455, 459
  crime, 460
  distributive justice, 455, 464
  economic theories, 457–8, 462
  Hart, HLA, 456, 459
  Kelsen, Hans, 456
  Mark, Karl, 457–8, 464
  meaning of justice, 454–6
  Mill, Jon Stuart, 457, 460
  natural law, 455, 456, 462, 492, 493
  Nozick, Robert, 458
  positivism, 455–7, 462
  procedural justice, 456, 459
  Rawls, John, 458
  substantive justice, 456, 459–60
  tort, 461
  utilitarianism, 456–7, 458, 460–4, 492,
      493

lawful chastisement, 223, 451
loss of chance, 367–8

making of without payment, 293–4, 301–4
  actus reus, 301–2, 303
  dishonesty, 303
  mens rea, 301, 302–3
  permanently, intention to avoid payment,
      303, 304, 329–30
  spot, payment on the, 301–3, 304
manslaughter
  causation, 133
  constructive or unlawful act manslaughter,
      177, 178–83, 185–8, 192, 475
  corporate killing, 189–90, 192, 460, 461
  diminished responsibility, 157, 165–9, 172,
      173
  gross carelessness, killing by, 189, 192
  gross negligence manslaughter, 139, 177,
      183–91, 474
  involuntary, 157, 189, 192
  motor, 185

manslaughter (*continued*)
  recklessness, 183, 189, 192
  result crimes, 133
  voluntary, 157–75
marital rape, 443, 486, 488
medical treatment
  consent, 223–4
  negligence, compensation for, 481
  refusal of, 137, 151, 466
  withdrawal of, 129, 131, 149, 471
mens rea, 139–47, 253–4. *See also under*
      particular offences
  fault, 473–7, 492, 498
  intention, 139–44, 151
  intoxication, 237, 238–9, 252
  knowledge, 139
  manslaughter, 133
  mistake, 245, 246, 248
  murder, 127, 133–4
  recklessness, 139, 144–6
  transferred malice, 146
mercy killing, 149
mere puffs, 7, 8, 31
misrepresentation, 4, 61, 74–80, 467
  change in previous statements, not admitting
      to, 73
  damages, 76, 77–9, 121, 477
  definition, 72–3
  exclusion of liability, reasonableness of, 79
  expenses, 78
  fact, statements of, 73–4
  fault, 477
  fraudulent misrepresentation, 75, 77–8, 121
  indemnity, 78–9
  inducement, 72, 74–5, 121
  innocent misrepresentation, 76, 78, 477
  intention, statements of, 74
  negligent misrepresentation, 75, 78, 121
  omission of material facts, 73
  opinions, 74
  partial disclosure, 73
  remedies, 76–9, 121
  rescission, 76, 78
    affirmation, 77
    damages, 77, 78
    impossibility, 77
    lapse of time, 77
    third party rights, 77

silence, 73
untrue statements, 73
utmost good faith, 73
voidable contracts, 61, 79
mistake, 61, 62–71 *see also* mistake in criminal
      law
  common mistake, 62, 63–5
  fault, 477
  fraud, 477
  fundamental breach, 62
  identity, 62, 66–8
  inducement, 68, 69
  mutual mistake, 62, 66
  non est factum, 69, 478
  quality, 63, 64–5, 66
  rectification, 68
  rescission, 64–5, 106
  subject matter, existence of, 63–4, 65
  unilateral, 63, 66–8
  void contracts, 61, 62–9, 487
mistake in criminal law, 4, 245–7
  actus reus, 245
  criminal damage, lawful excuse and, 246
  duress, 324
  intoxication, 239–40, 247–8, 252, 315
  justification, 246–7
  mens rea, 245, 246, 248
  rape, consent and, 246–7
  reasonableness, 246
  self-defence, 244, 246, 247, 248, 324
  theft, 267
mitigating and aggravating factors in
      sentencing, 475
M'Naughten's Rules, 229, 233
money transfer by deception, obtaining, 295
morality and law, 444–53, 492–3
  contraception to children, prescribing,
      445–6
  contract, 450, 452
  corrupt public morals, conspiracy to, 448
  crimes, 443–4, 450, 452
  designer babies, 449–50
  embryos in medical research, use of, 446
  homosexuality, 447–9, 451, 488
  judges, role of, 447
  marital rape, 443
  omissions, criminal liability for, 443
  outraging public decency, 449

morality and law (*continued*)
  prostitution, 447, 488
  sado-masochistic acts, 448–9
  tort, 451, 452
motor manslaughter 185
murder, 148–56
  actus reus, 127, 134, 146–55
  causation, 133, 149–52
  de minimis rule, 149
  duress, 317, 318, 324–5
  foreseeability, 151–2
  intention, 140–2
  manslaughter, 157
  mens rea, 146–7, 150–5, 460
  mercy killing, 149
  necessity, 318
  omissions, 148–9
  result crimes, 133
  sentencing, 149
  unlawful killing, 148
mercy killing, 149

natural law, 455, 456, 462, 492, 493
necessity, 317, 318–19, 325, 460
  circumstances, by, 317, 318, 319, 323
  criminal damage, 318
  duress, 317, 323
  murder, 318
negligence, 335–6 *see also* contributory
      negligence, duty of care, etc.
  medical negligence, 481
  misrepresentation, 75, 78, 121
  non est factum, 69
negligent misstatements, 345–8
  assumption of responsibility, 347–8, 351,
      372
  disclaimers, 346
  economic loss, 344–8, 372
  fair, just and reasonable test, 348–9
  foreseeability, 238–9
  knowledge, 346–7, 349, 350
  proximity, 238–9
  reasonable reliance, 347, 349, 350–1
  references, 346, 351
  special skill, 345–6, 349, 350–1
nervous shock *see* psychiatric harm
non est factum, 69, 478
novus actus interveniens. See intervening acts

nuisance, 333, 395, 396–406, 466
  abatement, 405
  acts of God, 479
  adoption of nuisance, 401–2
  causation, 403, 420
  class of people, 397
  creator of nuisance, 401–2
  damages, 404, 432
  fault, 478
  foreseeability, 402, 405
  frequency and duration, 399
  injunctions, 404–5, 422, 432, 461
  interest in land, 400–1, 402
  locality, 399
  malice, 400
  occupiers' liability, 396
  planning permission, 403
  prescription, defence of, 404
  private nuisance, 396, 397–8, 400–1, 420
  public nuisance, 396, 397, 401, 420, 478,
      487
  reasonableness, 398–400, 402, 405, 478
  Rylands v *Fletcher*, 396, 410, 413, 420–1,
      422
  sensitivity, 400
  standing, 400–1
  state of affairs, 399
  statutory authority, defence of, 403
  statutory nuisance, 396–7
  telephone calls, 401
  television reception, interference with, 398,
      421
  temporary nuisance, 399
  use or enjoyment of land, unreasonable
      interference with, 397–8
  usefulness of activity, 399

occupiers' liability, 333, 375–93, 461
  activities on property, 382
  breach of duty, 382, 389, 391
  causation, 382, 389
  children, 377–9, 385–9, 391–3, 437–8, 451,
      478, 487
  contributory negligence, 388, 390, 391, 393
  defences, 383, 388–9
  exclusions, unfair contract terms and, 382–3,
      391–2
  foreseeability, 378, 382, 391

occupiers' liability (*continued*)
  independent contractors, 379–81, 391, 393, 437
  lawful visitors, 377
  non-visitors, 385–93
  nuisance, 396
  occupier, meaning of, 377, 383
  professionals, 379, 383
  reasonableness, 386, 389, 391
  trespass, 375, 381, 385–6, 388, 392–3, 487
  visitors, 375–85, 391
  warnings, 377, 381–3, 387–93
offer, 3, 5, 6–14
  acceptance, 10, 12–13, 15–16, 120, 479
  advertisements, 7, 8
  auctions, 9
  bilateral offers, 6
  consideration, 6
  collateral contracts, 9
  counter-offers, 19–11
  death, 12–13
  display, goods on, 7–8
  information, supplying, 9, 11, 16
  invitations to treat, 7, 8
  lapse of time, 12
  mere puffs, 7, 8
  rejection, 10–11
  revocation, 11–12, 479
  rewards, 7
  tenders, 9
  termination, 10–13
  unilateral offers, 6, 12
omissions, 73, 129–31, 148–9, 178, 181, 201, 342, 443

Parliament, supremacy of, 456, 485
Pearson Commission, no-fault compensation and, 480–1
penalty clauses, 25–6, 114–15
performance, discharge by, 88–93
  conditions, time for performance and, 91
  damages, 91
  entire contracts, 88–90
  exact and complete performance, requirement for, 88–91
  frustration, 95–7
  improper performance, 103
  incomplete, 16–17

partial performance, 88, 90
prevention of performance, 90
severable or divisible contracts, 89–90
substantial performance, 89
tender of performance, 90–1
time of performance, 91
vicarious performance, 91–2
warranties, time for performance and, 91
police, immunity of, 340–1, 461, 468
positivism, 455–7, 462
postal rule, 18–19, 479, 487
precedent, 459, 466, 469, 484–7, 488–90, 494, 496–9
prescription, 404
privacy, 471
property by deception, obtaining, 294–5, 296, 300
prostitution, morality and, 447, 488
provocation, 157, 158–64, 172, 173, 486
  battered woman syndrome, 159–62
  cooling off period, 159–60, 162, 466
  diminished responsibility, 165–6, 169
  evidence, 159, 163
  harassment, 210
  intoxication, 161–2
  loss of self-control, 158, 159–63, 166
  reasonable person test, 158, 160–3, 166
  sudden and temporary loss of control, 159, 160, 162, 166
proximity
  duty of care, 339, 340, 343
  economic loss, 349
  negligent misstatements, 238–9
  psychiatric injury, 353–3, 356, 358, 359
psychiatric harm, 216, 335, 352–60, 372, 451, 487
  actual bodily harm, assault occasioning, 205
  communication of shock, 357–8
  floodgates argument, 352
  foreseeability, 352–4, 359
  grief, 358
  grievous bodily harm and wounding, 210
  immediate aftermath, 355, 357
  love and affection, close ties of, 354–7, 359
  primary and secondary victims, 354–6, 359, 438

psychiatric harm (*continued*)
   proximity, 352–3, 356, 358, 359
   reform, 258–9
   rescuers, 355–6, 359, 438
   sudden shock, 358, 359
public and private interests, 463–6, 468

rape, 246–7, 443, 486, 488
recklessness
   assault, 200, 205, 206
   burglary, 284–5
   consent, 224, 225
   criminal damage, 308, 310
   deception, 293, 295, 296, 299
   fault, 474
   grievous bodily harm and wounding, 211,
      212
   intoxication, 236, 237, 239
   manslaughter, 182, 183, 189, 192
   mens rea, 139, 144–6
   objective, 144–6
   reckless killing, 189
   robbery, 279
   subjective, 144–6, 486
rectification, 68, 116
remedies 470. *See also* damages, injunctions,
    rescission
   equitable, 115–16
   misrepresentation, 76–9, 121
   specific performance, 115, 460
remission of existing liability, securing, 297,
    300
remoteness, 110–12, 368–70
repudiation, 104, 105–6
rescission, 85, 115–16, 460, 478
   affirmation, 77
   conditions, breach of, 46–9, 86, 115
   damages, 77, 78
   fundamental breach, 106–7
   impossibility, 77
   lapse of time, 77
   misrepresentation, 76–8
   mistake, 64–5
   repudiation, 105–8
   warranties, breach of, 115
rescuers, 355–6, 359, 427, 429, 438
rewards, 7
road traffic accident, failure to report, 130

robbery, 259, 276–80, 288–9
   actus reus, 276–7, 279, 280
   dishonesty, 279
   fear, seeking to put any person in, 278–9
   immediacy requirement, 279
   mens rea, 276–7, 279–80, 330
   recklessness, 279
   use or threat of force, 276–8
Rylands v *Fletcher*, 333, 395, 407–13
   acts of God or strangers, 412, 479
   brings on to land, 408
   causation, 412
   common benefit, 412
   consent, 412
   contributory negligence, 412
   default of claimant, 412
   defences, 411–12, 420
   escape, 410, 413, 420
   fault, 479, 480
   foreseeability, 409, 411, 413, 480
   mischief, likely to cause, 409, 410, 412–13,
    420
   non-natural user, 407–11, 413, 420
   nuisance, 396, 410, 413, 420, 421, 422
   reform, 408
   statutory authority, defence of, 411
   strict liability, 411

sado-masochistic acts, 222, 448–9, 460, 466, 486
sale of goods, 41–2, 479
sale of land, formalities for, 99
self-defence, use of reasonable force and, 201,
    242–5
   another, defence of, 243
   crime prevention, 242–3
   diminished responsibility, 168
   excessive force, 244–5
   imminent threat, 243–4
   mistake, 244, 246–8, 324
sentencing
   aggravating and mitigating factors, 475
   aims of, 459, 470
   murder, 149
services by deception, obtaining, 295–6, 299,
    300
social and domestic agreements, 29–30, 120,
    487
specific performance, 115, 460

sports and games, 42, 222, 223, 427–8
standard forms, 16, 55
standard of care, 363–4, 372–3
statutory interpretation
    contract, 487
    crime, 486
    golden rule, 485, 490
    Hansard, 485
    Human Rights Act 1998, 486
    judicial creativity, 483–8, 494, 496–9
    literal rule, 485, 489, 490
    mischief rule, 485, 490
    purposive approach, 485, 490
    tort, 487–8
strict liability, 487–8
    fault, 475–7, 479–81
    regulatory offences, 476
    Rylands v *Fletcher*, 411
suicide
    assisted 129, 171, 221
    pacts, 157, 170–3

television reception, interference with, 398, 421
tenders, 9
terms, 37–45. *See also* conditions, implied terms, warranties
    breach, 37
    exclusion clauses, 38, 51–7, 79, 346, 450
    express, 37, 39–41
    innominate or intermediate terms, 37, 46–8, 460, 479
    representations, 460
terrorism, 469, 471–2
theft, 259, 269–75, 288–9
    actus reus, 260–8, 270, 274–5
    appropriation 132, 261–4, 268, 269–70, 272
    assumption of rights of owner, 261
    belonging to another, 264, 265–6, 268
    borrowing, 270
    consent, 261–4, 269–70
    deal with property in a certain, obligation to, 266–7
    deception, 263–4
    definition, 260
    dishonesty, 262–4, 269–75, 330
    intention permanently to deprive, 139–40, 273–5
    mens rea, 260–3, 266, 269–75

mistake, property received by, 267
overpayments, 267
property, meaning of, 264–5, 268
thin skull rule, 134, 136–7, 180, 354, 370, 466
tort, 333
    balancing conflicting interests and, 467–8
    fault and, 478–9, 480
    justice and, 461
    morality and, 451, 452
    statutory interpretation, 487–8
    see also individual units
torture, 471–2
trespass
    burglary, 282, 283–4, 286–7
    occupiers' liability, 375, 381, 385–6, 388, 392–3, 487

unfair contract terms, exclusion clauses and, 38, 54–6, 460, 467
    death or personal injury, exclusion of, 54, 55
    disclaimers, 346
    EC law, 55
    implied terms, 54
    negligence, 54
    occupiers' liability, 382–3, 391–2
    plain, intelligible language, 55
    reasonableness, 54, 55, 79
    standard terms, 55
unlawful act manslaughter. *See* constructive or unlawful act manslaughter
use of force. *See* self-defence, use of reasonable force and
utilitarianism, 456–7, 458, 460–4, 492, 493
utmost good faith, 73

vicarious liability, 395, 414–19
    agency workers, 416
    assault, 417–18, 422, 488
    authorized acts, 417
    course of employment, 416–18, 421, 480
    employers' liability, 395, 414–19,480
    fault, 480
    independent contractors, 415–16, 421
    precautions, cost of, 415
    seconded workers, 416
    test for employee status, 415–16, 421

vitiating factors. *See* misrepresentation,
    mistake
volenti non fit injuria, 424, 426–9
    implied consent, 427–8
    intervening acts, 428
    intoxication, 428
    knowledge of risk, 426–7
    real consent, 426
    rescuers, 427, 429
    road traffic cases, 427
    sports, 427–8
voluntary manslaughter, 157–75. *See also*
    diminished responsibility, provocation
    actus reus, 157
    mens rea, 157
    murder, 157
    suicide pacts, 157, 170–2, 173

wait or forgo payment, inducing a creditor to,
    297–8, 300
warnings, 377, 381–3, 387–93
warranties
    breach, 37, 46–9, 86, 107, 115, 467
    conditions and, difference between, 47
    damages, 46–8, 86, 107, 467
    performance, time for, 91
wounding. *See* grievous bodily harm and
    wounding